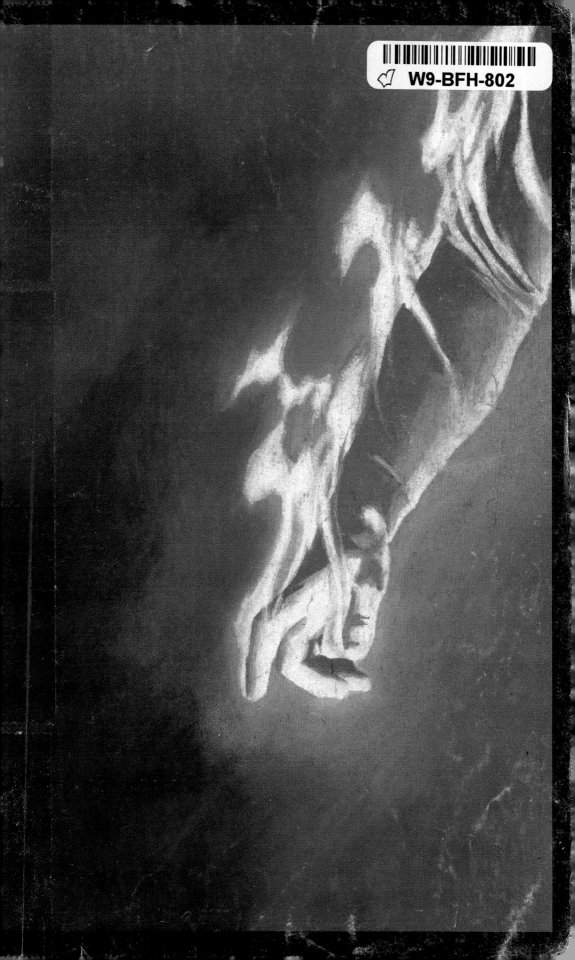

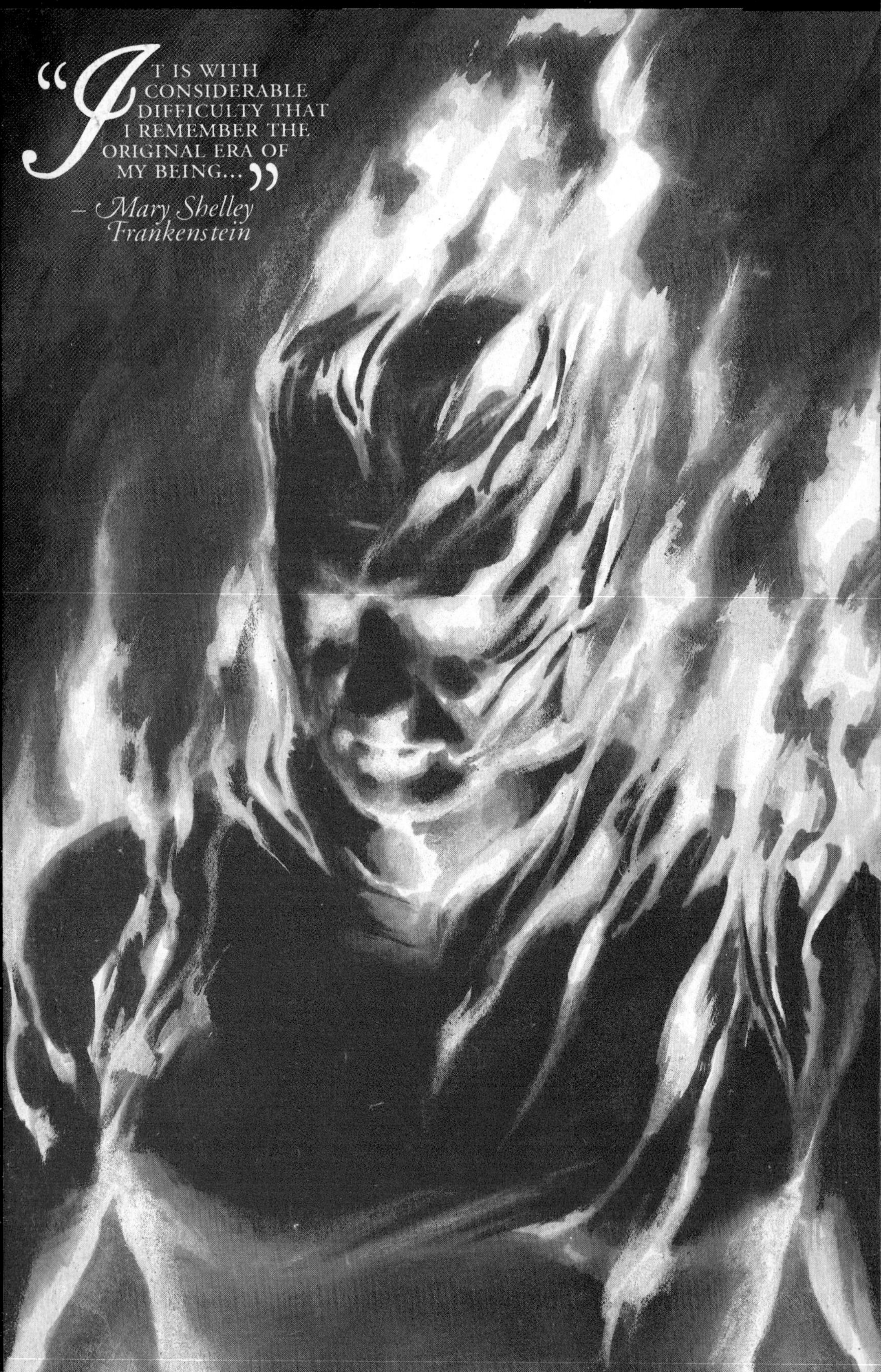
"IT IS WITH CONSIDERABLE DIFFICULTY THAT I REMEMBER THE ORIGINAL ERA OF MY BEING..."
– Mary Shelley
Frankenstein

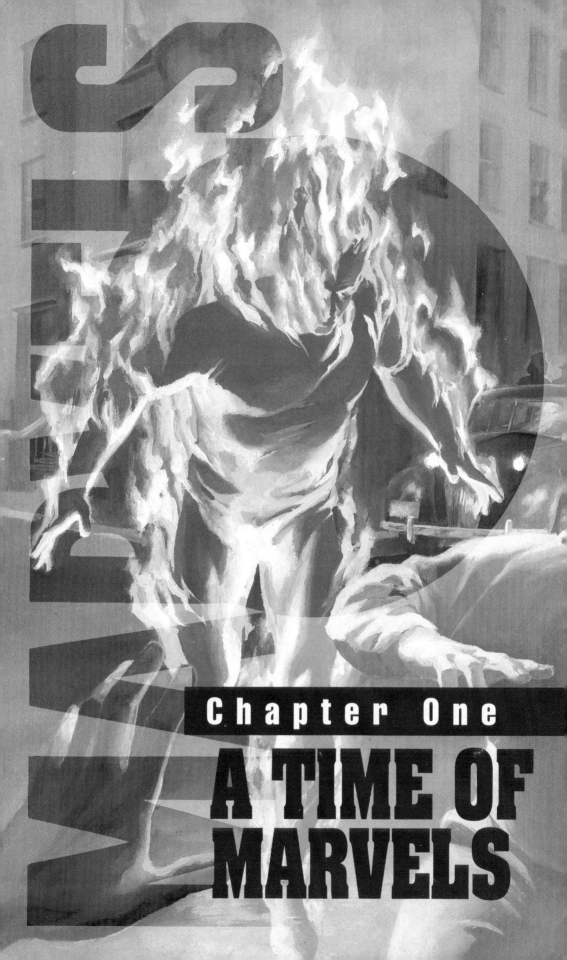

Chapter One
A TIME OF MARVELS

Spider-Man and Doctor Strange, whose unique genius helped to make those characters the unforgettable, legendary icons they are today.

Indeed, all the colorful, costumed cavorters depicted in this fabulous volume of **MARVELS** owe their enduring popularity to so many wonderful comic book superstars whose lives have touched yours and mine throughout the years, people like John Romita, John Buscema, Gene Colan, Joe Sinnott, Don Heck, John Severin, Wally Wood, Gil Kane, Dick Ayers, Larry Lieber, Marie Severin, Roy Thomas, Chris Claremont, John Byrne, Ross Andru — the list goes on endlessly.

That's why this book means so much to me. Kurt and Alex have taken characters who are the foundation of Marvel Comics, characters who have been part of my life, and possibly yours, for decades, characters on whom all the people mentioned above have lavished so much time, effort and enthusiasm for so many years, and they have presented them in a manner never seen before, a style breathtaking new and astonishingly realistic.

The absorbing chronicle you're about to read features virtually every one of Marvel Comics' major super heroes, as well as a number of vile and vicious villains who have become part of the fabric of comicdom's lore. And yet, perhaps for the first time in magazine history, these are not merely the adventures of the heroes and villains, but rather the adventures and logical reactions of the ordinary citizens whose lives are impacted by our super characters. In fact, the true hero of the **MARVELS** saga is a distinctly non-superpowered photojournalist through whose eyes the entire epic unfolds. Though the pages are filled with action and spectacle, the scenes are far different from those you'll see in any comic book, the emphasis is different, the tone is different, the approach is different. Kurt Busiek and Alex Ross have achieved a rare literary and artistic triumph by maintaining ever-mounting suspense and excitement without any of the usual life-and-death battles continuing for page after page, which you'll find in the average comic book. I've never read anything like the stories on the pages ahead, nor have I ever seen anything surpassing the spectacular artwork which brings each episode so glowingly to life, and I'm sure, after you've read them, you'll enthusiastically echo those sentiments.

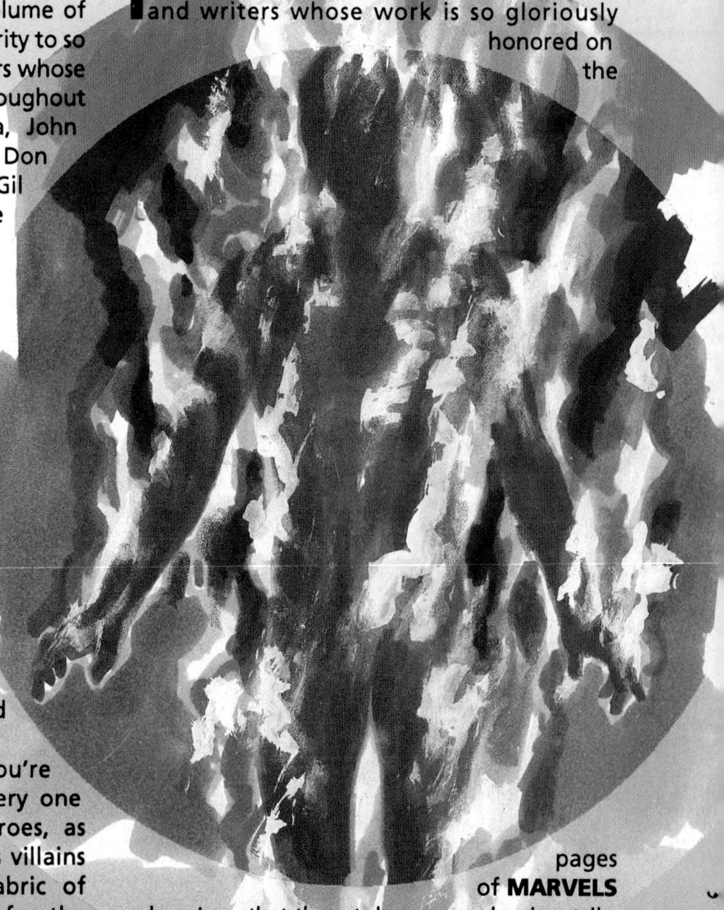

In closing, I feel I can speak for all the artists and writers whose work is so gloriously honored on the pages of **MARVELS** when I say that these tales are a glowing tribute to what has gone before, and an inspiring presage of what is yet to come. They have taken comics to the next level of entertainment by adding a dimension and a reality that has seldom, *if ever,* been seen in the medium. I've read these stories over and over, each time finding something new and surprising. Having them all together in one volume is the ultimate luxury, as well as the ultimate proof that tales told in illustrated format can favorably compete with *any* and *every* form of literature.

Excelsior!

Stan

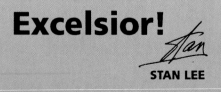

STAN LEE

Foreword by Stan Lee

It's unbelievable!

I was actually *asked* to write this foreword! As if I'd say no! As if I wouldn't have *fought* for the chance! As if I'd have let *anyone* else write the foreword to a series that I consider the most innovative, brilliantly conceived and skillfully executed concept to come along in years!

MARVELS is far more than just another comic book title. In fact, referring to it as merely a comic book would be like referring to World War Two as a disturbing little fracas. Artwise, scriptwise and formatwise, **MARVELS** is a giant leap forward, bringing us to a new plateau in the evolution of illustrated literature.

In case I'm not making myself clear, I think it's pretty cool.

You know, creating the Marvel Universe was considered to be somewhat daring and revolutionary when we first structured it many years ago. Never before had one comic book company's burgeoning cast of characters, both heroic and villainous, lived in the same world — mainly in the same city, New York — where they would meet and interface with each other just as we all do in our everyday lives. Never before had a comic book company striven so conscientiously to inject realism into its stories by using the names of real cities, real buildings, real vehicles and real events whenever possible. Thus the Marvel Universe was born. But, never before, not until Kurt Busiek and Alex Ross created **MARVELS**, had that universe seemed quite so undeniably authentic, so unquestionably credible, so eminently compelling.

Of all the countless graphic novels published during the last few decades, novels masterfully scripted and magnificently illustrated, none have brought the reader directly into the story the way **MARVELS** does, none have made the reader a part of the events that transpired the way **MARVELS** does, and none have made the reader feel as though he or she is on the scene, witnessing history in the making the way **MARVELS** does.

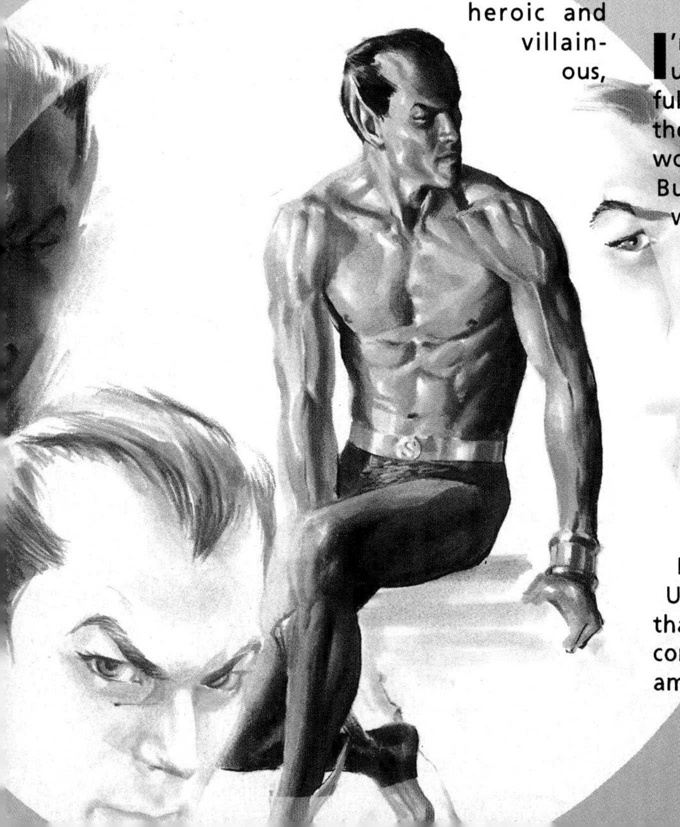

I'm sure you can readily understand my unbounded enthusiasm for these wonderfully rendered tales. You see, I was there at the beginning. I was lucky enough to have worked with such towering talents as Carl Burgos, creator of the Human Torch, and with Bill Everett who brought us the Sub-Mariner, as well as with Syd Shores, Al Avison, Joe Maneely, and all the other shining stars of the forties and fifties. No, I haven't forgotten the great Jack Kirby. He deserves a very special mention. Even in those early days, those glorious days when he, together with Joe Simon, brought us Captain America, he was in a class by himself, just as he was for the next half-century when we worked together on THE FANTASTIC FOUR, THE INCREDIBLE HULK, THE UNCANNY X-MEN and so many other titles that are still among the world's best-selling comic books. Then, of course, there was the amazing Steve Ditko, who breathed life into

Credits

Kurt Busiek Writer

Alex Ross Artist/Cover Artist

**Richard Starkings/
Comicraft** Lettering and Interior Design

Joe Kaufman Logo Design

Marc McLaurin Original Editor

Spencer Lamm Original Assistant Editor

Introduction **Stan Lee**

Commentaries **Kurt Busiek
Alex Ross
John Romita Sr.**

Afterword **Scott McCloud**

Matty Ryan Cover Redesign

Ben Abernathy Collections Editor

Bernadetter Thomas Manufacturing Manager

Bob Greenberger Director-Publishing Operations

Joe Quesada Editor in Chief

Bill Jemas President

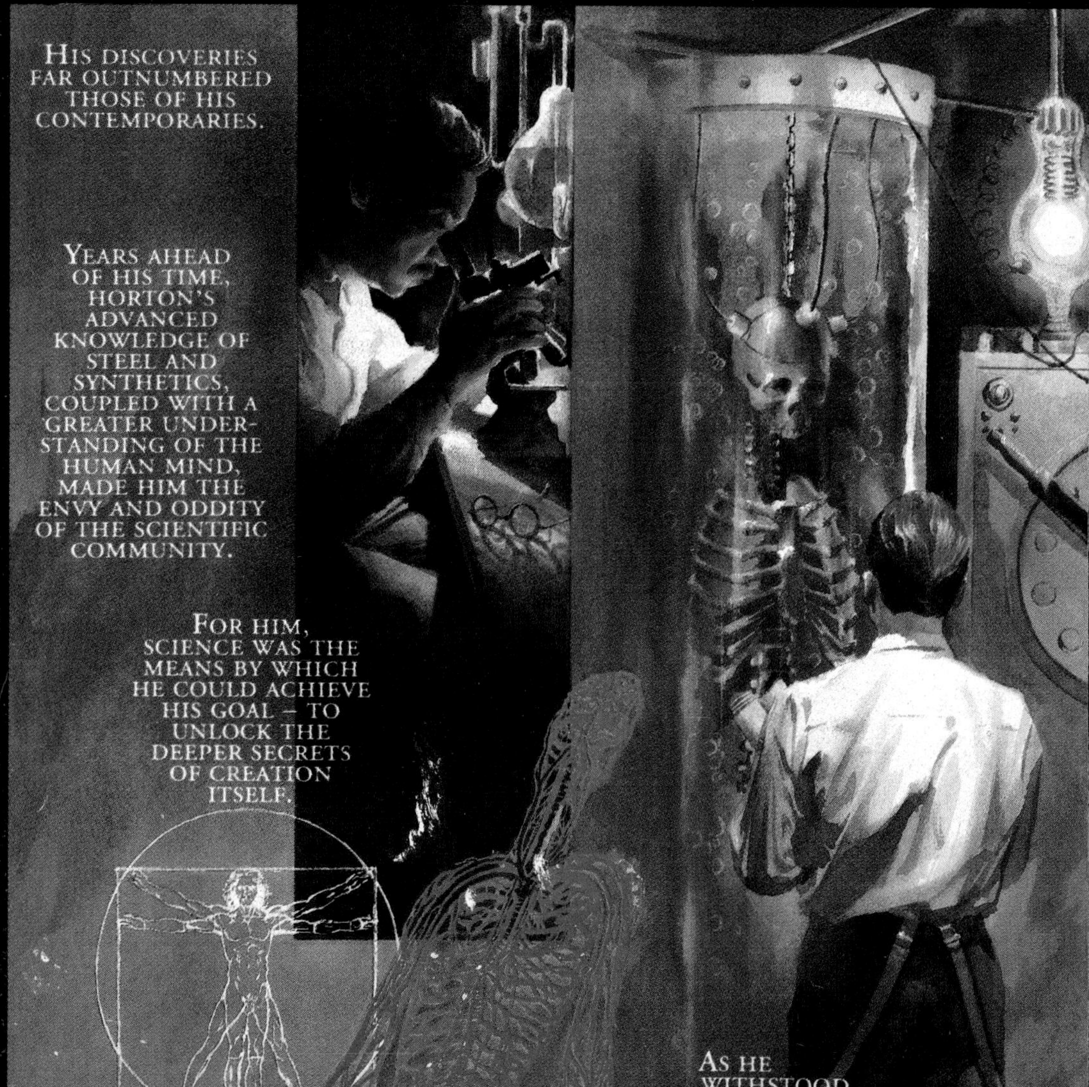

His discoveries far outnumbered those of his contemporaries.
Years ahead of his time, Horton's advanced knowledge of steel and synthetics, coupled with a greater under-standing of the human mind, made him the envy and oddity of the scientific community.
For him, science was the means by which he could achieve his goal — to unlock the deeper secrets of creation itself.
As he withstood the skepticism and jeers of his colleagues, he pooled his resources toward the realization of his goal.
The stress of his life's work would culminate in me.

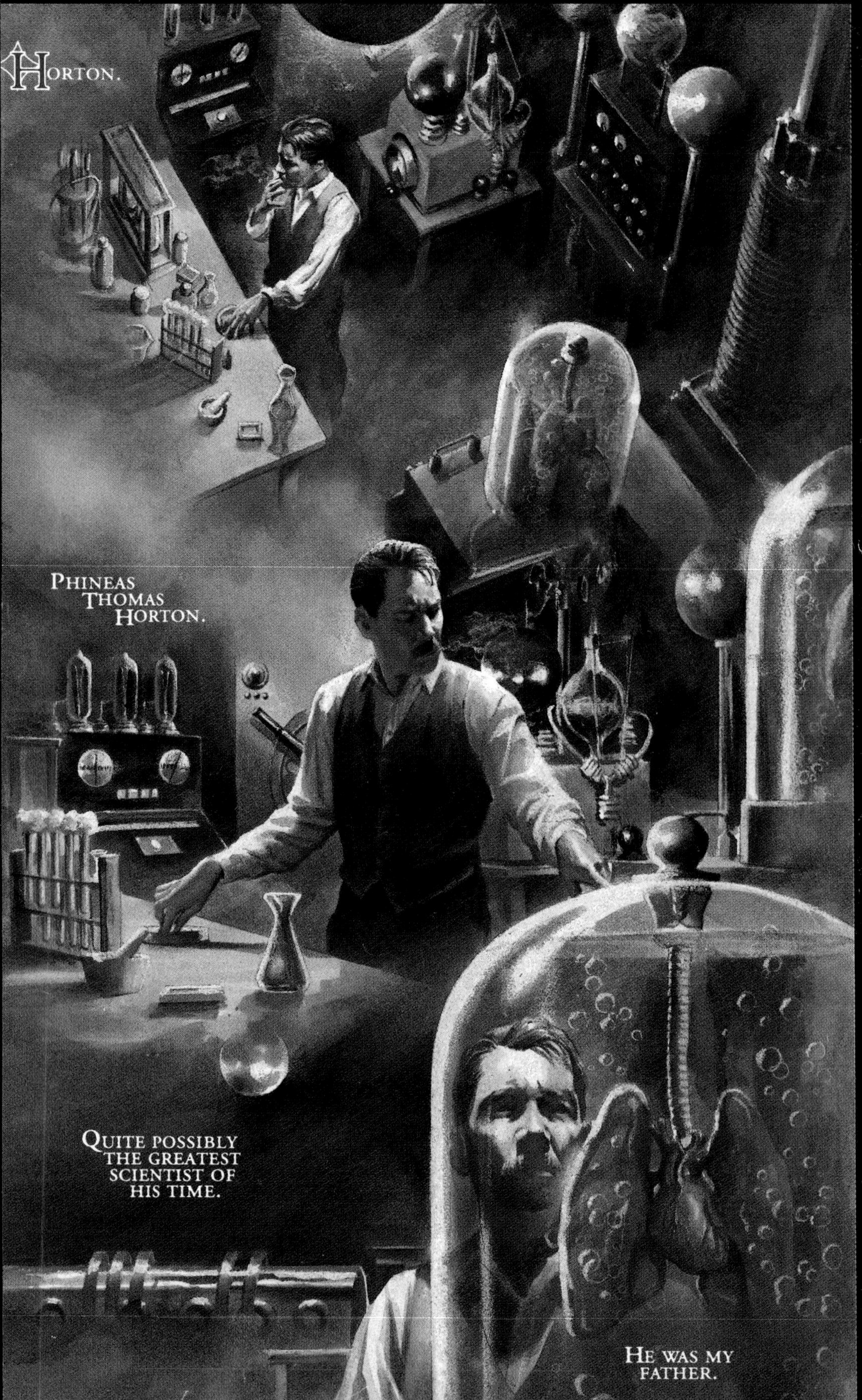
HORTON.
PHINEAS
THOMAS
HORTON.
QUITE POSSIBLY
THE GREATEST
SCIENTIST OF
HIS TIME.
HE WAS MY
FATHER.

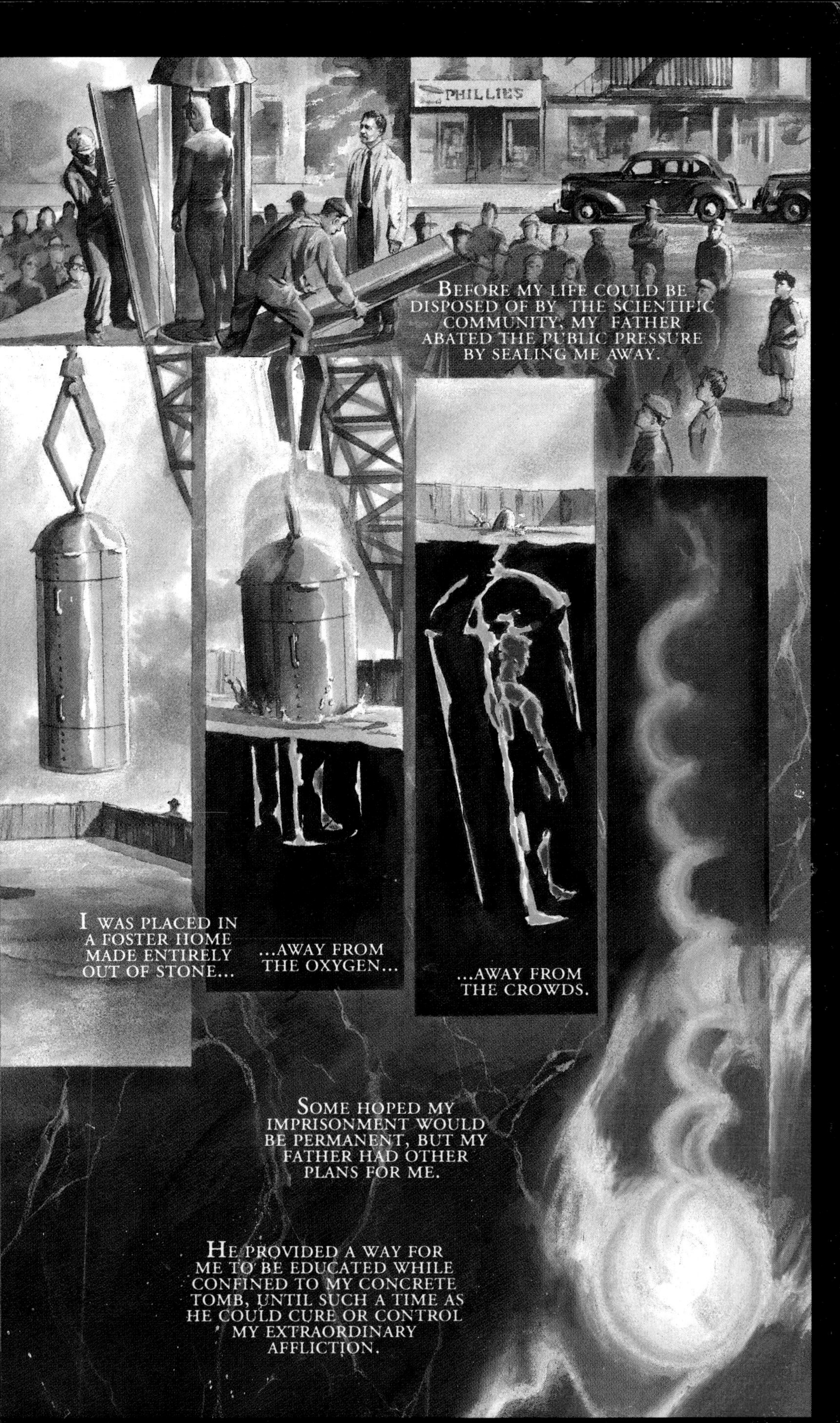

PHILLIES
Before my life could be disposed of by the scientific community, my father abated the public pressure by sealing me away.
I was placed in a foster home made entirely out of stone...
...away from the oxygen...
...away from the crowds.
Some hoped my imprisonment would be permanent, but my father had other plans for me.
He provided a way for me to be educated while confined to my concrete tomb, until such a time as he could cure or control my extraordinary affliction.

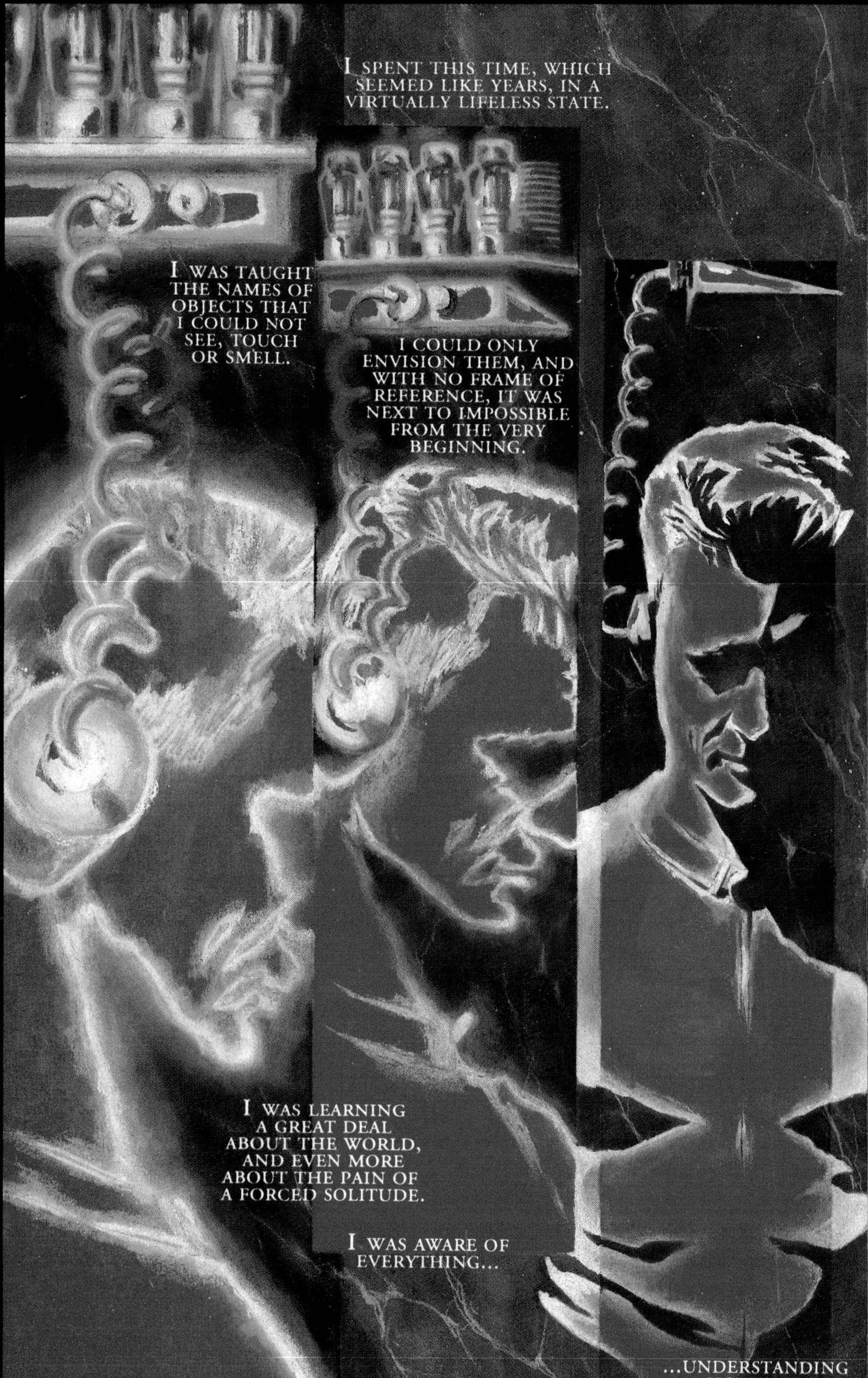
I SPENT THIS TIME, WHICH SEEMED LIKE YEARS, IN A VIRTUALLY LIFELESS STATE.
I WAS TAUGHT THE NAMES OF OBJECTS THAT I COULD NOT SEE, TOUCH OR SMELL.
I COULD ONLY ENVISION THEM, AND WITH NO FRAME OF REFERENCE, IT WAS NEXT TO IMPOSSIBLE FROM THE VERY BEGINNING.
I WAS LEARNING A GREAT DEAL ABOUT THE WORLD, AND EVEN MORE ABOUT THE PAIN OF A FORCED SOLITUDE.
I WAS AWARE OF EVERYTHING...
...UNDERSTANDING NOTHING.

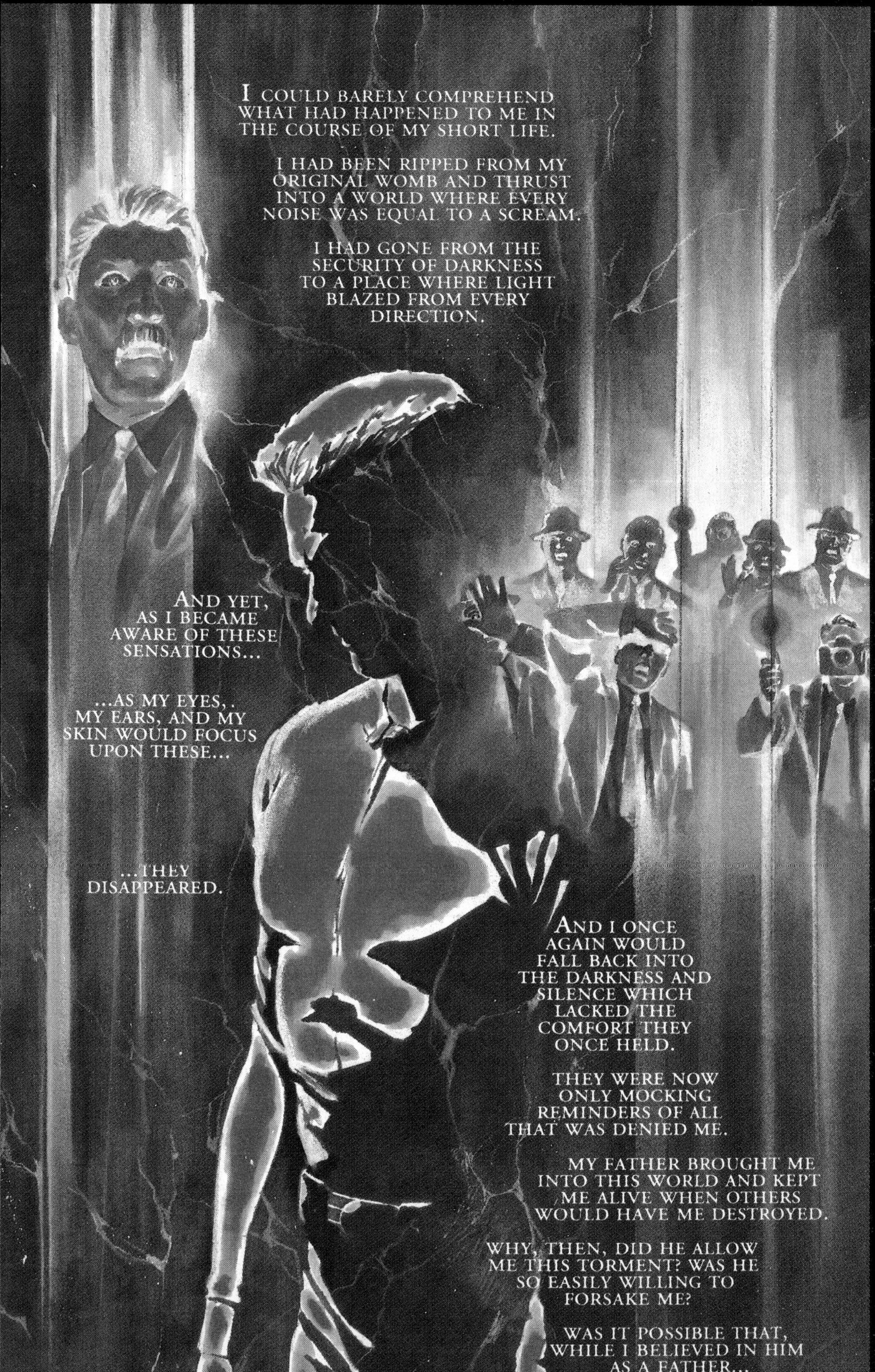
I COULD BARELY COMPREHEND WHAT HAD HAPPENED TO ME IN THE COURSE OF MY SHORT LIFE.
I HAD BEEN RIPPED FROM MY ORIGINAL WOMB AND THRUST INTO A WORLD WHERE EVERY NOISE WAS EQUAL TO A SCREAM.
I HAD GONE FROM THE SECURITY OF DARKNESS TO A PLACE WHERE LIGHT BLAZED FROM EVERY DIRECTION.
AND YET, AS I BECAME AWARE OF THESE SENSATIONS...
...AS MY EYES, MY EARS, AND MY SKIN WOULD FOCUS UPON THESE...
...THEY DISAPPEARED.
AND I ONCE AGAIN WOULD FALL BACK INTO THE DARKNESS AND SILENCE WHICH LACKED THE COMFORT THEY ONCE HELD.
THEY WERE NOW ONLY MOCKING REMINDERS OF ALL THAT WAS DENIED ME.
MY FATHER BROUGHT ME INTO THIS WORLD AND KEPT ME ALIVE WHEN OTHERS WOULD HAVE ME DESTROYED.
WHY, THEN, DID HE ALLOW ME THIS TORMENT? WAS HE SO EASILY WILLING TO FORSAKE ME?
WAS IT POSSIBLE THAT, WHILE I BELIEVED IN HIM AS A FATHER...
...HE DID NOT BELIEVE IN ME AS A SON?

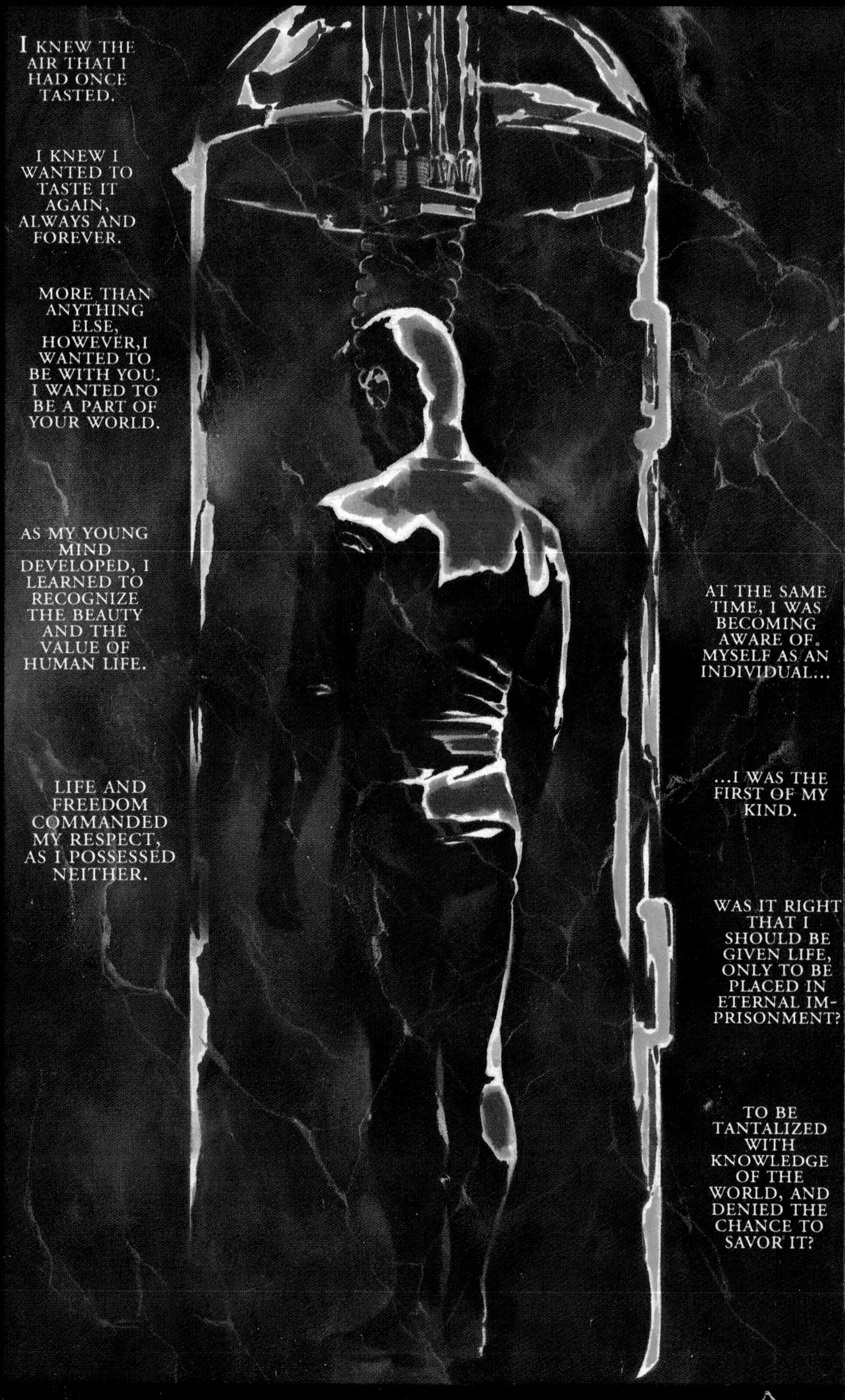
I KNEW THE AIR THAT I HAD ONCE TASTED.
I KNEW I WANTED TO TASTE IT AGAIN, ALWAYS AND FOREVER.
MORE THAN ANYTHING ELSE, HOWEVER,I WANTED TO BE WITH YOU. I WANTED TO BE A PART OF YOUR WORLD.
AS MY YOUNG MIND DEVELOPED, I LEARNED TO RECOGNIZE THE BEAUTY AND THE VALUE OF HUMAN LIFE.
LIFE AND FREEDOM COMMANDED MY RESPECT, AS I POSSESSED NEITHER.
AT THE SAME TIME, I WAS BECOMING AWARE OF MYSELF AS AN INDIVIDUAL...
...I WAS THE FIRST OF MY KIND.
WAS IT RIGHT THAT I SHOULD BE GIVEN LIFE, ONLY TO BE PLACED IN ETERNAL IMPRISONMENT?
TO BE TANTALIZED WITH KNOWLEDGE OF THE WORLD, AND DENIED THE CHANCE TO SAVOR IT?

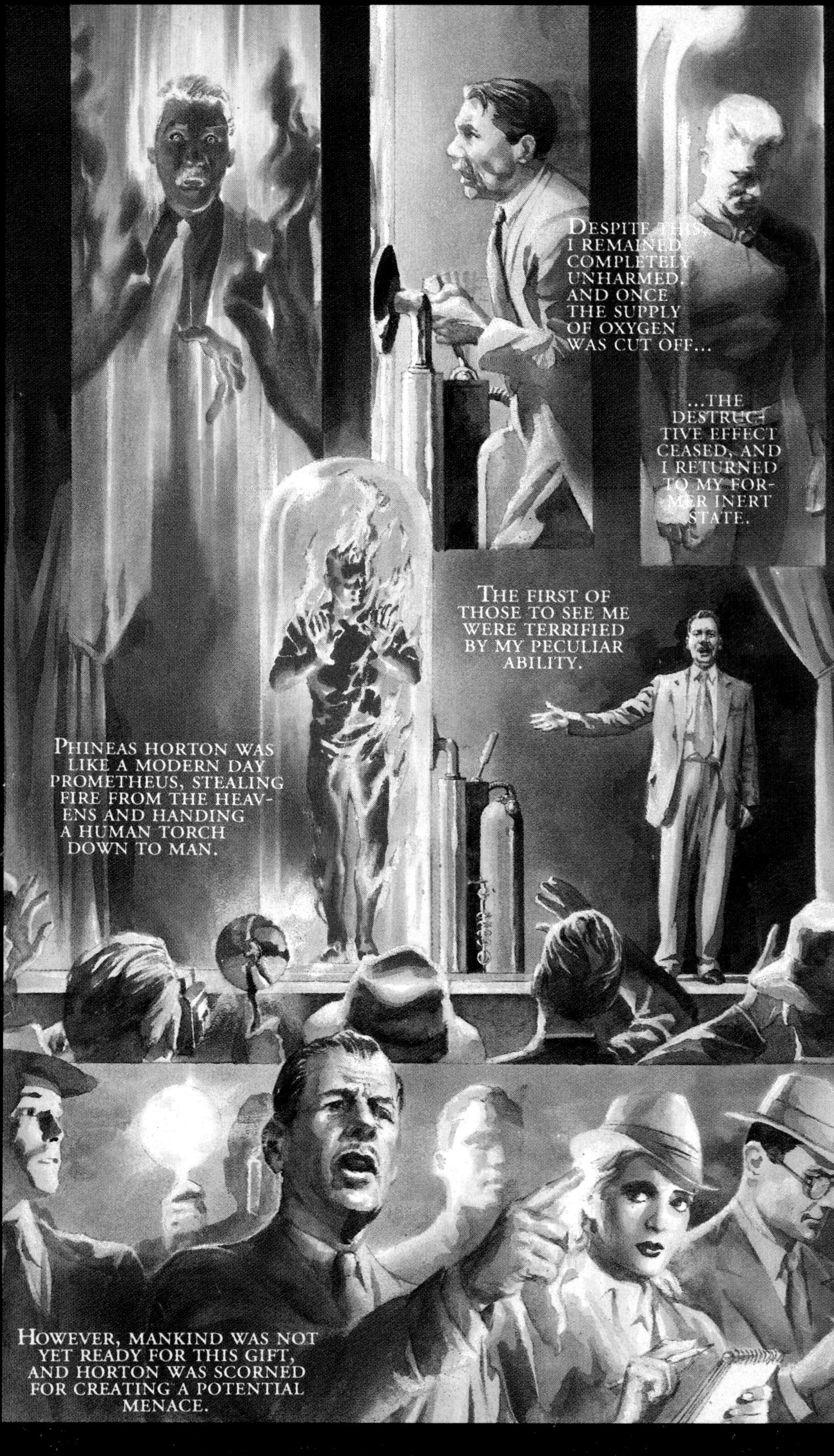
Despite this, I remained completely unharmed, and once the supply of oxygen was cut off...
...the destructive effect ceased, and I returned to my former inert state.
The first of those to see me were terrified by my peculiar ability.
Phineas Horton was like a modern day Prometheus, stealing fire from the heavens and handing a human torch down to man.
However, mankind was not yet ready for this gift, and Horton was scorned for creating a potential menace.

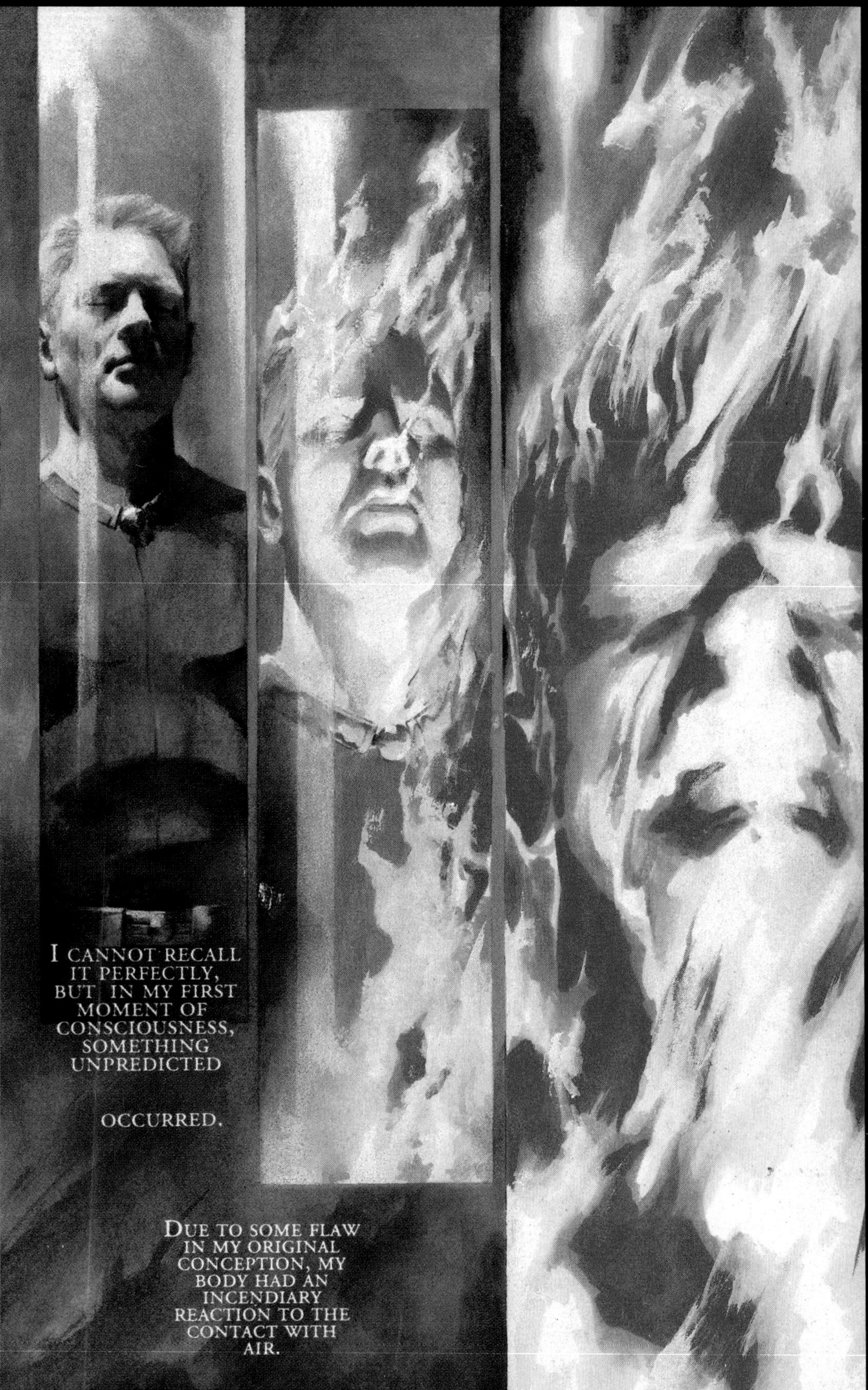
I CANNOT RECALL IT PERFECTLY, BUT IN MY FIRST MOMENT OF CONSCIOUSNESS, SOMETHING UNPREDICTED
OCCURRED.
DUE TO SOME FLAW IN MY ORIGINAL CONCEPTION, MY BODY HAD AN INCENDIARY REACTION TO THE CONTACT WITH AIR.

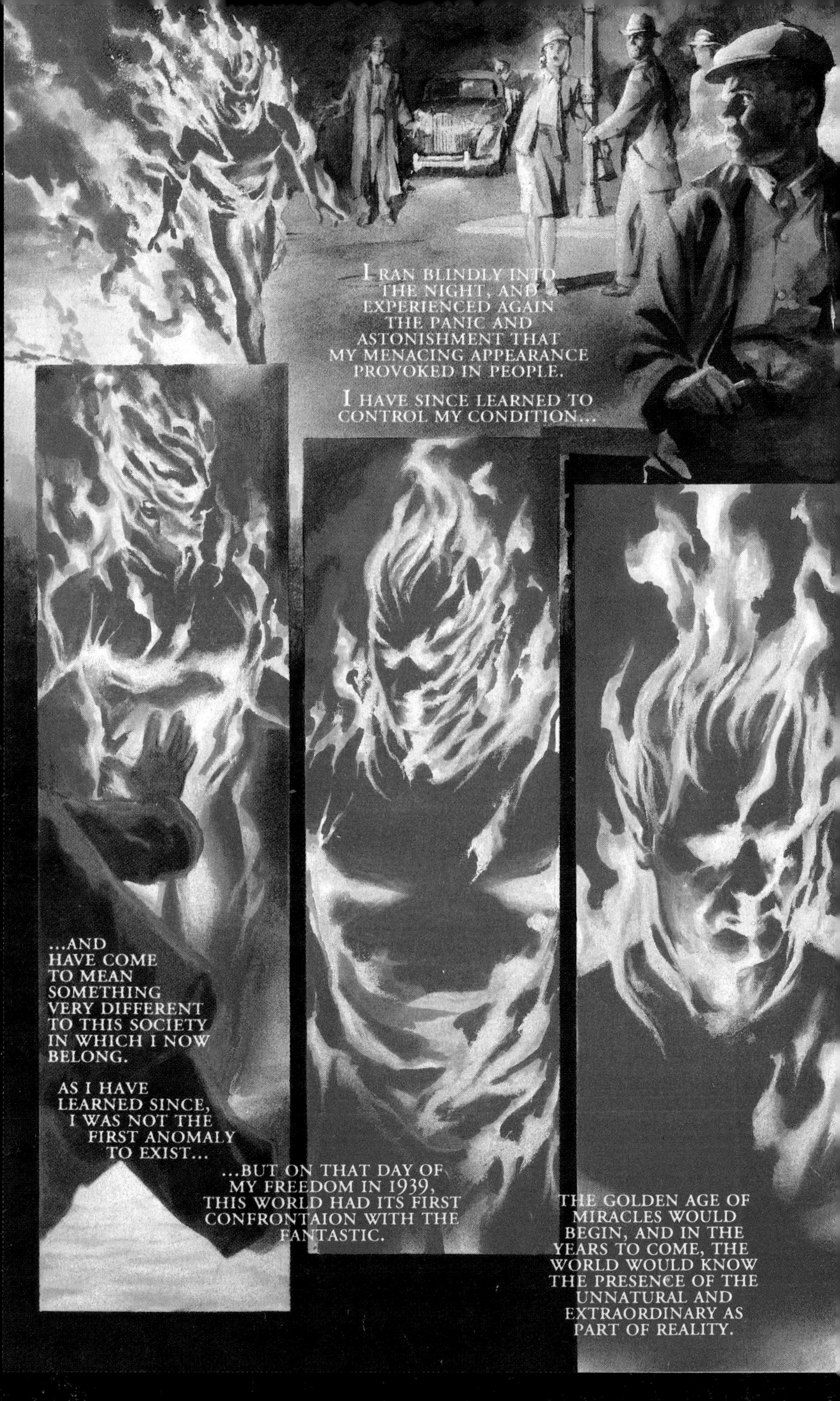
I RAN BLINDLY INTO THE NIGHT, AND EXPERIENCED AGAIN THE PANIC AND ASTONISHMENT THAT MY MENACING APPEARANCE PROVOKED IN PEOPLE.
I HAVE SINCE LEARNED TO CONTROL MY CONDITION...
...AND HAVE COME TO MEAN SOMETHING VERY DIFFERENT TO THIS SOCIETY IN WHICH I NOW BELONG.
AS I HAVE LEARNED SINCE, I WAS NOT THE FIRST ANOMALY TO EXIST...
...BUT ON THAT DAY OF MY FREEDOM IN 1939, THIS WORLD HAD ITS FIRST CONFRONTAION WITH THE FANTASTIC.
THE GOLDEN AGE OF MIRACLES WOULD BEGIN, AND IN THE YEARS TO COME, THE WORLD WOULD KNOW THE PRESENCE OF THE UNNATURAL AND EXTRAORDINARY AS PART OF REALITY.

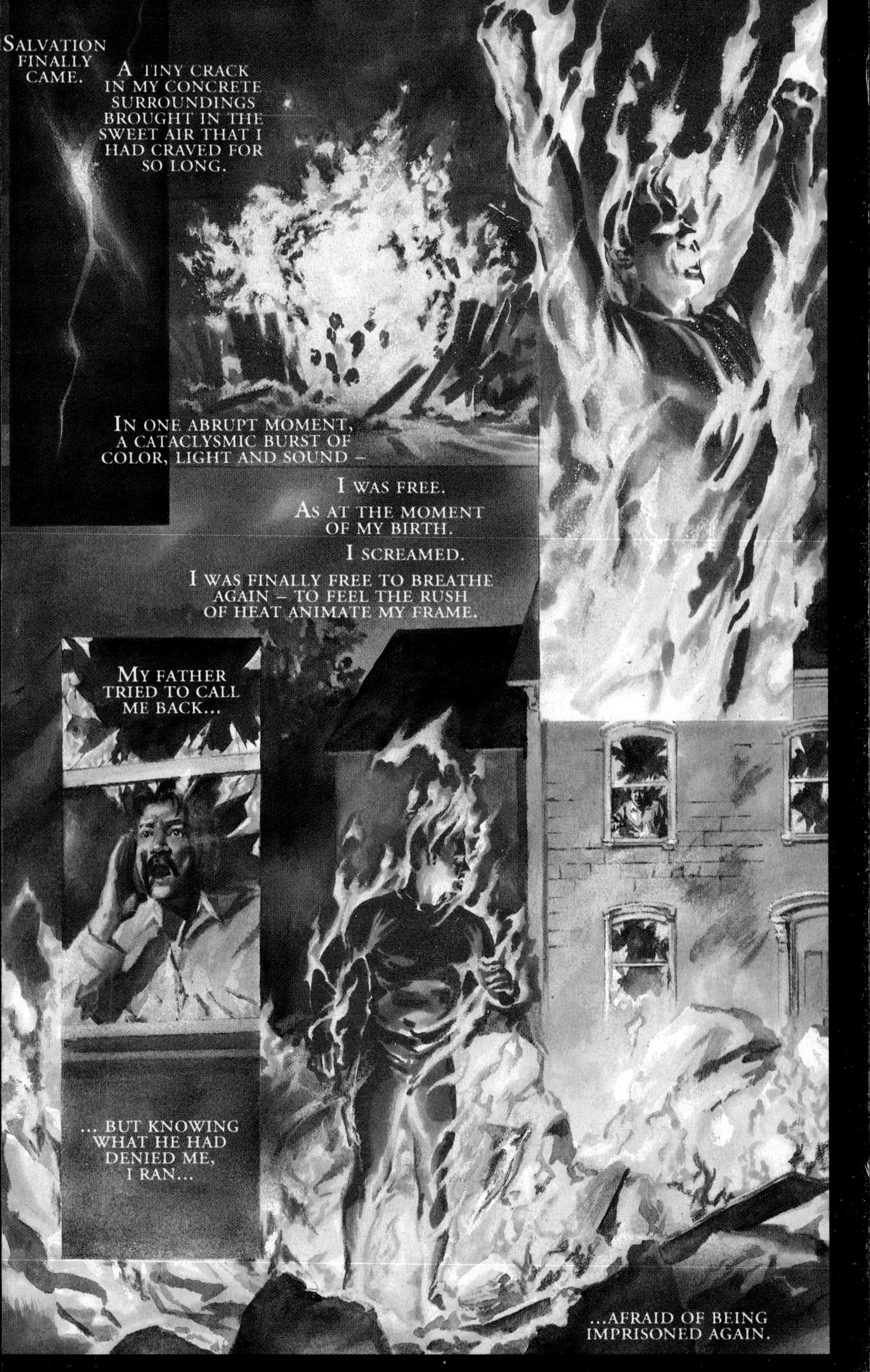
SALVATION FINALLY CAME.
A TINY CRACK IN MY CONCRETE SURROUNDINGS BROUGHT IN THE SWEET AIR THAT I HAD CRAVED FOR SO LONG.
IN ONE ABRUPT MOMENT, A CATACLYSMIC BURST OF COLOR, LIGHT AND SOUND –
I WAS FREE.
AS AT THE MOMENT OF MY BIRTH.
I SCREAMED.
I WAS FINALLY FREE TO BREATHE AGAIN – TO FEEL THE RUSH OF HEAT ANIMATE MY FRAME.
MY FATHER TRIED TO CALL ME BACK...
... BUT KNOWING WHAT HE HAD DENIED ME, I RAN...
...AFRAID OF BEING IMPRISONED AGAIN.

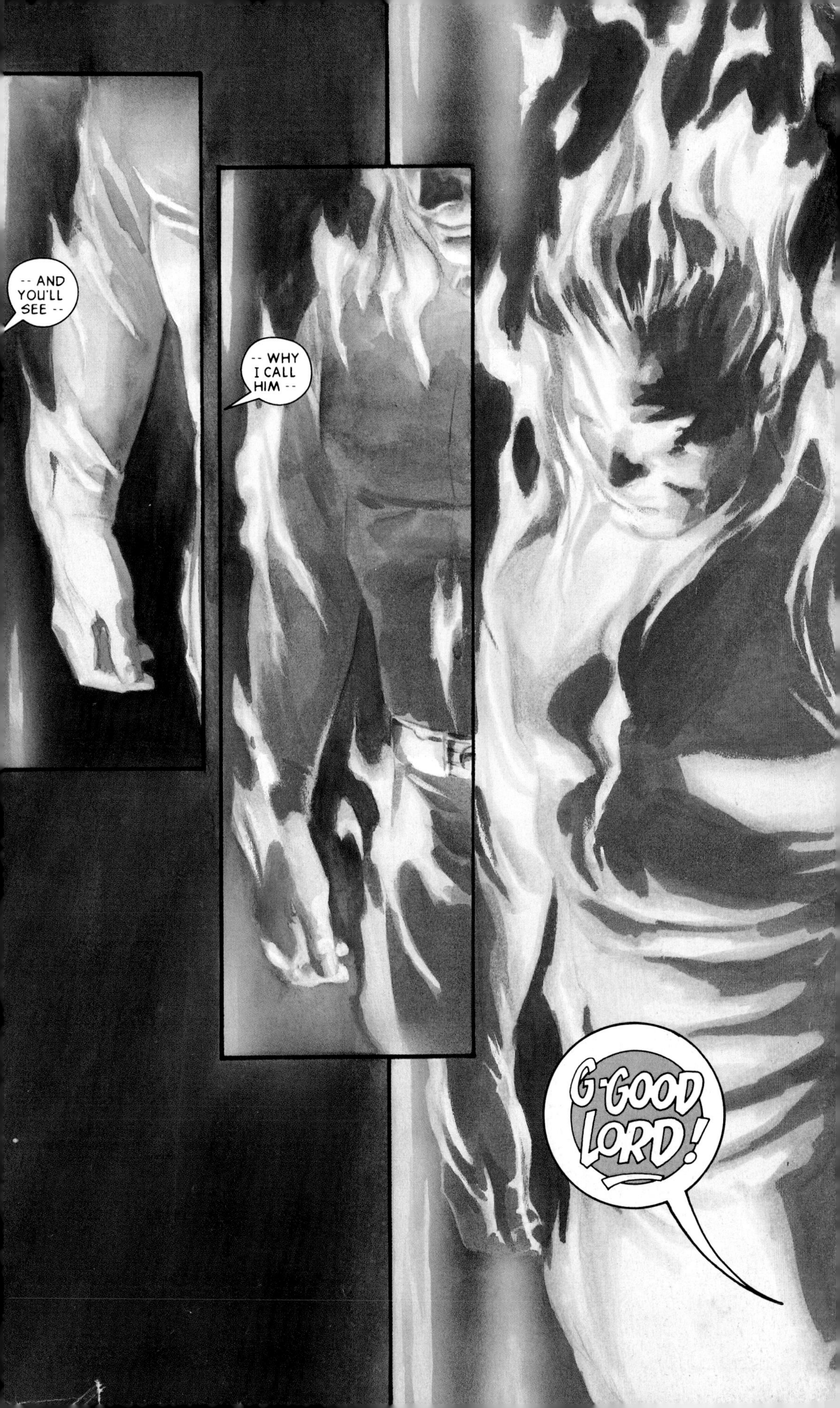
-- AND YOU'LL SEE --
-- WHY I CALL HIM --
G-GOOD LORD!

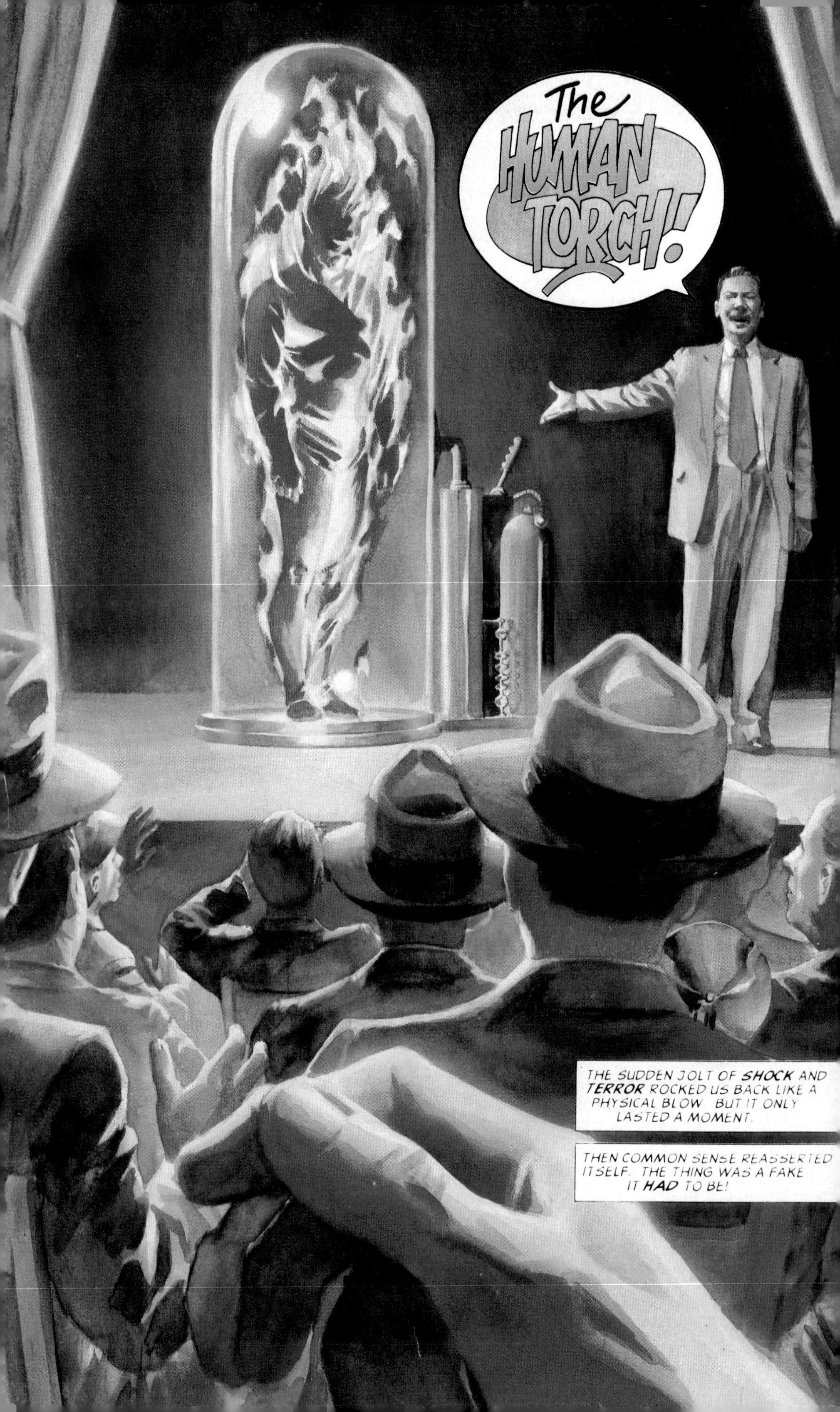
The HUMAN TORCH!
THE SUDDEN JOLT OF SHOCK AND TERROR ROCKED US BACK LIKE A PHYSICAL BLOW. BUT IT ONLY LASTED A MOMENT.
THEN COMMON SENSE REASSERTED ITSELF. THE THING WAS A FAKE. IT HAD TO BE!

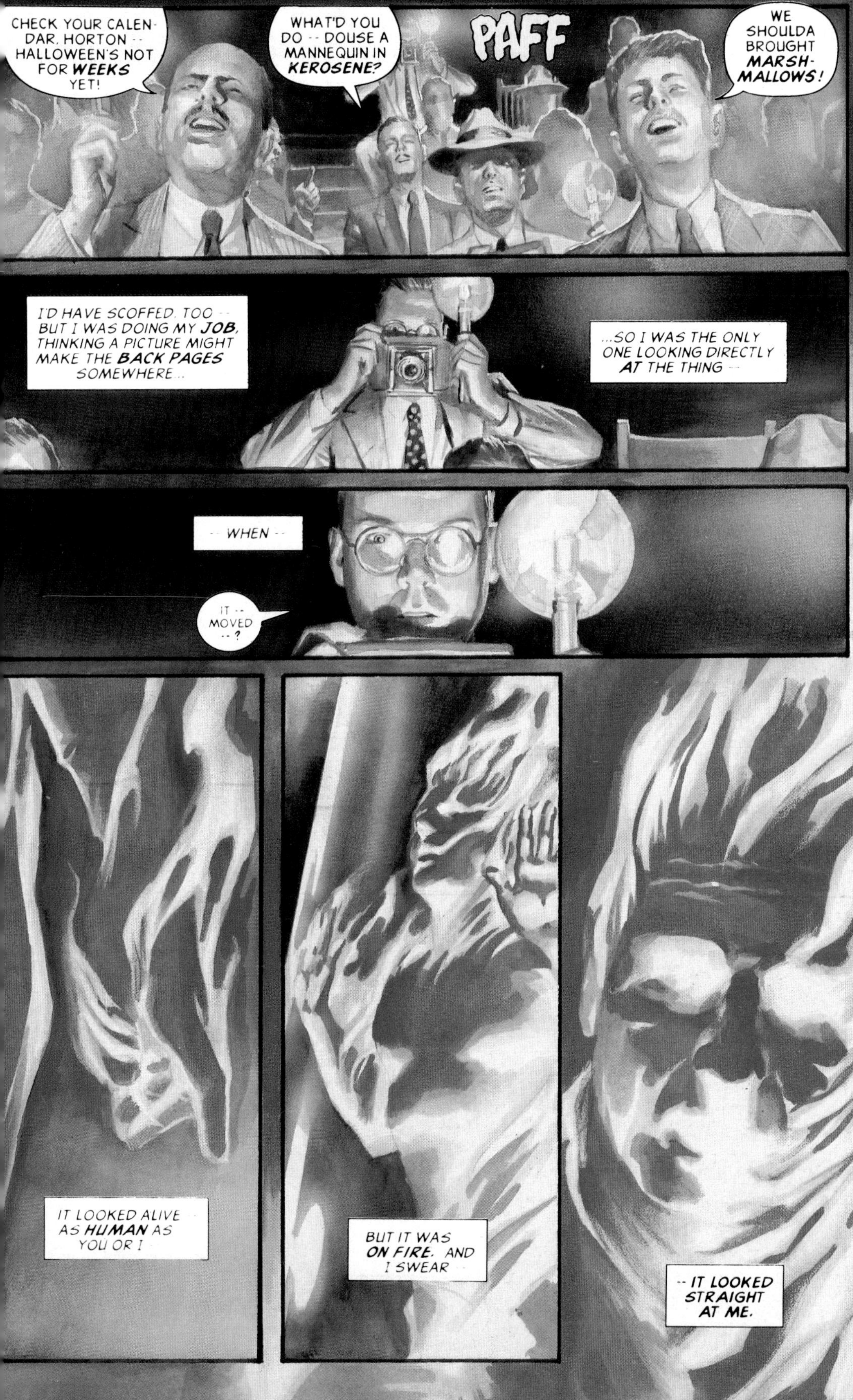
CHECK YOUR CALENDAR, HORTON -- HALLOWEEN'S NOT FOR **WEEKS** YET!
WHAT'D YOU DO -- DOUSE A MANNEQUIN IN **KEROSENE?**
PAFF
WE SHOULDA BROUGHT **MARSH-MALLOWS!**
*I'D HAVE SCOFFED, TOO -- BUT I WAS DOING MY **JOB**, THINKING A PICTURE MIGHT MAKE THE **BACK PAGES** SOMEWHERE...*
*...SO I WAS THE ONLY ONE LOOKING DIRECTLY **AT** THE THING --*
-- WHEN --
IT -- MOVED --?
*IT LOOKED ALIVE -- AS **HUMAN** AS YOU OR I*
*BUT IT WAS **ON FIRE**. AND I SWEAR*
-- IT LOOKED STRAIGHT AT ME.

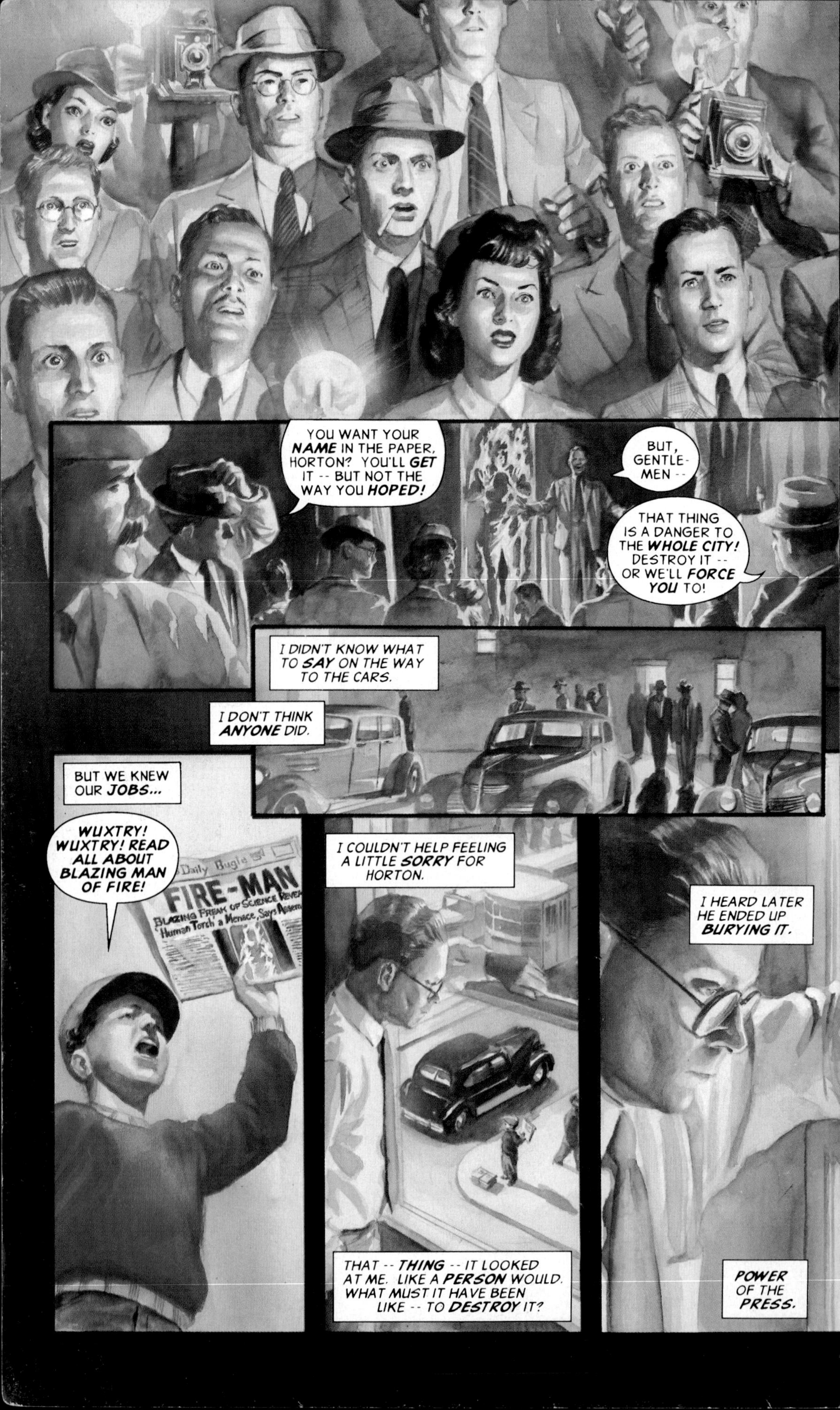
YOU WANT YOUR NAME IN THE PAPER, HORTON? YOU'LL GET IT -- BUT NOT THE WAY YOU HOPED!
BUT, GENTLE-MEN --
THAT THING IS A DANGER TO THE WHOLE CITY! DESTROY IT -- OR WE'LL FORCE YOU TO!
I DIDN'T KNOW WHAT TO SAY ON THE WAY TO THE CARS.
I DON'T THINK ANYONE DID.
BUT WE KNEW OUR JOBS...
WUXTRY! WUXTRY! READ ALL ABOUT BLAZING MAN OF FIRE!
Daily Bugle
FIRE-MAN
I COULDN'T HELP FEELING A LITTLE SORRY FOR HORTON.
THAT -- THING -- IT LOOKED AT ME. LIKE A PERSON WOULD. WHAT MUST IT HAVE BEEN LIKE -- TO DESTROY IT?
I HEARD LATER HE ENDED UP BURYING IT.
POWER OF THE PRESS.

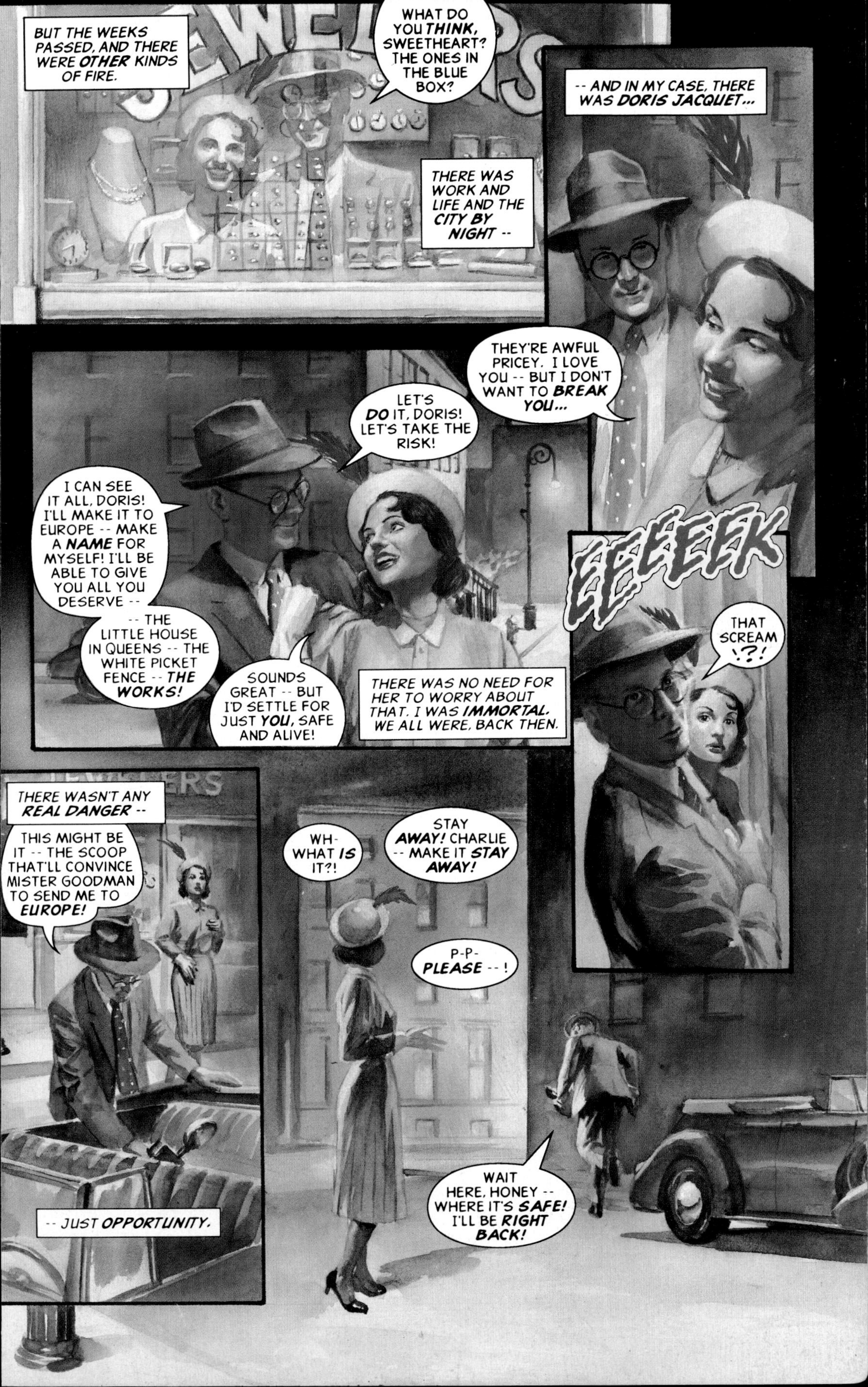

BUT THE WEEKS PASSED, AND THERE WERE OTHER KINDS OF FIRE.
WHAT DO YOU THINK, SWEETHEART? THE ONES IN THE BLUE BOX?
THERE WAS WORK AND LIFE AND THE CITY BY NIGHT --
-- AND IN MY CASE, THERE WAS DORIS JACQUET...
THEY'RE AWFUL PRICEY. I LOVE YOU -- BUT I DON'T WANT TO BREAK YOU...
LET'S DO IT, DORIS! LET'S TAKE THE RISK!
I CAN SEE IT ALL, DORIS! I'LL MAKE IT TO EUROPE -- MAKE A NAME FOR MYSELF! I'LL BE ABLE TO GIVE YOU ALL YOU DESERVE --
-- THE LITTLE HOUSE IN QUEENS -- THE WHITE PICKET FENCE -- THE WORKS!
SOUNDS GREAT -- BUT I'D SETTLE FOR JUST YOU, SAFE AND ALIVE!
THERE WAS NO NEED FOR HER TO WORRY ABOUT THAT. I WAS IMMORTAL. WE ALL WERE, BACK THEN.
EEEEEK
THAT SCREAM !?!
THERE WASN'T ANY REAL DANGER --
THIS MIGHT BE IT -- THE SCOOP THAT'LL CONVINCE MISTER GOODMAN TO SEND ME TO EUROPE!
-- JUST OPPORTUNITY.
WH- WHAT IS IT?!
STAY AWAY! CHARLIE -- MAKE IT STAY AWAY!
P-P- PLEASE -- !
WAIT HERE, HONEY -- WHERE IT'S SAFE! I'LL BE RIGHT BACK!

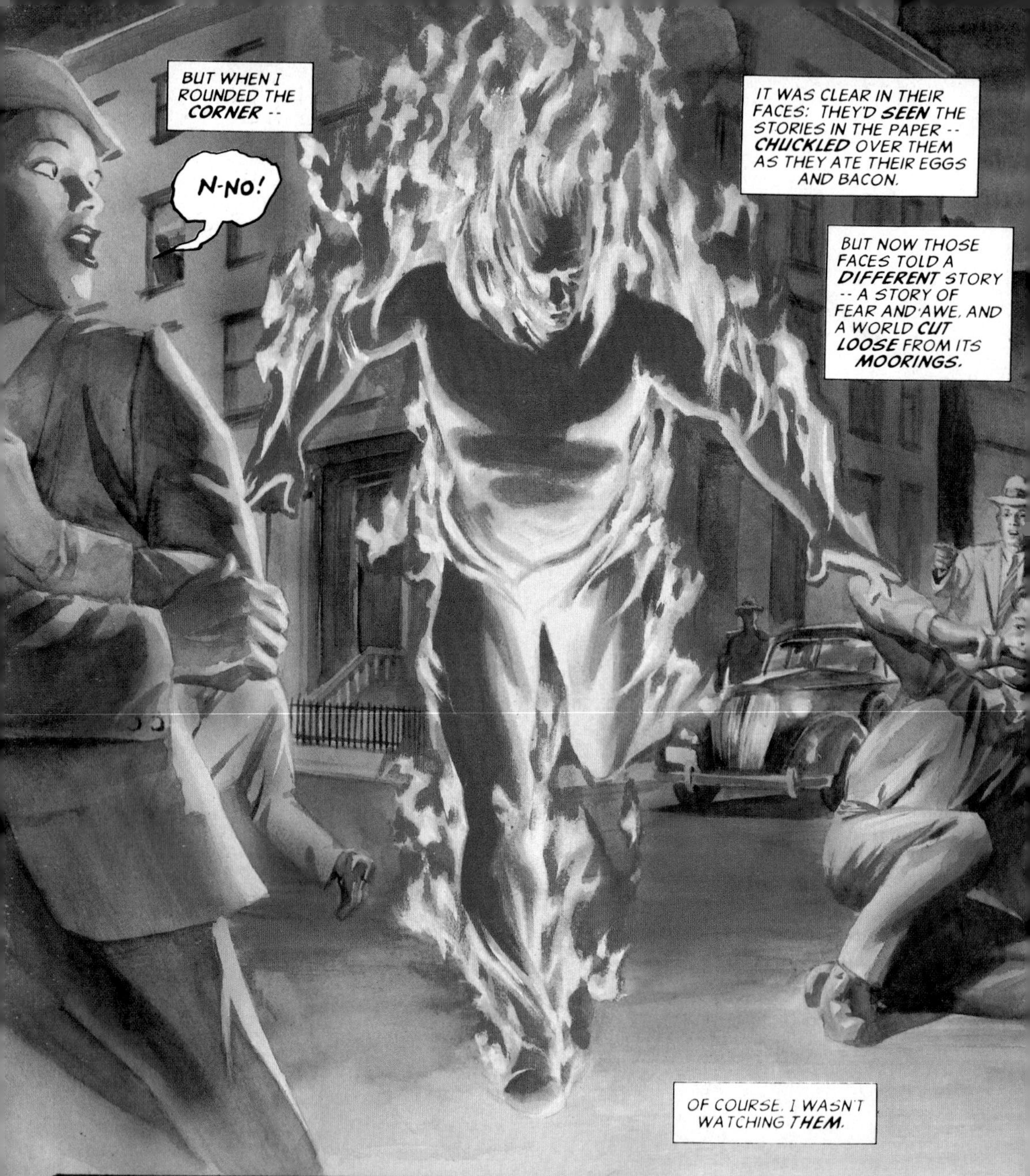
BUT WHEN I ROUNDED THE **CORNER** --
N-NO!
IT WAS CLEAR IN THEIR FACES: THEY'D **SEEN** THE STORIES IN THE PAPER -- **CHUCKLED** OVER THEM AS THEY ATE THEIR EGGS AND BACON.
BUT NOW THOSE FACES TOLD A **DIFFERENT** STORY -- A STORY OF FEAR AND AWE, AND A WORLD **CUT LOOSE** FROM ITS **MOORINGS.**
OF COURSE, I WASN'T WATCHING **THEM.**

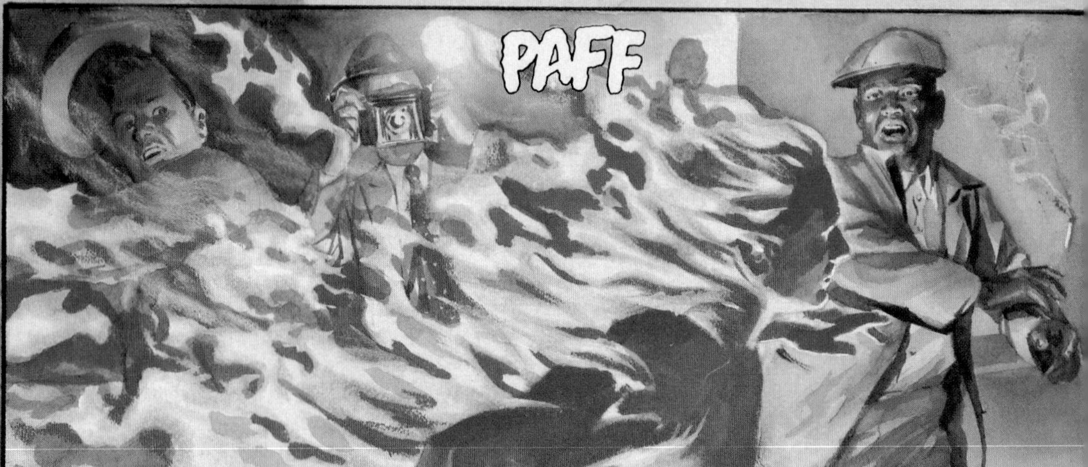
PAFF

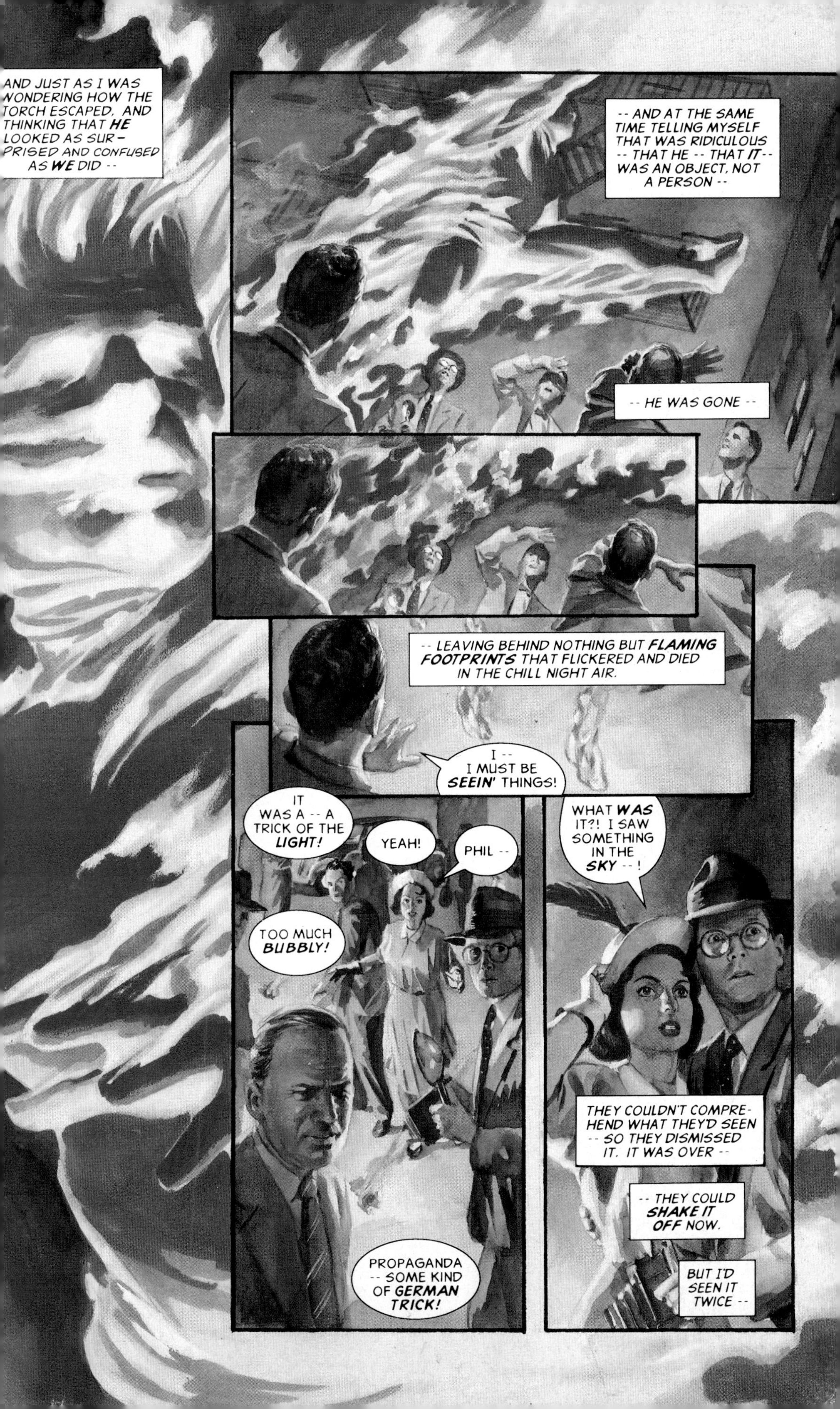

AND JUST AS I WAS WONDERING HOW THE TORCH ESCAPED, AND THINKING THAT **HE** LOOKED AS SUR-PRISED AND CONFUSED AS **WE** DID --
-- AND AT THE SAME TIME TELLING MYSELF THAT WAS RIDICULOUS -- THAT HE -- THAT **IT** -- WAS AN OBJECT, NOT A PERSON --
-- HE WAS GONE --
-- LEAVING BEHIND NOTHING BUT **FLAMING FOOTPRINTS** THAT FLICKERED AND DIED IN THE CHILL NIGHT AIR.
I -- I MUST BE **SEEIN'** THINGS!
IT WAS A -- A TRICK OF THE **LIGHT!**
YEAH!
PHIL --
TOO MUCH **BUBBLY!**
PROPAGANDA -- SOME KIND OF **GERMAN TRICK!**
WHAT **WAS** IT?! I SAW SOMETHING IN THE **SKY** --!
THEY COULDN'T COMPRE-HEND WHAT THEY'D SEEN -- SO THEY DISMISSED IT. IT WAS OVER --
-- THEY COULD **SHAKE IT OFF** NOW.
BUT I'D SEEN IT TWICE --

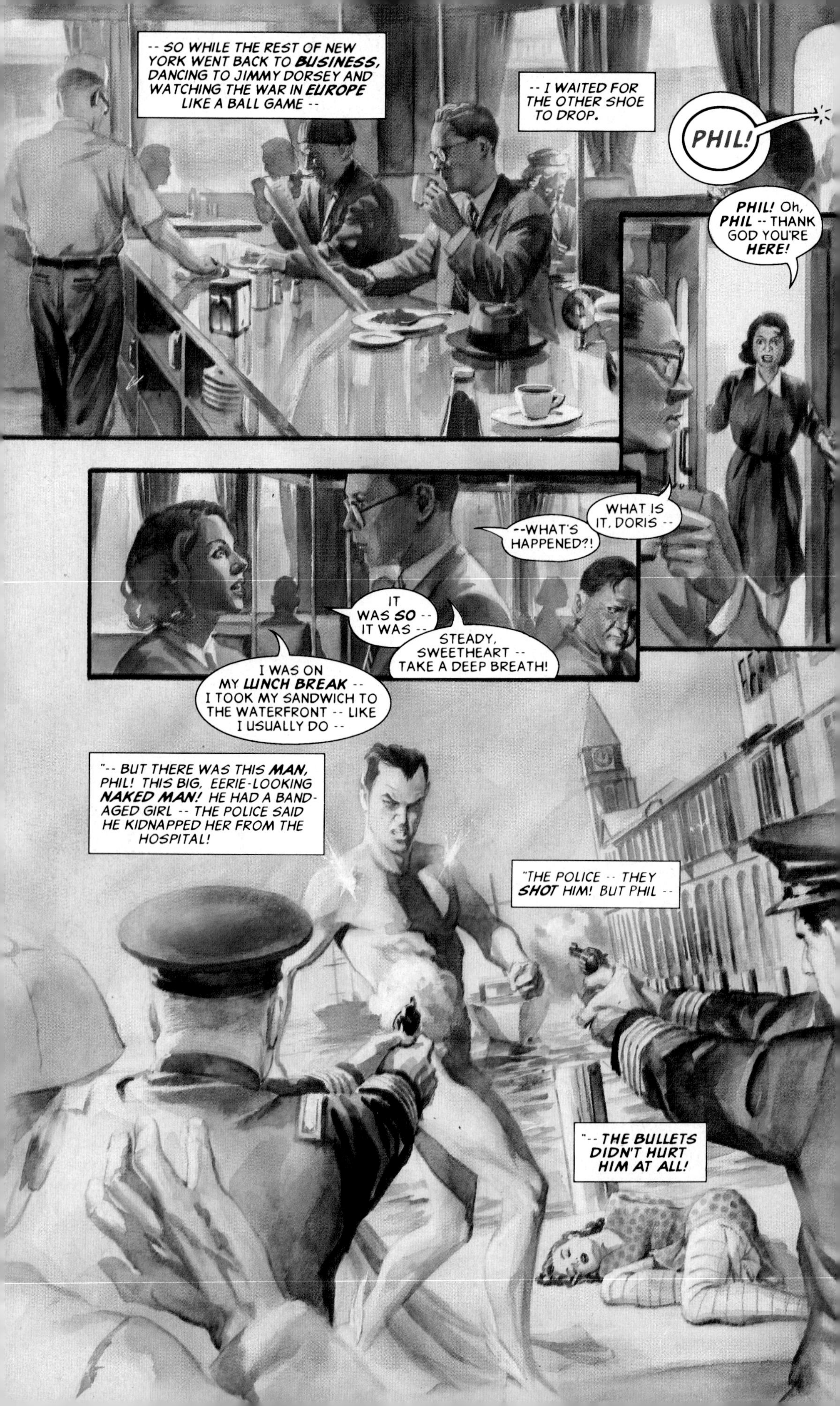
-- SO WHILE THE REST OF NEW YORK WENT BACK TO BUSINESS, DANCING TO JIMMY DORSEY AND WATCHING THE WAR IN EUROPE LIKE A BALL GAME --
-- I WAITED FOR THE OTHER SHOE TO DROP.
PHIL!
PHIL! Oh, PHIL -- THANK GOD YOU'RE HERE!
WHAT IS IT, DORIS --
--WHAT'S HAPPENED?!
IT WAS SO -- IT WAS --
STEADY, SWEETHEART -- TAKE A DEEP BREATH!
I WAS ON MY LUNCH BREAK -- I TOOK MY SANDWICH TO THE WATERFRONT -- LIKE I USUALLY DO --
"-- BUT THERE WAS THIS MAN, PHIL! THIS BIG, EERIE-LOOKING NAKED MAN! HE HAD A BAND-AGED GIRL -- THE POLICE SAID HE KIDNAPPED HER FROM THE HOSPITAL!
"THE POLICE -- THEY SHOT HIM! BUT PHIL --
"-- THE BULLETS DIDN'T HURT HIM AT ALL!

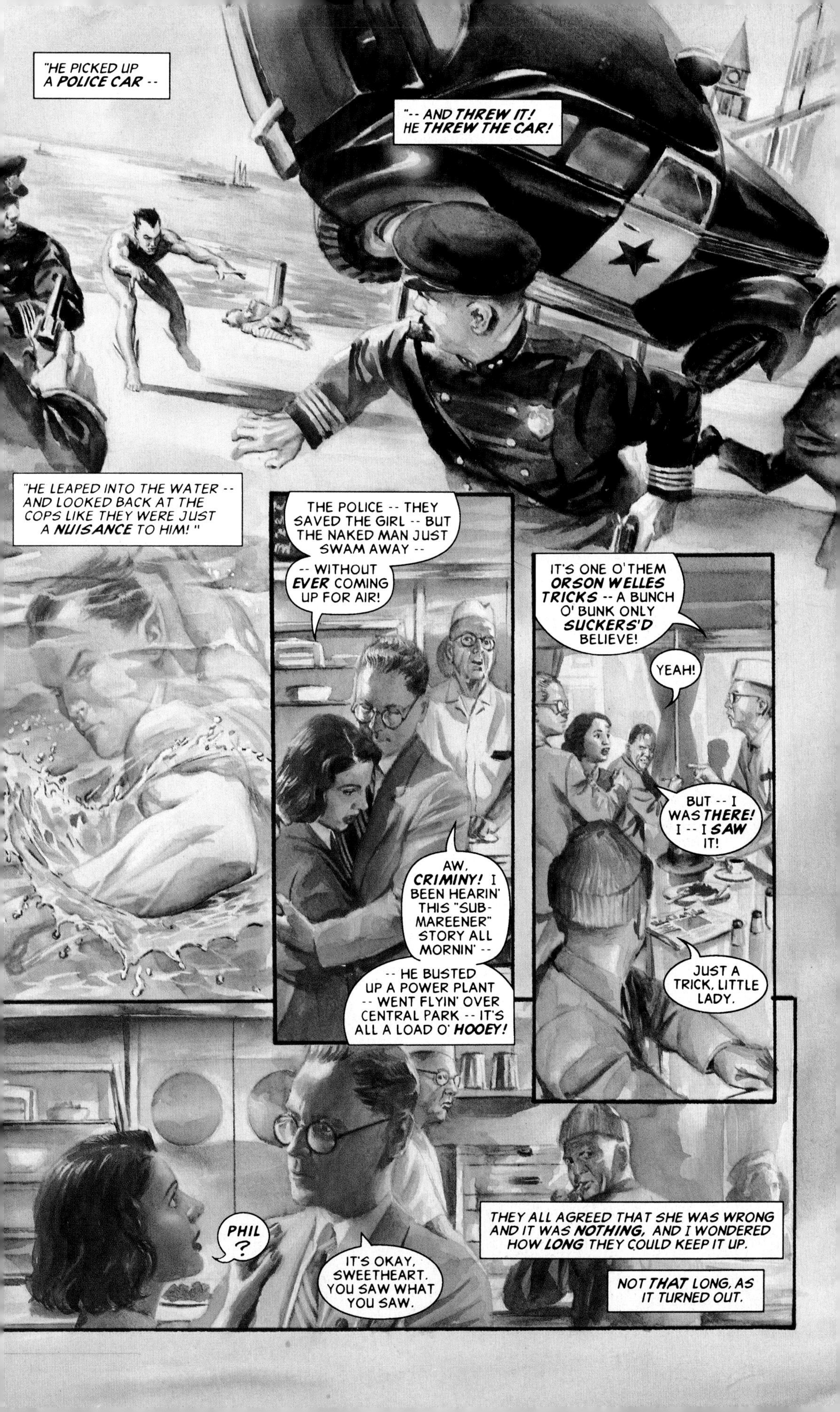
"HE PICKED UP A POLICE CAR --
"-- AND THREW IT! HE THREW THE CAR!
"HE LEAPED INTO THE WATER -- AND LOOKED BACK AT THE COPS LIKE THEY WERE JUST A NUISANCE TO HIM! "
THE POLICE -- THEY SAVED THE GIRL -- BUT THE NAKED MAN JUST SWAM AWAY --
-- WITHOUT EVER COMING UP FOR AIR!
AW, CRIMINY! I BEEN HEARIN' THIS "SUB-MAREENER" STORY ALL MORNIN' --
-- HE BUSTED UP A POWER PLANT -- WENT FLYIN' OVER CENTRAL PARK -- IT'S ALL A LOAD O' HOOEY!
IT'S ONE O'THEM ORSON WELLES TRICKS -- A BUNCH O' BUNK ONLY SUCKERS'D BELIEVE!
YEAH!
BUT -- I WAS THERE! I -- I SAW IT!
JUST A TRICK, LITTLE LADY.
PHIL?
IT'S OKAY, SWEETHEART. YOU SAW WHAT YOU SAW.
THEY ALL AGREED THAT SHE WAS WRONG AND IT WAS NOTHING, AND I WONDERED HOW LONG THEY COULD KEEP IT UP.
NOT THAT LONG, AS IT TURNED OUT.

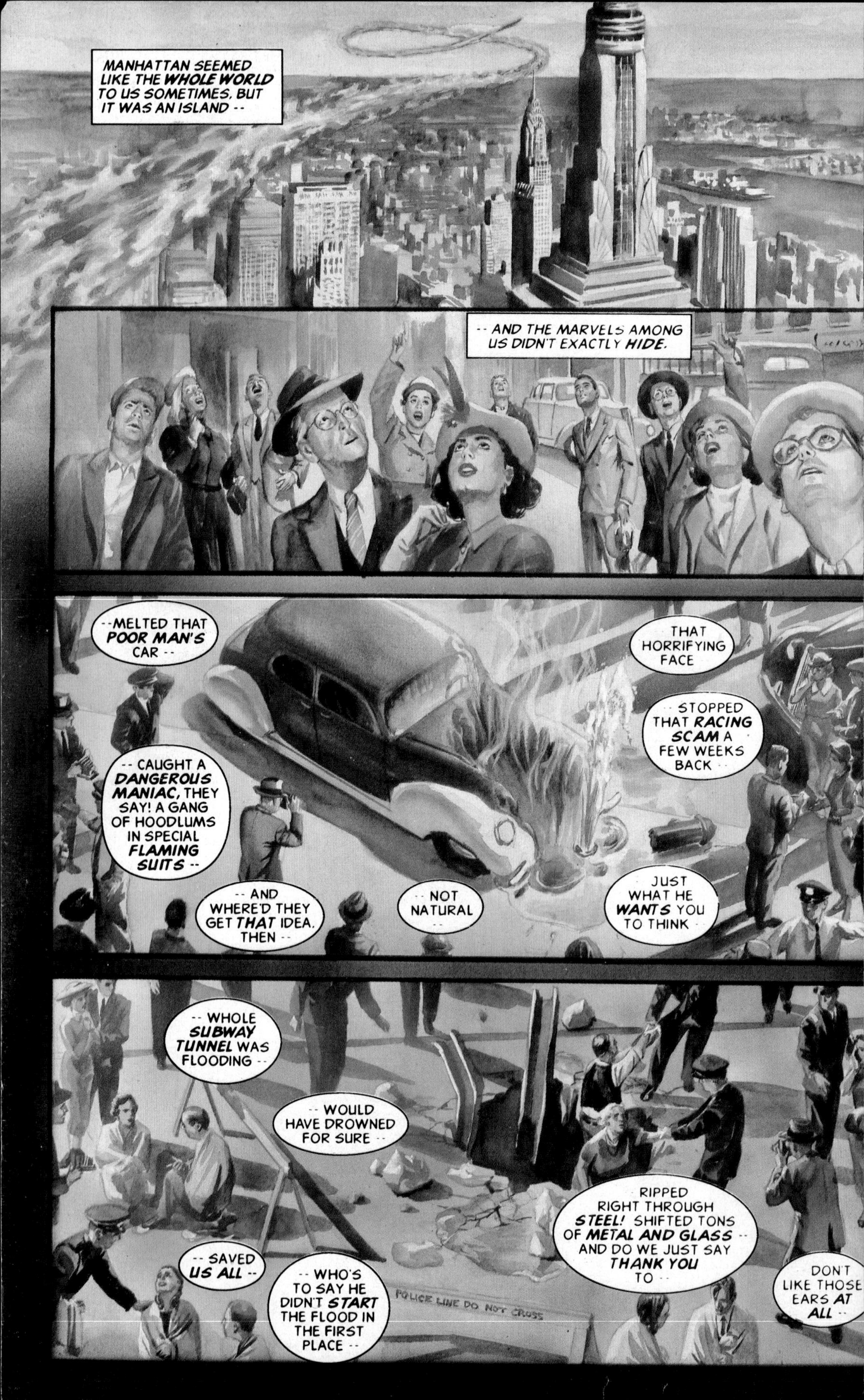
MANHATTAN SEEMED LIKE THE WHOLE WORLD TO US SOMETIMES, BUT IT WAS AN ISLAND --
-- AND THE MARVELS AMONG US DIDN'T EXACTLY HIDE.
--MELTED THAT POOR MAN'S CAR --
THAT HORRIFYING FACE
-- STOPPED THAT RACING SCAM A FEW WEEKS BACK --
-- CAUGHT A DANGEROUS MANIAC, THEY SAY! A GANG OF HOODLUMS IN SPECIAL FLAMING SUITS --
-- AND WHERE'D THEY GET THAT IDEA, THEN --
-- NOT NATURAL --
-- JUST WHAT HE WANTS YOU TO THINK
-- WHOLE SUBWAY TUNNEL WAS FLOODING --
-- WOULD HAVE DROWNED FOR SURE --
-- RIPPED RIGHT THROUGH STEEL! SHIFTED TONS OF METAL AND GLASS -- AND DO WE JUST SAY THANK YOU TO --
-- SAVED US ALL --
-- WHO'S TO SAY HE DIDN'T START THE FLOOD IN THE FIRST PLACE --
POLICE LINE DO NOT CROSS
DON'T LIKE THOSE EARS AT ALL --

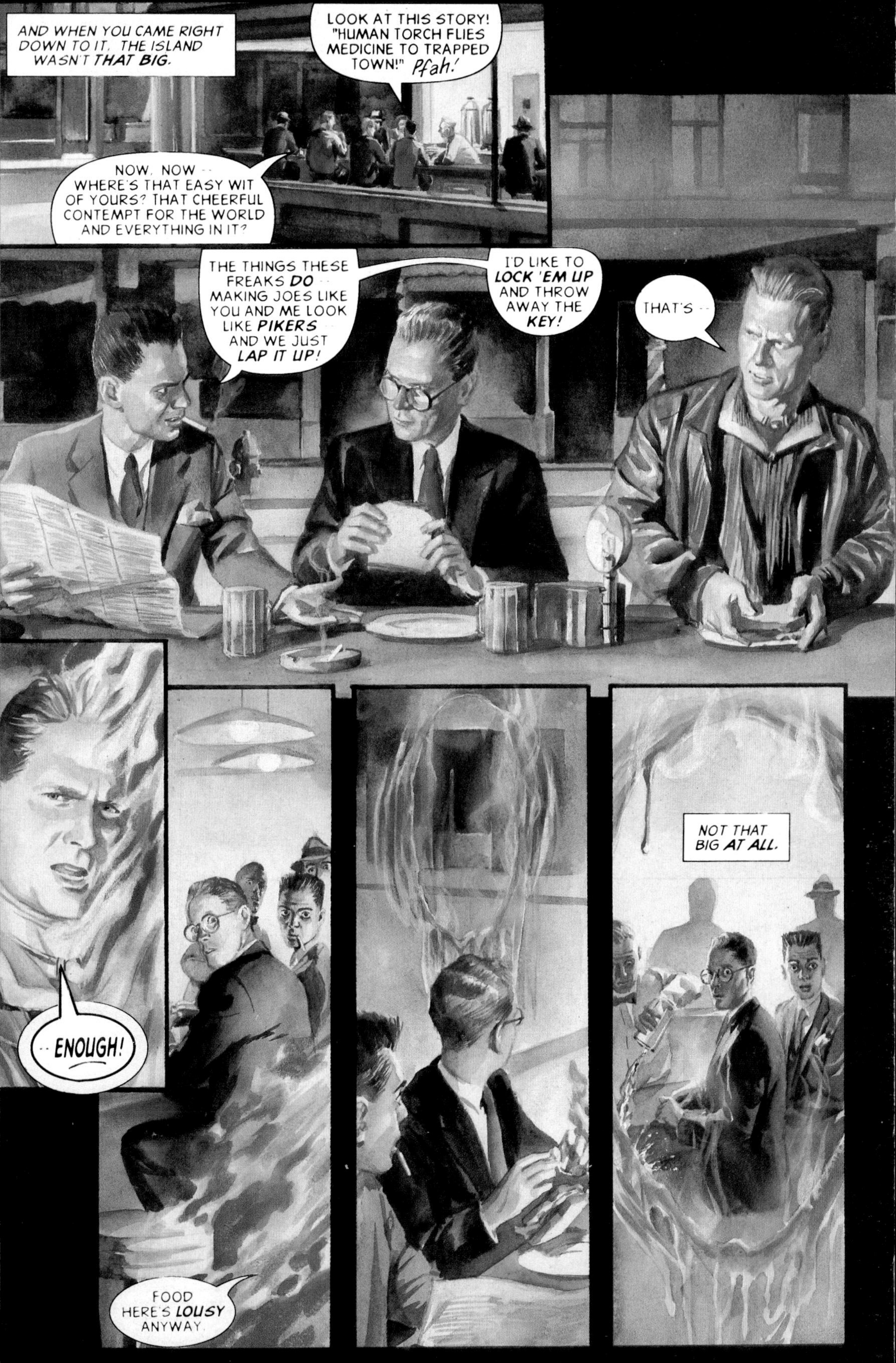
AND WHEN YOU CAME RIGHT DOWN TO IT, THE ISLAND WASN'T THAT BIG.
LOOK AT THIS STORY! "HUMAN TORCH FLIES MEDICINE TO TRAPPED TOWN!" Pfah!
NOW, NOW -- WHERE'S THAT EASY WIT OF YOURS? THAT CHEERFUL CONTEMPT FOR THE WORLD AND EVERYTHING IN IT?
THE THINGS THESE FREAKS DO -- MAKING JOES LIKE YOU AND ME LOOK LIKE PIKERS -- AND WE JUST LAP IT UP!
I'D LIKE TO LOCK 'EM UP AND THROW AWAY THE KEY!
THAT'S --
-- ENOUGH!
FOOD HERE'S LOUSY ANYWAY.
NOT THAT BIG AT ALL.

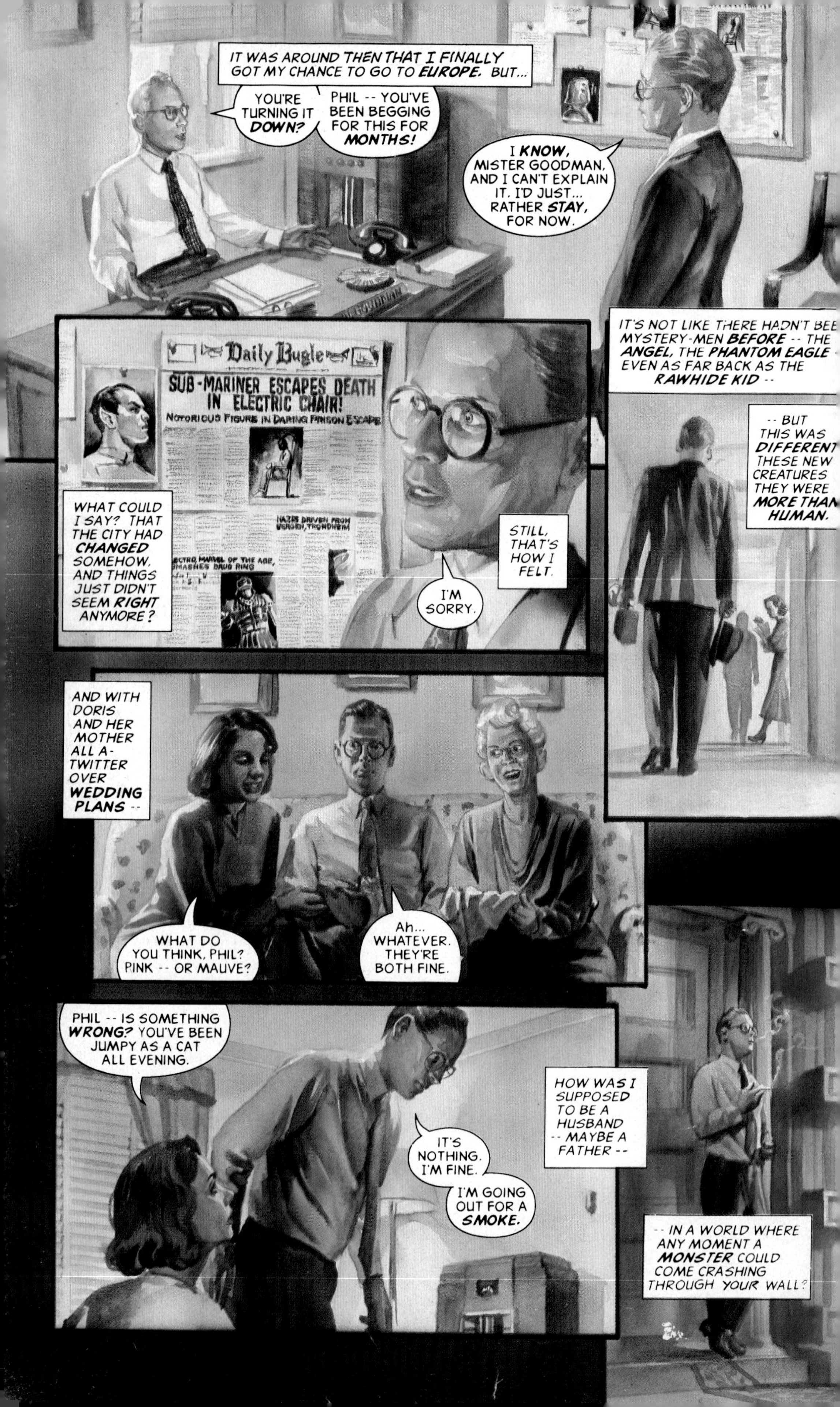

IT WAS AROUND THEN THAT I FINALLY GOT MY CHANCE TO GO TO EUROPE. BUT...
YOU'RE TURNING IT DOWN?
PHIL -- YOU'VE BEEN BEGGING FOR THIS FOR MONTHS!
I KNOW, MISTER GOODMAN, AND I CAN'T EXPLAIN IT. I'D JUST... RATHER STAY, FOR NOW.
Daily Bugle
SUB-MARINER ESCAPES DEATH IN ELECTRIC CHAIR!
NOTORIOUS FIGURE IN DARING PRISON ESCAPE
NAZIS DRIVEN FROM BERGEN, TRONDHEIM
WHAT COULD I SAY? THAT THE CITY HAD CHANGED SOMEHOW, AND THINGS JUST DIDN'T SEEM RIGHT ANYMORE?
I'M SORRY.
STILL, THAT'S HOW I FELT.
IT'S NOT LIKE THERE HADN'T BEE MYSTERY-MEN BEFORE -- THE ANGEL, THE PHANTOM EAGLE -- EVEN AS FAR BACK AS THE RAWHIDE KID --
-- BUT THIS WAS DIFFERENT THESE NEW CREATURES THEY WERE MORE THAN HUMAN.
AND WITH DORIS AND HER MOTHER ALL A-TWITTER OVER WEDDING PLANS --
WHAT DO YOU THINK, PHIL? PINK -- OR MAUVE?
Ah... WHATEVER. THEY'RE BOTH FINE.
PHIL -- IS SOMETHING WRONG? YOU'VE BEEN JUMPY AS A CAT ALL EVENING.
IT'S NOTHING. I'M FINE.
I'M GOING OUT FOR A SMOKE.
HOW WAS I SUPPOSED TO BE A HUSBAND -- MAYBE A FATHER --
-- IN A WORLD WHERE ANY MOMENT A MONSTER COULD COME CRASHING THROUGH YOUR WALL?

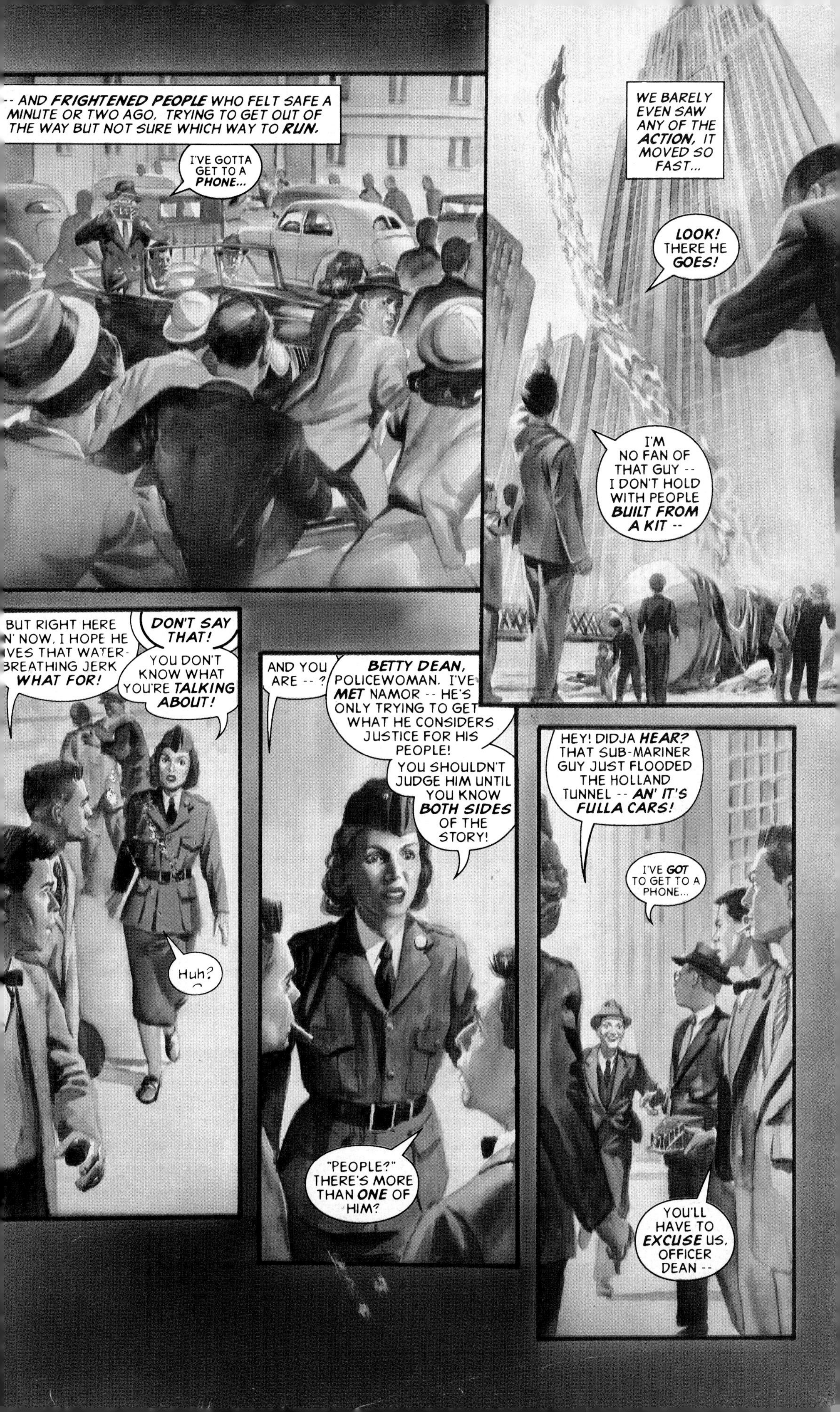
-- AND FRIGHTENED PEOPLE WHO FELT SAFE A MINUTE OR TWO AGO, TRYING TO GET OUT OF THE WAY BUT NOT SURE WHICH WAY TO RUN.
I'VE GOTTA GET TO A PHONE...
WE BARELY EVEN SAW ANY OF THE ACTION, IT MOVED SO FAST...
LOOK! THERE HE GOES!
I'M NO FAN OF THAT GUY -- I DON'T HOLD WITH PEOPLE BUILT FROM A KIT --
BUT RIGHT HERE N' NOW, I HOPE HE IVES THAT WATER-BREATHING JERK WHAT FOR!
DON'T SAY THAT!
YOU DON'T KNOW WHAT YOU'RE TALKING ABOUT!
Huh?
AND YOU ARE -- ?
BETTY DEAN, POLICEWOMAN. I'VE MET NAMOR -- HE'S ONLY TRYING TO GET WHAT HE CONSIDERS JUSTICE FOR HIS PEOPLE!
YOU SHOULDN'T JUDGE HIM UNTIL YOU KNOW BOTH SIDES OF THE STORY!
"PEOPLE?" THERE'S MORE THAN ONE OF HIM?
HEY! DIDJA HEAR? THAT SUB-MARINER GUY JUST FLOODED THE HOLLAND TUNNEL -- AN' IT'S FULLA CARS!
I'VE GOT TO GET TO A PHONE...
YOU'LL HAVE TO EXCUSE US, OFFICER DEAN --

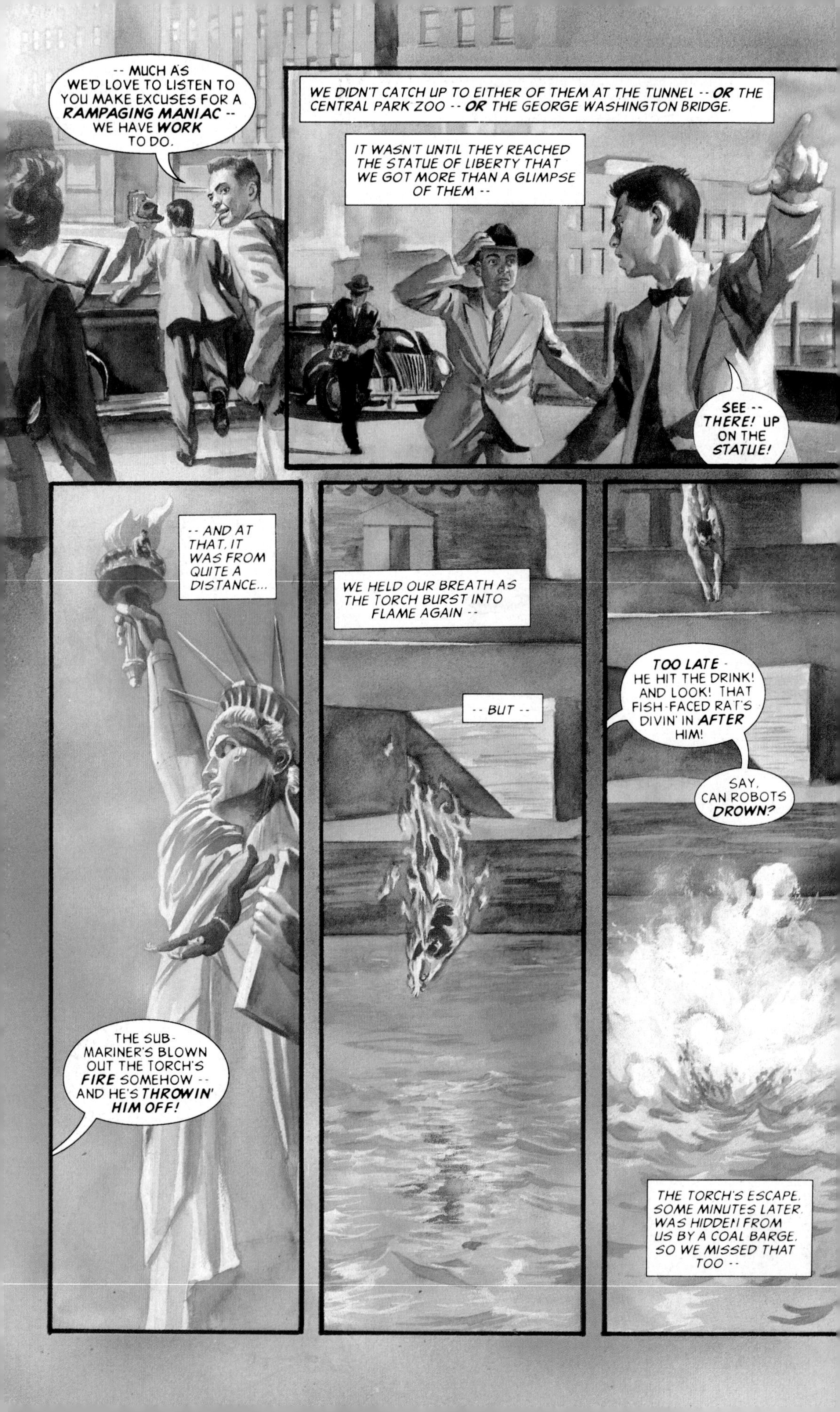
-- MUCH AS WE'D LOVE TO LISTEN TO YOU MAKE EXCUSES FOR A RAMPAGING MANIAC -- WE HAVE WORK TO DO.
WE DIDN'T CATCH UP TO EITHER OF THEM AT THE TUNNEL -- OR THE CENTRAL PARK ZOO -- OR THE GEORGE WASHINGTON BRIDGE.
IT WASN'T UNTIL THEY REACHED THE STATUE OF LIBERTY THAT WE GOT MORE THAN A GLIMPSE OF THEM --
SEE -- THERE! UP ON THE STATUE!
-- AND AT THAT, IT WAS FROM QUITE A DISTANCE...
THE SUB-MARINER'S BLOWN OUT THE TORCH'S FIRE SOMEHOW -- AND HE'S THROWIN' HIM OFF!
WE HELD OUR BREATH AS THE TORCH BURST INTO FLAME AGAIN --
-- BUT --
TOO LATE - HE HIT THE DRINK! AND LOOK! THAT FISH-FACED RAT'S DIVIN' IN AFTER HIM!
SAY, CAN ROBOTS DROWN?
THE TORCH'S ESCAPE, SOME MINUTES LATER, WAS HIDDEN FROM US BY A COAL BARGE, SO WE MISSED THAT TOO --

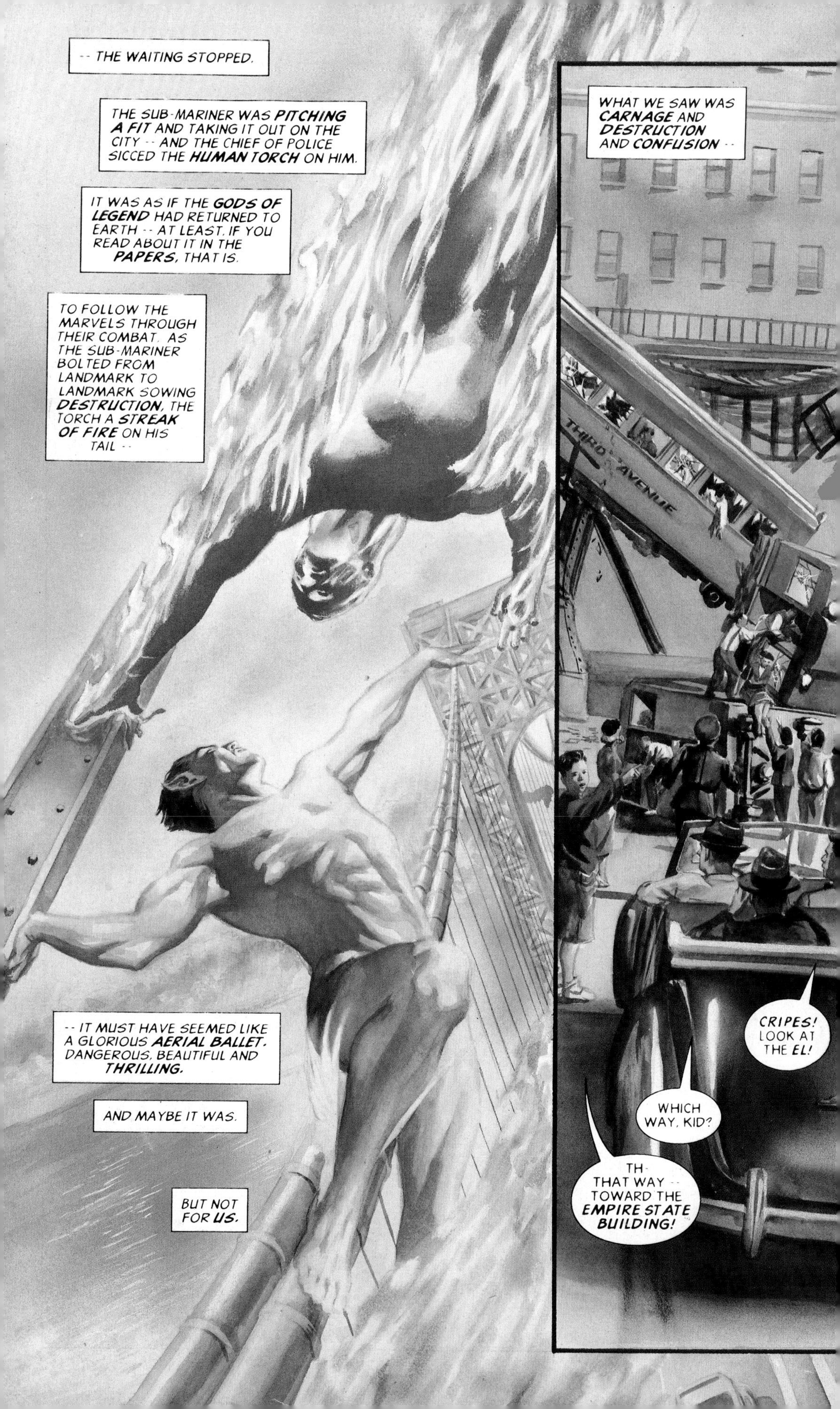
-- THE WAITING STOPPED.
THE SUB-MARINER WAS PITCHING A FIT AND TAKING IT OUT ON THE CITY -- AND THE CHIEF OF POLICE SICCED THE HUMAN TORCH ON HIM.
IT WAS AS IF THE GODS OF LEGEND HAD RETURNED TO EARTH -- AT LEAST, IF YOU READ ABOUT IT IN THE PAPERS, THAT IS.
TO FOLLOW THE MARVELS THROUGH THEIR COMBAT. AS THE SUB-MARINER BOLTED FROM LANDMARK TO LANDMARK SOWING DESTRUCTION, THE TORCH A STREAK OF FIRE ON HIS TAIL --
-- IT MUST HAVE SEEMED LIKE A GLORIOUS AERIAL BALLET. DANGEROUS, BEAUTIFUL AND THRILLING.
AND MAYBE IT WAS.
BUT NOT FOR US.
WHAT WE SAW WAS CARNAGE AND DESTRUCTION AND CONFUSION --
THIRD AVENUE
CRIPES! LOOK AT THE EL!
WHICH WAY, KID?
TH-THAT WAY -- TOWARD THE EMPIRE STATE BUILDING!

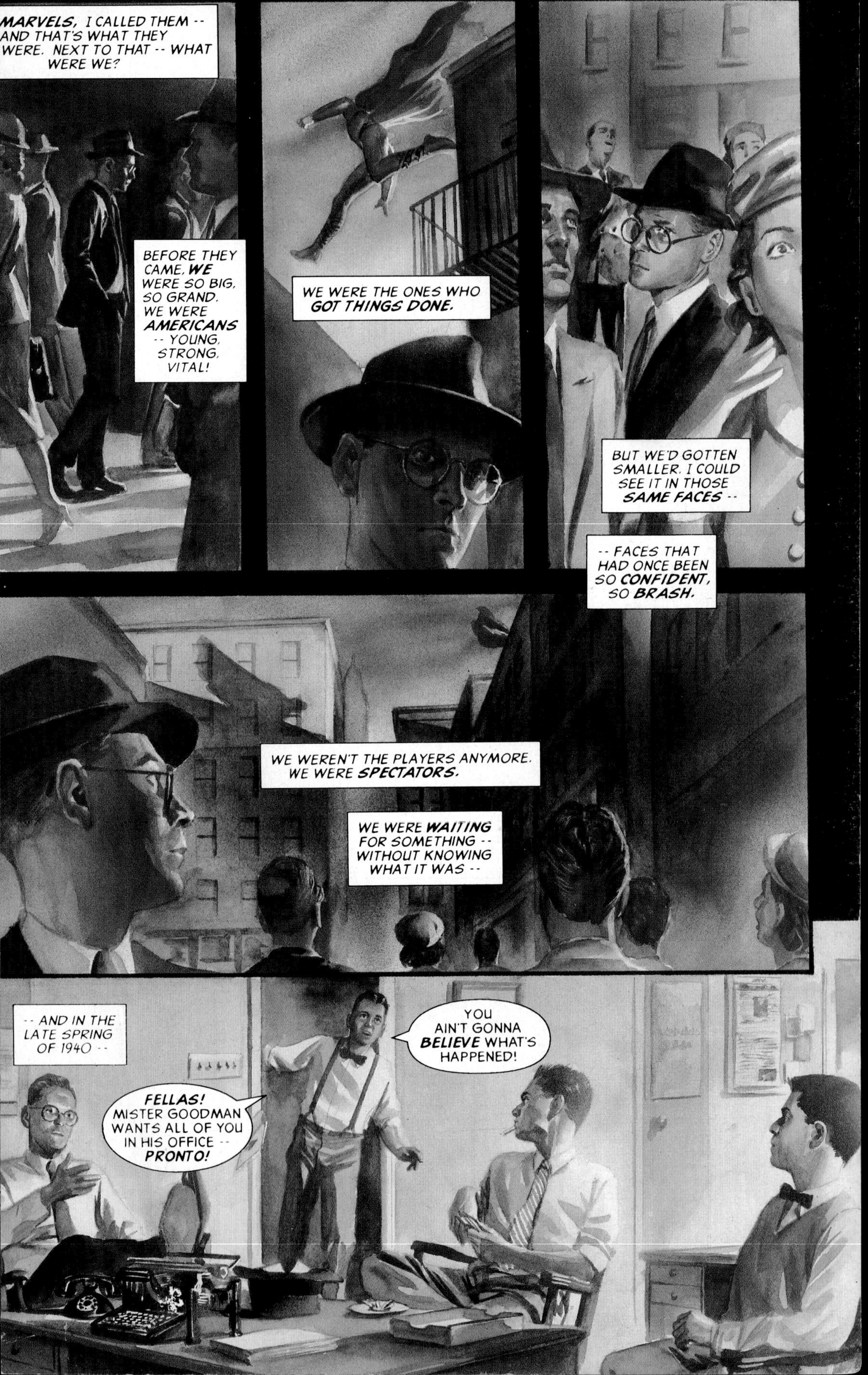
MARVELS, I CALLED THEM -- AND THAT'S WHAT THEY WERE. NEXT TO THAT -- WHAT WERE WE?
BEFORE THEY CAME, WE WERE SO BIG, SO GRAND. WE WERE AMERICANS -- YOUNG, STRONG, VITAL!
WE WERE THE ONES WHO GOT THINGS DONE.
BUT WE'D GOTTEN SMALLER. I COULD SEE IT IN THOSE SAME FACES --
-- FACES THAT HAD ONCE BEEN SO CONFIDENT, SO BRASH.
WE WEREN'T THE PLAYERS ANYMORE. WE WERE SPECTATORS.
WE WERE WAITING FOR SOMETHING -- WITHOUT KNOWING WHAT IT WAS --
-- AND IN THE LATE SPRING OF 1940 --
FELLAS! MISTER GOODMAN WANTS ALL OF YOU IN HIS OFFICE -- PRONTO!
YOU AIN'T GONNA BELIEVE WHAT'S HAPPENED!

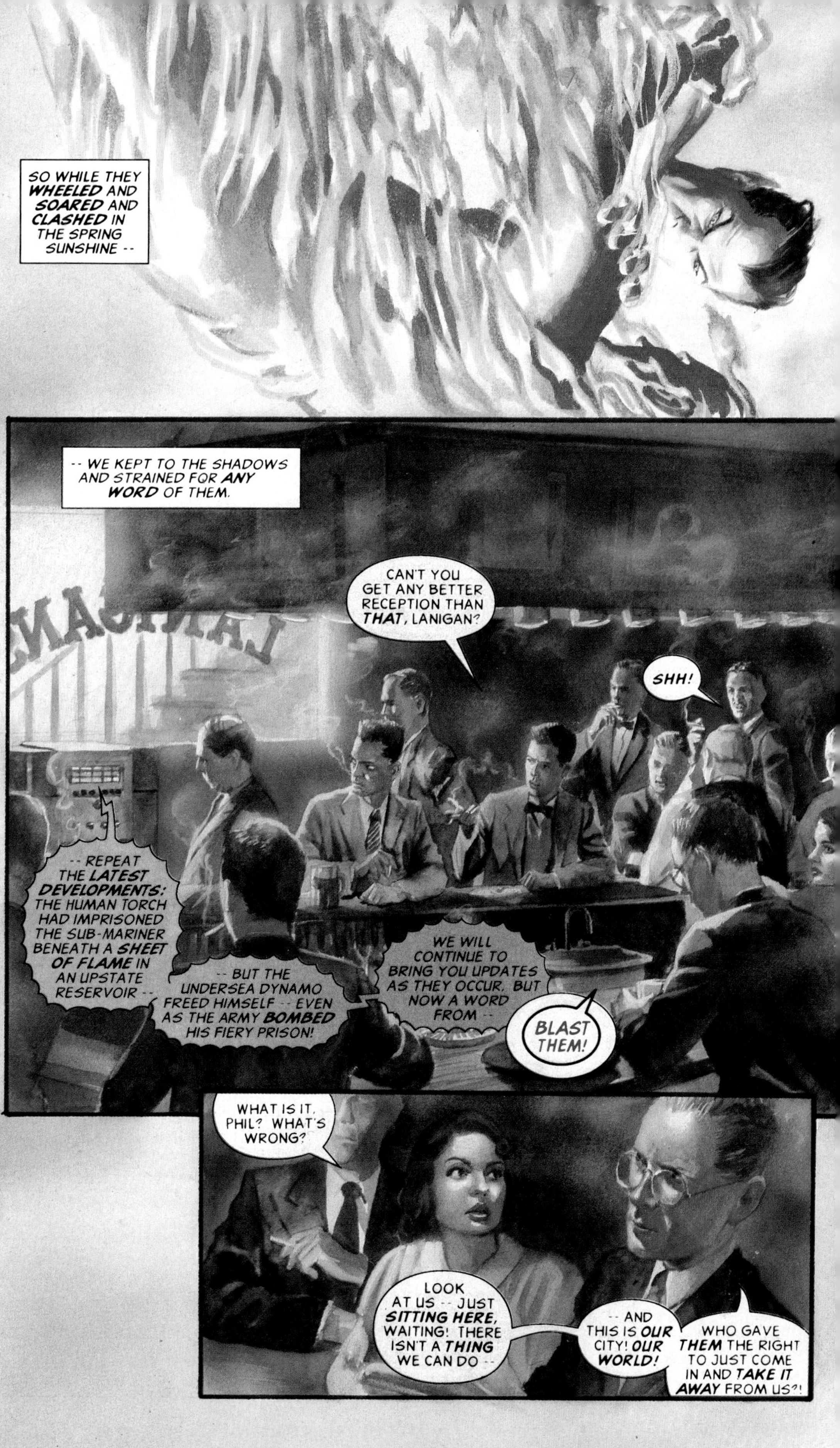

SO WHILE THEY WHEELED AND SOARED AND CLASHED IN THE SPRING SUNSHINE --
-- WE KEPT TO THE SHADOWS AND STRAINED FOR ANY WORD OF THEM.
CAN'T YOU GET ANY BETTER RECEPTION THAN THAT, LANIGAN?
SHH!
-- REPEAT THE LATEST DEVELOPMENTS: THE HUMAN TORCH HAD IMPRISONED THE SUB-MARINER BENEATH A SHEET OF FLAME IN AN UPSTATE RESERVOIR --
-- BUT THE UNDERSEA DYNAMO FREED HIMSELF -- EVEN AS THE ARMY BOMBED HIS FIERY PRISON!
WE WILL CONTINUE TO BRING YOU UPDATES AS THEY OCCUR. BUT NOW A WORD FROM --
BLAST THEM!
WHAT IS IT, PHIL? WHAT'S WRONG?
LOOK AT US -- JUST SITTING HERE, WAITING! THERE ISN'T A THING WE CAN DO --
-- AND THIS IS OUR CITY! OUR WORLD!
WHO GAVE THEM THE RIGHT TO JUST COME IN AND TAKE IT AWAY FROM US?!

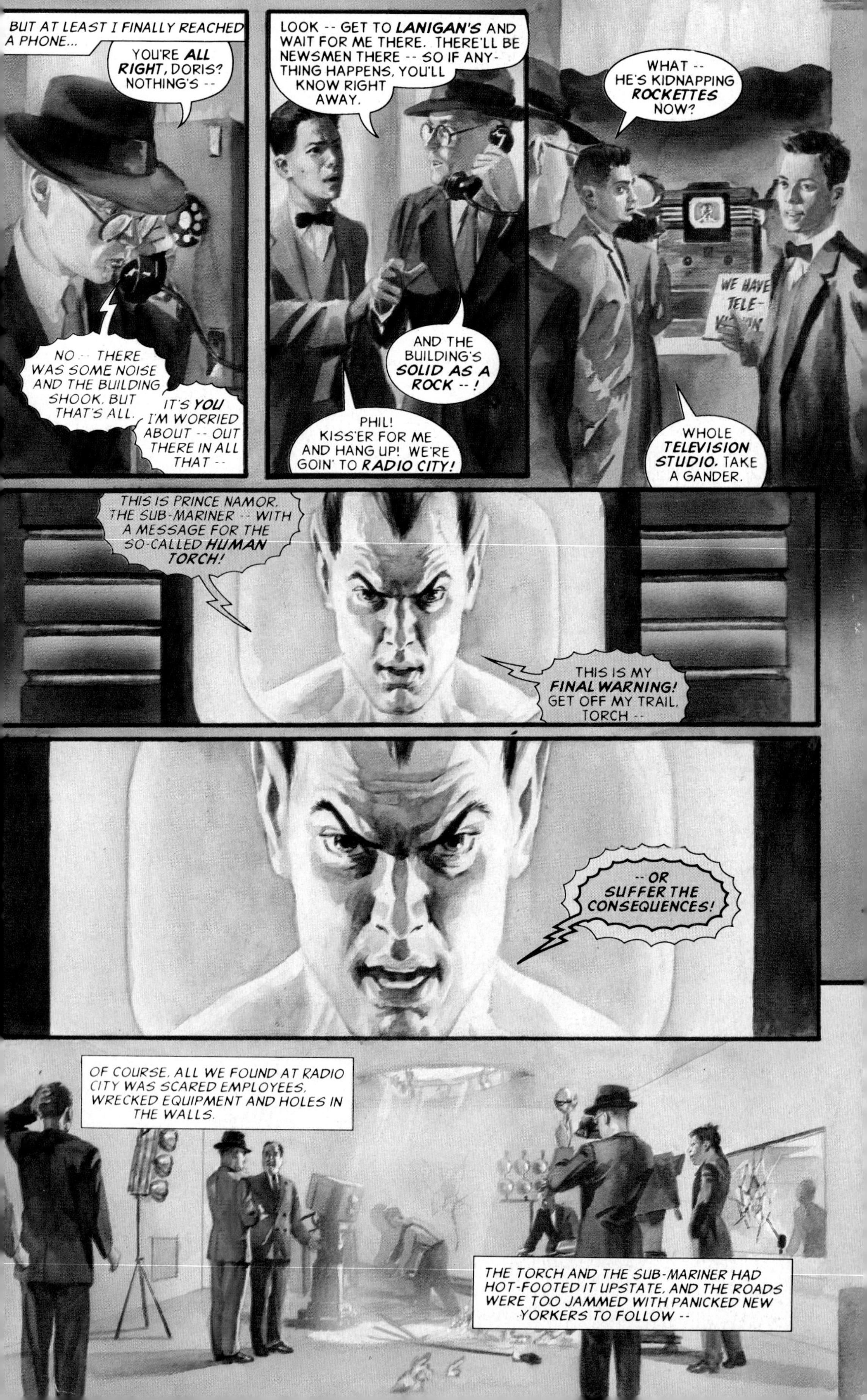

BUT AT LEAST I FINALLY REACHED A PHONE...
YOU'RE ALL RIGHT, DORIS? NOTHING'S --
NO -- THERE WAS SOME NOISE AND THE BUILDING SHOOK, BUT THAT'S ALL.
IT'S YOU I'M WORRIED ABOUT -- OUT THERE IN ALL THAT --
LOOK -- GET TO LANIGAN'S AND WAIT FOR ME THERE. THERE'LL BE NEWSMEN THERE -- SO IF ANYTHING HAPPENS, YOU'LL KNOW RIGHT AWAY.
AND THE BUILDING'S SOLID AS A ROCK -- !
PHIL! KISS'ER FOR ME AND HANG UP! WE'RE GOIN' TO RADIO CITY!
WHAT -- HE'S KIDNAPPING ROCKETTES NOW?
WHOLE TELEVISION STUDIO. TAKE A GANDER.
THIS IS PRINCE NAMOR, THE SUB-MARINER -- WITH A MESSAGE FOR THE SO-CALLED HUMAN TORCH!
THIS IS MY FINAL WARNING! GET OFF MY TRAIL, TORCH --
-- OR SUFFER THE CONSEQUENCES!
OF COURSE, ALL WE FOUND AT RADIO CITY WAS SCARED EMPLOYEES, WRECKED EQUIPMENT AND HOLES IN THE WALLS.
THE TORCH AND THE SUB-MARINER HAD HOT-FOOTED IT UPSTATE, AND THE ROADS WERE TOO JAMMED WITH PANICKED NEW YORKERS TO FOLLOW --

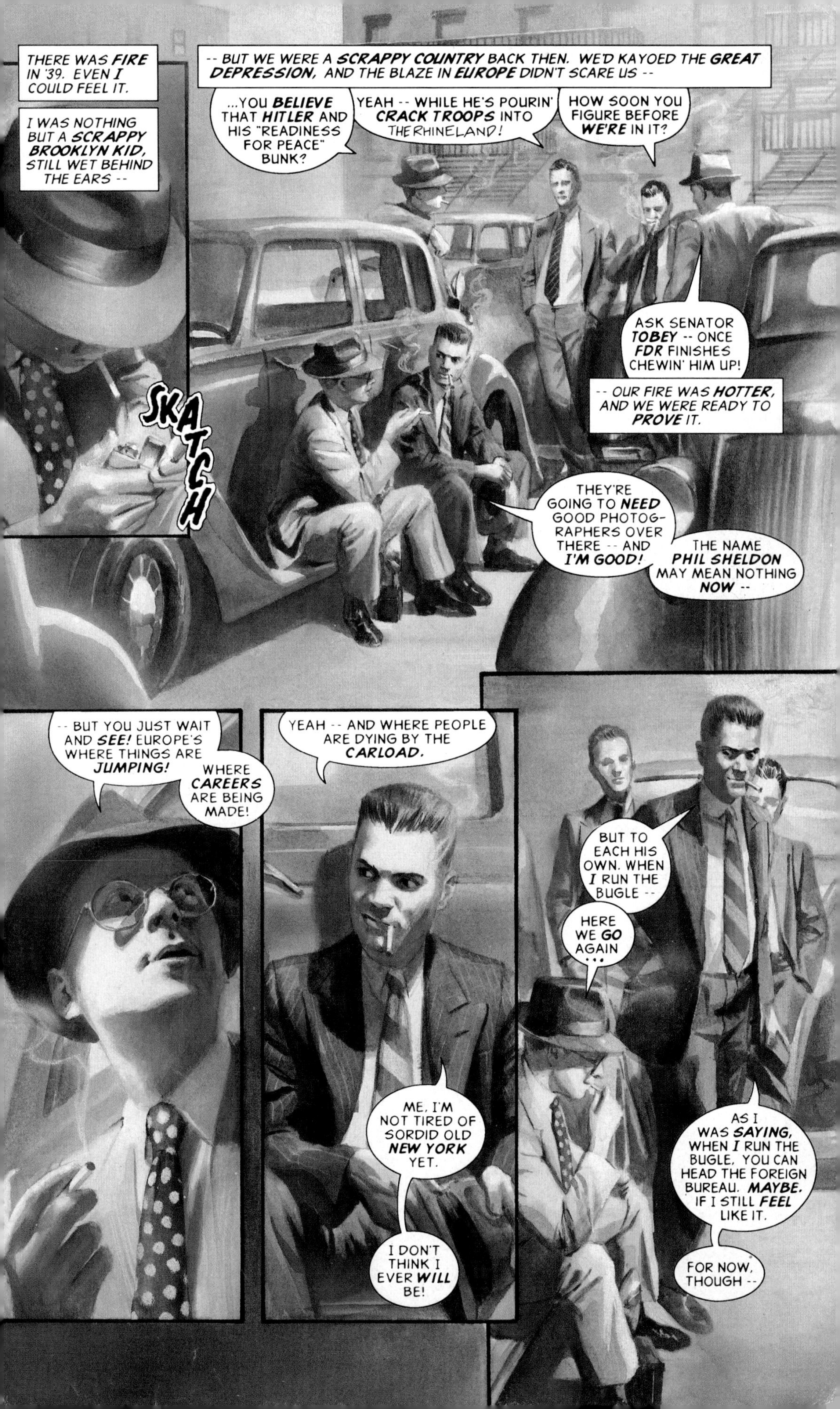
THERE WAS FIRE IN '39. EVEN I COULD FEEL IT.
I WAS NOTHING BUT A SCRAPPY BROOKLYN KID, STILL WET BEHIND THE EARS --
-- BUT WE WERE A SCRAPPY COUNTRY BACK THEN. WE'D KAYOED THE GREAT DEPRESSION, AND THE BLAZE IN EUROPE DIDN'T SCARE US --
...YOU BELIEVE THAT HITLER AND HIS "READINESS FOR PEACE" BUNK?
YEAH -- WHILE HE'S POURIN' CRACK TROOPS INTO THE RHINELAND!
HOW SOON YOU FIGURE BEFORE WE'RE IN IT?
SKATCH
ASK SENATOR TOBEY -- ONCE FDR FINISHES CHEWIN' HIM UP!
-- OUR FIRE WAS HOTTER, AND WE WERE READY TO PROVE IT.
THEY'RE GOING TO NEED GOOD PHOTOG-RAPHERS OVER THERE -- AND I'M GOOD!
THE NAME PHIL SHELDON MAY MEAN NOTHING NOW --
-- BUT YOU JUST WAIT AND SEE! EUROPE'S WHERE THINGS ARE JUMPING!
WHERE CAREERS ARE BEING MADE!
YEAH -- AND WHERE PEOPLE ARE DYING BY THE CARLOAD.
ME, I'M NOT TIRED OF SORDID OLD NEW YORK YET.
I DON'T THINK I EVER WILL BE!
BUT TO EACH HIS OWN. WHEN I RUN THE BUGLE --
HERE WE GO AGAIN . . .
AS I WAS SAYING, WHEN I RUN THE BUGLE, YOU CAN HEAD THE FOREIGN BUREAU. MAYBE. IF I STILL FEEL LIKE IT.
FOR NOW, THOUGH --

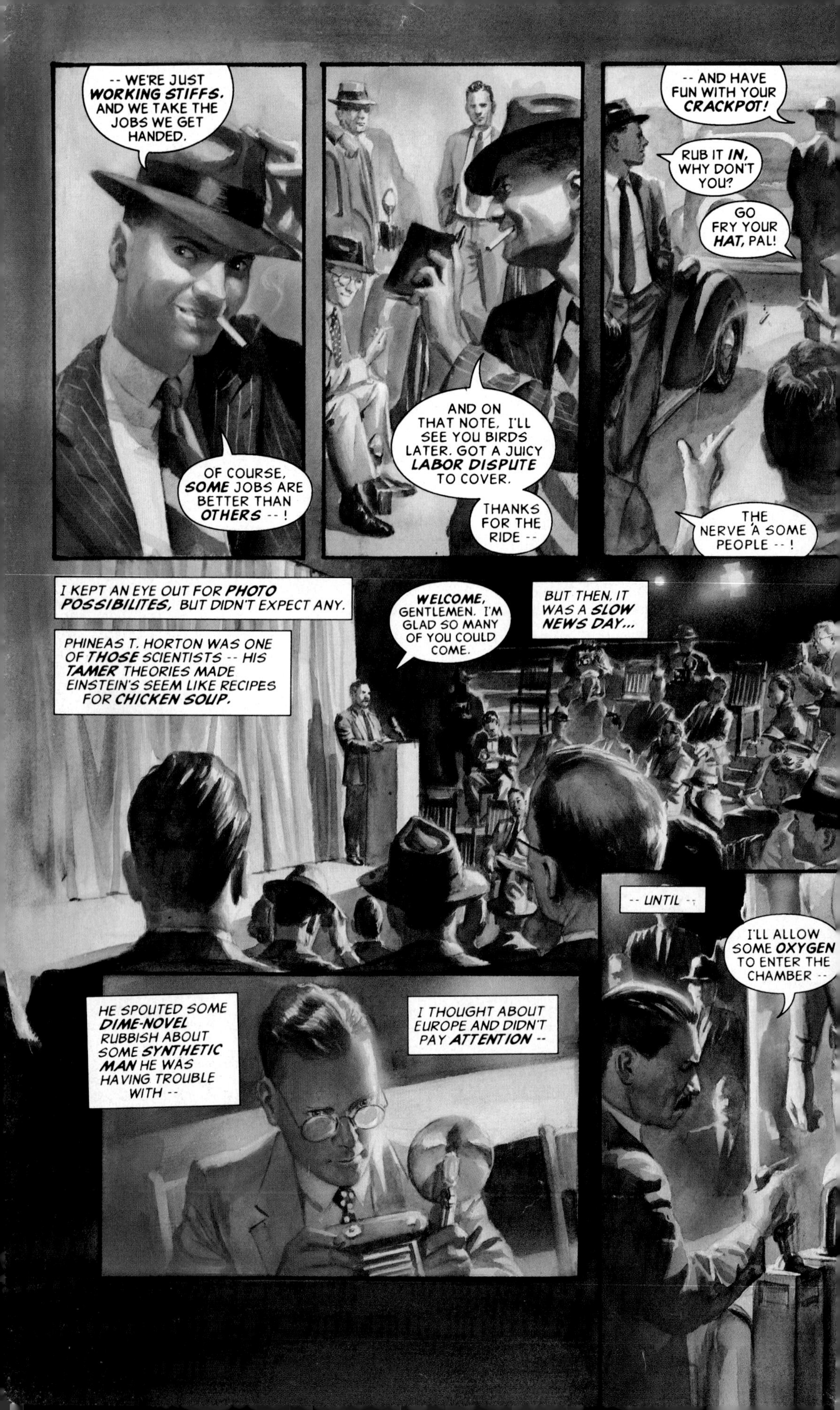
-- WE'RE JUST **WORKING STIFFS.** AND WE TAKE THE JOBS WE GET HANDED.
OF COURSE, **SOME** JOBS ARE BETTER THAN **OTHERS** -- !
AND ON THAT NOTE, I'LL SEE YOU BIRDS LATER. GOT A JUICY **LABOR DISPUTE** TO COVER.
THANKS FOR THE RIDE --
-- AND HAVE FUN WITH YOUR **CRACKPOT!**
RUB IT **IN,** WHY DON'T YOU?
GO FRY YOUR **HAT,** PAL!
THE NERVE 'A SOME PEOPLE -- !
I KEPT AN EYE OUT FOR **PHOTO POSSIBILITES,** BUT DIDN'T EXPECT ANY.
PHINEAS T. HORTON WAS ONE OF **THOSE** SCIENTISTS -- HIS **TAMER** THEORIES MADE EINSTEIN'S SEEM LIKE RECIPES FOR **CHICKEN SOUP.**
WELCOME, GENTLEMEN. I'M GLAD SO MANY OF YOU COULD COME.
BUT THEN, IT WAS A **SLOW NEWS DAY...**
HE SPOUTED SOME **DIME-NOVEL** RUBBISH ABOUT SOME **SYNTHETIC MAN** HE WAS HAVING TROUBLE WITH --
I THOUGHT ABOUT EUROPE AND DIDN'T PAY **ATTENTION** --
-- UNTIL --
I'LL ALLOW SOME **OXYGEN** TO ENTER THE CHAMBER --

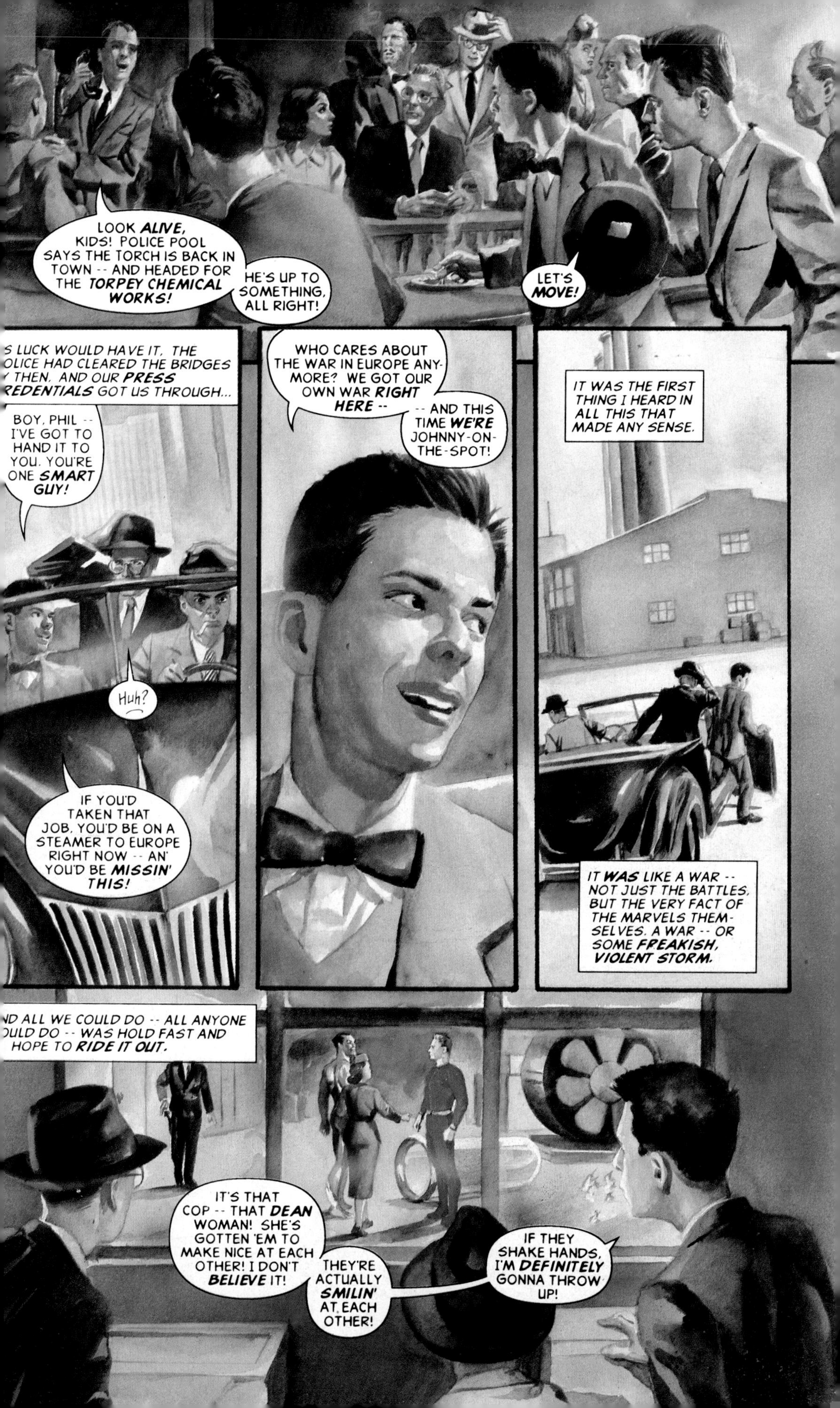

LOOK ALIVE, KIDS! POLICE POOL SAYS THE TORCH IS BACK IN TOWN -- AND HEADED FOR THE TORPEY CHEMICAL WORKS!
HE'S UP TO SOMETHING, ALL RIGHT!
LET'S MOVE!
S LUCK WOULD HAVE IT, THE OLICE HAD CLEARED THE BRIDGES THEN, AND OUR PRESS REDENTIALS GOT US THROUGH...
BOY, PHIL -- I'VE GOT TO HAND IT TO YOU. YOU'RE ONE SMART GUY!
Huh?
IF YOU'D TAKEN THAT JOB, YOU'D BE ON A STEAMER TO EUROPE RIGHT NOW -- AN' YOU'D BE MISSIN' THIS!
WHO CARES ABOUT THE WAR IN EUROPE ANY-MORE? WE GOT OUR OWN WAR RIGHT HERE --
-- AND THIS TIME WE'RE JOHNNY-ON-THE-SPOT!
IT WAS THE FIRST THING I HEARD IN ALL THIS THAT MADE ANY SENSE.
IT WAS LIKE A WAR -- NOT JUST THE BATTLES, BUT THE VERY FACT OF THE MARVELS THEM-SELVES. A WAR -- OR SOME FREAKISH, VIOLENT STORM.
ND ALL WE COULD DO -- ALL ANYONE OULD DO -- WAS HOLD FAST AND HOPE TO RIDE IT OUT.
IT'S THAT COP -- THAT DEAN WOMAN! SHE'S GOTTEN 'EM TO MAKE NICE AT EACH OTHER! I DON'T BELIEVE IT!
THEY'RE ACTUALLY SMILIN' AT EACH OTHER!
IF THEY SHAKE HANDS, I'M DEFINITELY GONNA THROW UP!

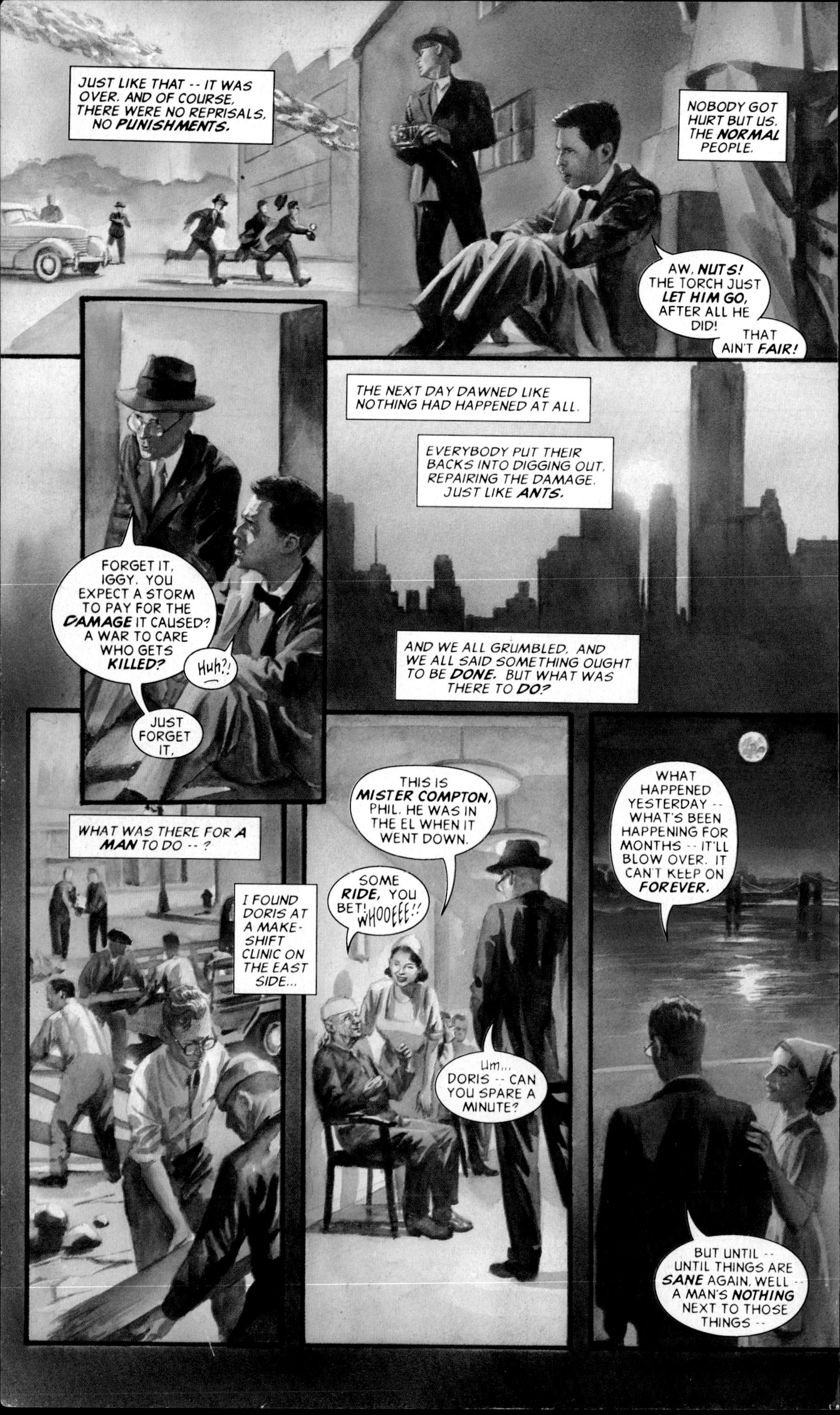

JUST LIKE THAT -- IT WAS OVER. AND OF COURSE, THERE WERE NO REPRISALS, NO PUNISHMENTS.
NOBODY GOT HURT BUT US. THE NORMAL PEOPLE.
AW, NUTS! THE TORCH JUST LET HIM GO, AFTER ALL HE DID!
THAT AIN'T FAIR!
FORGET IT, IGGY. YOU EXPECT A STORM TO PAY FOR THE DAMAGE IT CAUSED? A WAR TO CARE WHO GETS KILLED?
Huh?!
JUST FORGET IT.
THE NEXT DAY DAWNED LIKE NOTHING HAD HAPPENED AT ALL.
EVERYBODY PUT THEIR BACKS INTO DIGGING OUT, REPAIRING THE DAMAGE. JUST LIKE ANTS.
AND WE ALL GRUMBLED, AND WE ALL SAID SOMETHING OUGHT TO BE DONE. BUT WHAT WAS THERE TO DO?
WHAT WAS THERE FOR A MAN TO DO -- ?
I FOUND DORIS AT A MAKE-SHIFT CLINIC ON THE EAST SIDE...
THIS IS MISTER COMPTON, PHIL. HE WAS IN THE EL WHEN IT WENT DOWN.
SOME RIDE, YOU BET! WHOOEEE!!
Um... DORIS -- CAN YOU SPARE A MINUTE?
WHAT HAPPENED YESTERDAY -- WHAT'S BEEN HAPPENING FOR MONTHS -- IT'LL BLOW OVER. IT CAN'T KEEP ON FOREVER.
BUT UNTIL -- UNTIL THINGS ARE SANE AGAIN, WELL -- A MAN'S NOTHING NEXT TO THOSE THINGS --

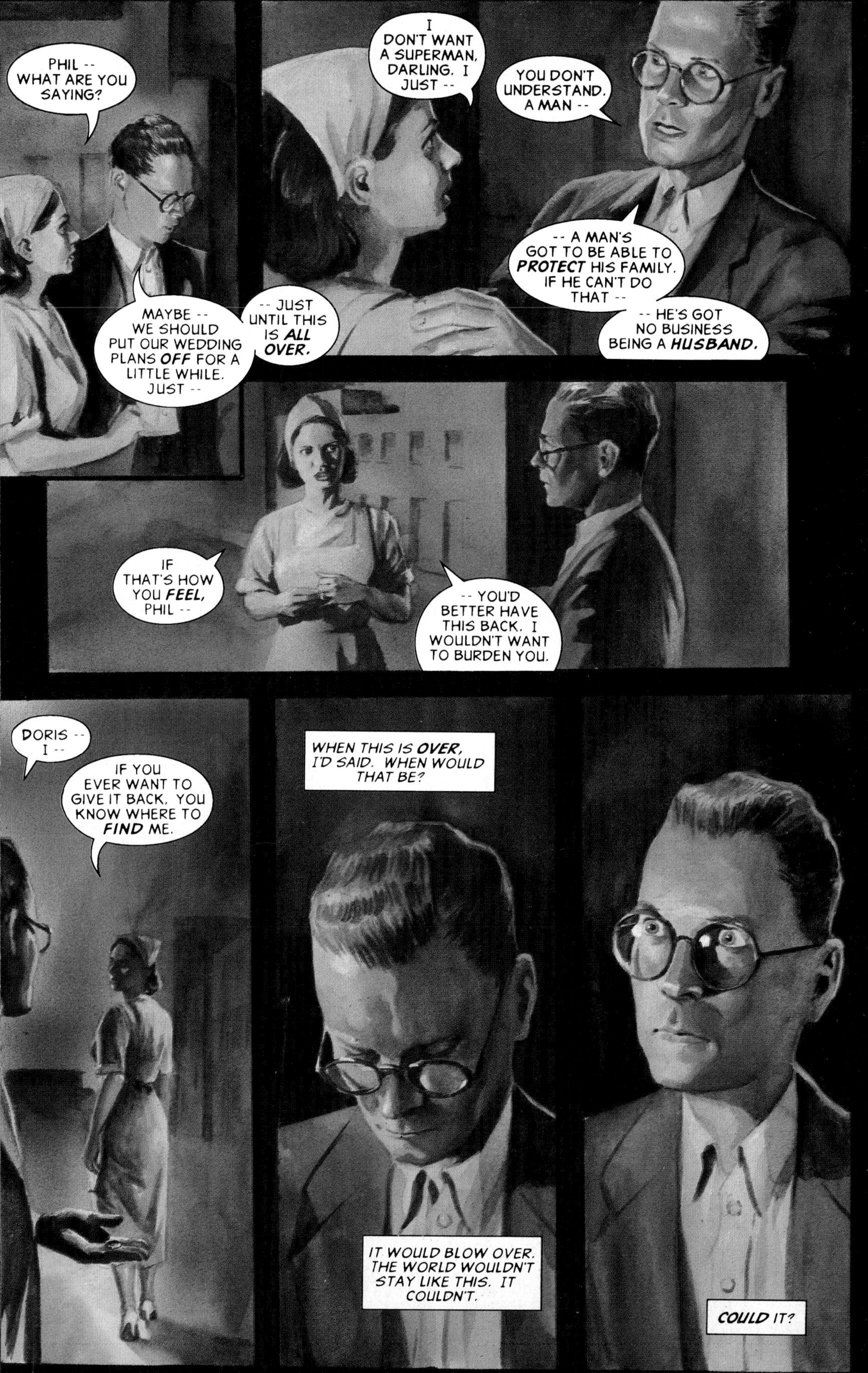
PHIL -- WHAT ARE YOU SAYING?
MAYBE -- WE SHOULD PUT OUR WEDDING PLANS **OFF** FOR A LITTLE WHILE. JUST --
-- JUST UNTIL THIS IS **ALL OVER.**
I DON'T WANT A SUPERMAN, DARLING. I JUST --
YOU DON'T UNDERSTAND. A MAN --
-- A MAN'S GOT TO BE ABLE TO **PROTECT** HIS FAMILY. IF HE CAN'T DO THAT --
-- HE'S GOT NO BUSINESS BEING A **HUSBAND.**
IF THAT'S HOW YOU **FEEL,** PHIL --
-- YOU'D BETTER HAVE THIS BACK. I WOULDN'T WANT TO BURDEN YOU.
DORIS -- I --
IF YOU EVER WANT TO GIVE IT BACK, YOU KNOW WHERE TO **FIND** ME.
*WHEN THIS IS **OVER**, I'D SAID. WHEN WOULD THAT BE?*
IT WOULD BLOW OVER. THE WORLD WOULDN'T STAY LIKE THIS. IT COULDN'T.
***COULD** IT?*

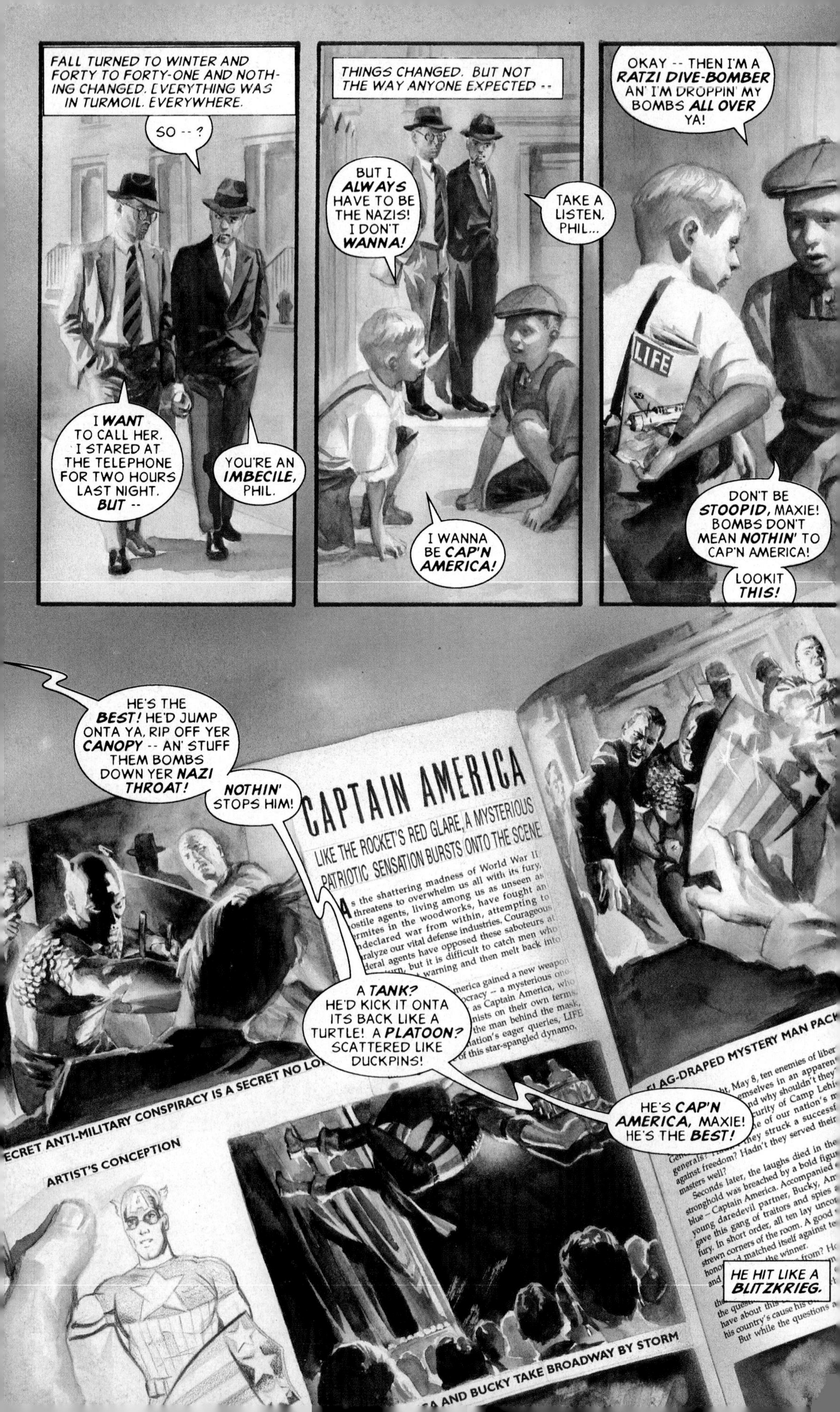

FALL TURNED TO WINTER AND FORTY TO FORTY-ONE AND NOTHING CHANGED. EVERYTHING WAS IN TURMOIL. EVERYWHERE.
SO -- ?
I WANT TO CALL HER. I STARED AT THE TELEPHONE FOR TWO HOURS LAST NIGHT. BUT --
YOU'RE AN IMBECILE, PHIL.
THINGS CHANGED. BUT NOT THE WAY ANYONE EXPECTED --
BUT I ALWAYS HAVE TO BE THE NAZIS! I DON'T WANNA!
TAKE A LISTEN, PHIL...
I WANNA BE CAP'N AMERICA!
OKAY -- THEN I'M A RATZI DIVE-BOMBER AN' I'M DROPPIN' MY BOMBS ALL OVER YA!
LIFE
DON'T BE STOOPID, MAXIE! BOMBS DON'T MEAN NOTHIN' TO CAP'N AMERICA!
LOOKIT THIS!
HE'S THE BEST! HE'D JUMP ONTA YA, RIP OFF YER CANOPY -- AN' STUFF THEM BOMBS DOWN YER NAZI THROAT!
NOTHIN' STOPS HIM!
CAPTAIN AMERICA
LIKE THE ROCKET'S RED GLARE, A MYSTERIOUS PATRIOTIC SENSATION BURSTS ONTO THE SCENE
A TANK? HE'D KICK IT ONTA ITS BACK LIKE A TURTLE! A PLATOON? SCATTERED LIKE DUCKPINS!
FLAG-DRAPED MYSTERY MAN PACK
May 8, ten enemies of liber
HE'S CAP'N AMERICA, MAXIE! HE'S THE BEST!
SECRET ANTI-MILITARY CONSPIRACY IS A SECRET NO LO
ARTIST'S CONCEPTION
HE HIT LIKE A BLITZKRIEG.
A AND BUCKY TAKE BROADWAY BY STORM

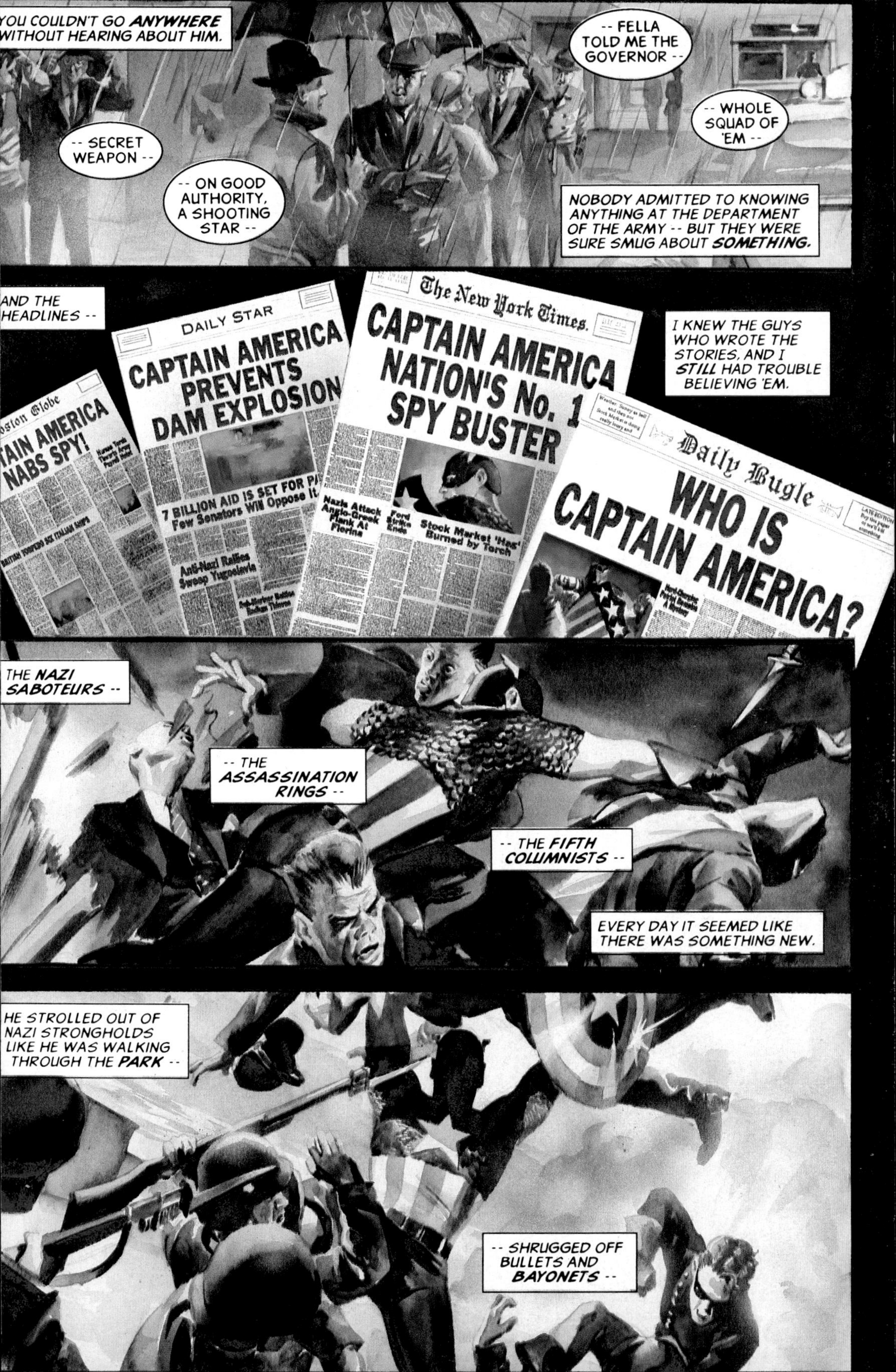

YOU COULDN'T GO ANYWHERE WITHOUT HEARING ABOUT HIM.
-- SECRET WEAPON --
-- ON GOOD AUTHORITY, A SHOOTING STAR --
-- FELLA TOLD ME THE GOVERNOR --
-- WHOLE SQUAD OF 'EM --
NOBODY ADMITTED TO KNOWING ANYTHING AT THE DEPARTMENT OF THE ARMY -- BUT THEY WERE SURE SMUG ABOUT SOMETHING.
AND THE HEADLINES --
CAPTAIN AMERICA NABS SPY!
DAILY STAR
CAPTAIN AMERICA PREVENTS DAM EXPLOSION
7 BILLION AID IS SET FOR PA
Few Senators Will Oppose It
Anti-Nazi Rallies Sweep Yugoslavia
The New York Times.
CAPTAIN AMERICA NATION'S No. 1 SPY BUSTER
Nazis Attack Anglo-Greek Flank At Florina
Ford Strike Ends
Stock Market 'Has' Burned by Torch
Daily Bugle
WHO IS CAPTAIN AMERICA?
I KNEW THE GUYS WHO WROTE THE STORIES, AND I STILL HAD TROUBLE BELIEVING 'EM.
THE NAZI SABOTEURS --
-- THE ASSASSINATION RINGS --
-- THE FIFTH COLUMNISTS --
EVERY DAY IT SEEMED LIKE THERE WAS SOMETHING NEW.
HE STROLLED OUT OF NAZI STRONGHOLDS LIKE HE WAS WALKING THROUGH THE PARK --
-- SHRUGGED OFF BULLETS AND BAYONETS --

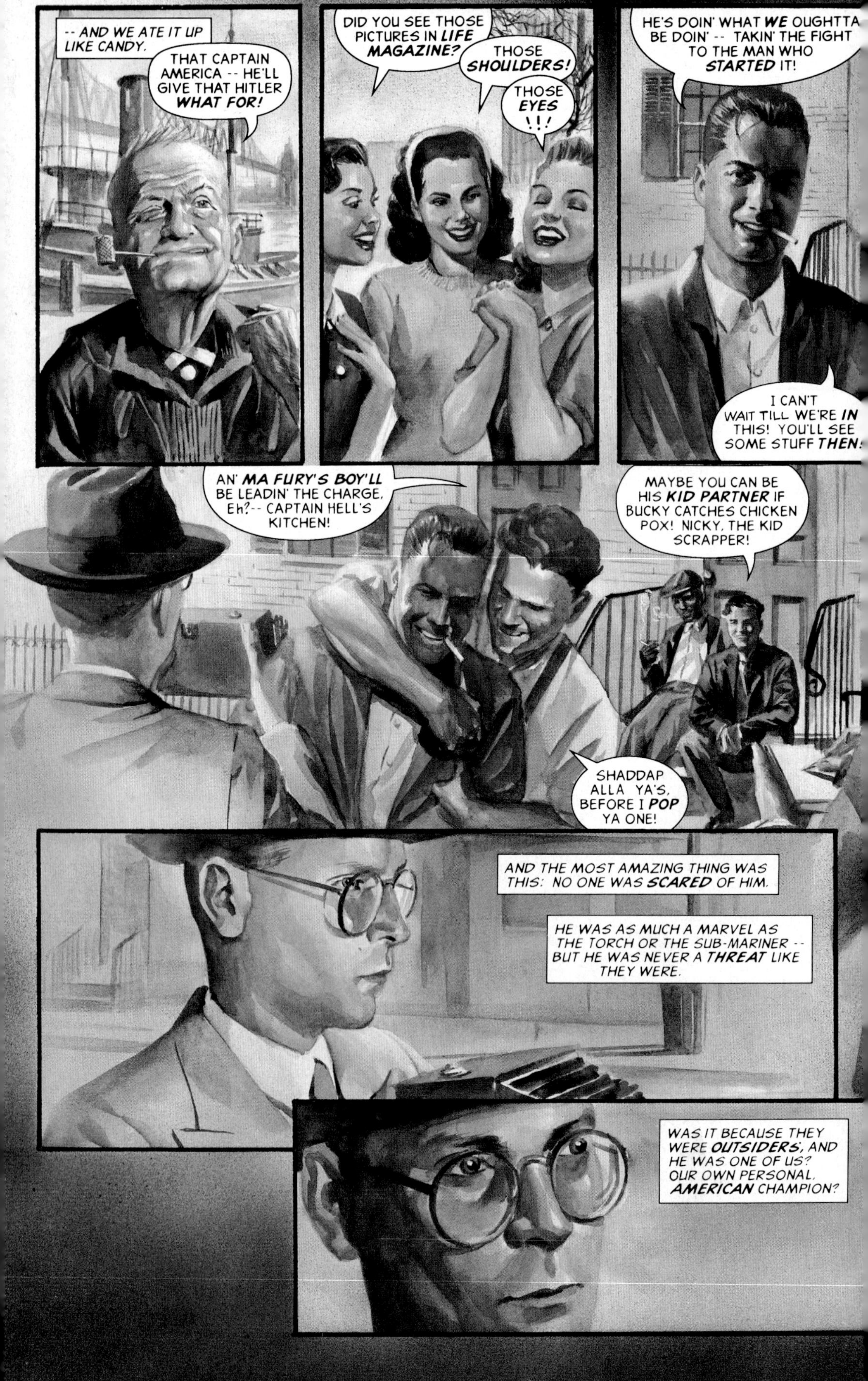

-- AND WE ATE IT UP LIKE CANDY.
THAT CAPTAIN AMERICA -- HE'LL GIVE THAT HITLER **WHAT FOR!**
DID YOU SEE THOSE PICTURES IN ***LIFE MAGAZINE?***
THOSE **SHOULDERS!**
THOSE ***EYES*** !!!
HE'S DOIN' WHAT ***WE*** OUGHTTA BE DOIN' -- TAKIN' THE FIGHT TO THE MAN WHO ***STARTED*** IT!
I CAN'T WAIT TILL WE'RE ***IN*** THIS! YOU'LL SEE SOME STUFF ***THEN***!
AN' ***MA FURY'S BOY'LL*** BE LEADIN' THE CHARGE, Eh?-- CAPTAIN HELL'S KITCHEN!
MAYBE YOU CAN BE HIS ***KID PARTNER*** IF BUCKY CATCHES CHICKEN POX! NICKY, THE KID SCRAPPER!
SHADDAP ALLA YA'S, BEFORE I ***POP*** YA ONE!
AND THE MOST AMAZING THING WAS THIS: NO ONE WAS ***SCARED*** OF HIM.
HE WAS AS MUCH A MARVEL AS THE TORCH OR THE SUB-MARINER -- BUT HE WAS NEVER A ***THREAT*** LIKE THEY WERE.
WAS IT BECAUSE THEY WERE ***OUTSIDERS***, AND HE WAS ONE OF US? OUR OWN PERSONAL, ***AMERICAN*** CHAMPION?

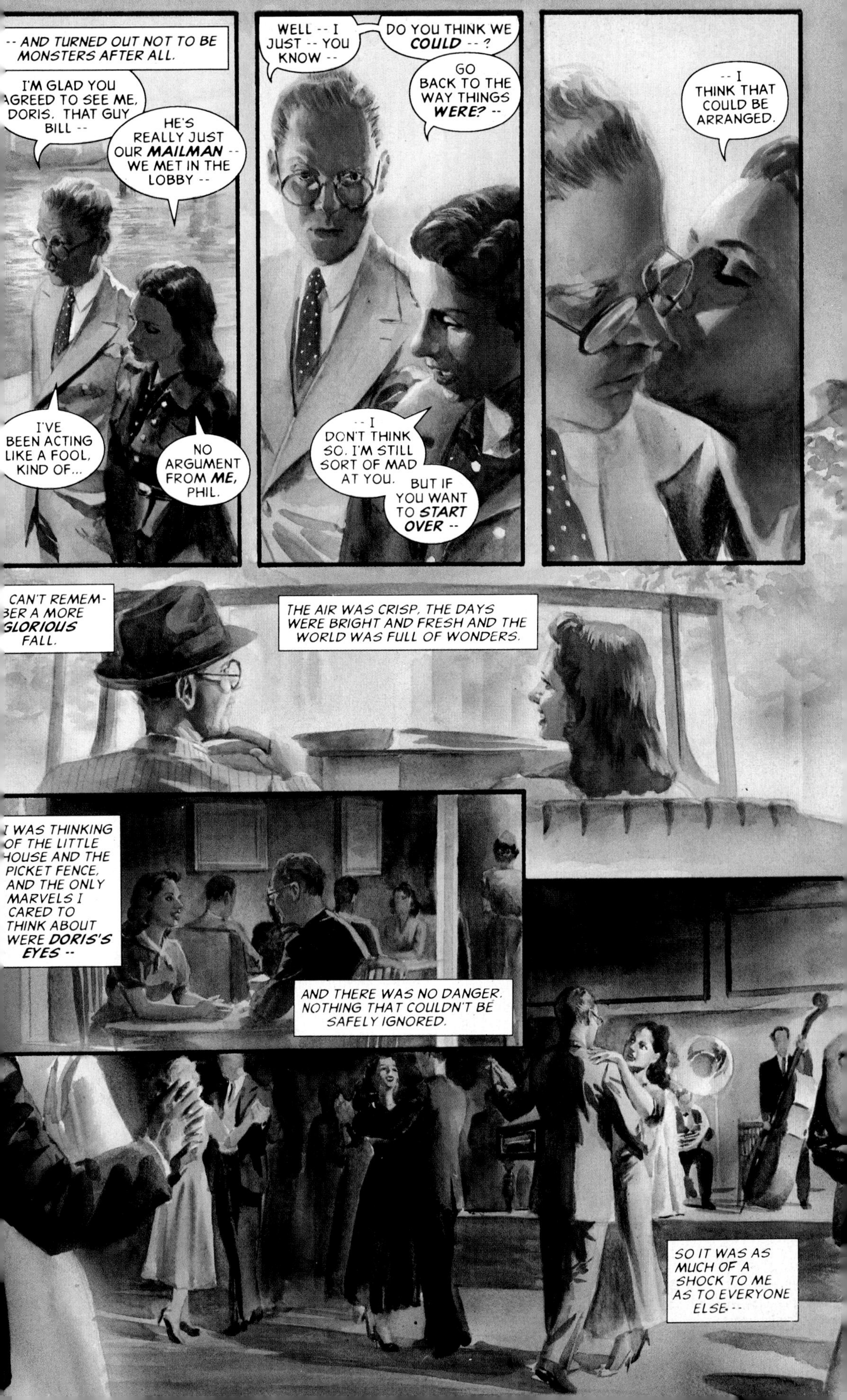
-- AND TURNED OUT NOT TO BE MONSTERS AFTER ALL.
I'M GLAD YOU AGREED TO SEE ME, DORIS. THAT GUY BILL --
HE'S REALLY JUST OUR MAILMAN -- WE MET IN THE LOBBY --
I'VE BEEN ACTING LIKE A FOOL, KIND OF...
NO ARGUMENT FROM ME, PHIL.
WELL -- I JUST -- YOU KNOW --
DO YOU THINK WE COULD -- ?
GO BACK TO THE WAY THINGS WERE? --
-- I DON'T THINK SO. I'M STILL SORT OF MAD AT YOU.
BUT IF YOU WANT TO START OVER --
-- I THINK THAT COULD BE ARRANGED.
CAN'T REMEMBER A MORE GLORIOUS FALL.
THE AIR WAS CRISP, THE DAYS WERE BRIGHT AND FRESH AND THE WORLD WAS FULL OF WONDERS.
I WAS THINKING OF THE LITTLE HOUSE AND THE PICKET FENCE, AND THE ONLY MARVELS I CARED TO THINK ABOUT WERE DORIS'S EYES --
AND THERE WAS NO DANGER. NOTHING THAT COULDN'T BE SAFELY IGNORED.
SO IT WAS AS MUCH OF A SHOCK TO ME AS TO EVERYONE ELSE --

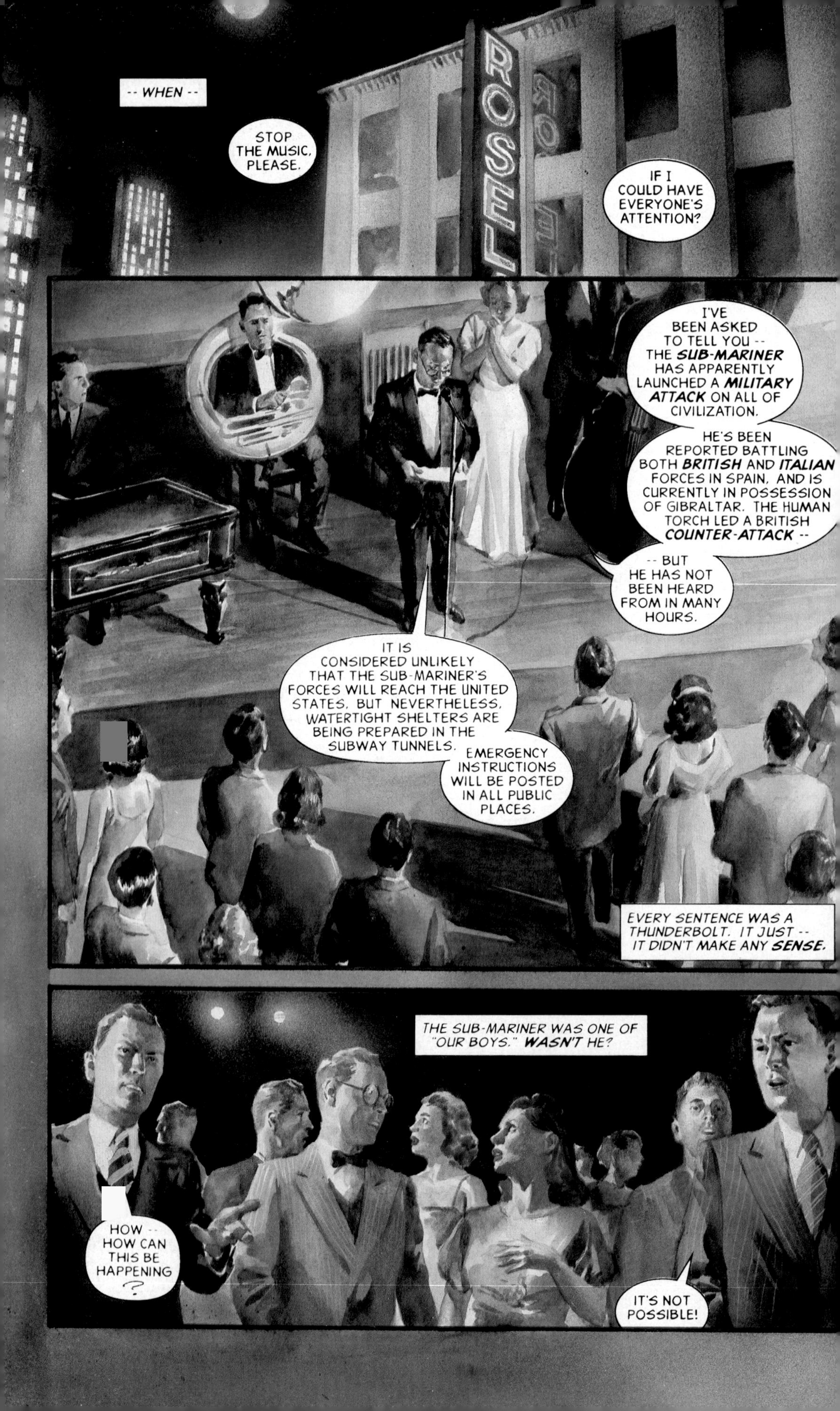
-- WHEN --
STOP THE MUSIC, PLEASE.
IF I COULD HAVE EVERYONE'S ATTENTION?
I'VE BEEN ASKED TO TELL YOU -- THE **SUB-MARINER** HAS APPARENTLY LAUNCHED A ***MILITARY ATTACK*** ON ALL OF CIVILIZATION.
HE'S BEEN REPORTED BATTLING BOTH ***BRITISH*** AND ***ITALIAN*** FORCES IN SPAIN, AND IS CURRENTLY IN POSSESSION OF GIBRALTAR. THE HUMAN TORCH LED A BRITISH ***COUNTER-ATTACK*** --
-- BUT HE HAS NOT BEEN HEARD FROM IN MANY HOURS.
IT IS CONSIDERED UNLIKELY THAT THE SUB-MARINER'S FORCES WILL REACH THE UNITED STATES, BUT NEVERTHELESS, WATERTIGHT SHELTERS ARE BEING PREPARED IN THE SUBWAY TUNNELS.
EMERGENCY INSTRUCTIONS WILL BE POSTED IN ALL PUBLIC PLACES.
EVERY SENTENCE WAS A THUNDERBOLT. IT JUST -- IT DIDN'T MAKE ANY ***SENSE.***
THE SUB-MARINER WAS ONE OF "OUR BOYS." ***WASN'T*** HE?
HOW -- HOW CAN THIS BE HAPPENING?
IT'S NOT POSSIBLE!

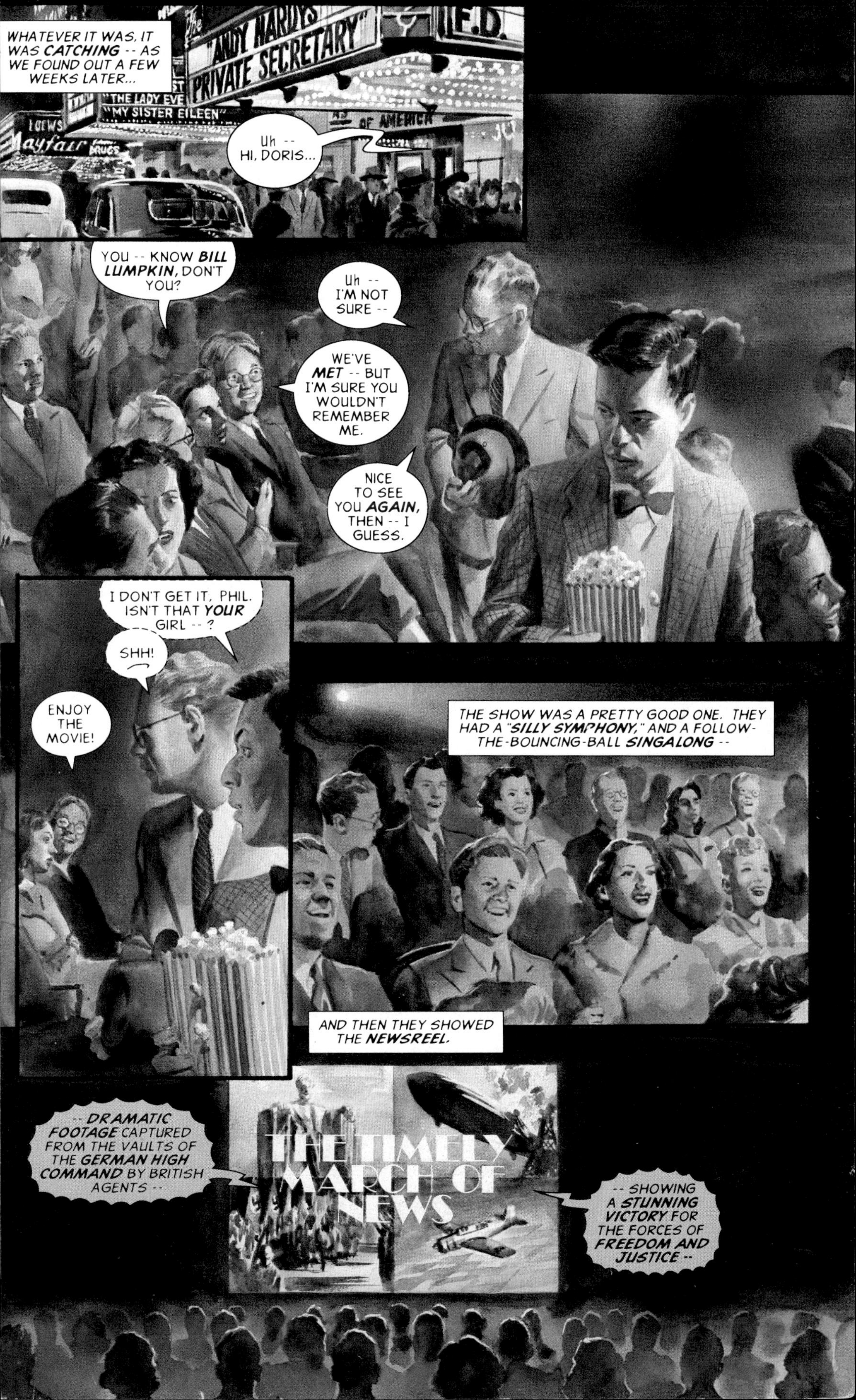
WHATEVER IT WAS, IT WAS CATCHING -- AS WE FOUND OUT A FEW WEEKS LATER...
"ANDY HARDY'S PRIVATE SECRETARY"
"THE LADY EVE"
"MY SISTER EILEEN"
LOEWS
Mayfair
Uh -- HI, DORIS...
YOU -- KNOW BILL LUMPKIN, DON'T YOU?
Uh -- I'M NOT SURE --
WE'VE MET -- BUT I'M SURE YOU WOULDN'T REMEMBER ME.
NICE TO SEE YOU AGAIN, THEN -- I GUESS.
I DON'T GET IT, PHIL. ISN'T THAT YOUR GIRL -- ?
SHH!
ENJOY THE MOVIE!
THE SHOW WAS A PRETTY GOOD ONE. THEY HAD A "SILLY SYMPHONY," AND A FOLLOW-THE-BOUNCING-BALL SINGALONG --
AND THEN THEY SHOWED THE NEWSREEL.
THE TIMELY MARCH OF NEWS
-- DRAMATIC FOOTAGE CAPTURED FROM THE VAULTS OF THE GERMAN HIGH COMMAND BY BRITISH AGENTS --
-- SHOWING A STUNNING VICTORY FOR THE FORCES OF FREEDOM AND JUSTICE --

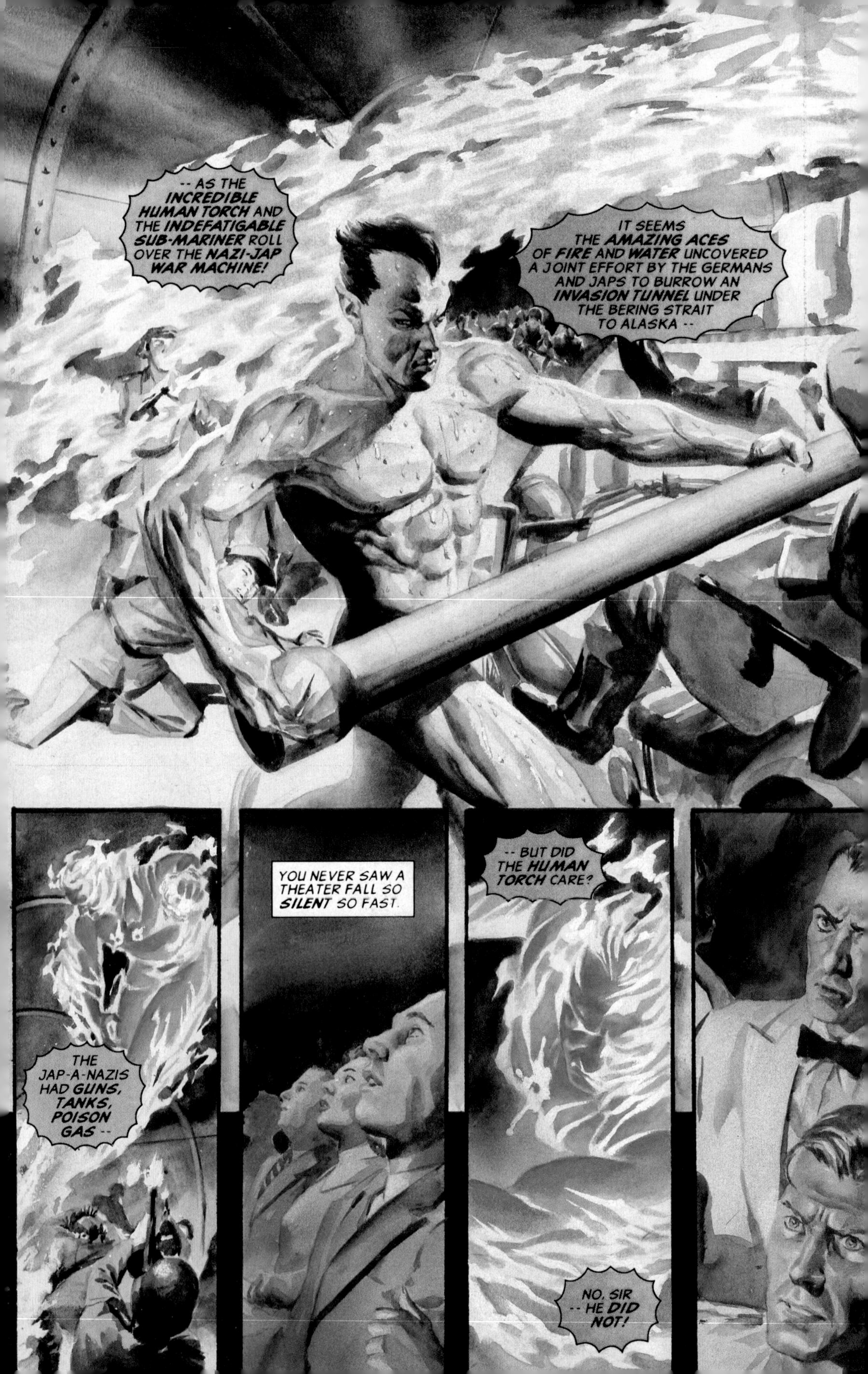
-- AS THE INCREDIBLE HUMAN TORCH AND THE INDEFATIGABLE SUB-MARINER ROLL OVER THE NAZI-JAP WAR MACHINE!
IT SEEMS THE AMAZING ACES OF FIRE AND WATER UNCOVERED A JOINT EFFORT BY THE GERMANS AND JAPS TO BURROW AN INVASION TUNNEL UNDER THE BERING STRAIT TO ALASKA --
THE JAP-A-NAZIS HAD GUNS, TANKS, POISON GAS --
YOU NEVER SAW A THEATER FALL SO SILENT SO FAST.
-- BUT DID THE HUMAN TORCH CARE?
NO, SIR -- HE DID NOT!

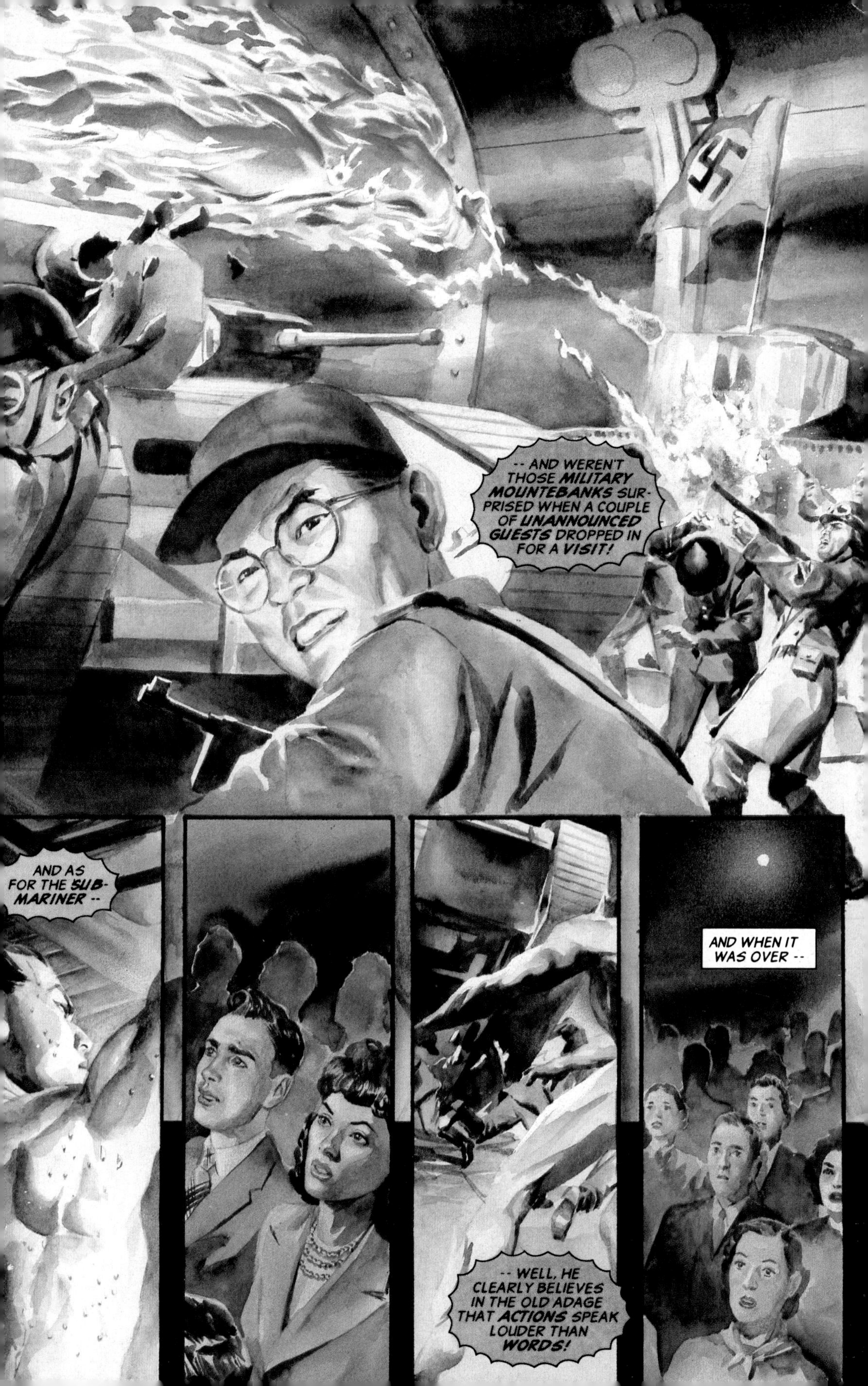
-- AND WEREN'T THOSE MILITARY MOUNTEBANKS SURPRISED WHEN A COUPLE OF UNANNOUNCED GUESTS DROPPED IN FOR A VISIT!
AND AS FOR THE SUB-MARINER --
-- WELL, HE CLEARLY BELIEVES IN THE OLD ADAGE THAT ACTIONS SPEAK LOUDER THAN WORDS!
AND WHEN IT WAS OVER --

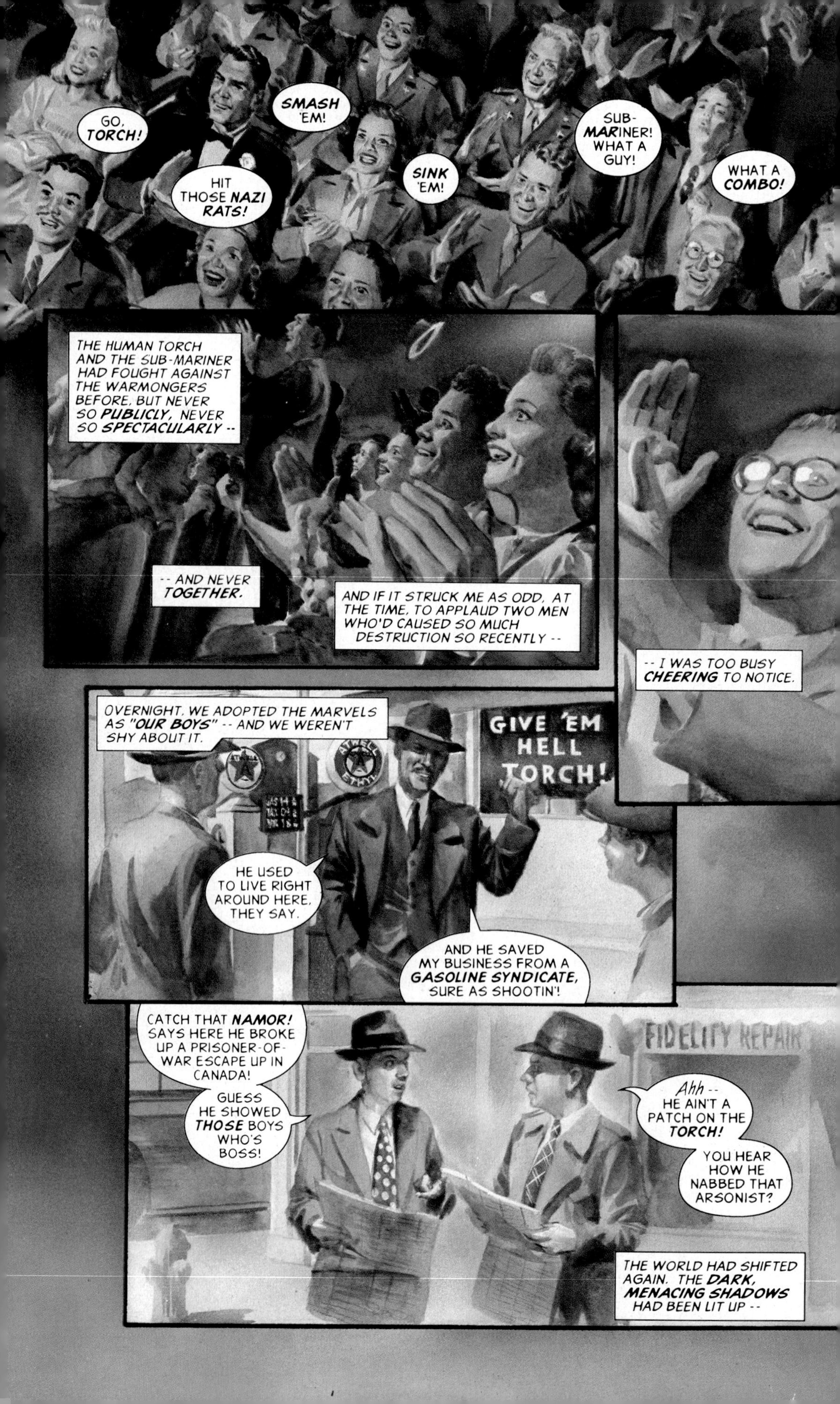

GO, TORCH!
HIT THOSE NAZI RATS!
SMASH 'EM!
SINK 'EM!
SUB-MARINER! WHAT A GUY!
WHAT A COMBO!
THE HUMAN TORCH AND THE SUB-MARINER HAD FOUGHT AGAINST THE WARMONGERS BEFORE, BUT NEVER SO PUBLICLY, NEVER SO SPECTACULARLY --
-- AND NEVER TOGETHER.
AND IF IT STRUCK ME AS ODD, AT THE TIME, TO APPLAUD TWO MEN WHO'D CAUSED SO MUCH DESTRUCTION SO RECENTLY --
-- I WAS TOO BUSY CHEERING TO NOTICE.
OVERNIGHT, WE ADOPTED THE MARVELS AS "OUR BOYS" -- AND WE WEREN'T SHY ABOUT IT.
GIVE 'EM HELL TORCH!
ATWELL ETHYL
HE USED TO LIVE RIGHT AROUND HERE, THEY SAY.
AND HE SAVED MY BUSINESS FROM A GASOLINE SYNDICATE, SURE AS SHOOTIN'!
CATCH THAT NAMOR! SAYS HERE HE BROKE UP A PRISONER-OF-WAR ESCAPE UP IN CANADA!
GUESS HE SHOWED THOSE BOYS WHO'S BOSS!
FIDELITY REPAIR
Ahh -- HE AIN'T A PATCH ON THE TORCH!
YOU HEAR HOW HE NABBED THAT ARSONIST?
THE WORLD HAD SHIFTED AGAIN. THE DARK, MENACING SHADOWS HAD BEEN LIT UP --

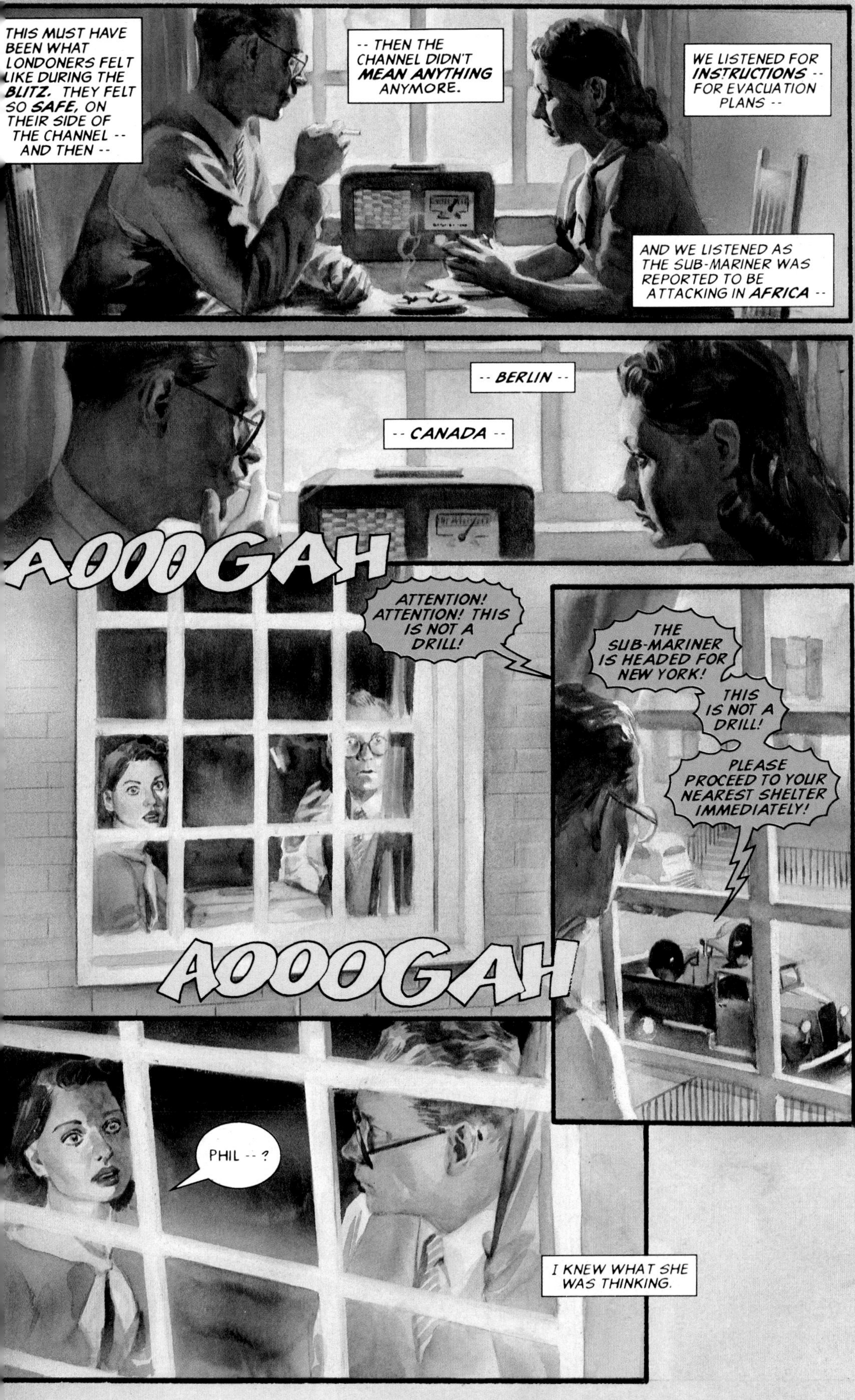
THIS MUST HAVE BEEN WHAT LONDONERS FELT LIKE DURING THE BLITZ. THEY FELT SO SAFE, ON THEIR SIDE OF THE CHANNEL -- AND THEN --
-- THEN THE CHANNEL DIDN'T MEAN ANYTHING ANYMORE.
WE LISTENED FOR INSTRUCTIONS -- FOR EVACUATION PLANS --
AND WE LISTENED AS THE SUB-MARINER WAS REPORTED TO BE ATTACKING IN AFRICA --
-- BERLIN --
-- CANADA --
AOOOGAH
ATTENTION! ATTENTION! THIS IS NOT A DRILL!
THE SUB-MARINER IS HEADED FOR NEW YORK!
THIS IS NOT A DRILL!
PLEASE PROCEED TO YOUR NEAREST SHELTER IMMEDIATELY!
AOOOGAH
PHIL -- ?
I KNEW WHAT SHE WAS THINKING.

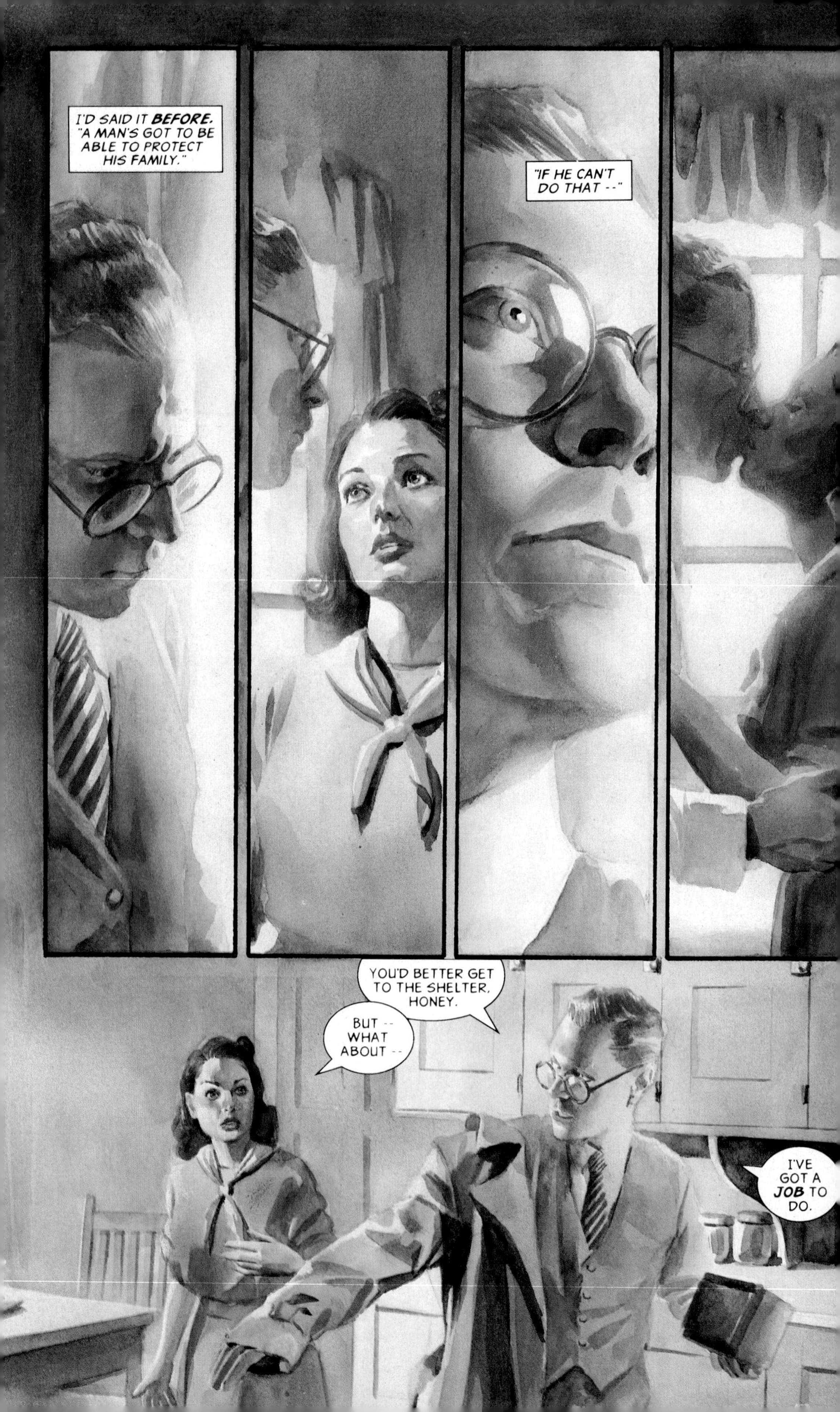

I'D SAID IT **BEFORE.**
"A MAN'S GOT TO BE ABLE TO PROTECT HIS FAMILY."
"IF HE CAN'T DO THAT --"
YOU'D BETTER GET TO THE SHELTER, HONEY.
BUT -- WHAT ABOUT --
I'VE GOT A **JOB** TO DO.

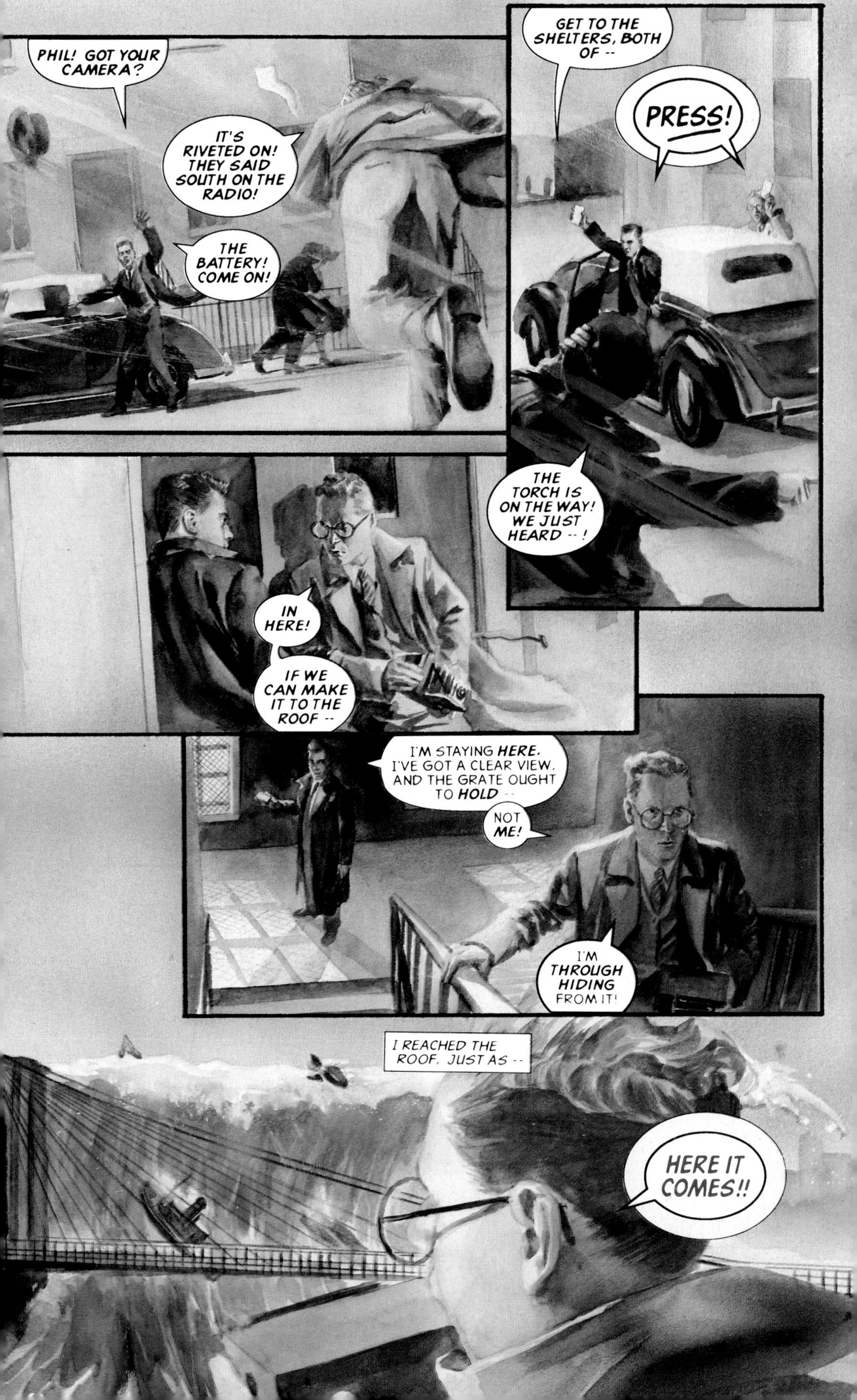
PHIL! GOT YOUR CAMERA?
IT'S RIVETED ON! THEY SAID SOUTH ON THE RADIO!
THE BATTERY! COME ON!
GET TO THE SHELTERS, BOTH OF --
PRESS!
THE TORCH IS ON THE WAY! WE JUST HEARD -- !
IN HERE!
IF WE CAN MAKE IT TO THE ROOF --
I'M STAYING HERE. I'VE GOT A CLEAR VIEW, AND THE GRATE OUGHT TO HOLD --
NOT ME!
I'M THROUGH HIDING FROM IT!
I REACHED THE ROOF, JUST AS --
HERE IT COMES!!

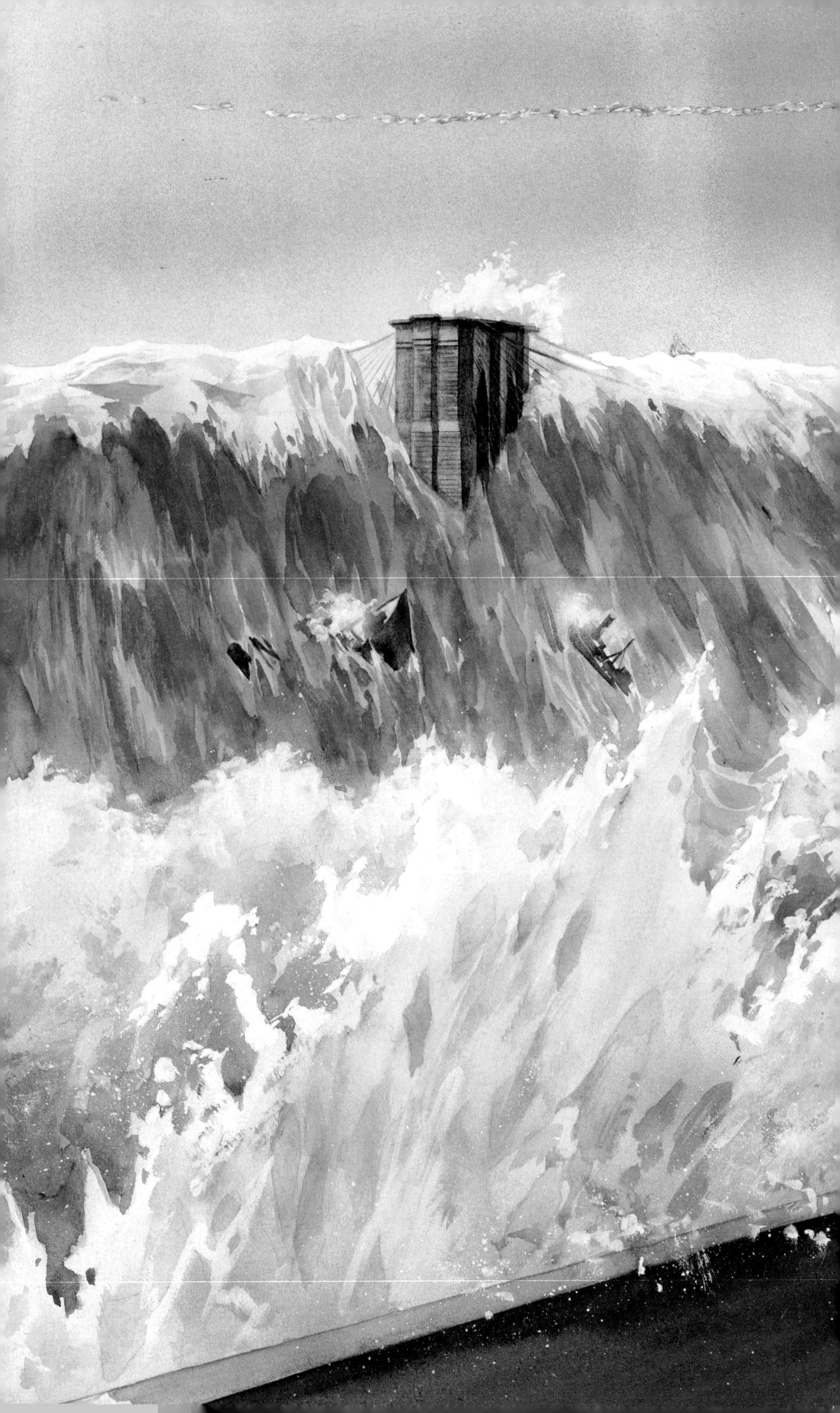

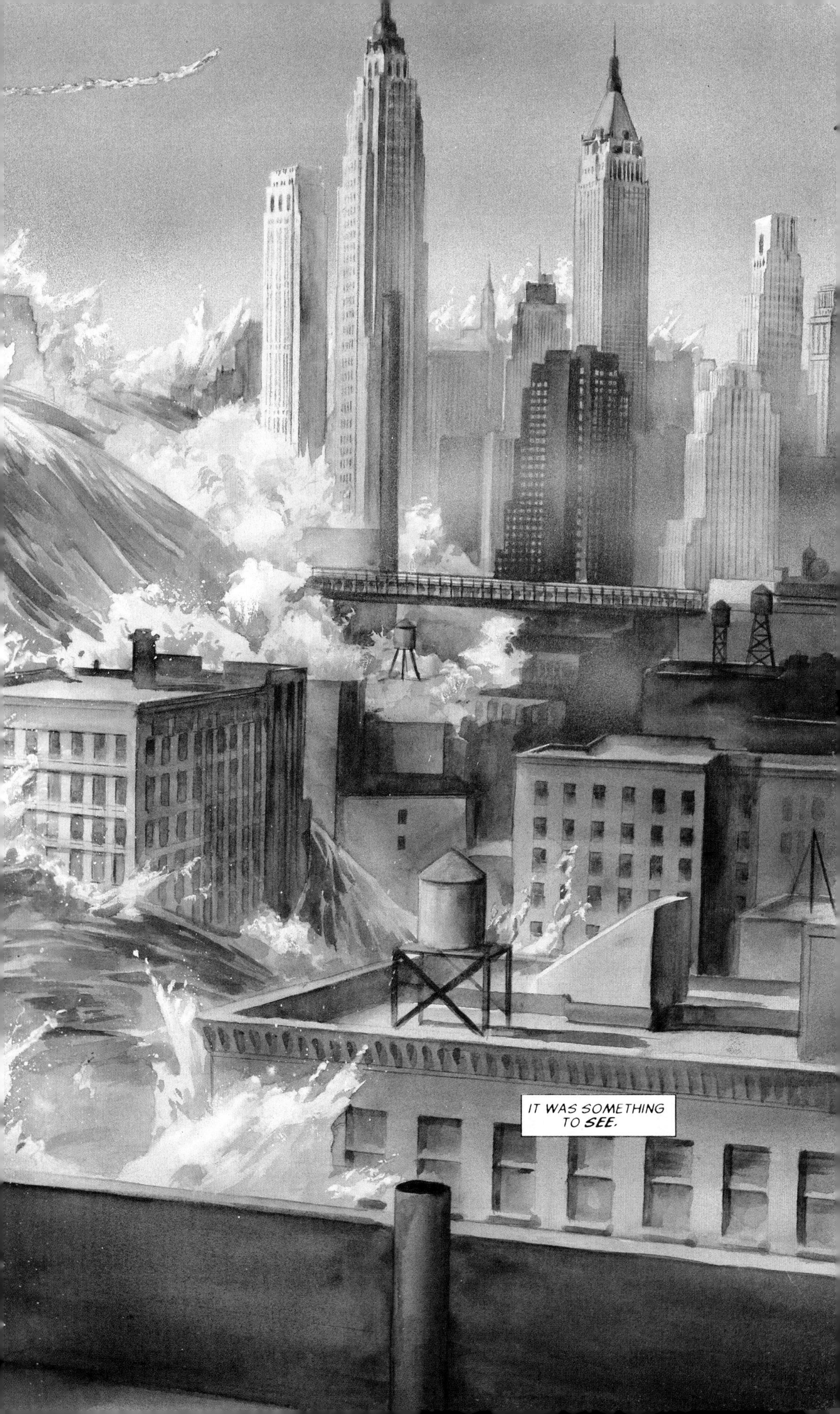
IT WAS SOMETHING TO SEE.

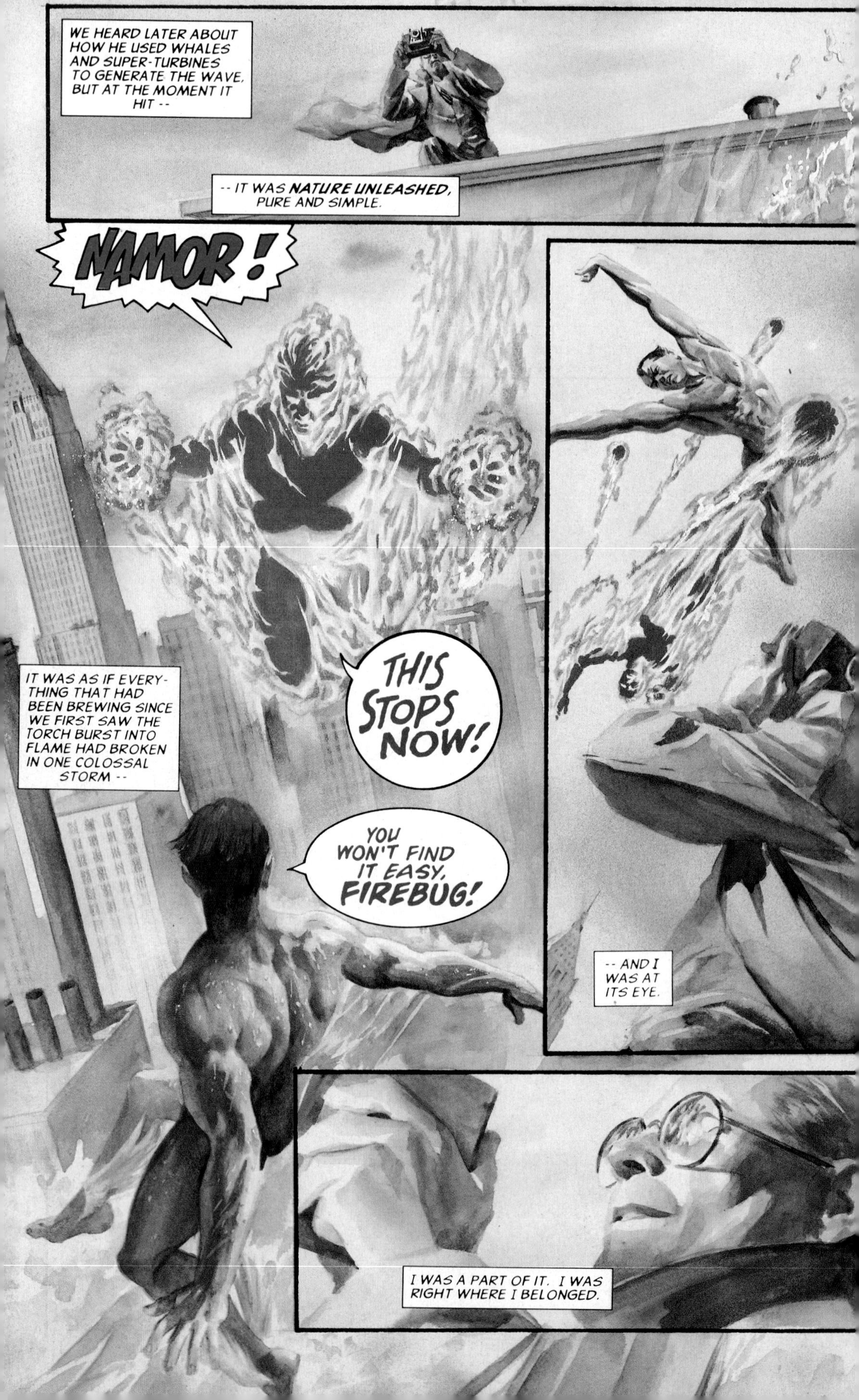

WE HEARD LATER ABOUT HOW HE USED WHALES AND SUPER-TURBINES TO GENERATE THE WAVE, BUT AT THE MOMENT IT HIT --
-- IT WAS NATURE UNLEASHED, PURE AND SIMPLE.
NAMOR!
THIS STOPS NOW!
IT WAS AS IF EVERY-THING THAT HAD BEEN BREWING SINCE WE FIRST SAW THE TORCH BURST INTO FLAME HAD BROKEN IN ONE COLOSSAL STORM --
YOU WON'T FIND IT EASY, FIREBUG!
-- AND I WAS AT ITS EYE.
I WAS A PART OF IT. I WAS RIGHT WHERE I BELONGED.

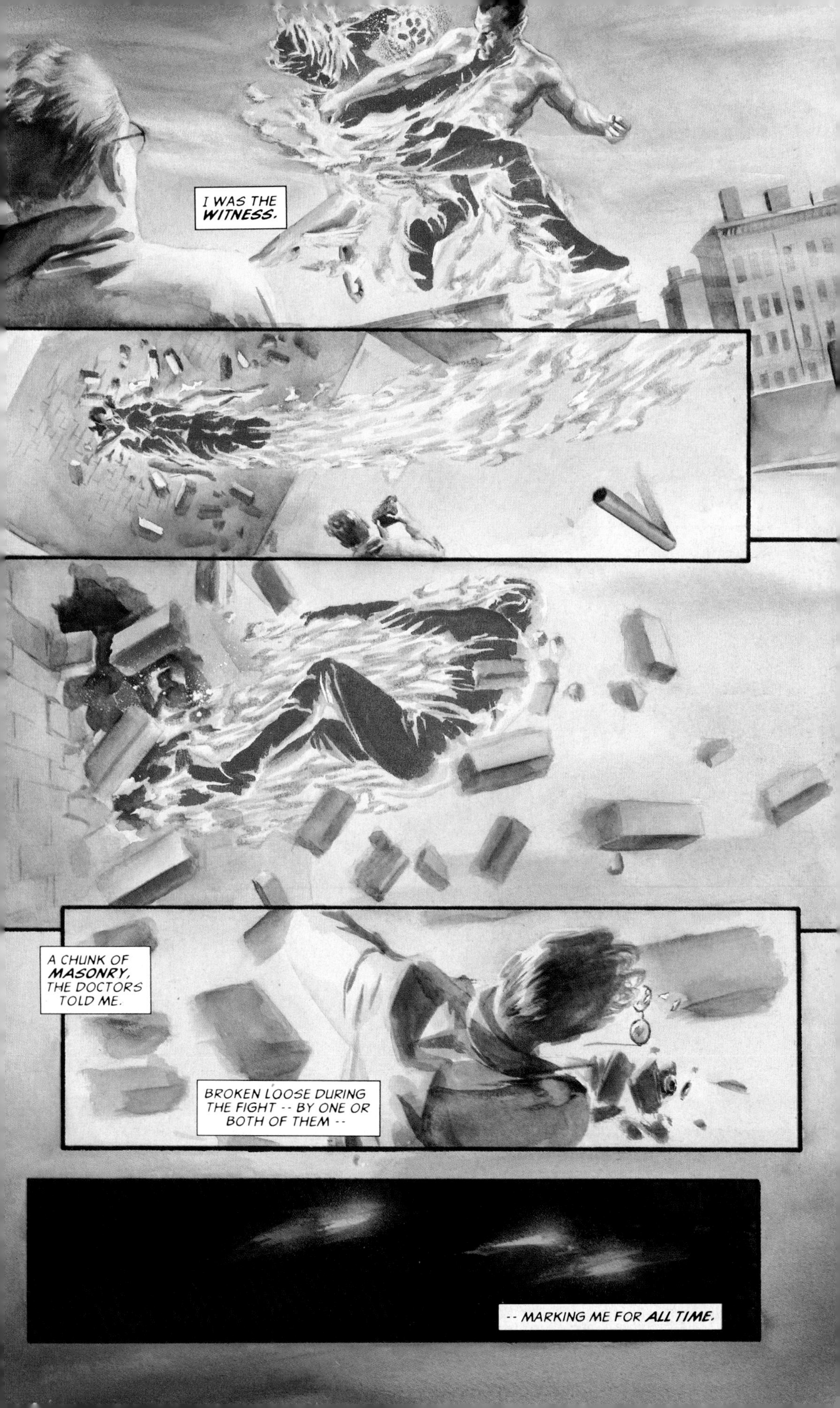
I WAS THE **WITNESS.**
A CHUNK OF **MASONRY,** THE DOCTORS TOLD ME.
BROKEN LOOSE DURING THE FIGHT -- BY ONE OR BOTH OF THEM --
-- MARKING ME FOR **ALL TIME.**

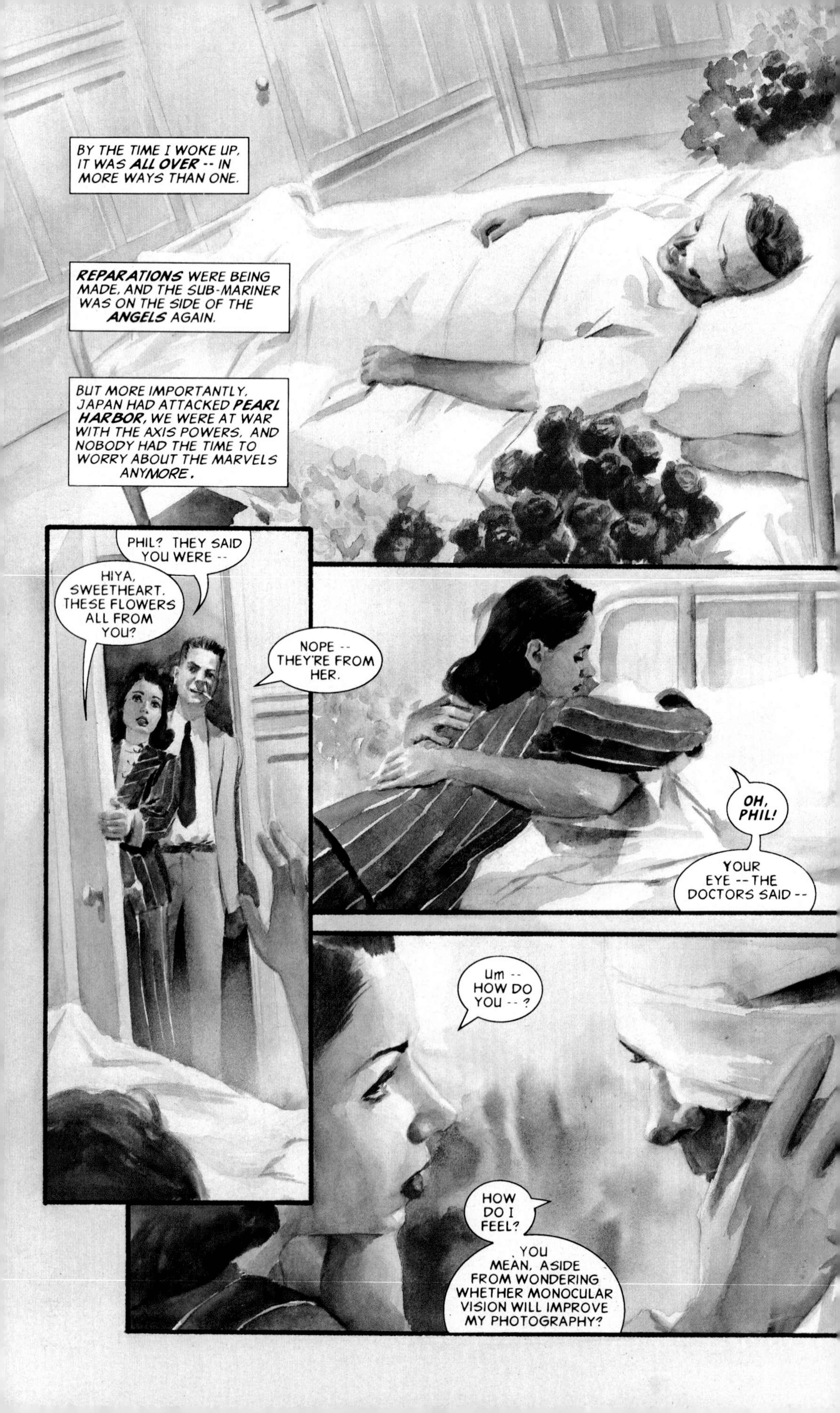

BY THE TIME I WOKE UP, IT WAS ALL OVER -- IN MORE WAYS THAN ONE.
REPARATIONS WERE BEING MADE, AND THE SUB-MARINER WAS ON THE SIDE OF THE ANGELS AGAIN.
BUT MORE IMPORTANTLY, JAPAN HAD ATTACKED PEARL HARBOR, WE WERE AT WAR WITH THE AXIS POWERS, AND NOBODY HAD THE TIME TO WORRY ABOUT THE MARVELS ANYMORE.
PHIL? THEY SAID YOU WERE --
HIYA, SWEETHEART. THESE FLOWERS ALL FROM YOU?
NOPE -- THEY'RE FROM HER.
OH, PHIL!
YOUR EYE -- THE DOCTORS SAID --
Um -- HOW DO YOU -- ?
HOW DO I FEEL?
YOU MEAN, ASIDE FROM WONDERING WHETHER MONOCULAR VISION WILL IMPROVE MY PHOTOGRAPHY?

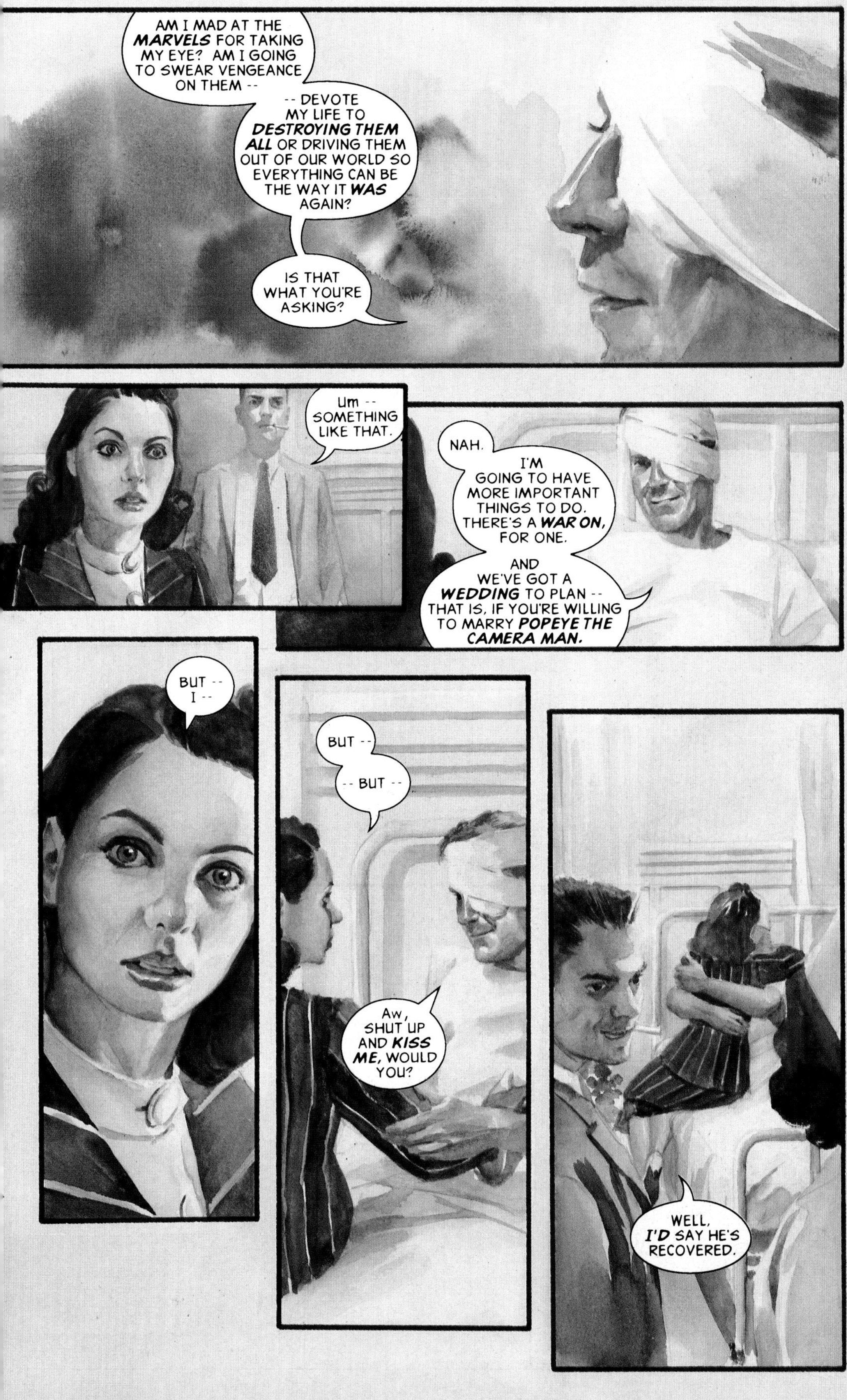
AM I MAD AT THE MARVELS FOR TAKING MY EYE? AM I GOING TO SWEAR VENGEANCE ON THEM --
-- DEVOTE MY LIFE TO DESTROYING THEM ALL OR DRIVING THEM OUT OF OUR WORLD SO EVERYTHING CAN BE THE WAY IT WAS AGAIN?
IS THAT WHAT YOU'RE ASKING?
Um -- SOMETHING LIKE THAT.
NAH.
I'M GOING TO HAVE MORE IMPORTANT THINGS TO DO. THERE'S A WAR ON, FOR ONE.
AND WE'VE GOT A WEDDING TO PLAN -- THAT IS, IF YOU'RE WILLING TO MARRY POPEYE THE CAMERA MAN.
BUT -- I --
BUT --
-- BUT --
Aw, SHUT UP AND KISS ME, WOULD YOU?
WELL, I'D SAY HE'S RECOVERED.

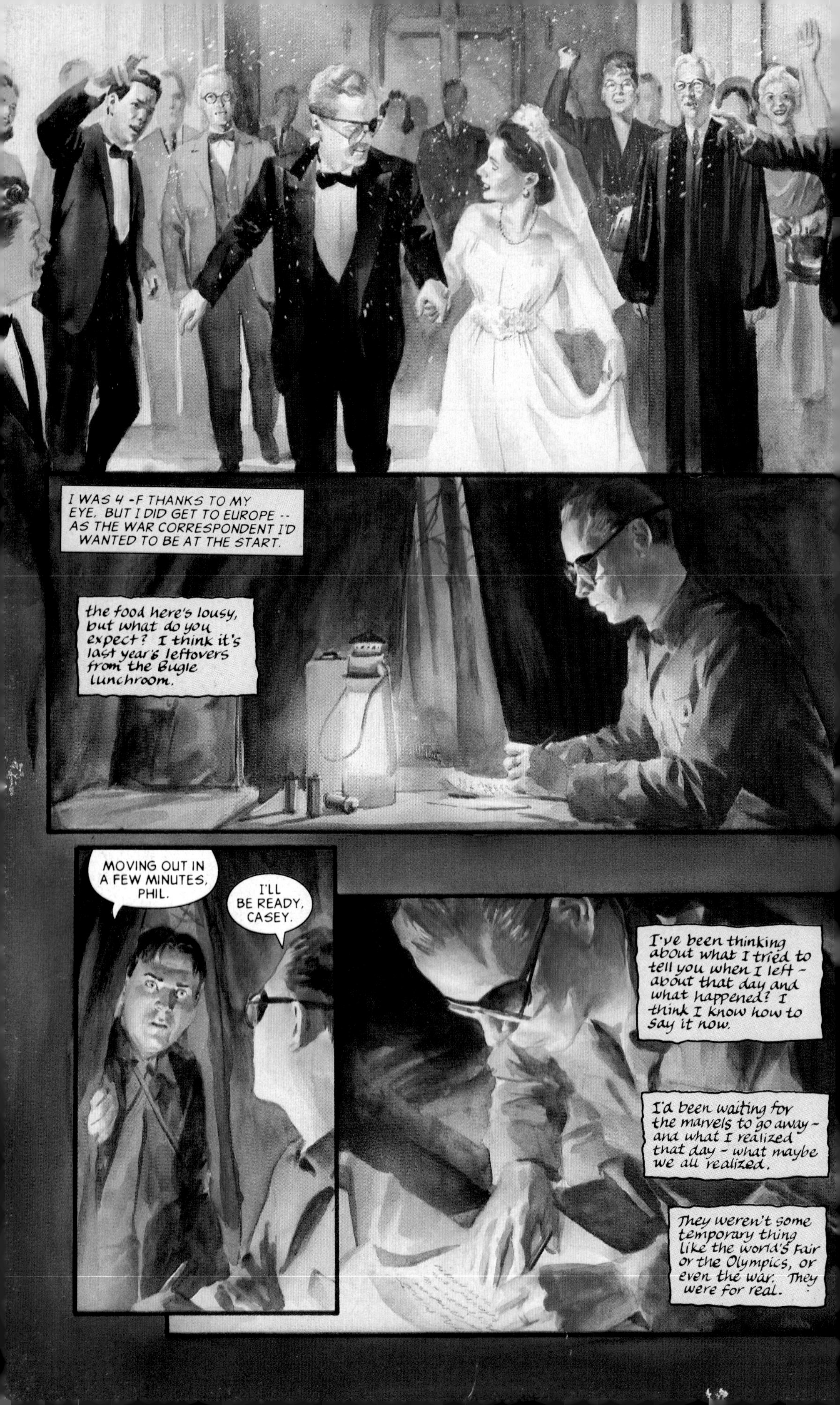

I WAS 4-F THANKS TO MY EYE, BUT I DID GET TO EUROPE -- AS THE WAR CORRESPONDENT I'D WANTED TO BE AT THE START.
the food here's lousy, but what do you expect? I think it's last year's leftovers from the Bugle lunchroom.
MOVING OUT IN A FEW MINUTES, PHIL.
I'LL BE READY, CASEY.
I've been thinking about what I tried to tell you when I left - about that day and what happened? I think I know how to say it now.
I'd been waiting for the marvels to go away - and what I realized that day - what maybe we all realized.
They weren't some temporary thing like the World's Fair or the Olympics, or even the war. They were for real.

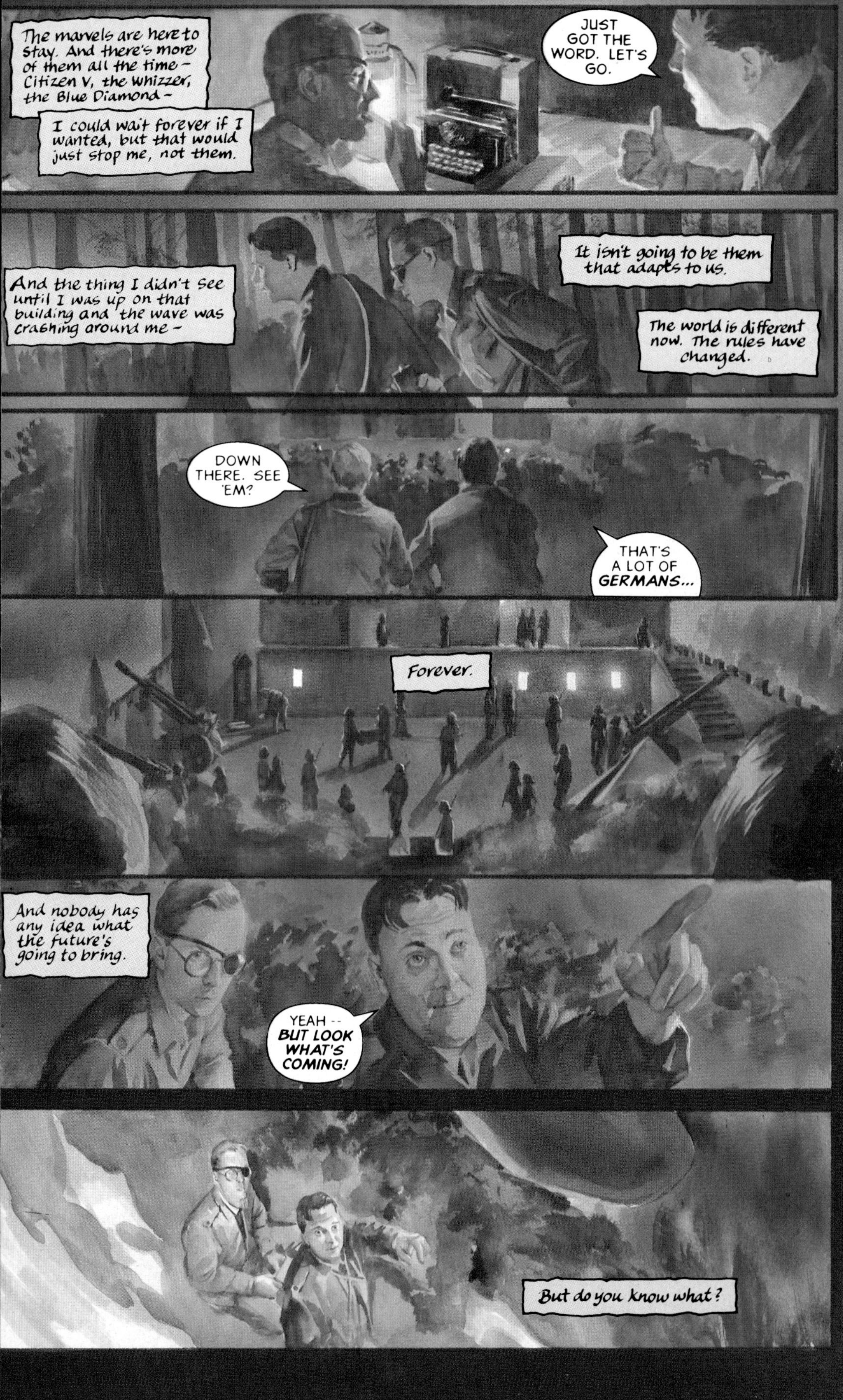
The marvels are here to stay. And there's more of them all the time - Citizen V, the Whizzer, the Blue Diamond -
I could wait forever if I wanted, but that would just stop me, not them.
JUST GOT THE WORD. LET'S GO.
And the thing I didn't see until I was up on that building and the wave was crashing around me -
It isn't going to be them that adapts to us.
The world is different now. The rules have changed.
DOWN THERE. SEE 'EM?
THAT'S A LOT OF GERMANS...
Forever.
And nobody has any idea what the future's going to bring.
YEAH -- BUT LOOK WHAT'S COMING!
But do you know what?

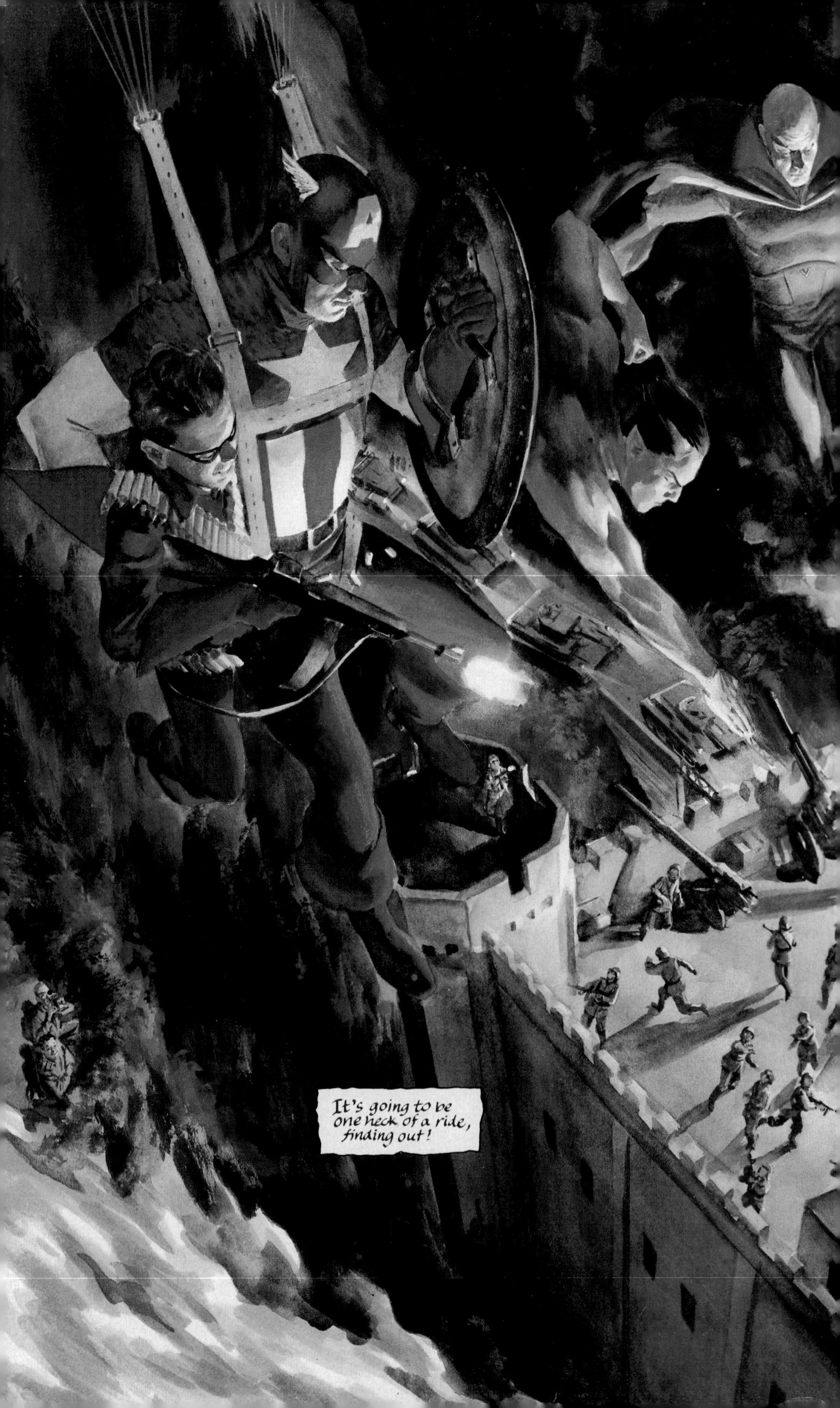
It's going to be one heck of a ride, finding out!

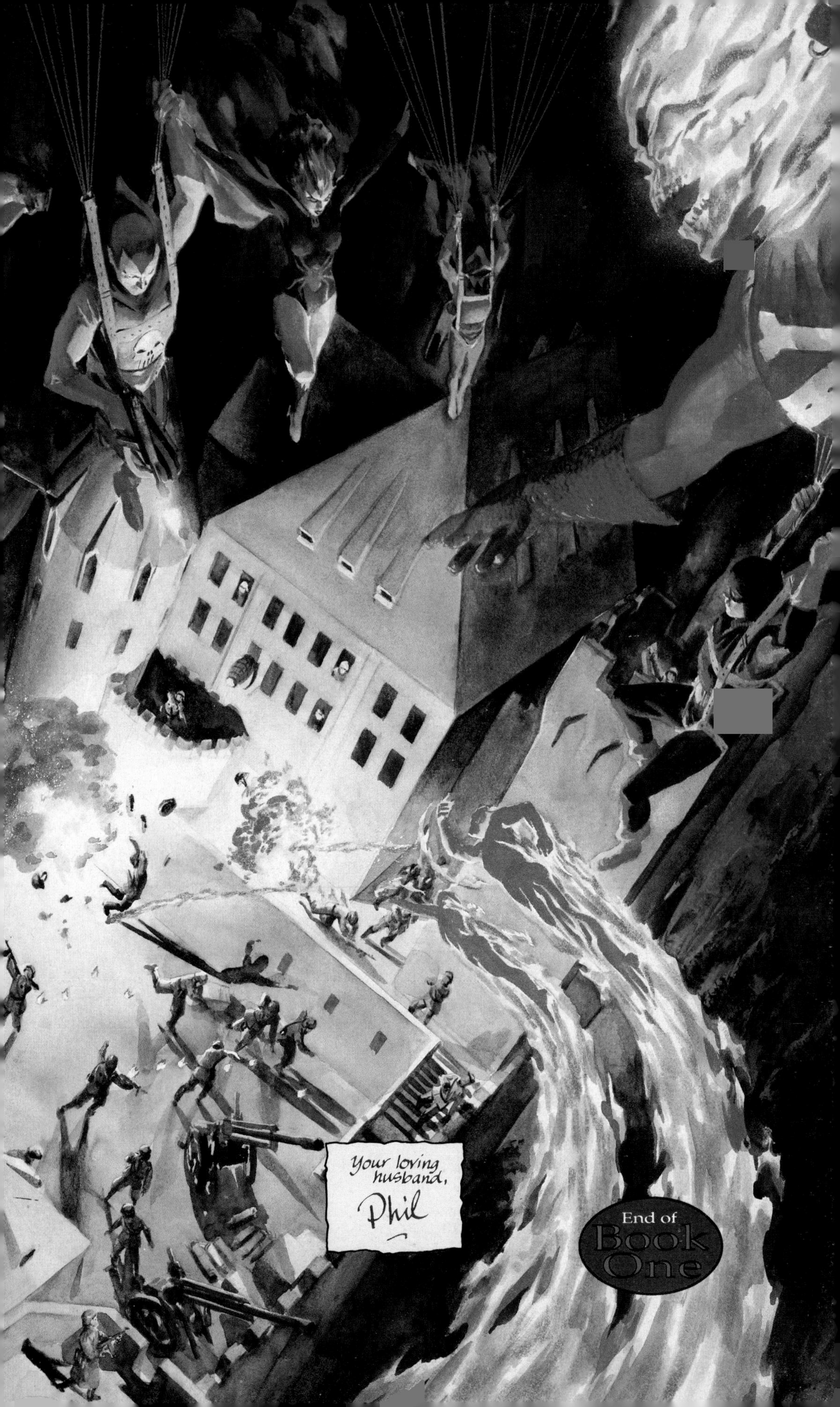
Your loving husband,
Phil
End of Book One

Commentary by Kurt Busiek

I never read these stories when they were first published.

Oh, maybe a few of them, here and there, slipped in among the stacks of RICHIE RICH and BATMAN in my friends' basements, or purchased furtively from the local drugstore, read hastily and then stuffed behind the big air-conditioning unit in the train station between the drugstore and my home (my parents did not allow comic books into the house), but I never read them in any organized manner, never got a sense of the Marvel Universe as a whole. And

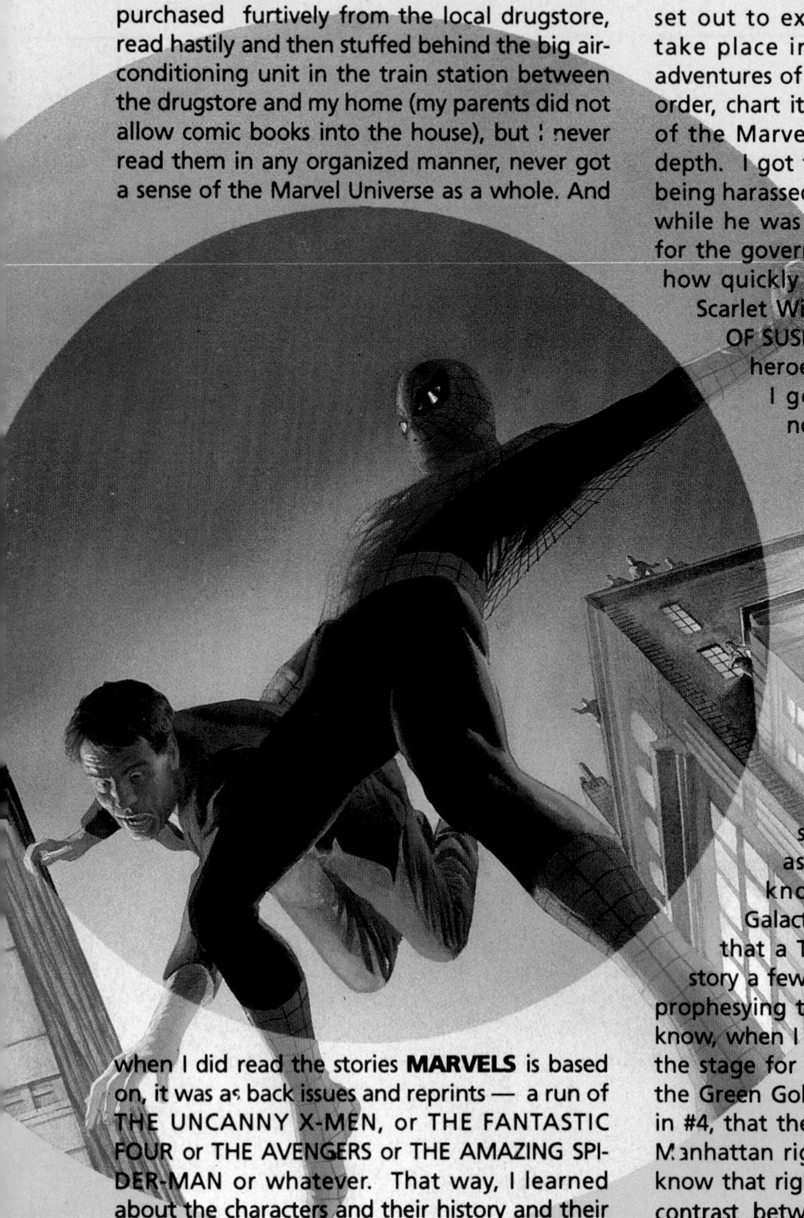

when I did read the stories **MARVELS** is based on, it was as back issues and reprints — a run of THE UNCANNY X-MEN, or THE FANTASTIC FOUR or THE AVENGERS or THE AMAZING SPIDER-MAN or whatever. That way, I learned about the characters and their history and their troubles, but seldom learned how those individual tracks fit together, seldom got a sense o what was happening in the other books at th time each series was progressing.

So when I came to do **MARVELS** an set out to explore the world these storie take place in, rather than the individua adventures of the heroes, I had to put it all i order, chart it out and see what the breadt of the Marvel Universe held alongside th depth. I got to discover that Tony Stark wa being harassed by the Senate in his own serie while he was busy helping create S.H.I.E.L.D for the government over in STRANGE TALES how quickly Hawkeye, Quicksilver and th Scarlet Witch went from villains in TALE OF SUSPENSE and UNCANNY X-MEN t heroes in AVENGERS, and more, an I got to use it, more often tha not, in the stories.

And the one thing continually discovered was this There's no substitute fo hands-on research.

I had all the fancy artisti goals. I knew my themes. knew the grand scope of th stories I wanted to tell. Bu without the details, it coul never have come through th way it did. Had I been able t go back in time and have thing set up for me, I couldn't hav asked for better. How was I t know, when I wanted to set u Galactus as an apocalyptic figure in #3 that a TALES TO ASTONISH/AVENGER story a few months prior had religious nut prophesying the coming end? How was I t know, when I wanted a wide-scale crisis to se the stage for the very human-scale drama o the Green Goblin's kidnapping of Gwen Stac in #4, that the forces of Atlantis had invade Manhattan right beforehand? How was I t know that right when I wanted to set up th contrast between the lionizing of the supe heroes and the demonizing of the mutant hat over in TALES TO ASTONISH, Benson's epartment Store was introducing a line of clothng inspired by the Wasp? *(Okay, so it was all a lot by The Magician to use the Wasp's vanity to mbush her, but it was there...)*

I mean, I knew the *stories*. I just didn't realize how they fit together.

And sometimes, even when I did now how the stories fit together, I didn't uspect how well. Take the climax of ook Two here, with the wedding of eed and Sue Richards and the debut f the mutant-hunting Sentinels. I new that the two stories had to appen reasonably close together since the Human Torch appearnce in X-MEN #13, one month efore the Sentinels showed up n publishing time, mentions the pcoming wedding), and I definitely wanted to juxtapose the wo events — the ultimate example of the FF as the "royalty" of he Marvel Universe and the ultinate expression of fear and hatred f the mutants — but when I went o figure out which came first, well...

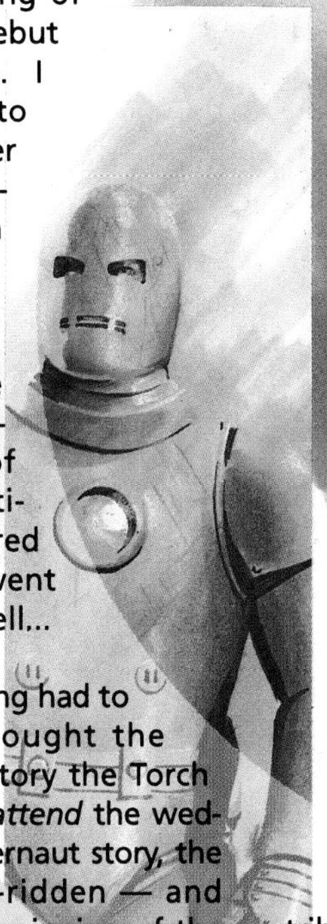

Here's how it works: The wedding had to happen after the X-Men fought the uggernaut, since that was the story the Torch uest-starred in. But the X-Men *attend* the wedling, and at the end of the Juggernaut story, the X-Men are all injured and bed-ridden — and hey're still recuperating at the beginning of the entinels story, so it can't happen between those wo issues. But they're all injured again by the end f the 3-part Sentinels story, and are hospitalized in he beginning of the next issue, which flows right nto a 2-part Magneto story — and by the time *hat's* over, we're 5 or 6 months beyond the wedling in publishing time. So it must happen *during* n issue, and as it turns out, the only time during hat stretch that the X-Men are uninjured and othrwise unoccupied is very early in the Sentinels tory — a period of less than two days.

So there I was, looking for the juxtaposiion of the two events — and wouldn't you know it, he only way for them to work out is *if they happen t almost the same time*. Whatever my lofty plans or the climax of **MARVELS** #2, it had just become ar more powerful, and all because of the minor letails of the source material.

I kept running into this as I researched nd wrote **MARVELS.** I'd need something — and *here* it was. I'd want to set up some emotional oint, some thematic symbol — and *there* was the vidence for it in Marvel history, as if it had been vaiting for me.

And that's the point of this piece, I guess. For all that **MARVELS** has won praise for its humanity, for its perspective, for its depiction of a complex and mostly-believable world, and for all that I'm willing to accept credit for what I contributed to the project (and for most of what Alex contributed, when he's not around to hear), it ultimately boils down to this: If it wasn't out there in the first place, it couldn't have ended up in here.

So I owe a major debt of thanks to my uncredited collaborators — Carl Burgos, Bill Everett, Joe Simon, Jack Kirby, Stan Lee, Steve Ditko, Don Heck, Gene Colan, Dick Ayers, Roy Thomas, John Romita, Gerry Conway, John Buscema, Mike Friedrich, Gil Kane, Steve Gerber, Neal Adams, Werner Roth, Wally Wood and so many others. Thanks to one and all for creating such an involving, entertaining and multi-faceted fantasy world. It's the height of fatuousness to say we couldn't have done it without you — we wouldn't have had anywhere to start. We wouldn't have had any reason to come up with the idea in the first place.

We wouldn't even be in this line of business.

Thanks, guys. It was a rare treat to revisit the world you built.

KURT

KURT BUSIEK

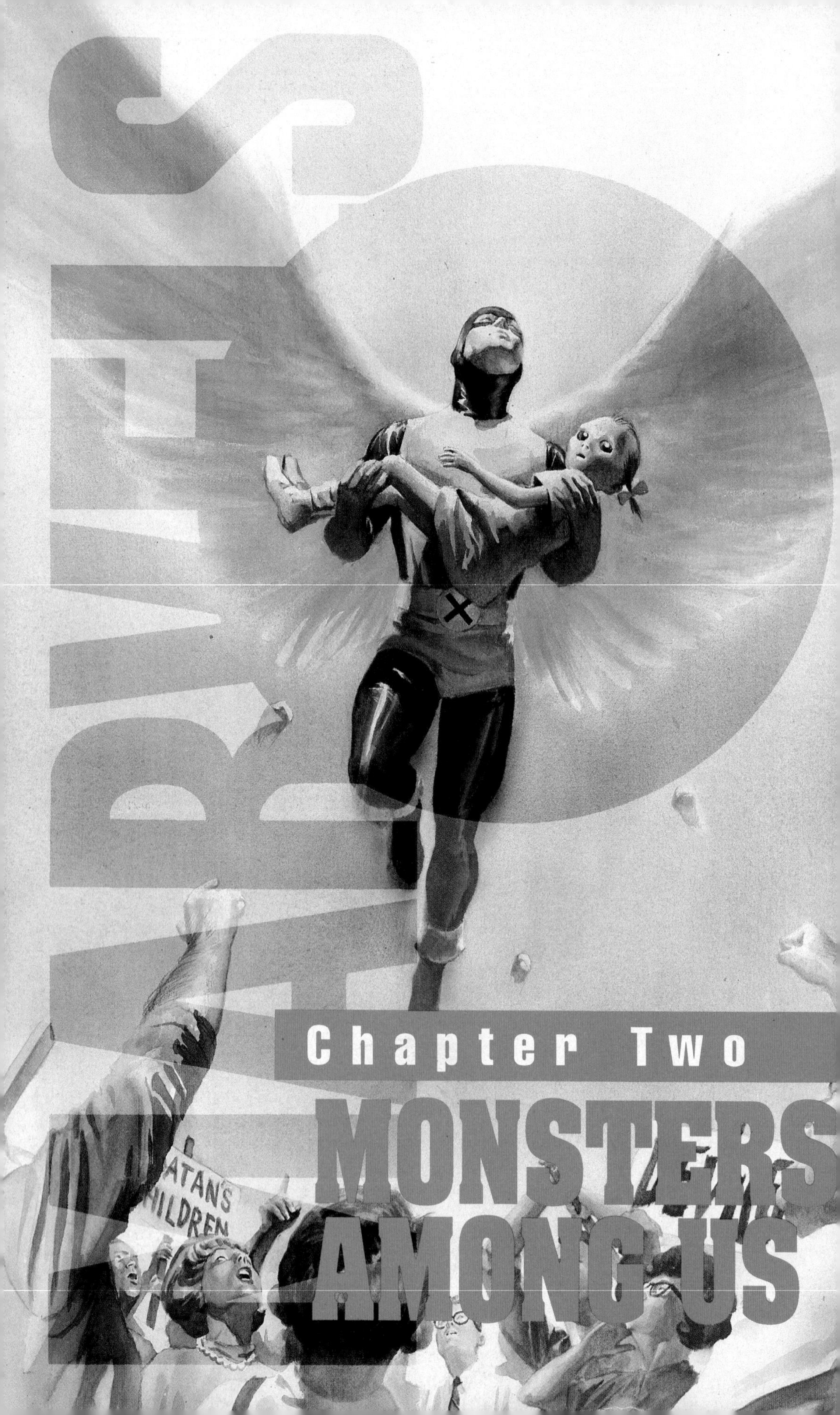

Chapter Two

MONSTERS AMONG US

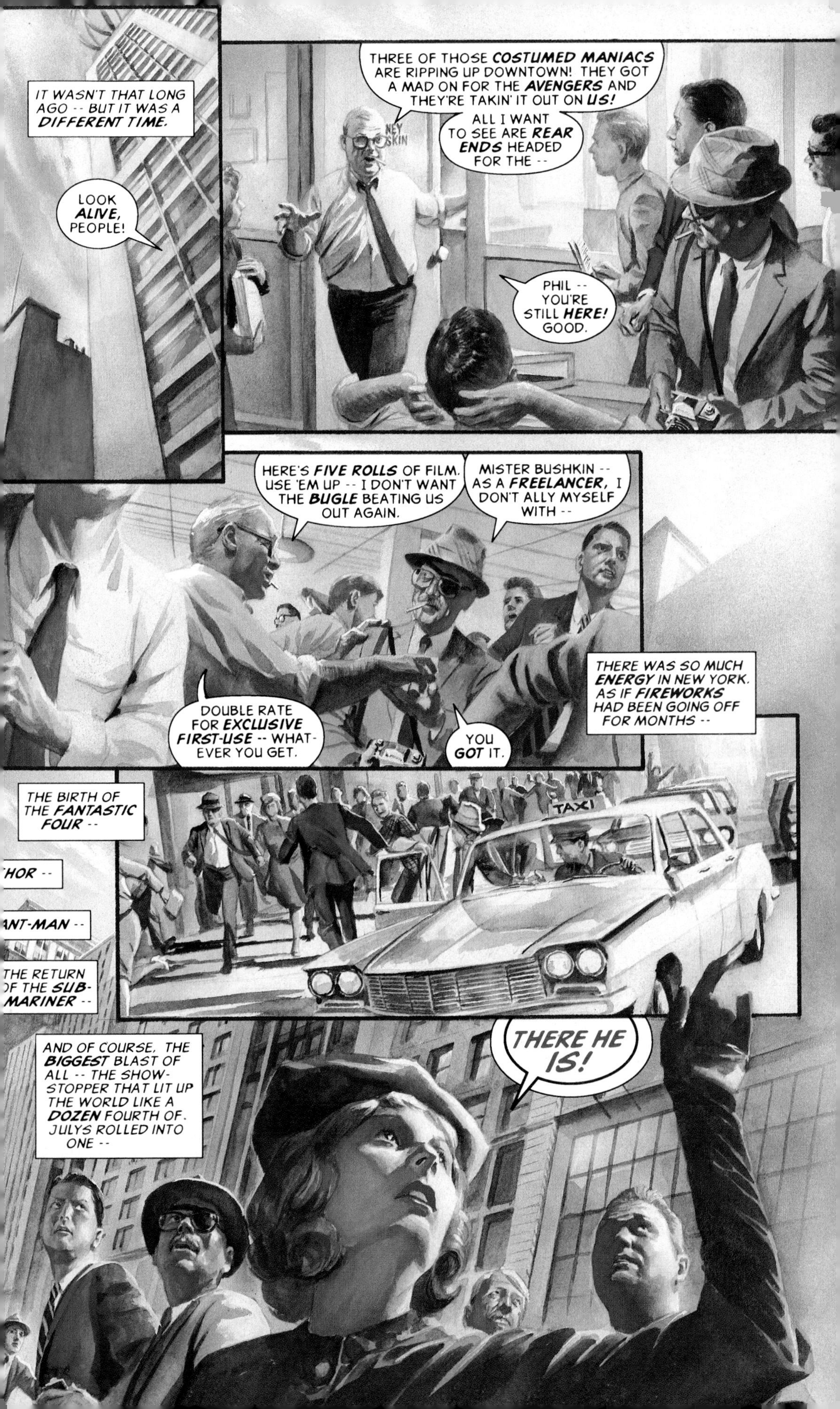
IT WASN'T THAT LONG AGO -- BUT IT WAS A DIFFERENT TIME.
LOOK ALIVE, PEOPLE!
THREE OF THOSE COSTUMED MANIACS ARE RIPPING UP DOWNTOWN! THEY GOT A MAD ON FOR THE AVENGERS AND THEY'RE TAKIN' IT OUT ON US!
ALL I WANT TO SEE ARE REAR ENDS HEADED FOR THE --
PHIL -- YOU'RE STILL HERE! GOOD.
HERE'S FIVE ROLLS OF FILM. USE 'EM UP -- I DON'T WANT THE BUGLE BEATING US OUT AGAIN.
MISTER BUSHKIN -- AS A FREELANCER, I DON'T ALLY MYSELF WITH --
DOUBLE RATE FOR EXCLUSIVE FIRST-USE -- WHATEVER YOU GET.
YOU GOT IT.
THERE WAS SO MUCH ENERGY IN NEW YORK. AS IF FIREWORKS HAD BEEN GOING OFF FOR MONTHS --
THE BIRTH OF THE FANTASTIC FOUR --
THOR --
ANT-MAN --
THE RETURN OF THE SUB-MARINER --
TAXI
AND OF COURSE, THE BIGGEST BLAST OF ALL -- THE SHOW-STOPPER THAT LIT UP THE WORLD LIKE A DOZEN FOURTH OF JULYS ROLLED INTO ONE --
THERE HE IS!

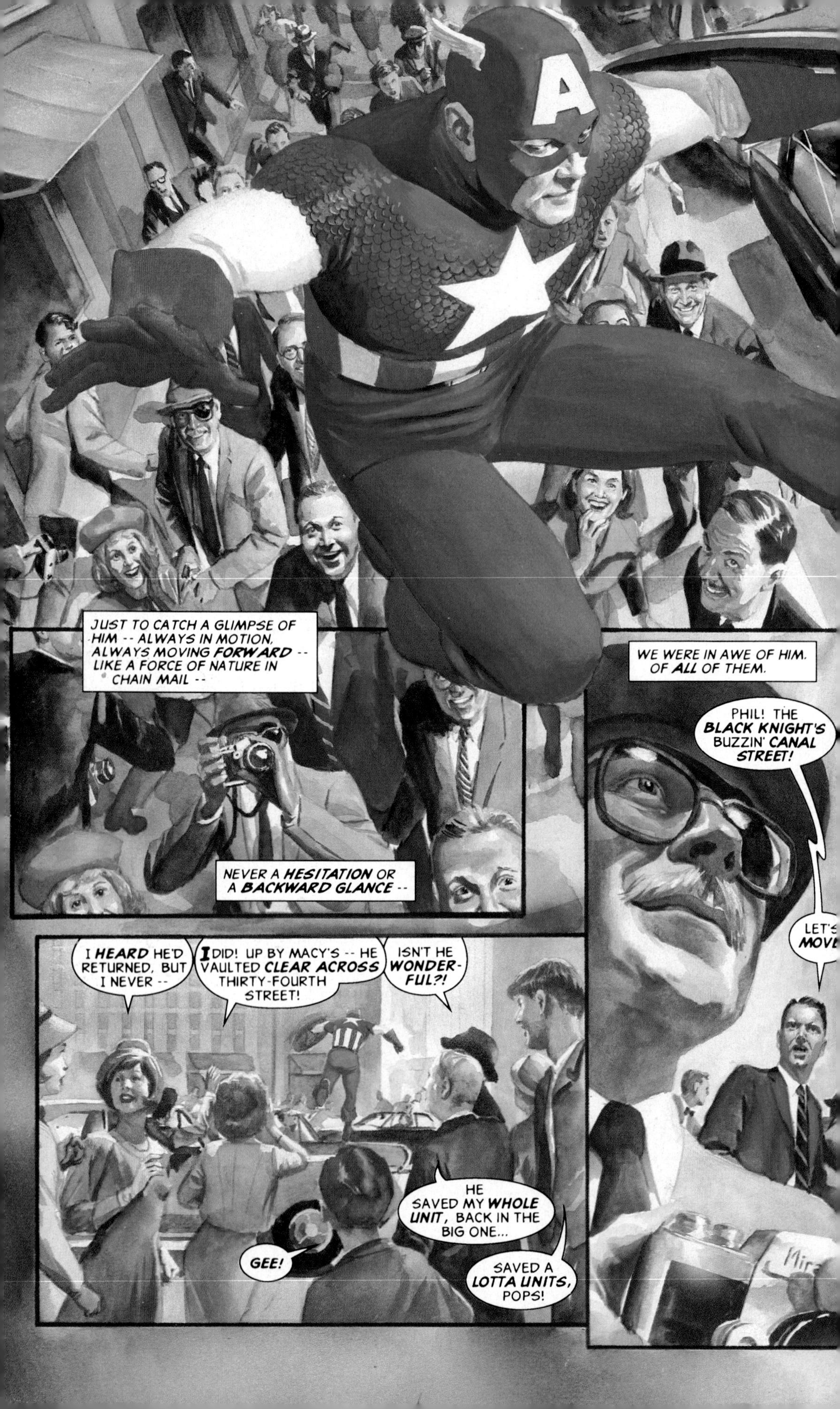

JUST TO CATCH A GLIMPSE OF HIM -- ALWAYS IN MOTION, ALWAYS MOVING FORWARD -- LIKE A FORCE OF NATURE IN CHAIN MAIL --
NEVER A HESITATION OR A BACKWARD GLANCE --
WE WERE IN AWE OF HIM. OF ALL OF THEM.
PHIL! THE BLACK KNIGHT'S BUZZIN' CANAL STREET!
LET'S MOVE
I HEARD HE'D RETURNED, BUT I NEVER --
I DID! UP BY MACY'S -- HE VAULTED CLEAR ACROSS THIRTY-FOURTH STREET!
ISN'T HE WONDERFUL?!
HE SAVED MY WHOLE UNIT, BACK IN THE BIG ONE...
GEE!
SAVED A LOTTA UNITS, POPS!

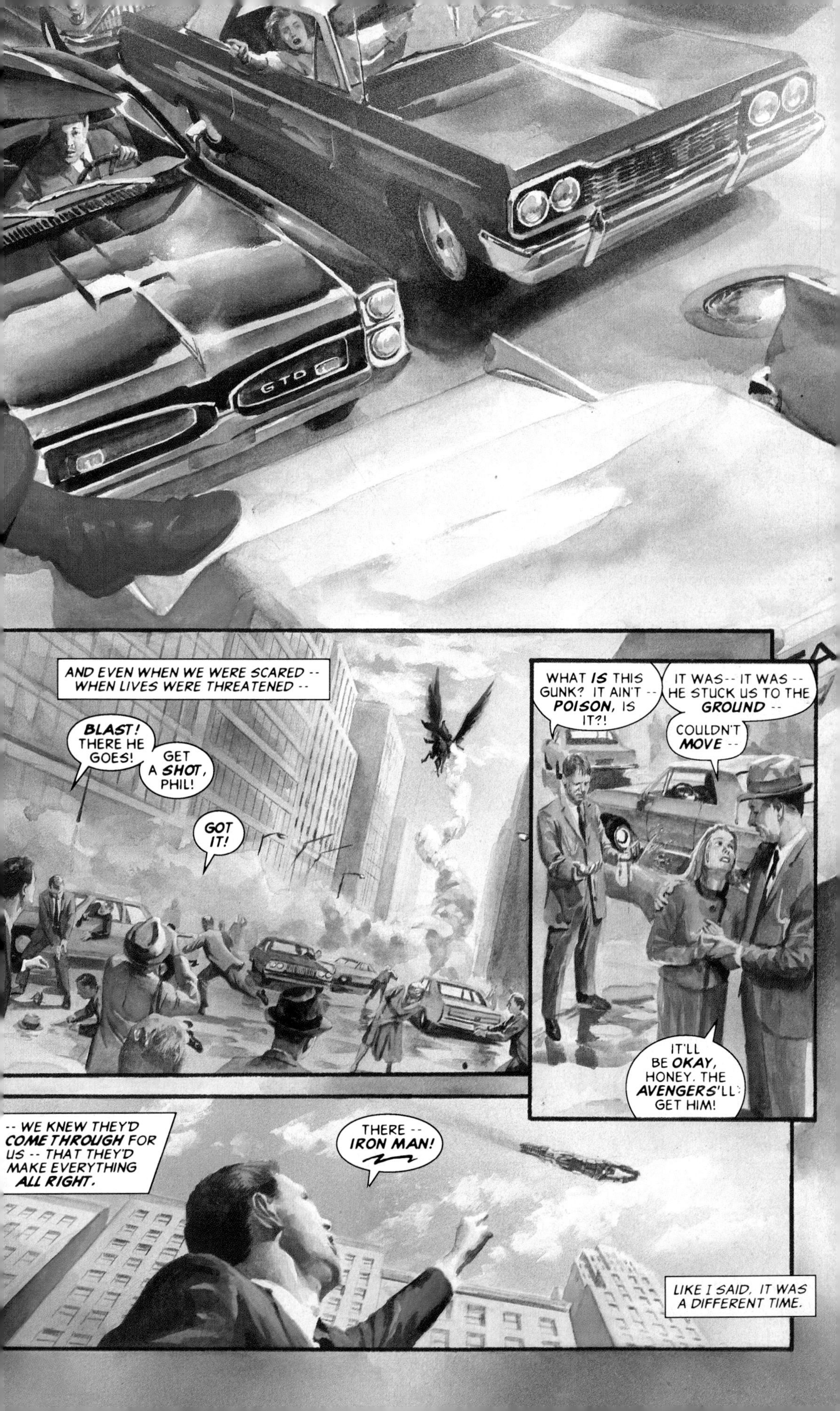
AND EVEN WHEN WE WERE SCARED -- WHEN LIVES WERE THREATENED --
BLAST! THERE HE GOES!
GET A SHOT, PHIL!
GOT IT!
WHAT IS THIS GUNK? IT AIN'T -- POISON, IS IT?!
IT WAS-- IT WAS -- HE STUCK US TO THE GROUND --
COULDN'T MOVE --
IT'LL BE OKAY, HONEY. THE AVENGERS'LL GET HIM!
-- WE KNEW THEY'D COME THROUGH FOR US -- THAT THEY'D MAKE EVERYTHING ALL RIGHT.
THERE -- IRON MAN!
LIKE I SAID, IT WAS A DIFFERENT TIME.

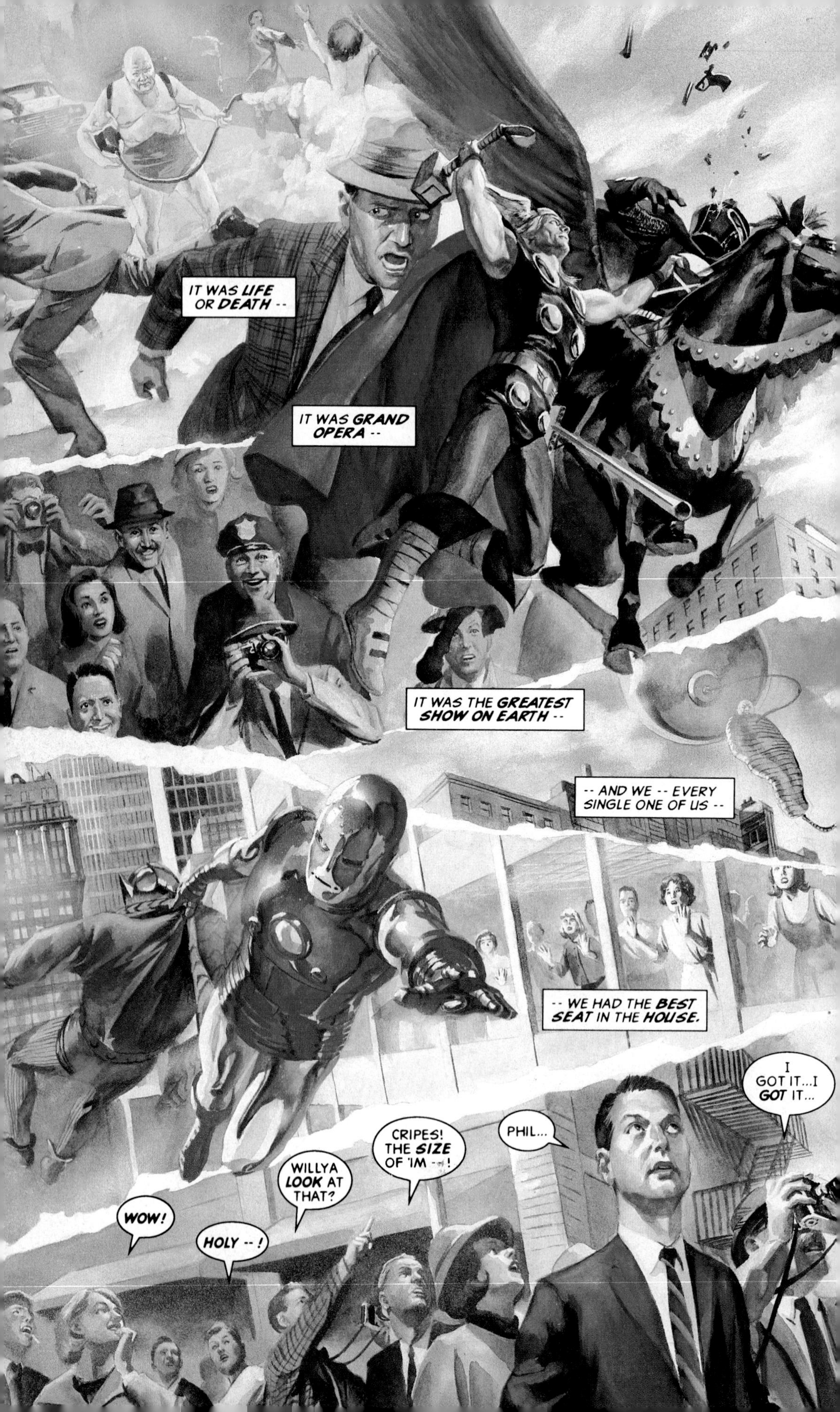
IT WAS LIFE OR DEATH --
IT WAS GRAND OPERA --
IT WAS THE GREATEST SHOW ON EARTH --
-- AND WE -- EVERY SINGLE ONE OF US --
-- WE HAD THE BEST SEAT IN THE HOUSE.
WOW!
HOLY -- !
WILLYA LOOK AT THAT?
CRIPES! THE SIZE OF 'IM --!
PHIL...
I GOT IT...I GOT IT...

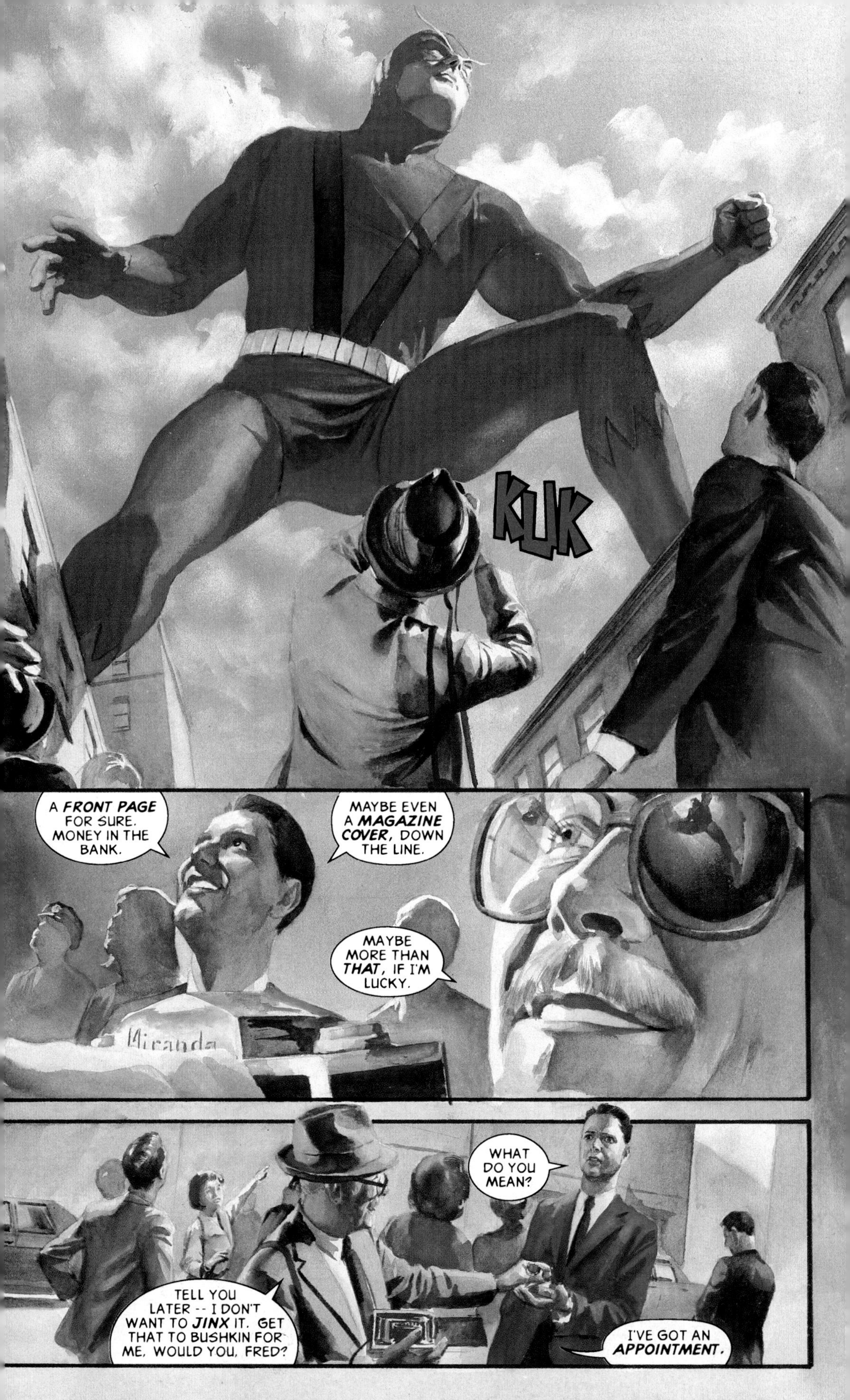
KLIK
A FRONT PAGE FOR SURE. MONEY IN THE BANK.
MAYBE EVEN A MAGAZINE COVER, DOWN THE LINE.
MAYBE MORE THAN THAT, IF I'M LUCKY.
Miranda
WHAT DO YOU MEAN?
TELL YOU LATER -- I DON'T WANT TO JINX IT. GET THAT TO BUSHKIN FOR ME, WOULD YOU, FRED?
I'VE GOT AN APPOINTMENT.

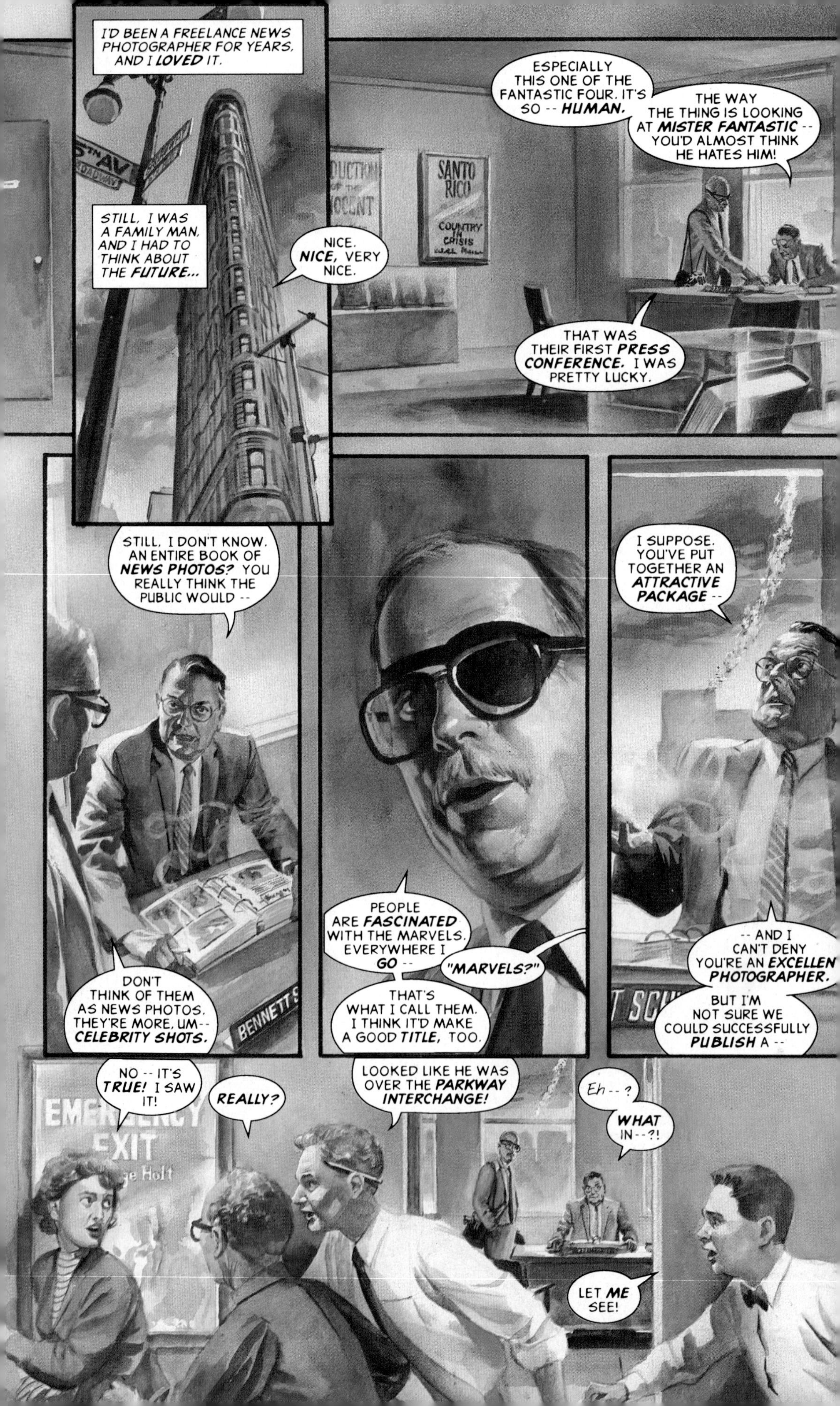

I'D BEEN A FREELANCE NEWS PHOTOGRAPHER FOR YEARS, AND I LOVED IT.
5TH AV
BROADWAY
STILL, I WAS A FAMILY MAN, AND I HAD TO THINK ABOUT THE FUTURE...
NICE. NICE, VERY NICE.
ESPECIALLY THIS ONE OF THE FANTASTIC FOUR. IT'S SO -- HUMAN.
THE WAY THE THING IS LOOKING AT MISTER FANTASTIC -- YOU'D ALMOST THINK HE HATES HIM!
SANTO RICO
COUNTRY IN CRISIS
THAT WAS THEIR FIRST PRESS CONFERENCE. I WAS PRETTY LUCKY.
STILL, I DON'T KNOW. AN ENTIRE BOOK OF NEWS PHOTOS? YOU REALLY THINK THE PUBLIC WOULD --
DON'T THINK OF THEM AS NEWS PHOTOS. THEY'RE MORE, UM-- CELEBRITY SHOTS.
BENNETT S
PEOPLE ARE FASCINATED WITH THE MARVELS. EVERYWHERE I GO --
"MARVELS?"
THAT'S WHAT I CALL THEM. I THINK IT'D MAKE A GOOD TITLE, TOO.
I SUPPOSE. YOU'VE PUT TOGETHER AN ATTRACTIVE PACKAGE --
-- AND I CAN'T DENY YOU'RE AN EXCELLEN PHOTOGRAPHER.
BUT I'M NOT SURE WE COULD SUCCESSFULLY PUBLISH A --
T SCH
EMERGENCY EXIT
NO -- IT'S TRUE! I SAW IT!
REALLY?
LOOKED LIKE HE WAS OVER THE PARKWAY INTERCHANGE!
Eh -- ?
WHAT IN --?!
LET ME SEE!

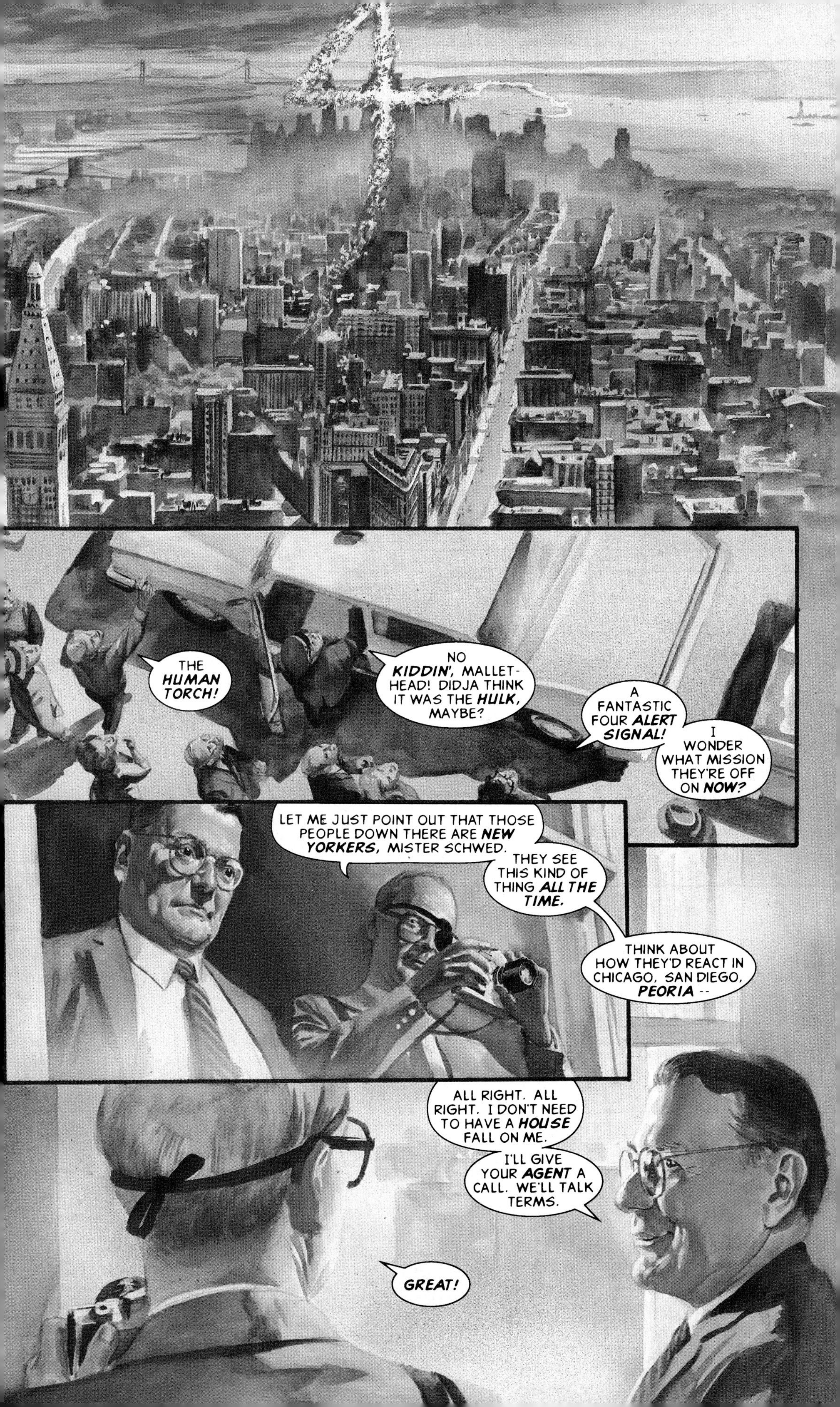
THE HUMAN TORCH!
NO KIDDIN', MALLET-HEAD! DIDJA THINK IT WAS THE HULK, MAYBE?
A FANTASTIC FOUR ALERT SIGNAL!
I WONDER WHAT MISSION THEY'RE OFF ON NOW?
LET ME JUST POINT OUT THAT THOSE PEOPLE DOWN THERE ARE NEW YORKERS, MISTER SCHWED.
THEY SEE THIS KIND OF THING ALL THE TIME.
THINK ABOUT HOW THEY'D REACT IN CHICAGO, SAN DIEGO, PEORIA --
ALL RIGHT. ALL RIGHT. I DON'T NEED TO HAVE A HOUSE FALL ON ME.
I'LL GIVE YOUR AGENT A CALL. WE'LL TALK TERMS.
GREAT!

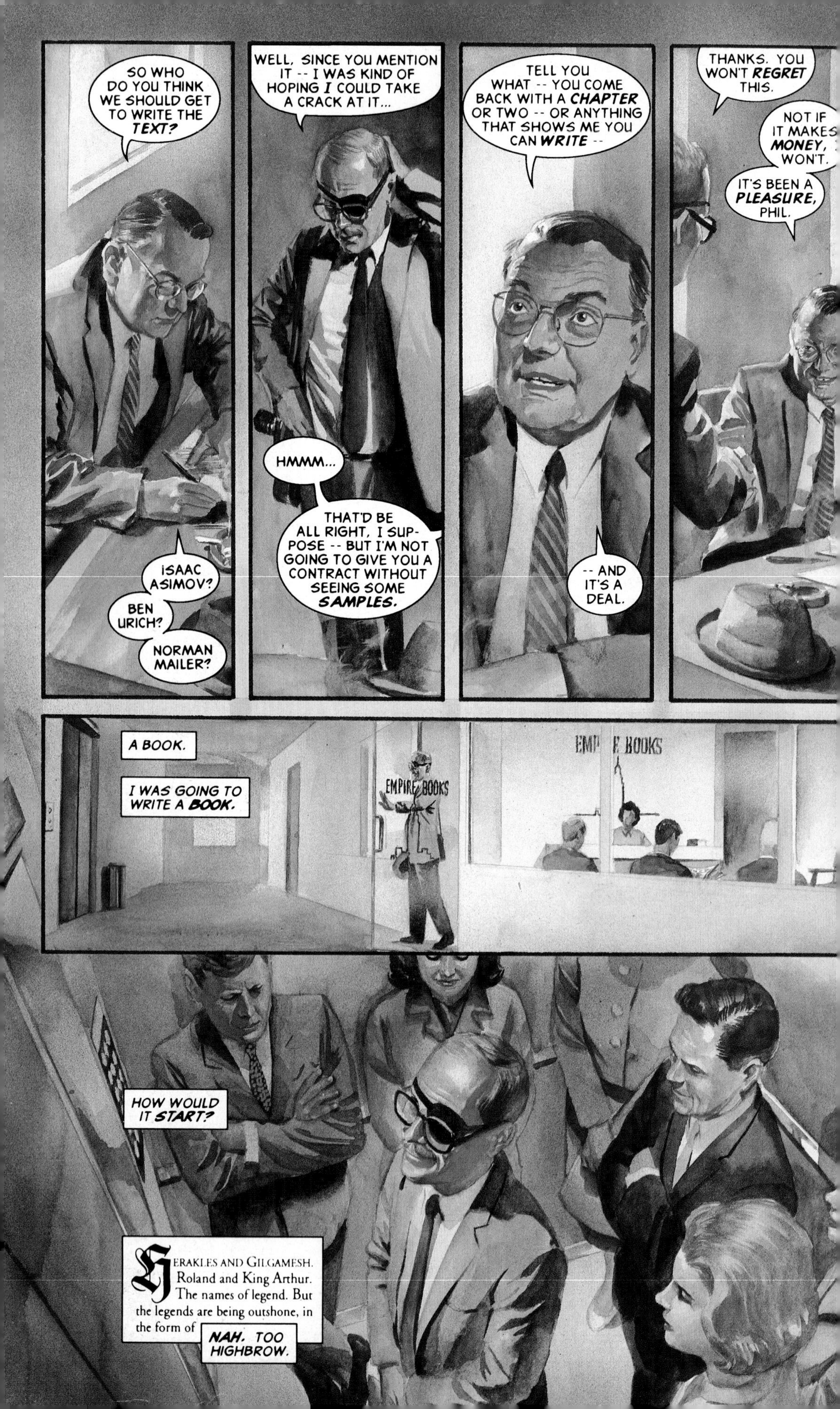

SO WHO DO YOU THINK WE SHOULD GET TO WRITE THE *TEXT?*
ISAAC ASIMOV?
BEN URICH?
NORMAN MAILER?
WELL, SINCE YOU MENTION IT -- I WAS KIND OF HOPING *I* COULD TAKE A CRACK AT IT...
HMMM...
THAT'D BE ALL RIGHT, I SUP-POSE -- BUT I'M NOT GOING TO GIVE YOU A CONTRACT WITHOUT SEEING SOME *SAMPLES.*
TELL YOU WHAT -- YOU COME BACK WITH A *CHAPTER* OR TWO -- OR ANYTHING THAT SHOWS ME YOU CAN *WRITE* --
-- AND IT'S A DEAL.
THANKS. YOU WON'T *REGRET* THIS.
NOT IF IT MAKES *MONEY,* WON'T.
IT'S BEEN A *PLEASURE,* PHIL.
A BOOK.
I WAS GOING TO WRITE A *BOOK.*
EMPIRE BOOKS
EMP E BOOKS
HOW WOULD IT *START?*
HERAKLES AND GILGAMESH. Roland and King Arthur. The names of legend. But the legends are being outshone, in the form of
NAH. TOO HIGHBROW.

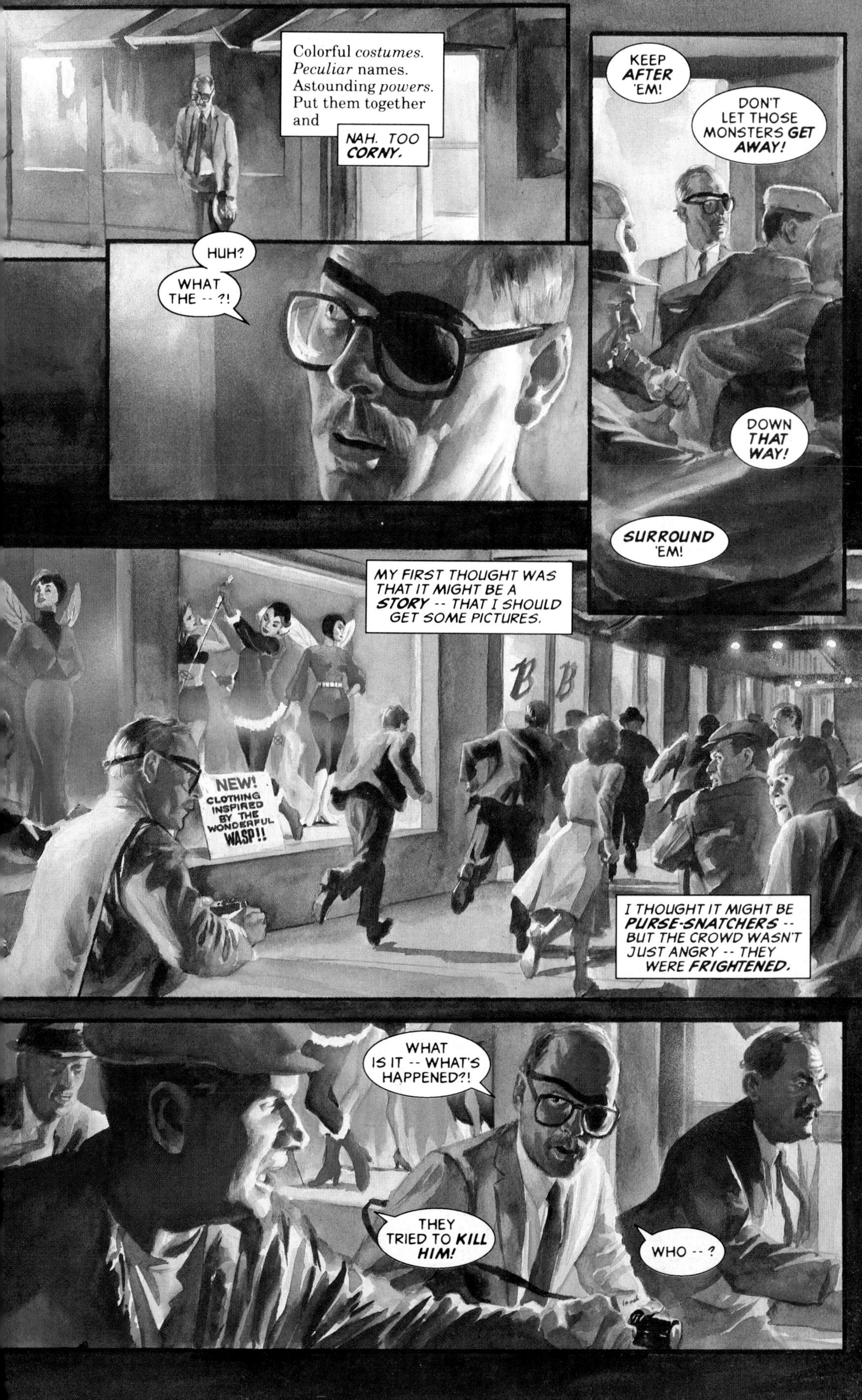
Colorful *costumes.* *Peculiar* names. Astounding *powers.* Put them together and
NAH. TOO **CORNY.**
KEEP **AFTER** 'EM!
DON'T LET THOSE MONSTERS **GET AWAY!**
HUH?
WHAT THE -- ?!
DOWN **THAT WAY!**
SURROUND 'EM!
MY FIRST THOUGHT WAS THAT IT **MIGHT** BE A **STORY** -- THAT I SHOULD GET SOME PICTURES.
B
B
NEW! CLOTHING INSPIRED BY THE WONDERFUL WASP!!
I THOUGHT IT MIGHT BE **PURSE-SNATCHERS** -- BUT THE CROWD WASN'T JUST ANGRY -- THEY WERE **FRIGHTENED.**
WHAT IS IT -- WHAT'S HAPPENED?!
THEY TRIED TO **KILL HIM!**
WHO -- ?

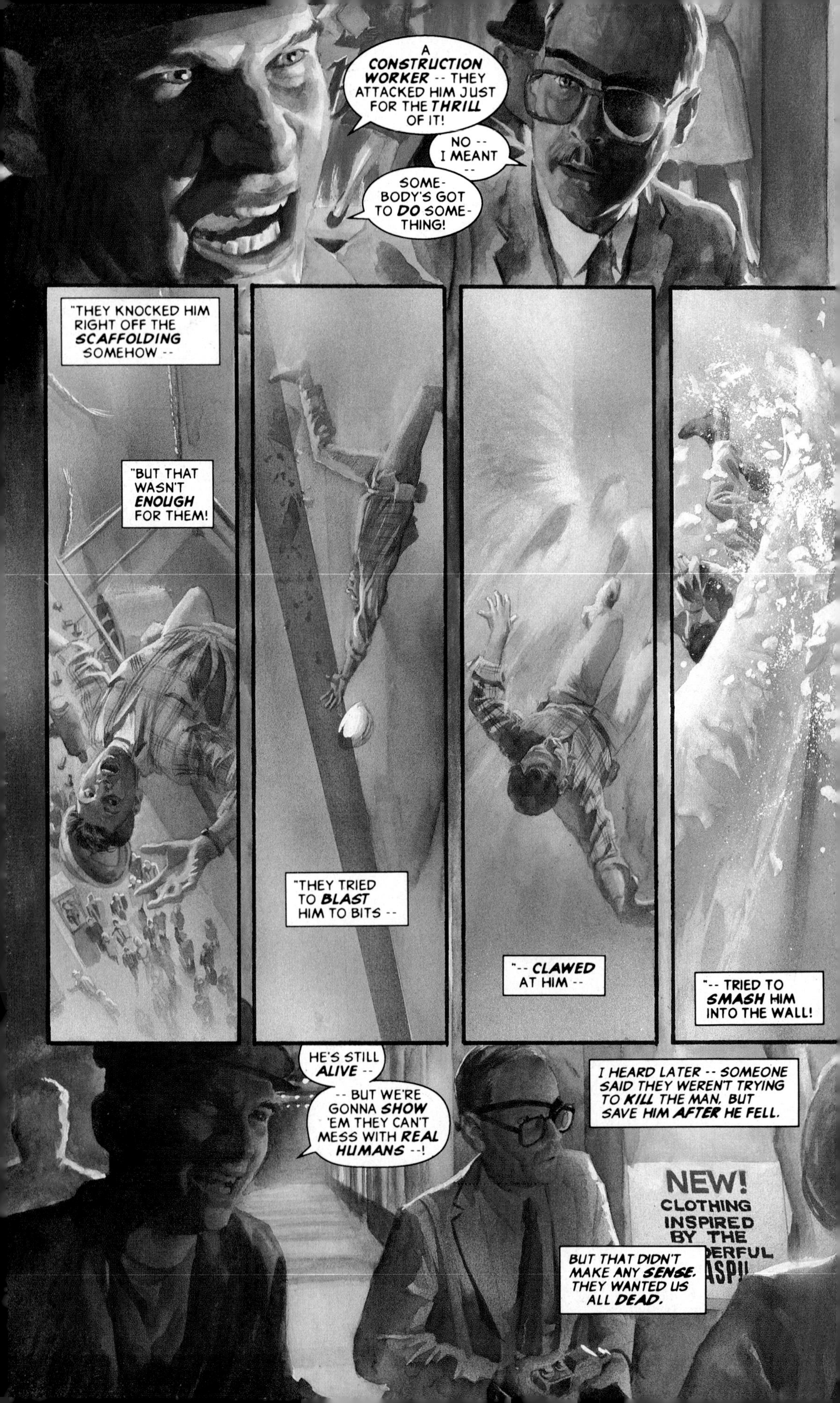

A CONSTRUCTION WORKER -- THEY ATTACKED HIM JUST FOR THE THRILL OF IT!
NO -- I MEANT --
SOME-BODY'S GOT TO DO SOME-THING!
"THEY KNOCKED HIM RIGHT OFF THE SCAFFOLDING SOMEHOW --
"BUT THAT WASN'T ENOUGH FOR THEM!
"THEY TRIED TO BLAST HIM TO BITS --
"-- CLAWED AT HIM --
"-- TRIED TO SMASH HIM INTO THE WALL!
HE'S STILL ALIVE --
-- BUT WE'RE GONNA SHOW 'EM THEY CAN'T MESS WITH REAL HUMANS --!
I HEARD LATER -- SOMEONE SAID THEY WEREN'T TRYING TO KILL THE MAN, BUT SAVE HIM AFTER HE FELL.
NEW! CLOTHING INSPIRED BY THE
BUT THAT DIDN'T MAKE ANY SENSE. THEY WANTED US ALL DEAD.

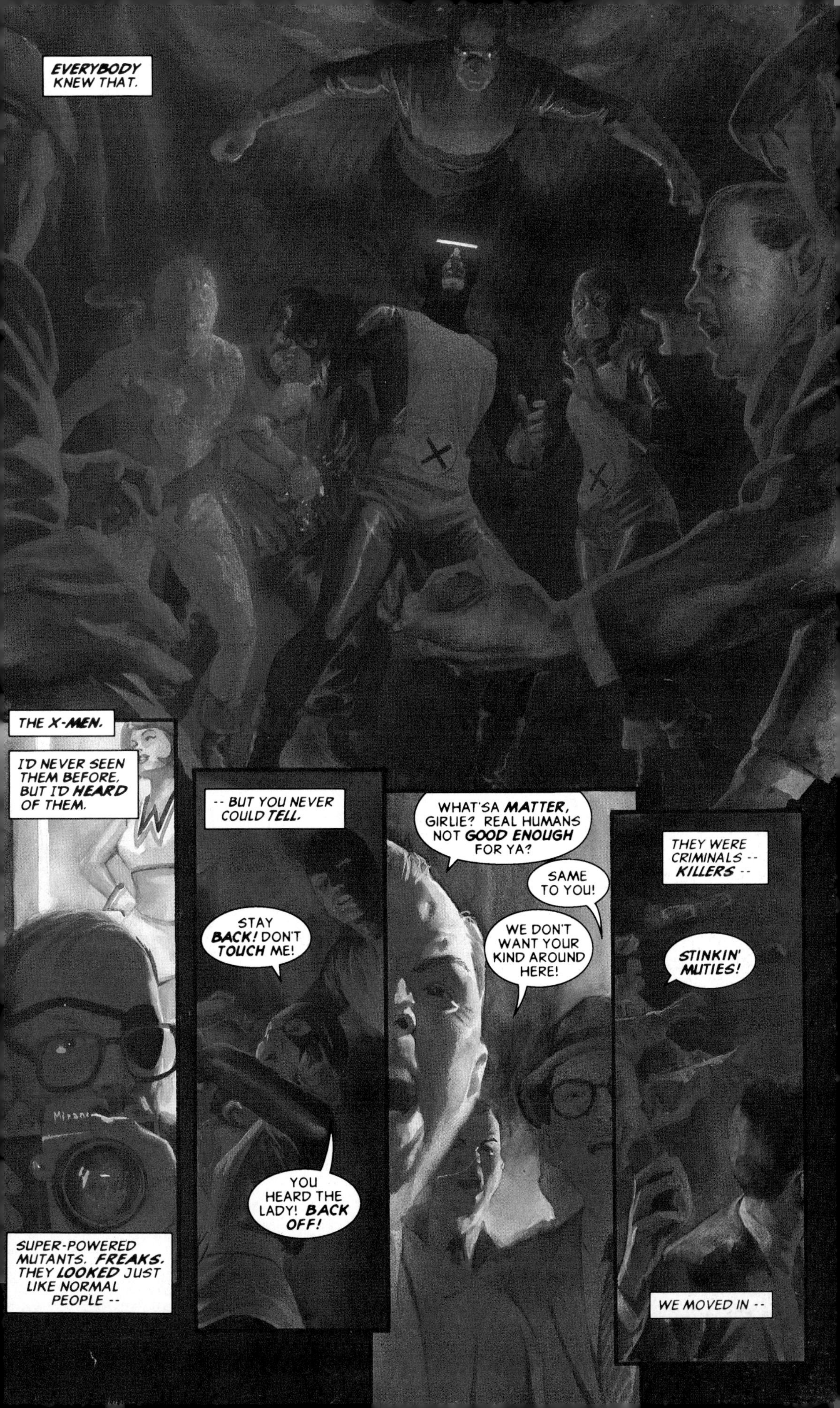

EVERYBODY KNEW THAT.
THE X-MEN.
I'D NEVER SEEN THEM BEFORE, BUT I'D HEARD OF THEM.
SUPER-POWERED MUTANTS. FREAKS. THEY LOOKED JUST LIKE NORMAL PEOPLE --
-- BUT YOU NEVER COULD TELL.
STAY BACK! DON'T TOUCH ME!
YOU HEARD THE LADY! BACK OFF!
WHAT'SA MATTER, GIRLIE? REAL HUMANS NOT GOOD ENOUGH FOR YA?
SAME TO YOU!
WE DON'T WANT YOUR KIND AROUND HERE!
THEY WERE CRIMINALS -- KILLERS --
STINKIN' MUTIES!
WE MOVED IN --

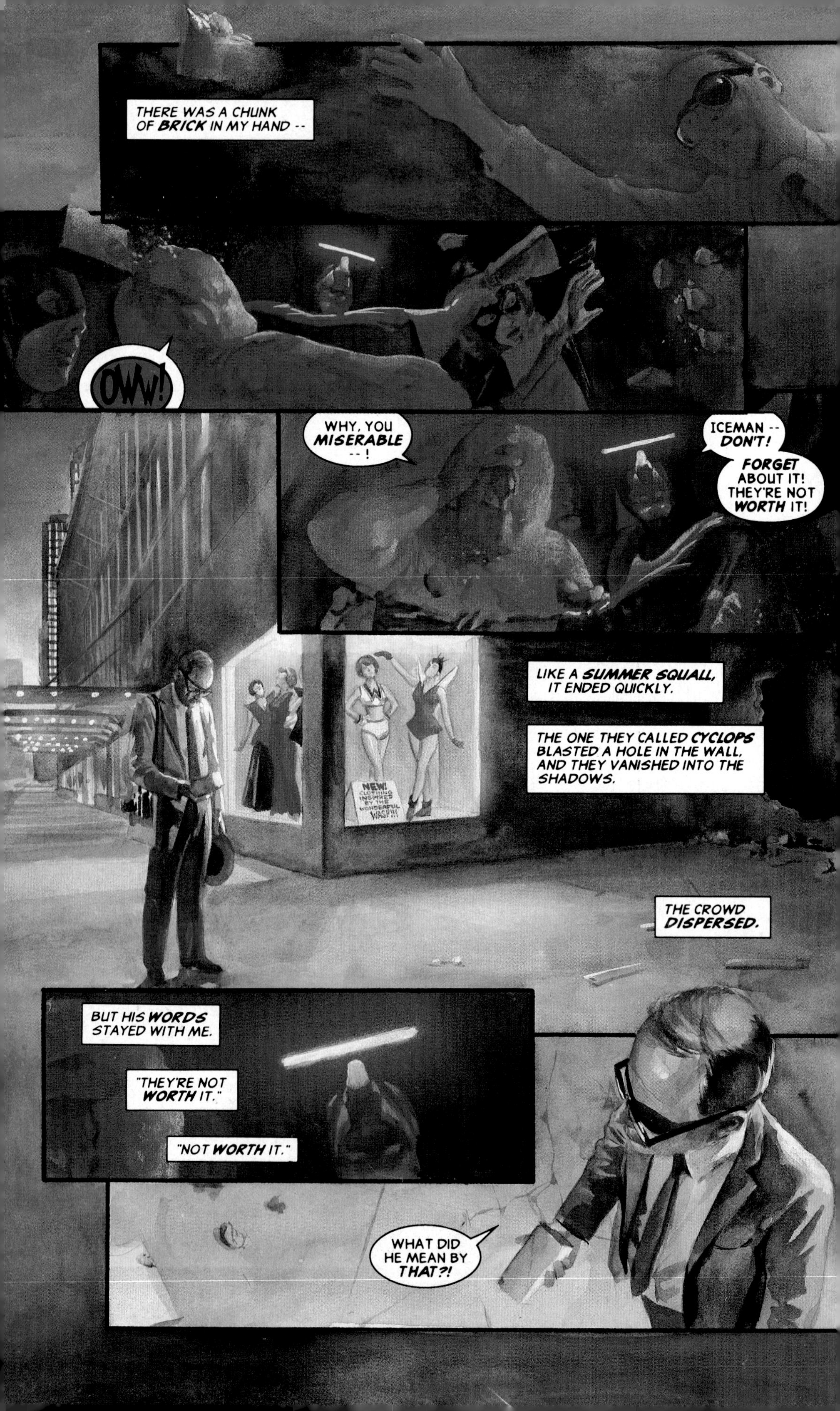
THERE WAS A CHUNK OF BRICK IN MY HAND --
OWW!
WHY, YOU MISERABLE --!
ICEMAN -- DON'T!
FORGET ABOUT IT! THEY'RE NOT WORTH IT!
NEW! CLOTHING INSPIRED BY THE WONDERFUL WASP!!!
LIKE A SUMMER SQUALL, IT ENDED QUICKLY.
THE ONE THEY CALLED CYCLOPS BLASTED A HOLE IN THE WALL, AND THEY VANISHED INTO THE SHADOWS.
THE CROWD DISPERSED.
BUT HIS WORDS STAYED WITH ME.
"THEY'RE NOT WORTH IT."
"NOT WORTH IT."
WHAT DID HE MEAN BY THAT?!

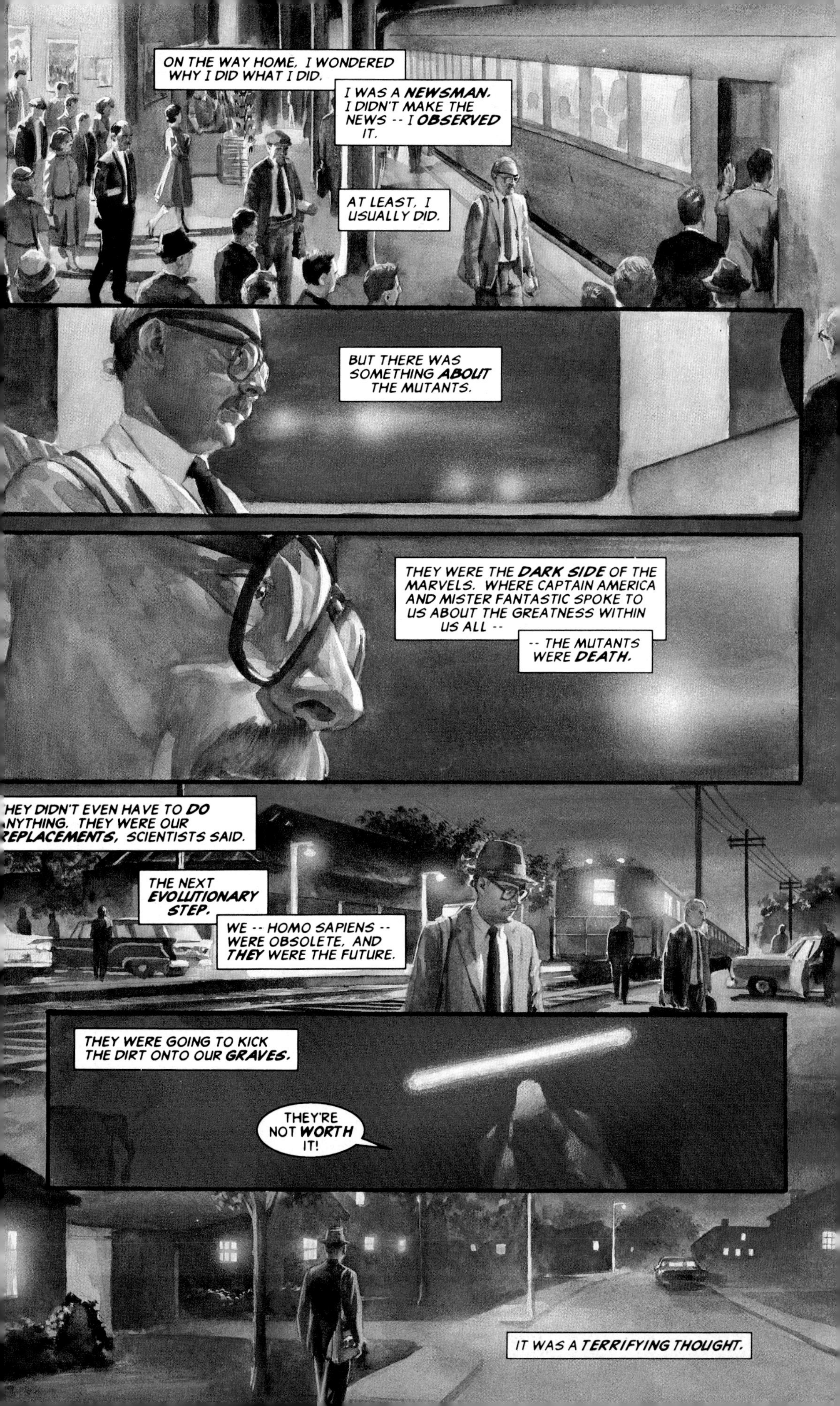
ON THE WAY HOME, I WONDERED WHY I DID WHAT I DID.
I WAS A NEWSMAN. I DIDN'T MAKE THE NEWS -- I OBSERVED IT.
AT LEAST, I USUALLY DID.
BUT THERE WAS SOMETHING ABOUT THE MUTANTS.
THEY WERE THE DARK SIDE OF THE MARVELS. WHERE CAPTAIN AMERICA AND MISTER FANTASTIC SPOKE TO US ABOUT THE GREATNESS WITHIN US ALL --
-- THE MUTANTS WERE DEATH.
HEY DIDN'T EVEN HAVE TO DO NYTHING. THEY WERE OUR REPLACEMENTS, SCIENTISTS SAID.
THE NEXT EVOLUTIONARY STEP.
WE -- HOMO SAPIENS -- WERE OBSOLETE, AND THEY WERE THE FUTURE.
THEY WERE GOING TO KICK THE DIRT ONTO OUR GRAVES.
THEY'RE NOT WORTH IT!
IT WAS A TERRIFYING THOUGHT.

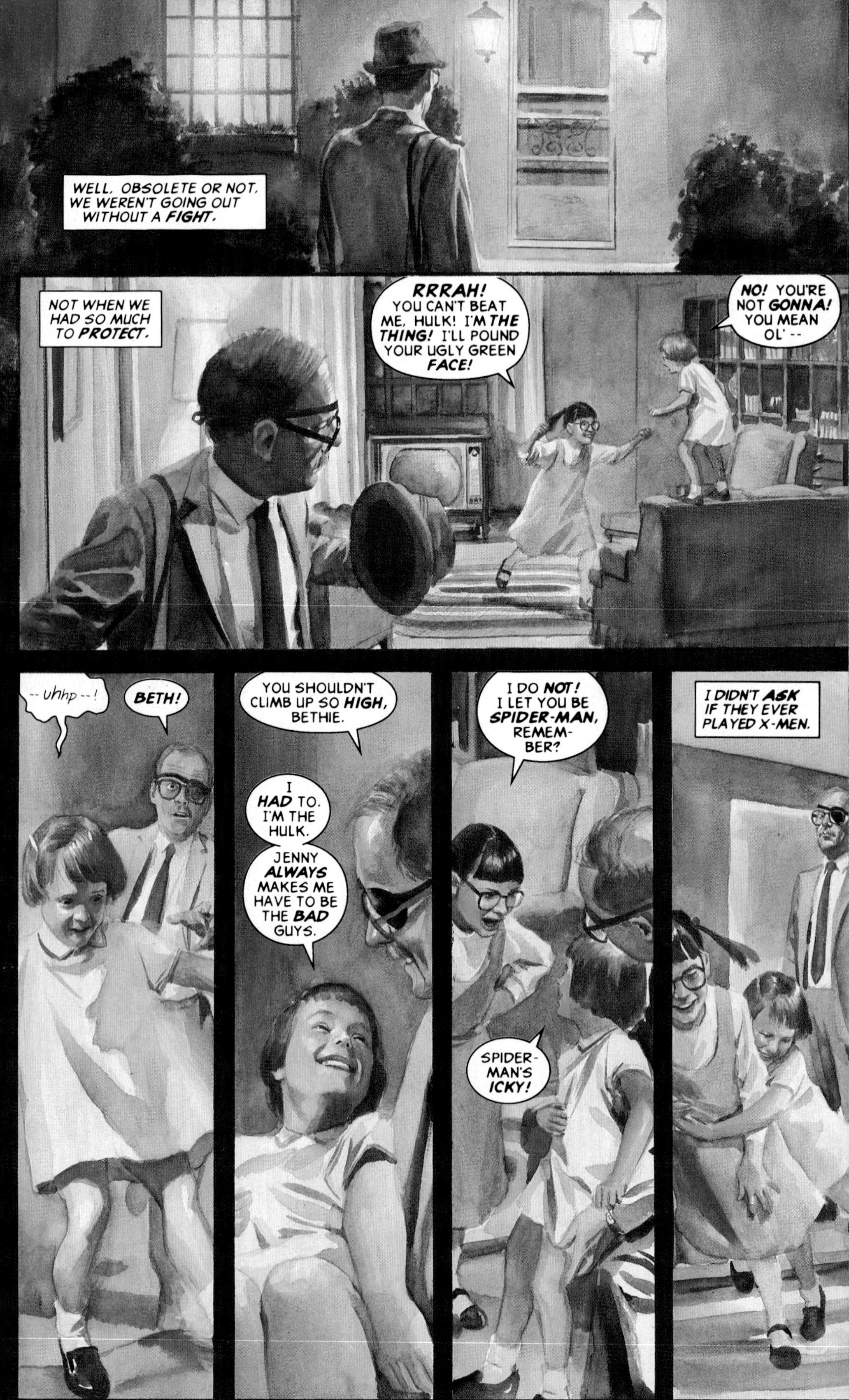
WELL, OBSOLETE OR NOT, WE WEREN'T GOING OUT WITHOUT A FIGHT.
NOT WHEN WE HAD SO MUCH TO PROTECT.
RRRAH! YOU CAN'T BEAT ME, HULK! I'M THE THING! I'LL POUND YOUR UGLY GREEN FACE!
NO! YOU'RE NOT GONNA! YOU MEAN OL' --
-- uhhp --!
BETH!
YOU SHOULDN'T CLIMB UP SO HIGH, BETHIE.
I HAD TO. I'M THE HULK.
JENNY ALWAYS MAKES ME HAVE TO BE THE BAD GUYS.
I DO NOT! I LET YOU BE SPIDER-MAN, REMEMBER?
SPIDER-MAN'S ICKY!
I DIDN'T ASK IF THEY EVER PLAYED X-MEN.

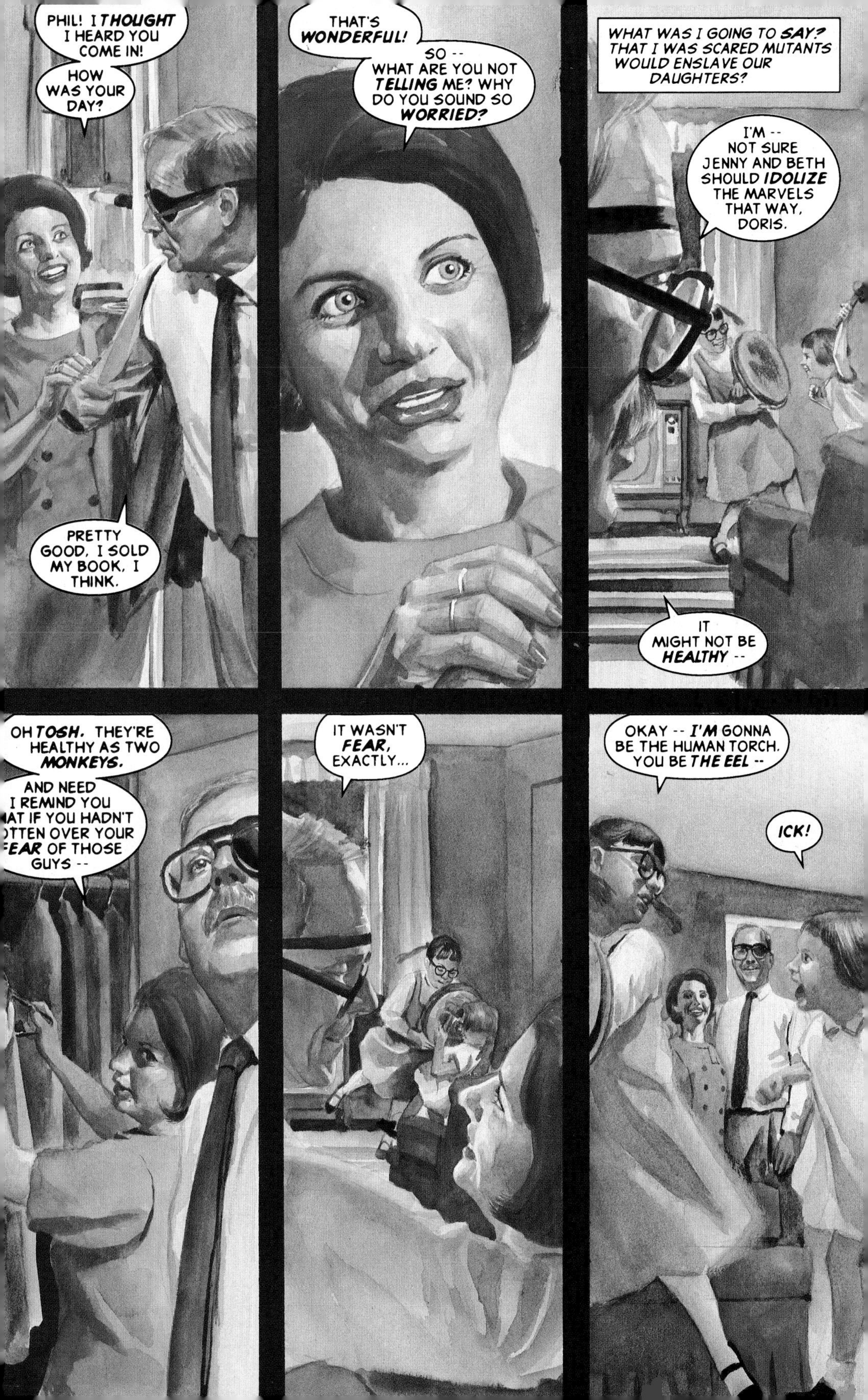
PHIL! I *THOUGHT* I HEARD YOU COME IN!
HOW WAS YOUR DAY?
PRETTY GOOD. I SOLD MY BOOK, I THINK.
THAT'S *WONDERFUL!*
SO -- WHAT ARE YOU NOT *TELLING* ME? WHY DO YOU SOUND SO *WORRIED?*
WHAT WAS I GOING TO *SAY?* THAT I WAS SCARED MUTANTS WOULD ENSLAVE OUR DAUGHTERS?
I'M -- NOT SURE JENNY AND BETH SHOULD *IDOLIZE* THE MARVELS THAT WAY, DORIS.
IT MIGHT NOT BE *HEALTHY* --
OH *TOSH.* THEY'RE HEALTHY AS TWO *MONKEYS.*
AND NEED I REMIND YOU
IT WASN'T *FEAR,* EXACTLY...
OKAY -- *I'M* GONNA BE THE HUMAN TORCH. YOU BE *THE EEL* --
ICK!

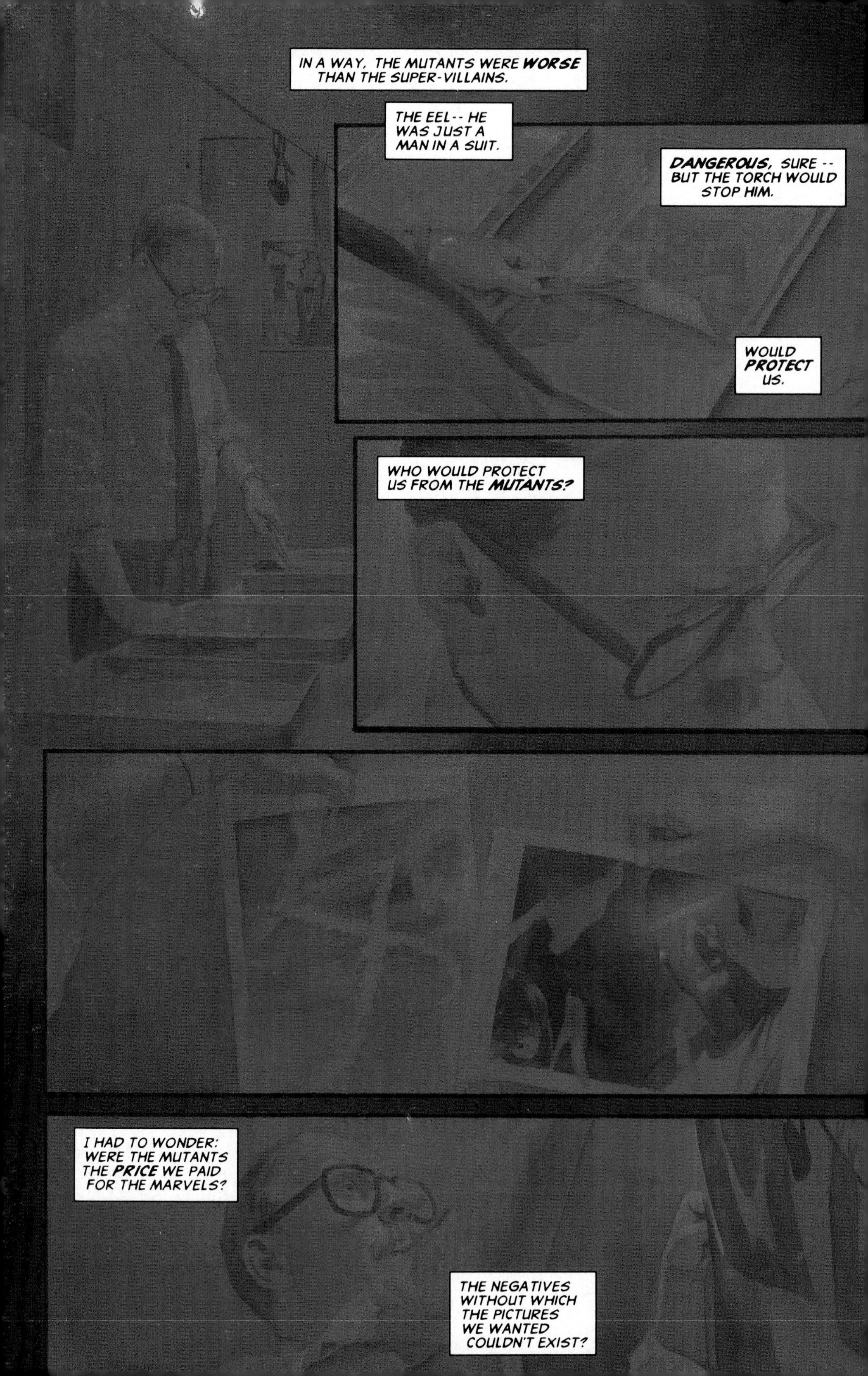
IN A WAY, THE MUTANTS WERE WORSE THAN THE SUPER-VILLAINS.
THE EEL-- HE WAS JUST A MAN IN A SUIT.
DANGEROUS, SURE -- BUT THE TORCH WOULD STOP HIM.
WOULD PROTECT US.
WHO WOULD PROTECT US FROM THE MUTANTS?
I HAD TO WONDER: WERE THE MUTANTS THE PRICE WE PAID FOR THE MARVELS?
THE NEGATIVES WITHOUT WHICH THE PICTURES WE WANTED COULDN'T EXIST?

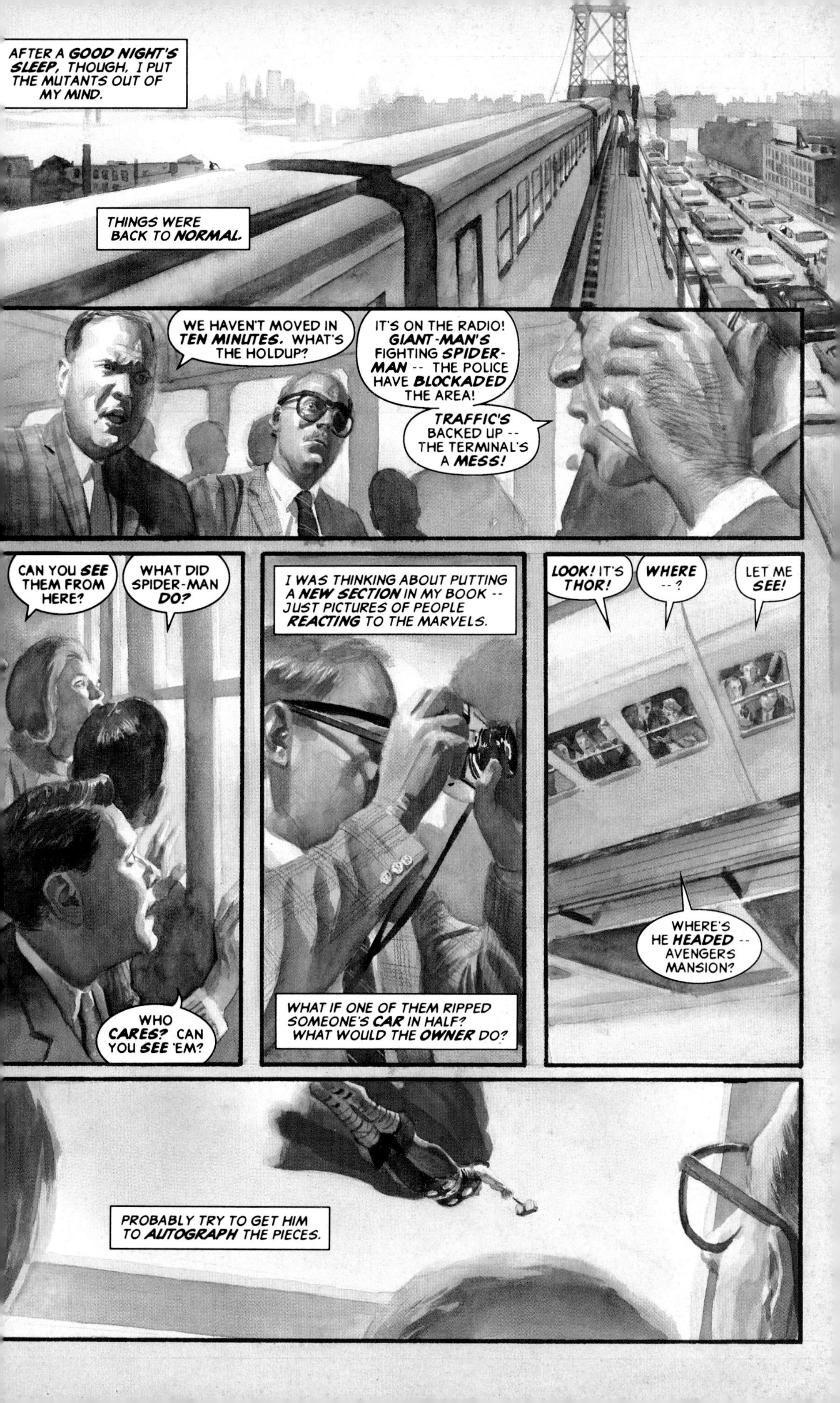

AFTER A GOOD NIGHT'S SLEEP, THOUGH, I PUT THE MUTANTS OUT OF MY MIND.
THINGS WERE BACK TO NORMAL.
WE HAVEN'T MOVED IN TEN MINUTES. WHAT'S THE HOLDUP?
IT'S ON THE RADIO! GIANT-MAN'S FIGHTING SPIDER-MAN -- THE POLICE HAVE BLOCKADED THE AREA!
TRAFFIC'S BACKED UP -- THE TERMINAL'S A MESS!
CAN YOU SEE THEM FROM HERE?
WHAT DID SPIDER-MAN DO?
WHO CARES? CAN YOU SEE 'EM?
I WAS THINKING ABOUT PUTTING A NEW SECTION IN MY BOOK -- JUST PICTURES OF PEOPLE REACTING TO THE MARVELS.
WHAT IF ONE OF THEM RIPPED SOMEONE'S CAR IN HALF? WHAT WOULD THE OWNER DO?
LOOK! IT'S THOR!
WHERE --?
LET ME SEE!
WHERE'S HE HEADED -- AVENGERS MANSION?
PROBABLY TRY TO GET HIM TO AUTOGRAPH THE PIECES.

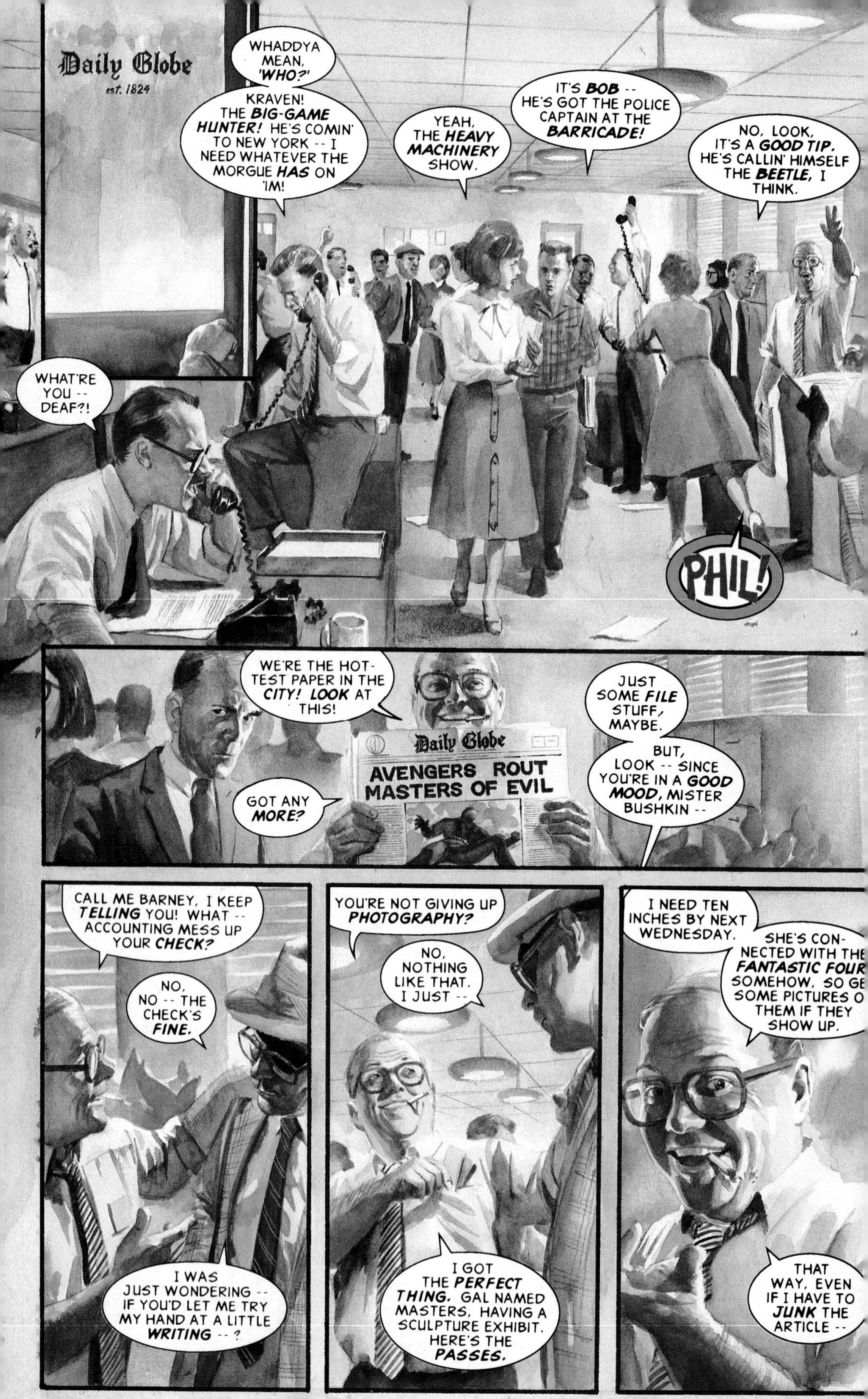
Daily Globe
est. 1824
WHADDYA MEAN, 'WHO?'
KRAVEN! THE BIG-GAME HUNTER! HE'S COMIN' TO NEW YORK -- I NEED WHATEVER THE MORGUE HAS ON 'IM!
YEAH, THE HEAVY MACHINERY SHOW.
IT'S BOB -- HE'S GOT THE POLICE CAPTAIN AT THE BARRICADE!
NO, LOOK, IT'S A GOOD TIP. HE'S CALLIN' HIMSELF THE BEETLE, I THINK.
WHAT'RE YOU -- DEAF?!
PHIL!
WE'RE THE HOT-TEST PAPER IN THE CITY! LOOK AT THIS!
Daily Globe
AVENGERS ROUT MASTERS OF EVIL
GOT ANY MORE?
JUST SOME FILE STUFF, MAYBE.
BUT, LOOK -- SINCE YOU'RE IN A GOOD MOOD, MISTER BUSHKIN --
CALL ME BARNEY, I KEEP TELLING YOU! WHAT -- ACCOUNTING MESS UP YOUR CHECK?
NO, NO -- THE CHECK'S FINE.
I WAS JUST WONDERING -- IF YOU'D LET ME TRY MY HAND AT A LITTLE WRITING -- ?
YOU'RE NOT GIVING UP PHOTOGRAPHY?
NO, NOTHING LIKE THAT. I JUST --
I GOT THE PERFECT THING. GAL NAMED MASTERS, HAVING A SCULPTURE EXHIBIT. HERE'S THE PASSES.
I NEED TEN INCHES BY NEXT WEDNESDAY.
SHE'S CON-NECTED WITH THE FANTASTIC FOUR SOMEHOW, SO GE SOME PICTURES O THEM IF THEY SHOW UP.
THAT WAY, EVEN IF I HAVE TO JUNK THE ARTICLE --

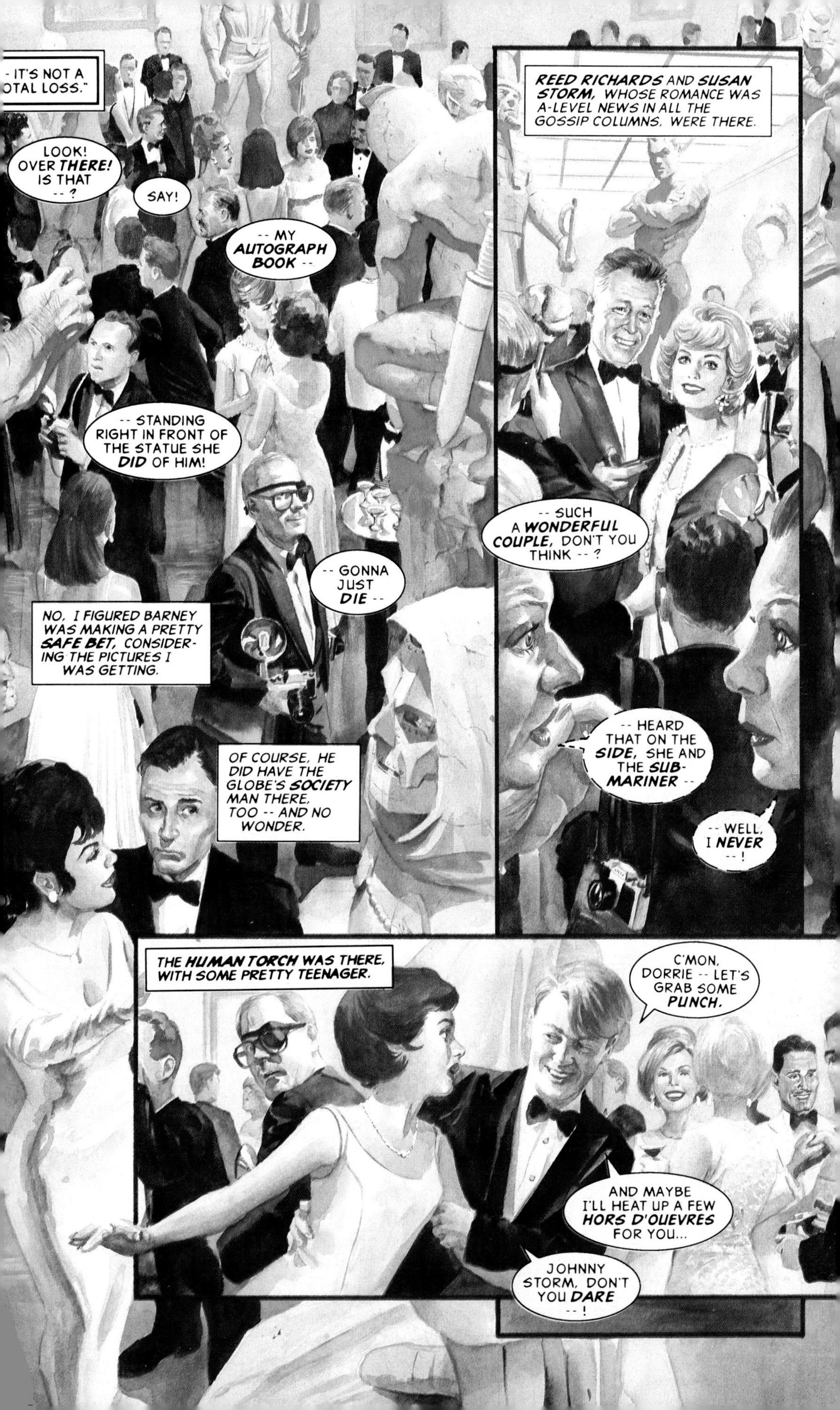

- IT'S NOT A
OTAL LOSS."
LOOK! OVER THERE! IS THAT -- ?
SAY!
-- MY AUTOGRAPH BOOK --
-- STANDING RIGHT IN FRONT OF THE STATUE SHE DID OF HIM!
-- GONNA JUST DIE --
NO, I FIGURED BARNEY WAS MAKING A PRETTY SAFE BET, CONSIDERING THE PICTURES I WAS GETTING.
OF COURSE, HE DID HAVE THE GLOBE'S SOCIETY MAN THERE, TOO -- AND NO WONDER.
REED RICHARDS AND SUSAN STORM, WHOSE ROMANCE WAS A-LEVEL NEWS IN ALL THE GOSSIP COLUMNS, WERE THERE.
-- SUCH A WONDERFUL COUPLE, DON'T YOU THINK -- ?
-- HEARD THAT ON THE SIDE, SHE AND THE SUB-MARINER --
-- WELL, I NEVER --!
THE HUMAN TORCH WAS THERE, WITH SOME PRETTY TEENAGER.
C'MON, DORRIE -- LET'S GRAB SOME PUNCH.
AND MAYBE I'LL HEAT UP A FEW HORS D'OUEVRES FOR YOU...
JOHNNY STORM, DON'T YOU DARE --!

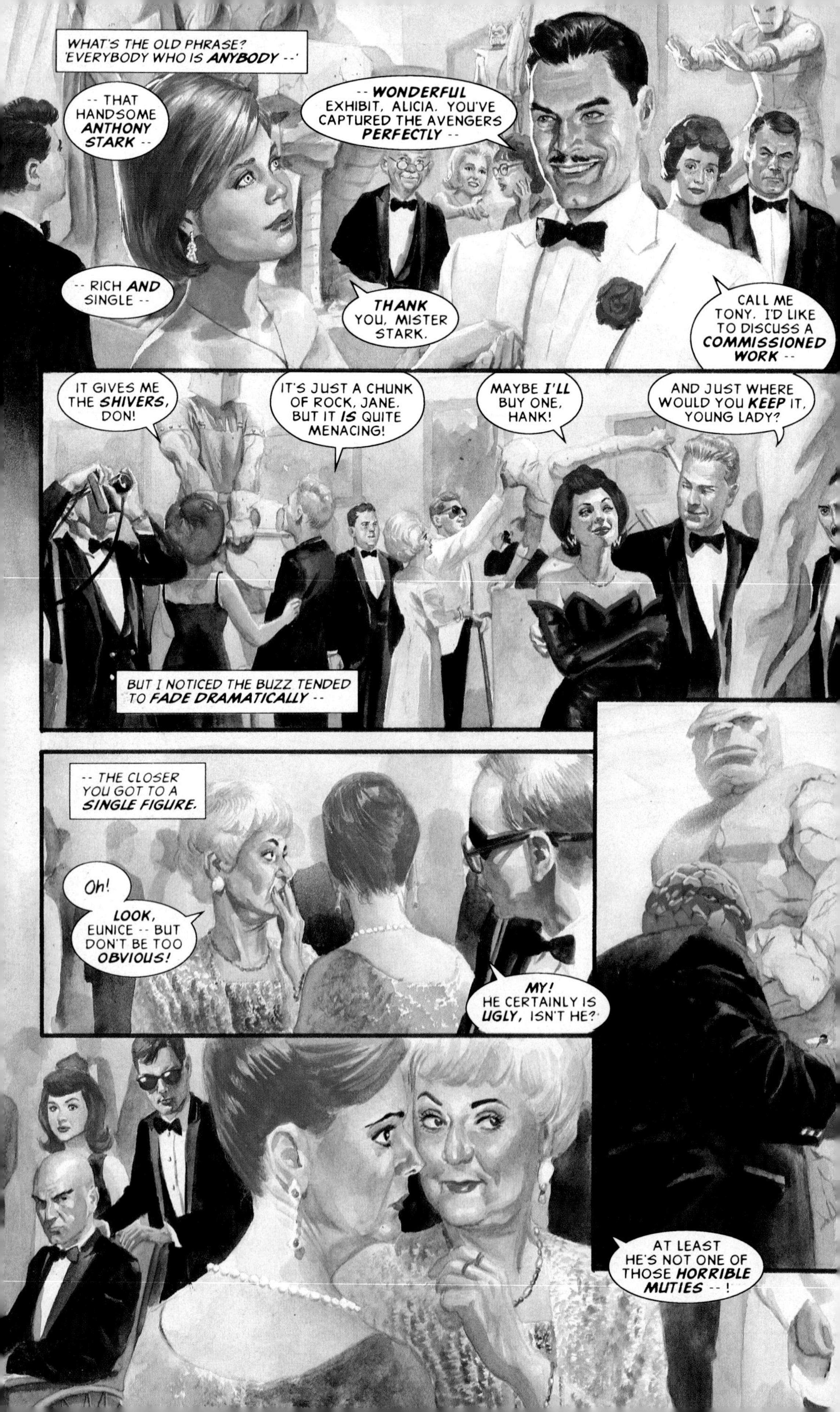
WHAT'S THE OLD PHRASE? 'EVERYBODY WHO IS ANYBODY --'
-- THAT HANDSOME ANTHONY STARK --
-- WONDERFUL EXHIBIT, ALICIA. YOU'VE CAPTURED THE AVENGERS PERFECTLY --
-- RICH AND SINGLE --
THANK YOU, MISTER STARK.
CALL ME TONY. I'D LIKE TO DISCUSS A COMMISSIONED WORK --
IT GIVES ME THE SHIVERS, DON!
IT'S JUST A CHUNK OF ROCK, JANE. BUT IT IS QUITE MENACING!
MAYBE I'LL BUY ONE, HANK!
AND JUST WHERE WOULD YOU KEEP IT, YOUNG LADY?
BUT I NOTICED THE BUZZ TENDED TO FADE DRAMATICALLY --
-- THE CLOSER YOU GOT TO A SINGLE FIGURE.
Oh!
LOOK, EUNICE -- BUT DON'T BE TOO OBVIOUS!
MY! HE CERTAINLY IS UGLY, ISN'T HE?
AT LEAST HE'S NOT ONE OF THOSE HORRIBLE MUTIES -- !

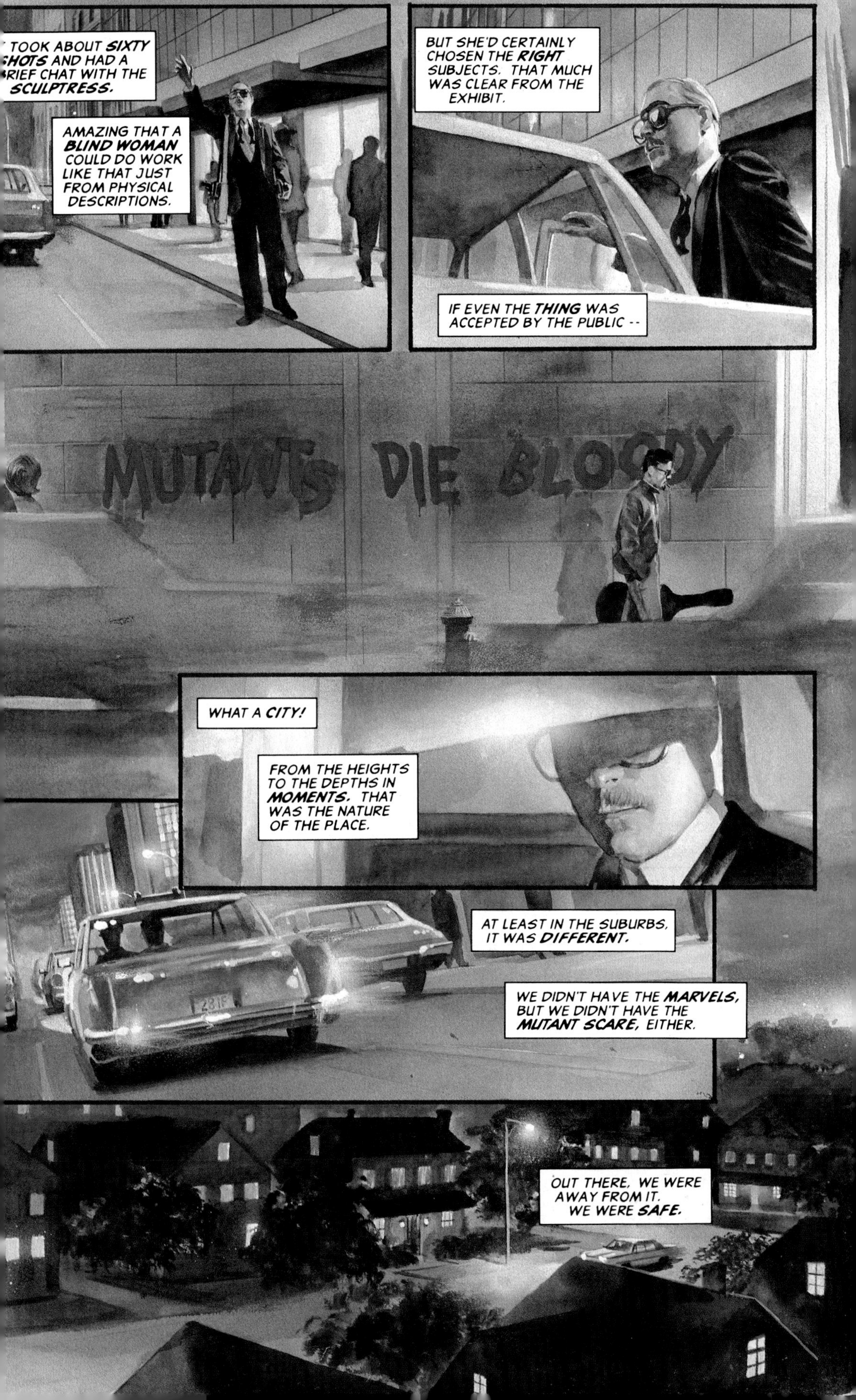

T TOOK ABOUT SIXTY SHOTS AND HAD A BRIEF CHAT WITH THE SCULPTRESS.
AMAZING THAT A BLIND WOMAN COULD DO WORK LIKE THAT JUST FROM PHYSICAL DESCRIPTIONS.
BUT SHE'D CERTAINLY CHOSEN THE RIGHT SUBJECTS. THAT MUCH WAS CLEAR FROM THE EXHIBIT.
IF EVEN THE THING WAS ACCEPTED BY THE PUBLIC --
MUTANTS DIE BLOODY
WHAT A CITY!
FROM THE HEIGHTS TO THE DEPTHS IN MOMENTS. THAT WAS THE NATURE OF THE PLACE.
AT LEAST IN THE SUBURBS, IT WAS DIFFERENT.
WE DIDN'T HAVE THE MARVELS, BUT WE DIDN'T HAVE THE MUTANT SCARE, EITHER.
OUT THERE, WE WERE AWAY FROM IT. WE WERE SAFE.

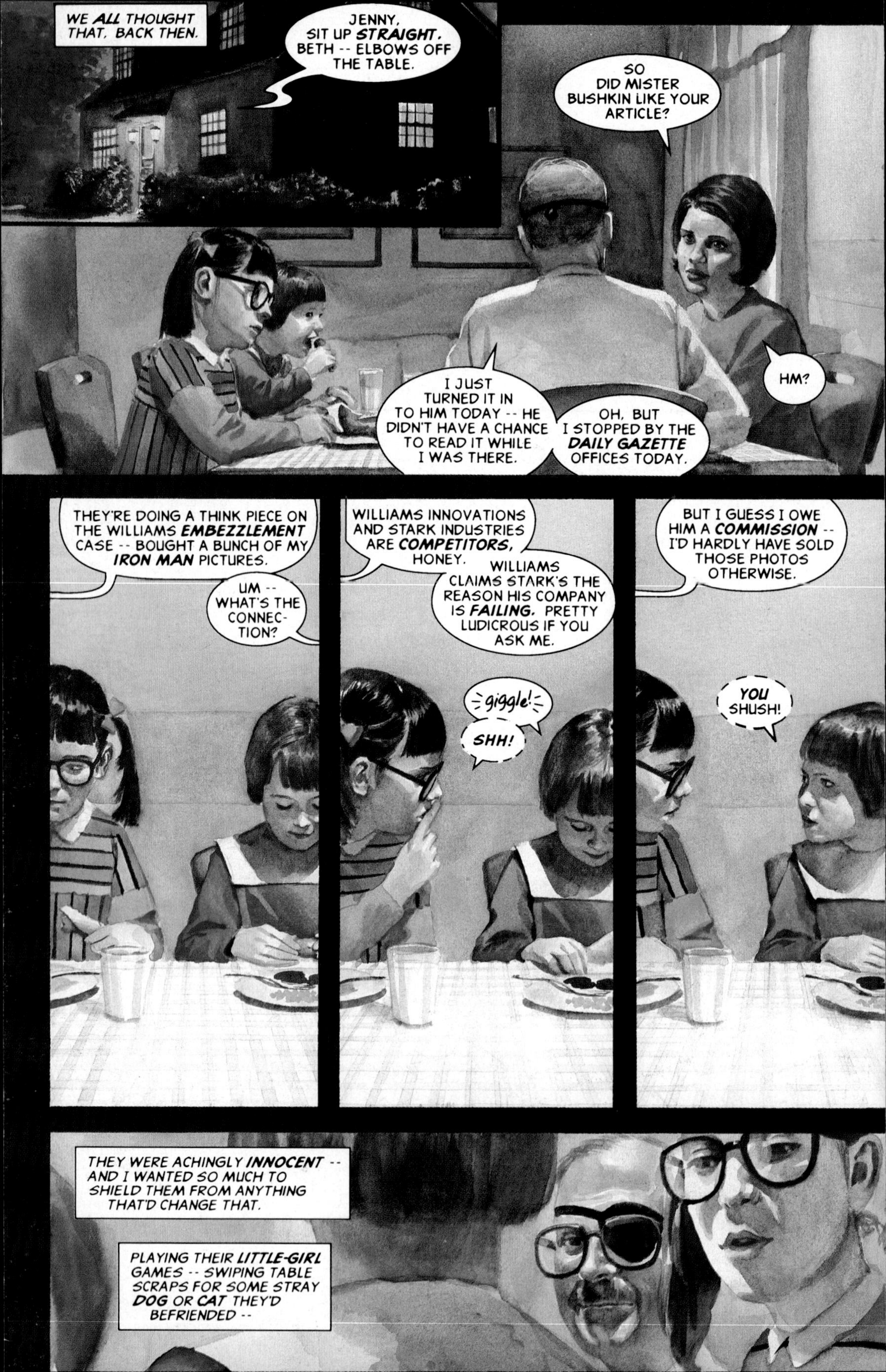

WE ALL THOUGHT THAT, BACK THEN.
JENNY, SIT UP STRAIGHT. BETH -- ELBOWS OFF THE TABLE.
SO DID MISTER BUSHKIN LIKE YOUR ARTICLE?
HM?
I JUST TURNED IT IN TO HIM TODAY -- HE DIDN'T HAVE A CHANCE TO READ IT WHILE I WAS THERE.
OH, BUT I STOPPED BY THE DAILY GAZETTE OFFICES TODAY.
THEY'RE DOING A THINK PIECE ON THE WILLIAMS EMBEZZLEMENT CASE -- BOUGHT A BUNCH OF MY IRON MAN PICTURES.
UM -- WHAT'S THE CONNEC-TION?
WILLIAMS INNOVATIONS AND STARK INDUSTRIES ARE COMPETITORS, HONEY.
WILLIAMS CLAIMS STARK'S THE REASON HIS COMPANY IS FAILING. PRETTY LUDICROUS IF YOU ASK ME.
giggle!
SHH!
BUT I GUESS I OWE HIM A COMMISSION -- I'D HARDLY HAVE SOLD THOSE PHOTOS OTHERWISE.
YOU SHUSH!
THEY WERE ACHINGLY INNOCENT -- AND I WANTED SO MUCH TO SHIELD THEM FROM ANYTHING THAT'D CHANGE THAT.
PLAYING THEIR LITTLE-GIRL GAMES -- SWIPING TABLE SCRAPS FOR SOME STRAY DOG OR CAT THEY'D BEFRIENDED --

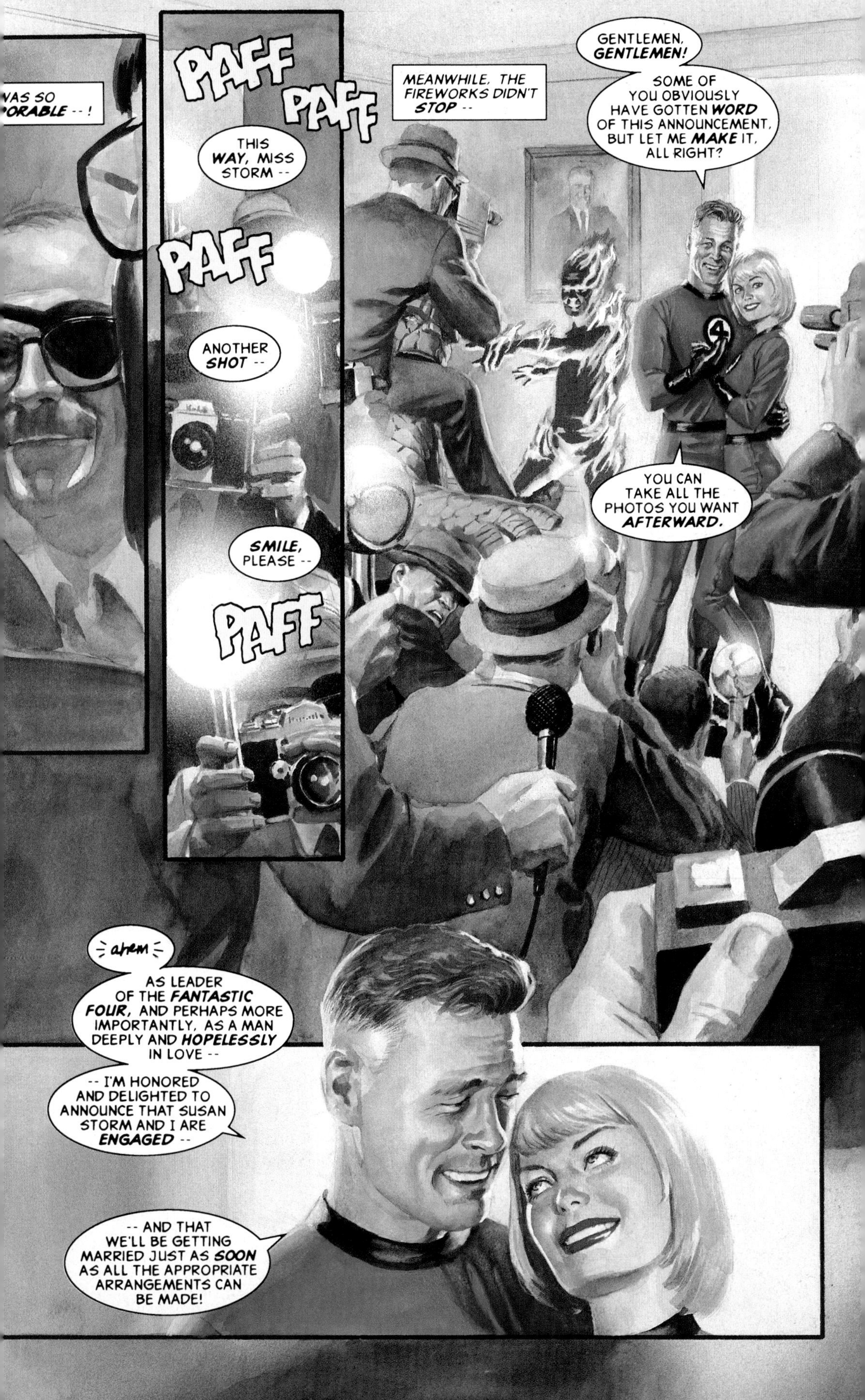

WAS SO
PORABLE --!
PAFF PAFF
THIS WAY, MISS STORM --
PAFF
ANOTHER SHOT --
SMILE, PLEASE --
PAFF
MEANWHILE, THE FIREWORKS DIDN'T STOP --
GENTLEMEN, GENTLEMEN!
SOME OF YOU OBVIOUSLY HAVE GOTTEN WORD OF THIS ANNOUNCEMENT, BUT LET ME MAKE IT, ALL RIGHT?
YOU CAN TAKE ALL THE PHOTOS YOU WANT AFTERWARD.
ahem
AS LEADER OF THE FANTASTIC FOUR, AND PERHAPS MORE IMPORTANTLY, AS A MAN DEEPLY AND HOPELESSLY IN LOVE --
-- I'M HONORED AND DELIGHTED TO ANNOUNCE THAT SUSAN STORM AND I ARE ENGAGED --
-- AND THAT WE'LL BE GETTING MARRIED JUST AS SOON AS ALL THE APPROPRIATE ARRANGEMENTS CAN BE MADE!

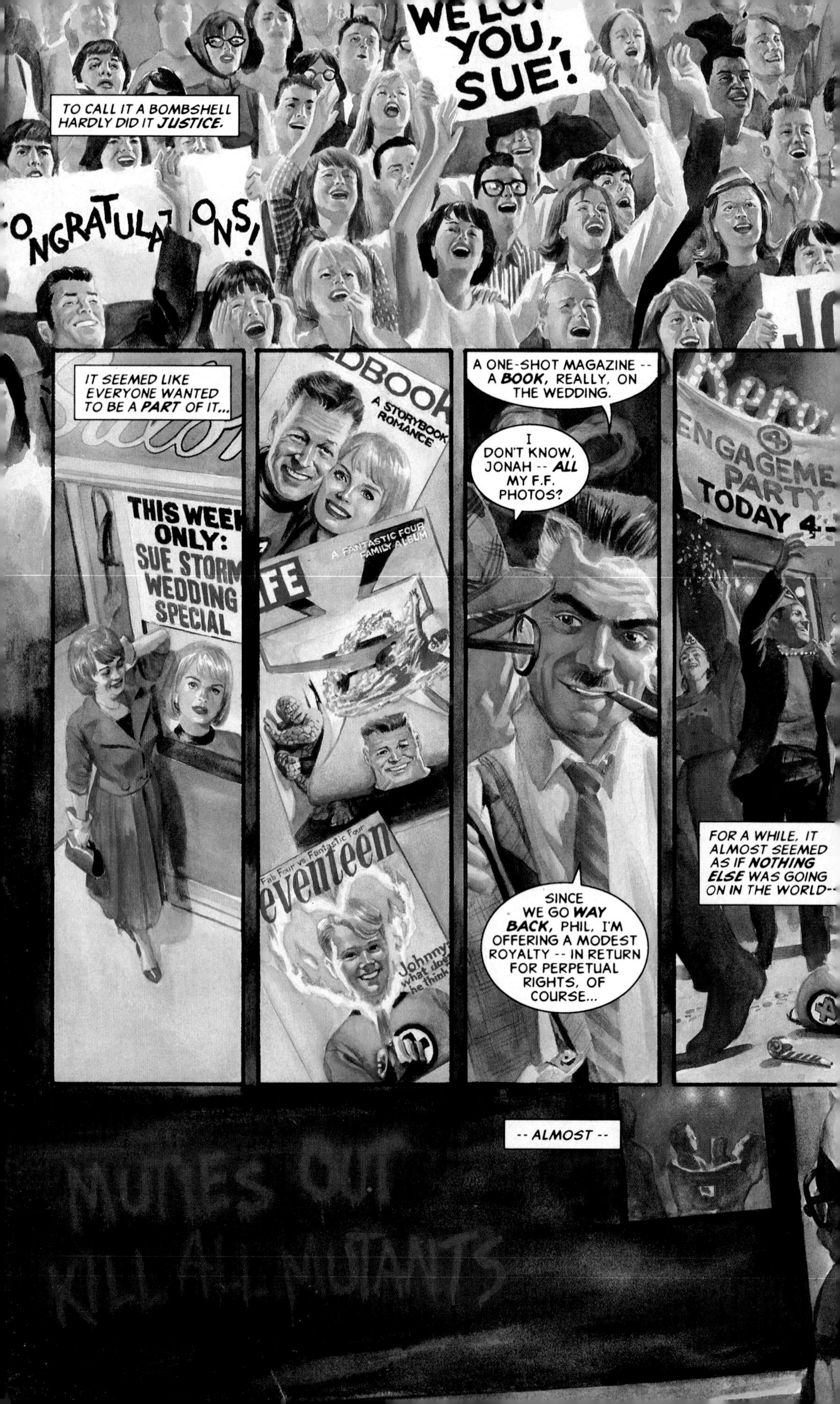

WE LO[...] YOU, SUE!
TO CALL IT A BOMBSHELL HARDLY DID IT JUSTICE.
ONGRATULA ONS!
IT SEEMED LIKE EVERYONE WANTED TO BE A PART OF IT...
THIS WEEK ONLY: SUE STORM WEDDING SPECIAL
A STORYBOOK ROMANCE
A FANTASTIC FOUR FAMILY ALBUM
FE
Fab Four vs. Fantastic Four
eventeen
A ONE-SHOT MAGAZINE -- A BOOK, REALLY, ON THE WEDDING.
I DON'T KNOW, JONAH -- ALL MY F.F. PHOTOS?
SINCE WE GO WAY BACK, PHIL, I'M OFFERING A MODEST ROYALTY -- IN RETURN FOR PERPETUAL RIGHTS, OF COURSE...
ENGAGEME PARTY TODAY 4
FOR A WHILE, IT ALMOST SEEMED AS IF NOTHING ELSE WAS GOING ON IN THE WORLD--
-- ALMOST --
MUTIES OUT
KILL ALL MUTANTS

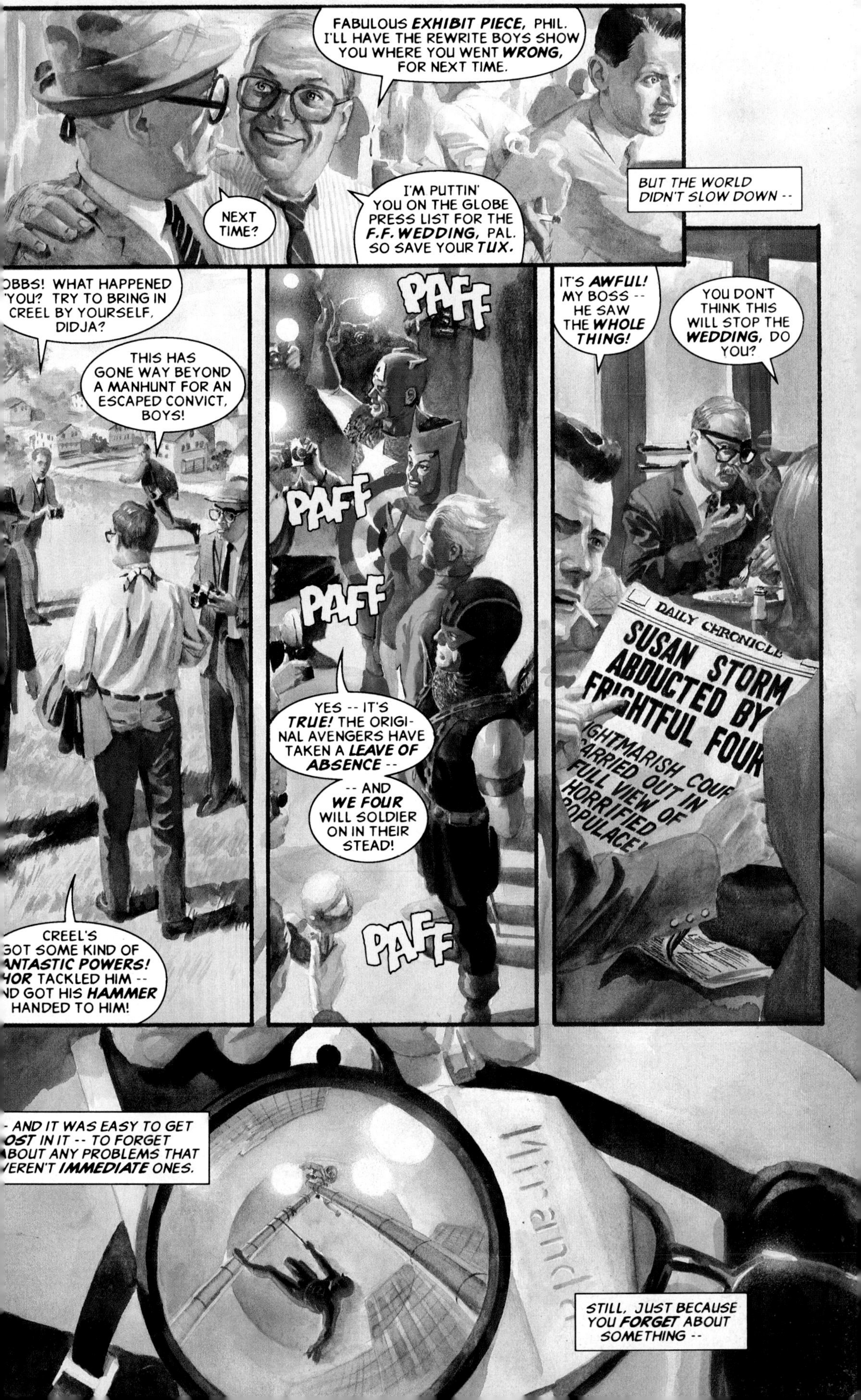

FABULOUS EXHIBIT PIECE, PHIL. I'LL HAVE THE REWRITE BOYS SHOW YOU WHERE YOU WENT WRONG, FOR NEXT TIME.
NEXT TIME?
I'M PUTTIN' YOU ON THE GLOBE PRESS LIST FOR THE F.F. WEDDING, PAL. SO SAVE YOUR TUX.
BUT THE WORLD DIDN'T SLOW DOWN --
OBBS! WHAT HAPPENED YOU? TRY TO BRING IN CREEL BY YOURSELF, DIDJA?
THIS HAS GONE WAY BEYOND A MANHUNT FOR AN ESCAPED CONVICT, BOYS!
CREEL'S GOT SOME KIND OF ANTASTIC POWERS! HOR TACKLED HIM -- ND GOT HIS HAMMER HANDED TO HIM!
PAFF
PAFF
PAFF
YES -- IT'S TRUE! THE ORIGINAL AVENGERS HAVE TAKEN A LEAVE OF ABSENCE --
-- AND WE FOUR WILL SOLDIER ON IN THEIR STEAD!
PAFF
IT'S AWFUL! MY BOSS -- HE SAW THE WHOLE THING!
YOU DON'T THINK THIS WILL STOP THE WEDDING, DO YOU?
DAILY CHRONICLE
SUSAN STORM ABDUCTED BY FRIGHTFUL FOUR
NIGHTMARISH COUP CARRIED OUT IN FULL VIEW OF HORRIFIED POPULACE!
- AND IT WAS EASY TO GET OST IN IT -- TO FORGET ABOUT ANY PROBLEMS THAT VEREN'T IMMEDIATE ONES.
Miranda
STILL, JUST BECAUSE YOU FORGET ABOUT SOMETHING --

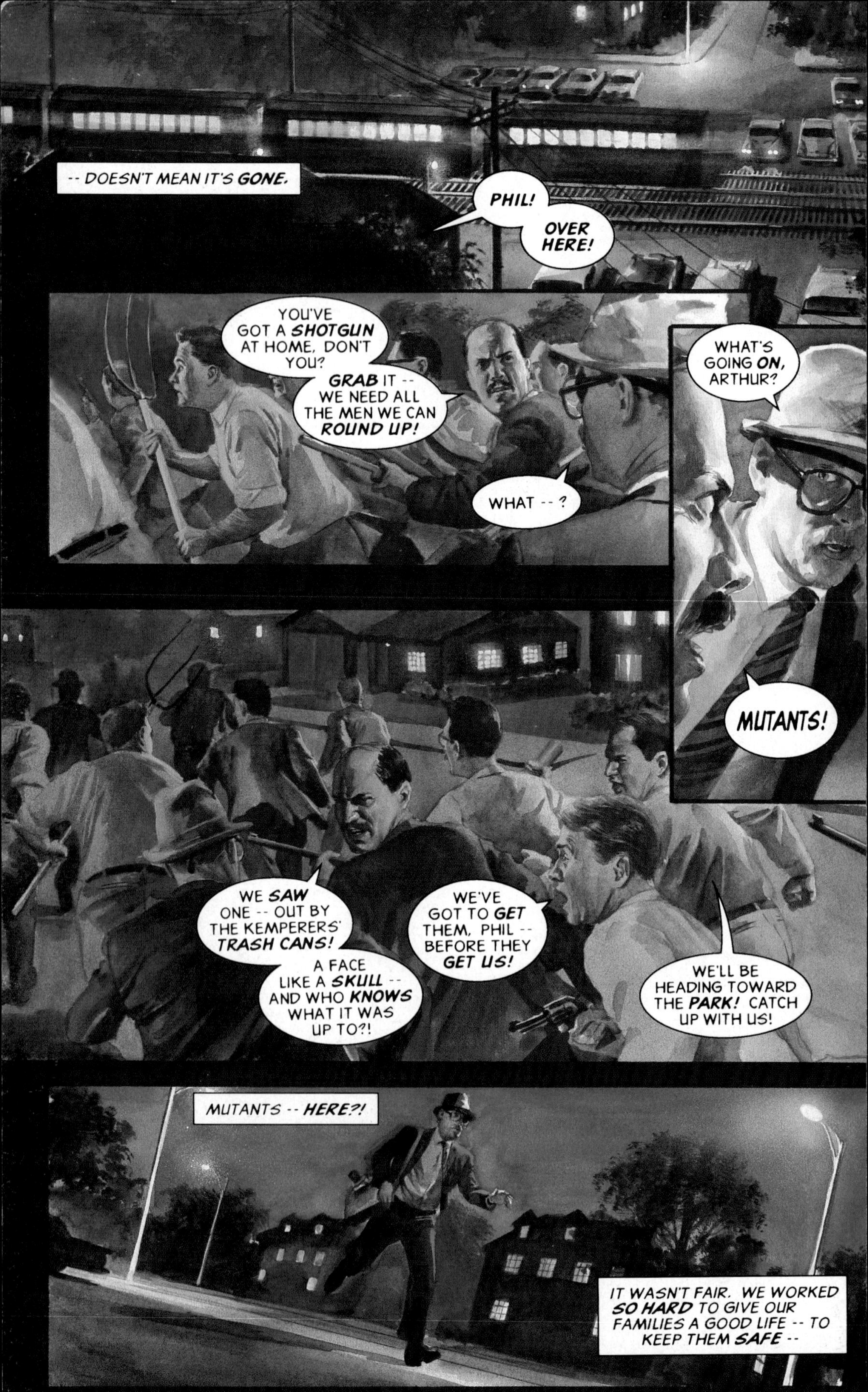

-- DOESN'T MEAN IT'S GONE.
PHIL!
OVER HERE!
YOU'VE GOT A SHOTGUN AT HOME, DON'T YOU?
GRAB IT -- WE NEED ALL THE MEN WE CAN ROUND UP!
WHAT -- ?
WHAT'S GOING ON, ARTHUR?
MUTANTS!
WE SAW ONE -- OUT BY THE KEMPERERS' TRASH CANS!
A FACE LIKE A SKULL -- AND WHO KNOWS WHAT IT WAS UP TO?!
WE'VE GOT TO GET THEM, PHIL -- BEFORE THEY GET US!
WE'LL BE HEADING TOWARD THE PARK! CATCH UP WITH US!
MUTANTS -- HERE?!
IT WASN'T FAIR. WE WORKED SO HARD TO GIVE OUR FAMILIES A GOOD LIFE -- TO KEEP THEM SAFE --

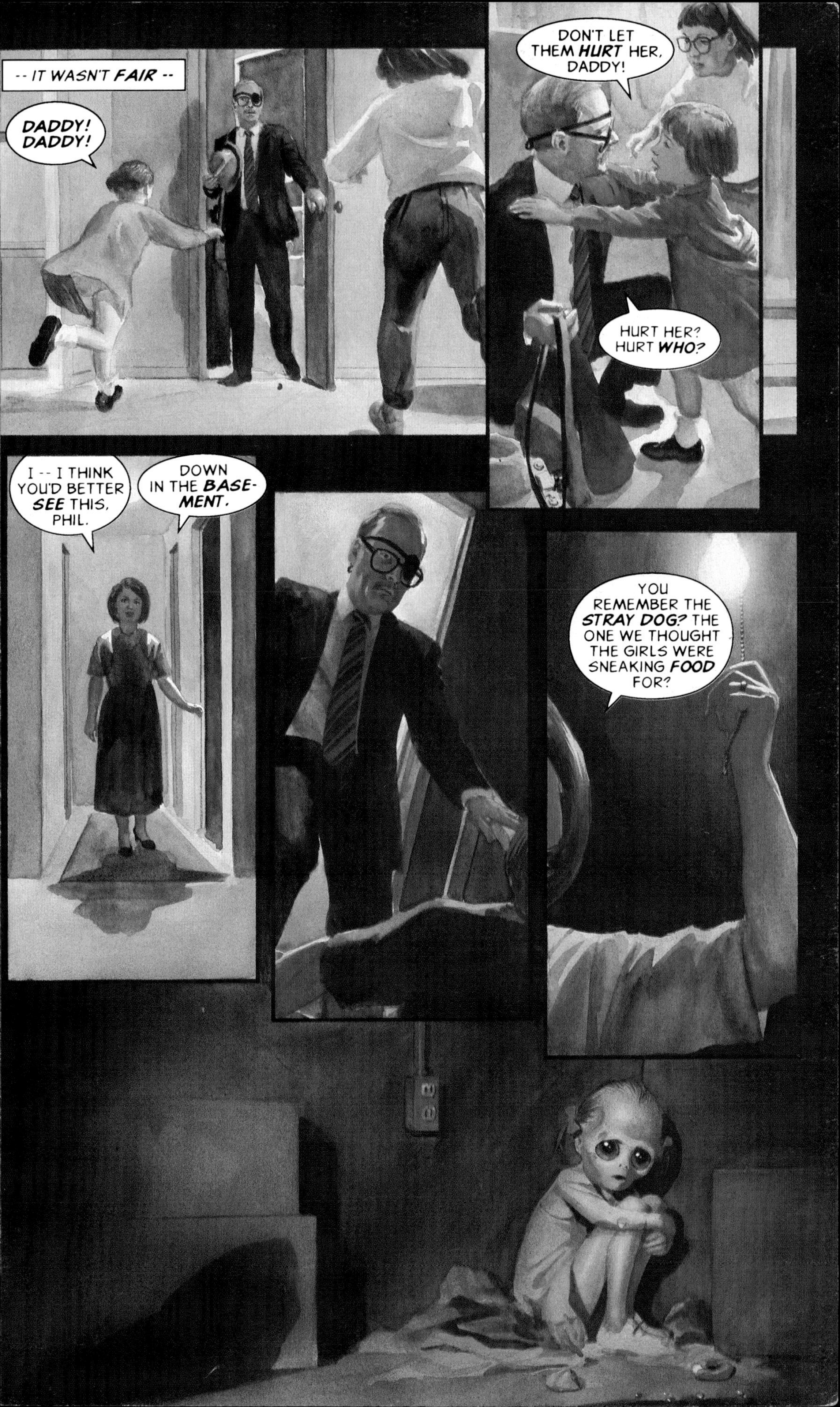
-- IT WASN'T FAIR --
DADDY! DADDY!
DON'T LET THEM HURT HER, DADDY!
HURT HER? HURT WHO?
I -- I THINK YOU'D BETTER SEE THIS, PHIL.
DOWN IN THE BASEMENT.
YOU REMEMBER THE STRAY DOG? THE ONE WE THOUGHT THE GIRLS WERE SNEAKING FOOD FOR?

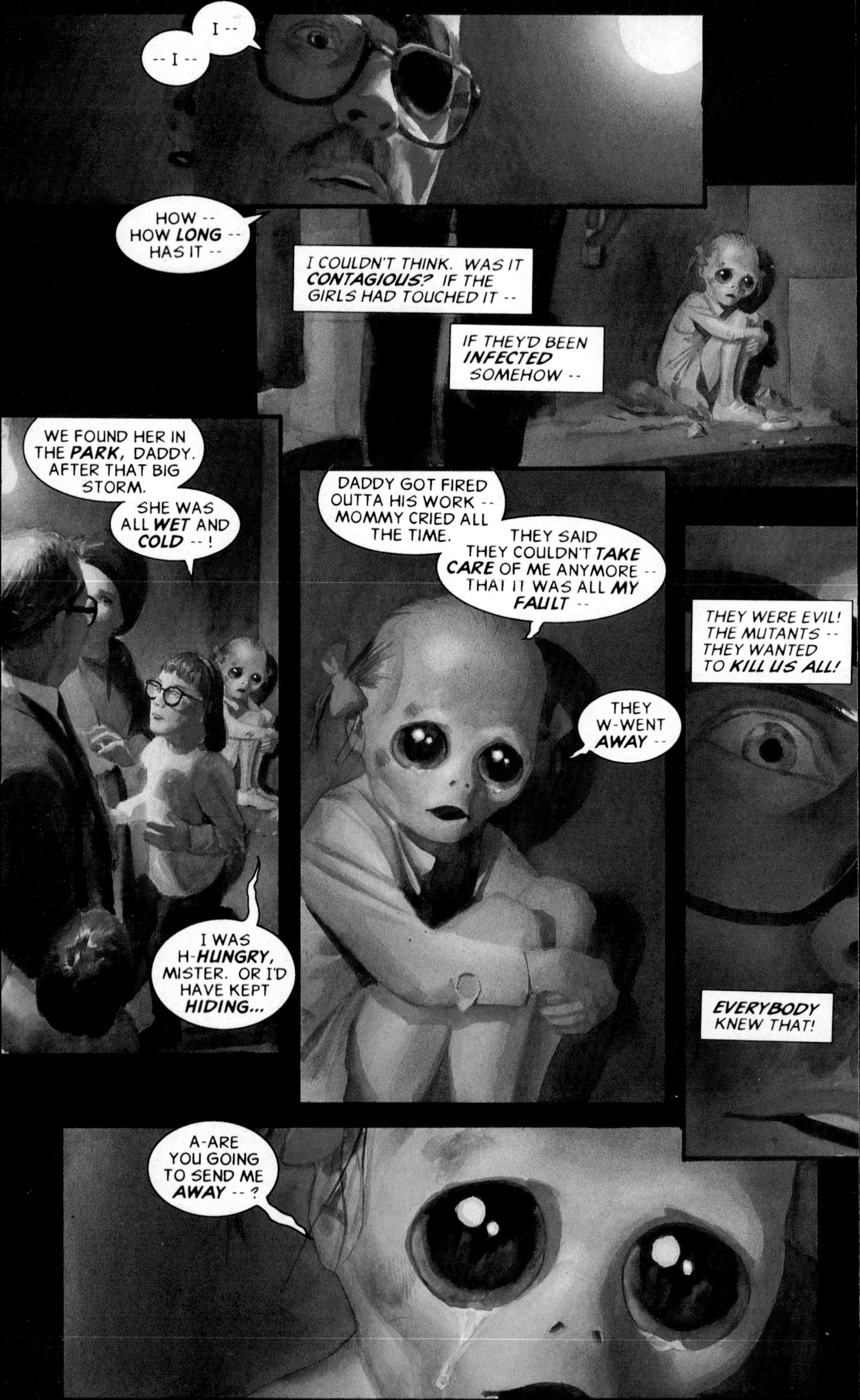
I --
-- I --
HOW -- HOW LONG -- HAS IT --
I COULDN'T THINK. WAS IT CONTAGIOUS? IF THE GIRLS HAD TOUCHED IT --
IF THEY'D BEEN INFECTED SOMEHOW --
WE FOUND HER IN THE PARK, DADDY. AFTER THAT BIG STORM.
SHE WAS ALL WET AND COLD --!
I WAS H-HUNGRY, MISTER. OR I'D HAVE KEPT HIDING...
DADDY GOT FIRED OUTTA HIS WORK -- MOMMY CRIED ALL THE TIME.
THEY SAID THEY COULDN'T TAKE CARE OF ME ANYMORE -- THAT IT WAS ALL MY FAULT --
THEY W-WENT AWAY --
THEY WERE EVIL! THE MUTANTS -- THEY WANTED TO KILL US ALL!
EVERYBODY KNEW THAT!
A-ARE YOU GOING TO SEND ME AWAY --?

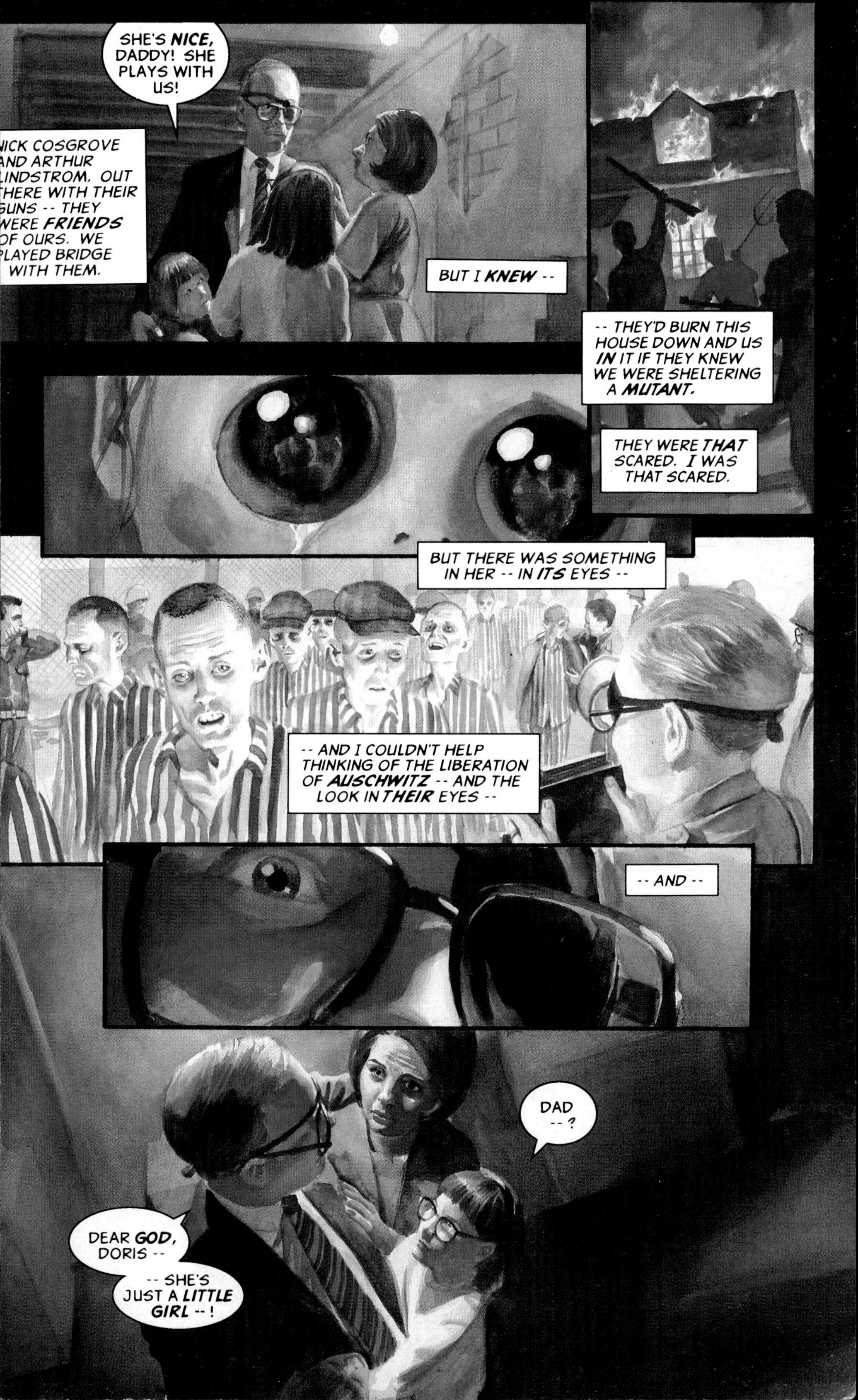
SHE'S NICE, DADDY! SHE PLAYS WITH US!
NICK COSGROVE AND ARTHUR LINDSTROM, OUT THERE WITH THEIR GUNS -- THEY WERE FRIENDS OF OURS. WE PLAYED BRIDGE WITH THEM.
BUT I KNEW --
-- THEY'D BURN THIS HOUSE DOWN AND US IN IT IF THEY KNEW WE WERE SHELTERING A MUTANT.
THEY WERE THAT SCARED. I WAS THAT SCARED.
BUT THERE WAS SOMETHING IN HER -- IN ITS EYES --
-- AND I COULDN'T HELP THINKING OF THE LIBERATION OF AUSCHWITZ -- AND THE LOOK IN THEIR EYES --
-- AND --
DAD --?
DEAR GOD, DORIS --
-- SHE'S JUST A LITTLE GIRL --!

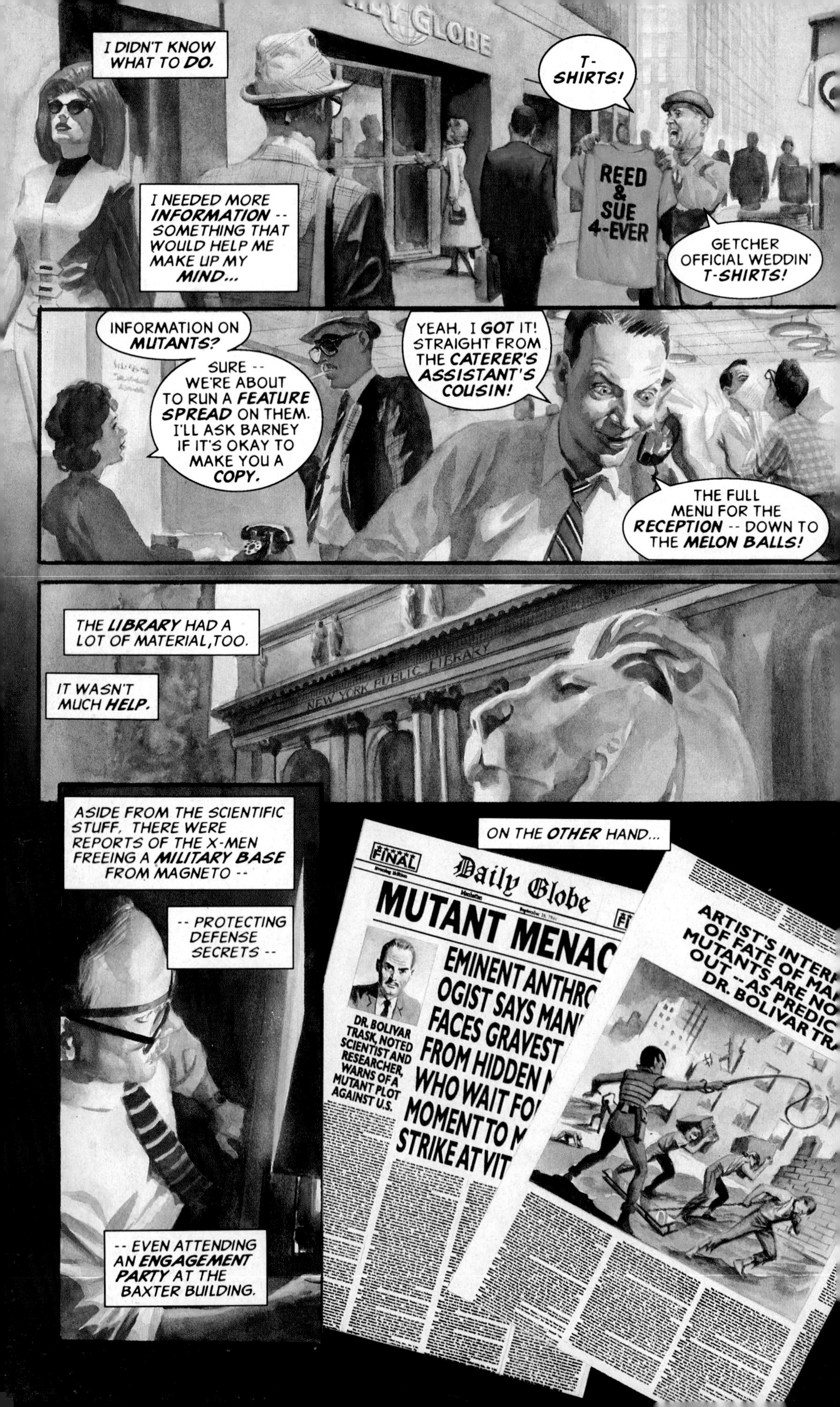
I DIDN'T KNOW WHAT TO DO.
GLOBE
T-SHIRTS!
REED & SUE 4-EVER
I NEEDED MORE INFORMATION -- SOMETHING THAT WOULD HELP ME MAKE UP MY MIND...
GETCHER OFFICIAL WEDDIN' T-SHIRTS!
INFORMATION ON MUTANTS?
SURE -- WE'RE ABOUT TO RUN A FEATURE SPREAD ON THEM. I'LL ASK BARNEY IF IT'S OKAY TO MAKE YOU A COPY.
YEAH, I GOT IT! STRAIGHT FROM THE CATERER'S ASSISTANT'S COUSIN!
THE FULL MENU FOR THE RECEPTION -- DOWN TO THE MELON BALLS!
THE LIBRARY HAD A LOT OF MATERIAL, TOO.
IT WASN'T MUCH HELP.
NEW YORK PUBLIC LIBRARY
ASIDE FROM THE SCIENTIFIC STUFF, THERE WERE REPORTS OF THE X-MEN FREEING A MILITARY BASE FROM MAGNETO --
-- PROTECTING DEFENSE SECRETS --
-- EVEN ATTENDING AN ENGAGEMENT PARTY AT THE BAXTER BUILDING.
ON THE OTHER HAND...
FINAL
Daily Globe
MUTANT MENAC
EMINENT ANTHRO OGIST SAYS MAN FACES GRAVEST FROM HIDDEN WHO WAIT FO MOMENT TO M STRIKE AT VIT
DR. BOLIVAR TRASK, NOTED SCIENTIST AND RESEARCHER, WARNS OF A MUTANT PLOT AGAINST U.S.
ARTIST'S INTER OF FATE OF MA MUTANTS ARE NO OUT -- AS PREDIC DR. BOLIVAR TR

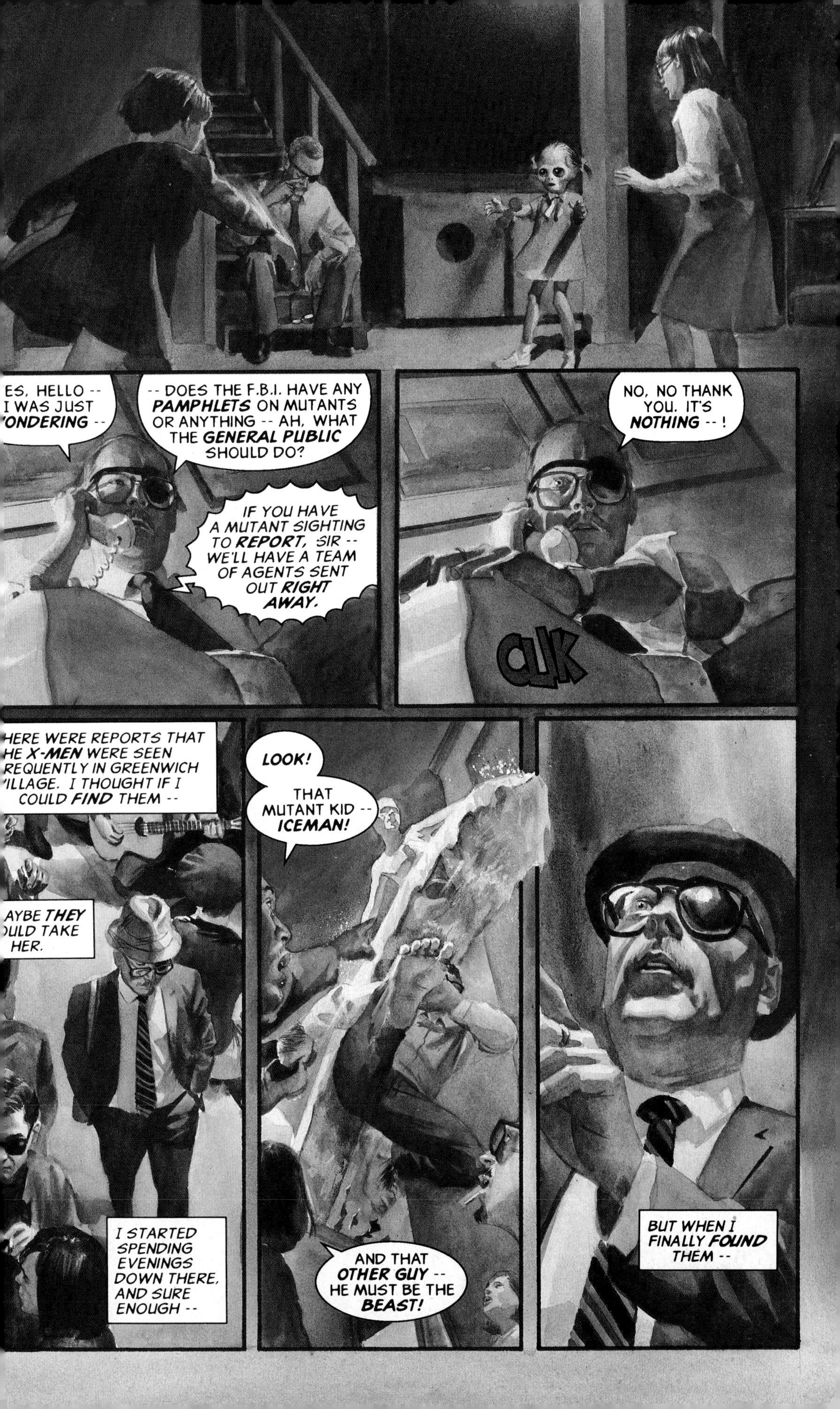

ES, HELLO -- I WAS JUST ONDERING --
-- DOES THE F.B.I. HAVE ANY PAMPHLETS ON MUTANTS OR ANYTHING -- AH, WHAT THE GENERAL PUBLIC SHOULD DO?
IF YOU HAVE A MUTANT SIGHTING TO REPORT, SIR -- WE'LL HAVE A TEAM OF AGENTS SENT OUT RIGHT AWAY.
NO, NO THANK YOU. IT'S NOTHING -- !
CLIK
HERE WERE REPORTS THAT HE X-MEN WERE SEEN REQUENTLY IN GREENWICH ILLAGE. I THOUGHT IF I COULD FIND THEM --
AYBE THEY OULD TAKE HER.
I STARTED SPENDING EVENINGS DOWN THERE, AND SURE ENOUGH --
LOOK!
THAT MUTANT KID -- ICEMAN!
AND THAT OTHER GUY -- HE MUST BE THE BEAST!
BUT WHEN I FINALLY FOUND THEM --

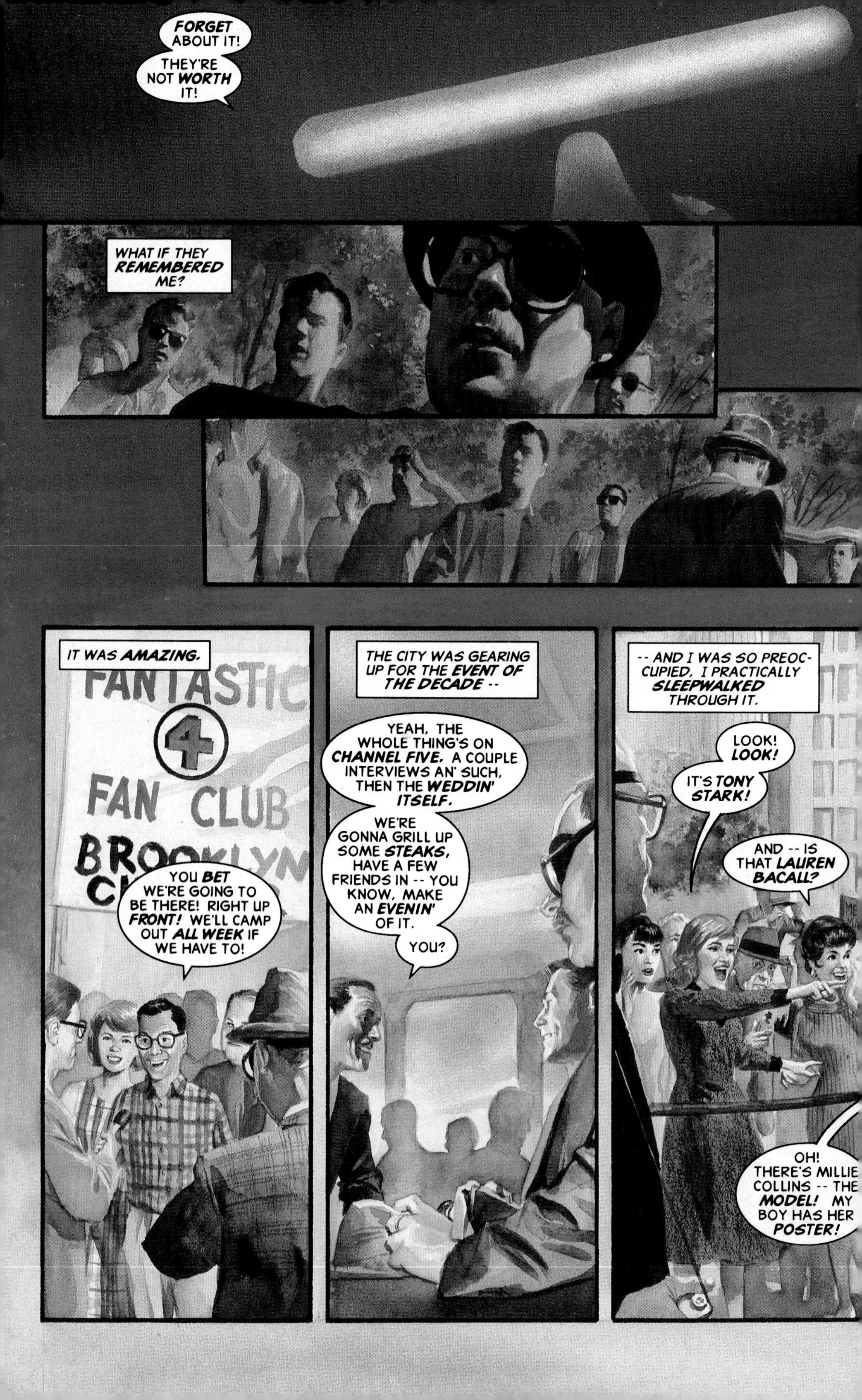
FORGET ABOUT IT!
THEY'RE NOT WORTH IT!
WHAT IF THEY REMEMBERED ME?
IT WAS AMAZING.
FANTASTIC 4 FAN CLUB BROOKLYN
YOU BET WE'RE GOING TO BE THERE! RIGHT UP FRONT! WE'LL CAMP OUT ALL WEEK IF WE HAVE TO!
THE CITY WAS GEARING UP FOR THE EVENT OF THE DECADE --
YEAH, THE WHOLE THING'S ON CHANNEL FIVE. A COUPLE INTERVIEWS AN' SUCH, THEN THE WEDDIN' ITSELF.
WE'RE GONNA GRILL UP SOME STEAKS, HAVE A FEW FRIENDS IN -- YOU KNOW, MAKE AN EVENIN' OF IT.
YOU?
-- AND I WAS SO PREOCCUPIED, I PRACTICALLY SLEEPWALKED THROUGH IT.
LOOK! LOOK!
IT'S TONY STARK!
AND -- IS THAT LAUREN BACALL?
OH! THERE'S MILLIE COLLINS -- THE MODEL! MY BOY HAS HER POSTER!

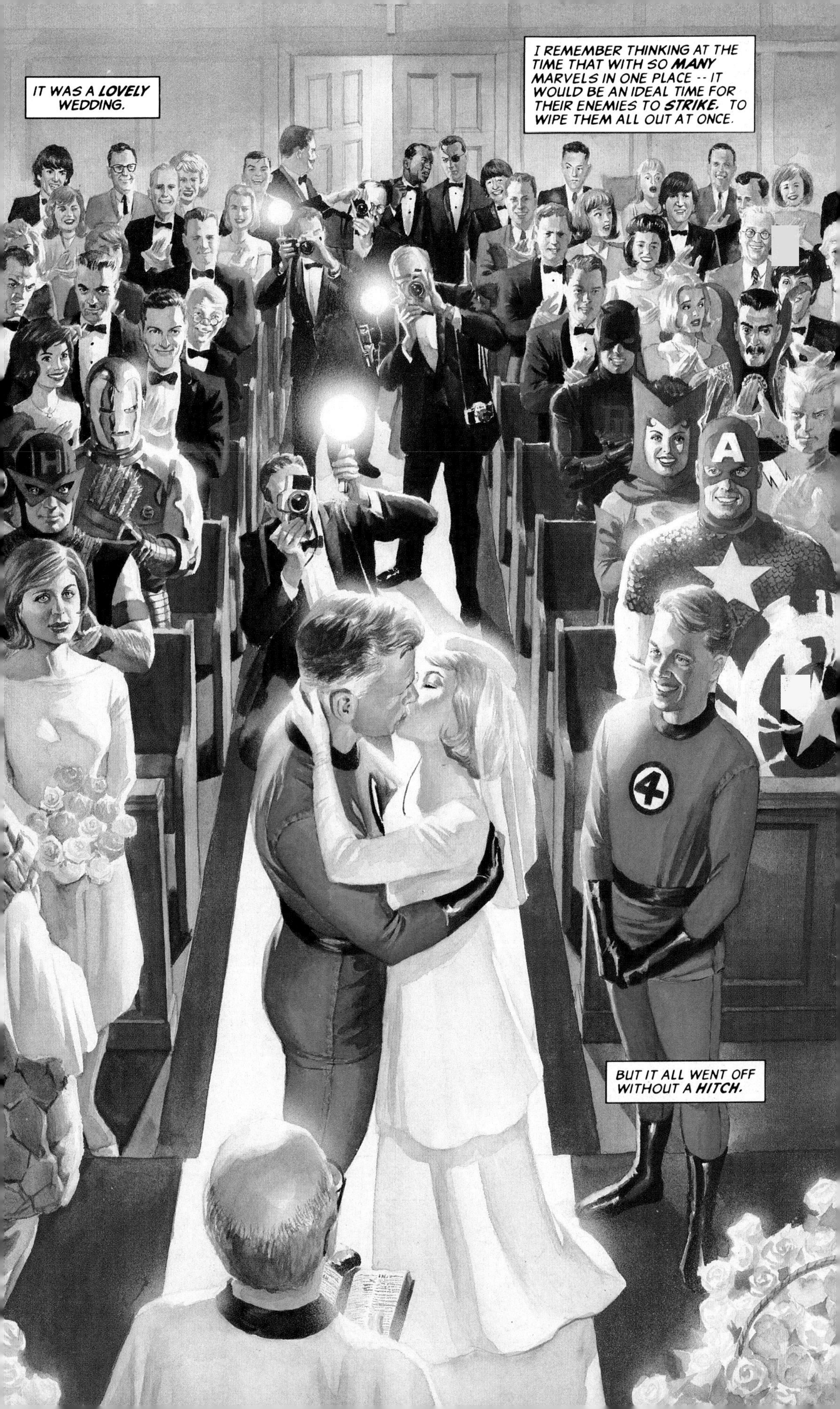
IT WAS A LOVELY WEDDING.
I REMEMBER THINKING AT THE TIME THAT WITH SO MANY MARVELS IN ONE PLACE -- IT WOULD BE AN IDEAL TIME FOR THEIR ENEMIES TO STRIKE. TO WIPE THEM ALL OUT AT ONCE.
BUT IT ALL WENT OFF WITHOUT A HITCH.

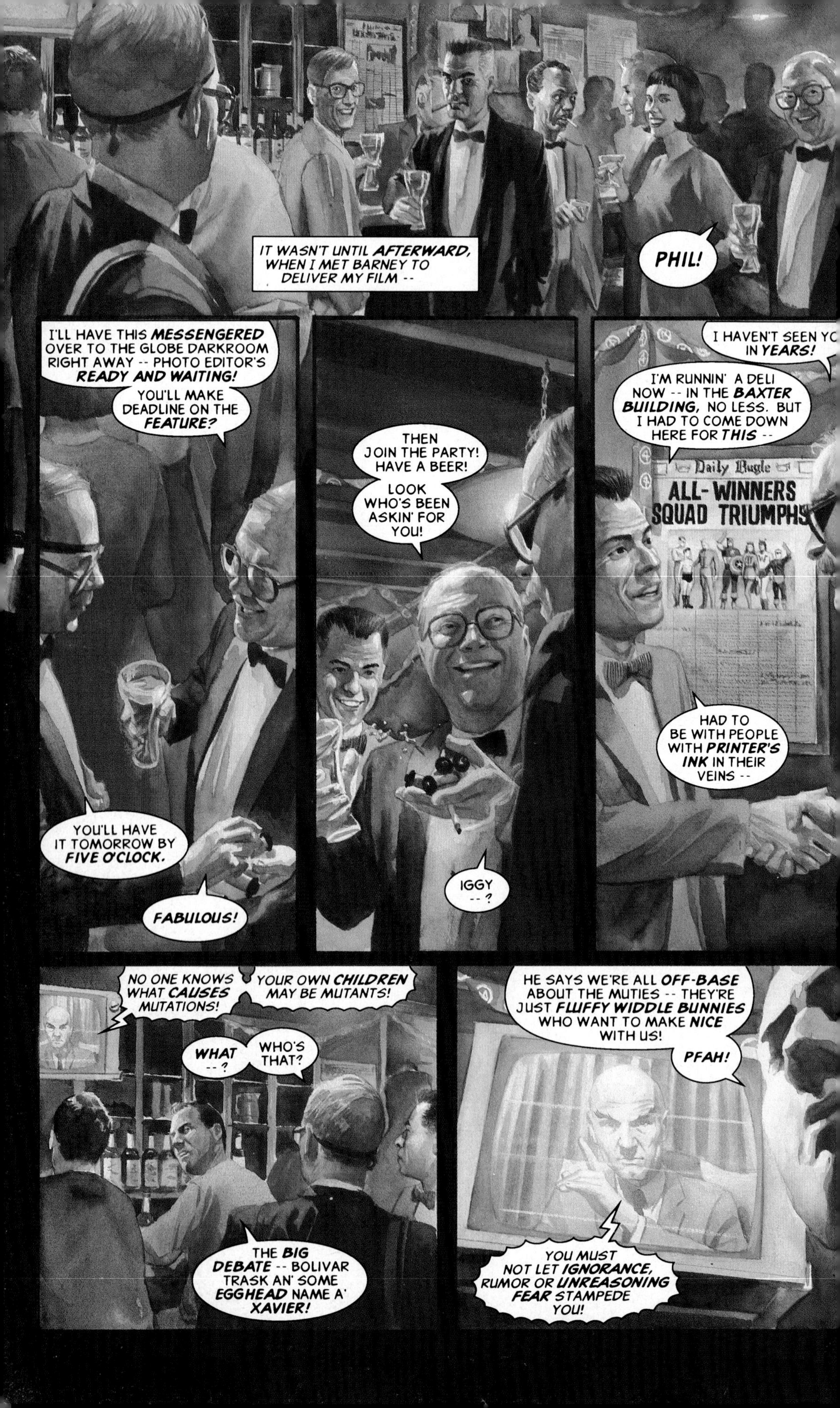
IT WASN'T UNTIL AFTERWARD, WHEN I MET BARNEY TO DELIVER MY FILM --
PHIL!
I'LL HAVE THIS MESSENGERED OVER TO THE GLOBE DARKROOM RIGHT AWAY -- PHOTO EDITOR'S READY AND WAITING!
YOU'LL MAKE DEADLINE ON THE FEATURE?
YOU'LL HAVE IT TOMORROW BY FIVE O'CLOCK.
FABULOUS!
THEN JOIN THE PARTY! HAVE A BEER!
LOOK WHO'S BEEN ASKIN' FOR YOU!
IGGY -- ?
I HAVEN'T SEEN YO IN YEARS!
I'M RUNNIN' A DELI NOW -- IN THE BAXTER BUILDING, NO LESS. BUT I HAD TO COME DOWN HERE FOR THIS --
Daily Bugle
ALL-WINNERS SQUAD TRIUMPHS
HAD TO BE WITH PEOPLE WITH PRINTER'S INK IN THEIR VEINS --
NO ONE KNOWS WHAT CAUSES MUTATIONS!
YOUR OWN CHILDREN MAY BE MUTANTS!
WHAT -- ?
WHO'S THAT?
THE BIG DEBATE -- BOLIVAR TRASK AN' SOME EGGHEAD NAME A' XAVIER!
HE SAYS WE'RE ALL OFF-BASE ABOUT THE MUTIES -- THEY'RE JUST FLUFFY WIDDLE BUNNIES WHO WANT TO MAKE NICE WITH US!
PFAH!
YOU MUST NOT LET IGNORANCE, RUMOR OR UNREASONING FEAR STAMPEDE YOU!

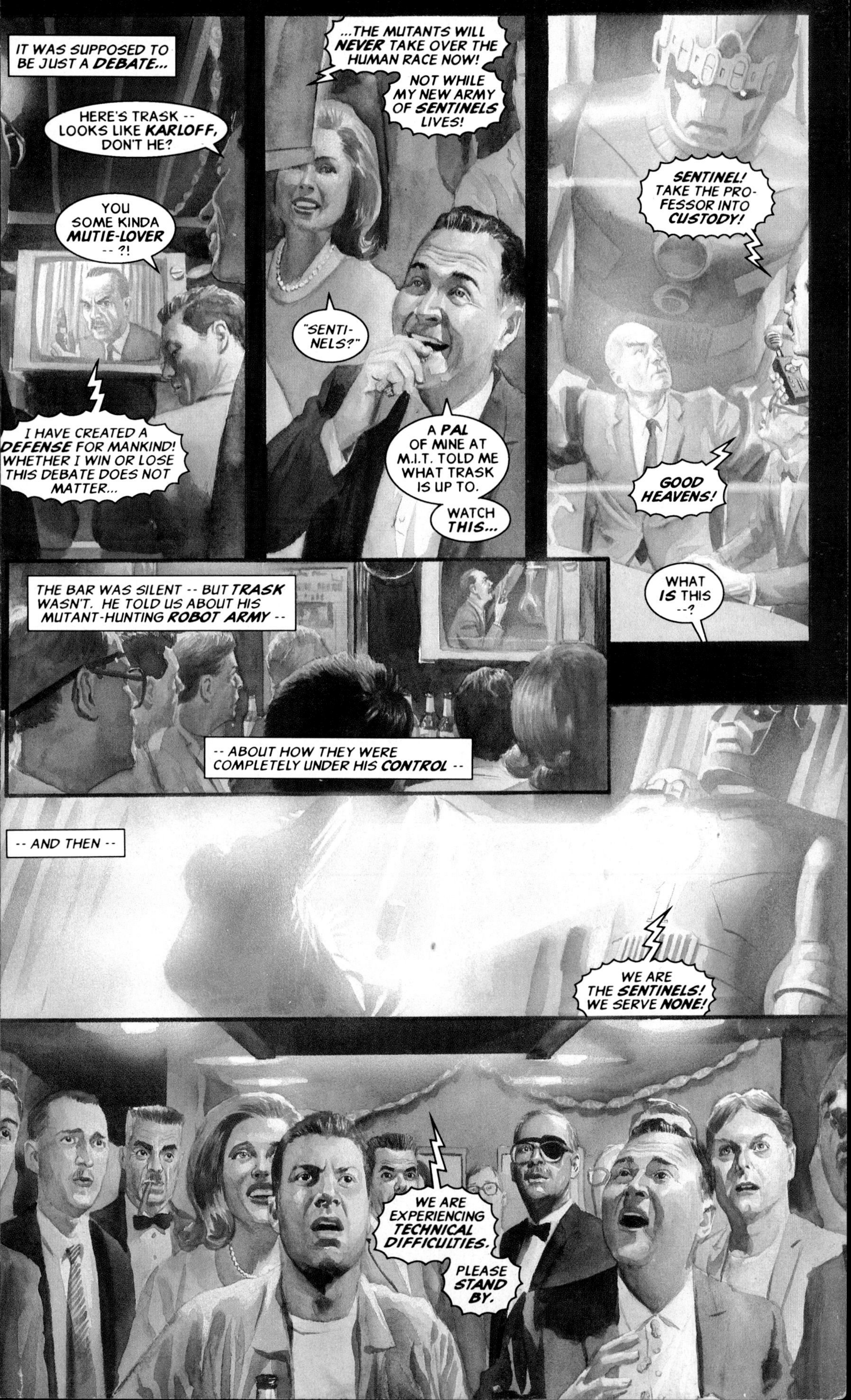
IT WAS SUPPOSED TO BE JUST A DEBATE...
HERE'S TRASK -- LOOKS LIKE KARLOFF, DON'T HE?
YOU SOME KINDA MUTIE-LOVER -- ?!
I HAVE CREATED A DEFENSE FOR MANKIND! WHETHER I WIN OR LOSE THIS DEBATE DOES NOT MATTER...
...THE MUTANTS WILL NEVER TAKE OVER THE HUMAN RACE NOW!
NOT WHILE MY NEW ARMY OF SENTINELS LIVES!
"SENTI-NELS?"
A PAL OF MINE AT M.I.T. TOLD ME WHAT TRASK IS UP TO.
WATCH THIS...
SENTINEL! TAKE THE PRO-FESSOR INTO CUSTODY!
GOOD HEAVENS!
WHAT IS THIS --?
THE BAR WAS SILENT -- BUT TRASK WASN'T. HE TOLD US ABOUT HIS MUTANT-HUNTING ROBOT ARMY --
-- ABOUT HOW THEY WERE COMPLETELY UNDER HIS CONTROL --
-- AND THEN --
WE ARE THE SENTINELS! WE SERVE NONE!
WE ARE EXPERIENCING TECHNICAL DIFFICULTIES.
PLEASE STAND BY.

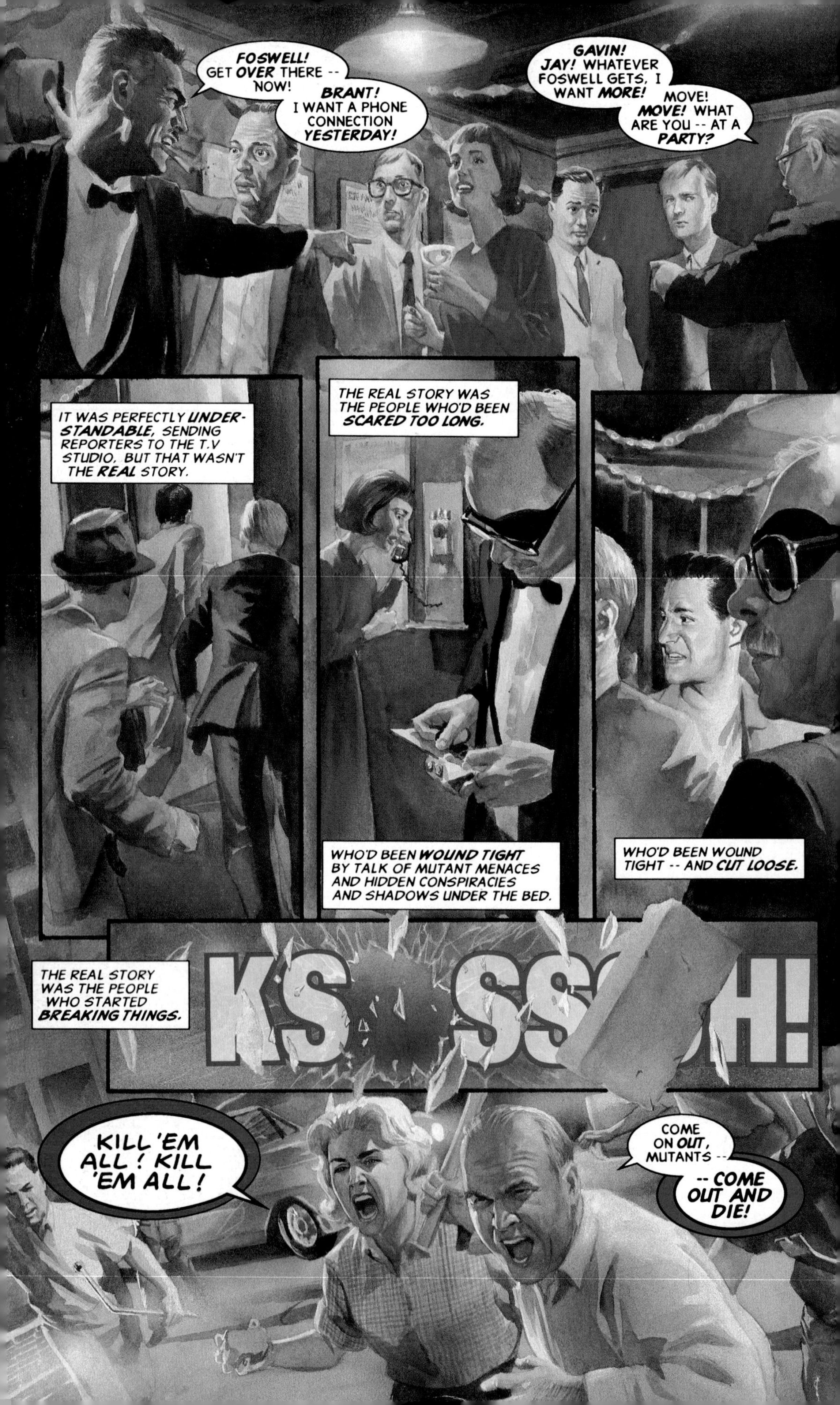

FOSWELL! GET OVER THERE -- NOW!
BRANT! I WANT A PHONE CONNECTION YESTERDAY!
GAVIN! JAY! WHATEVER FOSWELL GETS, I WANT MORE!
MOVE! MOVE! WHAT ARE YOU -- AT A PARTY?
IT WAS PERFECTLY UNDERSTANDABLE, SENDING REPORTERS TO THE T.V STUDIO, BUT THAT WASN'T THE REAL STORY.
THE REAL STORY WAS THE PEOPLE WHO'D BEEN SCARED TOO LONG.
WHO'D BEEN WOUND TIGHT BY TALK OF MUTANT MENACES AND HIDDEN CONSPIRACIES AND SHADOWS UNDER THE BED.
WHO'D BEEN WOUND TIGHT -- AND CUT LOOSE.
THE REAL STORY WAS THE PEOPLE WHO STARTED BREAKING THINGS.
KILL 'EM ALL! KILL 'EM ALL!
COME ON OUT, MUTANTS --
-- COME OUT AND DIE!

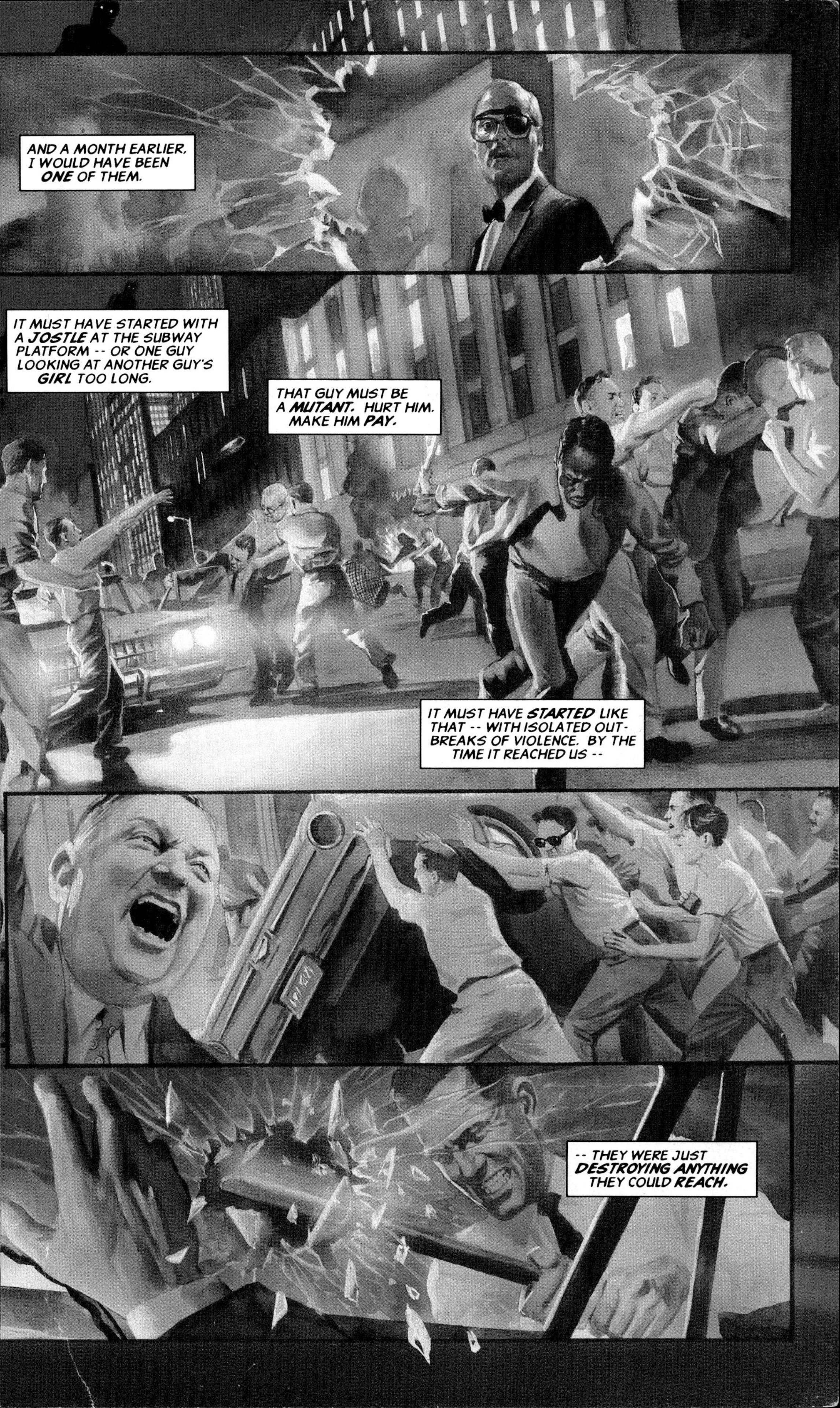
AND A MONTH EARLIER, I WOULD HAVE BEEN ONE OF THEM.
IT MUST HAVE STARTED WITH A JOSTLE AT THE SUBWAY PLATFORM -- OR ONE GUY LOOKING AT ANOTHER GUY'S GIRL TOO LONG.
THAT GUY MUST BE A MUTANT. HURT HIM. MAKE HIM PAY.
IT MUST HAVE STARTED LIKE THAT -- WITH ISOLATED OUT-BREAKS OF VIOLENCE. BY THE TIME IT REACHED US --
-- THEY WERE JUST DESTROYING ANYTHING THEY COULD REACH.

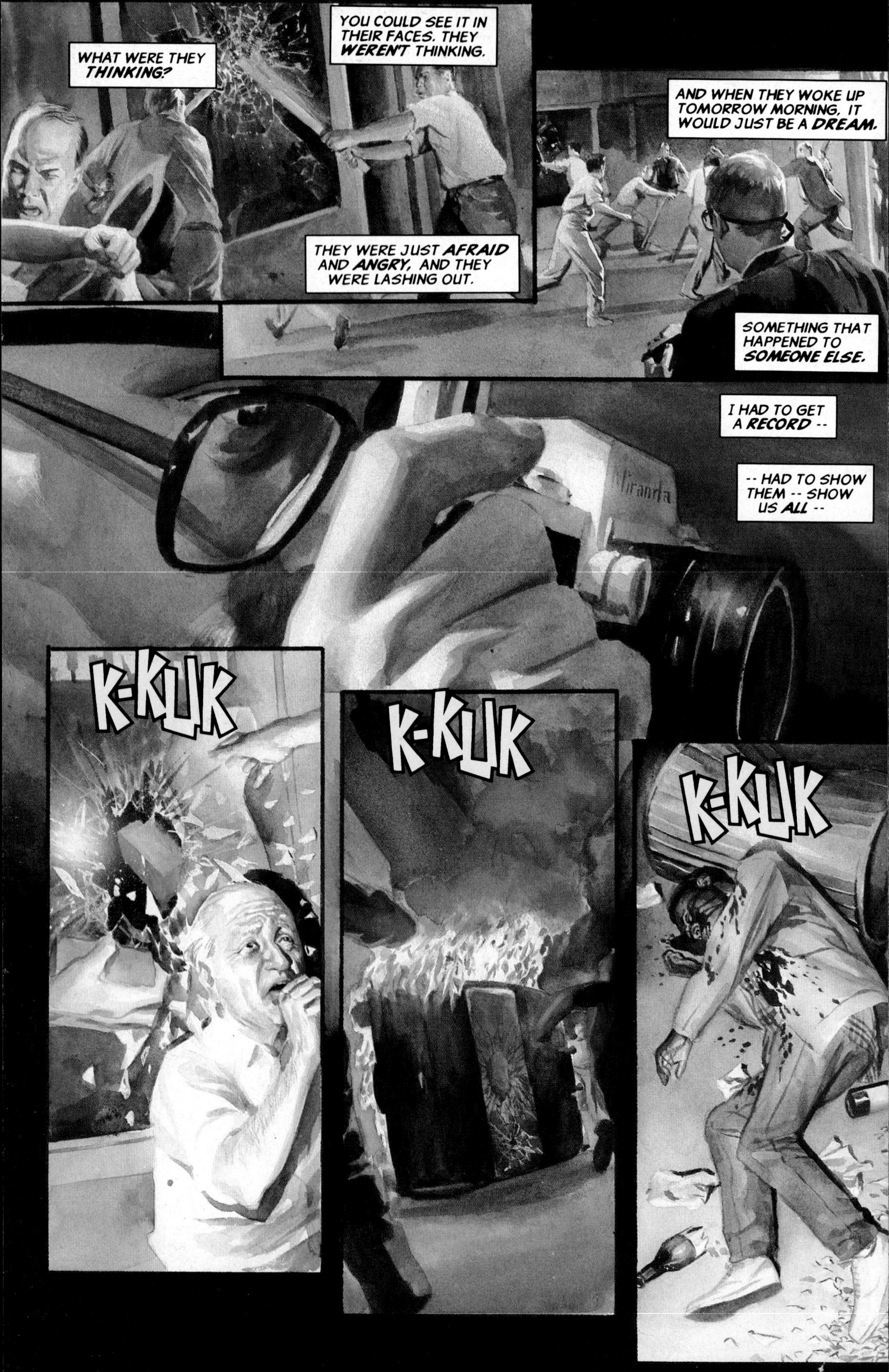

WHAT WERE THEY THINKING?
YOU COULD SEE IT IN THEIR FACES. THEY WEREN'T THINKING.
THEY WERE JUST AFRAID AND ANGRY, AND THEY WERE LASHING OUT.
AND WHEN THEY WOKE UP TOMORROW MORNING, IT WOULD JUST BE A DREAM.
SOMETHING THAT HAPPENED TO SOMEONE ELSE.
I HAD TO GET A RECORD --
-- HAD TO SHOW THEM -- SHOW US ALL --
Miranda
K-KLUK
K-KLUK
K-KLUK

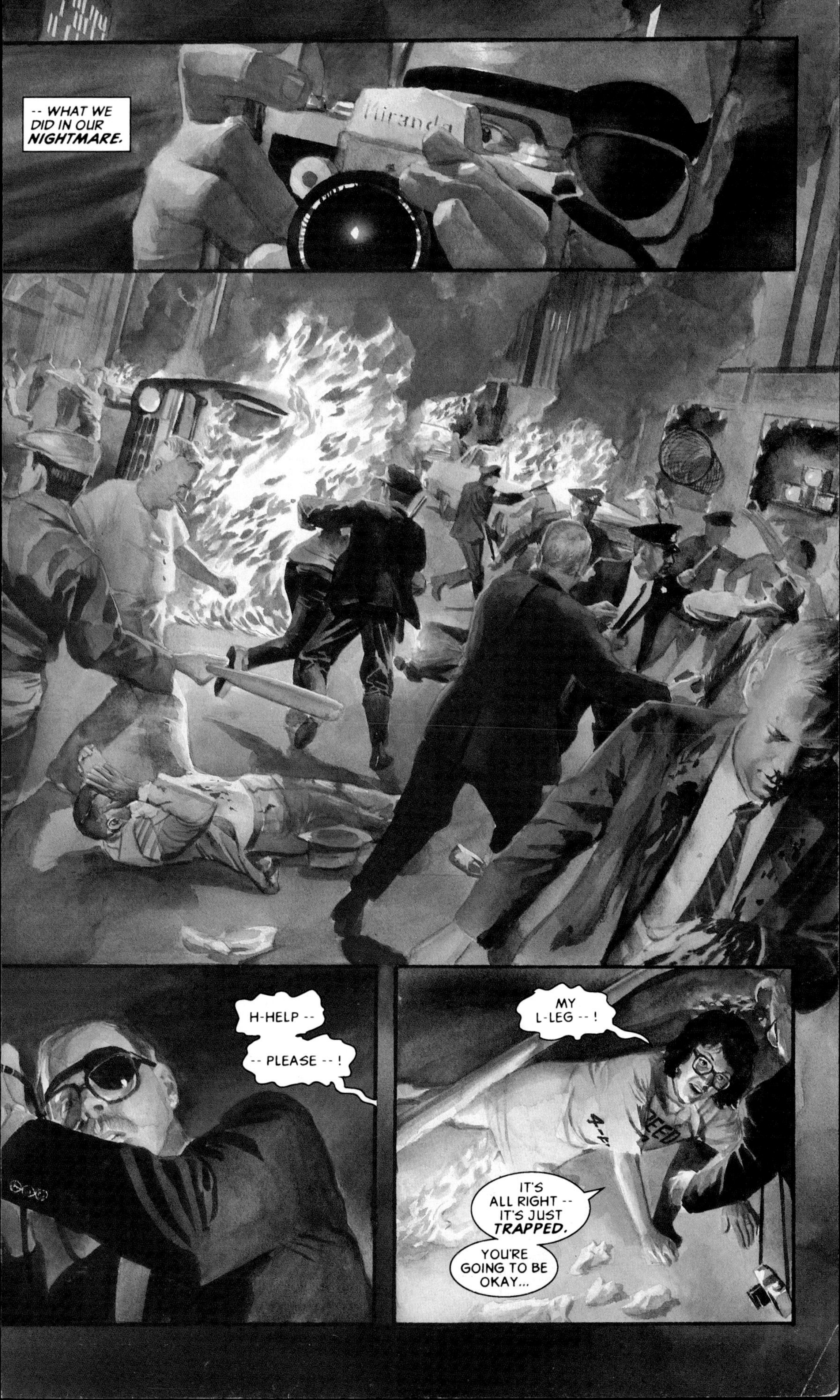
-- WHAT WE DID IN OUR NIGHTMARE.
Miranda
H-HELP --
-- PLEASE -- !
MY L-LEG -- !
IT'S ALL RIGHT -- IT'S JUST TRAPPED.
YOU'RE GOING TO BE OKAY...

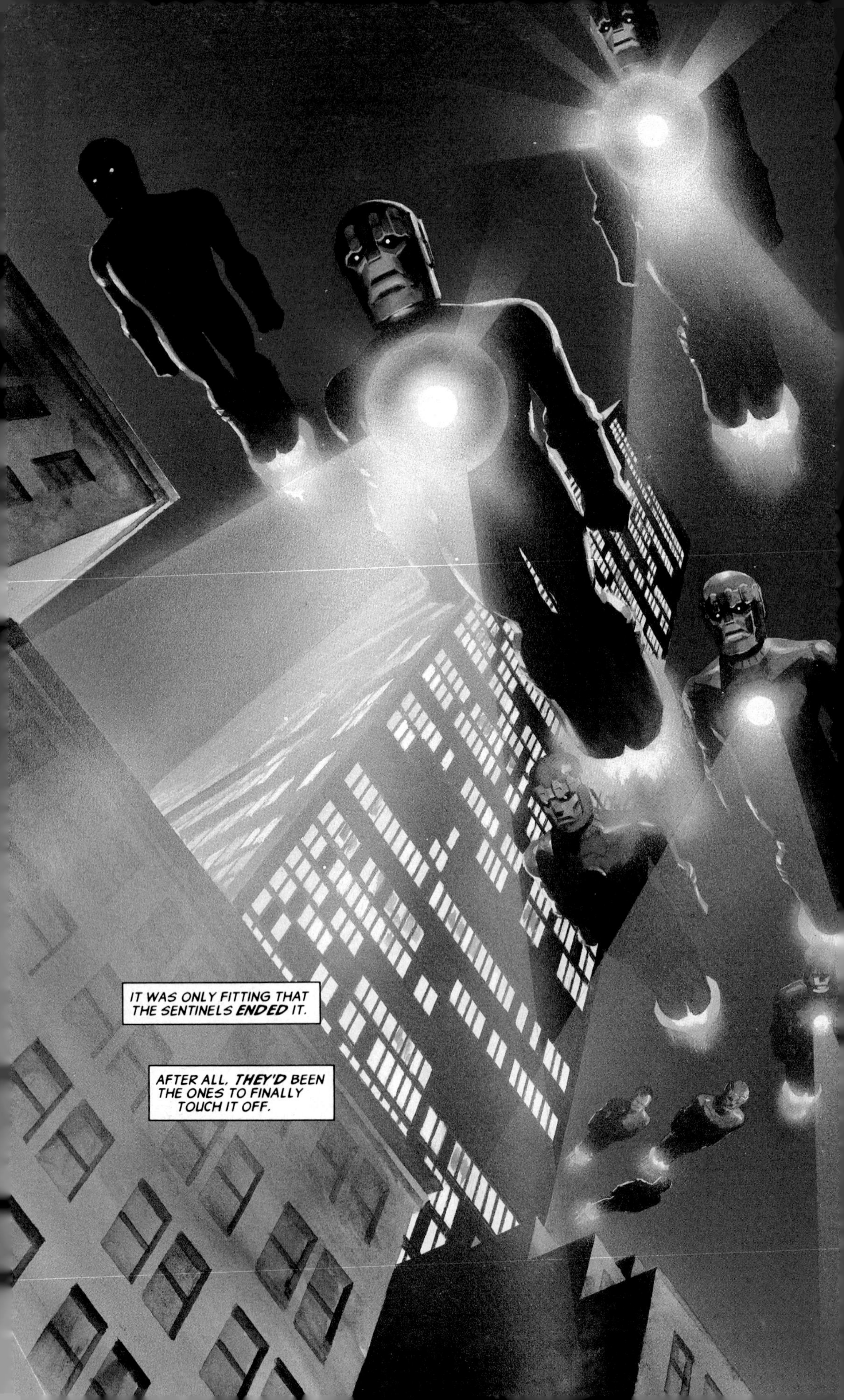
IT WAS ONLY FITTING THAT THE SENTINELS ENDED IT.
AFTER ALL, THEY'D BEEN THE ONES TO FINALLY TOUCH IT OFF.

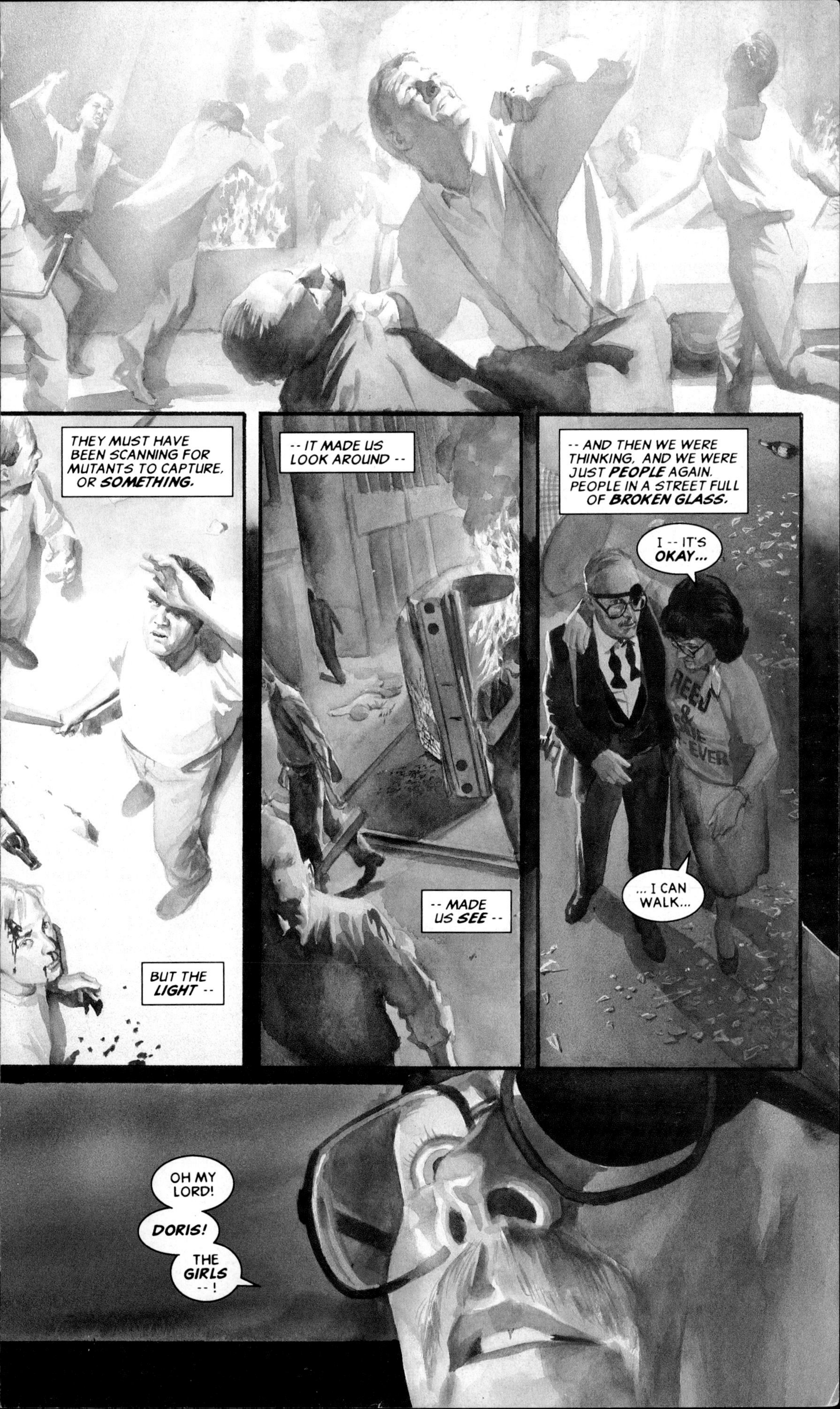
THEY MUST HAVE BEEN SCANNING FOR MUTANTS TO CAPTURE, OR SOMETHING.
BUT THE LIGHT --
-- IT MADE US LOOK AROUND --
-- MADE US SEE --
-- AND THEN WE WERE THINKING, AND WE WERE JUST PEOPLE AGAIN. PEOPLE IN A STREET FULL OF BROKEN GLASS.
I -- IT'S OKAY...
...I CAN WALK...
OH MY LORD!
DORIS!
THE GIRLS --!

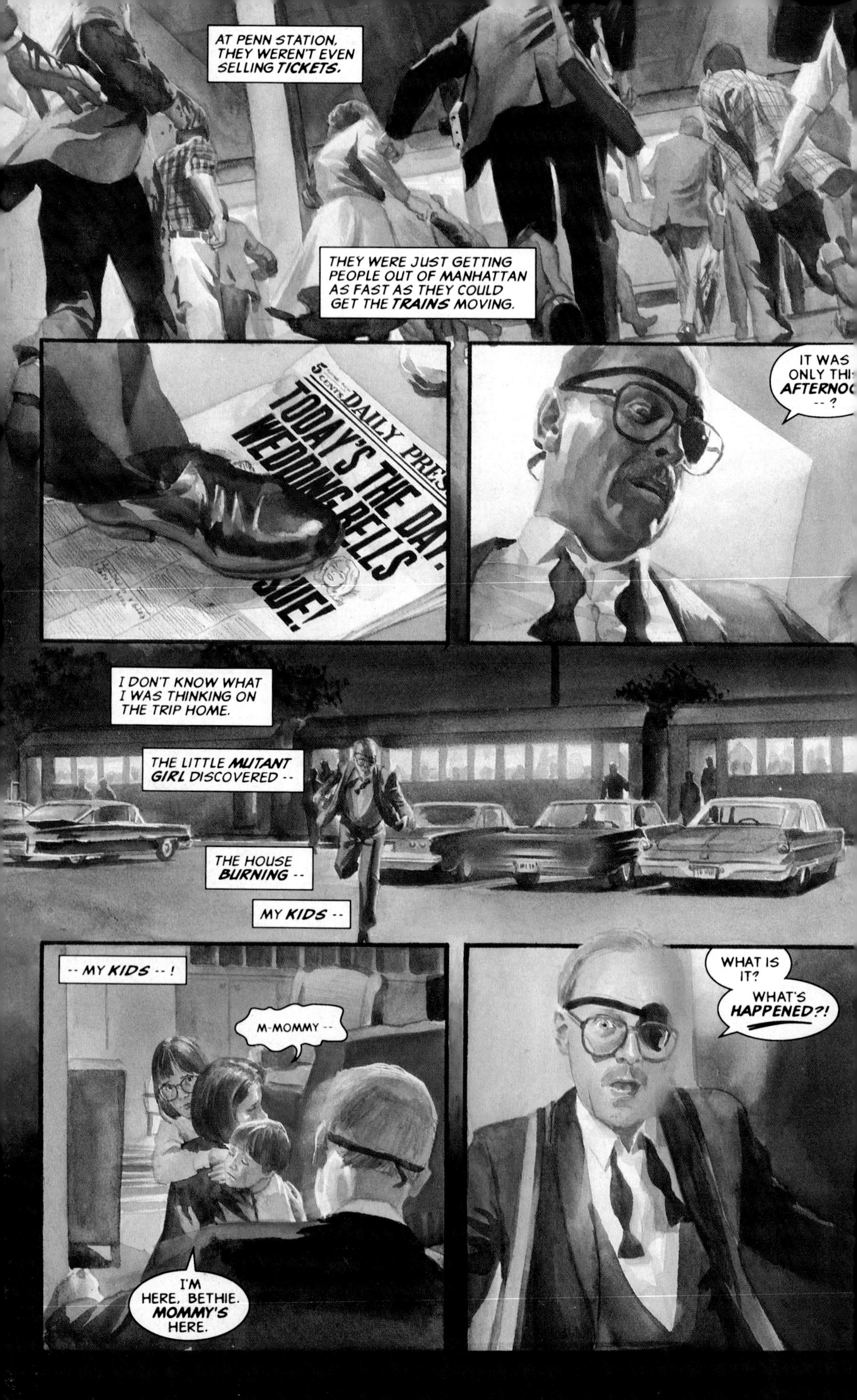
AT PENN STATION, THEY WEREN'T EVEN SELLING TICKETS.
THEY WERE JUST GETTING PEOPLE OUT OF MANHATTAN AS FAST AS THEY COULD GET THE TRAINS MOVING.
DAILY PRES
5 CENTS
TODAY'S THE DA
WEDDING BELLS
SUE!
IT WAS ONLY THI AFTERNO -- ?
I DON'T KNOW WHAT I WAS THINKING ON THE TRIP HOME.
THE LITTLE MUTANT GIRL DISCOVERED --
THE HOUSE BURNING --
MY KIDS --
-- MY KIDS -- !
M-MOMMY --
I'M HERE, BETHIE. MOMMY'S HERE.
WHAT IS IT?
WHAT'S HAPPENED?!

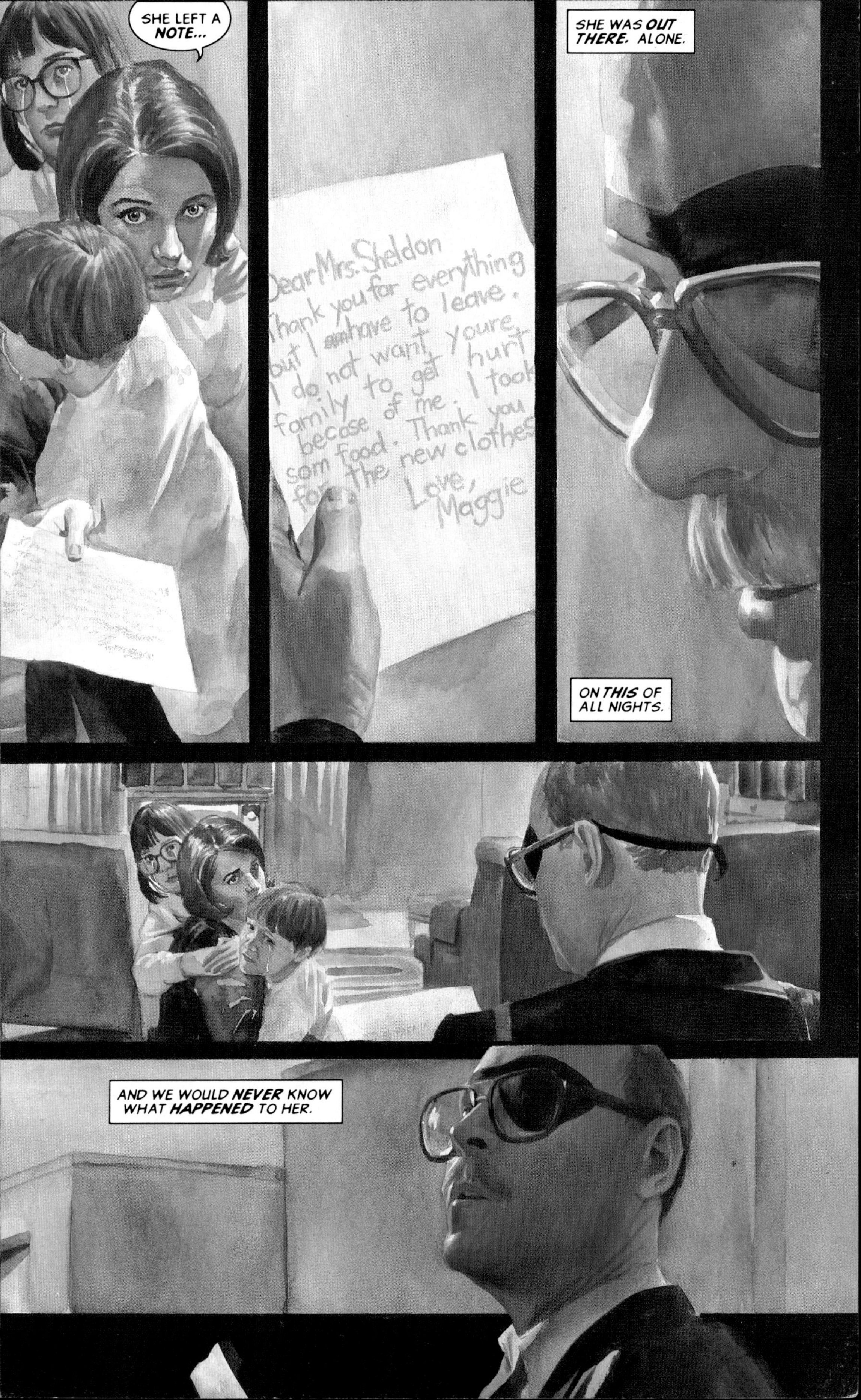
SHE LEFT A NOTE...
Dear Mrs. Sheldon
Thank you for everything
but I am have to leave.
I do not want youre
family to get hurt
becose of me. I took
som food. Thank you
for the new clothes
Love,
Maggie
SHE WAS OUT THERE. ALONE.
ON THIS OF ALL NIGHTS.
AND WE WOULD NEVER KNOW WHAT HAPPENED TO HER.

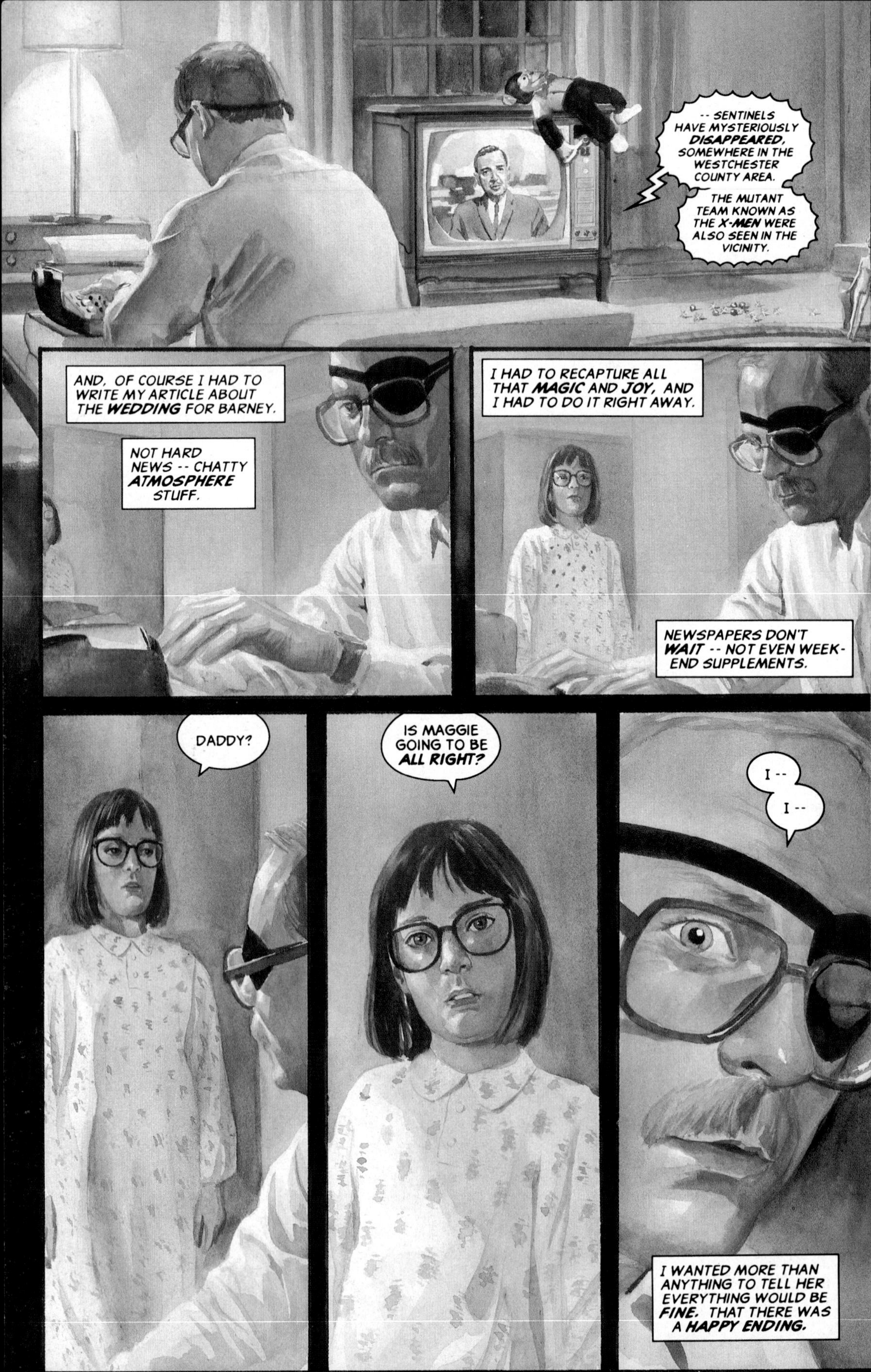
-- SENTINELS HAVE MYSTERIOUSLY DISAPPEARED, SOMEWHERE IN THE WESTCHESTER COUNTY AREA.
THE MUTANT TEAM KNOWN AS THE X-MEN WERE ALSO SEEN IN THE VICINITY.
AND, OF COURSE I HAD TO WRITE MY ARTICLE ABOUT THE WEDDING FOR BARNEY.
NOT HARD NEWS -- CHATTY ATMOSPHERE STUFF.
I HAD TO RECAPTURE ALL THAT MAGIC AND JOY, AND I HAD TO DO IT RIGHT AWAY.
NEWSPAPERS DON'T WAIT -- NOT EVEN WEEK-END SUPPLEMENTS.
DADDY?
IS MAGGIE GOING TO BE ALL RIGHT?
I --
I --
I WANTED MORE THAN ANYTHING TO TELL HER EVERYTHING WOULD BE FINE. THAT THERE WAS A HAPPY ENDING.

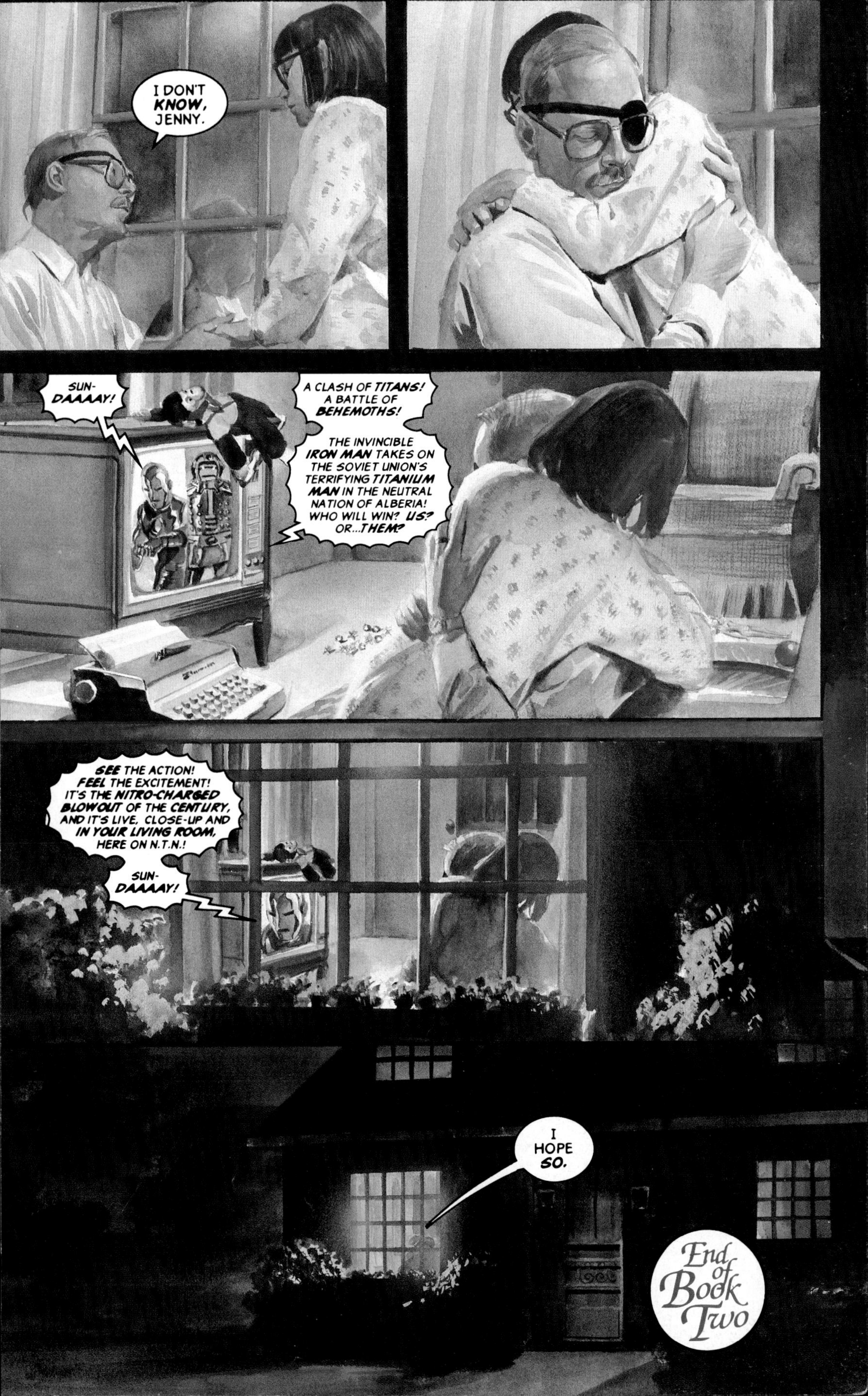
I DON'T KNOW, JENNY.
SUN-DAAAAY!
A CLASH OF TITANS! A BATTLE OF BEHEMOTHS!
THE INVINCIBLE IRON MAN TAKES ON THE SOVIET UNION'S TERRIFYING TITANIUM MAN IN THE NEUTRAL NATION OF ALBERIA! WHO WILL WIN? US? OR...THEM?
SEE THE ACTION! FEEL THE EXCITEMENT! IT'S THE NITRO-CHARGED BLOWOUT OF THE CENTURY, AND IT'S LIVE, CLOSE-UP AND IN YOUR LIVING ROOM, HERE ON N.T.N.!
SUN-DAAAAY!
I HOPE SO.
End of Book Two

Commentary by Alex Ross

The third chapter

of **MARVELS** is the one of which I feel most proud. Surprisingly to me, it became my favorite despite the fact that it had never been a part of the original proposal. Before I had even talked to Kurt about it, I conceived **MARVELS'** framework around a loose group of stories starting with the birth of the Human Torch and ending around the death of Gwen Stacy. Observing important events in Marvel history had not been my foremost intention, but as soon as that was determined to be part of our focus, I knew we had to restructure every-thing and toss out a lot of the short stories had wanted to tell. But the moment Kur mentioned the idea of covering the first coming of Galactus (The classic Fantastic Fou storyline from issues 48-50) I had a renewe faith in the concept. Luckily, my original ide was underdeveloped enough so that Kur was able to bring forth what I feel is th greatest moment of the series. The way tha Phil Sheldon feels a rising discontent with city's ungratefulness towards the supe heroes that builds to his rage in the las scene, set against the breathtaking events o Judgment Day, hit the spot for me as th most cohesive and driven storytelling tha Kurt has ever produced.

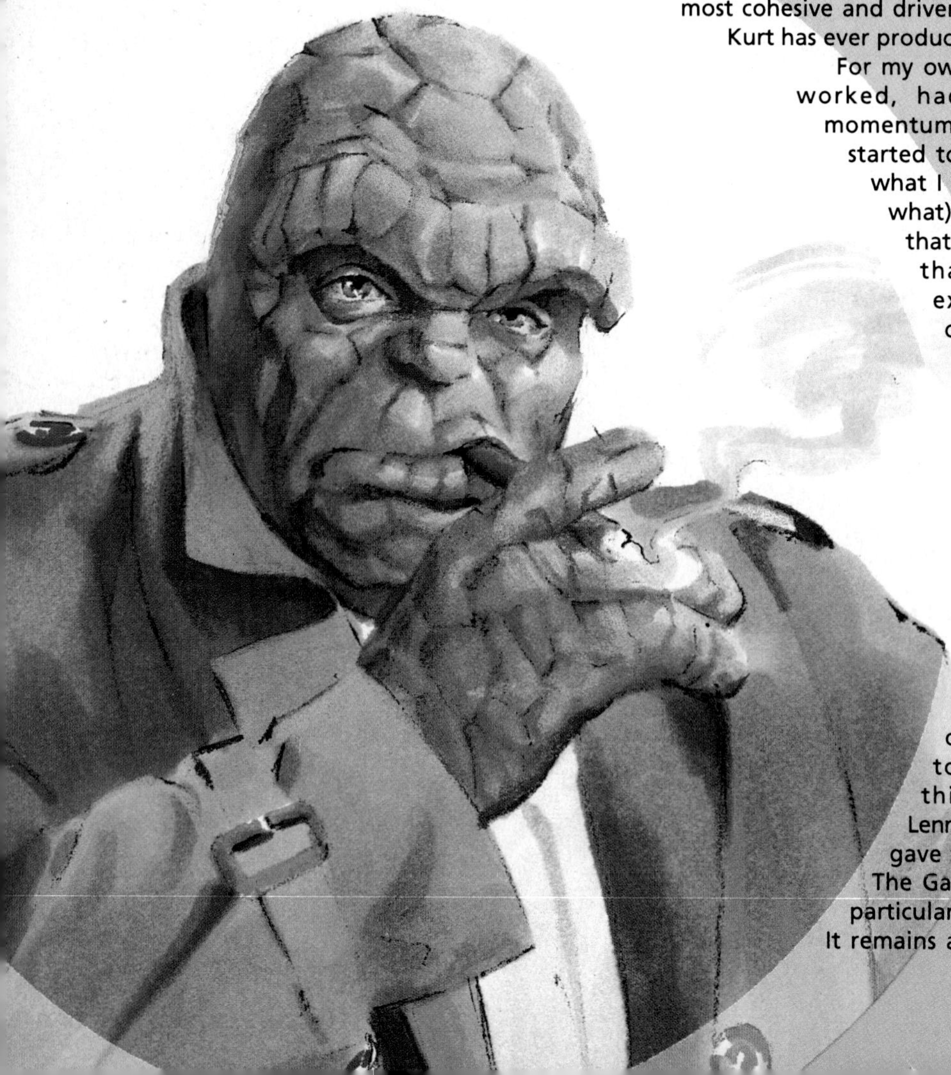

For my own part, the way worked, had gained som momentum by issue 3 and started to feel like I knev what I was doing (somewhat). Despite the fac that this was the stor that was the mos exciting to worl on, I was affecte by a psychological affliction tha I shall hereinafter describ as "Kirby Envy" Stan Le and Jack Kirby' partnership wa the best thing that happene to comics in th sixties. Both mer were at the to of their form an together gave t this medium wha Lennon and McCartne gave to popular music The Galactus storyline ir particular was a highpoint It remains a landmark in th

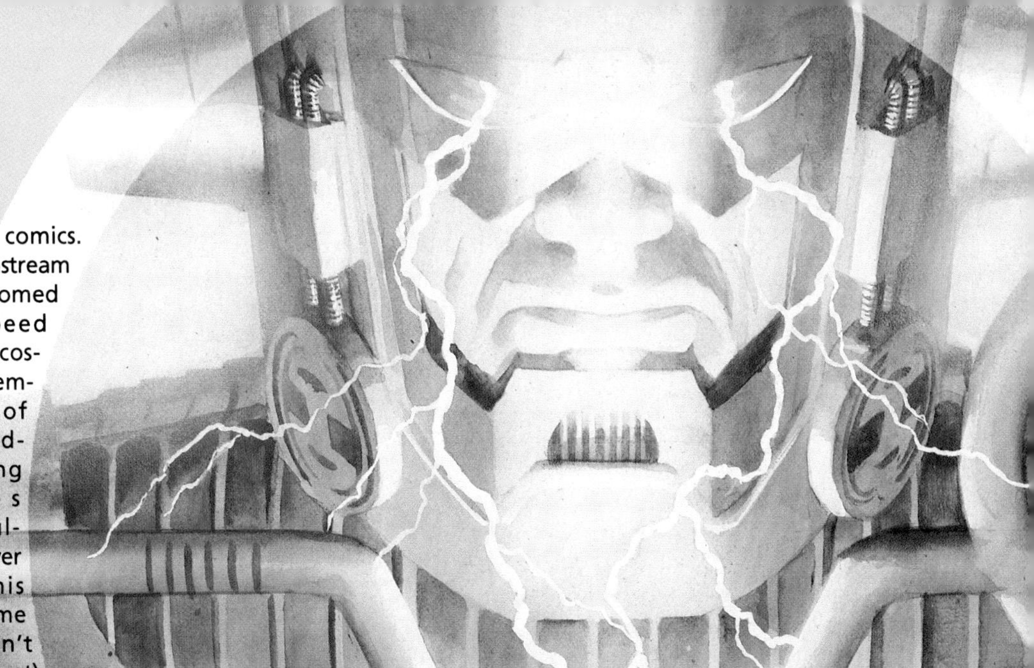

history of comics. Here mainstream comics zoomed up to speed with the cosmic contemplations of the mind-expanding sixties youth culture. I never knew this at the time (as I wasn't even alive yet) but I know now all the effects it had then, when Kirby conceived the Fantastic Four's ultimate foe as "God".

Grafting my style onto classic Kirby images has been one of the most delightful experiences of my life and easily one of the most intimidating. One artist can easily put more polish on another's work by having more time to fuss with it, especially when you're translating traditional pen and ink 4-color art to a more illustrative, painted approach, but to be able to capture the liveliness of Jack Kirby's drawing and the sheer energy of his storytelling is a near-impossible task. I've never cited Kirby as a direct influence on my art or on those artists whom I try to emulate, but that doesn't mean that I'm not mindful of the visual vocabulary he almost single-handedly created for comics.

My first encounter with his work, a short-lived SANDMAN series from the early 70's, struck me as bizarre and expressionistic, but oddly appealing. I soon became aware of his whole evolution through comics history, how he pushed his own boundaries creatively and artistically like no other. Also I encourage those who don't believe that Kirby dabbled in realism to look at FANTASTIC FOUR #11 where, in "A Visit With the Fantastic Four," we see realistic rendering come full blown from Kirby in a quiet, almost **MARVELS**-like story about the FF reading their mail.

The time I spent with Kirby's work studying scenes panel by panel to re-interpret sequences, could not have given me a more intimate respect for this man who was a titan in his field. I'm fortunate to have met Jack Kirby a year before his passing and grateful to Kurt Busiek and Marvel Comics for the opportunity to have walked over some of the same ground and enjoyed the beginnings of the universe he was instrumental in creating. This third chapter of **MARVELS** is very honestly intended as an expression of admiration for the single most creative and prolific individual in the history of comics.

God rest you, Jack.

Alex

ALEX ROSS

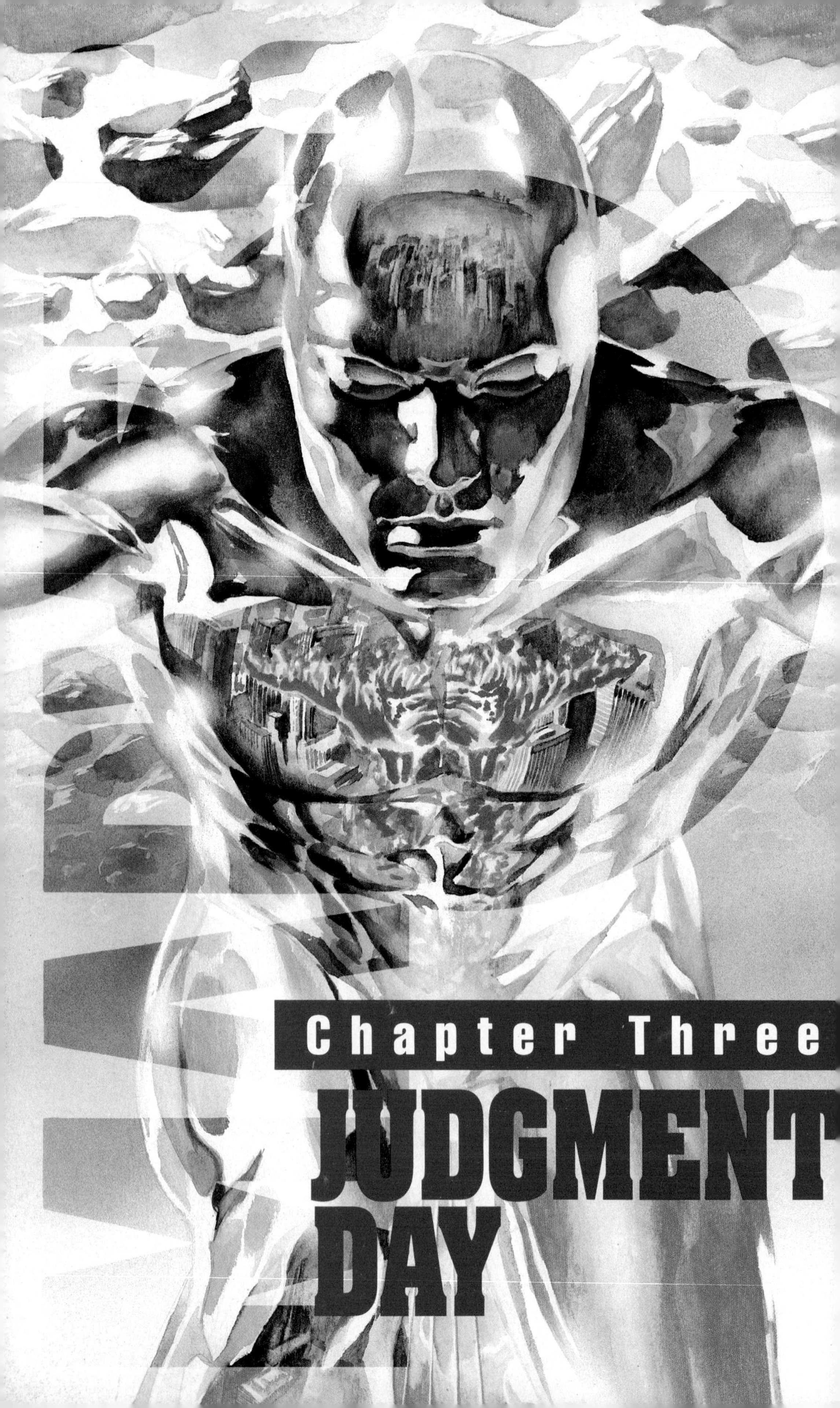

Chapter Three

JUDGMENT DAY

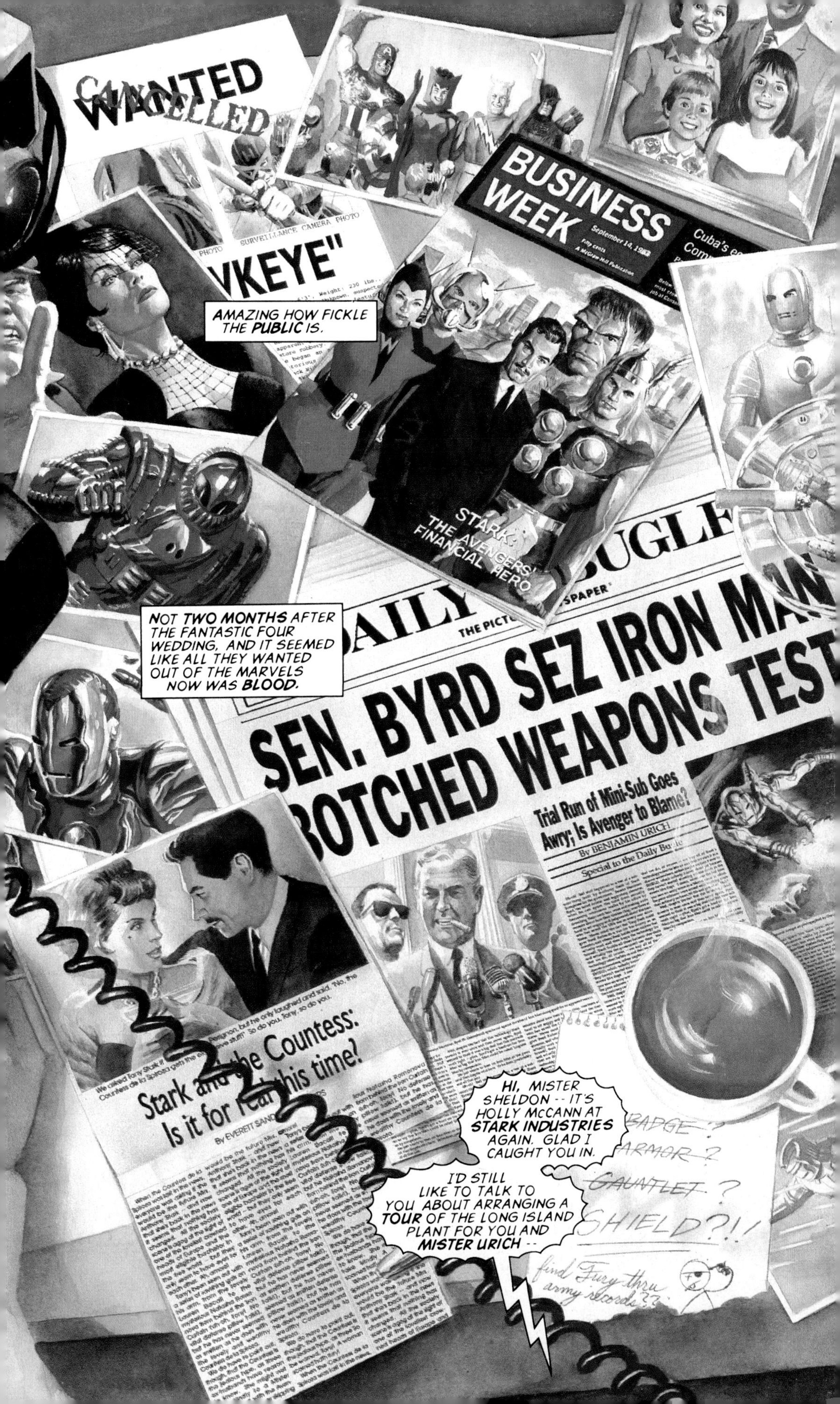
AMAZING HOW FICKLE THE PUBLIC IS.
NOT TWO MONTHS AFTER THE FANTASTIC FOUR WEDDING, AND IT SEEMED LIKE ALL THEY WANTED OUT OF THE MARVELS NOW WAS BLOOD.
HI, MISTER SHELDON -- IT'S HOLLY McCANN AT STARK INDUSTRIES AGAIN. GLAD I CAUGHT YOU IN.
I'D STILL LIKE TO TALK TO YOU ABOUT ARRANGING A TOUR OF THE LONG ISLAND PLANT FOR YOU AND MISTER URICH --
BUSINESS WEEK
STARK: THE AVENGERS' FINANCIAL HERO
SEN. BYRD SEZ IRON MAN BOTCHED WEAPONS TEST
Trial Run of Mini-Sub Goes Awry; Is Avenger to Blame?
By BENJAMIN URICH
Special to the Daily Bugle
Stark and the Countess: Is it for real this time?
By EVERETT SAND
BADGE?
ARMOR?
GAUNTLET?
SHIELD?!!
find Fury thru army records??

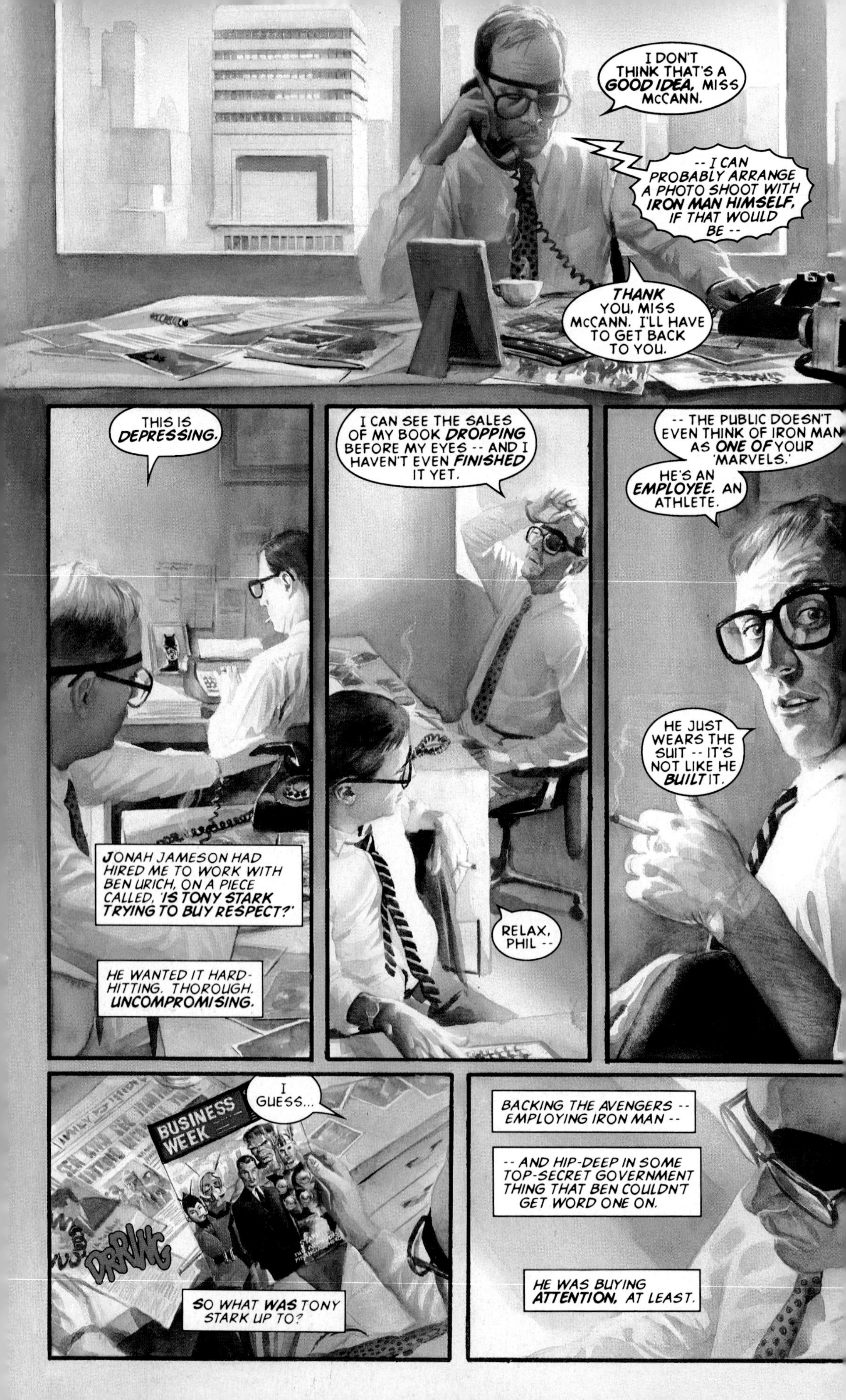

I DON'T THINK THAT'S A GOOD IDEA, MISS McCANN.
-- I CAN PROBABLY ARRANGE A PHOTO SHOOT WITH IRON MAN HIMSELF, IF THAT WOULD BE --
THANK YOU, MISS McCANN. I'LL HAVE TO GET BACK TO YOU.
THIS IS DEPRESSING.
JONAH JAMESON HAD HIRED ME TO WORK WITH BEN URICH, ON A PIECE CALLED, 'IS TONY STARK TRYING TO BUY RESPECT?'
HE WANTED IT HARD-HITTING. THOROUGH. UNCOMPROMISING.
I CAN SEE THE SALES OF MY BOOK DROPPING BEFORE MY EYES -- AND I HAVEN'T EVEN FINISHED IT YET.
RELAX, PHIL --
-- THE PUBLIC DOESN'T EVEN THINK OF IRON MAN AS ONE OF YOUR 'MARVELS.'
HE'S AN EMPLOYEE. AN ATHLETE.
HE JUST WEARS THE SUIT -- IT'S NOT LIKE HE BUILT IT.
I GUESS...
BUSINESS WEEK
DRRRING
SO WHAT WAS TONY STARK UP TO?
BACKING THE AVENGERS -- EMPLOYING IRON MAN --
-- AND HIP-DEEP IN SOME TOP-SECRET GOVERNMENT THING THAT BEN COULDN'T GET WORD ONE ON.
HE WAS BUYING ATTENTION, AT LEAST.

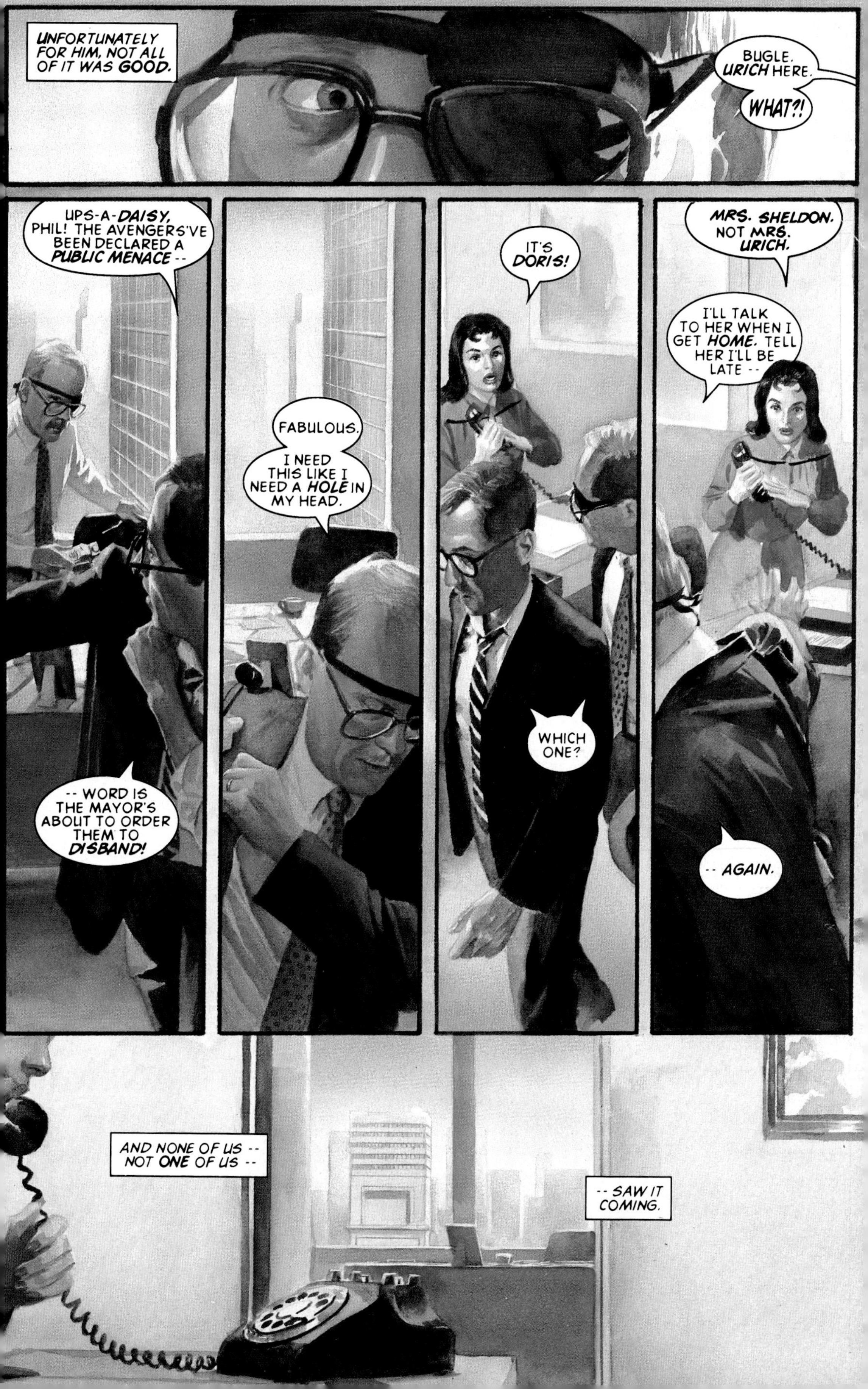
UNFORTUNATELY FOR HIM, NOT ALL OF IT WAS GOOD.
BUGLE. URICH HERE.
WHAT?!
UPS-A-DAISY, PHIL! THE AVENGERS'VE BEEN DECLARED A PUBLIC MENACE --
-- WORD IS THE MAYOR'S ABOUT TO ORDER THEM TO DISBAND!
FABULOUS.
I NEED THIS LIKE I NEED A HOLE IN MY HEAD.
IT'S DORIS!
WHICH ONE?
MRS. SHELDON. NOT MRS. URICH.
I'LL TALK TO HER WHEN I GET HOME. TELL HER I'LL BE LATE --
-- AGAIN.
AND NONE OF US -- NOT ONE OF US --
-- SAW IT COMING.

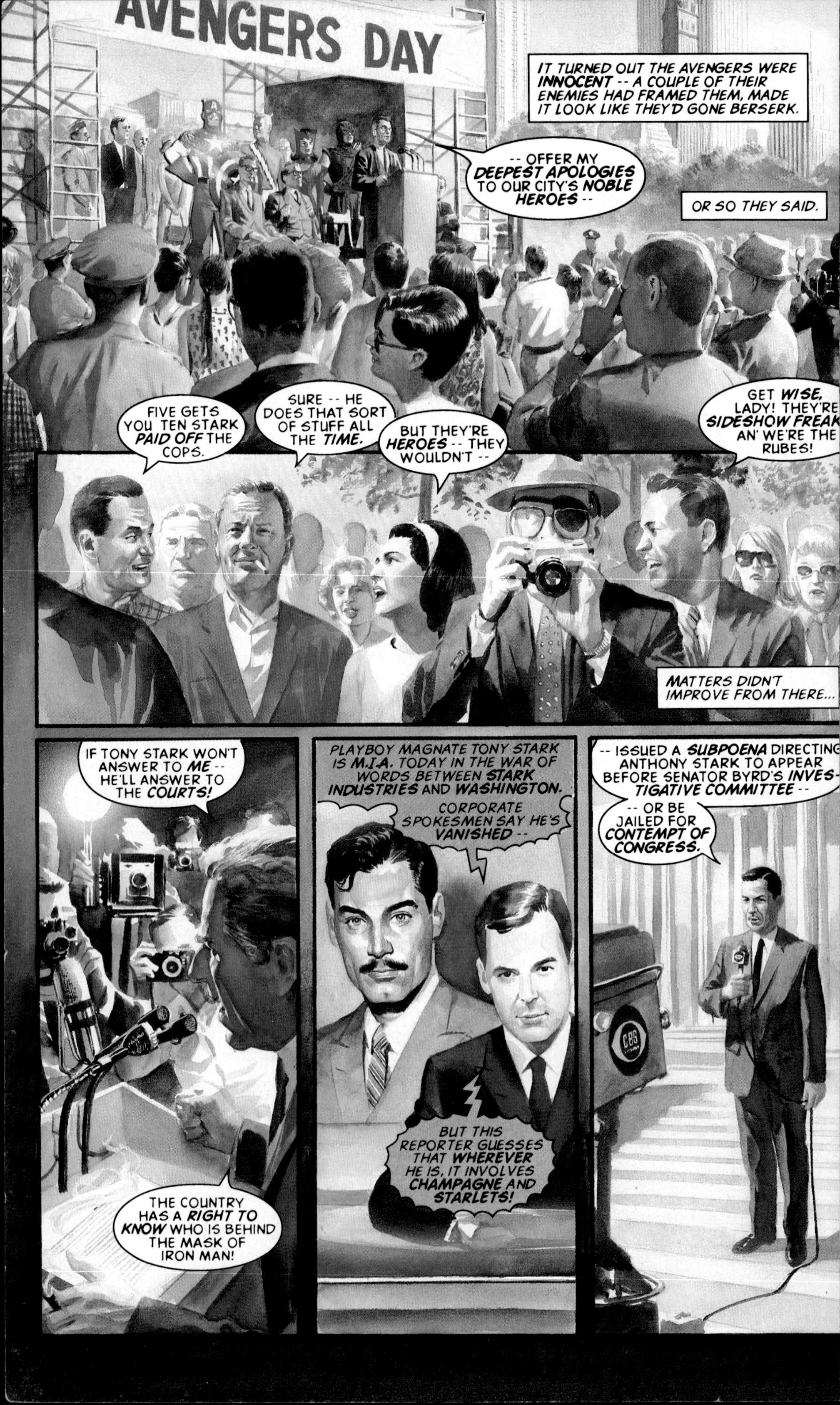
AVENGERS DAY
IT TURNED OUT THE AVENGERS WERE INNOCENT -- A COUPLE OF THEIR ENEMIES HAD FRAMED THEM, MADE IT LOOK LIKE THEY'D GONE BERSERK.
-- OFFER MY DEEPEST APOLOGIES TO OUR CITY'S NOBLE HEROES --
OR SO THEY SAID.
FIVE GETS YOU TEN STARK PAID OFF THE COPS.
SURE -- HE DOES THAT SORT OF STUFF ALL THE TIME.
BUT THEY'RE HEROES -- THEY WOULDN'T --
GET WISE, LADY! THEY'RE SIDESHOW FREAK AN' WE'RE THE RUBES!
MATTERS DIDN'T IMPROVE FROM THERE...
IF TONY STARK WON'T ANSWER TO ME -- HE'LL ANSWER TO THE COURTS!
THE COUNTRY HAS A RIGHT TO KNOW WHO IS BEHIND THE MASK OF IRON MAN!
PLAYBOY MAGNATE TONY STARK IS M.I.A. TODAY IN THE WAR OF WORDS BETWEEN STARK INDUSTRIES AND WASHINGTON.
CORPORATE SPOKESMEN SAY HE'S VANISHED --
BUT THIS REPORTER GUESSES THAT WHEREVER HE IS, IT INVOLVES CHAMPAGNE AND STARLETS!
-- ISSUED A SUBPOENA DIRECTING ANTHONY STARK TO APPEAR BEFORE SENATOR BYRD'S INVESTIGATIVE COMMITTEE --
-- OR BE JAILED FOR CONTEMPT OF CONGRESS.
CBS

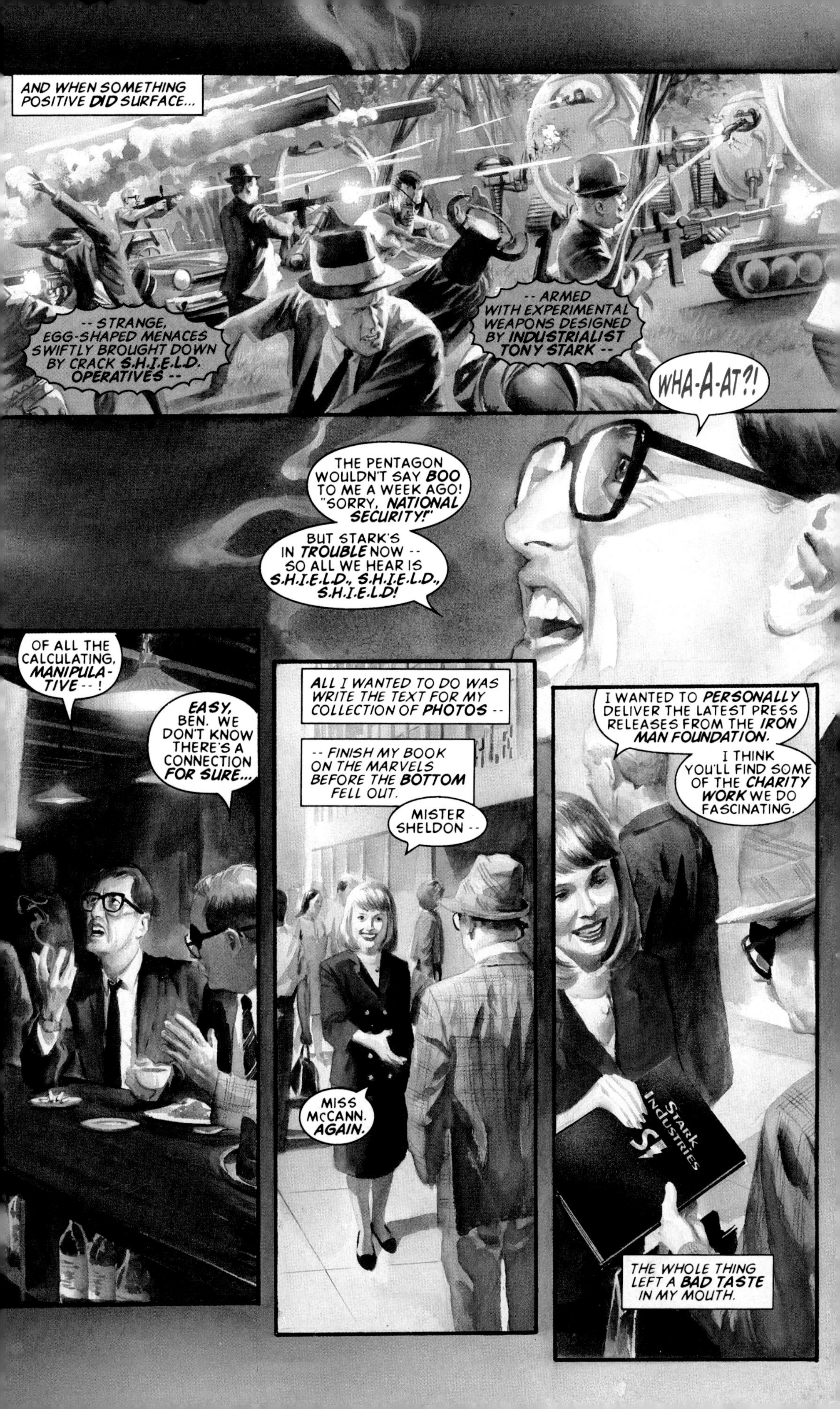
AND WHEN SOMETHING POSITIVE DID SURFACE...
-- STRANGE, EGG-SHAPED MENACES SWIFTLY BROUGHT DOWN BY CRACK S.H.I.E.L.D. OPERATIVES --
-- ARMED WITH EXPERIMENTAL WEAPONS DESIGNED BY INDUSTRIALIST TONY STARK --
WHA-A-AT?!
THE PENTAGON WOULDN'T SAY BOO TO ME A WEEK AGO! "SORRY, NATIONAL SECURITY!"
BUT STARK'S IN TROUBLE NOW -- SO ALL WE HEAR IS S.H.I.E.L.D., S.H.I.E.L.D., S.H.I.E.L.D!
OF ALL THE CALCULATING, MANIPULATIVE -- !
EASY, BEN. WE DON'T KNOW THERE'S A CONNECTION FOR SURE...
ALL I WANTED TO DO WAS WRITE THE TEXT FOR MY COLLECTION OF PHOTOS --
-- FINISH MY BOOK ON THE MARVELS BEFORE THE BOTTOM FELL OUT.
MISTER SHELDON --
MISS McCANN. AGAIN.
I WANTED TO PERSONALLY DELIVER THE LATEST PRESS RELEASES FROM THE IRON MAN FOUNDATION.
I THINK YOU'LL FIND SOME OF THE CHARITY WORK WE DO FASCINATING.
Stark Industries
THE WHOLE THING LEFT A BAD TASTE IN MY MOUTH.

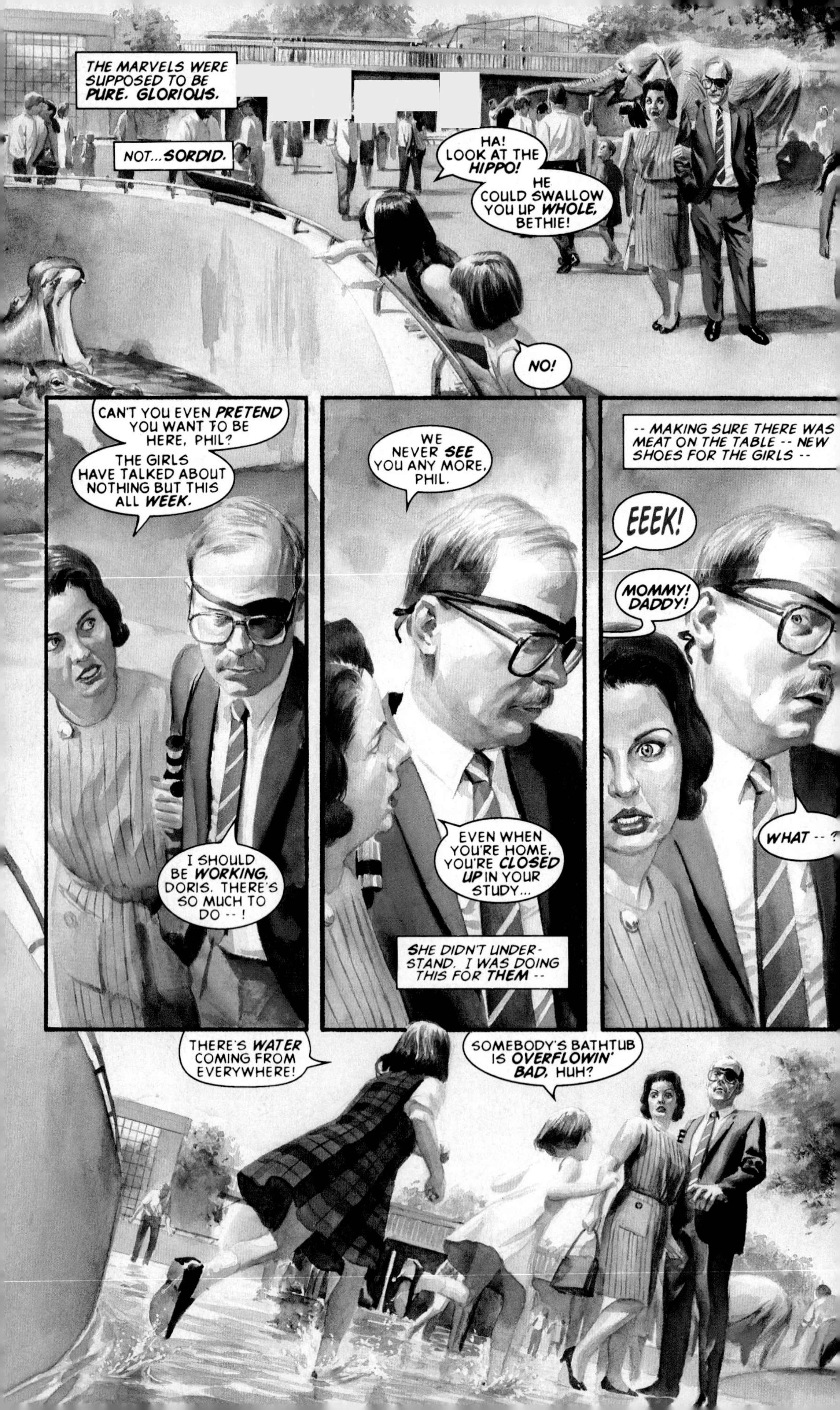

THE MARVELS WERE SUPPOSED TO BE PURE. GLORIOUS.
NOT...SORDID.
HA! LOOK AT THE HIPPO!
HE COULD SWALLOW YOU UP WHOLE, BETHIE!
NO!
CAN'T YOU EVEN PRETEND YOU WANT TO BE HERE, PHIL?
THE GIRLS HAVE TALKED ABOUT NOTHING BUT THIS ALL WEEK.
I SHOULD BE WORKING, DORIS. THERE'S SO MUCH TO DO --!
WE NEVER SEE YOU ANY MORE, PHIL.
EVEN WHEN YOU'RE HOME, YOU'RE CLOSED UP IN YOUR STUDY...
SHE DIDN'T UNDERSTAND. I WAS DOING THIS FOR THEM --
-- MAKING SURE THERE WAS MEAT ON THE TABLE -- NEW SHOES FOR THE GIRLS --
EEEK!
MOMMY! DADDY!
WHAT --?
THERE'S WATER COMING FROM EVERYWHERE!
SOMEBODY'S BATHTUB IS OVERFLOWIN' BAD, HUH?

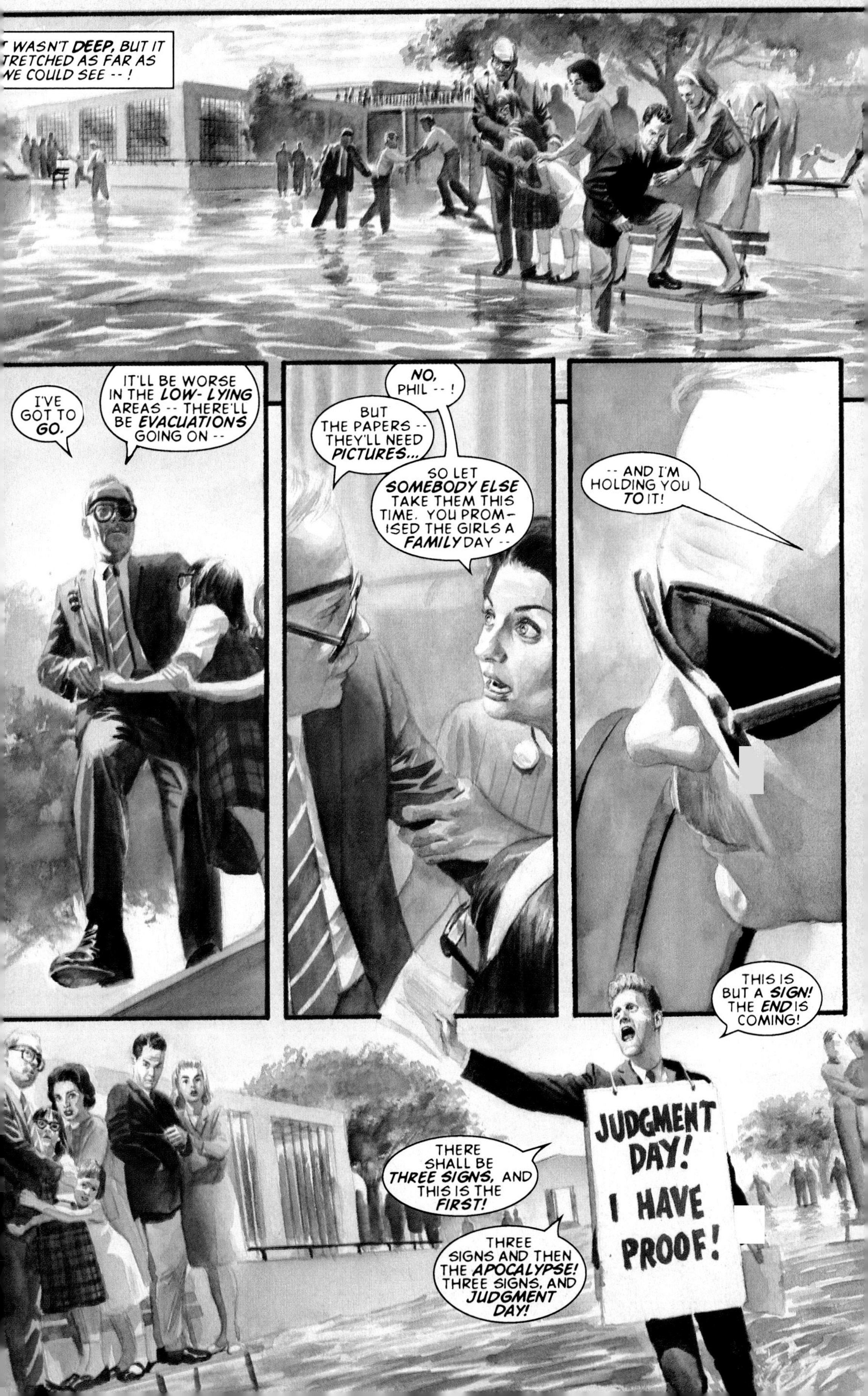

T WASN'T DEEP, BUT IT
TRETCHED AS FAR AS
WE COULD SEE -- !
I'VE GOT TO GO.
IT'LL BE WORSE IN THE LOW- LYING AREAS -- THERE'LL BE EVACUATIONS GOING ON --
NO, PHIL -- !
BUT THE PAPERS -- THEY'LL NEED PICTURES...
SO LET SOMEBODY ELSE TAKE THEM THIS TIME. YOU PROMISED THE GIRLS A FAMILY DAY --
-- AND I'M HOLDING YOU TO IT!
THIS IS BUT A SIGN! THE END IS COMING!
THERE SHALL BE THREE SIGNS, AND THIS IS THE FIRST!
THREE SIGNS AND THEN THE APOCALYPSE! THREE SIGNS, AND JUDGMENT DAY!
JUDGMENT DAY! I HAVE PROOF!

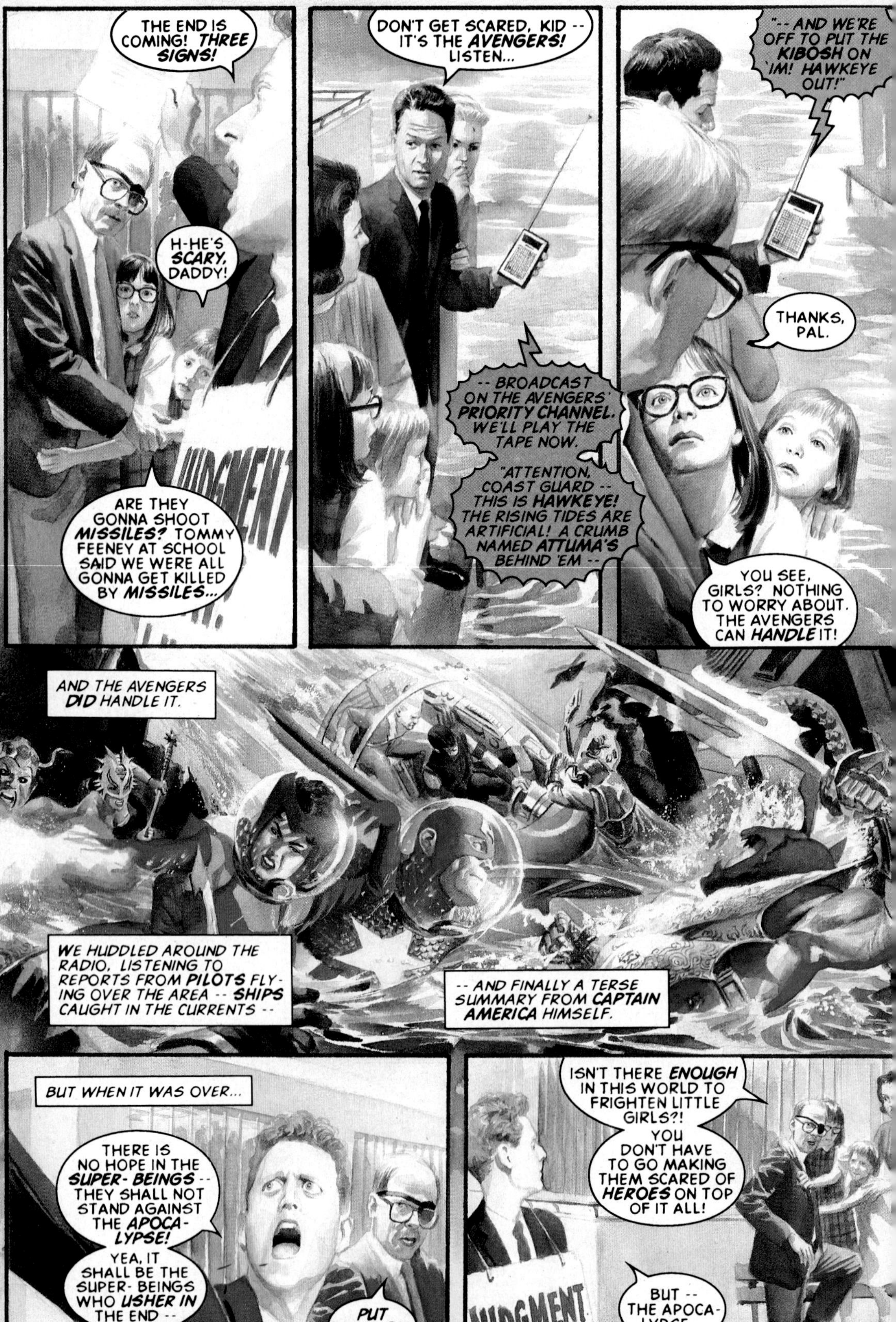
THE END IS COMING! THREE SIGNS!
H-HE'S SCARY, DADDY!
ARE THEY GONNA SHOOT MISSILES? TOMMY FEENEY AT SCHOOL SAID WE WERE ALL GONNA GET KILLED BY MISSILES...
JUDGMENT
DON'T GET SCARED, KID -- IT'S THE AVENGERS! LISTEN...
-- BROADCAST ON THE AVENGERS' PRIORITY CHANNEL. WE'LL PLAY THE TAPE NOW.
"ATTENTION, COAST GUARD -- THIS IS HAWKEYE! THE RISING TIDES ARE ARTIFICIAL! A CRUMB NAMED ATTUMA'S BEHIND 'EM --
"-- AND WE'RE OFF TO PUT THE KIBOSH ON 'IM! HAWKEYE OUT!"
THANKS, PAL.
YOU SEE, GIRLS? NOTHING TO WORRY ABOUT. THE AVENGERS CAN HANDLE IT!
AND THE AVENGERS DID HANDLE IT.
WE HUDDLED AROUND THE RADIO, LISTENING TO REPORTS FROM PILOTS FLYING OVER THE AREA -- SHIPS CAUGHT IN THE CURRENTS --
-- AND FINALLY A TERSE SUMMARY FROM CAPTAIN AMERICA HIMSELF.
BUT WHEN IT WAS OVER...
THERE IS NO HOPE IN THE SUPER-BEINGS -- THEY SHALL NOT STAND AGAINST THE APOCALYPSE! YEA, IT SHALL BE THE SUPER-BEINGS WHO USHER IN THE END --
PUT A LID ON IT!
ISN'T THERE ENOUGH IN THIS WORLD TO FRIGHTEN LITTLE GIRLS?! YOU DON'T HAVE TO GO MAKING THEM SCARED OF HEROES ON TOP OF IT ALL!
BUT -- THE APOCALYPSE --
JUDGMENT DAY!

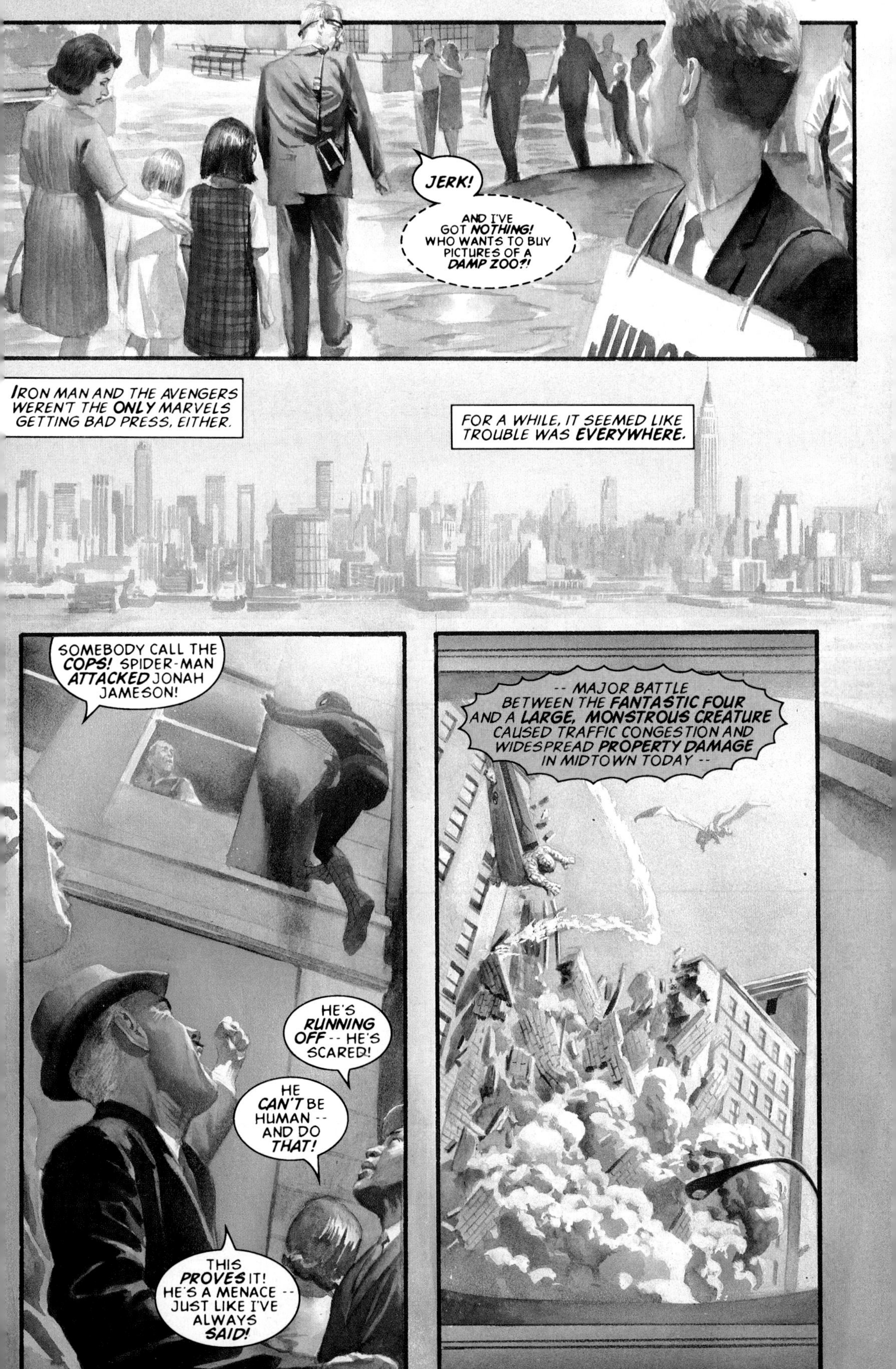
JERK!
AND I'VE GOT NOTHING! WHO WANTS TO BUY PICTURES OF A DAMP ZOO?!
IRON MAN AND THE AVENGERS WEREN'T THE ONLY MARVELS GETTING BAD PRESS, EITHER.
FOR A WHILE, IT SEEMED LIKE TROUBLE WAS EVERYWHERE.
SOMEBODY CALL THE COPS! SPIDER-MAN ATTACKED JONAH JAMESON!
HE'S RUNNING OFF -- HE'S SCARED!
HE CAN'T BE HUMAN -- AND DO THAT!
THIS PROVES IT! HE'S A MENACE -- JUST LIKE I'VE ALWAYS SAID!
-- MAJOR BATTLE BETWEEN THE FANTASTIC FOUR AND A LARGE, MONSTROUS CREATURE CAUSED TRAFFIC CONGESTION AND WIDESPREAD PROPERTY DAMAGE IN MIDTOWN TODAY --

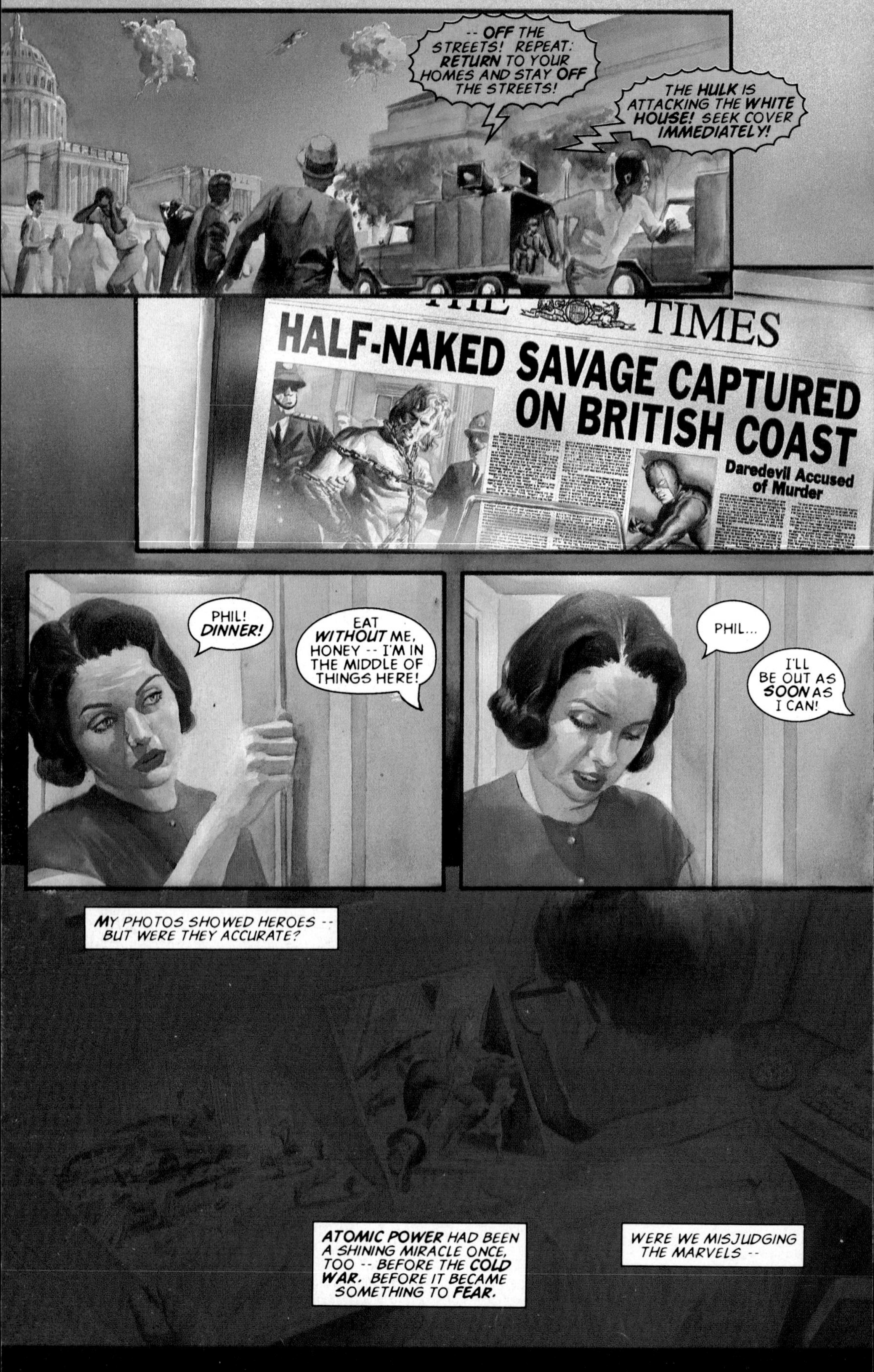
-- OFF THE STREETS! REPEAT: RETURN TO YOUR HOMES AND STAY OFF THE STREETS!
THE HULK IS ATTACKING THE WHITE HOUSE! SEEK COVER IMMEDIATELY!
TIMES
HALF-NAKED SAVAGE CAPTURED ON BRITISH COAST
Daredevil Accused of Murder
PHIL! DINNER!
EAT WITHOUT ME, HONEY -- I'M IN THE MIDDLE OF THINGS HERE!
PHIL...
I'LL BE OUT AS SOON AS I CAN!
MY PHOTOS SHOWED HEROES -- BUT WERE THEY ACCURATE?
ATOMIC POWER HAD BEEN A SHINING MIRACLE ONCE, TOO -- BEFORE THE COLD WAR. BEFORE IT BECAME SOMETHING TO FEAR.
WERE WE MISJUDGING THE MARVELS --

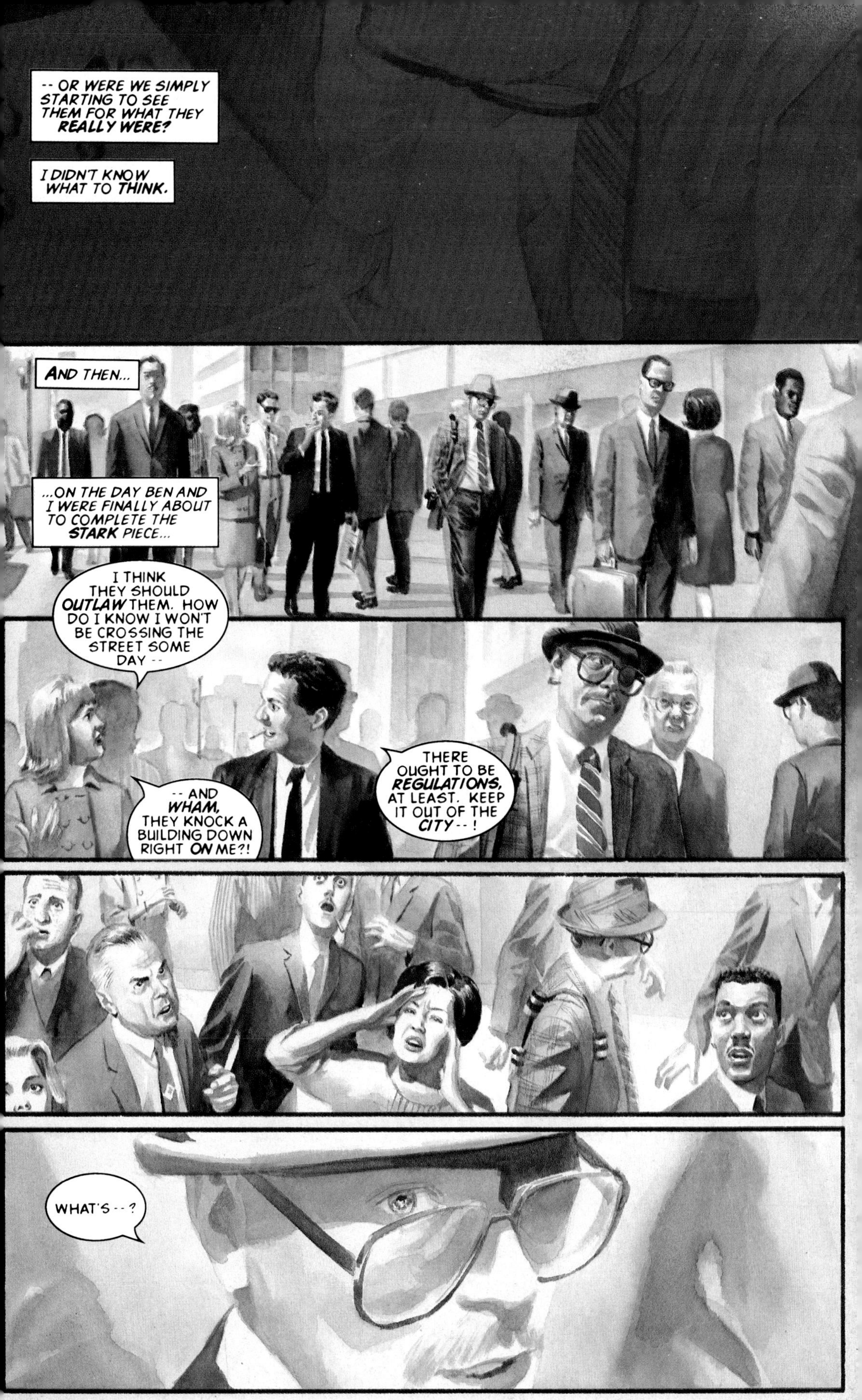
-- OR WERE WE SIMPLY STARTING TO SEE THEM FOR WHAT THEY REALLY WERE?
I DIDN'T KNOW WHAT TO THINK.
AND THEN...
...ON THE DAY BEN AND I WERE FINALLY ABOUT TO COMPLETE THE STARK PIECE...
I THINK THEY SHOULD OUTLAW THEM. HOW DO I KNOW I WON'T BE CROSSING THE STREET SOME DAY --
-- AND WHAM, THEY KNOCK A BUILDING DOWN RIGHT ON ME?!
THERE OUGHT TO BE REGULATIONS, AT LEAST. KEEP IT OUT OF THE CITY -- !
WHAT'S -- ?

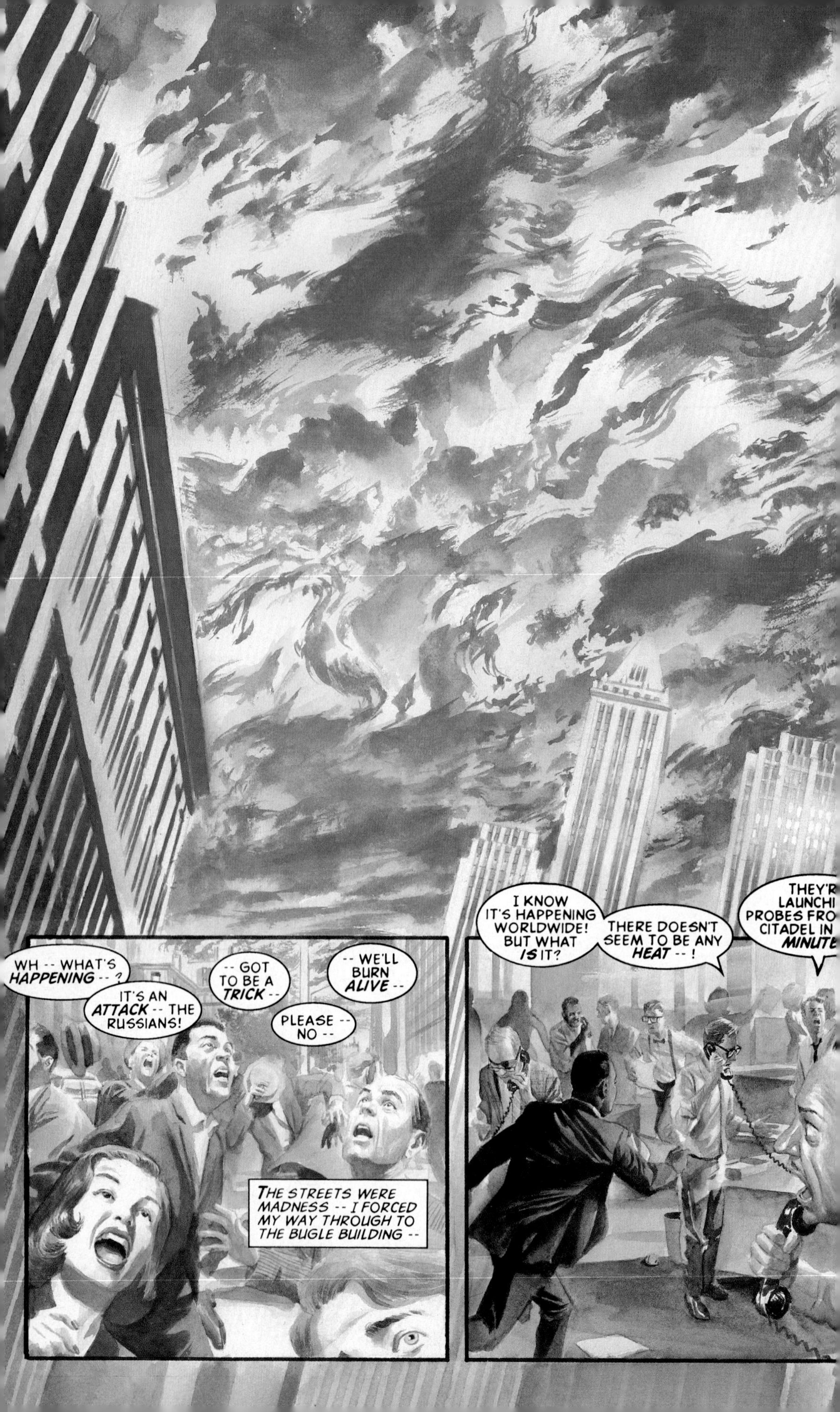
WH -- WHAT'S HAPPENING -- ?
IT'S AN ATTACK -- THE RUSSIANS!
-- GOT TO BE A TRICK --
-- WE'LL BURN ALIVE --
PLEASE -- NO --
THE STREETS WERE MADNESS -- I FORCED MY WAY THROUGH TO THE BUGLE BUILDING --
I KNOW IT'S HAPPENING WORLDWIDE! BUT WHAT IS IT?
THERE DOESN'T SEEM TO BE ANY HEAT -- !
THEY'R LAUNCHI PROBES FRO CITADEL IN MINUTE

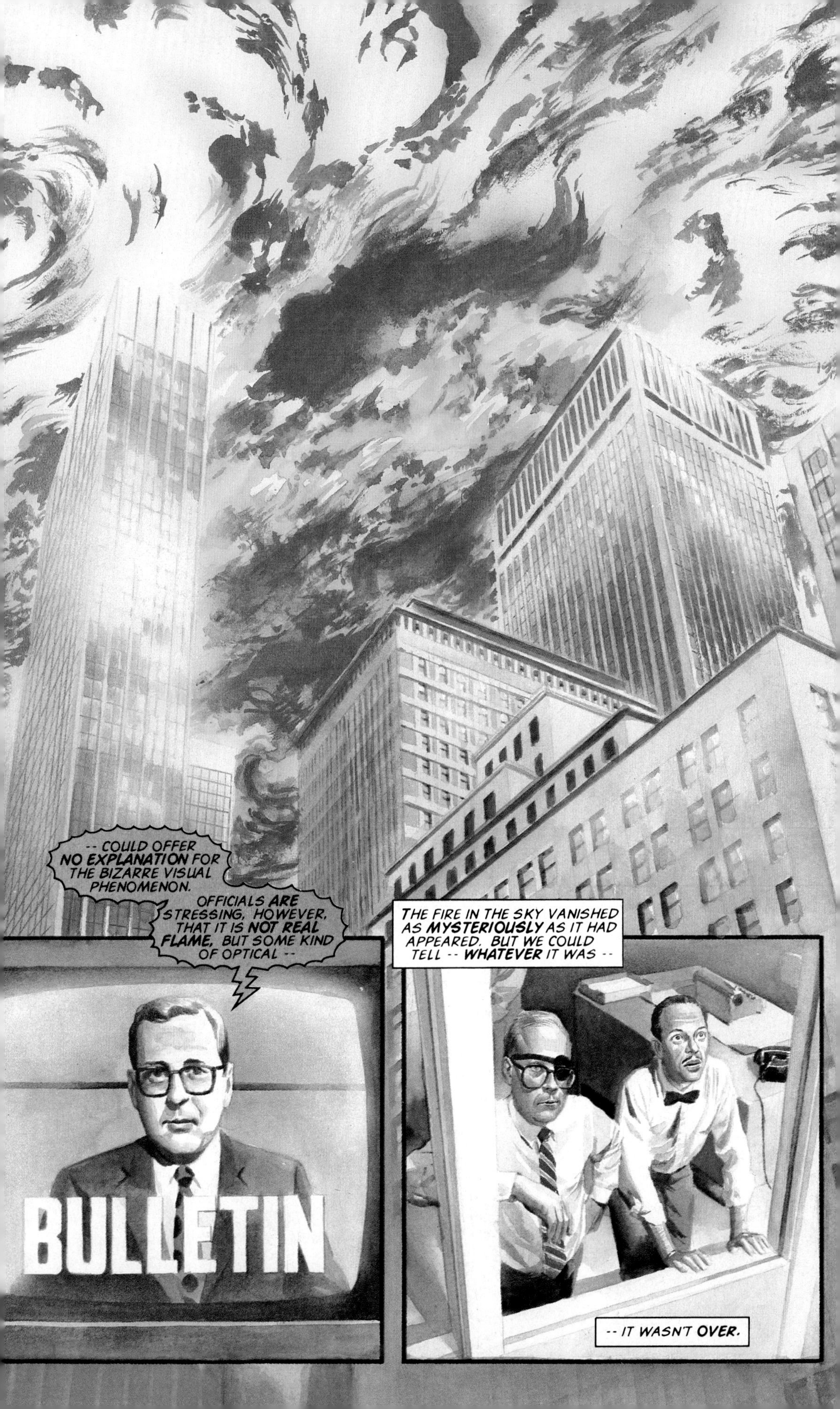
-- COULD OFFER NO EXPLANATION FOR THE BIZARRE VISUAL PHENOMENON.
OFFICIALS ARE STRESSING, HOWEVER, THAT IT IS NOT REAL FLAME, BUT SOME KIND OF OPTICAL --
THE FIRE IN THE SKY VANISHED AS MYSTERIOUSLY AS IT HAD APPEARED. BUT WE COULD TELL -- WHATEVER IT WAS --
BULLETIN
-- IT WASN'T OVER.

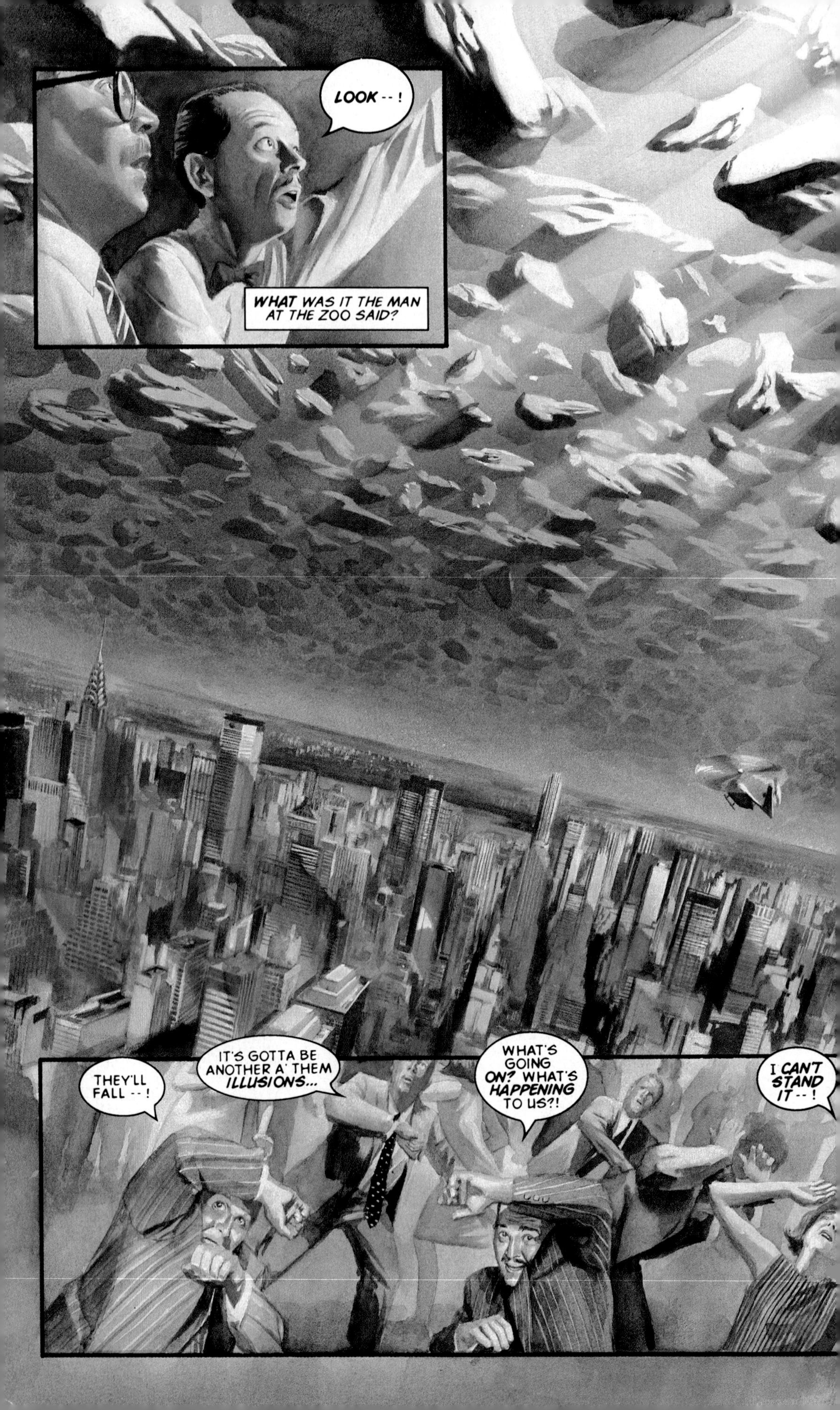
LOOK -- !
WHAT WAS IT THE MAN AT THE ZOO SAID?
THEY'LL FALL --!
IT'S GOTTA BE ANOTHER A' THEM ILLUSIONS...
WHAT'S GOING ON? WHAT'S HAPPENING TO US?!
I CAN'T STAND IT -- !

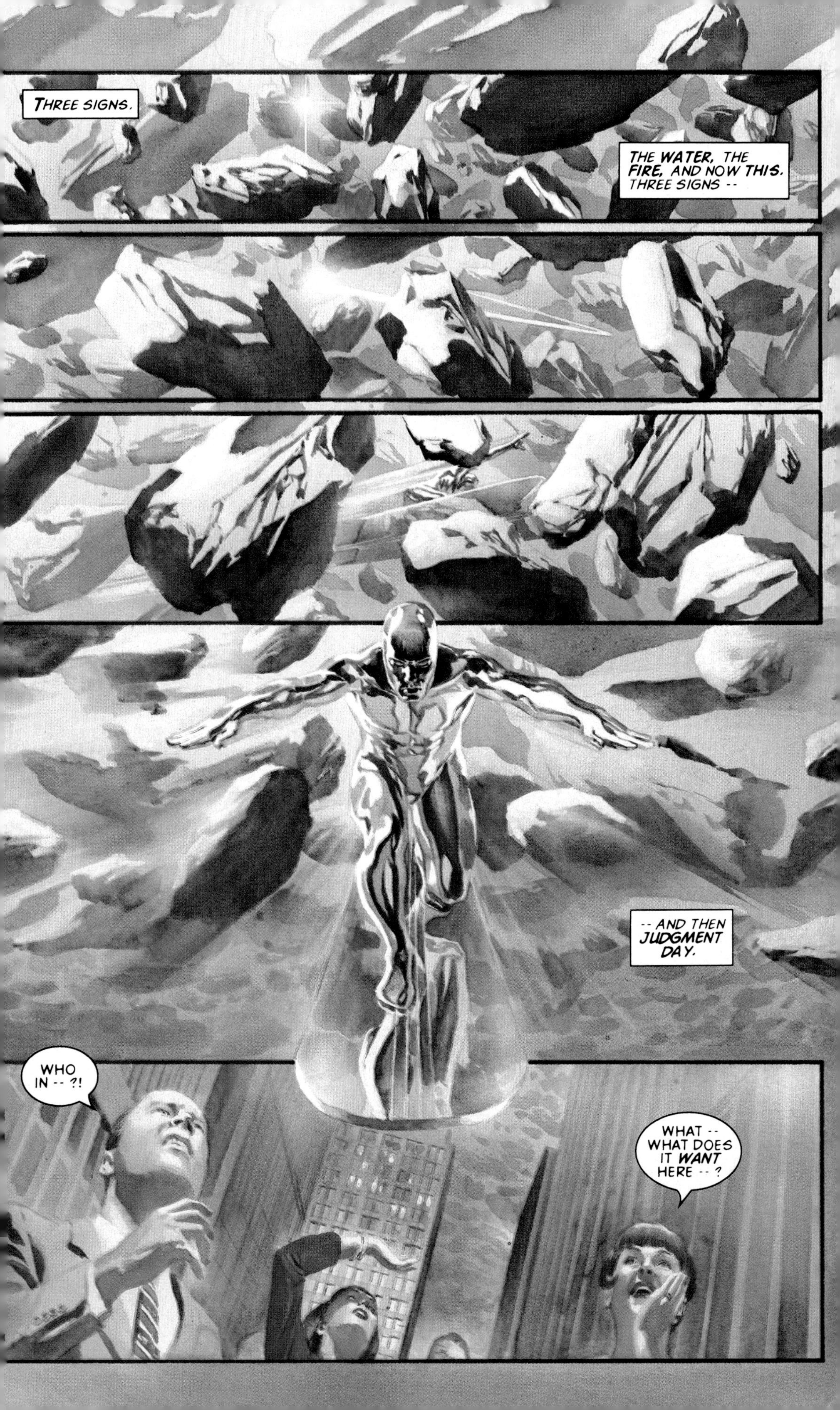

THREE SIGNS.
THE **WATER,** THE **FIRE,** AND NOW **THIS.** THREE SIGNS --
-- AND THEN **JUDGMENT DAY.**
WHO IN -- ?!
WHAT -- WHAT DOES IT **WANT** HERE -- ?

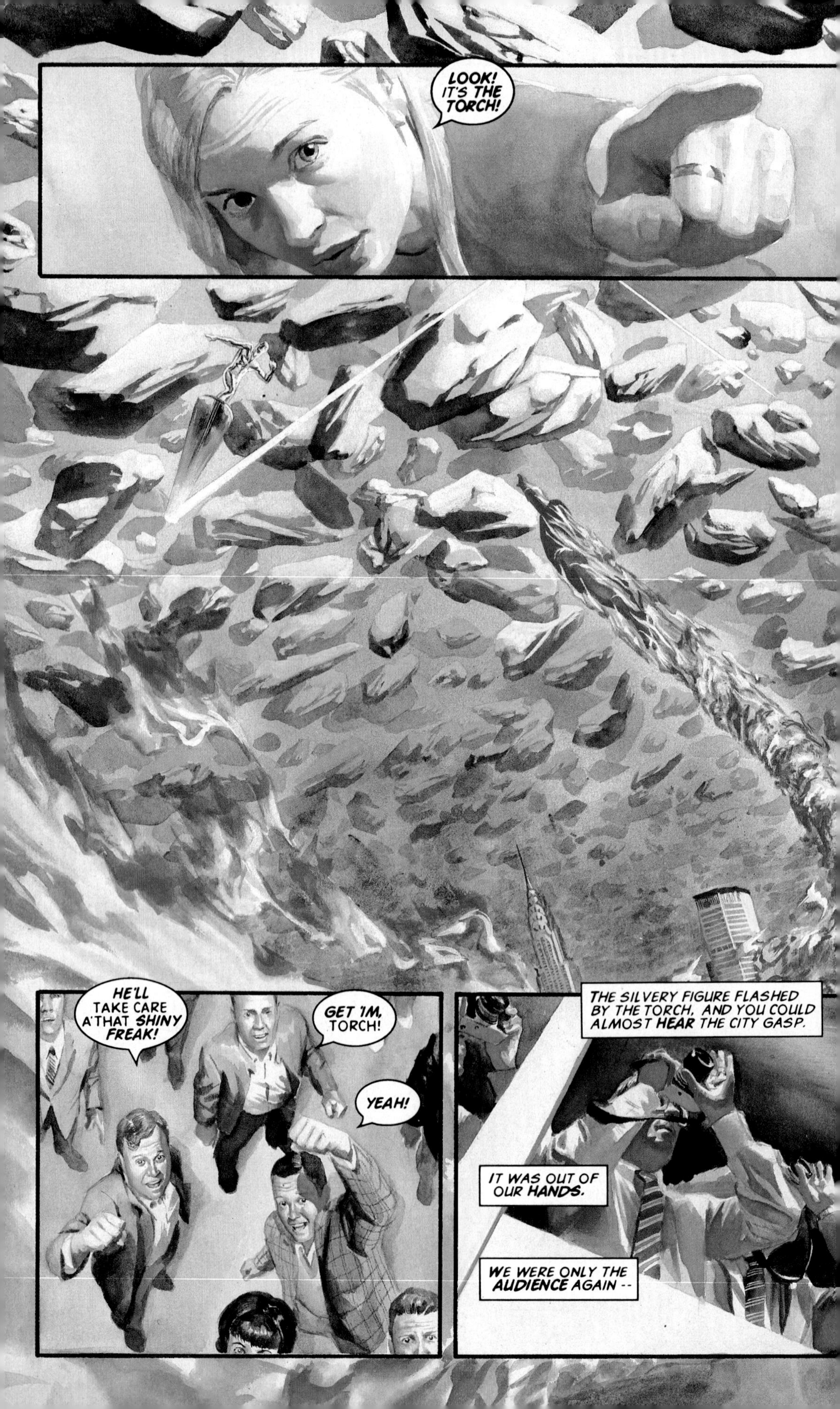
LOOK! IT'S THE TORCH!
HE'LL TAKE CARE A'THAT SHINY FREAK!
GET 'IM, TORCH!
YEAH!
THE SILVERY FIGURE FLASHED BY THE TORCH, AND YOU COULD ALMOST HEAR THE CITY GASP.
IT WAS OUT OF OUR HANDS.
WE WERE ONLY THE AUDIENCE AGAIN --

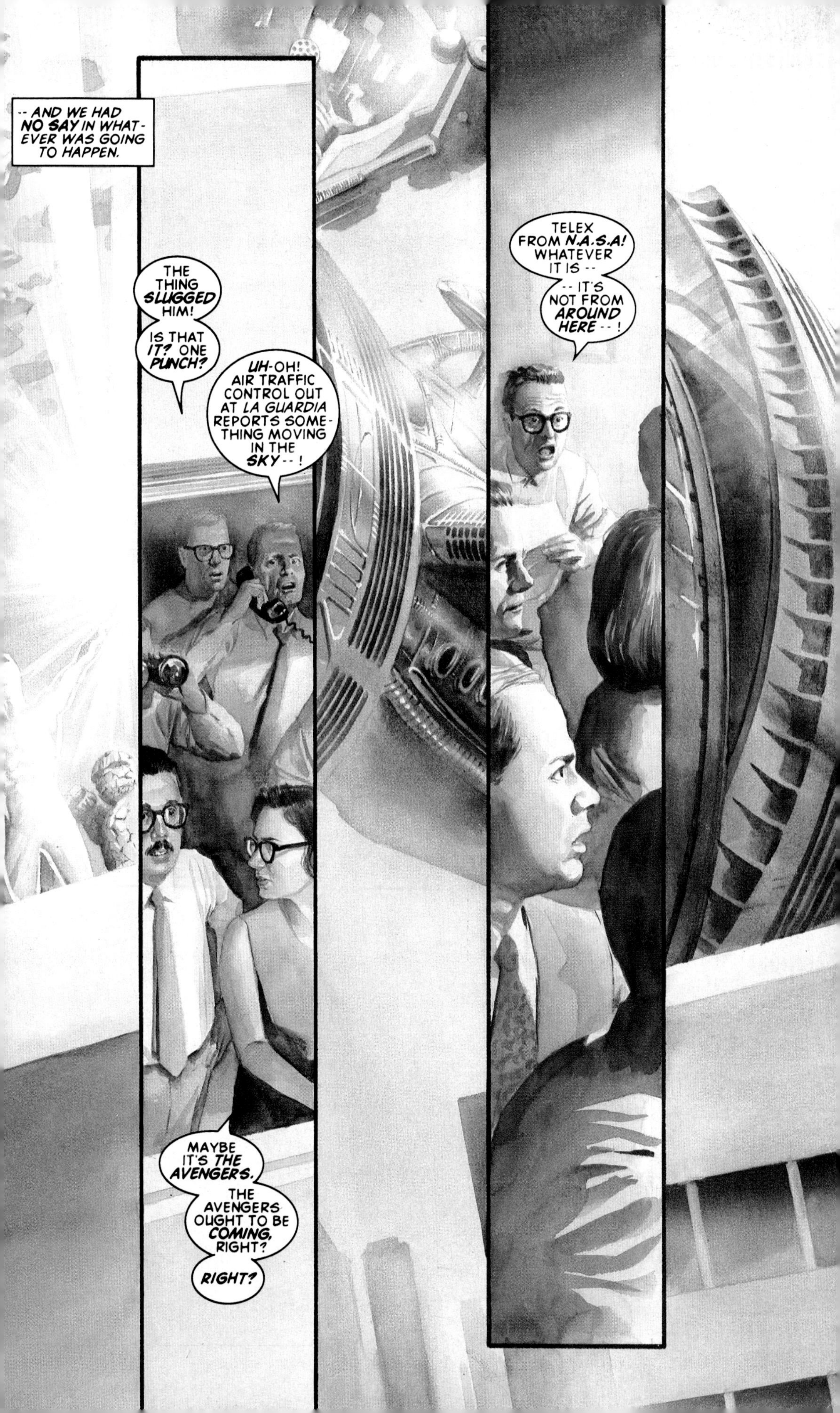
-- AND WE HAD NO SAY IN WHATEVER WAS GOING TO HAPPEN.
THE THING SLUGGED HIM!
IS THAT IT? ONE PUNCH?
UH-OH! AIR TRAFFIC CONTROL OUT AT LA GUARDIA REPORTS SOMETHING MOVING IN THE SKY -- !
MAYBE IT'S THE AVENGERS.
THE AVENGERS OUGHT TO BE COMING, RIGHT?
RIGHT?
TELEX FROM N.A.S.A! WHATEVER IT IS --
-- IT'S NOT FROM AROUND HERE -- !

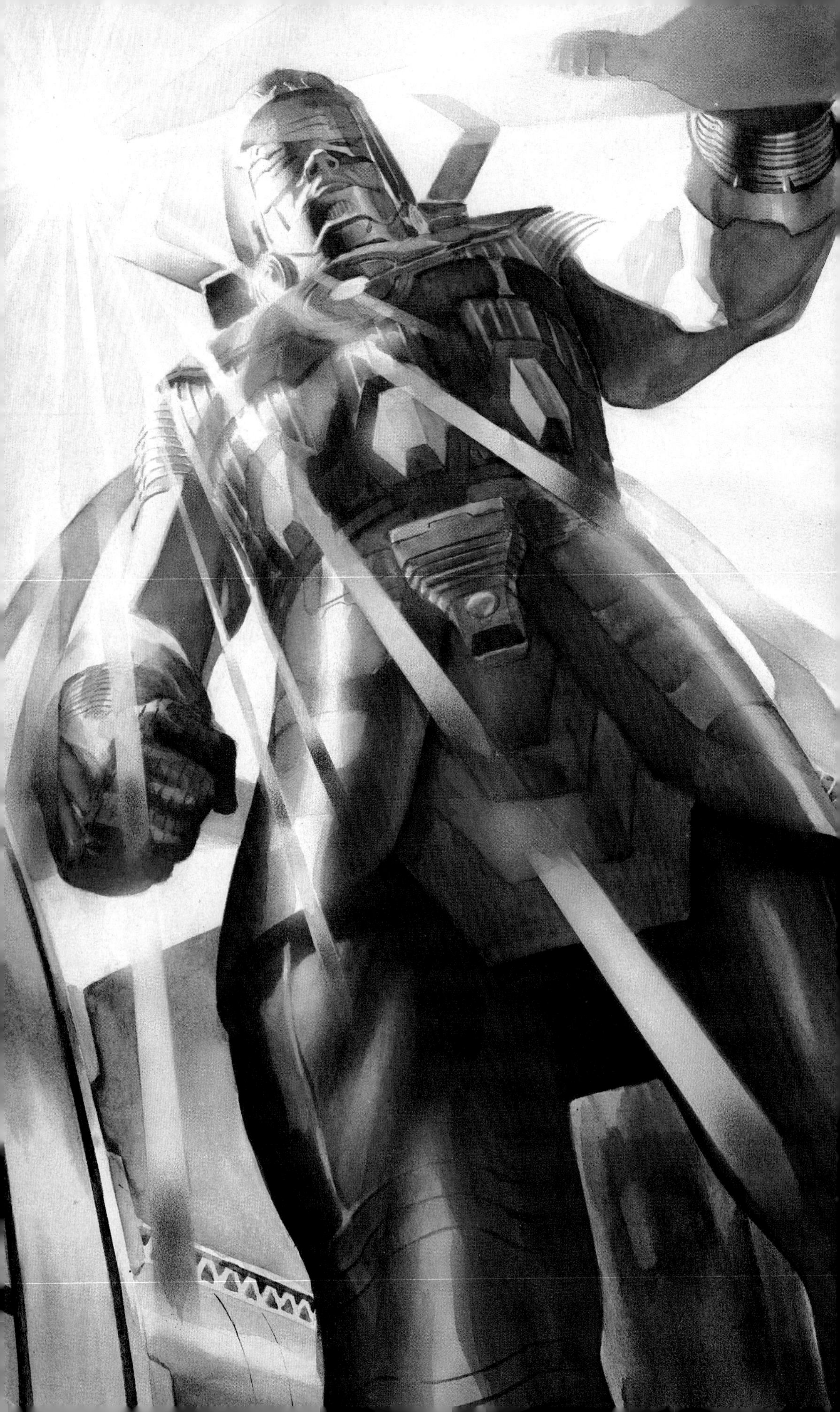

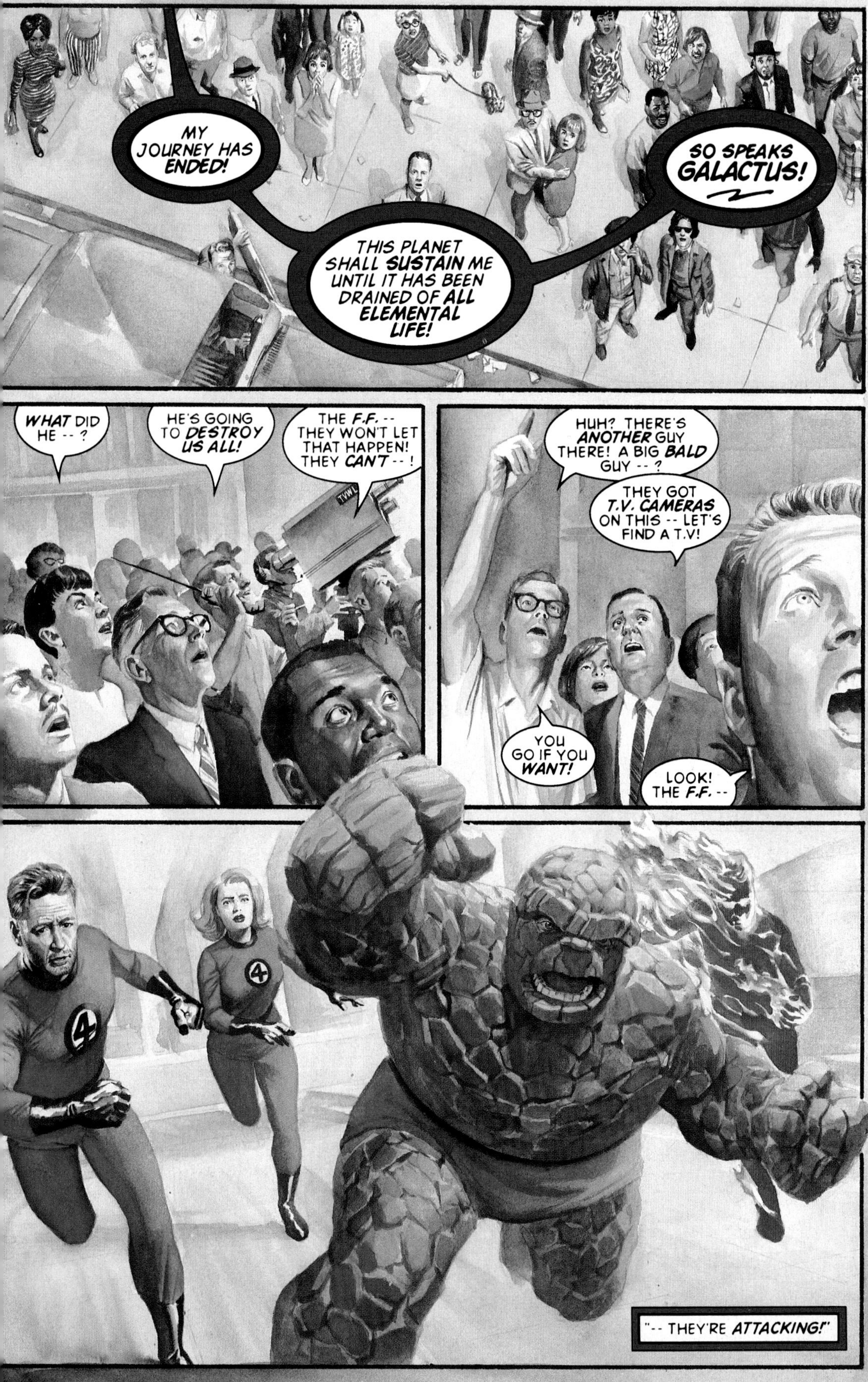
MY JOURNEY HAS ENDED!
THIS PLANET SHALL SUSTAIN ME UNTIL IT HAS BEEN DRAINED OF ALL ELEMENTAL LIFE!
SO SPEAKS GALACTUS!
WHAT DID HE -- ?
HE'S GOING TO DESTROY US ALL!
THE F.F. -- THEY WON'T LET THAT HAPPEN! THEY CAN'T -- !
TVWL
HUH? THERE'S ANOTHER GUY THERE! A BIG BALD GUY -- ?
THEY GOT T.V. CAMERAS ON THIS -- LET'S FIND A T.V!
YOU GO IF YOU WANT!
LOOK! THE F.F. --
"-- THEY'RE ATTACKING!"

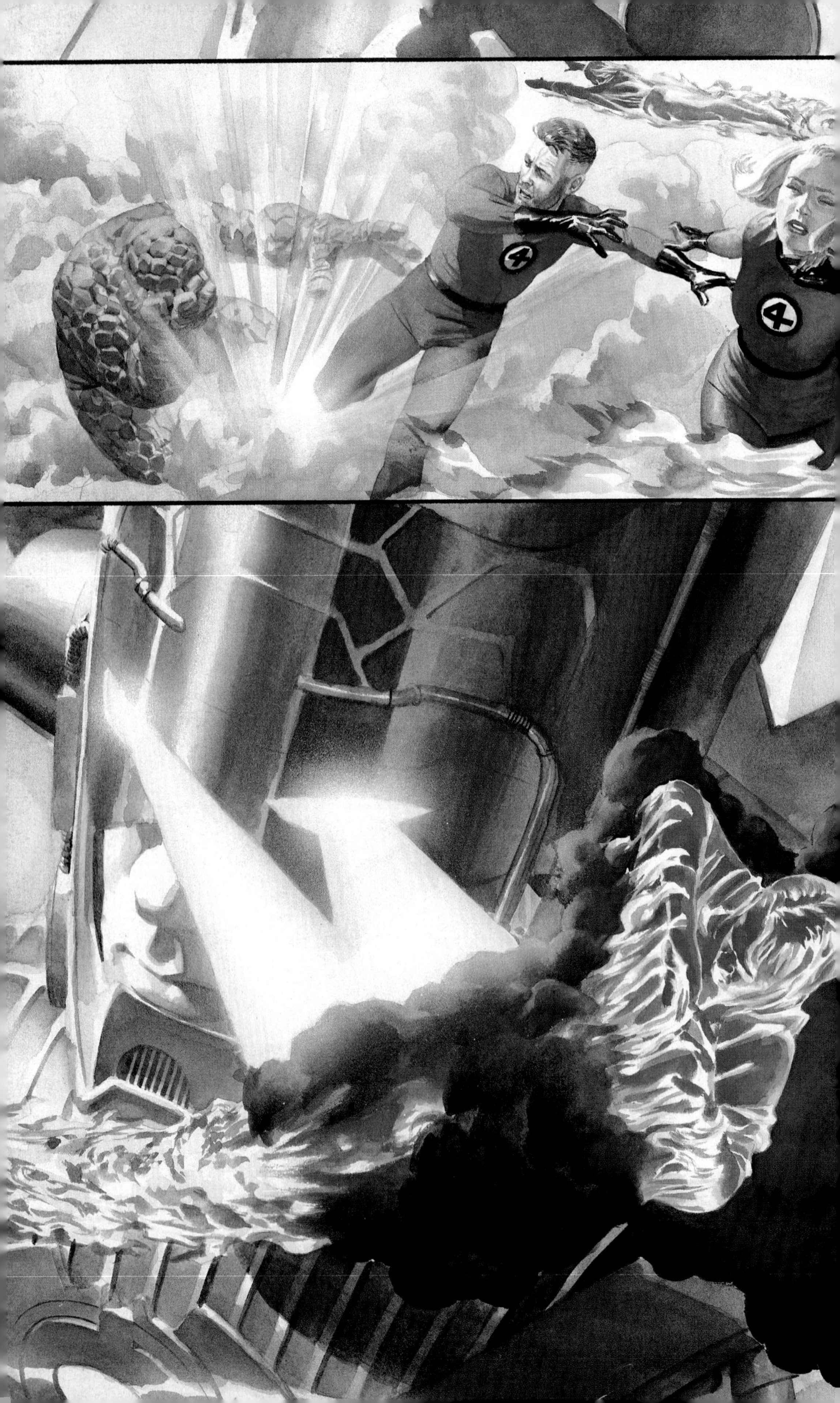

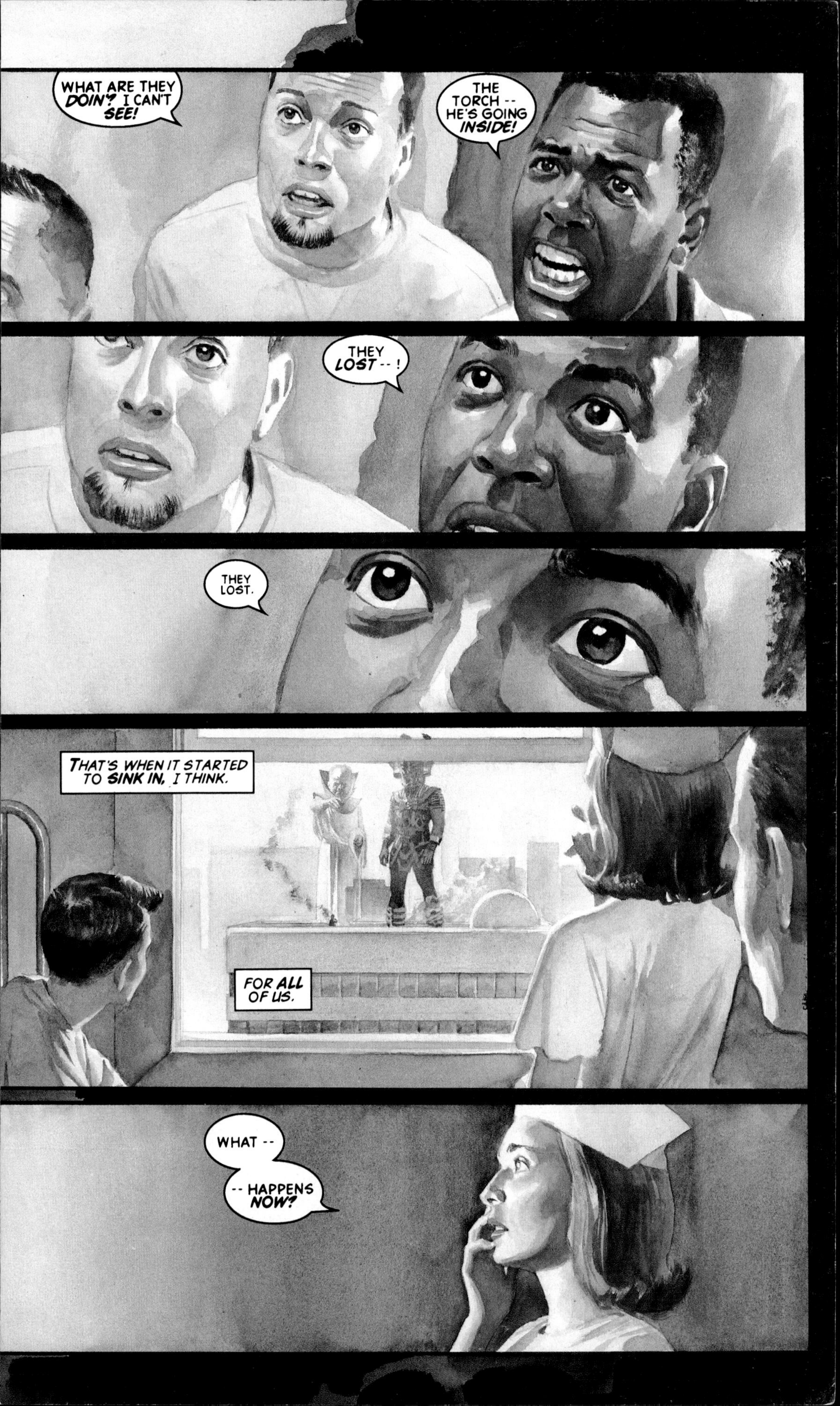
WHAT ARE THEY DOIN'? I CAN'T SEE!
THE TORCH -- HE'S GOING INSIDE!
THEY LOST -- !
THEY LOST.
THAT'S WHEN IT STARTED TO SINK IN, I THINK.
FOR ALL OF US.
WHAT --
-- HAPPENS NOW?

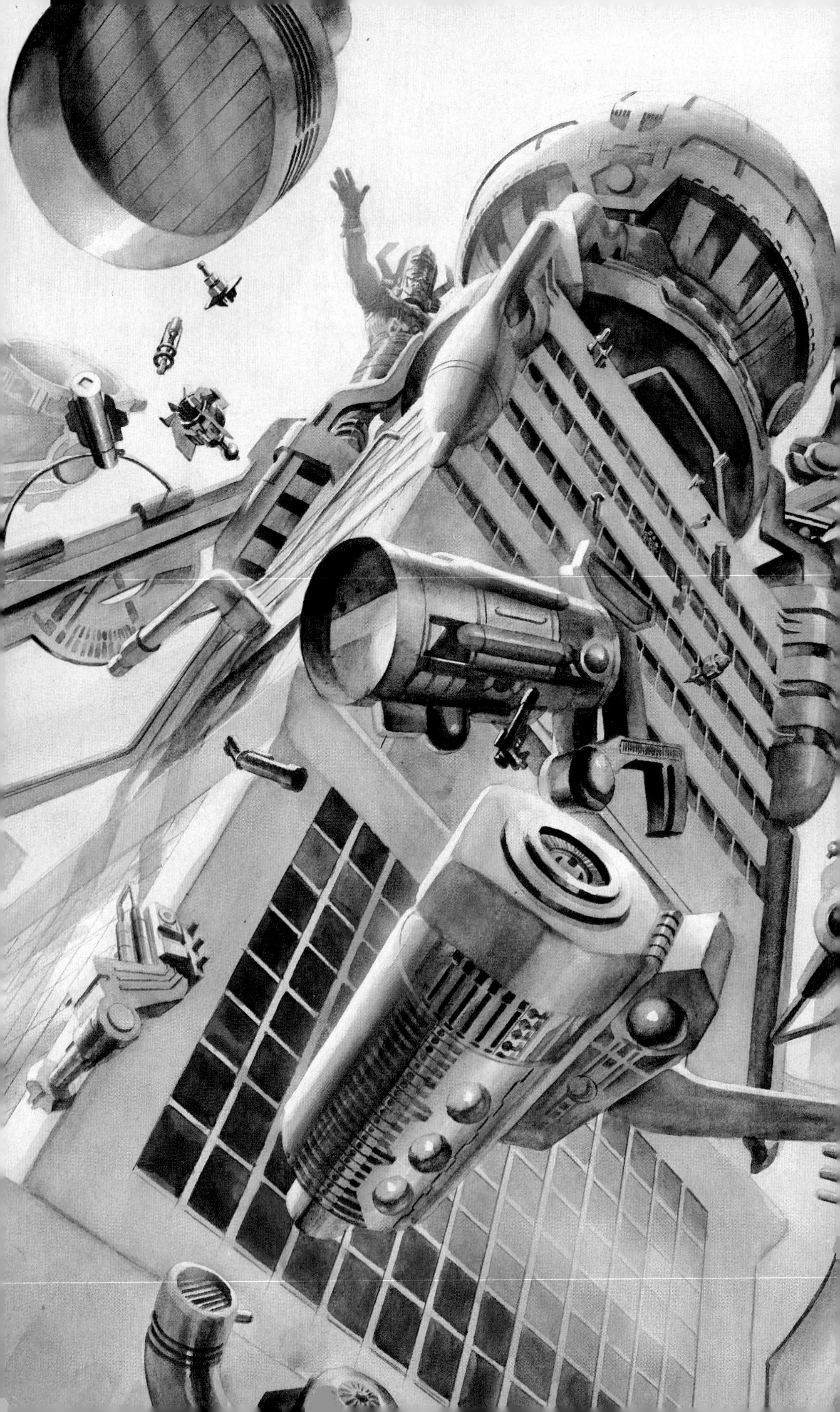

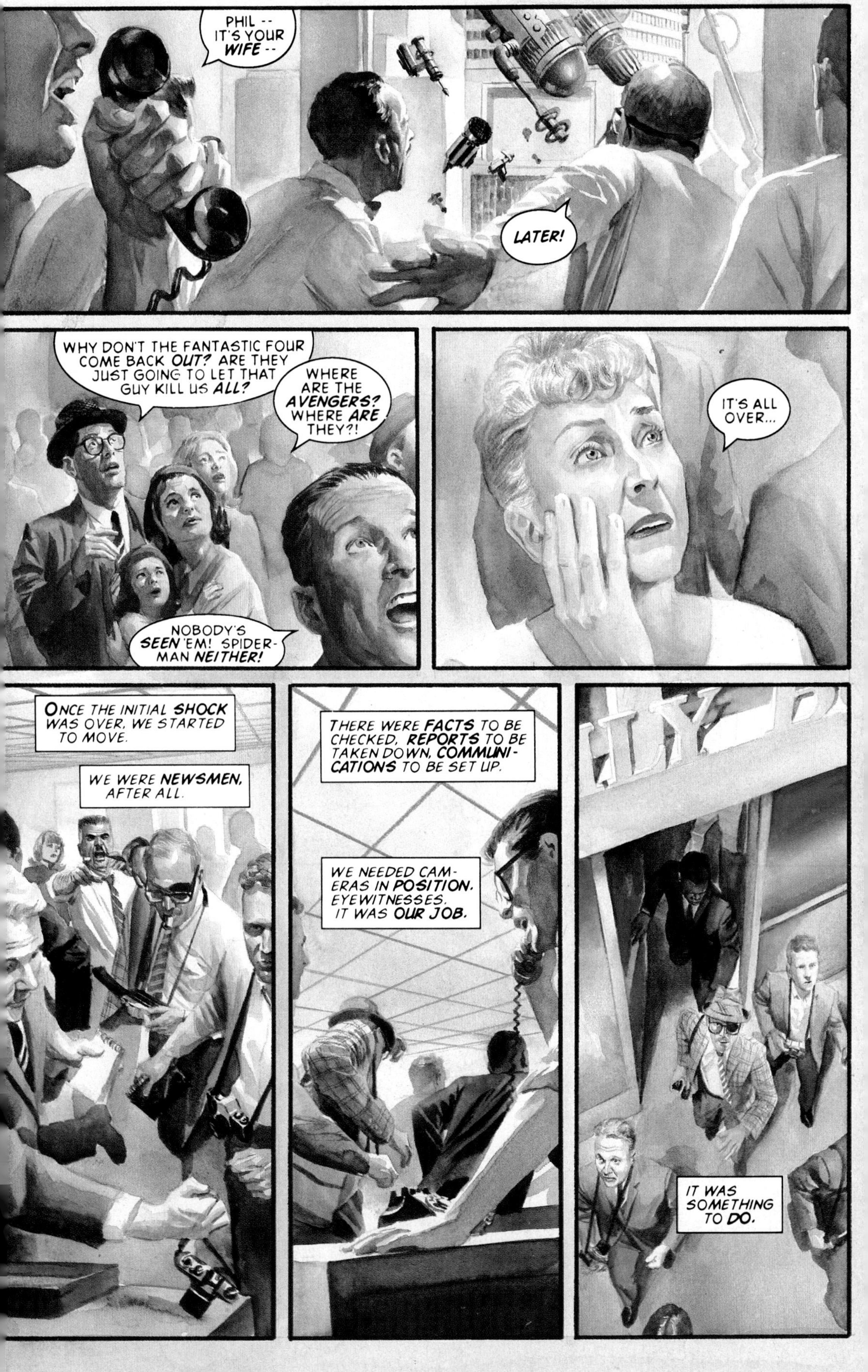
PHIL -- IT'S YOUR WIFE --
LATER!
WHY DON'T THE FANTASTIC FOUR COME BACK OUT? ARE THEY JUST GOING TO LET THAT GUY KILL US ALL?
WHERE ARE THE AVENGERS? WHERE ARE THEY?!
NOBODY'S SEEN 'EM! SPIDER-MAN NEITHER!
IT'S ALL OVER...
ONCE THE INITIAL SHOCK WAS OVER, WE STARTED TO MOVE.
WE WERE NEWSMEN, AFTER ALL.
THERE WERE FACTS TO BE CHECKED, REPORTS TO BE TAKEN DOWN, COMMUNICATIONS TO BE SET UP.
WE NEEDED CAMERAS IN POSITION, EYEWITNESSES. IT WAS OUR JOB.
IT WAS SOMETHING TO DO.

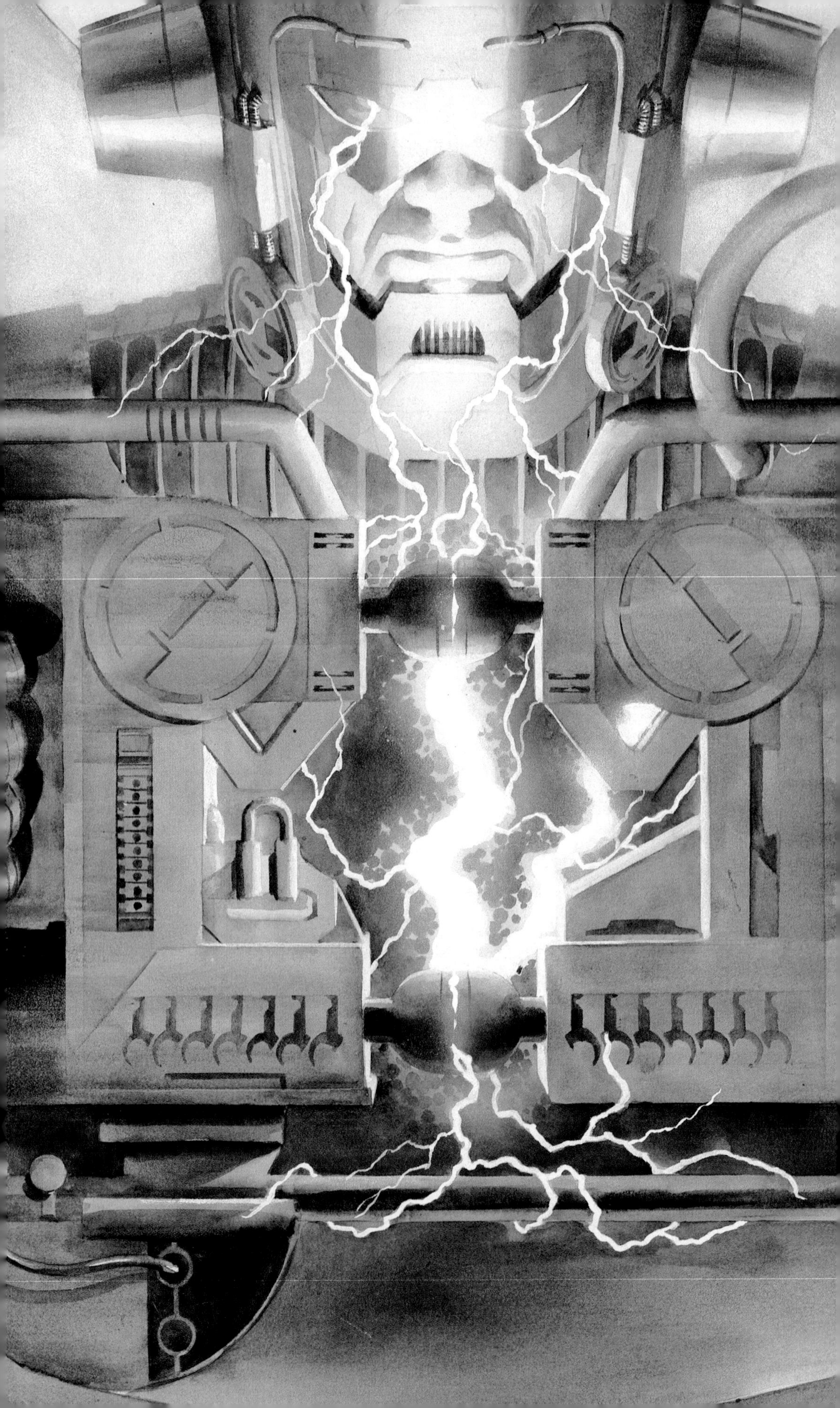

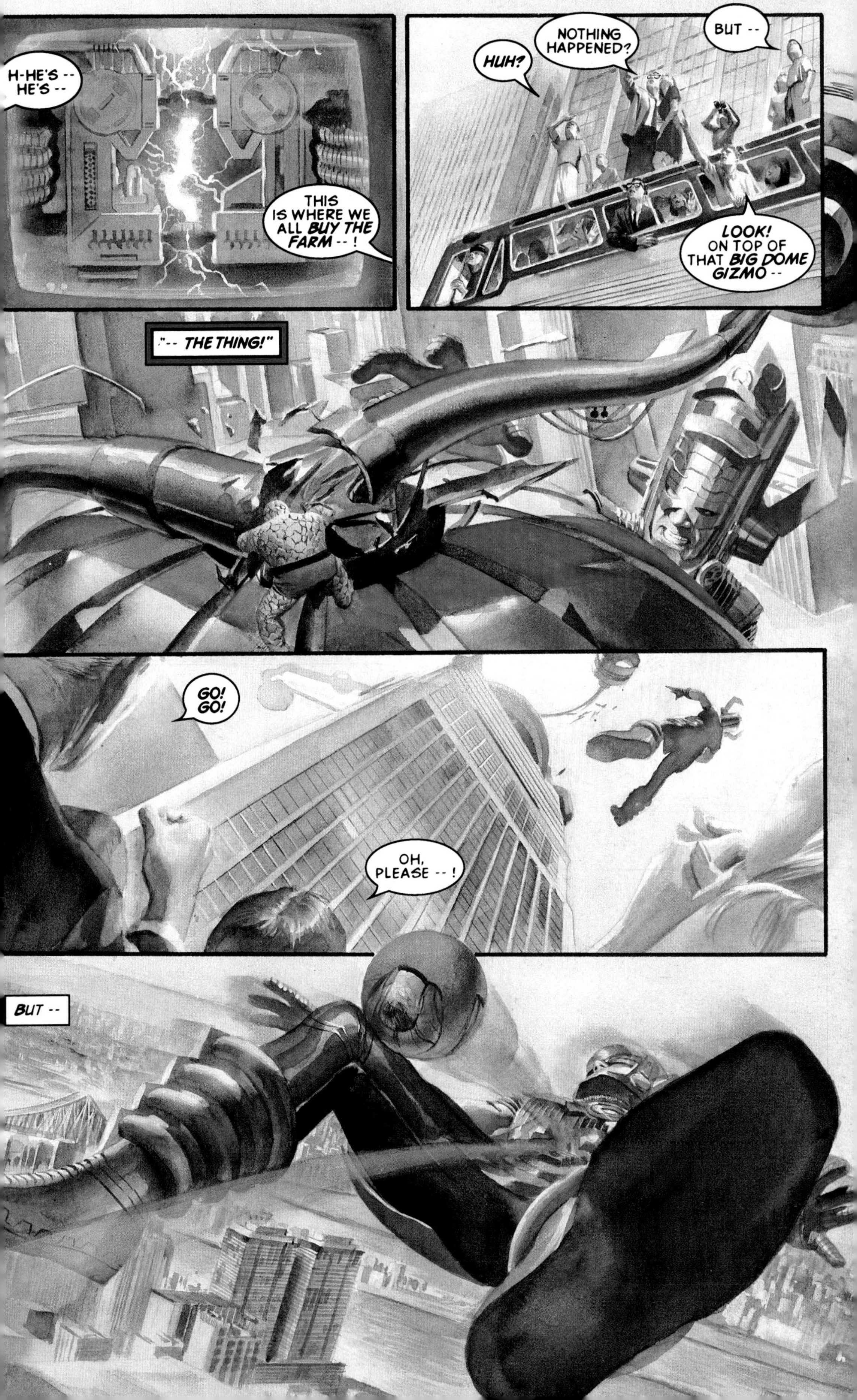
H-HE'S -- HE'S --
THIS IS WHERE WE ALL *BUY THE FARM* -- !
HUH?
NOTHING HAPPENED?
BUT --
LOOK! ON TOP OF THAT *BIG DOME GIZMO* --
"-- *THE THING!*"
GO! GO!
OH, PLEASE -- !
BUT --

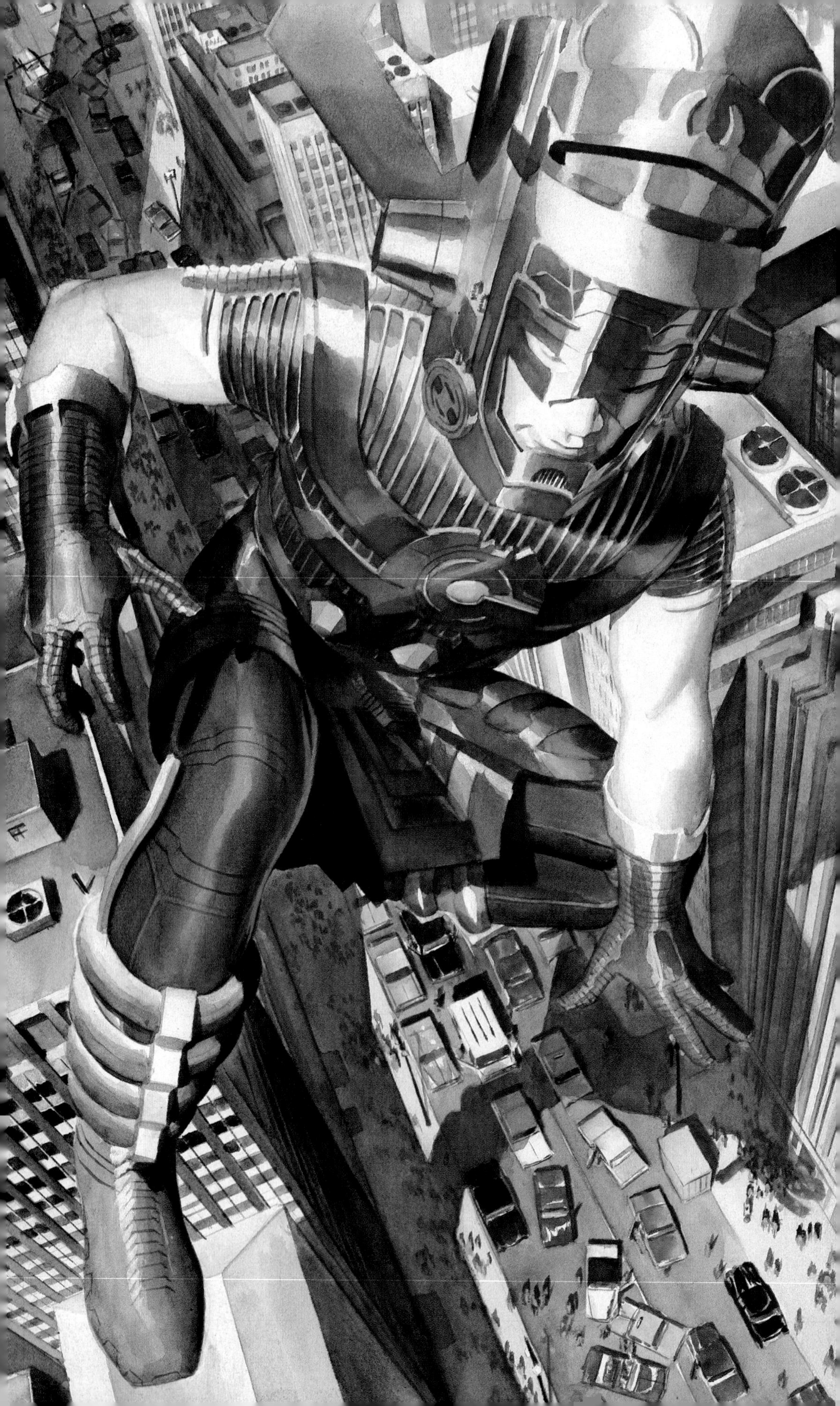

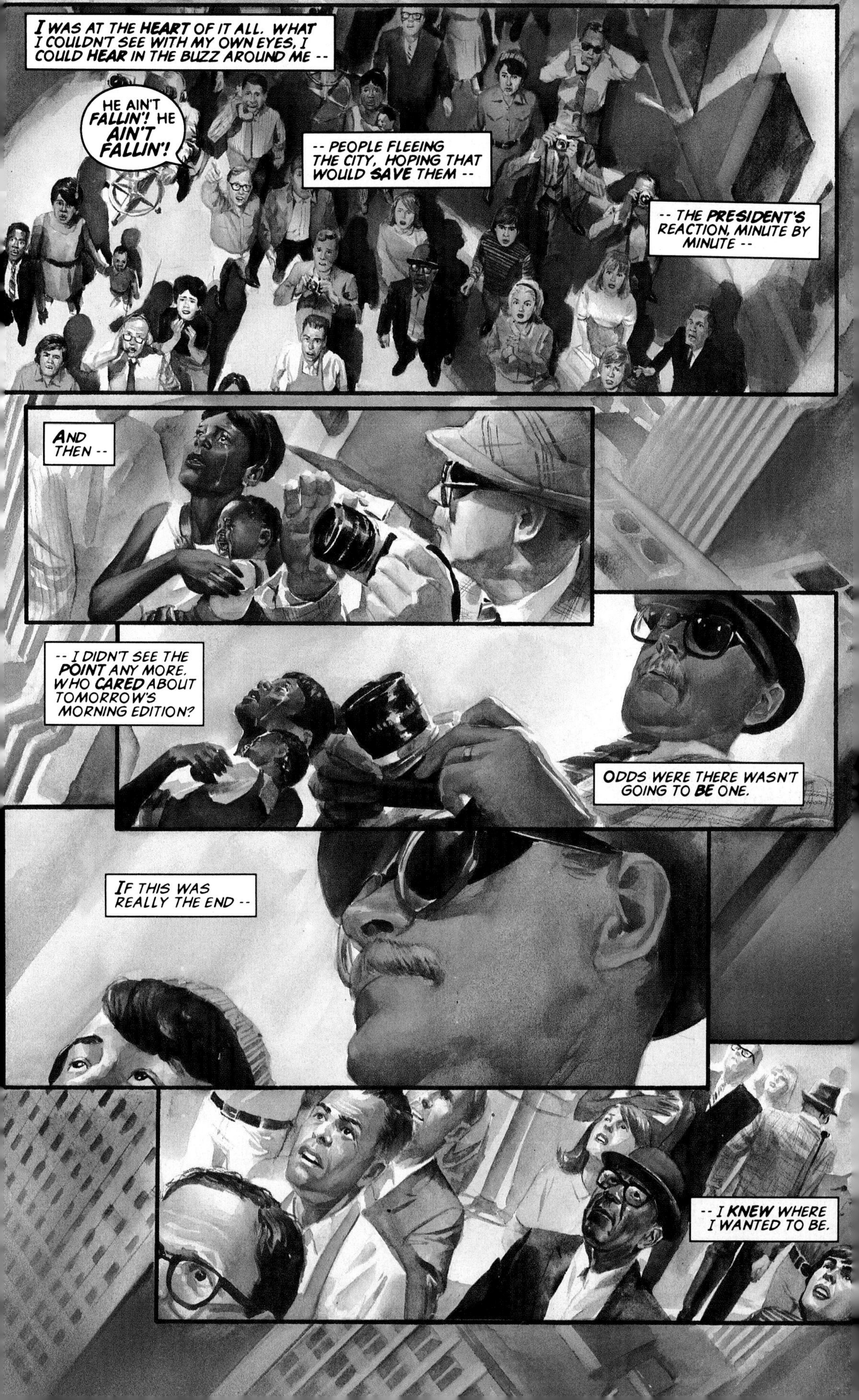

I WAS AT THE HEART OF IT ALL. WHAT I COULDN'T SEE WITH MY OWN EYES, I COULD HEAR IN THE BUZZ AROUND ME --
HE AIN'T FALLIN'! HE AIN'T FALLIN'!
-- PEOPLE FLEEING THE CITY, HOPING THAT WOULD SAVE THEM --
-- THE PRESIDENT'S REACTION, MINUTE BY MINUTE --
AND THEN --
-- I DIDN'T SEE THE POINT ANY MORE. WHO CARED ABOUT TOMORROW'S MORNING EDITION?
ODDS WERE THERE WASN'T GOING TO BE ONE.
IF THIS WAS REALLY THE END --
-- I KNEW WHERE I WANTED TO BE.

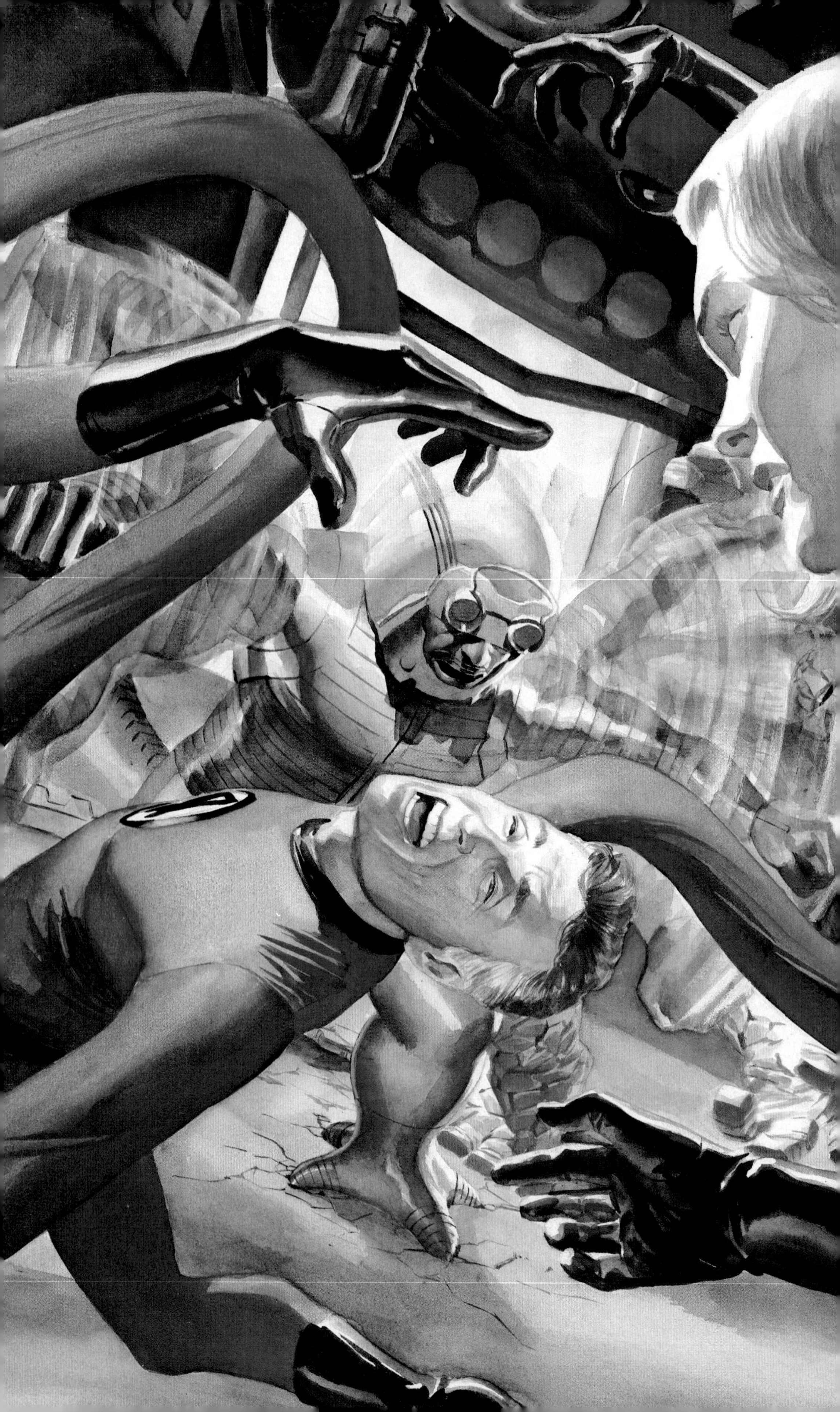

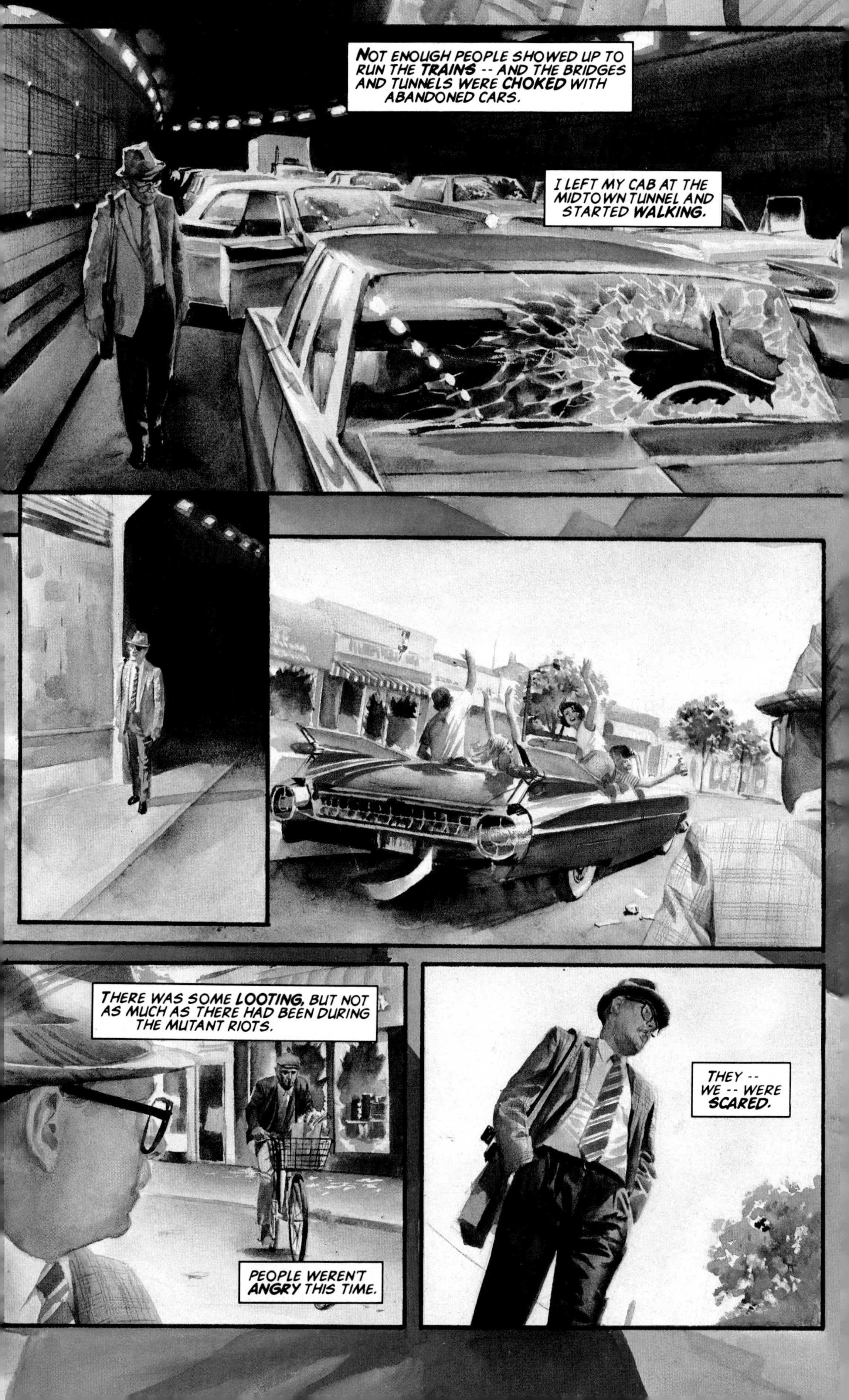
NOT ENOUGH PEOPLE SHOWED UP TO RUN THE TRAINS -- AND THE BRIDGES AND TUNNELS WERE CHOKED WITH ABANDONED CARS.
I LEFT MY CAB AT THE MIDTOWN TUNNEL AND STARTED WALKING.
THERE WAS SOME LOOTING, BUT NOT AS MUCH AS THERE HAD BEEN DURING THE MUTANT RIOTS.
PEOPLE WEREN'T ANGRY THIS TIME.
THEY -- WE -- WERE SCARED.

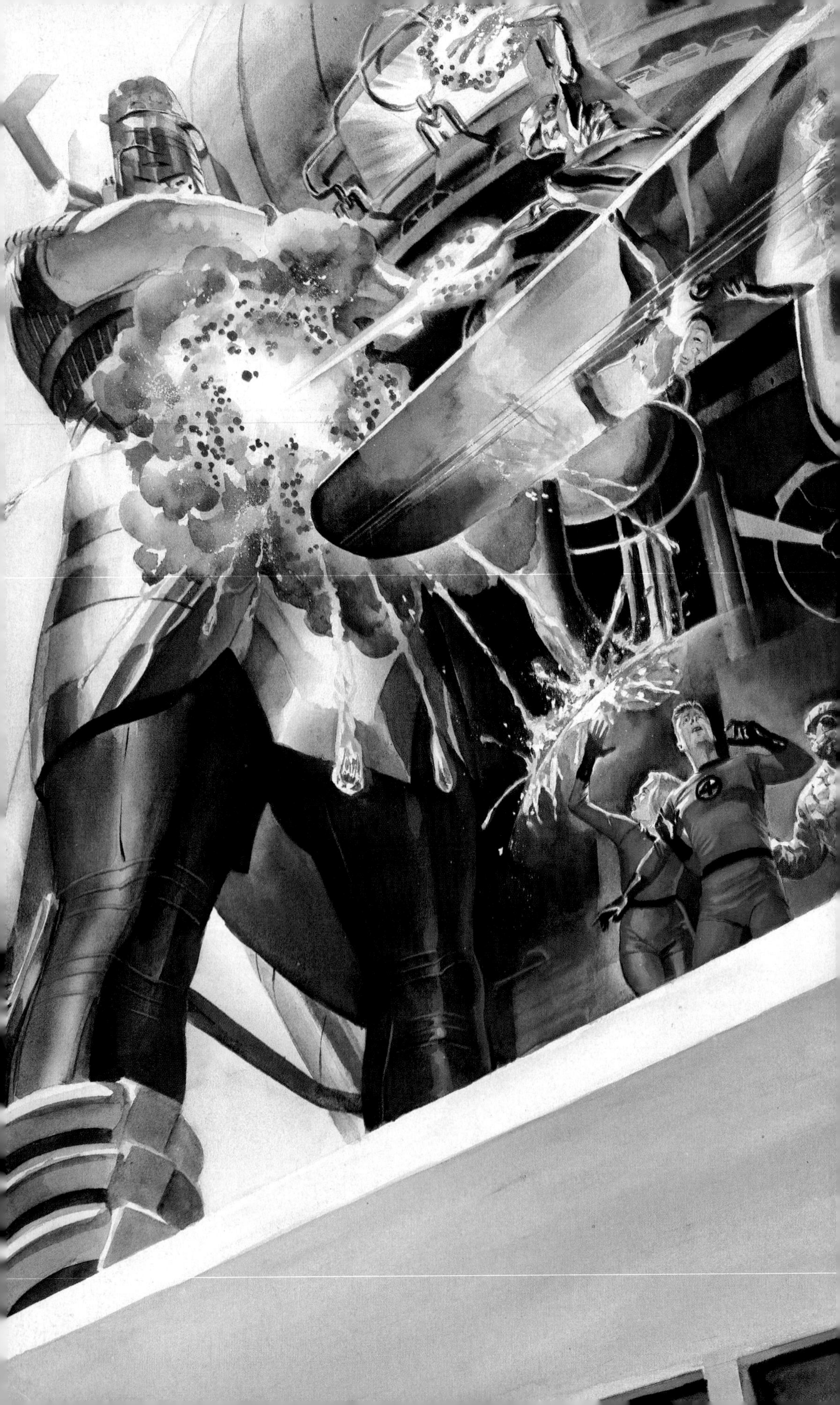

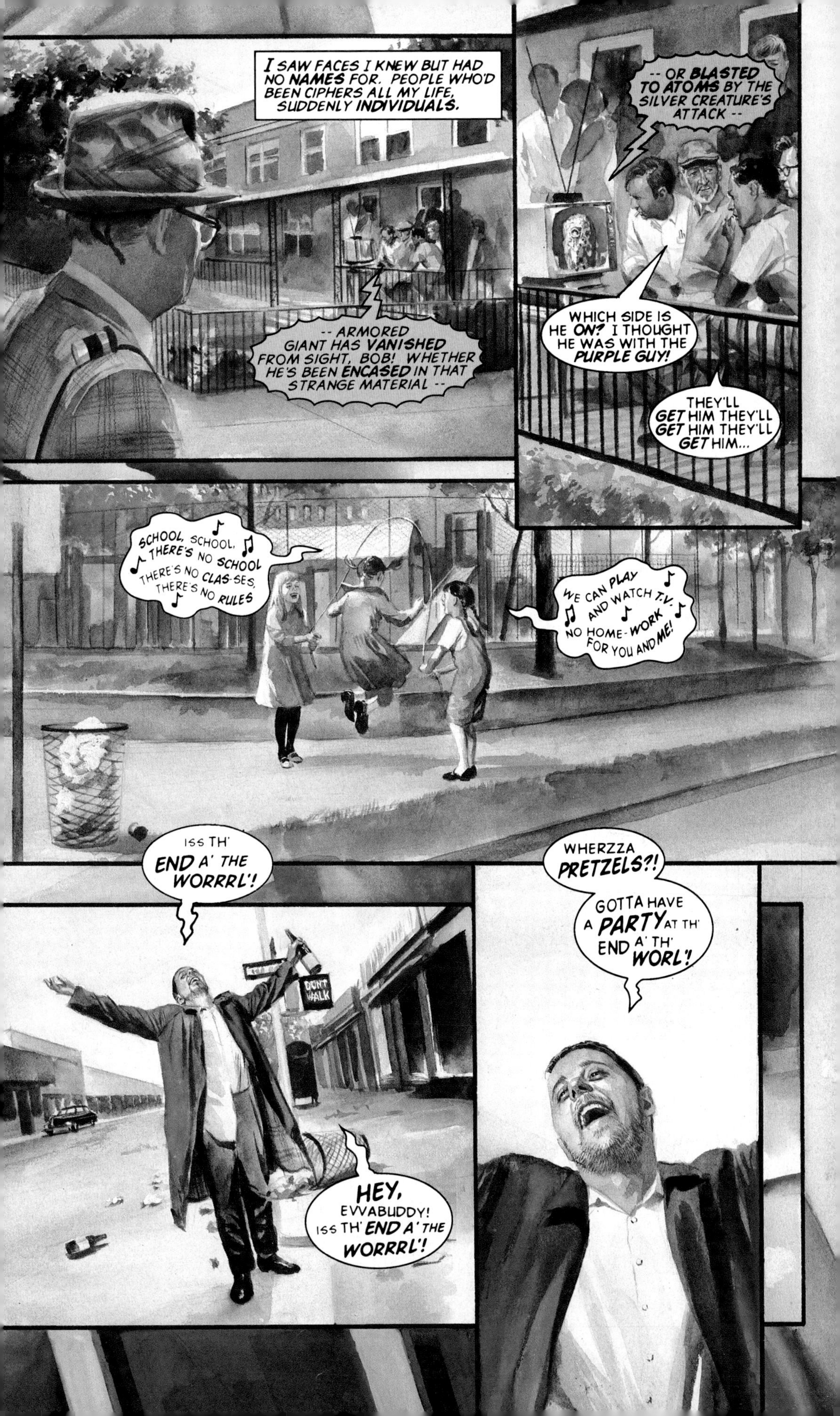
I SAW FACES I KNEW BUT HAD NO NAMES FOR. PEOPLE WHO'D BEEN CIPHERS ALL MY LIFE, SUDDENLY INDIVIDUALS.
-- ARMORED GIANT HAS VANISHED FROM SIGHT, BOB! WHETHER HE'S BEEN ENCASED IN THAT STRANGE MATERIAL --
-- OR BLASTED TO ATOMS BY THE SILVER CREATURE'S ATTACK --
WHICH SIDE IS HE ON? I THOUGHT HE WAS WITH THE PURPLE GUY!
THEY'LL GET HIM THEY'LL GET HIM THEY'LL GET HIM...
SCHOOL, SCHOOL, THERE'S NO SCHOOL THERE'S NO CLAS-SES, THERE'S NO RULES
WE CAN PLAY AND WATCH T.V. NO HOME-WORK FOR YOU AND ME!
ISS TH' END A' THE WORRRL'!
DON'T WALK
HEY, EVVABUDDY! ISS TH' END A' THE WORRRL'!
WHERZZA PRETZELS?!
GOTTA HAVE A PARTY AT TH' END A' TH' WORL'!

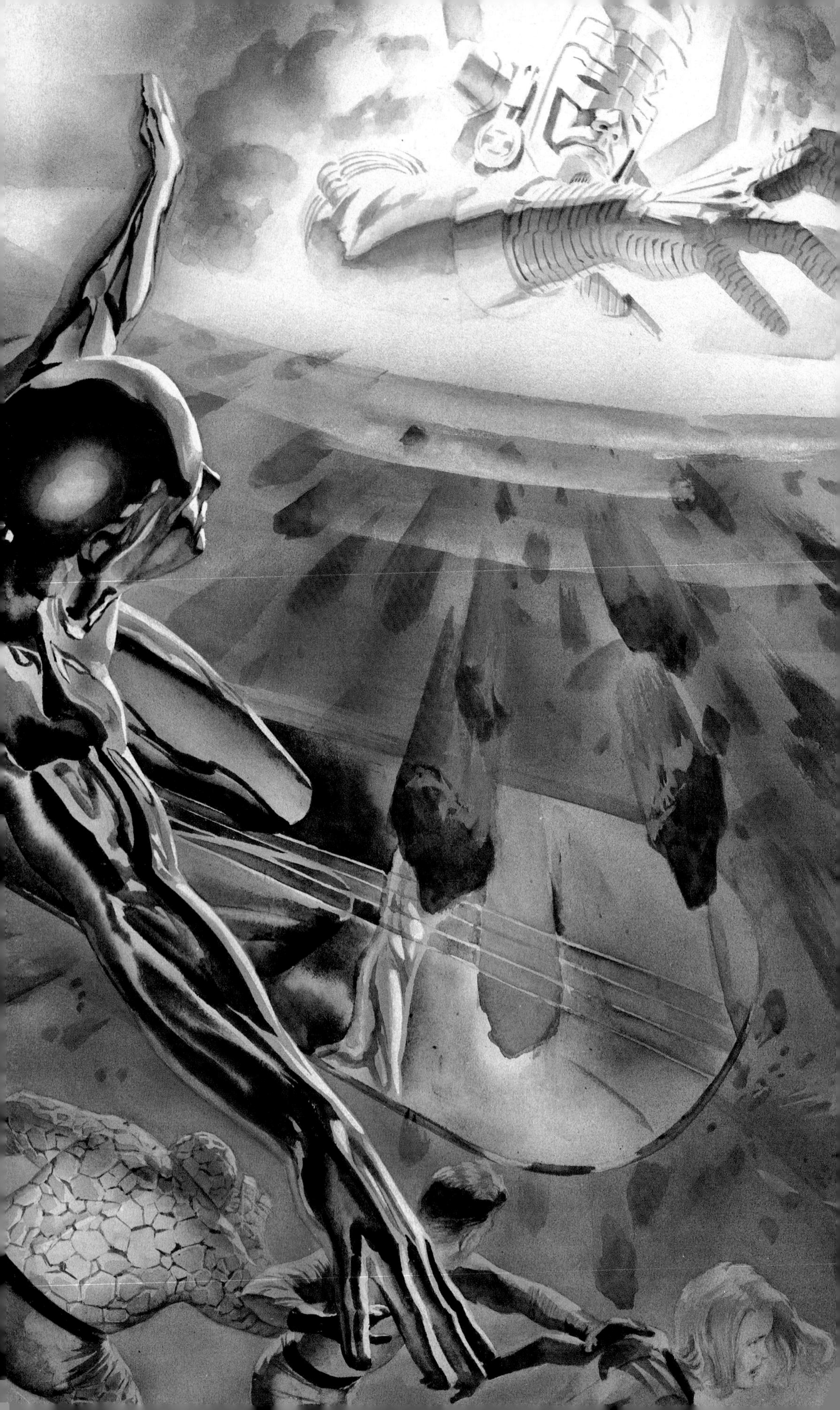

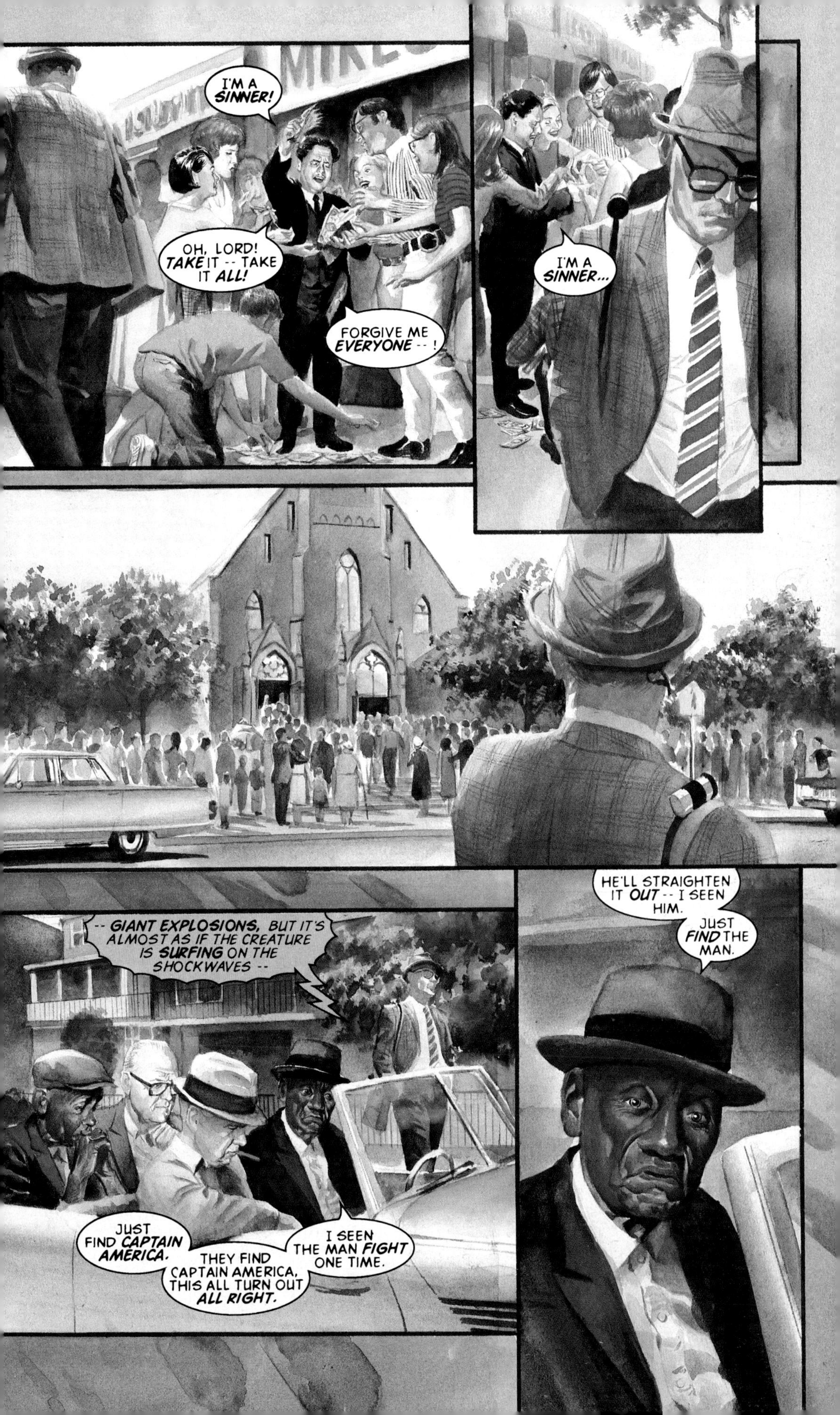
I'M A SINNER!
OH, LORD! TAKE IT -- TAKE IT ALL!
FORGIVE ME EVERYONE -- !
I'M A SINNER...
-- GIANT EXPLOSIONS, BUT IT'S ALMOST AS IF THE CREATURE IS SURFING ON THE SHOCKWAVES --
JUST FIND CAPTAIN AMERICA.
THEY FIND CAPTAIN AMERICA, THIS ALL TURN OUT ALL RIGHT.
I SEEN THE MAN FIGHT ONE TIME.
HE'LL STRAIGHTEN IT OUT -- I SEEN HIM.
JUST FIND THE MAN.

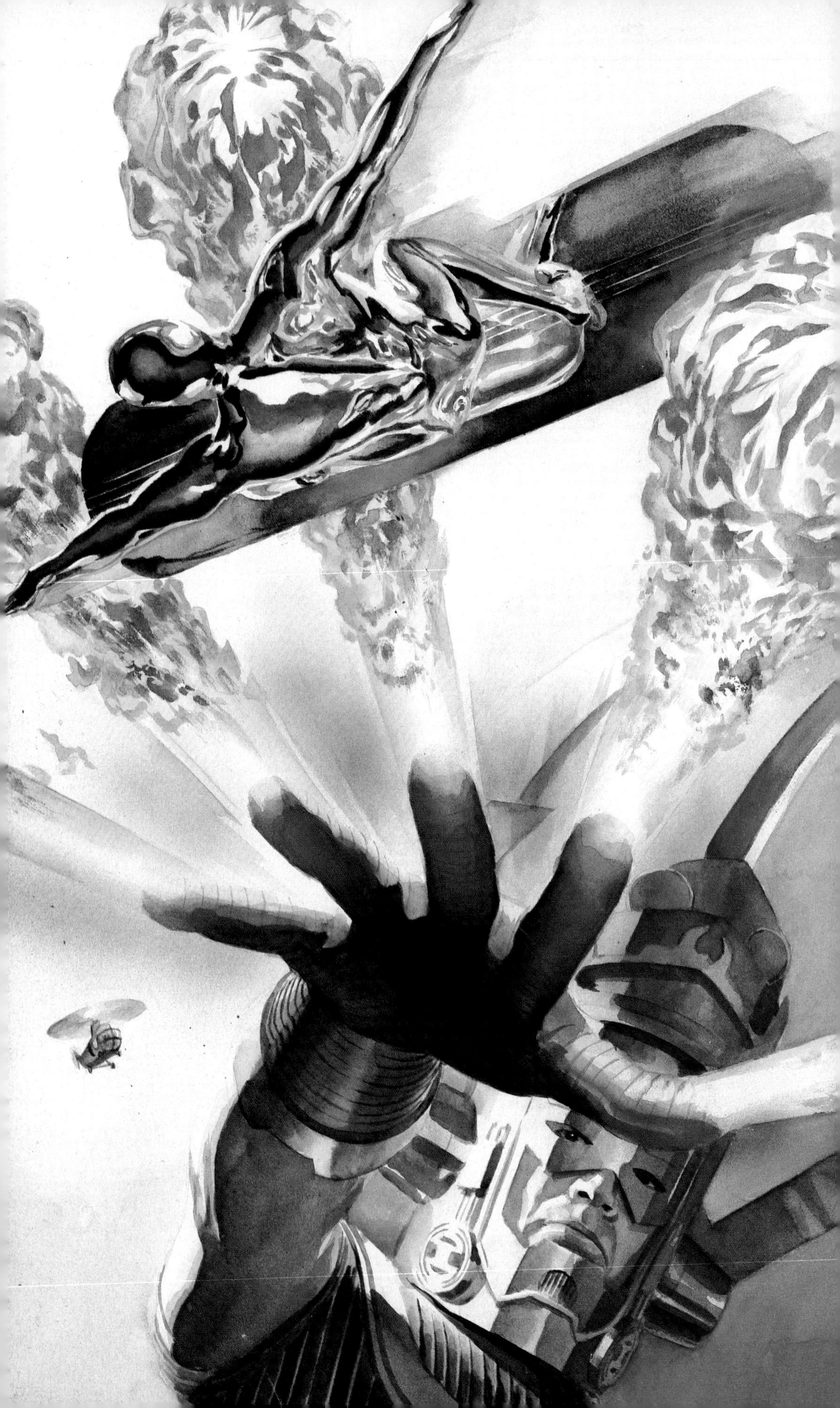

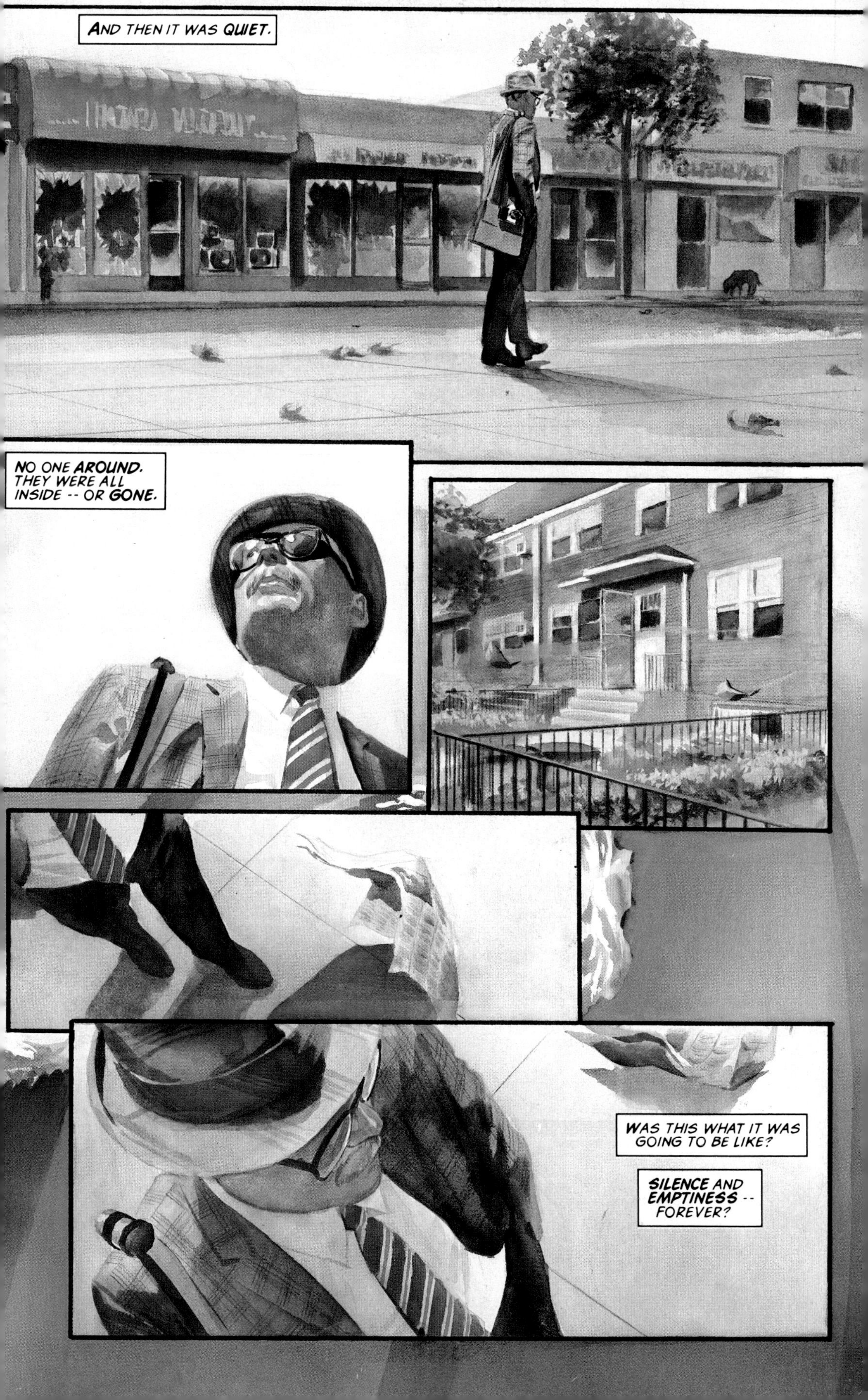
AND THEN IT WAS QUIET.
NO ONE AROUND. THEY WERE ALL INSIDE -- OR GONE.
WAS THIS WHAT IT WAS GOING TO BE LIKE?
SILENCE AND EMPTINESS -- FOREVER?

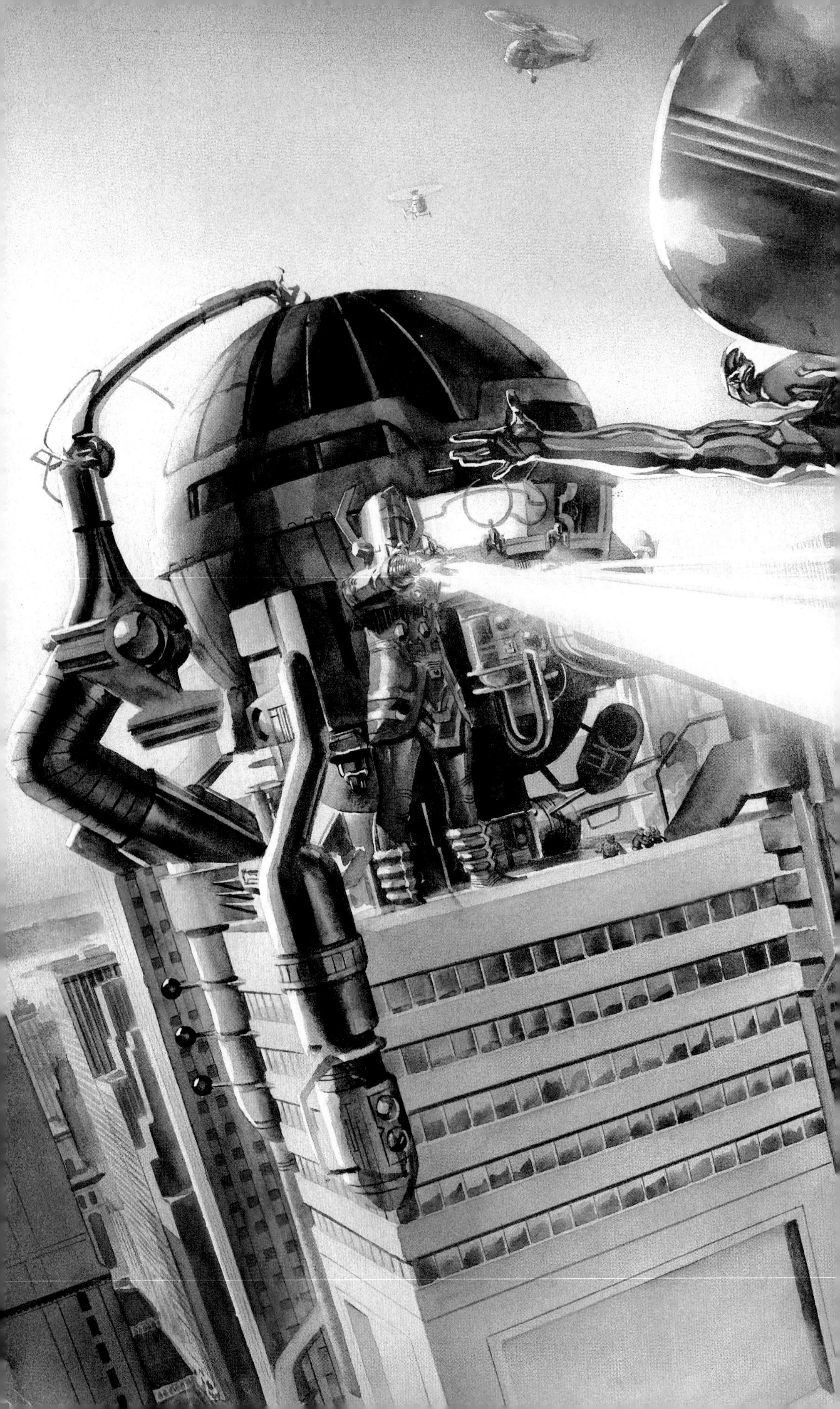

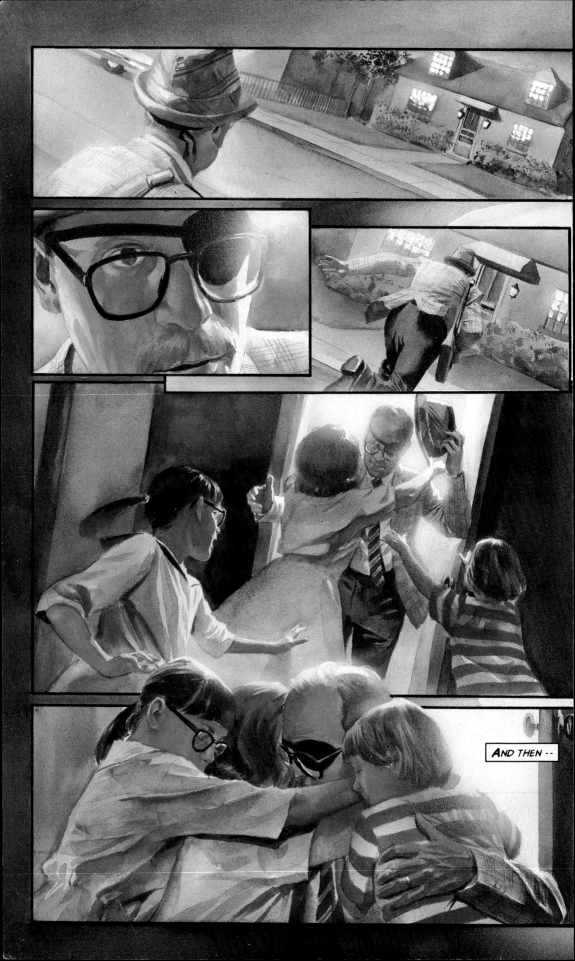

AND THEN --

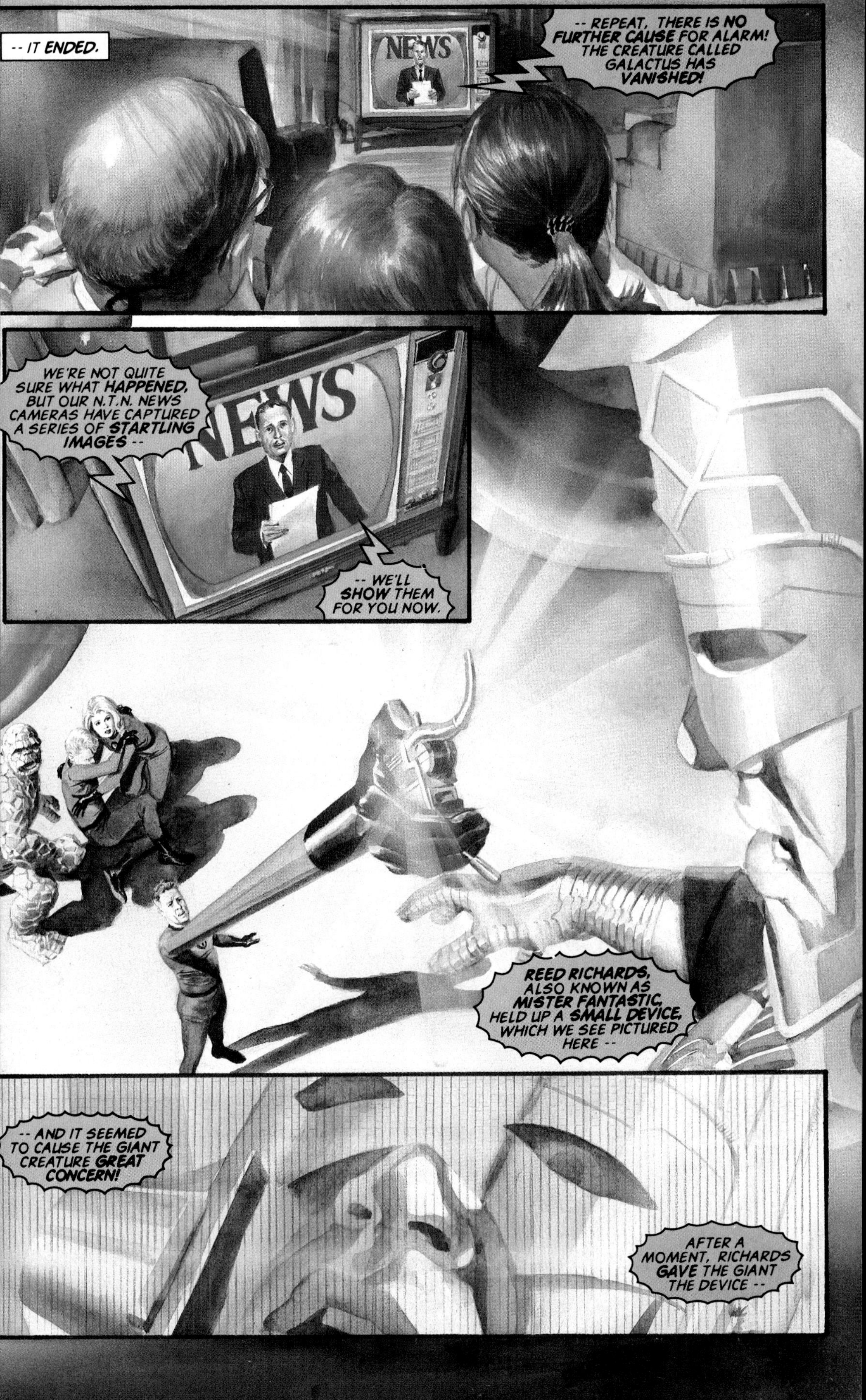
-- IT ENDED.
-- REPEAT, THERE IS NO FURTHER CAUSE FOR ALARM! THE CREATURE CALLED GALACTUS HAS VANISHED!
NEWS
WE'RE NOT QUITE SURE WHAT HAPPENED, BUT OUR N.T.N. NEWS CAMERAS HAVE CAPTURED A SERIES OF STARTLING IMAGES --
NEWS
-- WE'LL SHOW THEM FOR YOU NOW.
REED RICHARDS, ALSO KNOWN AS MISTER FANTASTIC, HELD UP A SMALL DEVICE, WHICH WE SEE PICTURED HERE --
-- AND IT SEEMED TO CAUSE THE GIANT CREATURE GREAT CONCERN!
AFTER A MOMENT, RICHARDS GAVE THE GIANT THE DEVICE --

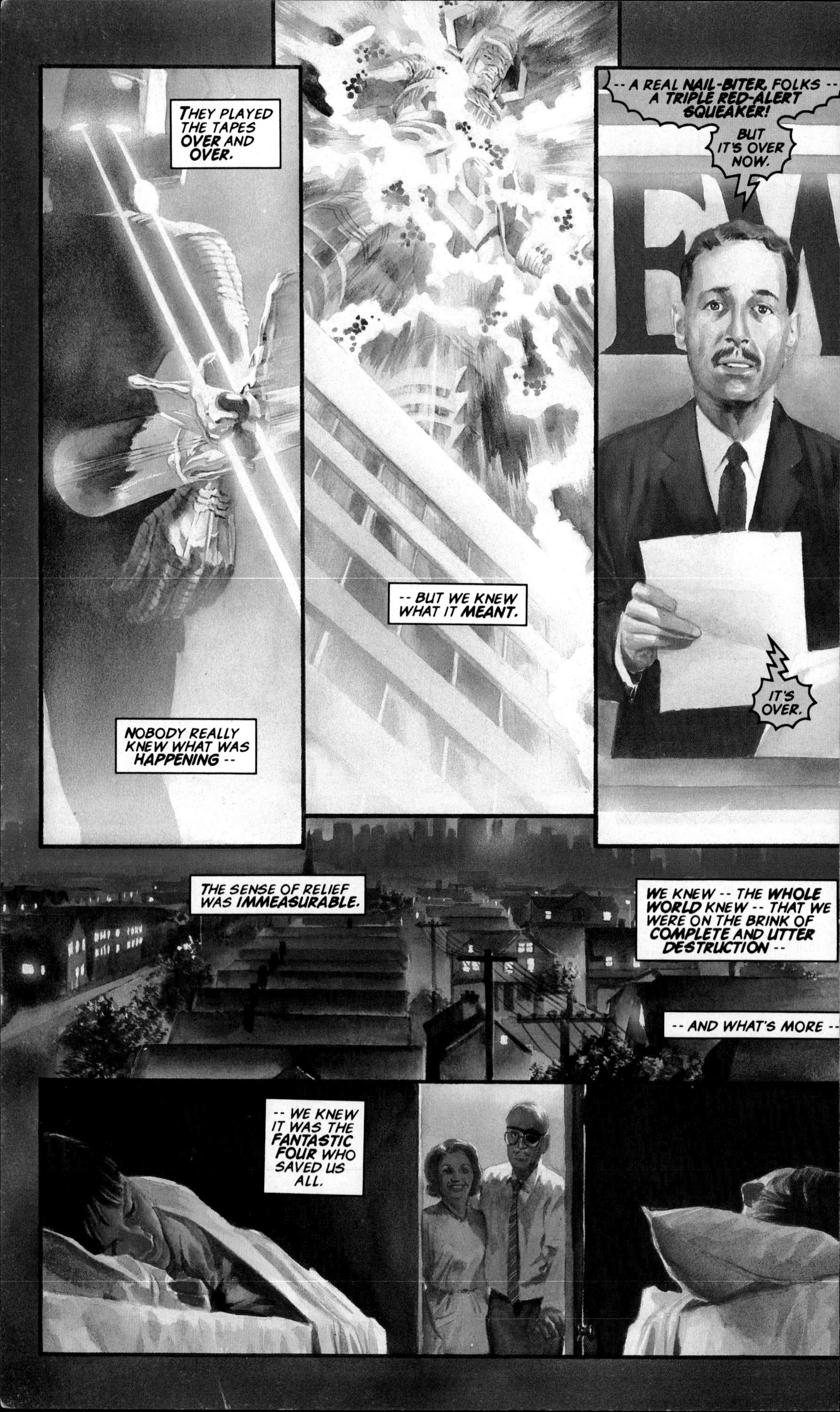
THEY PLAYED THE TAPES OVER AND OVER.
NOBODY REALLY KNEW WHAT WAS HAPPENING --
-- BUT WE KNEW WHAT IT MEANT.
-- A REAL NAIL-BITER, FOLKS -- A TRIPLE RED-ALERT SQUEAKER!
BUT IT'S OVER NOW.
IT'S OVER.
THE SENSE OF RELIEF WAS IMMEASURABLE.
WE KNEW -- THE WHOLE WORLD KNEW -- THAT WE WERE ON THE BRINK OF COMPLETE AND UTTER DESTRUCTION --
-- AND WHAT'S MORE --
-- WE KNEW IT WAS THE FANTASTIC FOUR WHO SAVED US ALL.

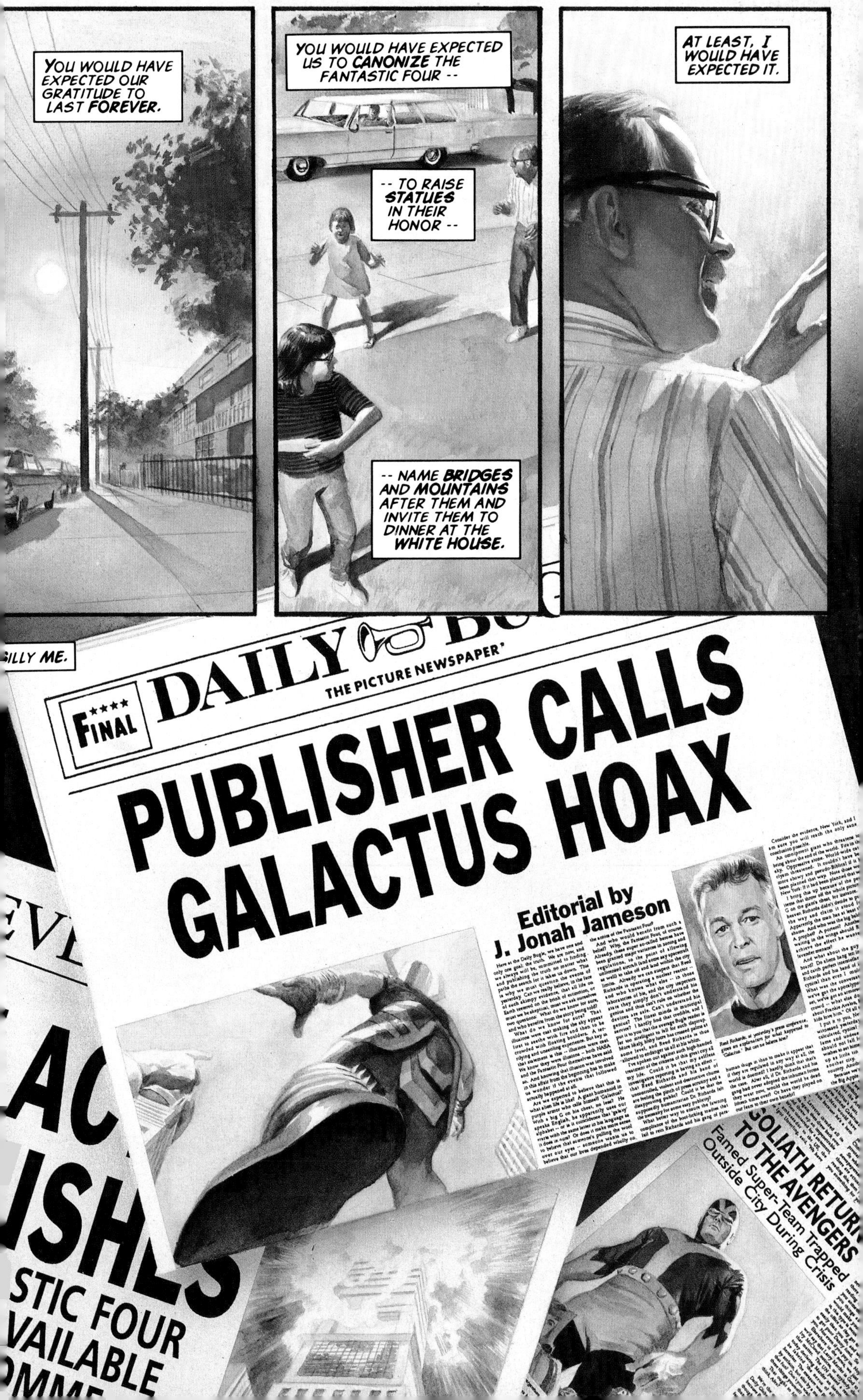

YOU WOULD HAVE EXPECTED OUR GRATITUDE TO LAST FOREVER.
YOU WOULD HAVE EXPECTED US TO CANONIZE THE FANTASTIC FOUR --
-- TO RAISE STATUES IN THEIR HONOR --
-- NAME BRIDGES AND MOUNTAINS AFTER THEM AND INVITE THEM TO DINNER AT THE WHITE HOUSE.
AT LEAST, I WOULD HAVE EXPECTED IT.
SILLY ME.
DAILY
THE PICTURE NEWSPAPER
FINAL
PUBLISHER CALLS GALACTUS HOAX
Editorial by J. Jonah Jameson
GOLIATH RETURNS TO THE AVENGERS
Famed Super-Team Trapped Outside City During Crisis
STIC FOUR
VAILABLE

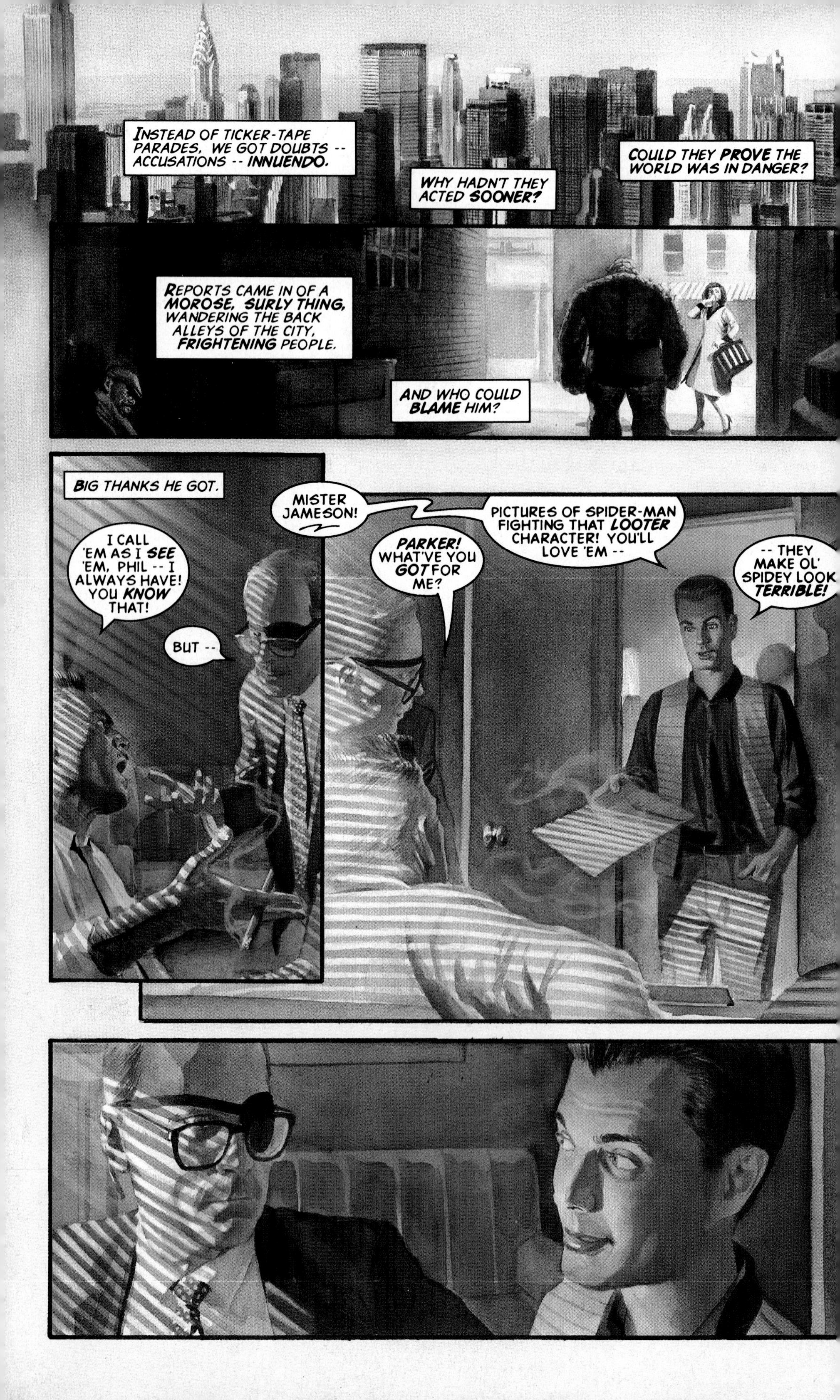

INSTEAD OF TICKER-TAPE PARADES, WE GOT DOUBTS -- ACCUSATIONS -- INNUENDO.
WHY HADN'T THEY ACTED SOONER?
COULD THEY PROVE THE WORLD WAS IN DANGER?
REPORTS CAME IN OF A MOROSE, SURLY THING, WANDERING THE BACK ALLEYS OF THE CITY, FRIGHTENING PEOPLE.
AND WHO COULD BLAME HIM?
BIG THANKS HE GOT.
I CALL 'EM AS I SEE 'EM, PHIL -- I ALWAYS HAVE! YOU KNOW THAT!
BUT --
MISTER JAMESON!
PARKER! WHAT'VE YOU GOT FOR ME?
PICTURES OF SPIDER-MAN FIGHTING THAT LOOTER CHARACTER! YOU'LL LOVE 'EM --
-- THEY MAKE OL' SPIDEY LOOK TERRIBLE!

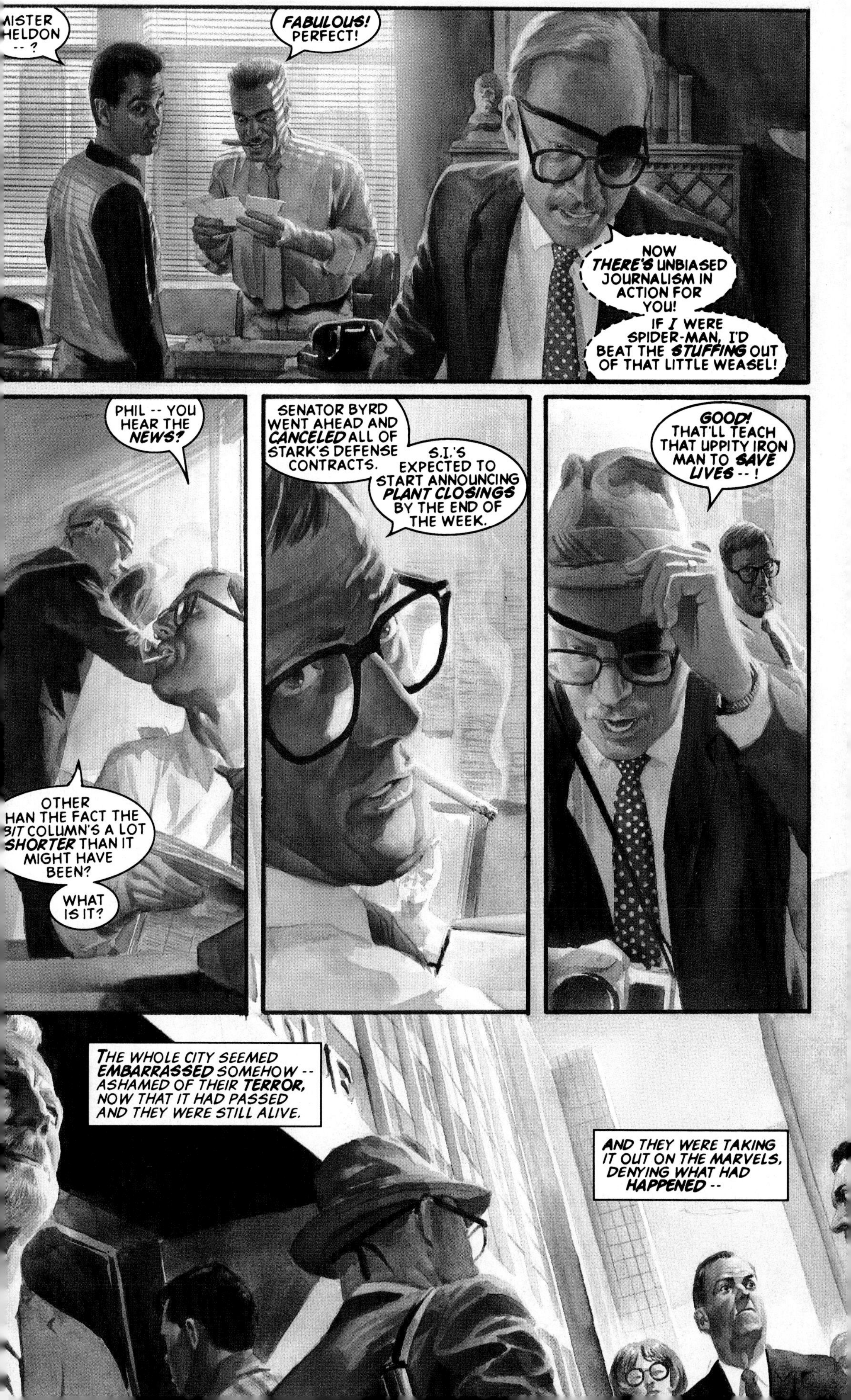

ISTER HELDON -- ?
FABULOUS! PERFECT!
NOW THERE'S UNBIASED JOURNALISM IN ACTION FOR YOU!
IF I WERE SPIDER-MAN, I'D BEAT THE STUFFING OUT OF THAT LITTLE WEASEL!
PHIL -- YOU HEAR THE NEWS?
OTHER HAN THE FACT THE BIT COLUMN'S A LOT SHORTER THAN IT MIGHT HAVE BEEN?
WHAT IS IT?
SENATOR BYRD WENT AHEAD AND CANCELED ALL OF STARK'S DEFENSE CONTRACTS.
S.I.'S EXPECTED TO START ANNOUNCING PLANT CLOSINGS BY THE END OF THE WEEK.
GOOD! THAT'LL TEACH THAT UPPITY IRON MAN TO SAVE LIVES -- !
THE WHOLE CITY SEEMED EMBARRASSED SOMEHOW -- ASHAMED OF THEIR TERROR, NOW THAT IT HAD PASSED AND THEY WERE STILL ALIVE.
AND THEY WERE TAKING IT OUT ON THE MARVELS, DENYING WHAT HAD HAPPENED --

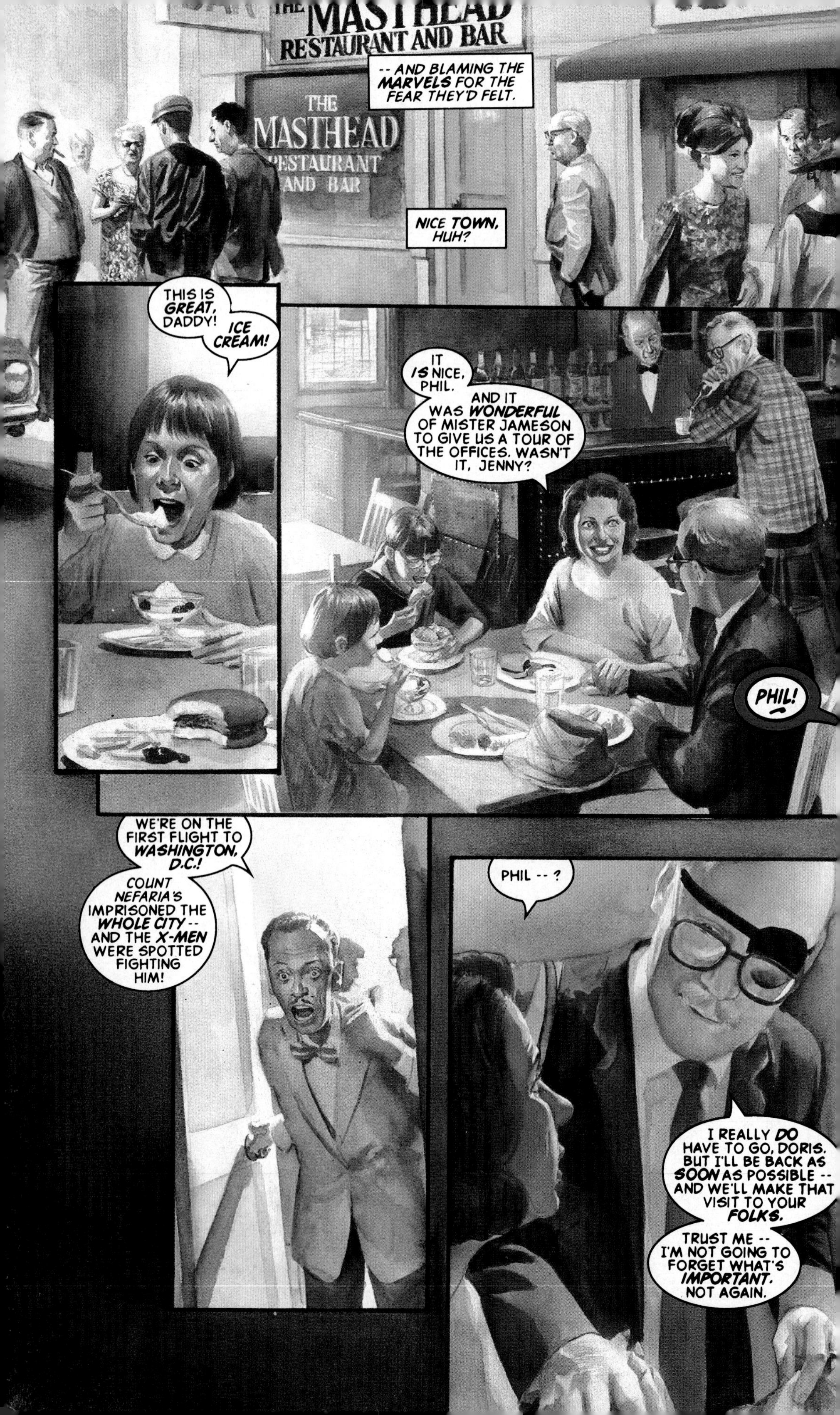
THE MASTHEAD RESTAURANT AND BAR
-- AND BLAMING THE MARVELS FOR THE FEAR THEY'D FELT.
THE MASTHEAD RESTAURANT AND BAR
NICE TOWN, HUH?
THIS IS GREAT, DADDY!
ICE CREAM!
IT IS NICE, PHIL.
AND IT WAS WONDERFUL OF MISTER JAMESON TO GIVE US A TOUR OF THE OFFICES. WASN'T IT, JENNY?
PHIL!
WE'RE ON THE FIRST FLIGHT TO WASHINGTON, D.C.!
COUNT NEFARIA'S IMPRISONED THE WHOLE CITY -- AND THE X-MEN WERE SPOTTED FIGHTING HIM!
PHIL -- ?
I REALLY DO HAVE TO GO, DORIS. BUT I'LL BE BACK AS SOON AS POSSIBLE -- AND WE'LL MAKE THAT VISIT TO YOUR FOLKS.
TRUST ME -- I'M NOT GOING TO FORGET WHAT'S IMPORTANT. NOT AGAIN.

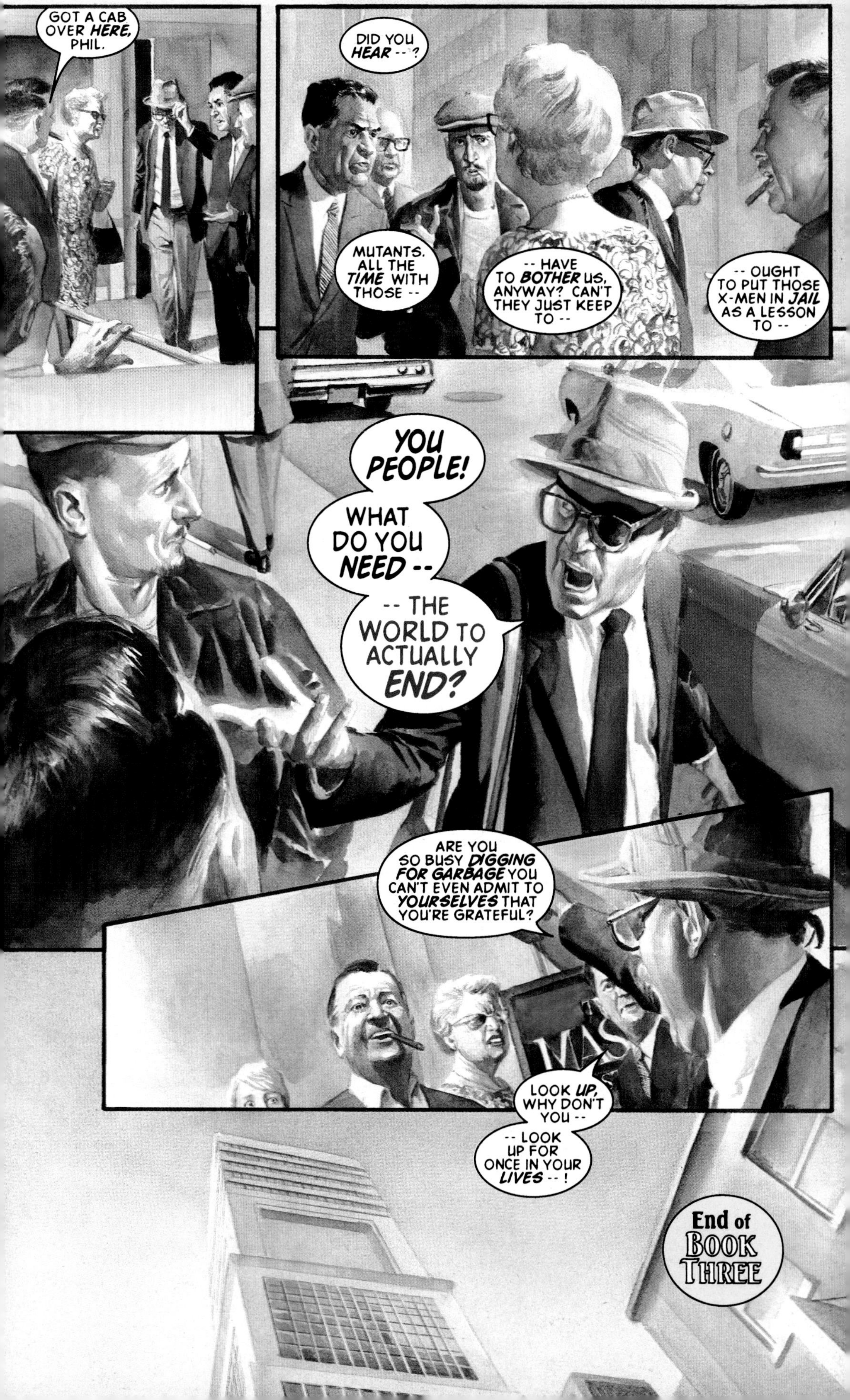
GOT A CAB OVER HERE, PHIL.
DID YOU HEAR --?
MUTANTS. ALL THE TIME WITH THOSE --
-- HAVE TO BOTHER US, ANYWAY? CAN'T THEY JUST KEEP TO --
-- OUGHT TO PUT THOSE X-MEN IN JAIL AS A LESSON TO --
YOU PEOPLE!
WHAT DO YOU NEED --
-- THE WORLD TO ACTUALLY END?
ARE YOU SO BUSY DIGGING FOR GARBAGE YOU CAN'T EVEN ADMIT TO YOURSELVES THAT YOU'RE GRATEFUL?
LOOK UP, WHY DON'T YOU --
-- LOOK UP FOR ONCE IN YOUR LIVES -- !
End of BOOK THREE

Commentary by John Romita

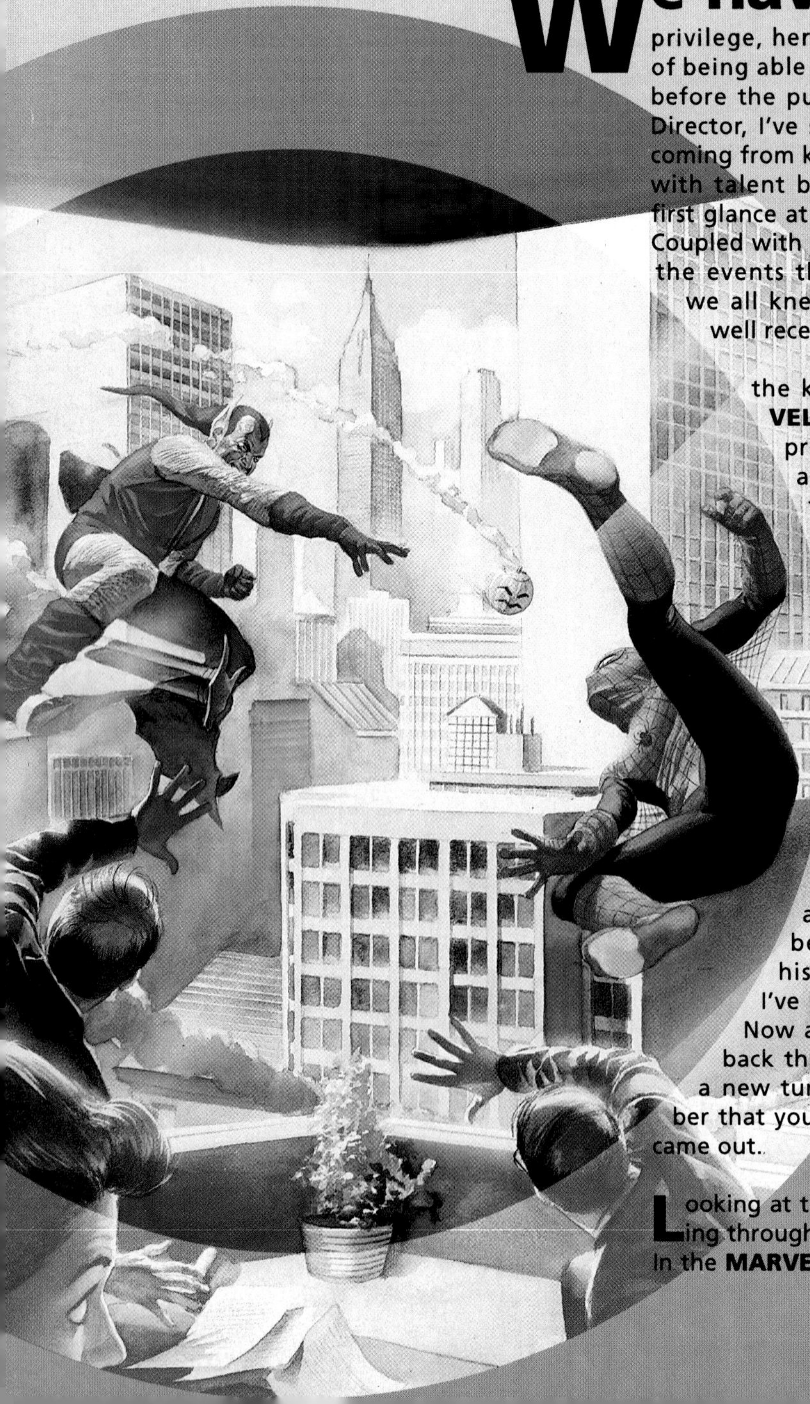

We have a specia
privilege, here around the Marvel offices of being able to see the artwork in person before the public has a chance to. As Ar Director, I've seen a lot of amazing talen coming from kids (and I use the term loosely with talent beyond their years. From my first glance at Alex's work, I was impressed Coupled with the feeling that Kurt put into the events through Phil Sheldon's eyes we all knew that **MARVELS** would be well received.

As a concept, I feel tha the kind of approach that **MARVELS** takes is a dramatic step. predict that this kind of visua approach of really making the fantastic feel like real life will be used more and more, until "normal" book look weak by comparison Computer graphics will be an added impetus.

The medium o comics is growing by leap and bounds, and those who remember the ultimate goal of comics — to tell a story — will always be at the head of the pack **MARVELS** does that with amazing grace. There have been many milestones in the history of Marvel Comics, and I've been here for a few of them Now all of you can be here to look back through these pages, and mark a new turning point. You can remember that you were there when **MARVELS** came out.

Looking at this series, I felt like I was looking through a photo album of old friends In the **MARVELS** series, Alex and Kurt hit a of the important points that I remember in the history of the Marvel Universe. But one event in the final issue touched me especially. That was the death of Gwen Stacy.

There is no great behind-the-scenes drama to tell about that event. Just the usual old tale about the "threatening" mail that came in following it. Mostly the mail was just heartfelt sadness at Gwen's passing. And the recollection that Gerry Conway, the writer at the time, was probably blamed more than he deserved.

My memory of it was a meeting with Gerry, myself, and probably Roy Thomas, in which we discussed giving the readers a "wake-up call" kind of shock that we felt THE AMAZING SPIDER-MAN book could use. I recall Aunt May's death was one option, and I suggested it should be Gwen. That's what we ended up going with. To this day, others, like Stan, think I was wrong. But in the end, it had the effect we wanted. The event was designed to affect readers profoundly, but I was surprised by the quality of Gerry's writing, and still consider it some of the best storytelling, art and writing that I can remember. Gil Kane's pencils were great. It was a turning point of sorts for all comics, and I don't think any character's death has so much affected so many readers since.

Now, Alex and Kurt tell that story from a new viewpoint, without the super hero trappings and fantastic action-adventure, instead pared down to the real human drama of an innocent death. When I was asked to be a part of this by posing for the part of the cabbie who drives Phil after Green Goblin, I loved it. The cameo was lots of fun. I only regret hamming it up so much for the photos.

Still, it is always great being a part of Marvel History. And it was great to see Gwen, one more time.

John Romita

JOHN ROMITA

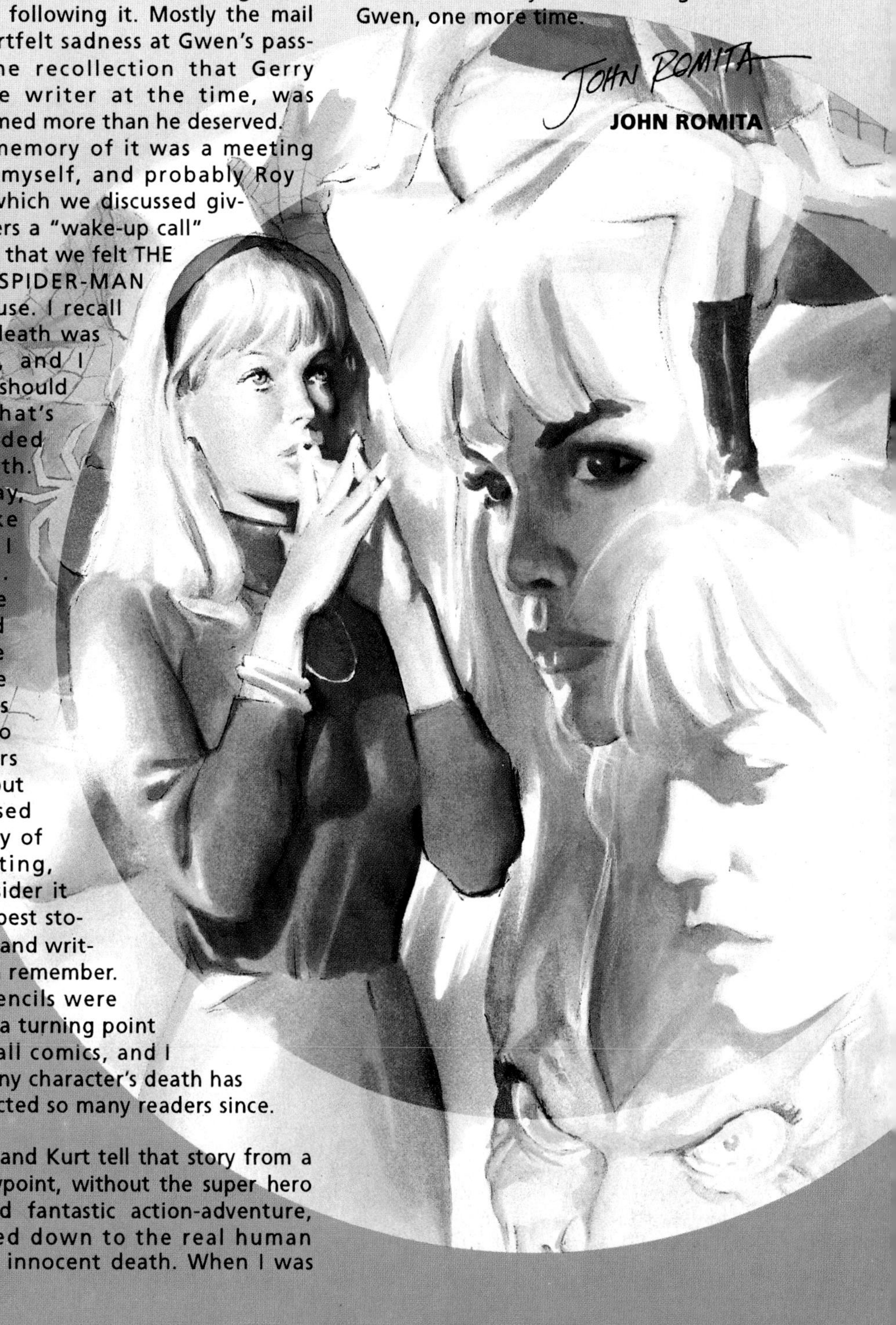

Chapter Four

THE DAY SHE DIED

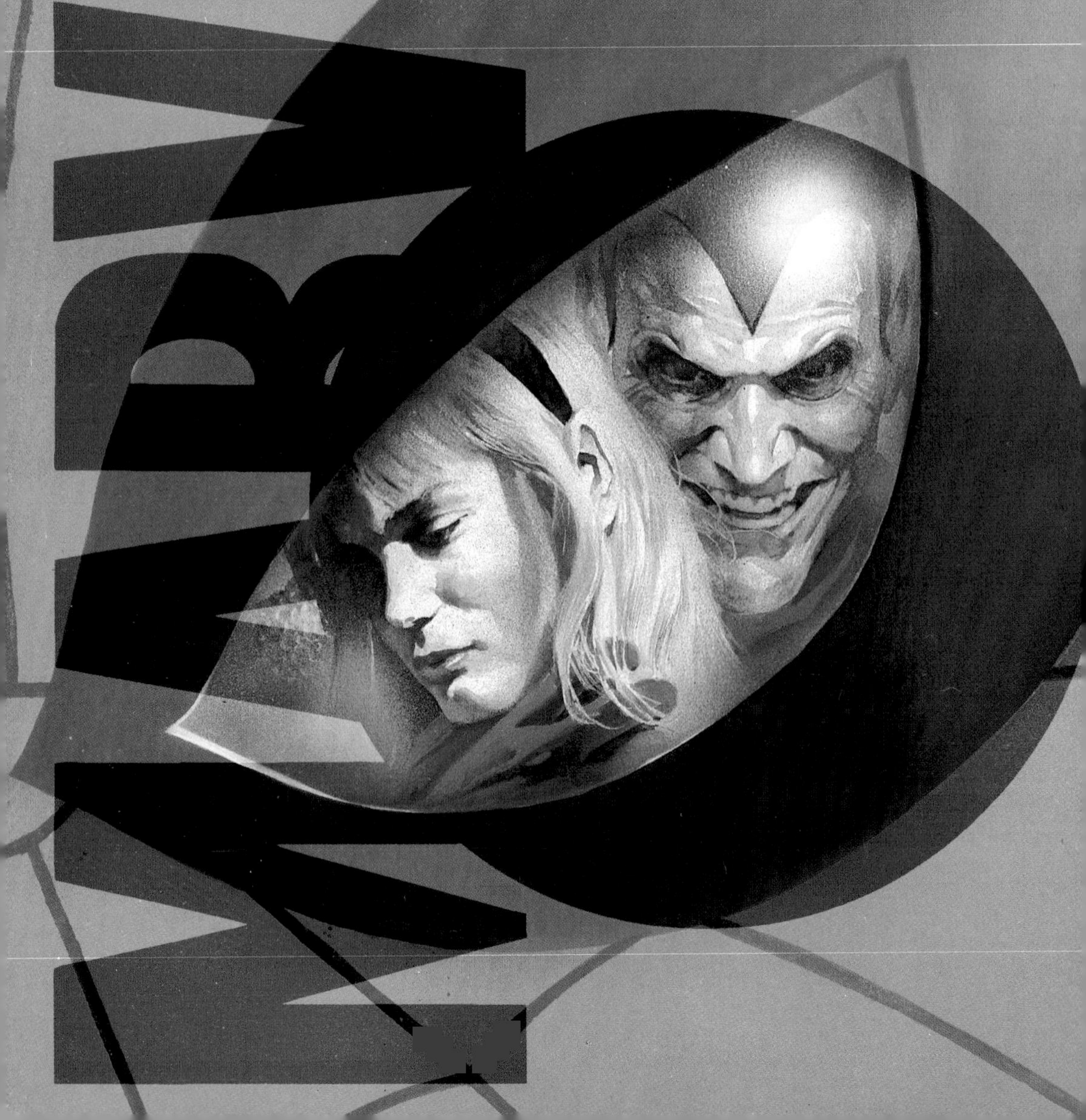

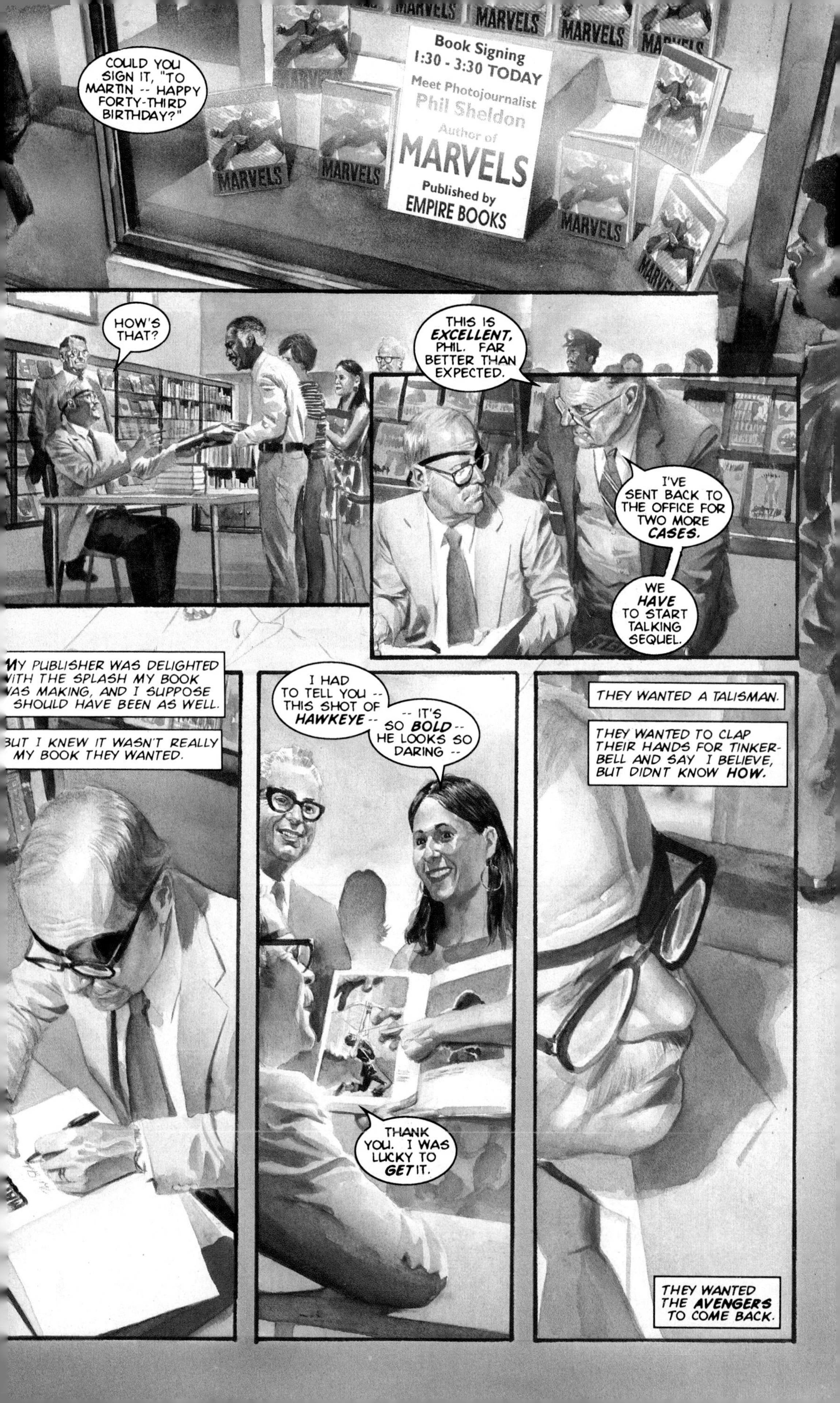
MARVELS
Book Signing
1:30 - 3:30 TODAY
Meet Photojournalist
Phil Sheldon
Author of
MARVELS
Published by
EMPIRE BOOKS
COULD YOU SIGN IT, "TO MARTIN -- HAPPY FORTY-THIRD BIRTHDAY?"
HOW'S THAT?
THIS IS EXCELLENT, PHIL. FAR BETTER THAN EXPECTED.
I'VE SENT BACK TO THE OFFICE FOR TWO MORE CASES.
WE HAVE TO START TALKING SEQUEL.
MY PUBLISHER WAS DELIGHTED WITH THE SPLASH MY BOOK WAS MAKING, AND I SUPPOSE I SHOULD HAVE BEEN AS WELL.
BUT I KNEW IT WASN'T REALLY MY BOOK THEY WANTED.
I HAD TO TELL YOU -- THIS SHOT OF HAWKEYE --
-- IT'S SO BOLD -- HE LOOKS SO DARING --
THANK YOU. I WAS LUCKY TO GET IT.
THEY WANTED A TALISMAN.
THEY WANTED TO CLAP THEIR HANDS FOR TINKER-BELL AND SAY I BELIEVE, BUT DIDNT KNOW HOW.
THEY WANTED THE AVENGERS TO COME BACK.

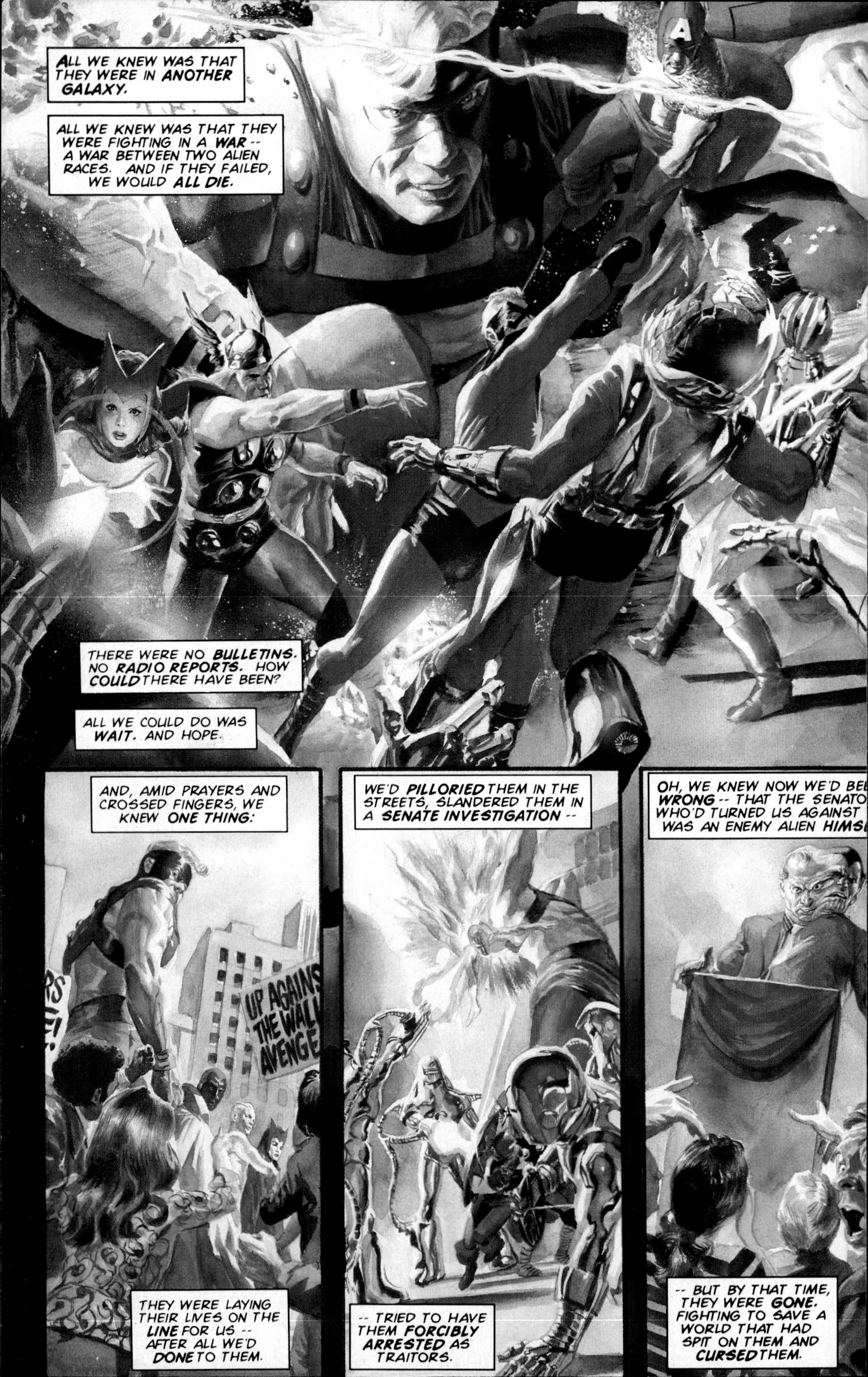
ALL WE KNEW WAS THAT THEY WERE IN ANOTHER GALAXY.
ALL WE KNEW WAS THAT THEY WERE FIGHTING IN A WAR -- A WAR BETWEEN TWO ALIEN RACES. AND IF THEY FAILED, WE WOULD ALL DIE.
THERE WERE NO BULLETINS. NO RADIO REPORTS. HOW COULD THERE HAVE BEEN?
ALL WE COULD DO WAS WAIT. AND HOPE.
AND, AMID PRAYERS AND CROSSED FINGERS, WE KNEW ONE THING:
UP AGAINS THE WALL AVENGE
THEY WERE LAYING THEIR LIVES ON THE LINE FOR US -- AFTER ALL WE'D DONE TO THEM.
WE'D PILLORIED THEM IN THE STREETS, SLANDERED THEM IN A SENATE INVESTIGATION --
-- TRIED TO HAVE THEM FORCIBLY ARRESTED AS TRAITORS.
OH, WE KNEW NOW WE'D BE WRONG -- THAT THE SENATO WHO'D TURNED US AGAINST WAS AN ENEMY ALIEN HIMS
-- BUT BY THAT TIME, THEY WERE GONE. FIGHTING TO SAVE A WORLD THAT HAD SPIT ON THEM AND CURSED THEM.

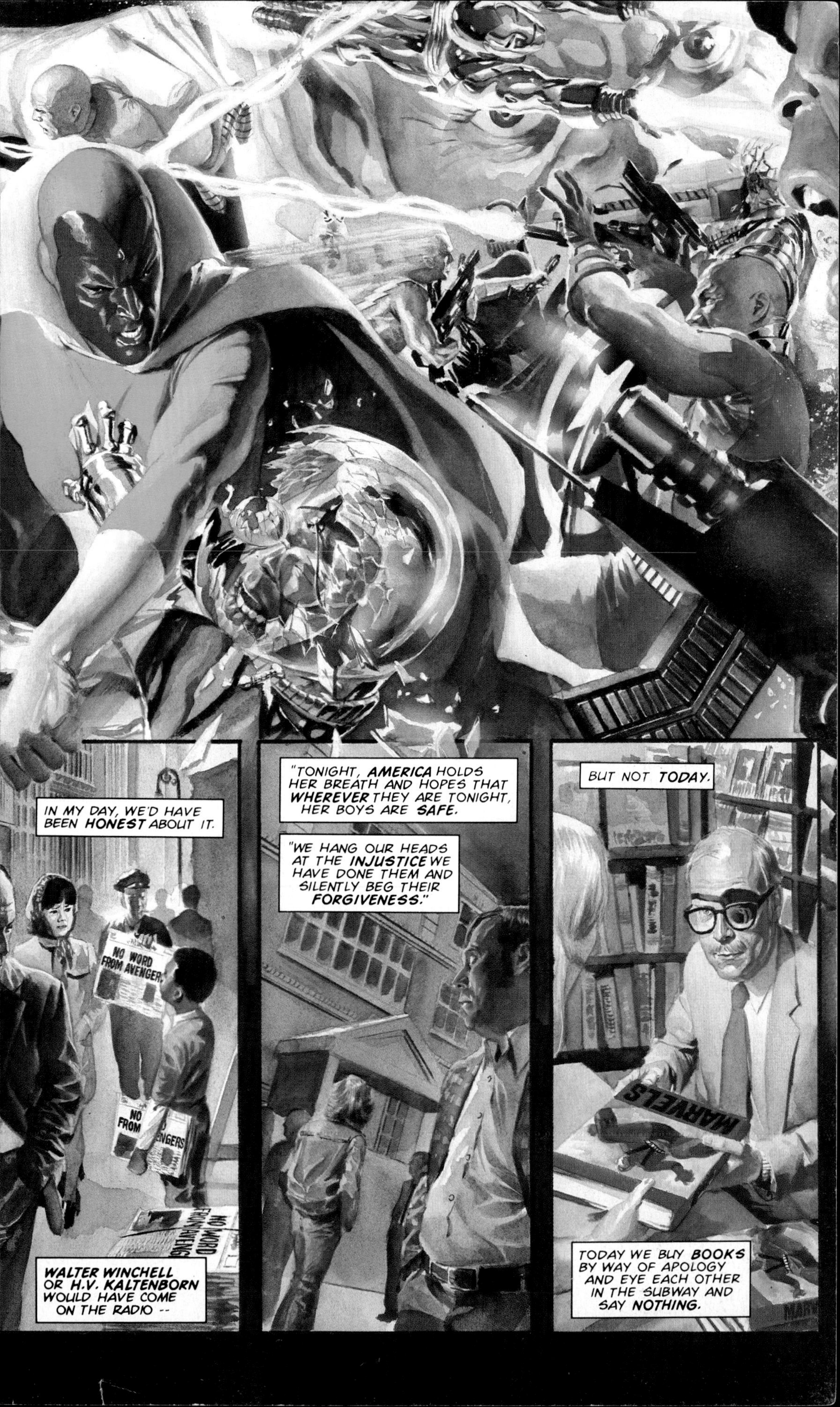

IN MY DAY, WE'D HAVE BEEN HONEST ABOUT IT.
NO WORD FROM AVENGER
WALTER WINCHELL OR H.V. KALTENBORN WOULD HAVE COME ON THE RADIO --
"TONIGHT, AMERICA HOLDS HER BREATH AND HOPES THAT WHEREVER THEY ARE TONIGHT, HER BOYS ARE SAFE.
"WE HANG OUR HEADS AT THE INJUSTICE WE HAVE DONE THEM AND SILENTLY BEG THEIR FORGIVENESS."
BUT NOT TODAY.
MARVELS
TODAY WE BUY BOOKS BY WAY OF APOLOGY AND EYE EACH OTHER IN THE SUBWAY AND SAY NOTHING.

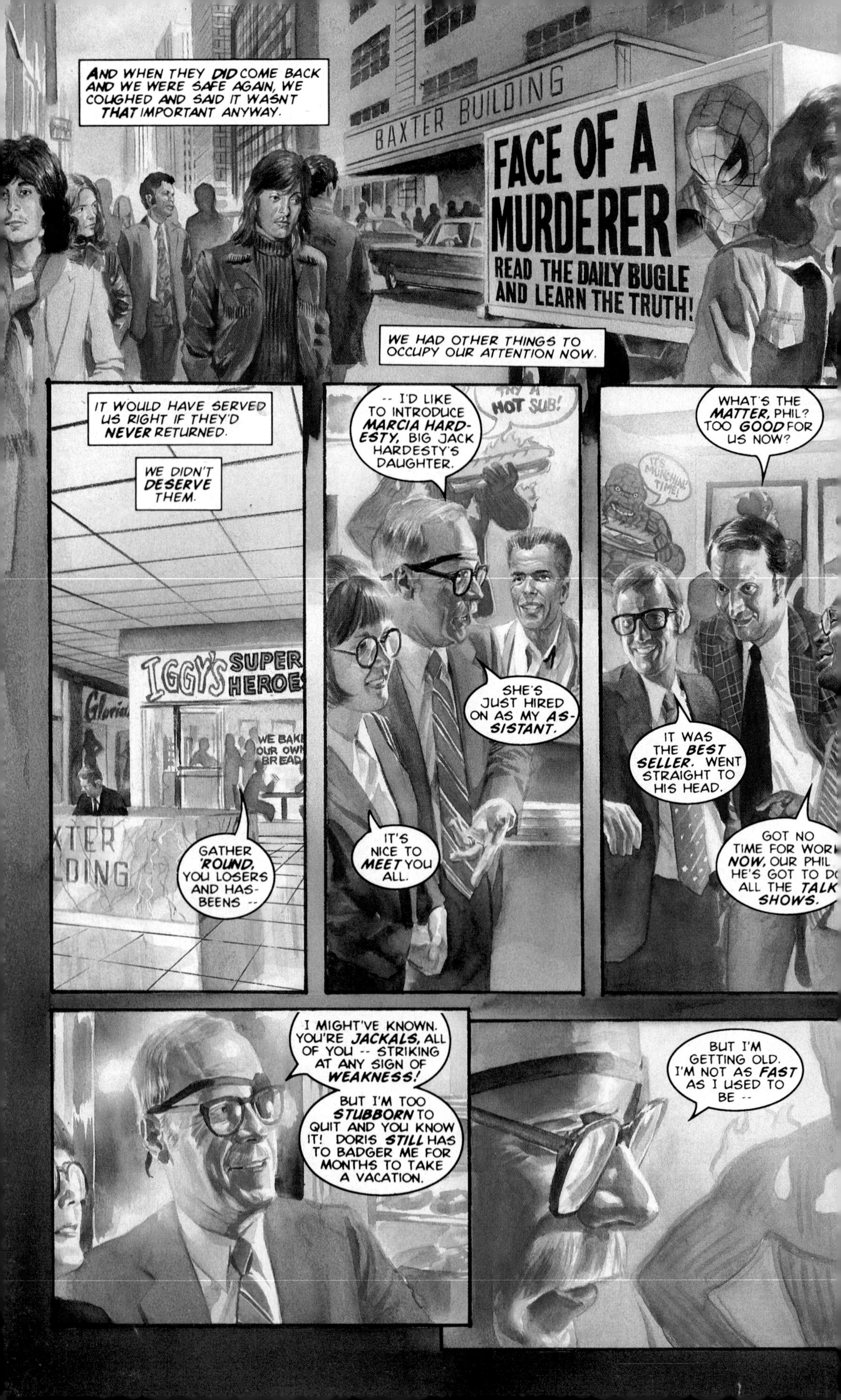

AND WHEN THEY DID COME BACK AND WE WERE SAFE AGAIN, WE COUGHED AND SAID IT WASN'T THAT IMPORTANT ANYWAY.
BAXTER BUILDING
FACE OF A MURDERER
READ THE DAILY BUGLE AND LEARN THE TRUTH!
WE HAD OTHER THINGS TO OCCUPY OUR ATTENTION NOW.
IT WOULD HAVE SERVED US RIGHT IF THEY'D NEVER RETURNED.
WE DIDN'T DESERVE THEM.
IGGY'S SUPER HEROES
WE BAKE OUR OWN BREAD
GATHER 'ROUND, YOU LOSERS AND HAS-BEENS --
-- I'D LIKE TO INTRODUCE MARCIA HARDESTY, BIG JACK HARDESTY'S DAUGHTER.
HOT SUB!
SHE'S JUST HIRED ON AS MY ASSISTANT.
IT'S NICE TO MEET YOU ALL.
WHAT'S THE MATTER, PHIL? TOO GOOD FOR US NOW?
IT'S MUNCHIN' TIME!
IT WAS THE BEST SELLER. WENT STRAIGHT TO HIS HEAD.
GOT NO TIME FOR WORK NOW, OUR PHIL. HE'S GOT TO DO ALL THE TALK SHOWS.
I MIGHT'VE KNOWN. YOU'RE JACKALS, ALL OF YOU -- STRIKING AT ANY SIGN OF WEAKNESS!
BUT I'M TOO STUBBORN TO QUIT AND YOU KNOW IT! DORIS STILL HAS TO BADGER ME FOR MONTHS TO TAKE A VACATION.
BUT I'M GETTING OLD. I'M NOT AS FAST AS I USED TO BE --

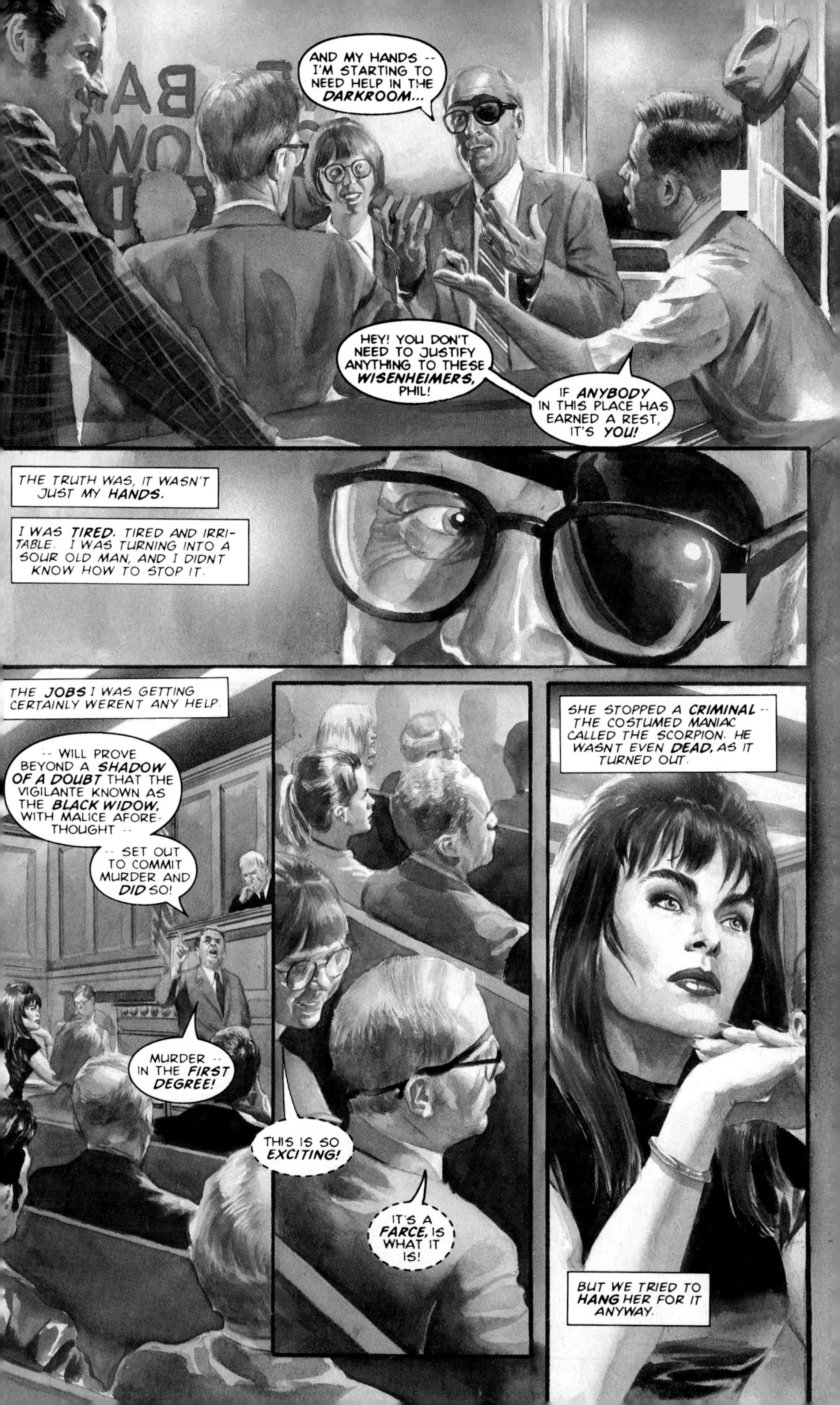
AND MY HANDS -- I'M STARTING TO NEED HELP IN THE DARKROOM...
HEY! YOU DON'T NEED TO JUSTIFY ANYTHING TO THESE WISENHEIMERS, PHIL!
IF ANYBODY IN THIS PLACE HAS EARNED A REST, IT'S YOU!
THE TRUTH WAS, IT WASN'T JUST MY HANDS.
I WAS TIRED. TIRED AND IRRITABLE. I WAS TURNING INTO A SOUR OLD MAN, AND I DIDNT KNOW HOW TO STOP IT.
THE JOBS I WAS GETTING CERTAINLY WERENT ANY HELP.
-- WILL PROVE BEYOND A SHADOW OF A DOUBT THAT THE VIGILANTE KNOWN AS THE BLACK WIDOW, WITH MALICE AFORE-THOUGHT --
-- SET OUT TO COMMIT MURDER AND DID SO!
MURDER -- IN THE FIRST DEGREE!
THIS IS SO EXCITING!
IT'S A FARCE, IS WHAT IT IS!
SHE STOPPED A CRIMINAL -- THE COSTUMED MANIAC CALLED THE SCORPION. HE WASN'T EVEN DEAD, AS IT TURNED OUT.
BUT WE TRIED TO HANG HER FOR IT ANYWAY.

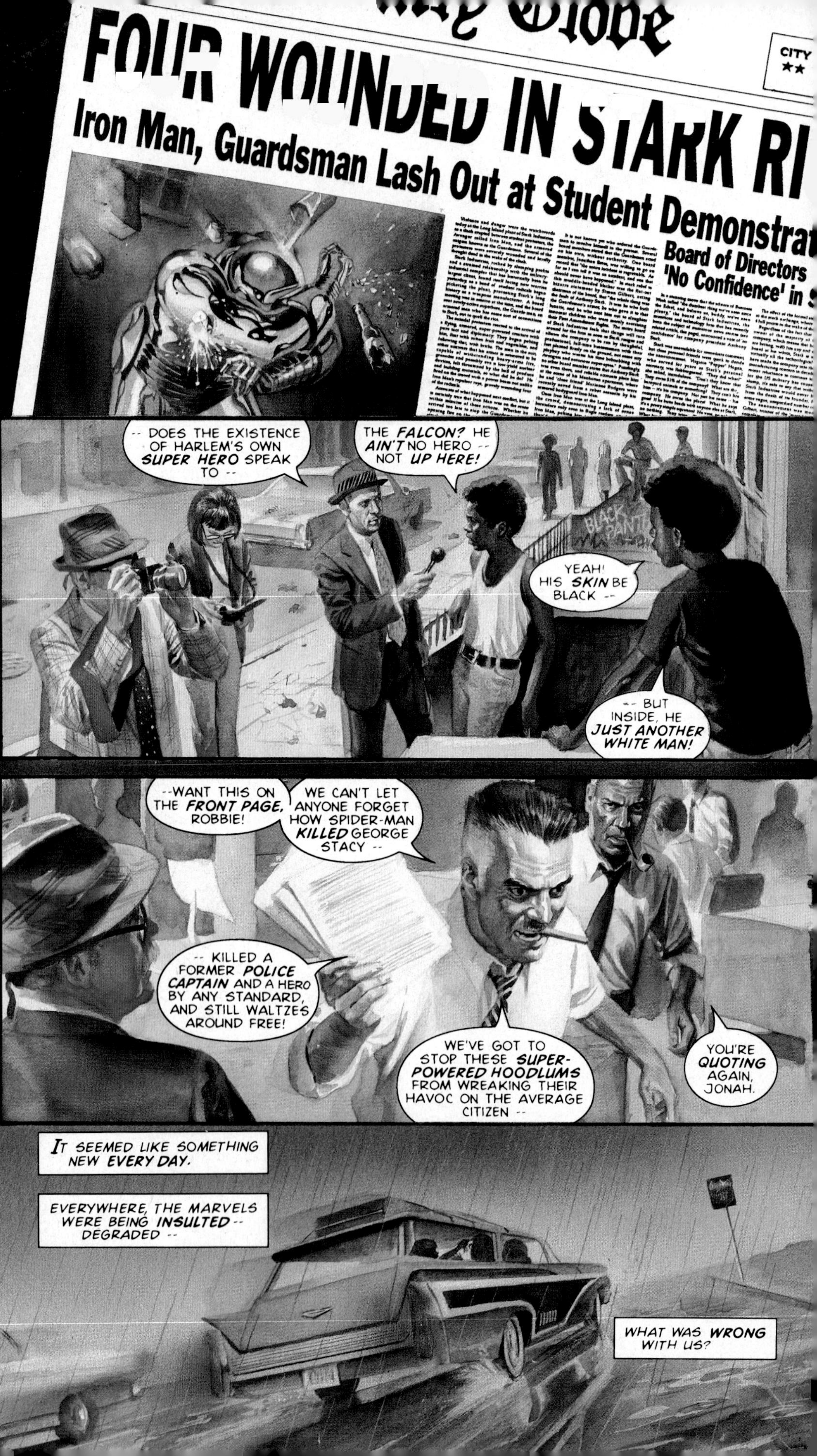

CITY ★★
FOUR WOUNDED IN STARK RI
Iron Man, Guardsman Lash Out at Student Demonstrat
Board of Directors
'No Confidence' in
-- DOES THE EXISTENCE OF HARLEM'S OWN SUPER HERO SPEAK TO --
THE FALCON? HE AIN'T NO HERO -- NOT UP HERE!
YEAH! HIS SKIN BE BLACK --
-- BUT INSIDE, HE JUST ANOTHER WHITE MAN!
--WANT THIS ON THE FRONT PAGE, ROBBIE!
WE CAN'T LET ANYONE FORGET HOW SPIDER-MAN KILLED GEORGE STACY --
-- KILLED A FORMER POLICE CAPTAIN AND A HERO BY ANY STANDARD, AND STILL WALTZES AROUND FREE!
WE'VE GOT TO STOP THESE SUPER-POWERED HOODLUMS FROM WREAKING THEIR HAVOC ON THE AVERAGE CITIZEN --
YOU'RE QUOTING AGAIN, JONAH.
IT SEEMED LIKE SOMETHING NEW EVERY DAY.
EVERYWHERE, THE MARVELS WERE BEING INSULTED -- DEGRADED --
WHAT WAS WRONG WITH US?

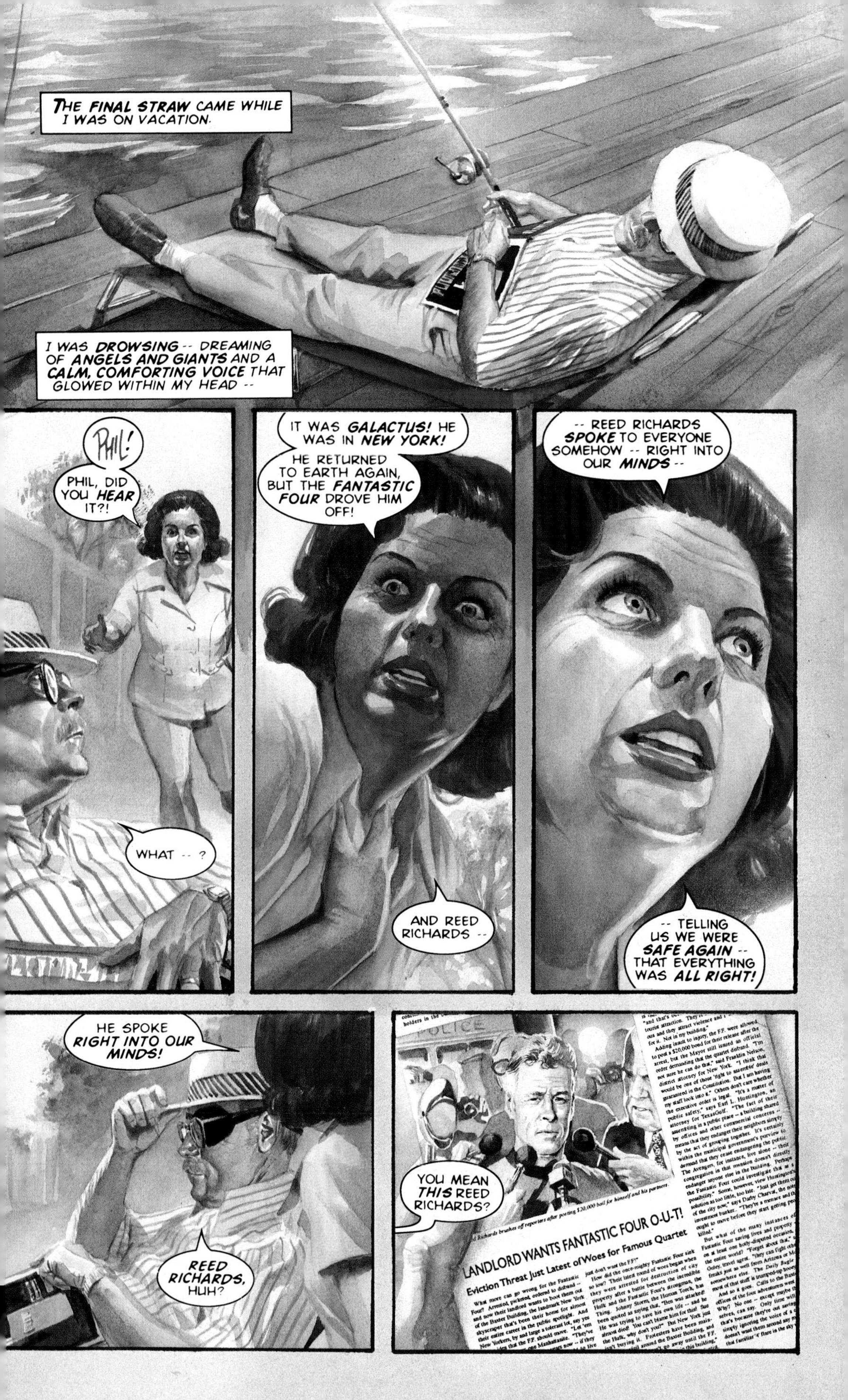

THE FINAL STRAW CAME WHILE I WAS ON VACATION.
I WAS DROWSING -- DREAMING OF ANGELS AND GIANTS AND A CALM, COMFORTING VOICE THAT GLOWED WITHIN MY HEAD --
PHIL!
PHIL, DID YOU HEAR IT?!
WHAT -- ?
IT WAS GALACTUS! HE WAS IN NEW YORK!
HE RETURNED TO EARTH AGAIN, BUT THE FANTASTIC FOUR DROVE HIM OFF!
AND REED RICHARDS --
-- REED RICHARDS SPOKE TO EVERYONE SOMEHOW -- RIGHT INTO OUR MINDS --
-- TELLING US WE WERE SAFE AGAIN -- THAT EVERYTHING WAS ALL RIGHT!
HE SPOKE RIGHT INTO OUR MINDS!
REED RICHARDS, HUH?
YOU MEAN THIS REED RICHARDS?
POLICE
LANDLORD WANTS FANTASTIC FOUR O-U-T!
Eviction Threat Just Latest of Woes for Famous Quartet

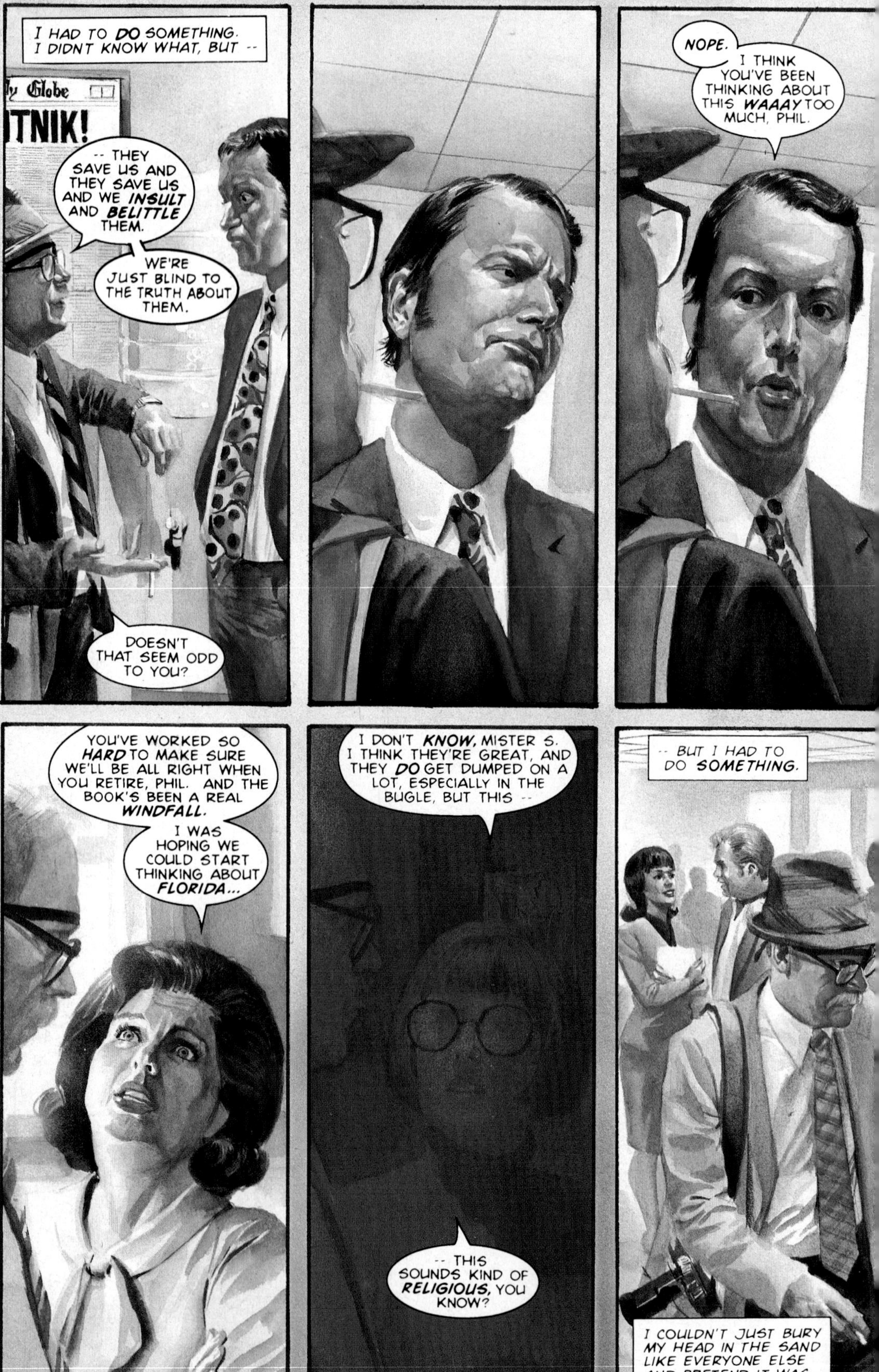
I HAD TO DO SOMETHING. I DIDN'T KNOW WHAT, BUT --
-- THEY SAVE US AND THEY SAVE US AND WE INSULT AND BELITTLE THEM.
WE'RE JUST BLIND TO THE TRUTH ABOUT THEM.
DOESN'T THAT SEEM ODD TO YOU?
NOPE.
I THINK YOU'VE BEEN THINKING ABOUT THIS WAAAY TOO MUCH, PHIL.
YOU'VE WORKED SO HARD TO MAKE SURE WE'LL BE ALL RIGHT WHEN YOU RETIRE, PHIL. AND THE BOOK'S BEEN A REAL WINDFALL.
I WAS HOPING WE COULD START THINKING ABOUT FLORIDA...
I DON'T KNOW, MISTER S. I THINK THEY'RE GREAT, AND THEY DO GET DUMPED ON A LOT, ESPECIALLY IN THE BUGLE, BUT THIS --
-- THIS SOUNDS KIND OF RELIGIOUS, YOU KNOW?
-- BUT I HAD TO DO SOMETHING.
I COULDN'T JUST BURY MY HEAD IN THE SAND LIKE EVERYONE ELSE AND PRETEND IT WAS OKAY TO --

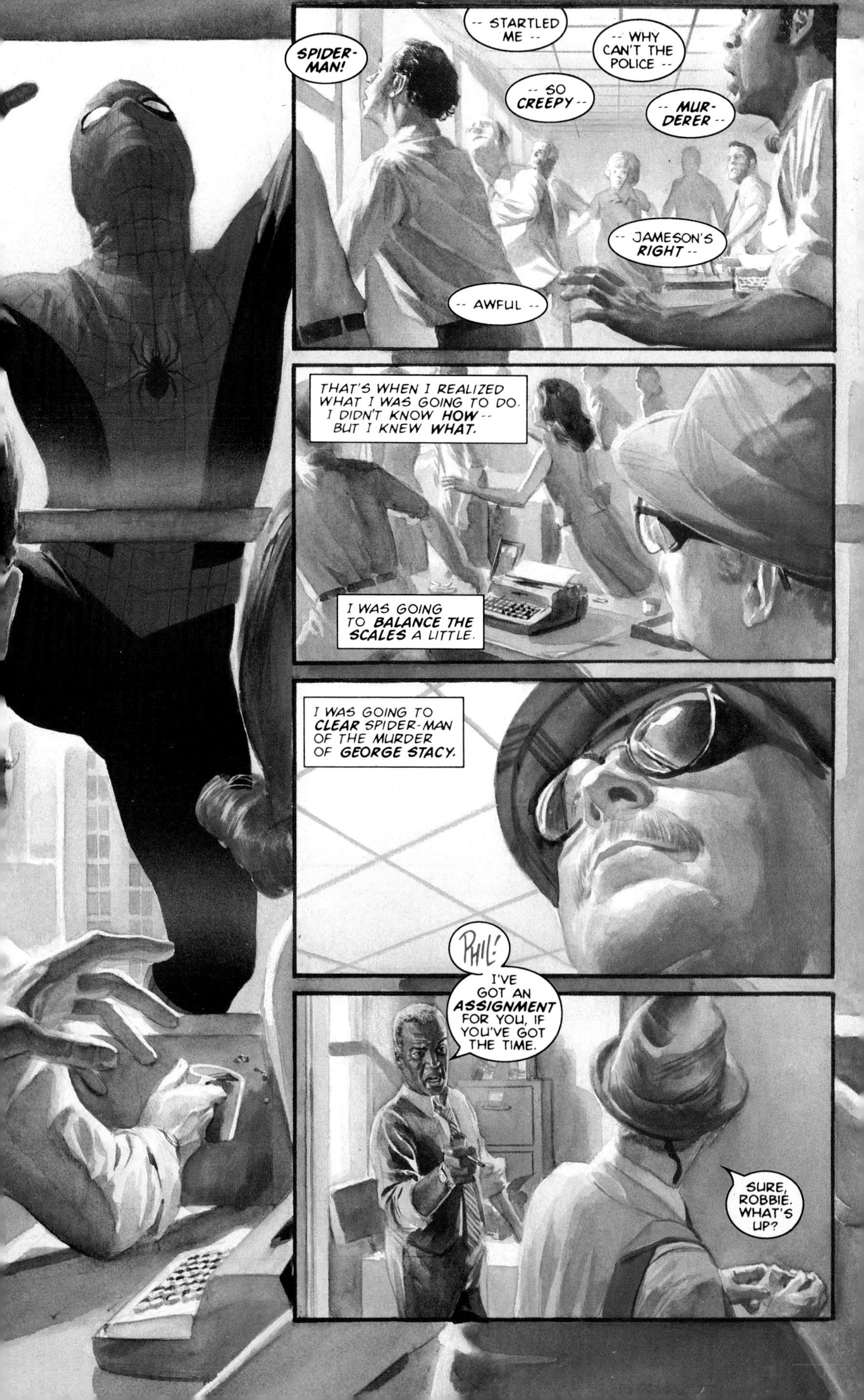
SPIDER-MAN!
-- STARTLED ME --
-- WHY CAN'T THE POLICE --
-- SO CREEPY --
-- MURDERER --
-- JAMESON'S RIGHT --
-- AWFUL --
THAT'S WHEN I REALIZED WHAT I WAS GOING TO DO. I DIDN'T KNOW HOW -- BUT I KNEW WHAT.
I WAS GOING TO BALANCE THE SCALES A LITTLE.
I WAS GOING TO CLEAR SPIDER-MAN OF THE MURDER OF GEORGE STACY.
PHIL!
I'VE GOT AN ASSIGNMENT FOR YOU, IF YOU'VE GOT THE TIME.
SURE, ROBBIE. WHAT'S UP?

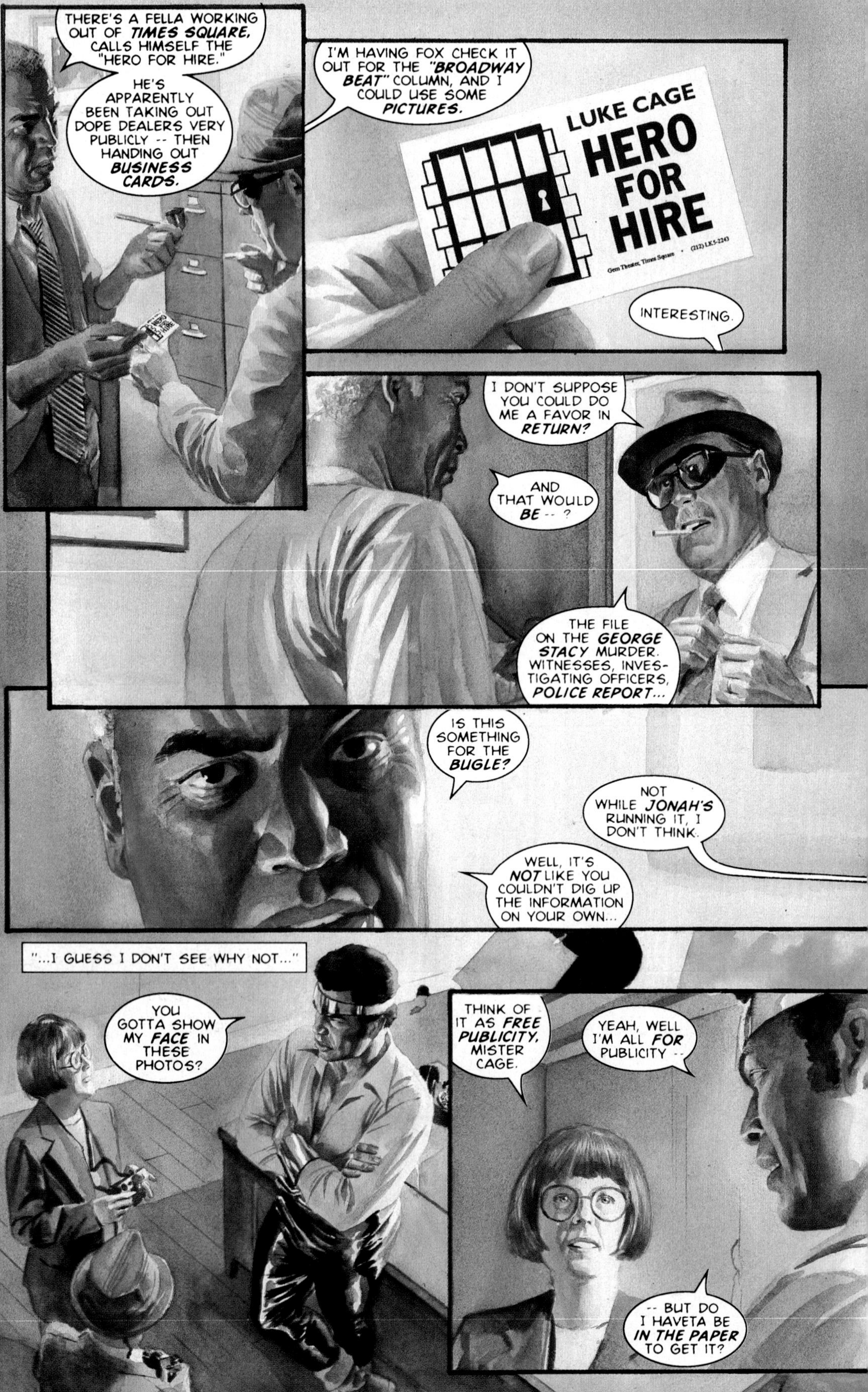

THERE'S A FELLA WORKING OUT OF TIMES SQUARE, CALLS HIMSELF THE "HERO FOR HIRE."
HE'S APPARENTLY BEEN TAKING OUT DOPE DEALERS VERY PUBLICLY -- THEN HANDING OUT BUSINESS CARDS.
I'M HAVING FOX CHECK IT OUT FOR THE "BROADWAY BEAT" COLUMN, AND I COULD USE SOME PICTURES.
LUKE CAGE
HERO FOR HIRE
Gem Theater, Times Square • (212) LK5-2243
INTERESTING.
I DON'T SUPPOSE YOU COULD DO ME A FAVOR IN RETURN?
AND THAT WOULD BE -- ?
THE FILE ON THE GEORGE STACY MURDER. WITNESSES, INVESTIGATING OFFICERS, POLICE REPORT...
IS THIS SOMETHING FOR THE BUGLE?
NOT WHILE JONAH'S RUNNING IT, I DON'T THINK.
WELL, IT'S NOT LIKE YOU COULDN'T DIG UP THE INFORMATION ON YOUR OWN...
"...I GUESS I DON'T SEE WHY NOT..."
YOU GOTTA SHOW MY FACE IN THESE PHOTOS?
THINK OF IT AS FREE PUBLICITY, MISTER CAGE.
YEAH, WELL I'M ALL FOR PUBLICITY --
-- BUT DO I HAVETA BE IN THE PAPER TO GET IT?

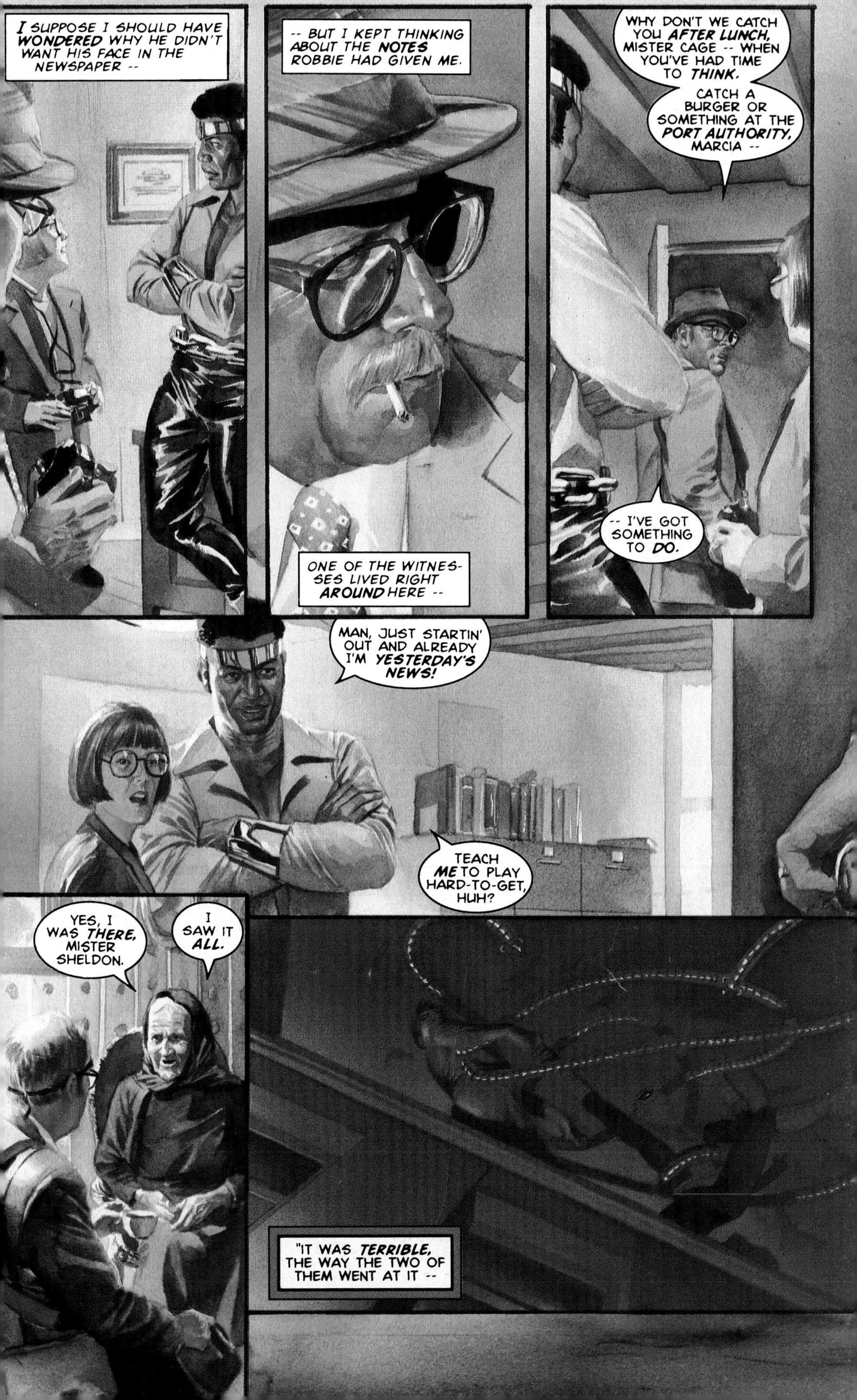
I SUPPOSE I SHOULD HAVE WONDERED WHY HE DIDN'T WANT HIS FACE IN THE NEWSPAPER --
-- BUT I KEPT THINKING ABOUT THE NOTES ROBBIE HAD GIVEN ME.
ONE OF THE WITNESSES LIVED RIGHT AROUND HERE --
WHY DON'T WE CATCH YOU AFTER LUNCH, MISTER CAGE -- WHEN YOU'VE HAD TIME TO THINK.
CATCH A BURGER OR SOMETHING AT THE PORT AUTHORITY, MARCIA --
-- I'VE GOT SOMETHING TO DO.
MAN, JUST STARTIN' OUT AND ALREADY I'M YESTERDAY'S NEWS!
TEACH ME TO PLAY HARD-TO-GET, HUH?
YES, I WAS THERE, MISTER SHELDON.
I SAW IT ALL.
"IT WAS TERRIBLE, THE WAY THE TWO OF THEM WENT AT IT --

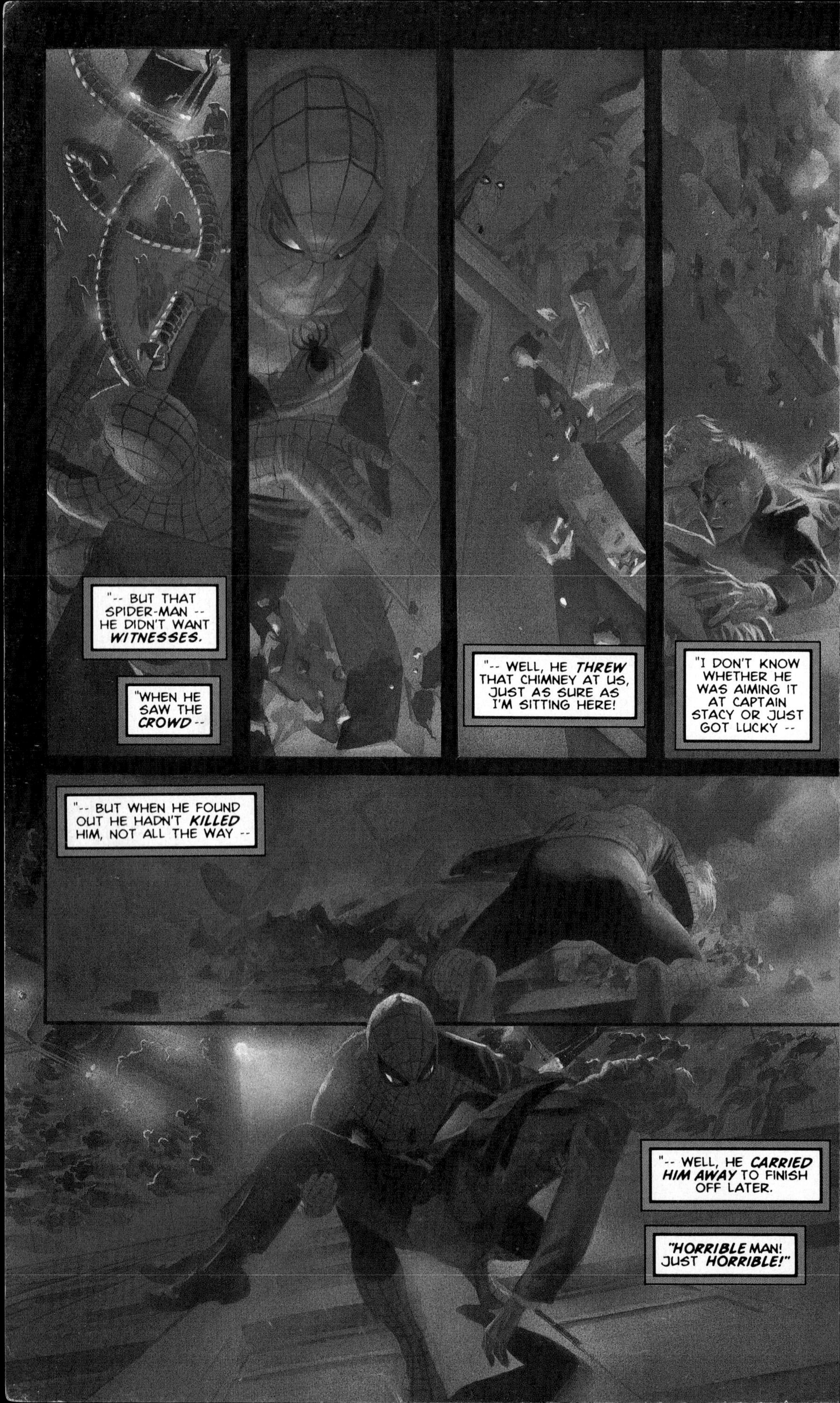
"-- BUT THAT SPIDER-MAN -- HE DIDN'T WANT *WITNESSES.*
"WHEN HE SAW THE *CROWD* --
"-- WELL, HE *THREW* THAT CHIMNEY AT US, JUST AS SURE AS I'M SITTING HERE!
"I DON'T KNOW WHETHER HE WAS AIMING IT AT CAPTAIN STACY OR JUST GOT LUCKY --
"-- BUT WHEN HE FOUND OUT HE HADN'T *KILLED* HIM, NOT ALL THE WAY --
"-- WELL, HE *CARRIED HIM AWAY* TO FINISH OFF LATER.
"*HORRIBLE* MAN! JUST *HORRIBLE!*"

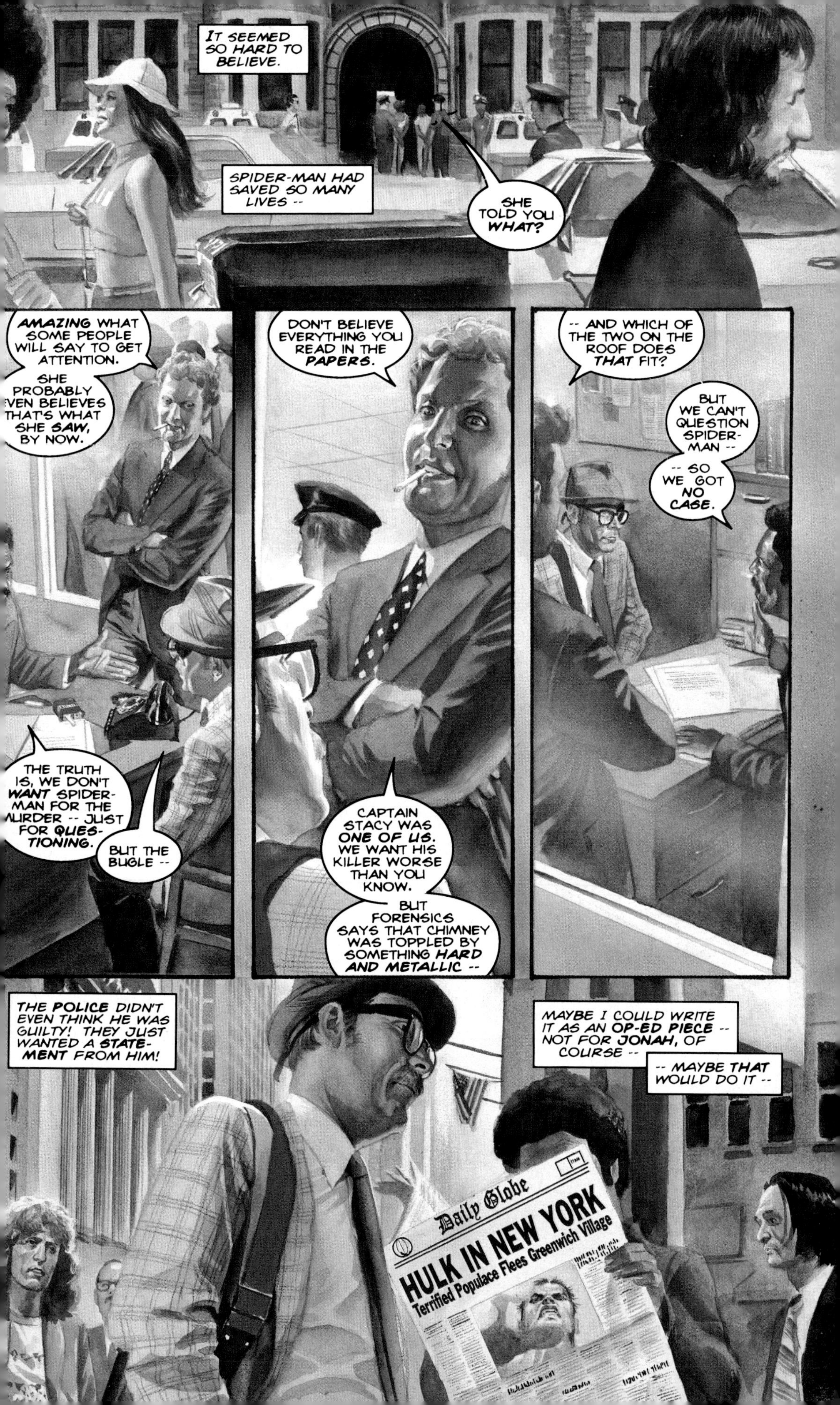
IT SEEMED SO HARD TO BELIEVE.
SPIDER-MAN HAD SAVED SO MANY LIVES --
SHE TOLD YOU WHAT?
AMAZING WHAT SOME PEOPLE WILL SAY TO GET ATTENTION.
SHE PROBABLY EVEN BELIEVES THAT'S WHAT SHE SAW, BY NOW.
THE TRUTH IS, WE DON'T WANT SPIDER-MAN FOR THE MURDER -- JUST FOR QUESTIONING.
BUT THE BUGLE --
DON'T BELIEVE EVERYTHING YOU READ IN THE PAPERS.
CAPTAIN STACY WAS ONE OF US. WE WANT HIS KILLER WORSE THAN YOU KNOW.
BUT FORENSICS SAYS THAT CHIMNEY WAS TOPPLED BY SOMETHING HARD AND METALLIC --
-- AND WHICH OF THE TWO ON THE ROOF DOES THAT FIT?
BUT WE CAN'T QUESTION SPIDER-MAN --
-- SO WE GOT NO CASE.
THE POLICE DIDN'T EVEN THINK HE WAS GUILTY! THEY JUST WANTED A STATEMENT FROM HIM!
MAYBE I COULD WRITE IT AS AN OP-ED PIECE -- NOT FOR JONAH, OF COURSE --
-- MAYBE THAT WOULD DO IT --
Daily Globe
HULK IN NEW YORK
Terrified Populace Flees Greenwich Village

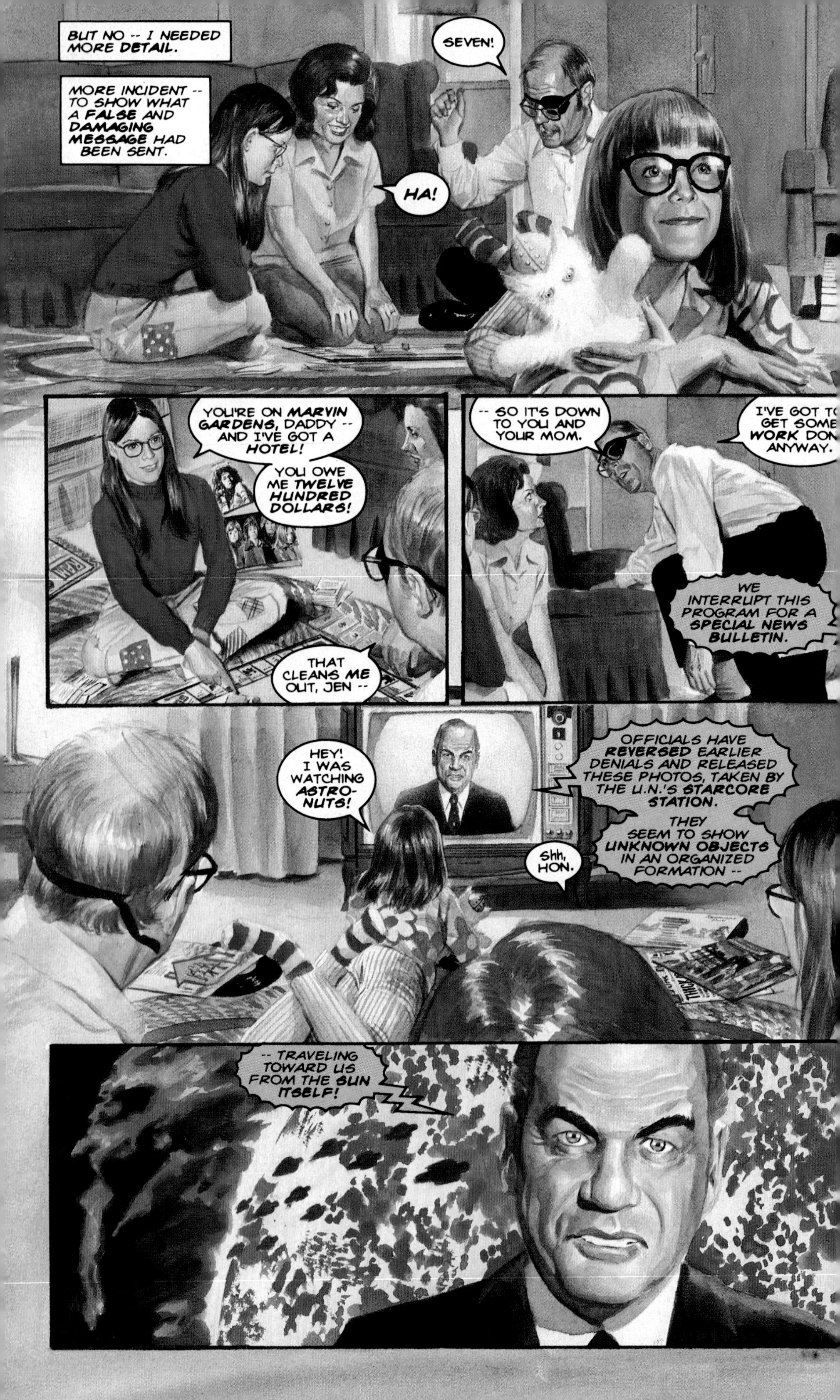

BUT NO -- I NEEDED MORE DETAIL.
MORE INCIDENT -- TO SHOW WHAT A FALSE AND DAMAGING MESSAGE HAD BEEN SENT.
SEVEN!
HA!
YOU'RE ON MARVIN GARDENS, DADDY -- AND I'VE GOT A HOTEL!
YOU OWE ME TWELVE HUNDRED DOLLARS!
THAT CLEANS ME OUT, JEN --
-- SO IT'S DOWN TO YOU AND YOUR MOM.
I'VE GOT TO GET SOME WORK DON ANYWAY.
WE INTERRUPT THIS PROGRAM FOR A SPECIAL NEWS BULLETIN.
HEY! I WAS WATCHING ASTRO-NUTS!
OFFICIALS HAVE REVERSED EARLIER DENIALS AND RELEASED THESE PHOTOS, TAKEN BY THE U.N.'S STARCORE STATION.
THEY SEEM TO SHOW UNKNOWN OBJECTS IN AN ORGANIZED FORMATION --
Shh, HON.
-- TRAVELING TOWARD US FROM THE SUN ITSELF!

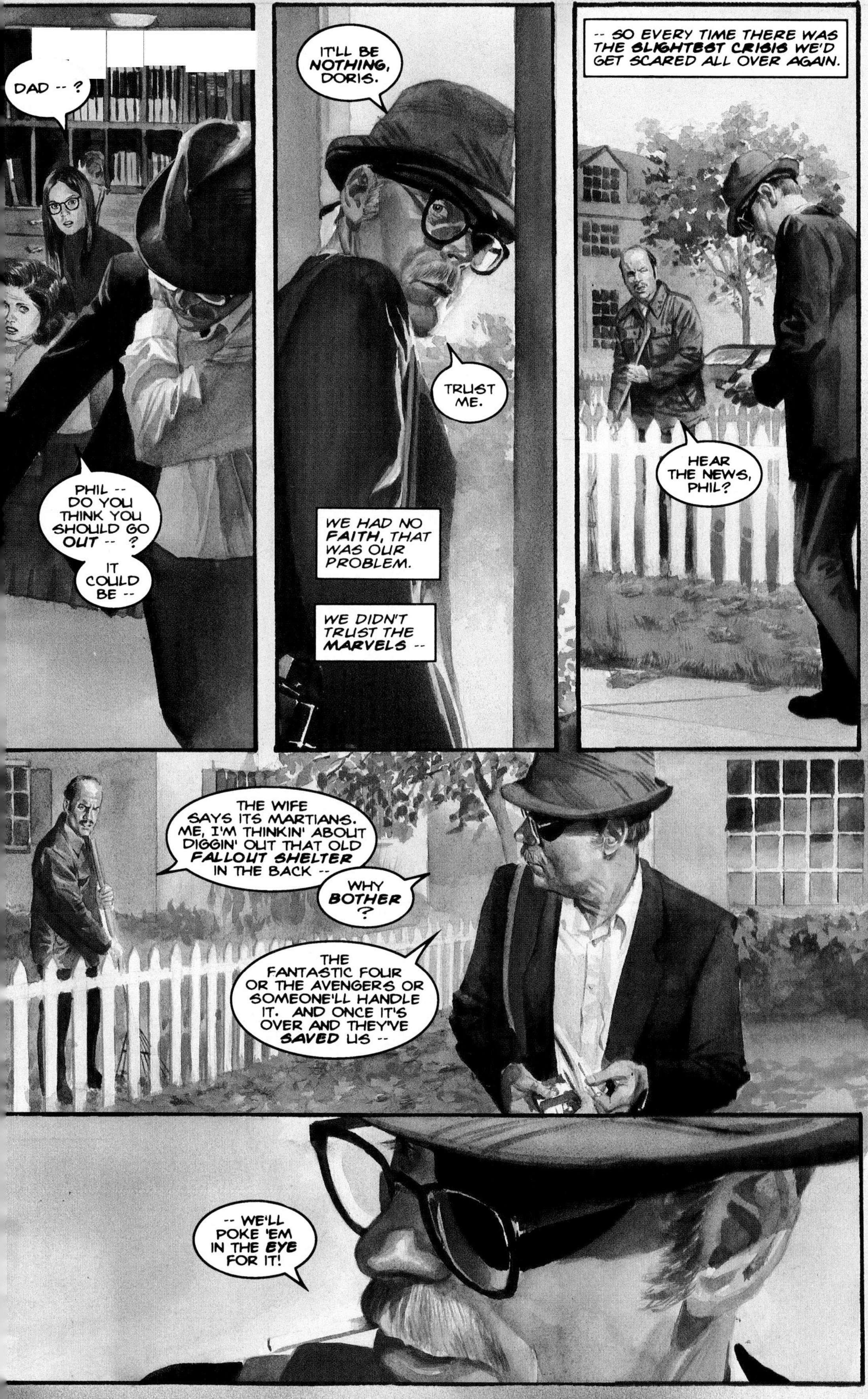
DAD -- ?
PHIL -- DO YOU THINK YOU SHOULD GO OUT -- ?
IT COULD BE --
IT'LL BE NOTHING, DORIS.
TRUST ME.
WE HAD NO FAITH, THAT WAS OUR PROBLEM.
WE DIDN'T TRUST THE MARVELS --
-- SO EVERY TIME THERE WAS THE SLIGHTEST CRISIS WE'D GET SCARED ALL OVER AGAIN.
HEAR THE NEWS, PHIL?
THE WIFE SAYS ITS MARTIANS. ME, I'M THINKIN' ABOUT DIGGIN' OUT THAT OLD FALLOUT SHELTER IN THE BACK --
WHY BOTHER?
THE FANTASTIC FOUR OR THE AVENGERS OR SOMEONE'LL HANDLE IT. AND ONCE IT'S OVER AND THEY'VE SAVED US --
-- WE'LL POKE 'EM IN THE EYE FOR IT!

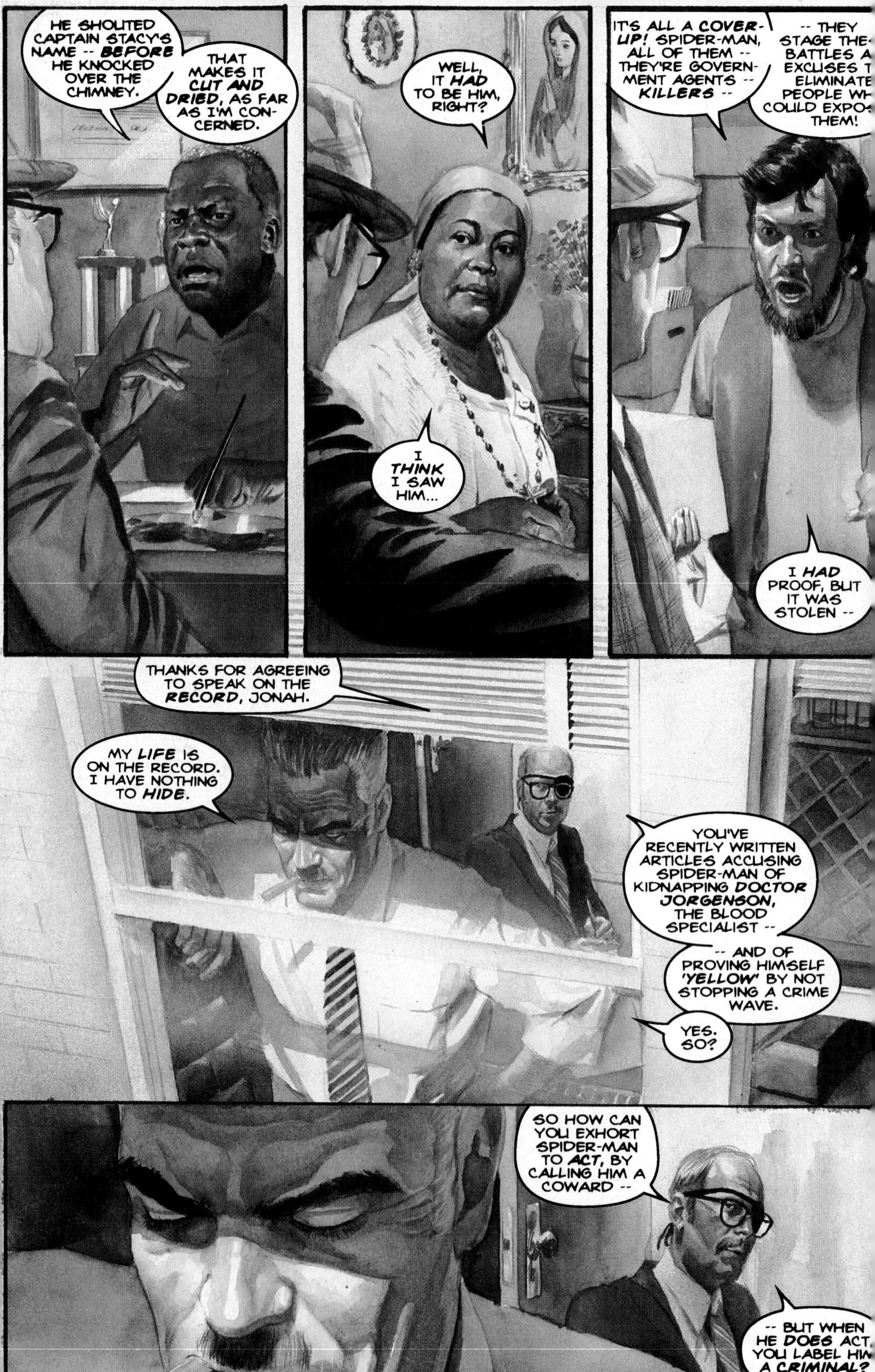
HE SHOUTED CAPTAIN STACY'S NAME -- BEFORE HE KNOCKED OVER THE CHIMNEY.
THAT MAKES IT CUT AND DRIED, AS FAR AS I'M CONCERNED.
WELL, IT HAD TO BE HIM, RIGHT?
I THINK I SAW HIM...
IT'S ALL A COVER-UP! SPIDER-MAN, ALL OF THEM -- THEY'RE GOVERNMENT AGENTS -- KILLERS --
-- THEY STAGE THE BATTLES A EXCUSES T ELIMINATE PEOPLE WH COULD EXPO THEM!
I HAD PROOF, BUT IT WAS STOLEN --
THANKS FOR AGREEING TO SPEAK ON THE RECORD, JONAH.
MY LIFE IS ON THE RECORD. I HAVE NOTHING TO HIDE.
YOU'VE RECENTLY WRITTEN ARTICLES ACCUSING SPIDER-MAN OF KIDNAPPING DOCTOR JORGENSON, THE BLOOD SPECIALIST --
-- AND OF PROVING HIMSELF 'YELLOW' BY NOT STOPPING A CRIME WAVE.
YES. SO?
SO HOW CAN YOU EXHORT SPIDER-MAN TO ACT, BY CALLING HIM A COWARD --
-- BUT WHEN HE DOES ACT, YOU LABEL HIM A CRIMINAL?

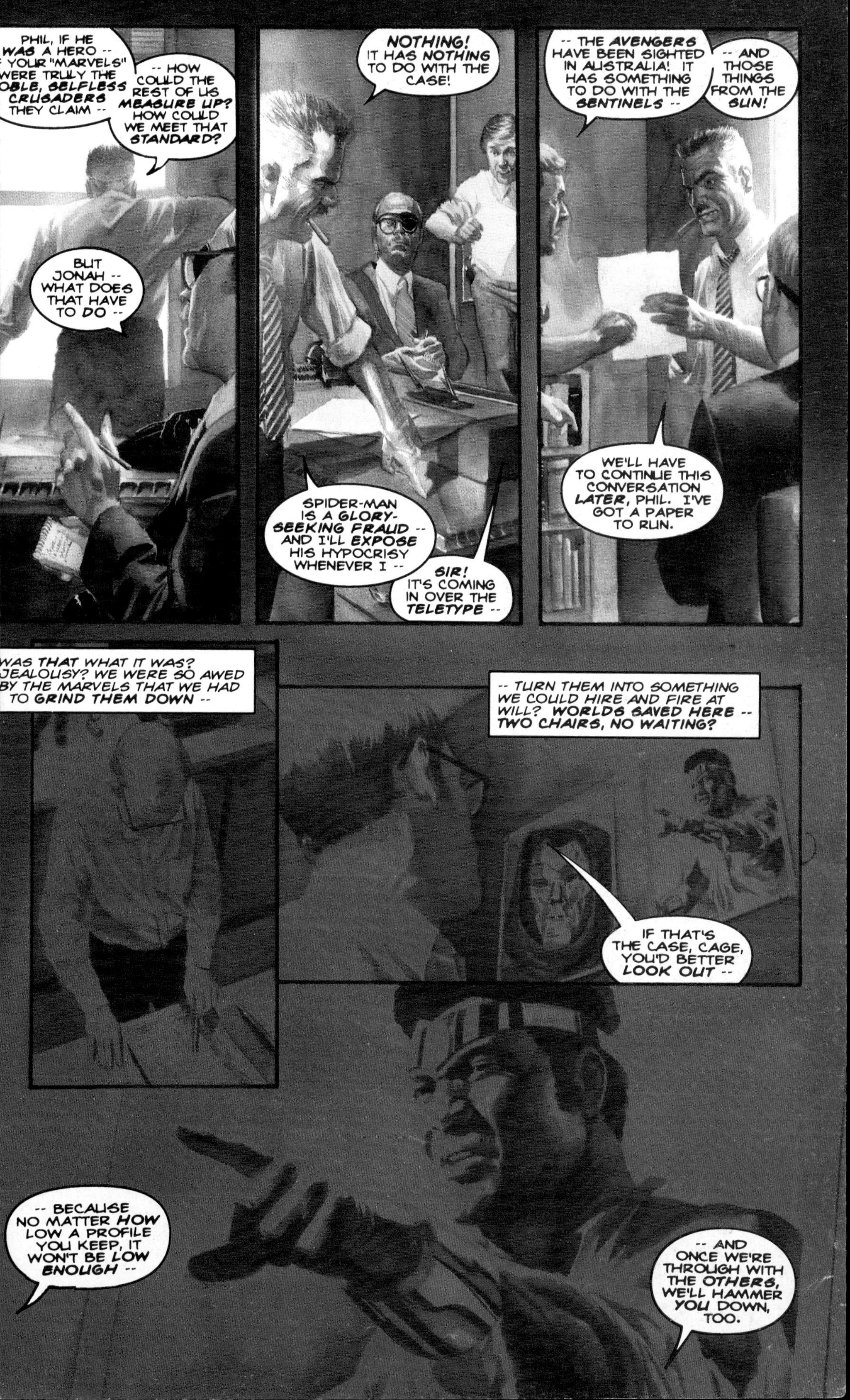
PHIL, IF HE WAS A HERO -- IF YOUR "MARVELS" WERE TRULY THE NOBLE, SELFLESS CRUSADERS THEY CLAIM --
-- HOW COULD THE REST OF US MEASURE UP? HOW COULD WE MEET THAT STANDARD?
BUT JONAH -- WHAT DOES THAT HAVE TO DO --
NOTHING! IT HAS NOTHING TO DO WITH THE CASE!
SPIDER-MAN IS A GLORY-SEEKING FRAUD -- AND I'LL EXPOSE HIS HYPOCRISY WHENEVER I --
SIR! IT'S COMING IN OVER THE TELETYPE --
-- THE AVENGERS HAVE BEEN SIGHTED IN AUSTRALIA! IT HAS SOMETHING TO DO WITH THE SENTINELS --
-- AND THOSE THINGS FROM THE SUN!
WE'LL HAVE TO CONTINUE THIS CONVERSATION LATER, PHIL. I'VE GOT A PAPER TO RUN.
WAS THAT WHAT IT WAS? JEALOUSY? WE WERE SO AWED BY THE MARVELS THAT WE HAD TO GRIND THEM DOWN --
-- TURN THEM INTO SOMETHING WE COULD HIRE AND FIRE AT WILL? WORLDS SAVED HERE -- TWO CHAIRS, NO WAITING?
IF THAT'S THE CASE, CAGE, YOU'D BETTER LOOK OUT --
-- BECAUSE NO MATTER HOW LOW A PROFILE YOU KEEP, IT WON'T BE LOW ENOUGH --
-- AND ONCE WE'RE THROUGH WITH THE OTHERS, WE'LL HAMMER YOU DOWN, TOO.

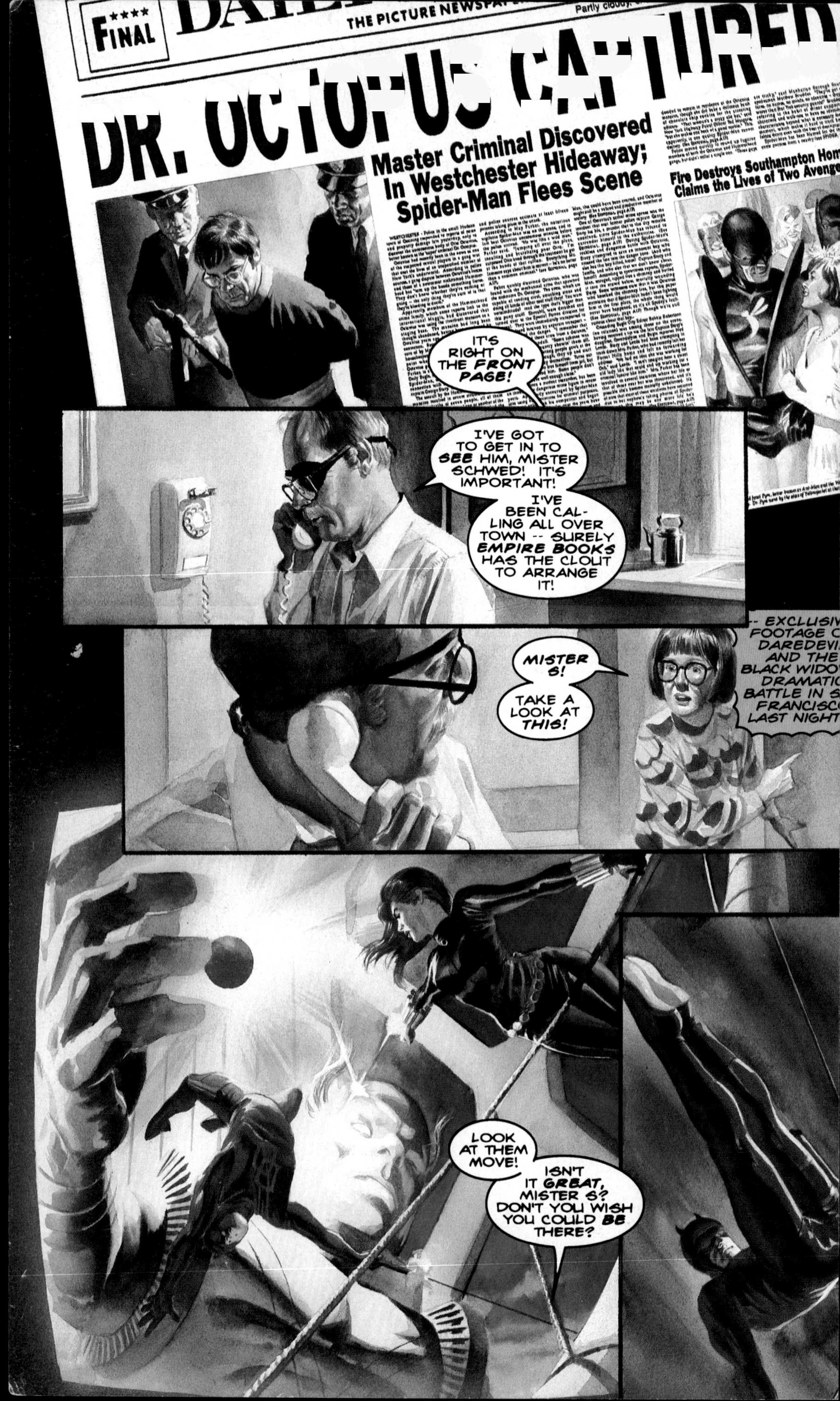
FINAL
THE PICTURE NEWSPA
Partly cloudy
Master Criminal Discovered In Westchester Hideaway; Spider-Man Flees Scene
Fire Destroys Southampton Hom
Claims the Lives of Two Avenge
IT'S RIGHT ON THE FRONT PAGE!
I'VE GOT TO GET IN TO SEE HIM, MISTER SCHWED! IT'S IMPORTANT!
I'VE BEEN CAL-LING ALL OVER TOWN -- SURELY EMPIRE BOOKS HAS THE CLOUT TO ARRANGE IT!
MISTER S!
TAKE A LOOK AT THIS!
-- EXCLUSIV FOOTAGE O DAREDEVI AND THE BLACK WIDO DRAMATI BATTLE IN S FRANCISC LAST NIGHT
LOOK AT THEM MOVE!
ISN'T IT GREAT, MISTER S? DON'T YOU WISH YOU COULD BE THERE?

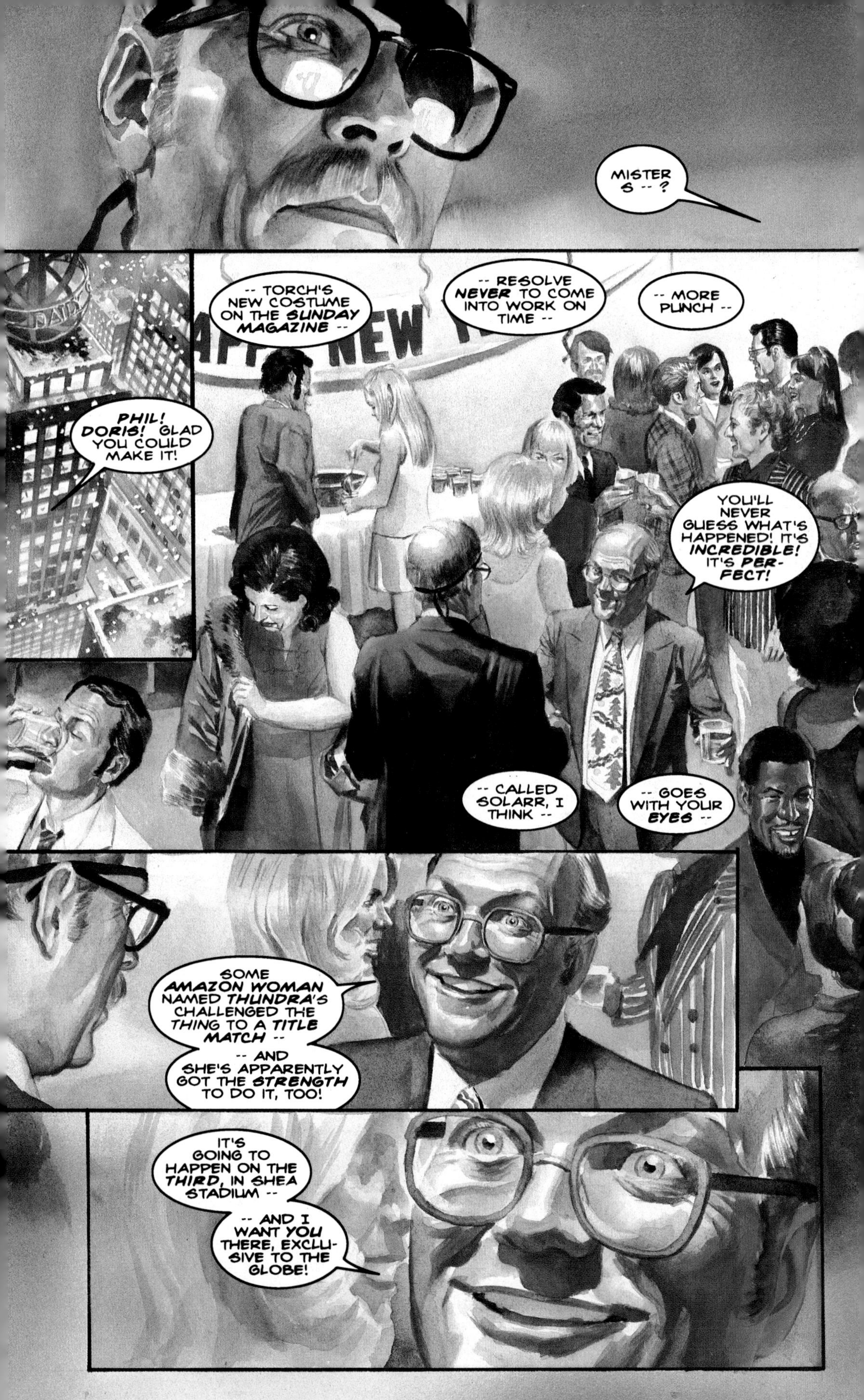

MISTER S -- ?
-- TORCH'S NEW COSTUME ON THE SUNDAY MAGAZINE --
-- RESOLVE NEVER TO COME INTO WORK ON TIME --
-- MORE PUNCH --
PHIL! DORIS! GLAD YOU COULD MAKE IT!
YOU'LL NEVER GUESS WHAT'S HAPPENED! IT'S INCREDIBLE! IT'S PER-FECT!
-- CALLED SOLARR, I THINK --
-- GOES WITH YOUR EYES --
SOME AMAZON WOMAN NAMED THUNDRA'S CHALLENGED THE THING TO A TITLE MATCH --
-- AND SHE'S APPARENTLY GOT THE STRENGTH TO DO IT, TOO!
IT'S GOING TO HAPPEN ON THE THIRD, IN SHEA STADIUM --
-- AND I WANT YOU THERE, EXCLU-SIVE TO THE GLOBE!

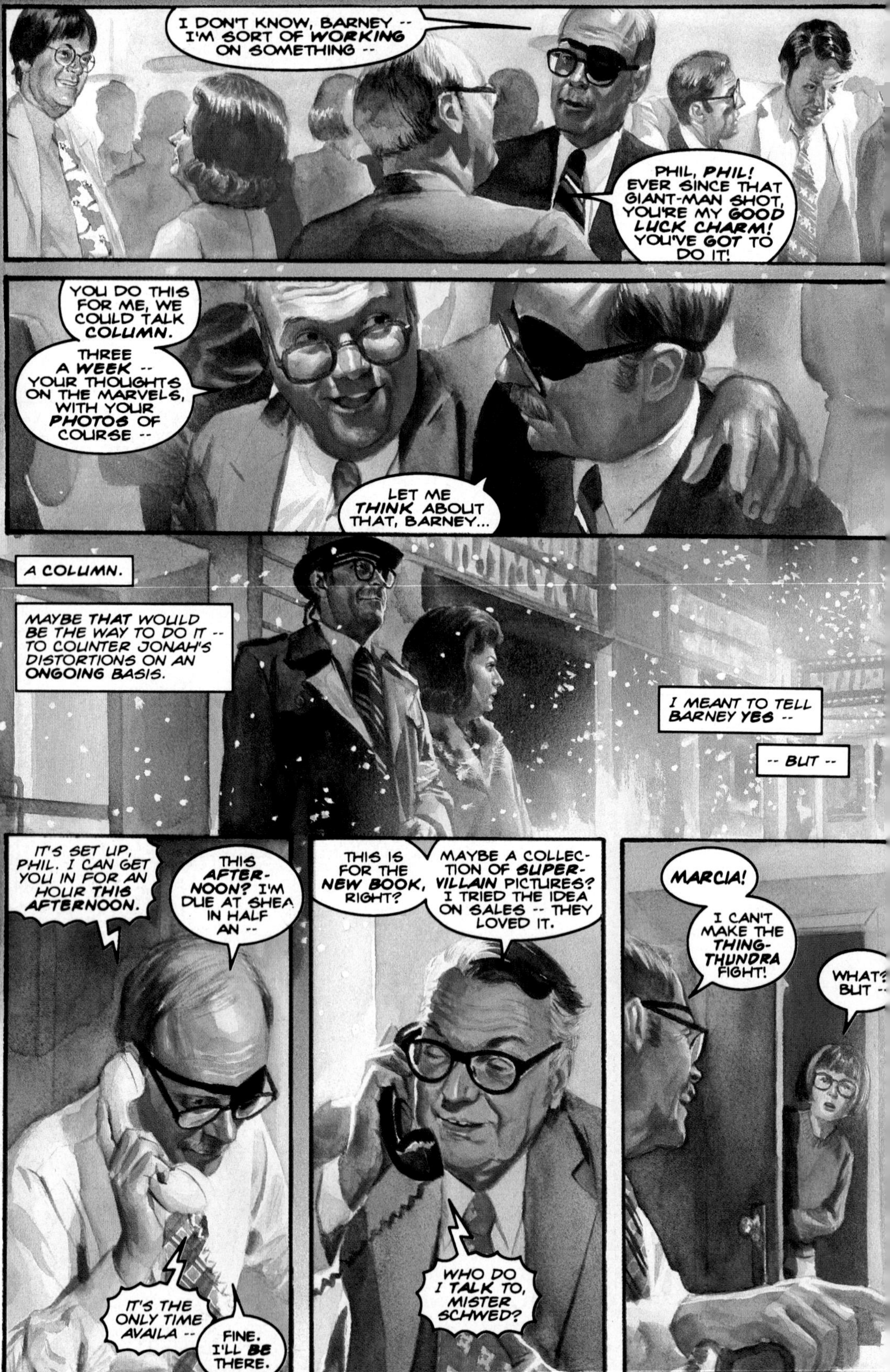
I DON'T KNOW, BARNEY -- I'M SORT OF WORKING ON SOMETHING --
PHIL, PHIL! EVER SINCE THAT GIANT-MAN SHOT, YOU'RE MY GOOD LUCK CHARM! YOU'VE GOT TO DO IT!
YOU DO THIS FOR ME, WE COULD TALK COLUMN.
THREE A WEEK -- YOUR THOUGHTS ON THE MARVELS, WITH YOUR PHOTOS OF COURSE --
LET ME THINK ABOUT THAT, BARNEY...
A COLUMN.
MAYBE THAT WOULD BE THE WAY TO DO IT -- TO COUNTER JONAH'S DISTORTIONS ON AN ONGOING BASIS.
I MEANT TO TELL BARNEY YES --
-- BUT --
IT'S SET UP, PHIL. I CAN GET YOU IN FOR AN HOUR THIS AFTERNOON.
THIS AFTERNOON? I'M DUE AT SHEA IN HALF AN --
IT'S THE ONLY TIME AVAILA --
FINE. I'LL BE THERE.
THIS IS FOR THE NEW BOOK, RIGHT?
MAYBE A COLLECTION OF SUPER-VILLAIN PICTURES? I TRIED THE IDEA ON SALES -- THEY LOVED IT.
WHO DO I TALK TO, MISTER SCHWED?
MARCIA!
I CAN'T MAKE THE THING-THUNDRA FIGHT!
WHAT? BUT --

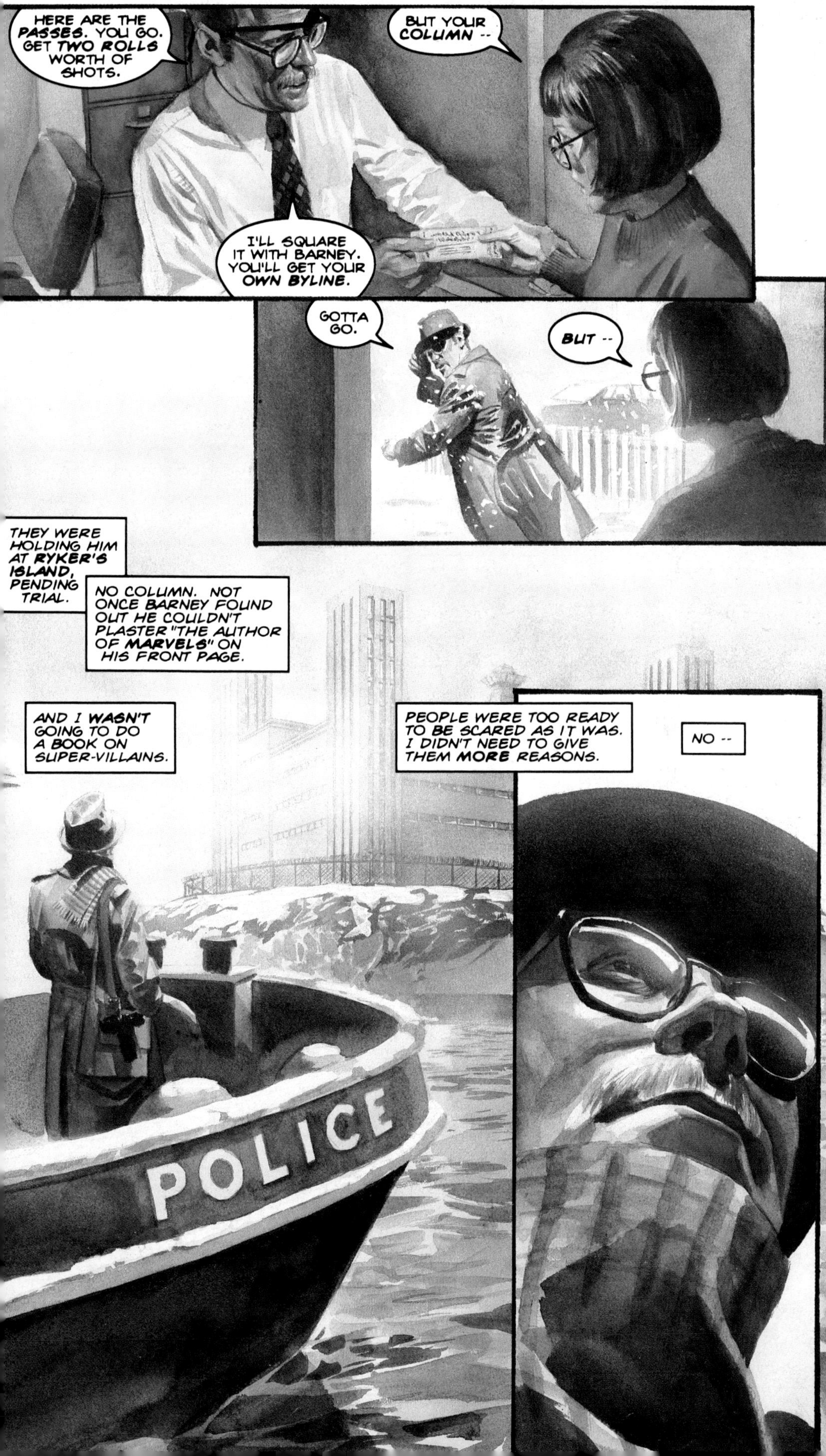
HERE ARE THE PASSES. YOU GO. GET TWO ROLLS WORTH OF SHOTS.
BUT YOUR COLUMN --
I'LL SQUARE IT WITH BARNEY. YOU'LL GET YOUR OWN BYLINE.
GOTTA GO.
BUT --
THEY WERE HOLDING HIM AT RYKER'S ISLAND, PENDING TRIAL.
NO COLUMN. NOT ONCE BARNEY FOUND OUT HE COULDN'T PLASTER "THE AUTHOR OF MARVELS" ON HIS FRONT PAGE.
AND I WASN'T GOING TO DO A BOOK ON SUPER-VILLAINS.
PEOPLE WERE TOO READY TO BE SCARED AS IT WAS. I DIDN'T NEED TO GIVE THEM MORE REASONS.
NO --
POLICE

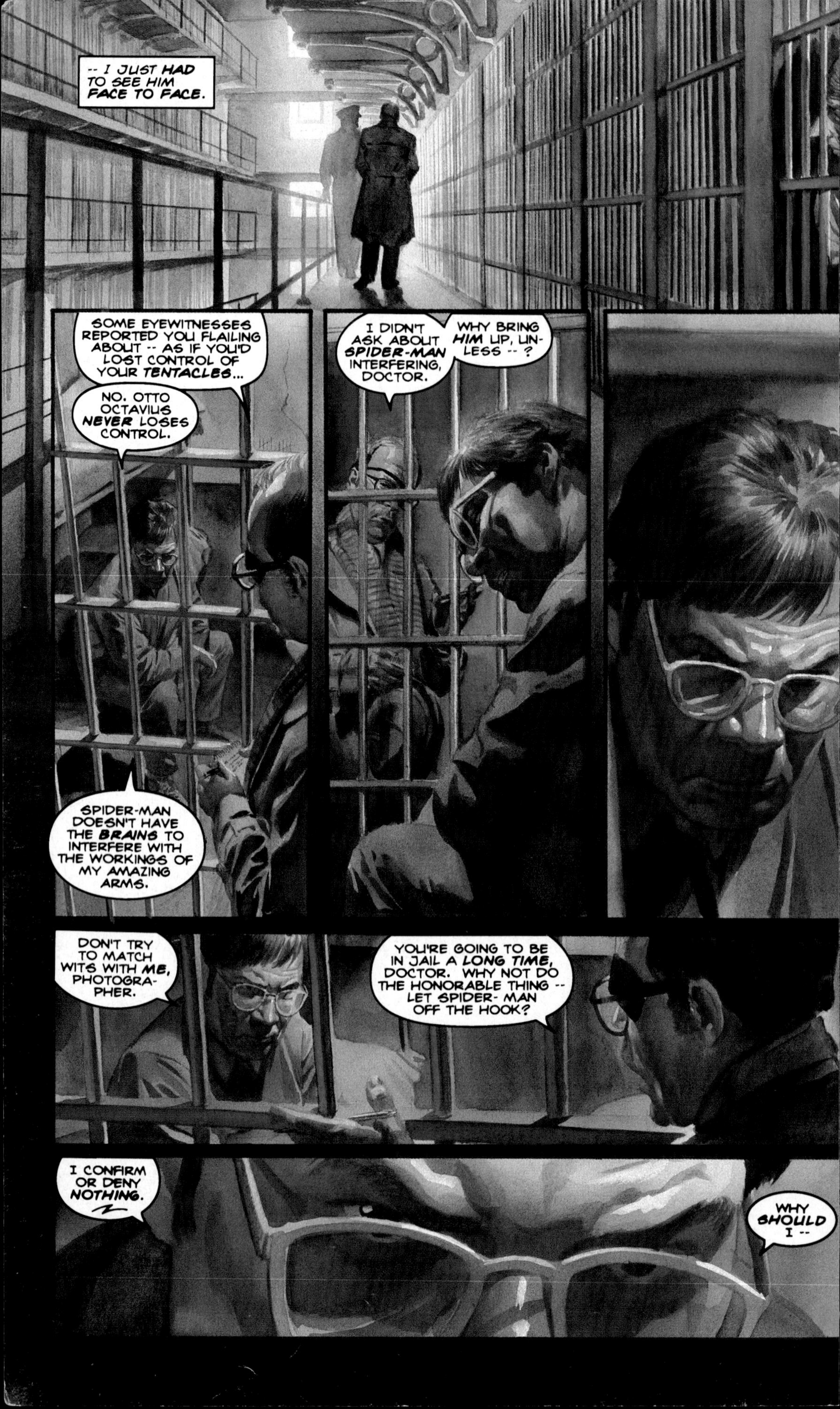
-- I JUST HAD TO SEE HIM FACE TO FACE.
SOME EYEWITNESSES REPORTED YOU FLAILING ABOUT -- AS IF YOU'D LOST CONTROL OF YOUR TENTACLES...
NO. OTTO OCTAVIUS NEVER LOSES CONTROL.
SPIDER-MAN DOESN'T HAVE THE BRAINS TO INTERFERE WITH THE WORKINGS OF MY AMAZING ARMS.
I DIDN'T ASK ABOUT SPIDER-MAN INTERFERING, DOCTOR.
WHY BRING HIM UP, UNLESS -- ?
DON'T TRY TO MATCH WITS WITH ME, PHOTOGRAPHER.
YOU'RE GOING TO BE IN JAIL A LONG TIME, DOCTOR. WHY NOT DO THE HONORABLE THING -- LET SPIDER-MAN OFF THE HOOK?
I CONFIRM OR DENY NOTHING.
WHY SHOULD I --

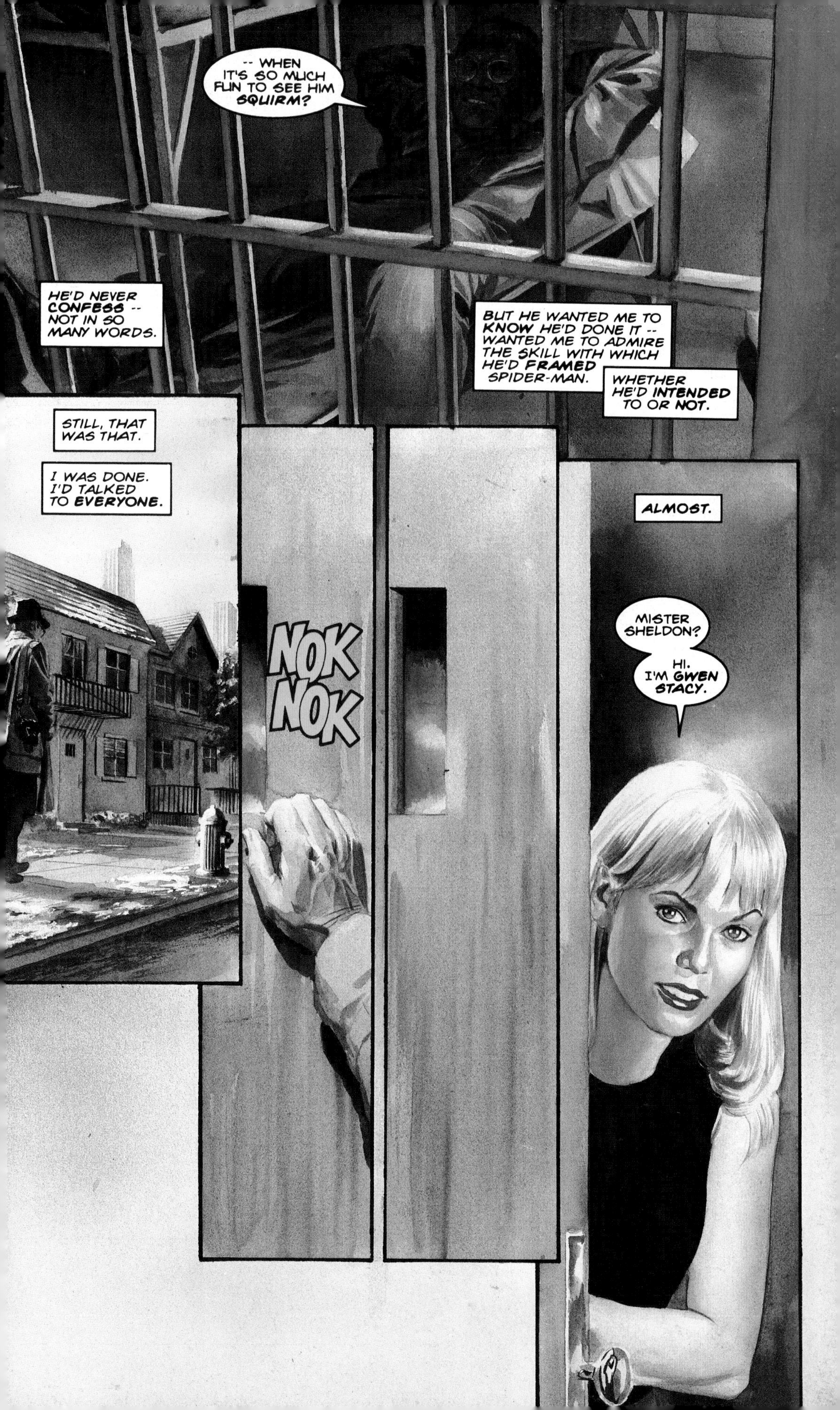
-- WHEN IT'S SO MUCH FUN TO SEE HIM SQUIRM?
HE'D NEVER CONFESS -- NOT IN SO MANY WORDS.
BUT HE WANTED ME TO KNOW HE'D DONE IT -- WANTED ME TO ADMIRE THE SKILL WITH WHICH HE'D FRAMED SPIDER-MAN.
WHETHER HE'D INTENDED TO OR NOT.
STILL, THAT WAS THAT.
I WAS DONE. I'D TALKED TO EVERYONE.
NOK NOK
ALMOST.
MISTER SHELDON?
HI. I'M GWEN STACY.

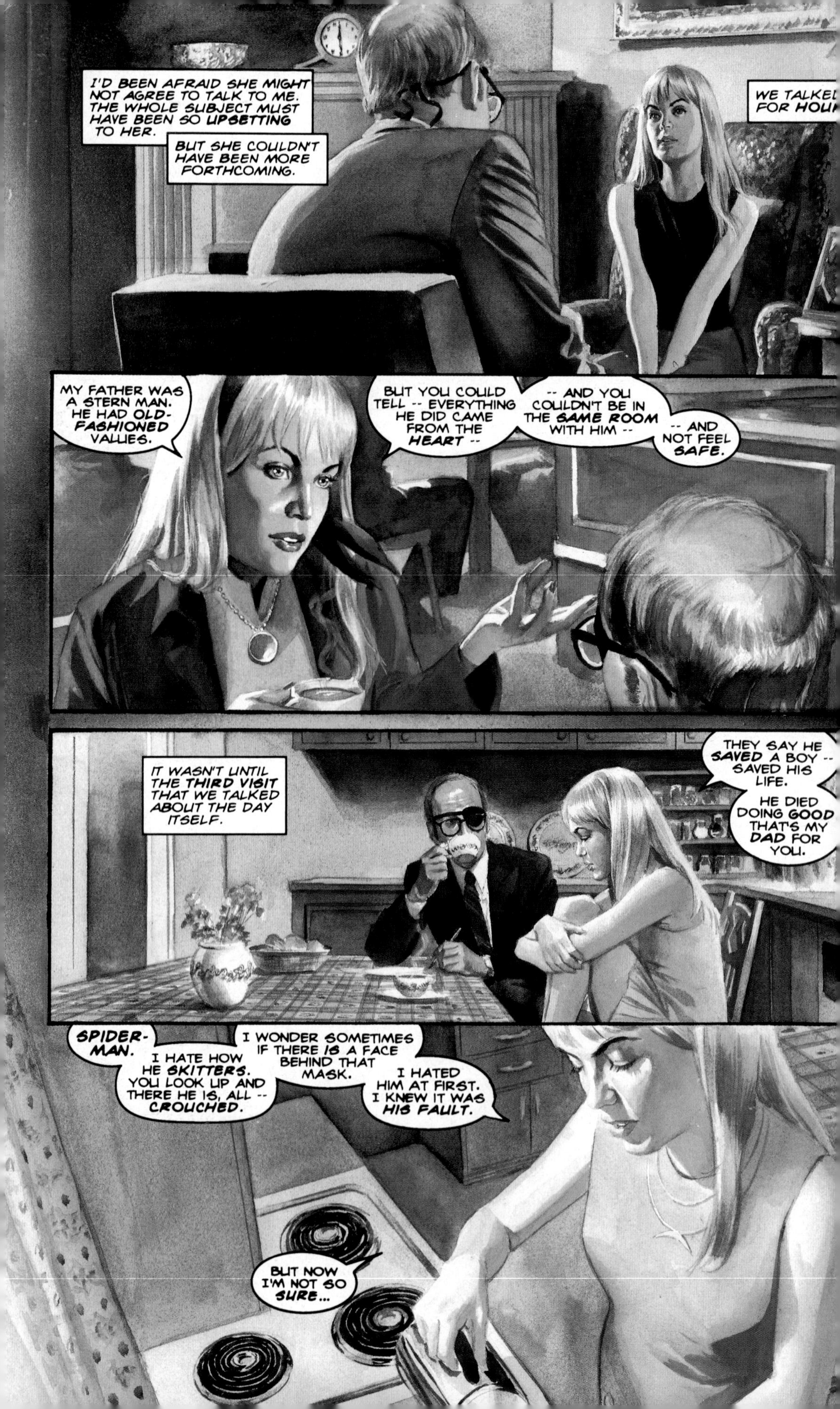
I'D BEEN AFRAID SHE MIGHT NOT AGREE TO TALK TO ME. THE WHOLE SUBJECT MUST HAVE BEEN SO UPSETTING TO HER.
BUT SHE COULDN'T HAVE BEEN MORE FORTHCOMING.
WE TALKED FOR HOU
MY FATHER WAS A STERN MAN. HE HAD OLD-FASHIONED VALUES.
BUT YOU COULD TELL -- EVERYTHING HE DID CAME FROM THE HEART --
-- AND YOU COULDN'T BE IN THE SAME ROOM WITH HIM --
-- AND NOT FEEL SAFE.
IT WASN'T UNTIL THE THIRD VISIT THAT WE TALKED ABOUT THE DAY ITSELF.
THEY SAY HE SAVED A BOY -- SAVED HIS LIFE.
HE DIED DOING GOOD THAT'S MY DAD FOR YOU.
SPIDER-MAN.
I HATE HOW HE SKITTERS. YOU LOOK UP AND THERE HE IS, ALL -- CROUCHED.
I WONDER SOMETIMES IF THERE IS A FACE BEHIND THAT MASK.
I HATED HIM AT FIRST. I KNEW IT WAS HIS FAULT.
BUT NOW I'M NOT SO SURE...

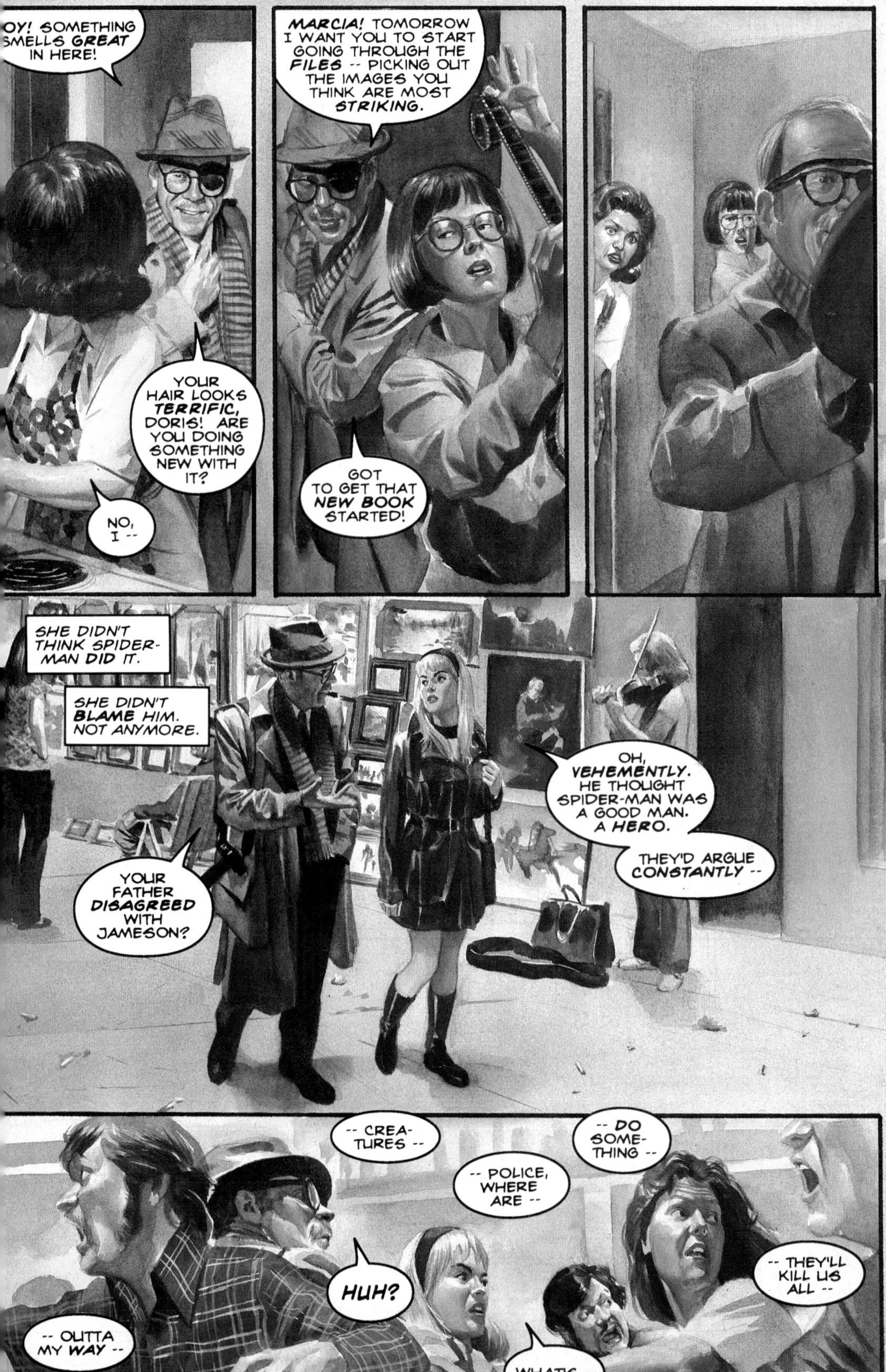
OY! SOMETHING SMELLS GREAT IN HERE!
YOUR HAIR LOOKS TERRIFIC, DORIS! ARE YOU DOING SOMETHING NEW WITH IT?
NO, I --
MARCIA! TOMORROW I WANT YOU TO START GOING THROUGH THE FILES -- PICKING OUT THE IMAGES YOU THINK ARE MOST STRIKING.
GOT TO GET THAT NEW BOOK STARTED!
SHE DIDN'T THINK SPIDER-MAN DID IT.
SHE DIDN'T BLAME HIM. NOT ANYMORE.
YOUR FATHER DISAGREED WITH JAMESON?
OH, VEHEMENTLY. HE THOUGHT SPIDER-MAN WAS A GOOD MAN. A HERO.
THEY'D ARGUE CONSTANTLY --
-- CREATURES --
-- DO SOMETHING --
-- POLICE, WHERE ARE --
HUH?
-- THEY'LL KILL US ALL --
-- OUTTA MY WAY --
WHAT'S --

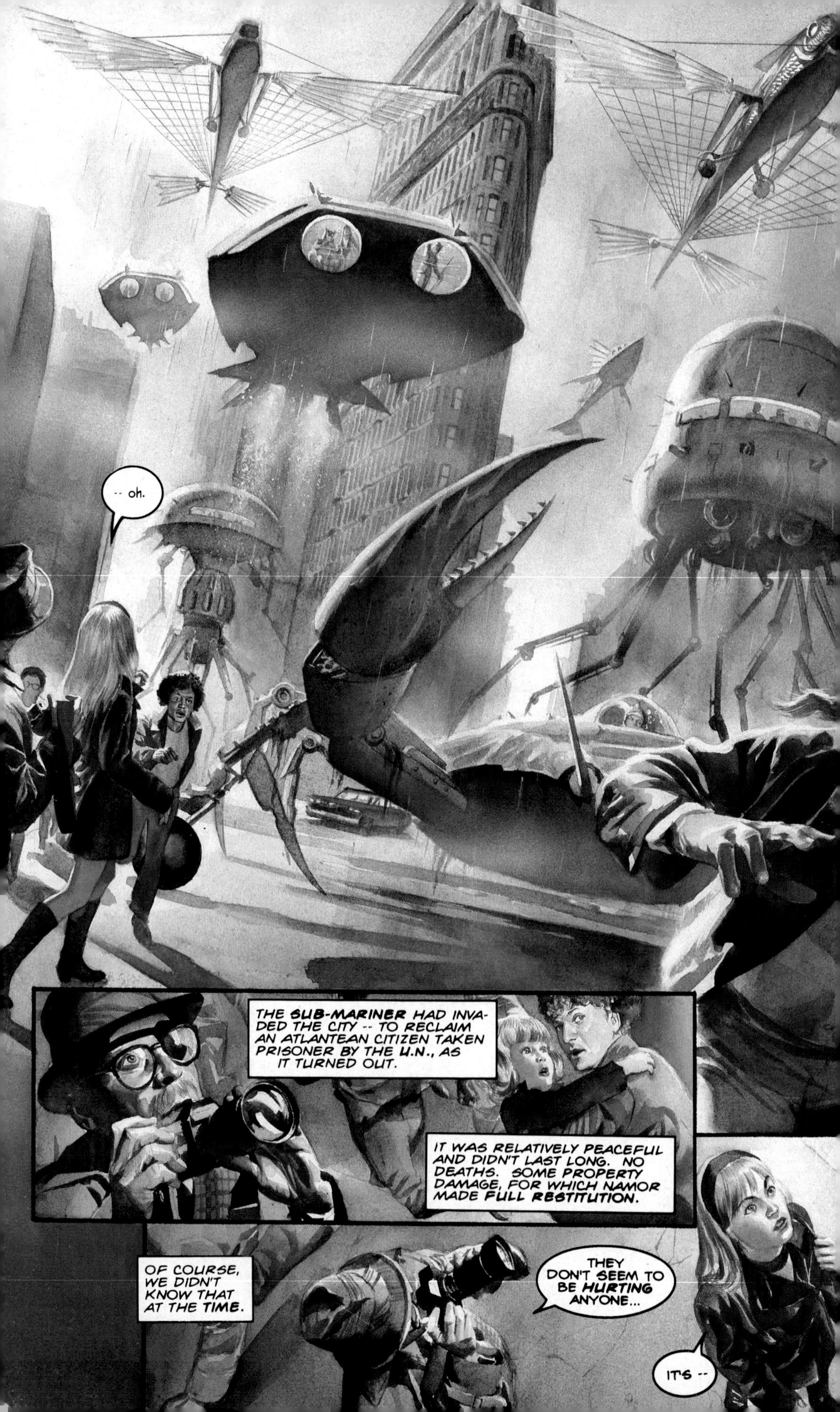
-- oh.
THE SUB-MARINER HAD INVADED THE CITY -- TO RECLAIM AN ATLANTEAN CITIZEN TAKEN PRISONER BY THE U.N., AS IT TURNED OUT.
IT WAS RELATIVELY PEACEFUL AND DIDN'T LAST LONG. NO DEATHS. SOME PROPERTY DAMAGE, FOR WHICH NAMOR MADE FULL RESTITUTION.
OF COURSE, WE DIDN'T KNOW THAT AT THE TIME.
THEY DON'T SEEM TO BE HURTING ANYONE...
IT'S --

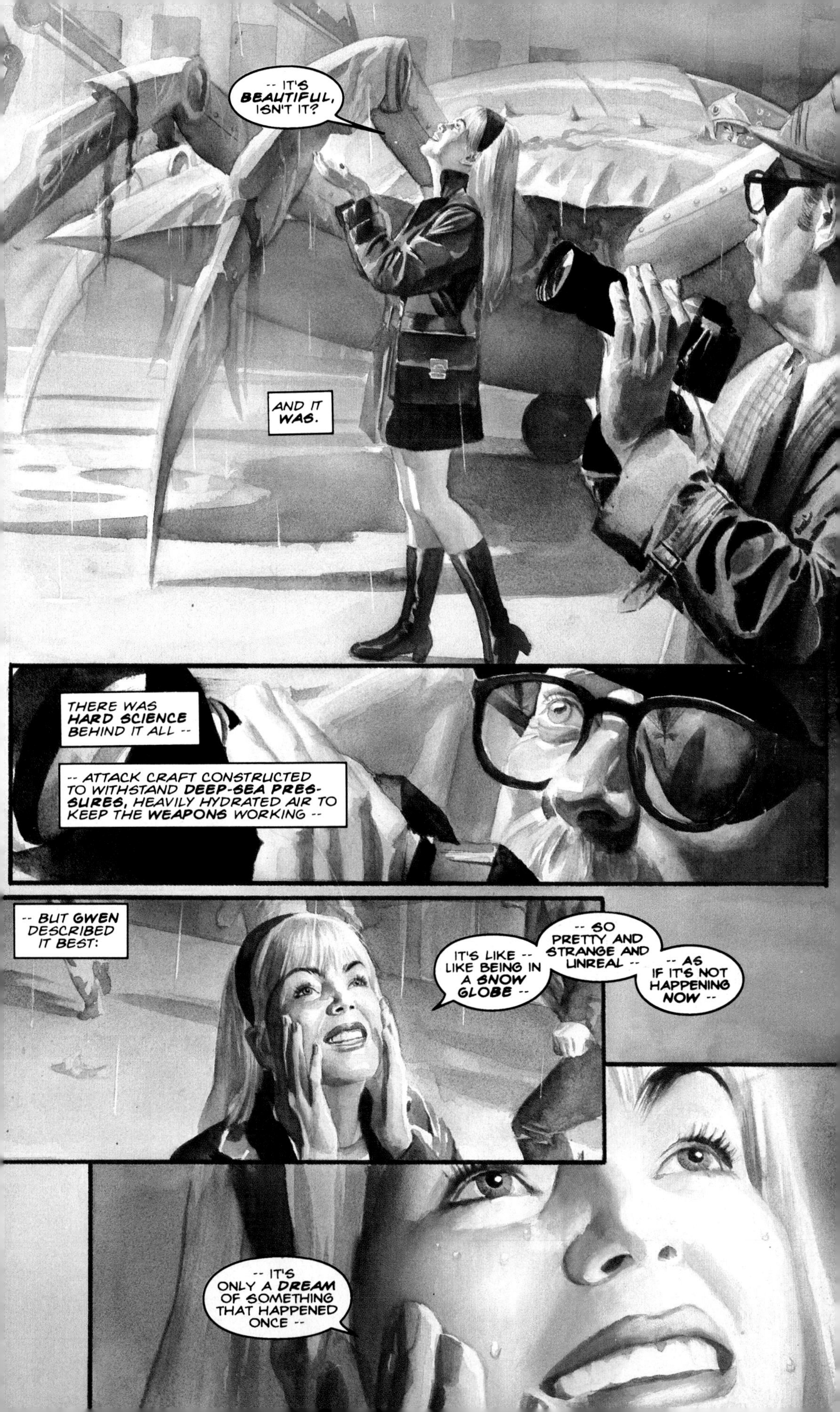
-- IT'S BEAUTIFUL, ISN'T IT?
AND IT WAS.
THERE WAS HARD SCIENCE BEHIND IT ALL --
-- ATTACK CRAFT CONSTRUCTED TO WITHSTAND DEEP-SEA PRES-SURES, HEAVILY HYDRATED AIR TO KEEP THE WEAPONS WORKING --
-- BUT GWEN DESCRIBED IT BEST:
IT'S LIKE -- LIKE BEING IN A SNOW GLOBE --
-- SO PRETTY AND STRANGE AND UNREAL --
-- AS IF IT'S NOT HAPPENING NOW --
-- IT'S ONLY A DREAM OF SOMETHING THAT HAPPENED ONCE --

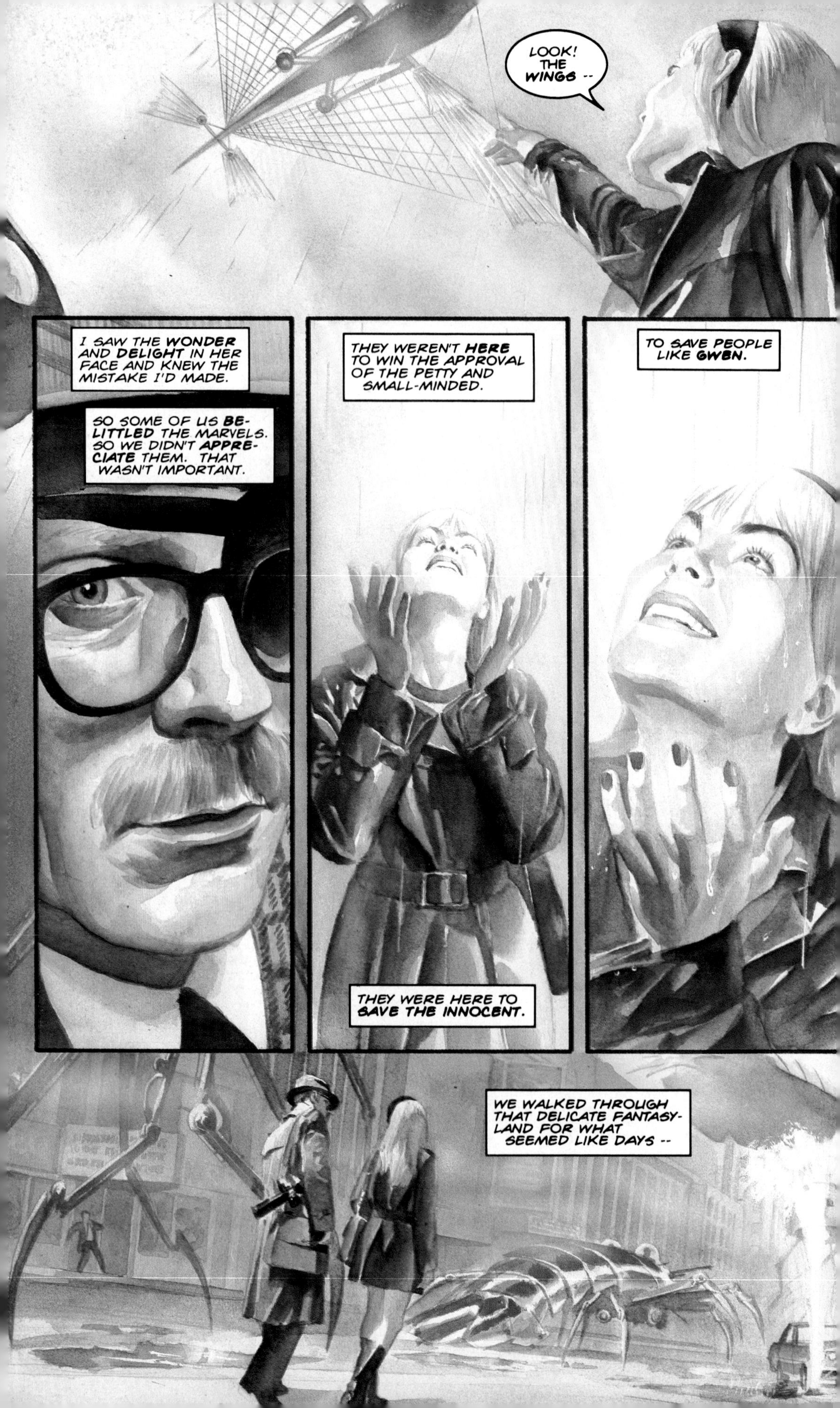
LOOK! THE WINGS --
I SAW THE WONDER AND DELIGHT IN HER FACE AND KNEW THE MISTAKE I'D MADE.
SO SOME OF US BE-LITTLED THE MARVELS. SO WE DIDN'T APPRE-CIATE THEM. THAT WASN'T IMPORTANT.
THEY WEREN'T HERE TO WIN THE APPROVAL OF THE PETTY AND SMALL-MINDED.
THEY WERE HERE TO SAVE THE INNOCENT.
TO SAVE PEOPLE LIKE GWEN.
WE WALKED THROUGH THAT DELICATE FANTASY-LAND FOR WHAT SEEMED LIKE DAYS --

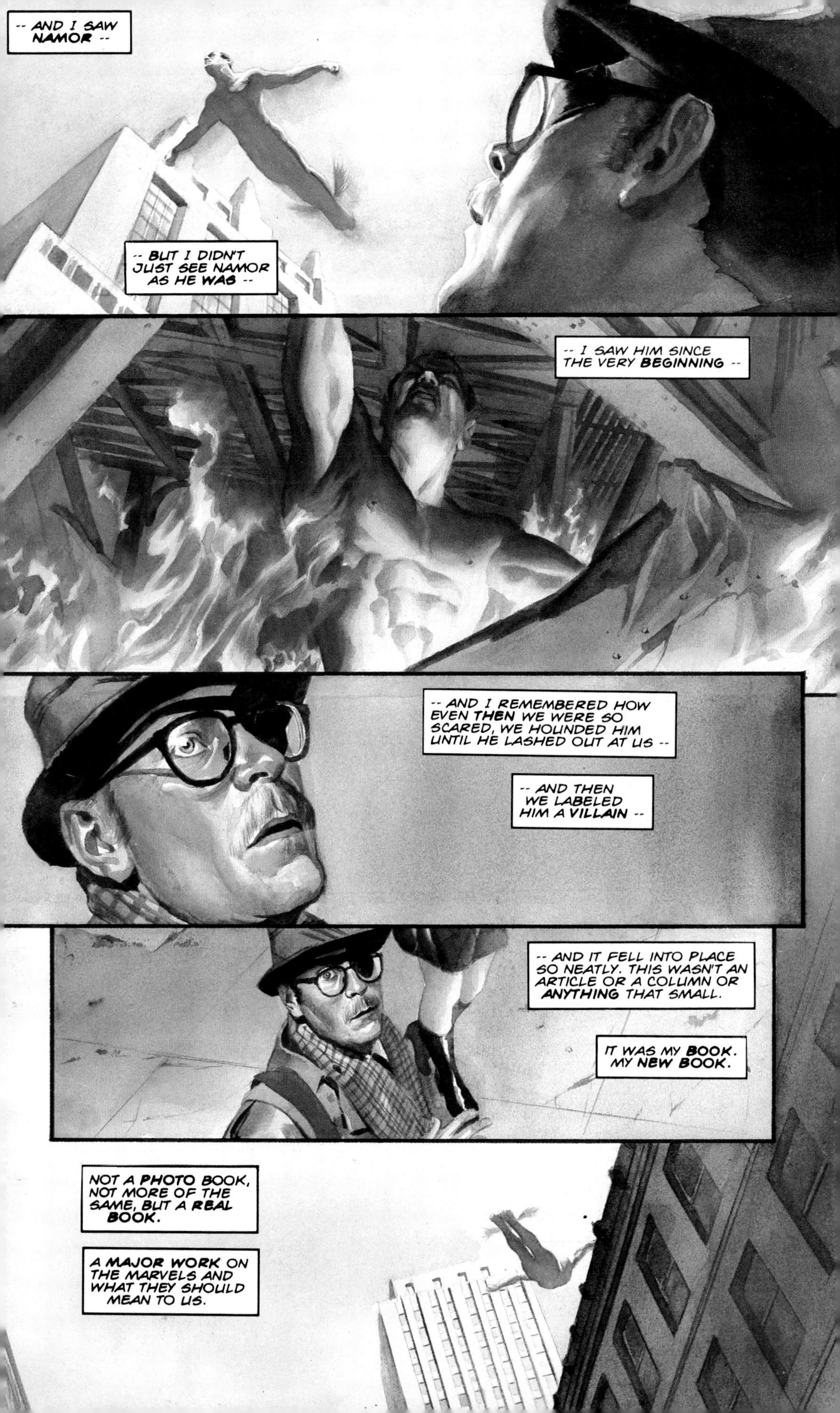

-- AND I SAW NAMOR --
-- BUT I DIDN'T JUST SEE NAMOR AS HE WAS --
-- I SAW HIM SINCE THE VERY BEGINNING --
-- AND I REMEMBERED HOW EVEN THEN WE WERE SO SCARED, WE HOUNDED HIM UNTIL HE LASHED OUT AT US --
-- AND THEN WE LABELED HIM A VILLAIN --
-- AND IT FELL INTO PLACE SO NEATLY. THIS WASN'T AN ARTICLE OR A COLUMN OR ANYTHING THAT SMALL.
IT WAS MY BOOK. MY NEW BOOK.
NOT A PHOTO BOOK, NOT MORE OF THE SAME, BUT A REAL BOOK.
A MAJOR WORK ON THE MARVELS AND WHAT THEY SHOULD MEAN TO US.

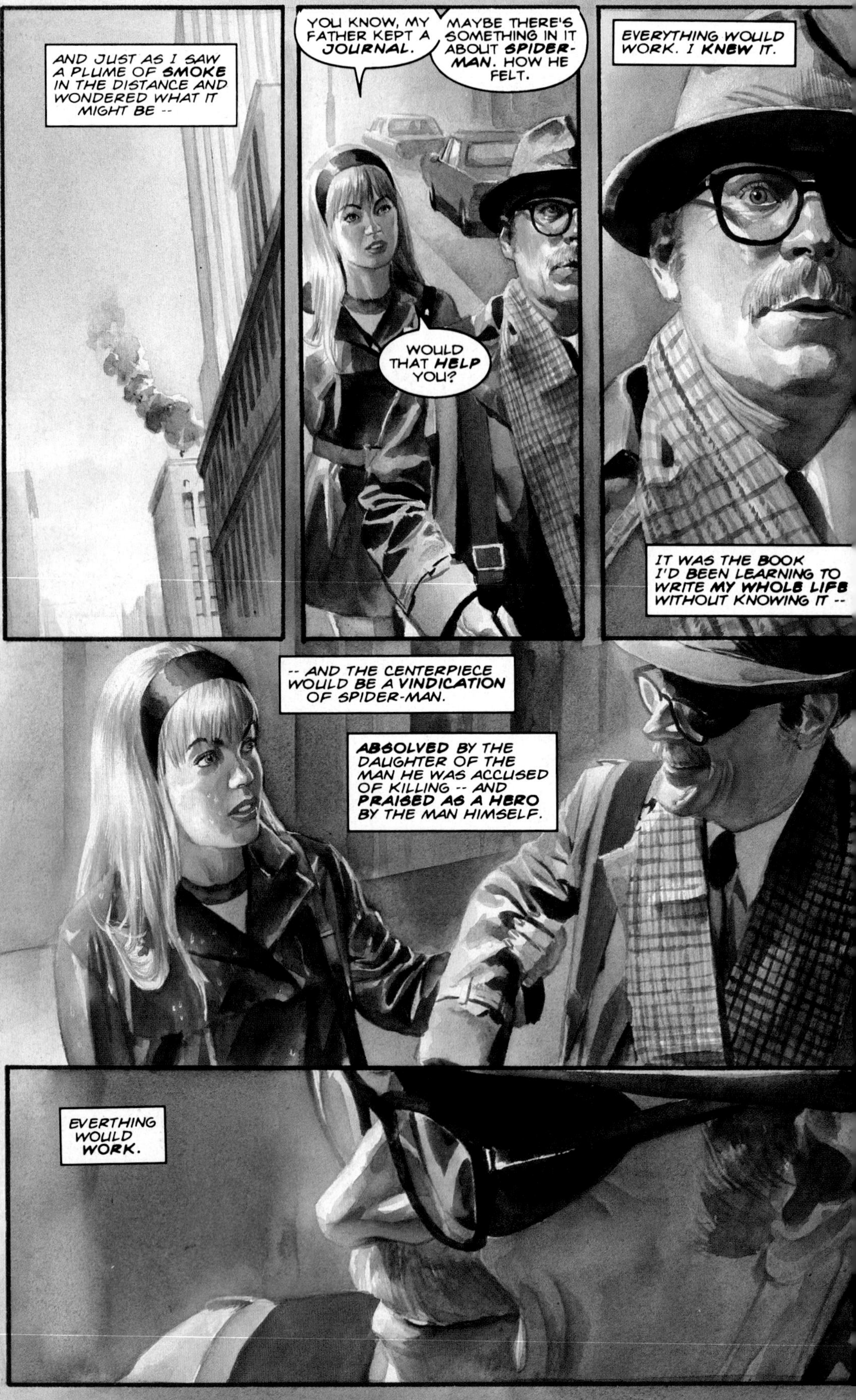
AND JUST AS I SAW A PLUME OF SMOKE IN THE DISTANCE AND WONDERED WHAT IT MIGHT BE --
YOU KNOW, MY FATHER KEPT A JOURNAL.
MAYBE THERE'S SOMETHING IN IT ABOUT SPIDER-MAN. HOW HE FELT.
WOULD THAT HELP YOU?
EVERYTHING WOULD WORK. I KNEW IT.
IT WAS THE BOOK I'D BEEN LEARNING TO WRITE MY WHOLE LIFE WITHOUT KNOWING IT --
-- AND THE CENTERPIECE WOULD BE A VINDICATION OF SPIDER-MAN.
ABSOLVED BY THE DAUGHTER OF THE MAN HE WAS ACCUSED OF KILLING -- AND PRAISED AS A HERO BY THE MAN HIMSELF.
EVERTHING WOULD WORK.

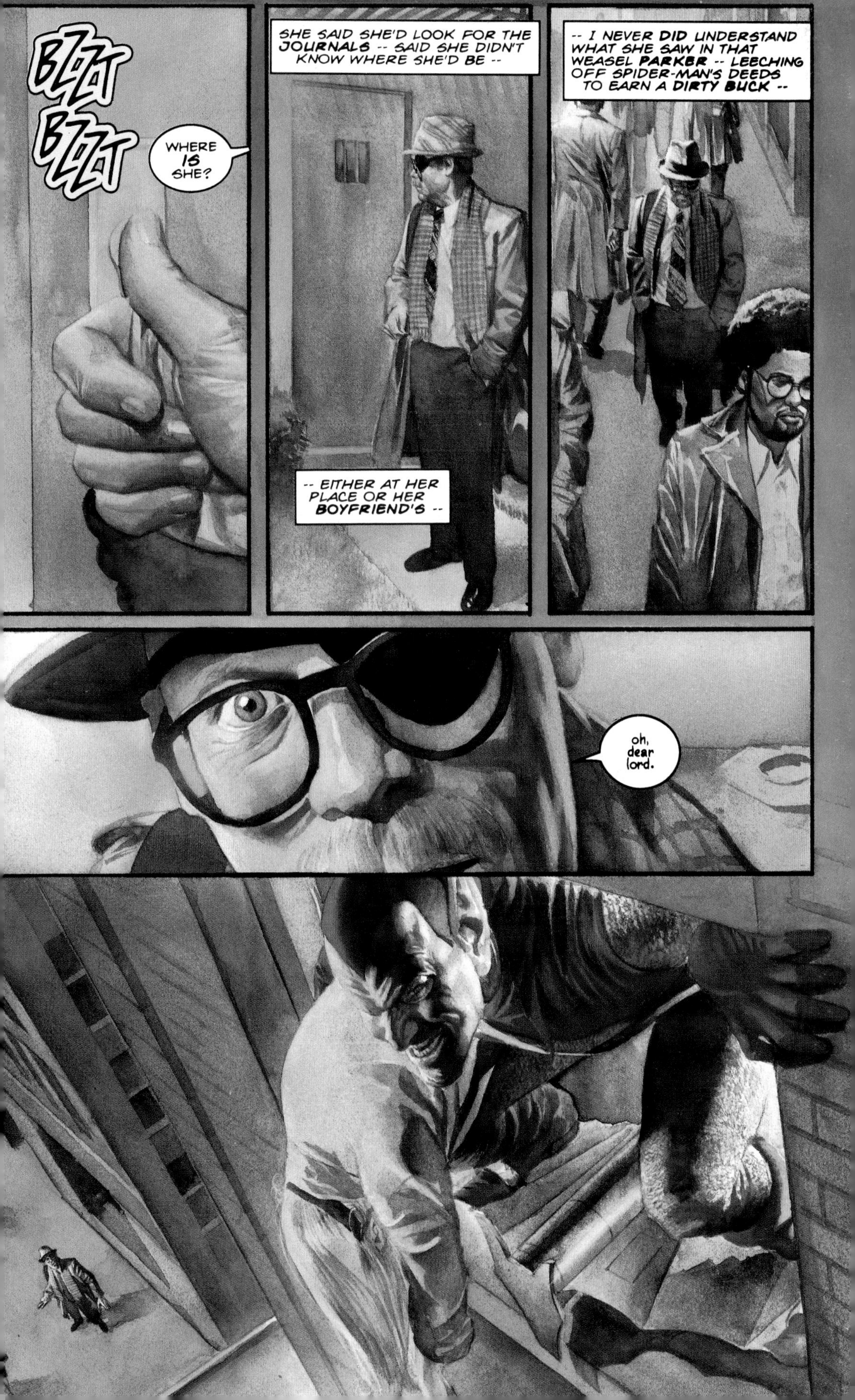

BZZZT
BZZZT
WHERE IS SHE?
SHE SAID SHE'D LOOK FOR THE JOURNALS -- SAID SHE DIDN'T KNOW WHERE SHE'D BE --
-- EITHER AT HER PLACE OR HER BOYFRIEND'S --
-- I NEVER DID UNDERSTAND WHAT SHE SAW IN THAT WEASEL PARKER -- LEECHING OFF SPIDER-MAN'S DEEDS TO EARN A DIRTY BUCK --
oh, dear lord.

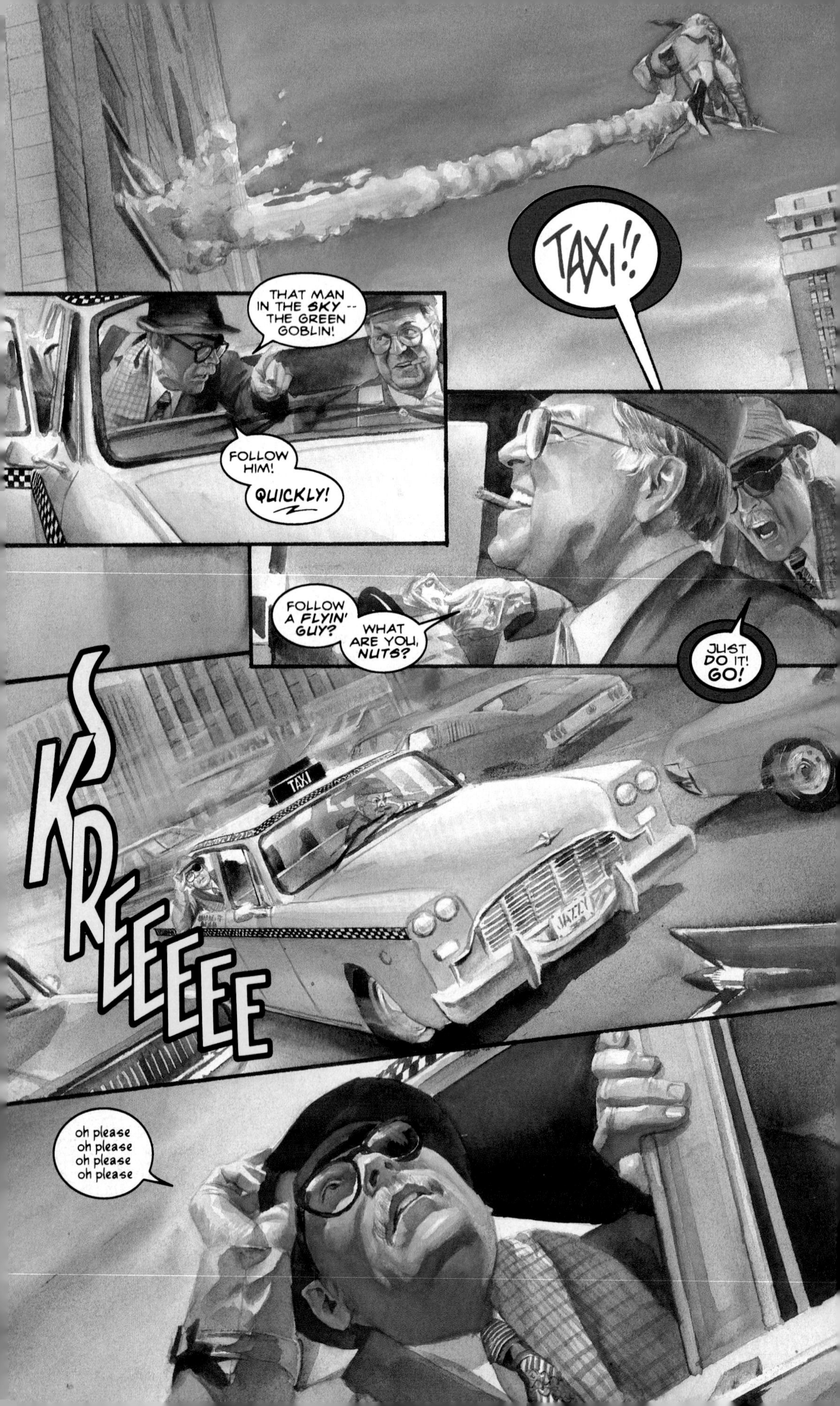
TAXI!!
THAT MAN IN THE SKY -- THE GREEN GOBLIN!
FOLLOW HIM!
QUICKLY!
FOLLOW A FLYIN' GUY?
WHAT ARE YOU, NUTS?
JUST DO IT! GO!
TAXI
JAZZY
SKREEEEE
oh please oh please oh please oh please

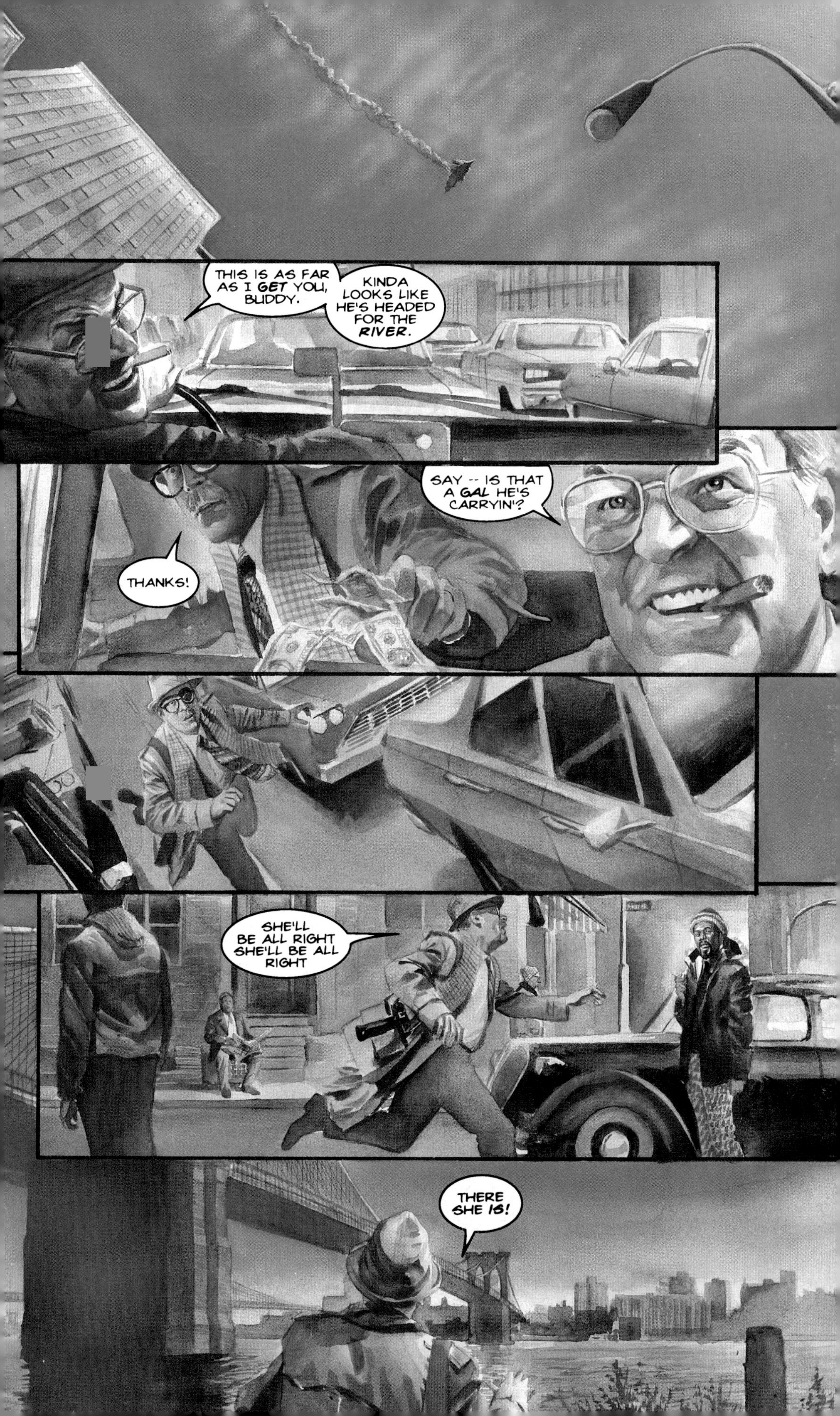

THIS IS AS FAR AS I GET YOU, BUDDY.
KINDA LOOKS LIKE HE'S HEADED FOR THE RIVER.
SAY -- IS THAT A GAL HE'S CARRYIN'?
THANKS!
SHE'LL BE ALL RIGHT SHE'LL BE ALL RIGHT
THERE SHE IS!

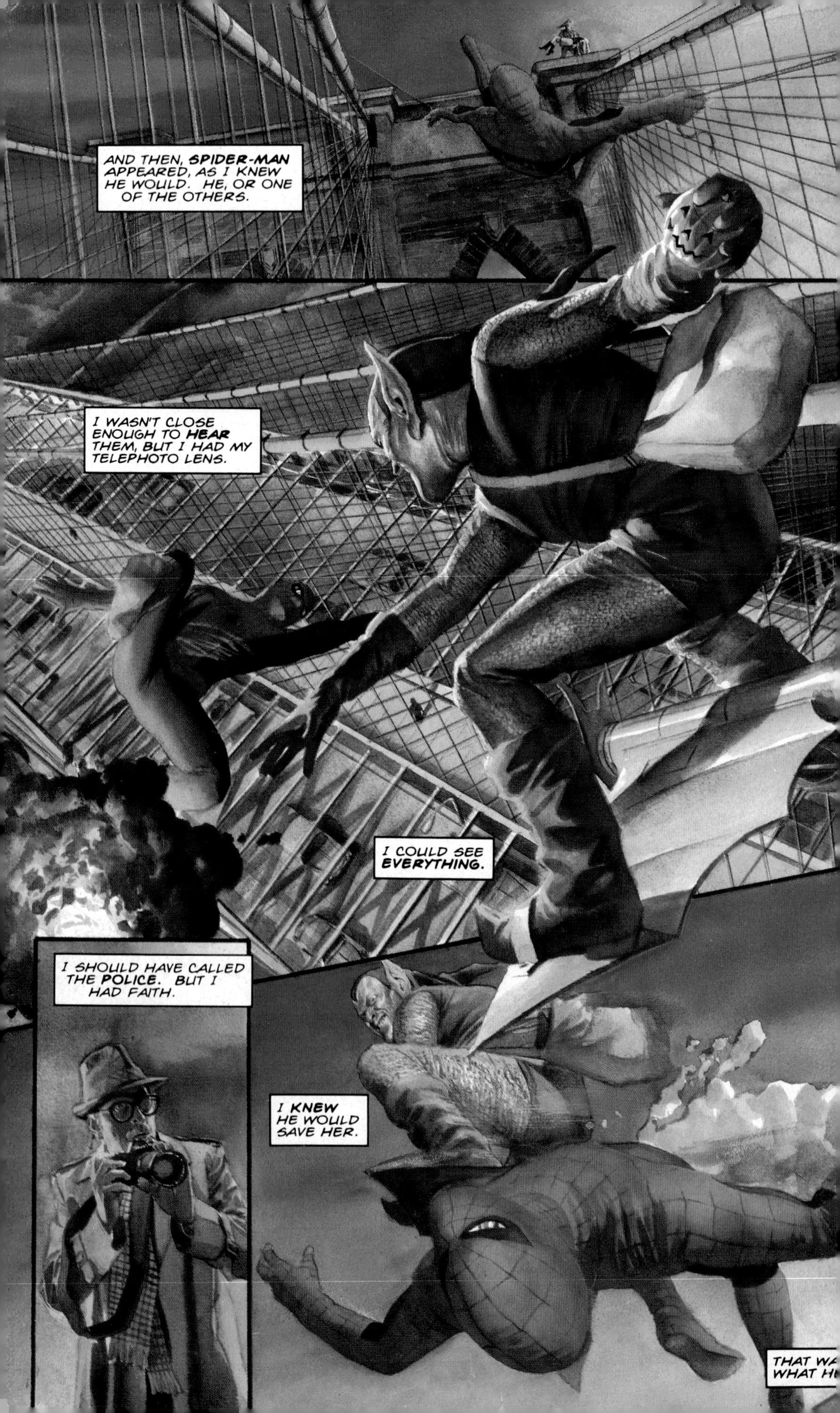
AND THEN, SPIDER-MAN APPEARED, AS I KNEW HE WOULD. HE, OR ONE OF THE OTHERS.
I WASN'T CLOSE ENOUGH TO HEAR THEM, BUT I HAD MY TELEPHOTO LENS.
I COULD SEE EVERYTHING.
I SHOULD HAVE CALLED THE POLICE. BUT I HAD FAITH.
I KNEW HE WOULD SAVE HER.

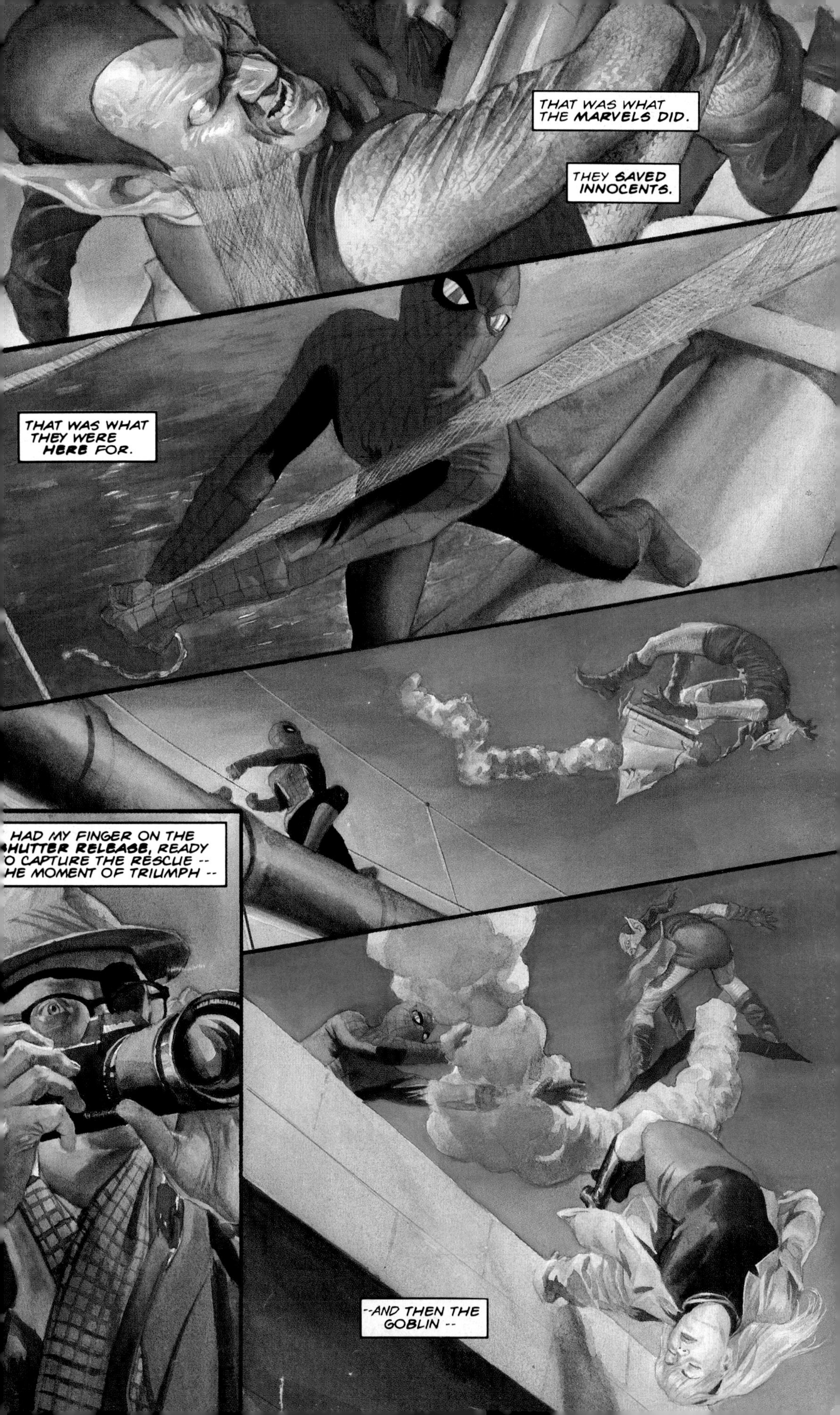
THAT WAS WHAT THE MARVELS DID.
THEY SAVED INNOCENTS.
THAT WAS WHAT THEY WERE HERE FOR.
HAD MY FINGER ON THE SHUTTER RELEASE, READY O CAPTURE THE RESCUE -- HE MOMENT OF TRIUMPH --
--AND THEN THE GOBLIN --

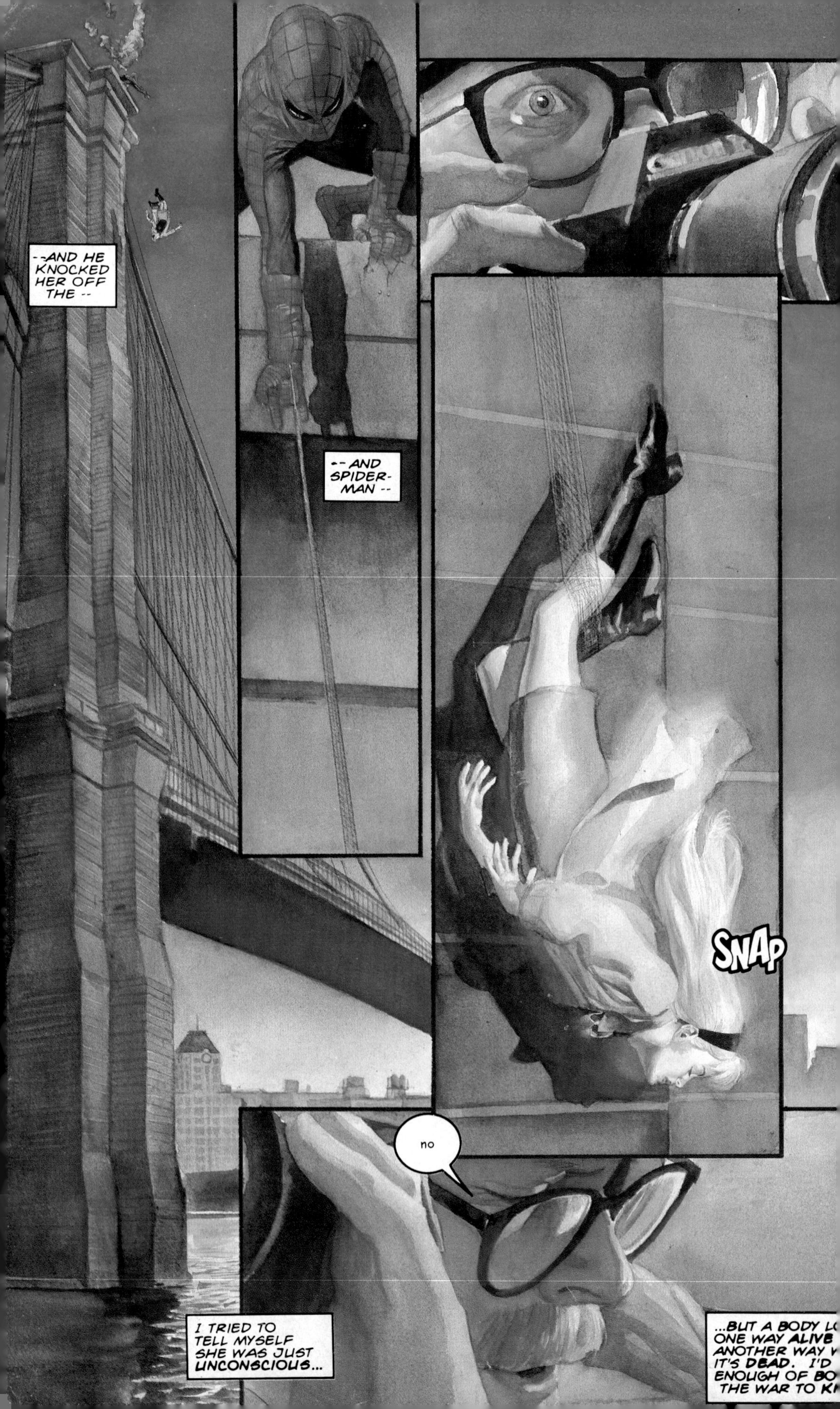
--AND HE KNOCKED HER OFF THE --
--AND SPIDER-MAN --
SNAP
no
I TRIED TO TELL MYSELF SHE WAS JUST UNCONSCIOUS...
...BUT A BODY L
ONE WAY ALIVE
ANOTHER WAY
IT'S DEAD. I'D
ENOUGH OF BO
THE WAR TO K

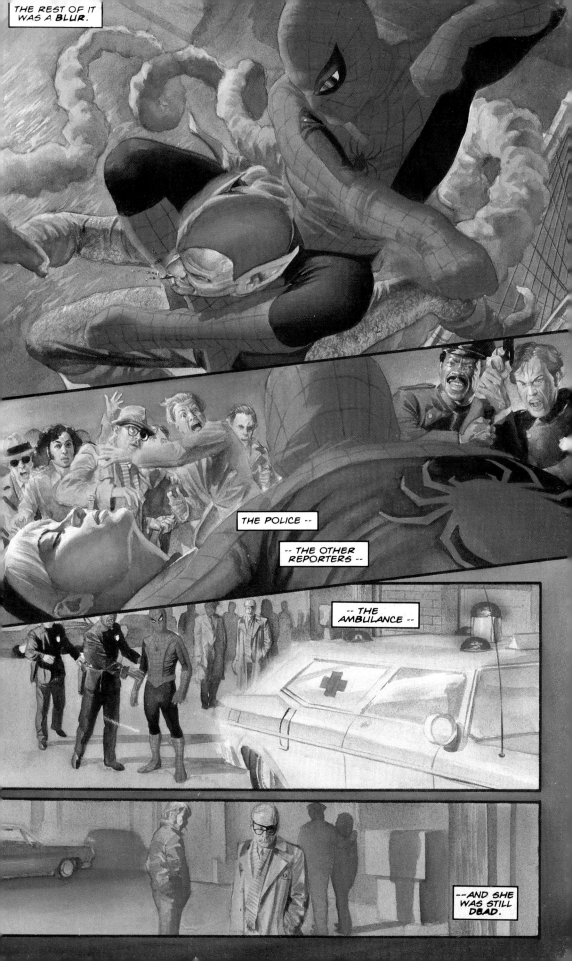

THE REST OF IT WAS A BLUR.

THE POLICE --

-- THE OTHER REPORTERS --

-- THE AMBULANCE --

--AND SHE WAS STILL DEAD.

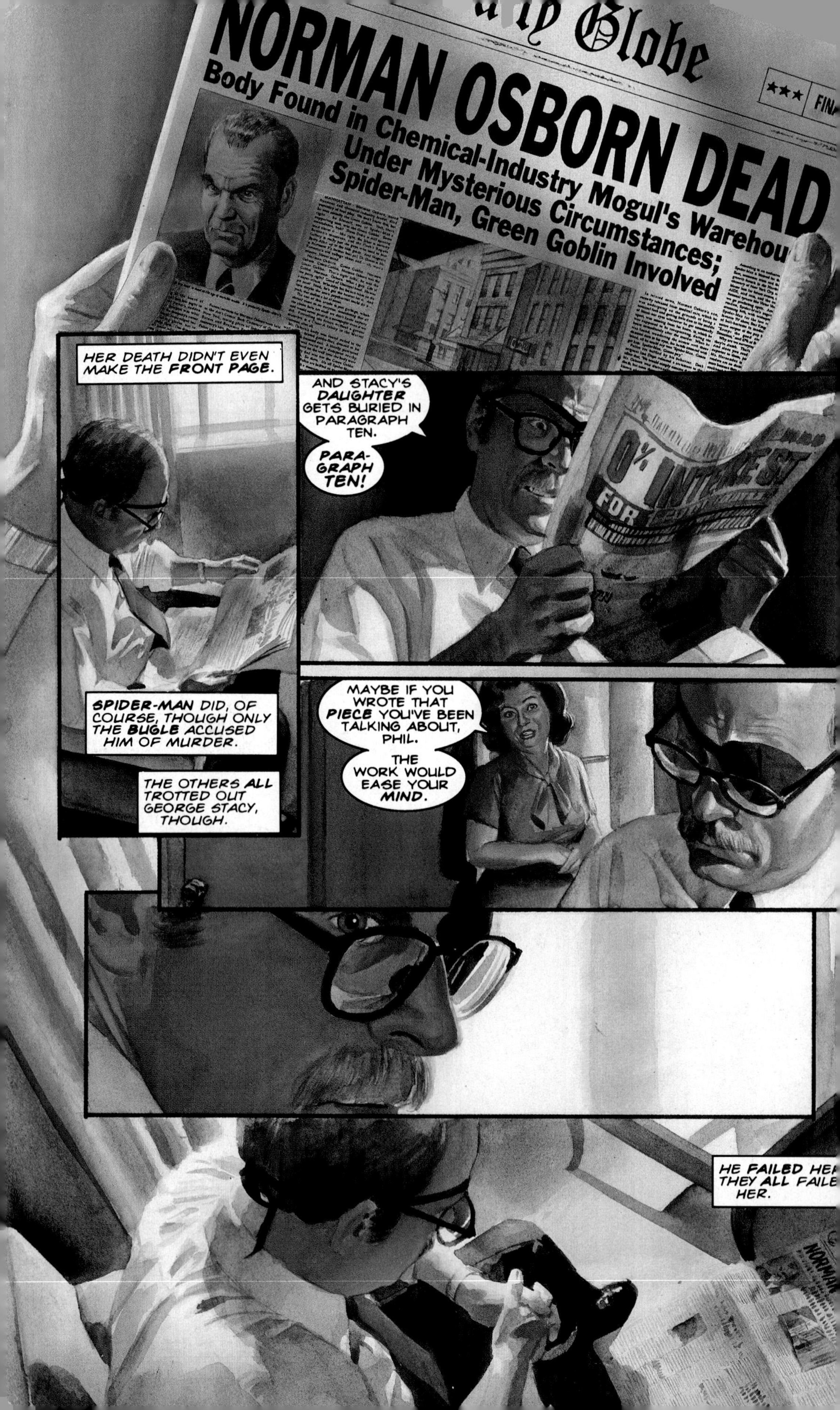

Globe
NORMAN OSBORN DEAD
Body Found in Chemical-Industry Mogul's Warehou
Under Mysterious Circumstances;
Spider-Man, Green Goblin Involved
HER DEATH DIDN'T EVEN MAKE THE FRONT PAGE.
AND STACY'S DAUGHTER GETS BURIED IN PARAGRAPH TEN.
PARAGRAPH TEN!
0% INTEREST
FOR
SPIDER-MAN DID, OF COURSE, THOUGH ONLY THE BUGLE ACCUSED HIM OF MURDER.
THE OTHERS ALL TROTTED OUT GEORGE STACY, THOUGH.
MAYBE IF YOU WROTE THAT PIECE YOU'VE BEEN TALKING ABOUT, PHIL.
THE WORK WOULD EASE YOUR MIND.
HE FAILED HE
THEY ALL FAILE
HER.

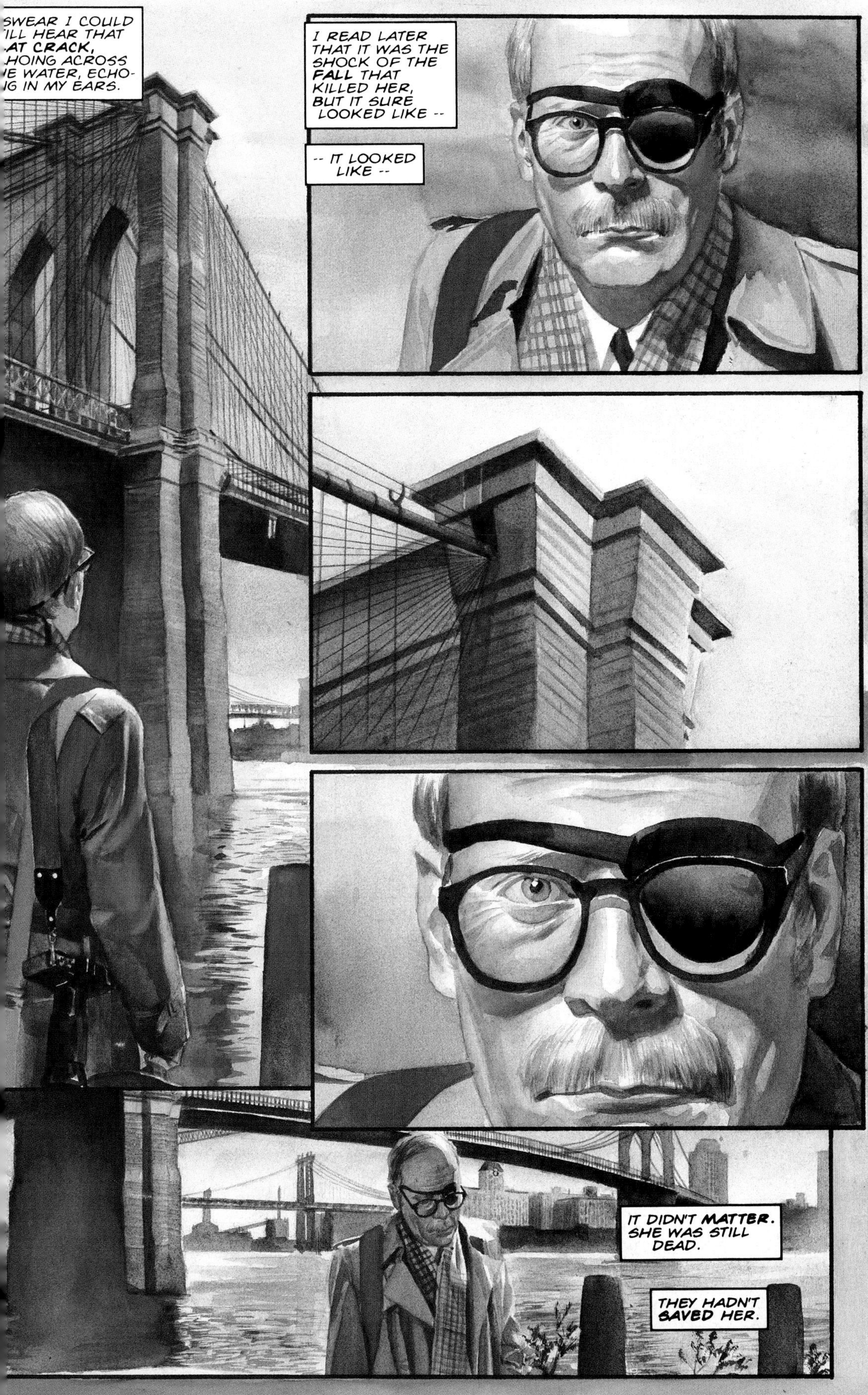
SWEAR I COULD
ILL HEAR THAT
AT CRACK,
HOING ACROSS
E WATER, ECHO-
G IN MY EARS.
I READ LATER THAT IT WAS THE SHOCK OF THE FALL THAT KILLED HER, BUT IT SURE LOOKED LIKE --
-- IT LOOKED LIKE --
IT DIDN'T MATTER. SHE WAS STILL DEAD.
THEY HADN'T SAVED HER.

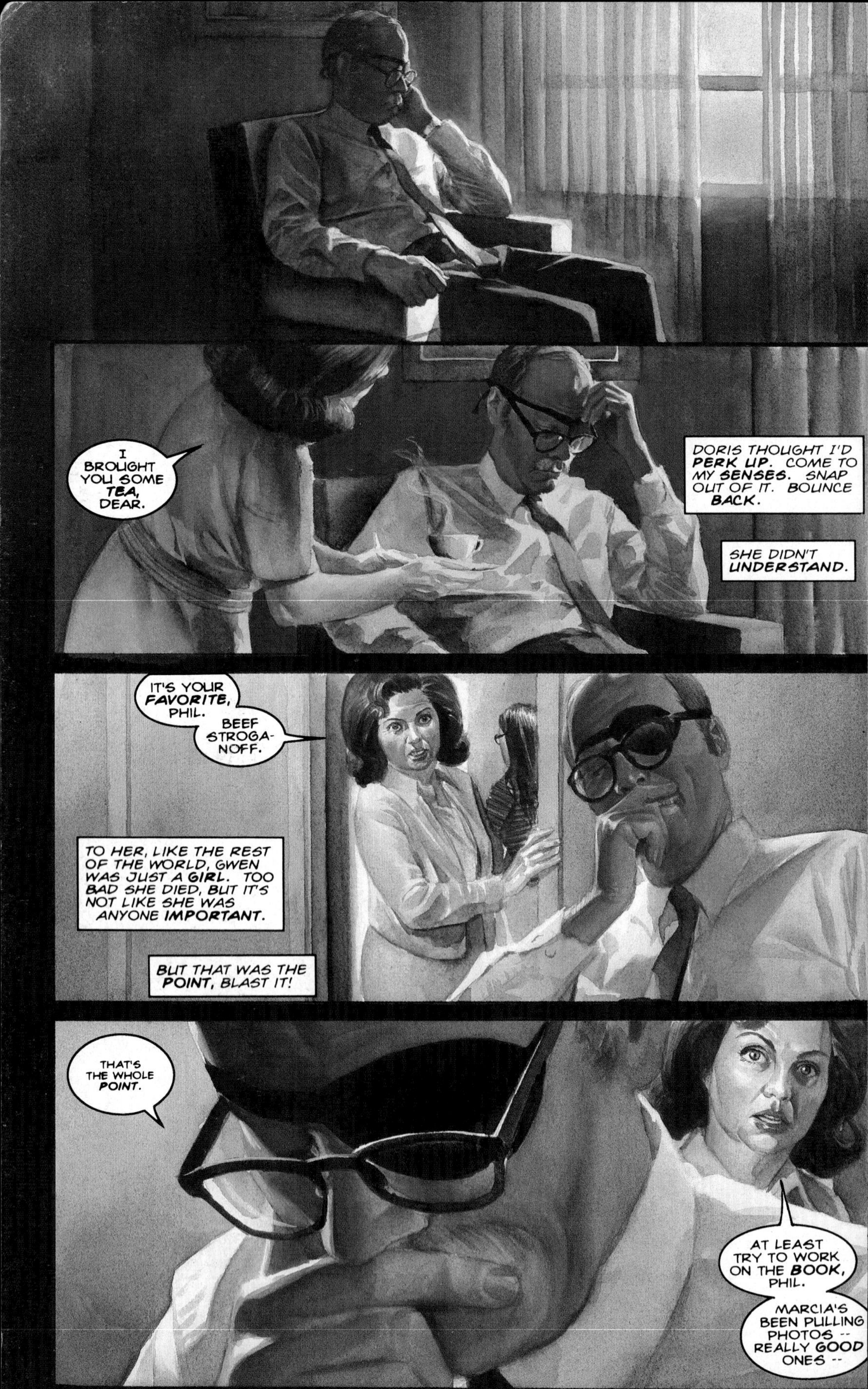
I BROUGHT YOU SOME TEA, DEAR.
DORIS THOUGHT I'D PERK UP. COME TO MY SENSES. SNAP OUT OF IT. BOUNCE BACK.
SHE DIDN'T UNDERSTAND.
IT'S YOUR FAVORITE, PHIL.
BEEF STROGA-NOFF.
TO HER, LIKE THE REST OF THE WORLD, GWEN WAS JUST A GIRL. TOO BAD SHE DIED, BUT IT'S NOT LIKE SHE WAS ANYONE IMPORTANT.
BUT THAT WAS THE POINT, BLAST IT!
THAT'S THE WHOLE POINT.
AT LEAST TRY TO WORK ON THE BOOK, PHIL.
MARCIA'S BEEN PULLING PHOTOS -- REALLY GOOD ONES --

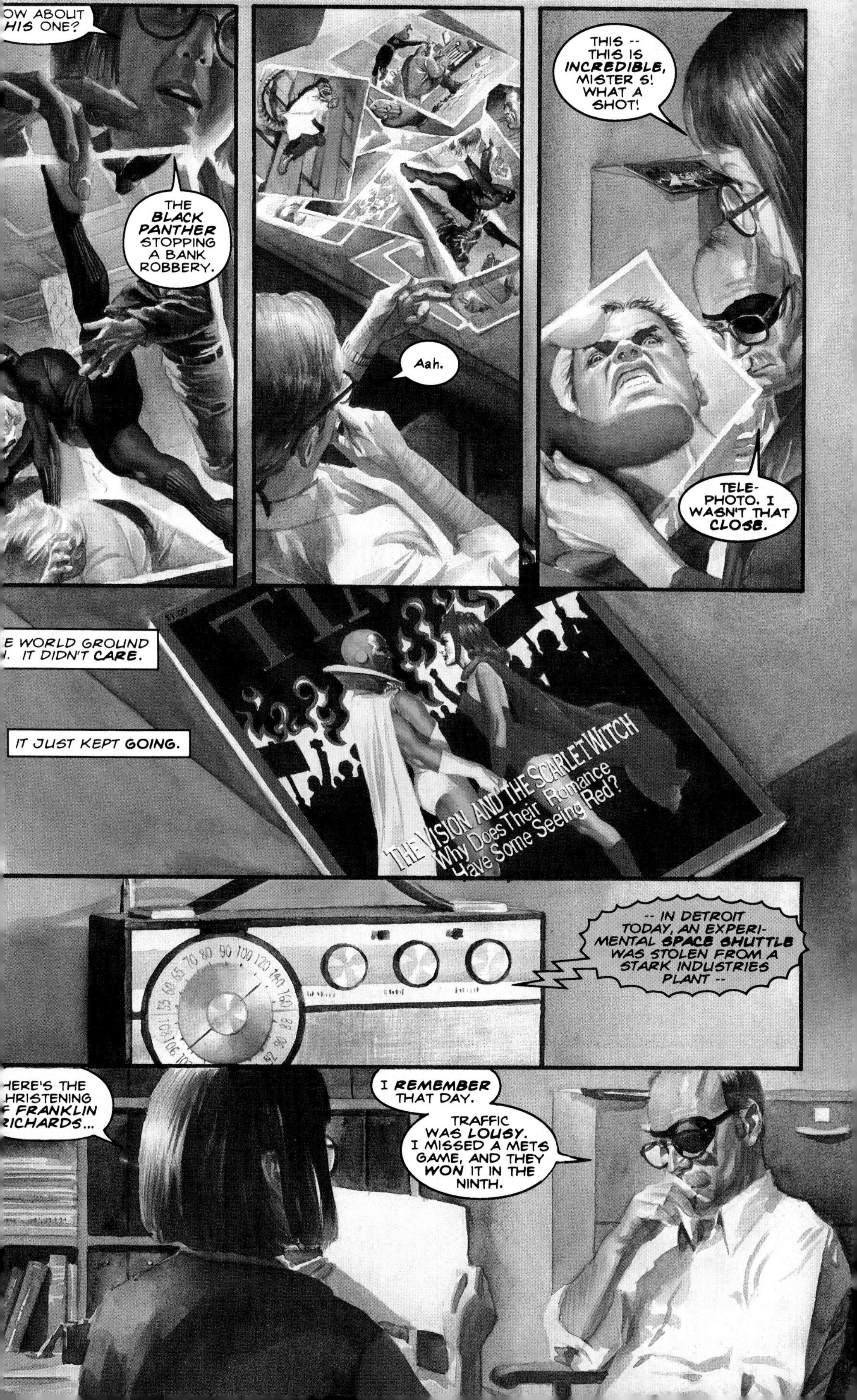
OW ABOUT HIS ONE?
THE BLACK PANTHER STOPPING A BANK ROBBERY.
Aah.
THIS -- THIS IS INCREDIBLE, MISTER S! WHAT A SHOT!
TELE-PHOTO. I WASN'T THAT CLOSE.
E WORLD GROUND I. IT DIDN'T CARE.
IT JUST KEPT GOING.
THE VISION AND THE SCARLET WITCH
Why Does Their Romance Have Some Seeing Red?
-- IN DETROIT TODAY, AN EXPERI-MENTAL SPACE SHUTTLE WAS STOLEN FROM A STARK INDUSTRIES PLANT --
HERE'S THE HRISTENING F FRANKLIN RICHARDS...
I REMEMBER THAT DAY.
TRAFFIC WAS LOUSY. I MISSED A METS GAME, AND THEY WON IT IN THE NINTH.

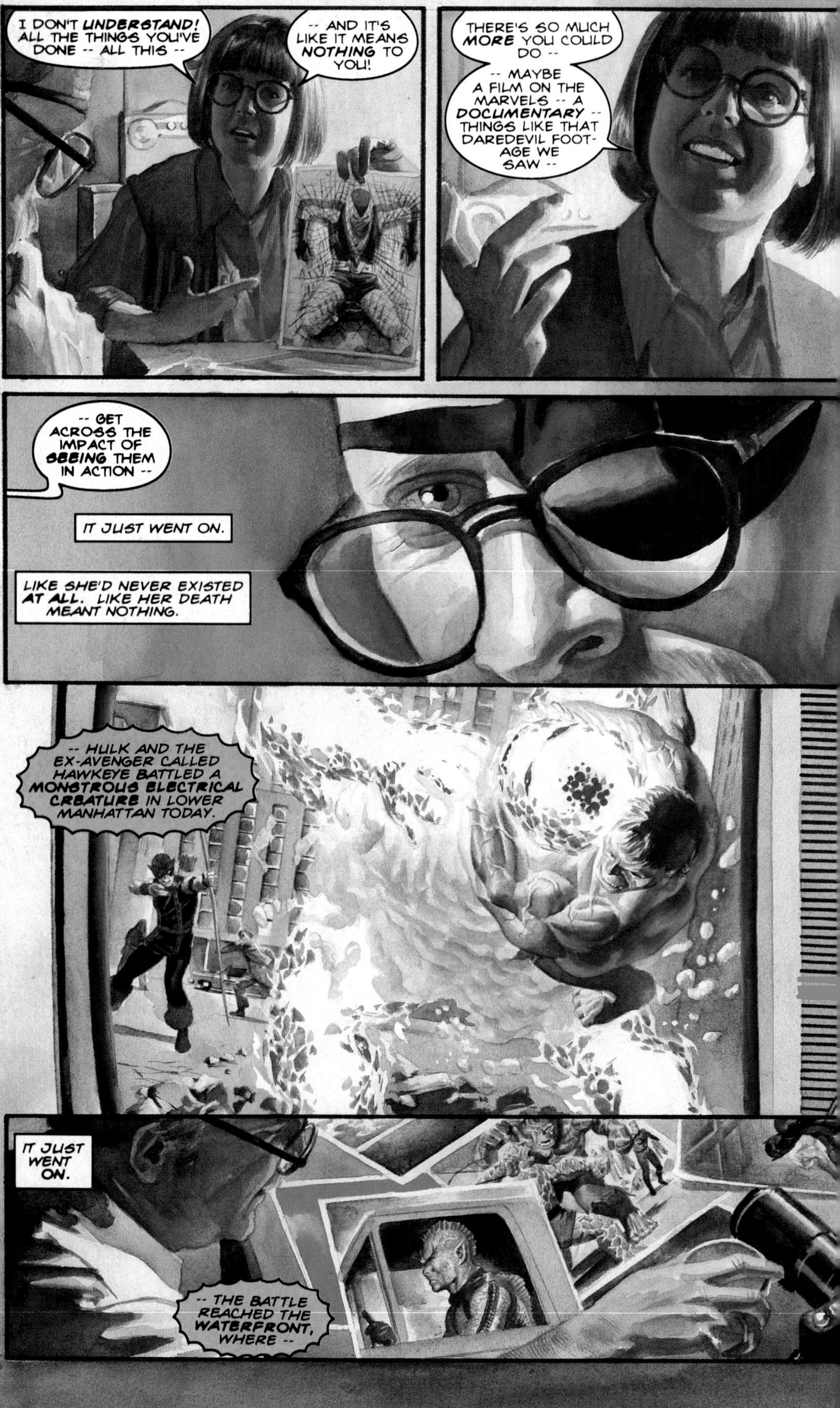
I DON'T UNDERSTAND! ALL THE THINGS YOU'VE DONE -- ALL THIS --
-- AND IT'S LIKE IT MEANS NOTHING TO YOU!
THERE'S SO MUCH MORE YOU COULD DO --
-- MAYBE A FILM ON THE MARVELS -- A DOCUMENTARY -- THINGS LIKE THAT DAREDEVIL FOOTAGE WE SAW --
-- GET ACROSS THE IMPACT OF SEEING THEM IN ACTION --
IT JUST WENT ON.
LIKE SHE'D NEVER EXISTED AT ALL. LIKE HER DEATH MEANT NOTHING.
-- HULK AND THE EX-AVENGER CALLED HAWKEYE BATTLED A MONSTROUS ELECTRICAL CREATURE IN LOWER MANHATTAN TODAY.
IT JUST WENT ON.
-- THE BATTLE REACHED THE WATERFRONT, WHERE --

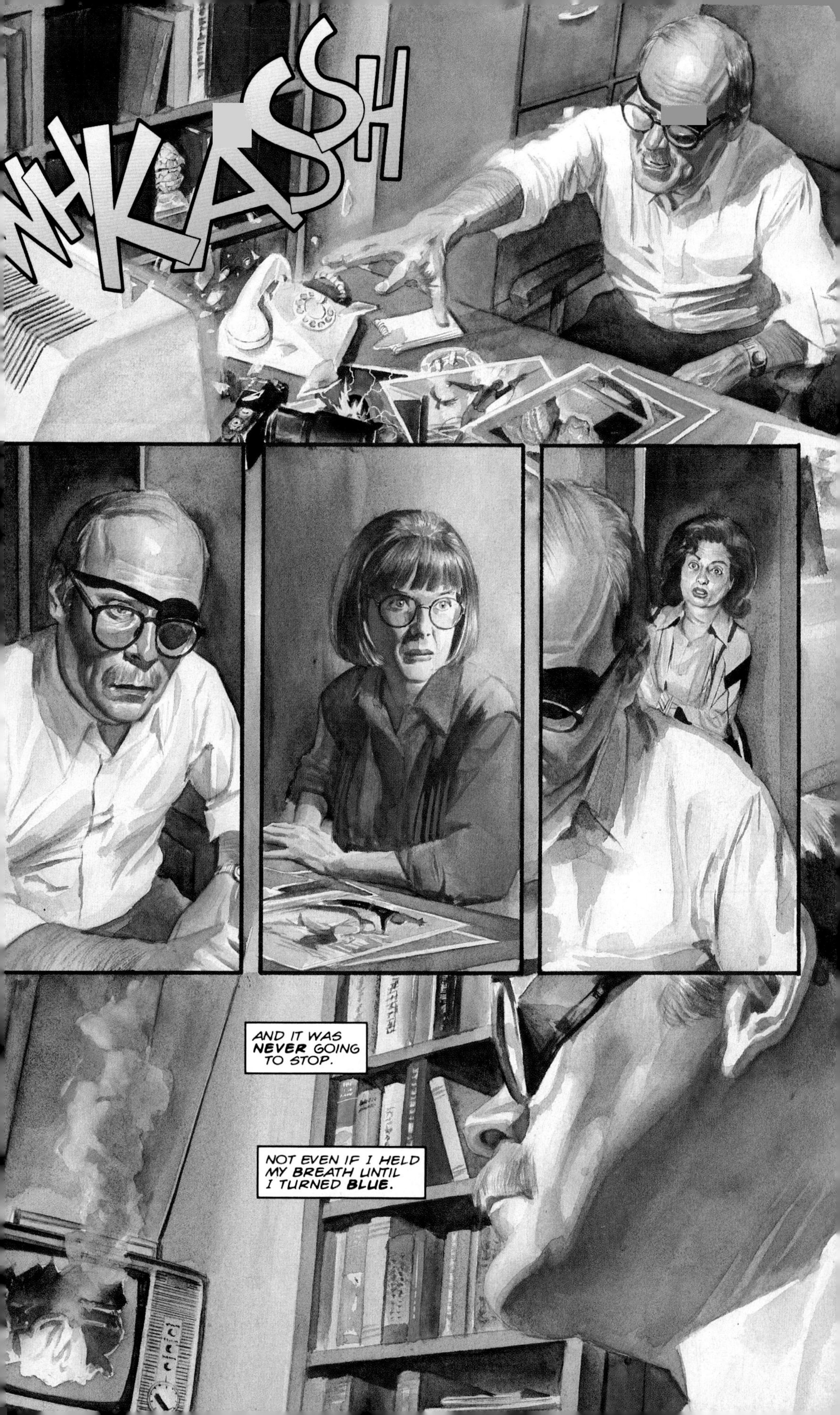
WHKASH
AND IT WAS NEVER GOING TO STOP.
NOT EVEN IF I HELD MY BREATH UNTIL I TURNED BLUE.

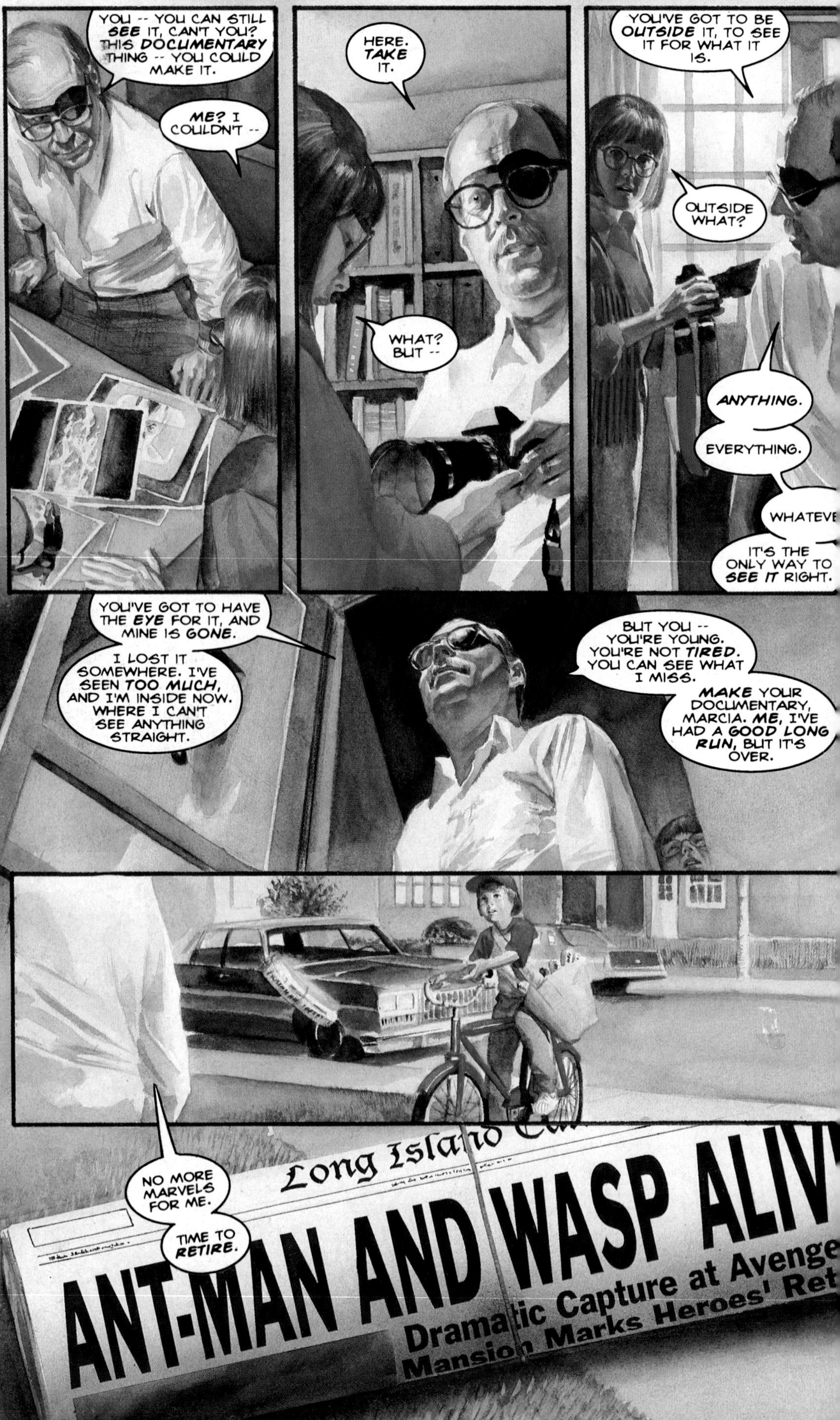
YOU -- YOU CAN STILL SEE IT, CAN'T YOU? THIS DOCUMENTARY THING -- YOU COULD MAKE IT.
ME? I COULDN'T --
HERE. TAKE IT.
WHAT? BUT --
YOU'VE GOT TO BE OUTSIDE IT, TO SEE IT FOR WHAT IT IS.
OUTSIDE WHAT?
ANYTHING.
EVERYTHING.
WHATEV
IT'S THE ONLY WAY TO SEE IT RIGHT.
YOU'VE GOT TO HAVE THE EYE FOR IT, AND MINE IS GONE.
I LOST IT SOMEWHERE. I'VE SEEN TOO MUCH, AND I'M INSIDE NOW. WHERE I CAN'T SEE ANYTHING STRAIGHT.
BUT YOU -- YOU'RE YOUNG. YOU'RE NOT TIRED. YOU CAN SEE WHAT I MISS.
MAKE YOUR DOCUMENTARY, MARCIA. ME, I'VE HAD A GOOD LONG RUN, BUT IT'S OVER.
NO MORE MARVELS FOR ME.
TIME TO RETIRE.
Long Island
ANT-MAN AND WASP ALIV
Dramatic Capture at Avenge
Mansion Marks Heroes' Ret

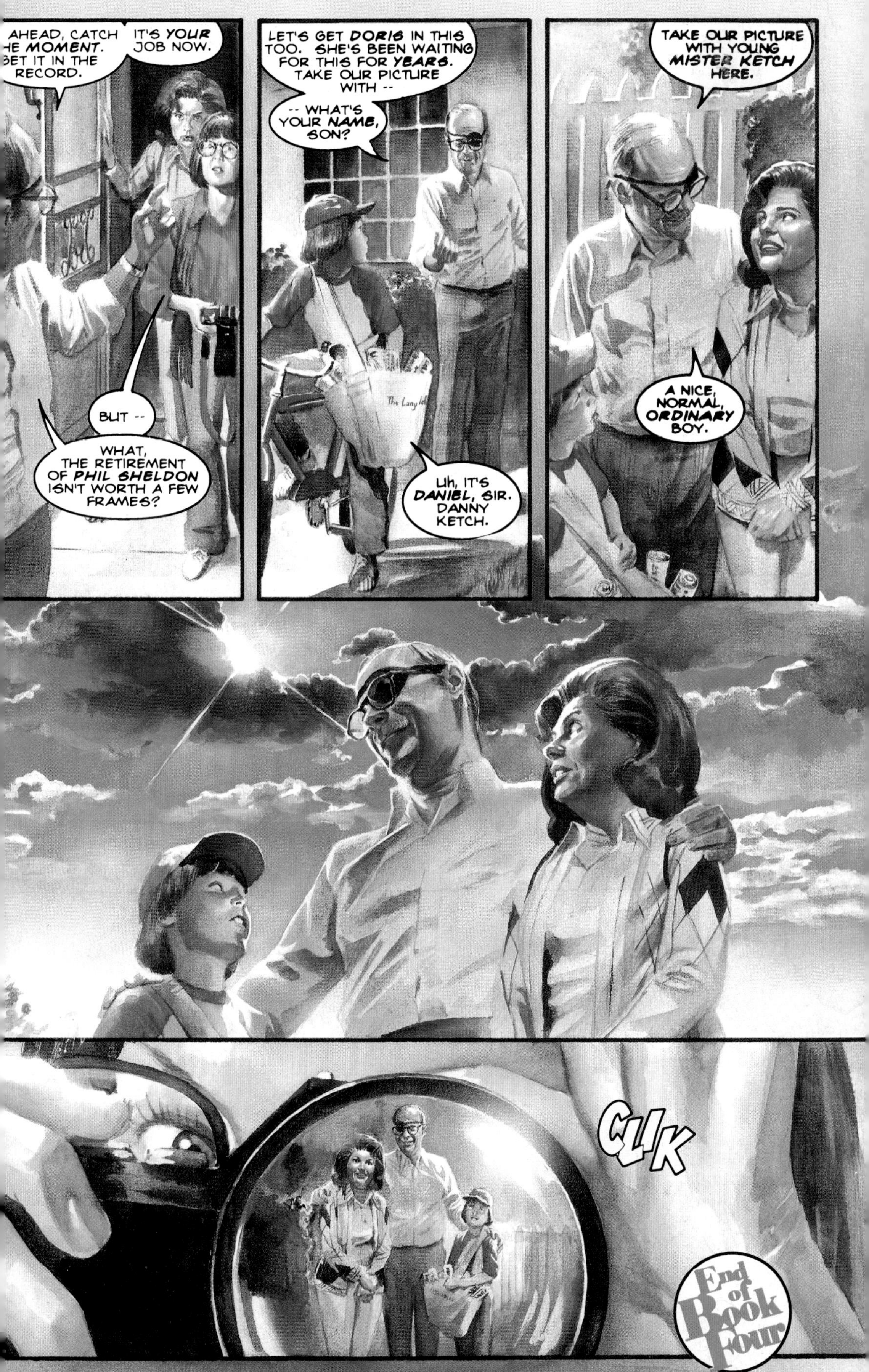

AHEAD, CATCH HE MOMENT. GET IT IN THE RECORD.
IT'S YOUR JOB NOW.
BUT --
WHAT, THE RETIREMENT OF PHIL SHELDON ISN'T WORTH A FEW FRAMES?
LET'S GET DORIS IN THIS TOO. SHE'S BEEN WAITING FOR THIS FOR YEARS. TAKE OUR PICTURE WITH --
-- WHAT'S YOUR NAME, SON?
Uh, IT'S DANIEL, SIR. DANNY KETCH.
TAKE OUR PICTURE WITH YOUNG MISTER KETCH HERE.
A NICE, NORMAL, ORDINARY BOY.
CLIK
End of Book Four

Understanding Marvel

Scott McCloud

Kurt and I had a deal. Kurt and I went to junior high school together back in Lexington, Massachusetts where we both grew up. The deal was that Kurt would come over to my house after school and he would play a game of chess with me (something I was obsessed with at the time) and, in exchange, I would play a game of pool with Kurt on our basement pool table.

Kurt and I had a lot in common. We both liked science fiction, weird British comedy, role-playing games... We were both nerds, basically. Still, there was one thing we did *not* have in common: comic books. Kurt loved comic books but I couldn't stand the things. It took him a while, but Kurt eventually force-fed me enough good back issues that I not only renounced my low opinion of comics, I decided that I wanted to draw them. Lucky for Kurt, since he wanted to be a writer.

Together we produced *The Battle of Lexington,* in which ten Marvel super heroes beat the crap out of each other and destroyed our high school, town library and several historic landmarks in 60 pages of lovingly rendered pencil artwork. Alex Ross, I wasn't, and never could be, but Kurt and I made it feel as realistic as we could.

That was the point after all: to make it *REAL.*

Kurt and I had another deal.

Within two years of graduating college, we were both working comics professionals, but somehow we had drifted about as far apart as two people can drift in the comics world. Kurt was deep in the heart of mainstream super hero comics, working to change comics within the "system" as it were. I was off in the independents with my creator-owned series, trying to change comics from the outside. I was getting good reviews, but couldn't sell a comic to save my life. Kurt was writing popular titles, but being ignored by the critics.

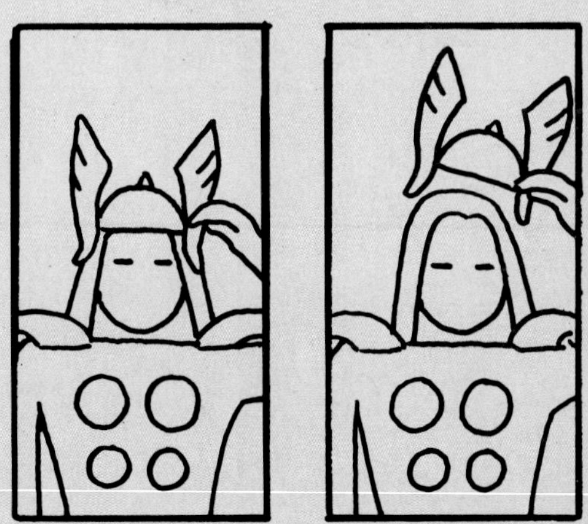

So Kurt suggested the deal. I could get all the good reviews, the awards, lecture at the Smithsonian, whatever, but I could never have anything of mine become insanely popular. Kurt, on the other hand, could write the insanely popular series, become filthy rich, but he could never win any awards or get good reviews or anything – that was *my* turf.

And that's just how it turned out in the end. My latest book, UNDERSTANDING COMICS was a big hit with the critics. It won three Harvey Awards, an Eisner Award, all that good stuff. I got all the ego gratification I could ask for. It sold well, sure, but it wasn't *insanely* popular, so I held up my end of the bargain.

Meanwhile, **MARVELS** *is* insanely popular. Everybody loves **MARVELS.** Even black-and-white small press guys like me loved the book. Kurt and Alex's masterpiece sold out in unbelievable quantities for such a high ticket item. Now Kurt gets to sit back and relax as **MARVELS** racks up all the honors he could ever have hoped for: blockbuster sales, great reviews, three Harvey awards, three Eisner aw...

Hey, wait a minute.

Busiek, you cheater!!

Scott

SCOTT McCLOUD

Sources

BOOK ONE

p.2-6
orton's press conference
Marvel Comics #1

p.8-9
orch in streets
Marvel Comics #1

p.10-11
amor in NYC
Marvel Mystery Comics #2

.12
lelted car/"Hoodlums in Flaming
uits"
Marvel Mystery Comics #4
That racing scam"
Marvel Mystery Comics #2
ubway rescue
Marvel Mystery Comics #5

.13
Human Torch Flies Medicine
to Trapped Town"
Marvel Mystery Comics #5

.14
amor and Electro headlines
Marvel Mystery Comics #6
Var news headline from New York
imes]

.15
hat's the Golden Age Angel. It's not
uperman.

p. 16-22
orch/Namor clash
Marvel Mystery Comics #7-10

.24
FE Magazine events
Captain America Comics #1

.25
aptain America headlines
Captain America Comics #1
Human Torch Thwarts Army Payroll
eist"
Marvel Mystery Comics #18
Sub-Mariner Battles Radium Thieves"
Sub-Mariner #1/Marvel Mystery #20
Stock Market 'Hag' Burned by Torch"
Marvel Mystery Comics #19
Other news headlines from New
ork Times]
aptain America Homefront Action
Captain America Comics #1
aptain America in Nazi Camp
Captain America Comics #2

p.28-29
orch & Namor in Bering tunnel
Marvel Mystery Comics #17

.30
Saved my business from a gasoline
yndicate"
Marvel Mystery Comics #10
Broke up a prisoner-of-war escape
p in Canada"
Sub-Mariner #2
Nabbed that arsonist"
Marvel Mystery Comics 20

p.32-39
orch/Namor battle
Human Torch #5 (Fall 1941)

p.44-45
or the record, clockwise from top
ft, they're: Bucky, Captain America,
amor, Aarkus the Vision (from
arvel Mystery Comics), The Mighty
estroyer (*Mystic Comics*) the
olden Age Black Widow (*Mystic*),
he Thunderer (*Daring Mystery*
omics), The Blazing Skull (*Mystic*),
he Black Marvel (*Mystic*), The
uman Torch and Toro.

BOOK TWO

p.1
"The Birth of the Fantastic Four —"
Fantastic Four #1
"Thor—"
Journey into Mystery #83-85
"Giant-Man —"
Tales to Astonish #49
"The Return of the Sub-Mariner—"
Fantastic Four #4
Return of Captain America
Avengers #4

pp.2-5
Masters of Evil battle
Avengers #6

p.6
"Santo Rico: Country in Crisis"
Tales to Astonish #54

p.7
Human Torch's '4' signal
Strange Tales #123

pp.9-12
Benson's Department Store/
Wasp display
Tales to Astonish #58

p.14
Hulk/Thing battle
Fantastic Four #25-26

p.15
Human Torch/Eel battle
Strange Tales #117

p.17
Giant-Man/Spider-Man battle
Tales to Astonish #57

p.18
Kraven coming to New York
Amazing Spider-Man #15
"Heavy Machinery Show"
Journey into Mystery #105
"At the barricade"
Tales to Astonish #57
"Callin' himself the Beetle"
Strange Tales #123

p.22
"WIlliams embezzlement case"
Avengers #9

p.23
FF engagement announcement
Fantastic Four #36

p.24
LIFE cover photo
Fantastic Four #24

p.25
Manhunt for Crusher Creel
Journey into Mystery #114
Avengers press conference
Avengers #16
"Susan Storm Abducted by Frightful
Four"
Fantastic Four #38
Daredevil/Stiltman battle
Daredevil #8

p.30
Globe "Mutant Menace" feature
X-Men #14

pp.32-33
Richards' wedding
Fantastic Four Annual #3

pp.34-35
Xavier/Trask "debate"
X-Men #14

pp.40-41
Sentinels over New York
X-Men #14

p.42
"Today's the Day"
Fantastic Four Annual #3

p.44
"Sentinels have mysteriously dis-
appeared"
X-Men #14

p.45
Iron Man/Titanium Man fight promo
Tales of Suspense #69

BOOK THREE

p.1
Widow & Ivan
Tales to Astonish #52
Avengers press conference photo
Avengers #16
"Stark and the Countess"
Tales of Suspense #69-72
"Sen. Byrd Sez Iron Man Botched
Weapons Test"
Tales of Suspense #66

p.3
Avengers declared Public Menace
Avengers #21

P.4
Avengers innocent/"Avengers Day"
Avengers #22
Byrd's demands for Iron Man's ID/
Stark missing
Tales of Suspense #72
Byrd's subpoena issued
Tales of Suspense #74

P.5
S.H.I.E.L.D. vs. Egg-craft
Strange Tales #144-145

pp.6-8
Attuma floods eastern seaboard,
fights Avengers
Avengers #27

p. 9
"Spider-Man attacked Jonah Jameson!"
Amazing Spider-Man #34
FF/Dragon Man battle wrecks buildings
Fantastic Four #45

p.10
Hulk in Washington DC
Tales to Astonish #75
Ka-Zar/Daredevil in England
Daredevil #14
Hercules photo
Journey into Mystery #125
Cap/Batroc battle photo
Tales of Suspense #75

pp.12-40
Galactus events
Fantastic Four #48-50

p.41
"Galactus Hoax"/"Galactus
Vanishes"
Fantastic Four #50
"Goliath Returns to Avengers"
Avengers #28-31

p.42
Thing wandering alleys
Fantastic Four #50
"Spider-Man fighting that
Looter character"
Amazing Spider-Man #36

p.43
Byrd cancels Stark's defense contracts
Tales of Suspense #77

p.44
Count Nefaria imprisons
Washington, DC
X-Men #23

BOOK FOUR

pp.2-3
Kree/Skrull War
Avengers #92-97

p.5
Black Widow trial
Daredevil #83

p.6
"Four Wounded in Stark Riot"
Iron Man #45-46

Attitude toward Falcon in Harlem
Captain America #151

"How Spider-Man killed George Stacy"
Amazing Spider-Man #90
Editorial in Bugle
Daredevil #84

p.7
Galactus in New York again
Fantastic Four #120-123
"Landlord Wants Fantastic Four O-U-T!"
Fantastic Four#120
FF arrested, picketed, out on bail
Fantastic Four #113-116

p.10
Cage taking out dope dealers
Hero for Hire #1
"I'm having Fox check it out"
Hero for Hire #4

pp.11-12
Spider-Man/Dr. Octopus battle
Amazing Spider-Man #90

p.13
"Hulk in New York"
Marvel Feature #2

p.14
Astro-Nuts/Xemnu TV show
Marvel Feature #3
News of Sentinels approaching
Avengers #102

p.16
"Accusing Spider-Man of
Kidnapping Dr. Jorgenson"
Marvel Team-Up #4
"not stopping a crime wave"
Amazing Spider-Man #112

p.17
Avengers in Australia
Avengers #104

p.18
"Dr. Octopus Captured"
Amazing Spider-Man #115
Fire destroys Pym home
Marvel Feature #6
File photo of Pym wedding
Avengers #60
Daredevil & Black Widow vs.
Indestructible Man
Daredevil #94

p. 19
"Torch's new costume"
Fantastic Four #132-133
"— called Solarr, I think —"
Captain America #160
Thundra's challenge
Fantastic Four#133

p.22
"As if you'd lost control of your
Tentacles"
Amazing Spider-Man #90

pp.26-30
Atlantean Invasion
Sub-Mariner #60

pp.31-37
Kidnapping & death of Gwen Stacy
Amazing Spider-Man #121-122

p.38
Death of Norman Osborn discovered
Amazing Spider-Man #123

p.41
Black Panther photo
Avengers #77
Lizard photo
Amazing Spider-Man #44
Spider-Man/Rhino fight
Amazing Spider-Man #43
Vision/Scarlet Witch romance public
Avengers #113

p.42
Shocker photo
Amazing Spider-Man #72
Hulk & Hawkeye vs. Zzzax
Incredible Hulk #166/
Avengers #114
Triton in truck photo
Avengers #95
Thing/Hulk battle photo
Fantastic Four #25

p.44
"Ant-Man and Wasp Alive!"
Marvel Feature #10

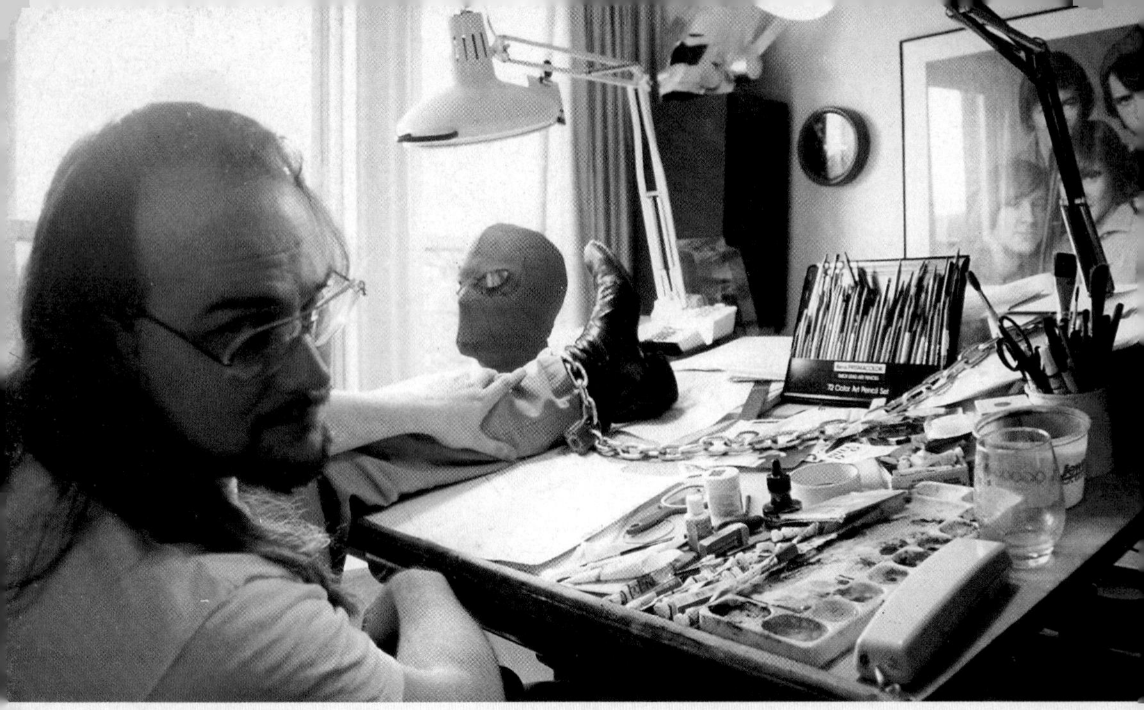

"I wear the chain I forged in life"

—Charles Dickens, *A Christmas Carol*

Being shackled to your drawing board is pretty much the status quo for comic book freelanc and MARVELS provided me with that complete deprivation from freedom as well. My enjoyment in working on the series was easily balanced by my exasperation with not being able to do anything *but* work on the series. These 180 pages of story took over a year to complete, with four months spent on each issue and relatively no days off. The extensive research and referencing I did was a large pain, but it was also the thing that kept my interest in the project consistently strong. Over-thinking how to translate these characters and stories visually and trying to figure out how they might actually work made this series come alive for me. I would consider how much pre-production thought goes into big budget films of this genre, and try to put in as much of that attention myself. With comics you have an unlimited budget and you can use as many special effects, props, and actors as you want. Using my friends as models, along with various period references of places, objects, and people, was a way for me to have a stronger identification with the subject matter. My hope was to give the material a life that the reader could be as absorbed by as I was.

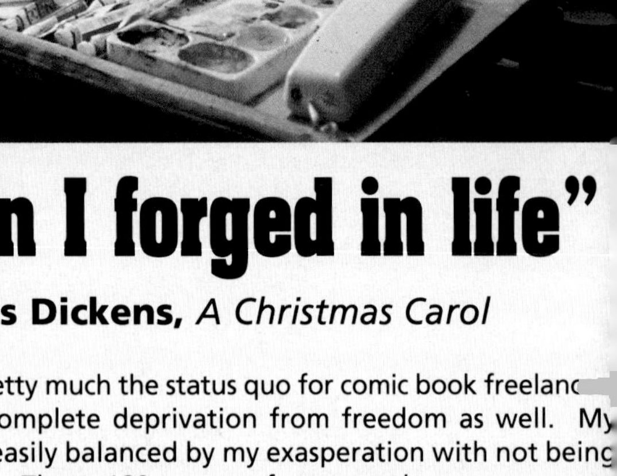

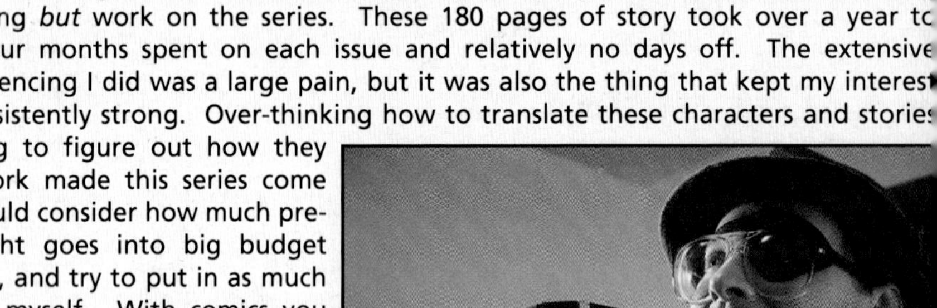
A *FRONT PAGE* FOR SURE. MONEY IN THE BANK.
MAYBE EVEN A ***MAGAZINE COVER***, DOWN THE LINE.
MAYBE MORE THAN ***THAT***, IF I'M LUCKY.

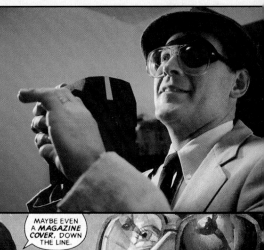

A slight alteration easily transformed Mark Braun into either an older or younger Phil Sheldon. ➲

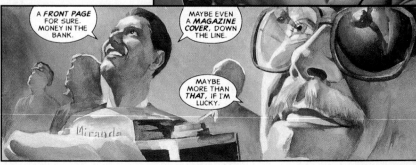

Overthinking Things

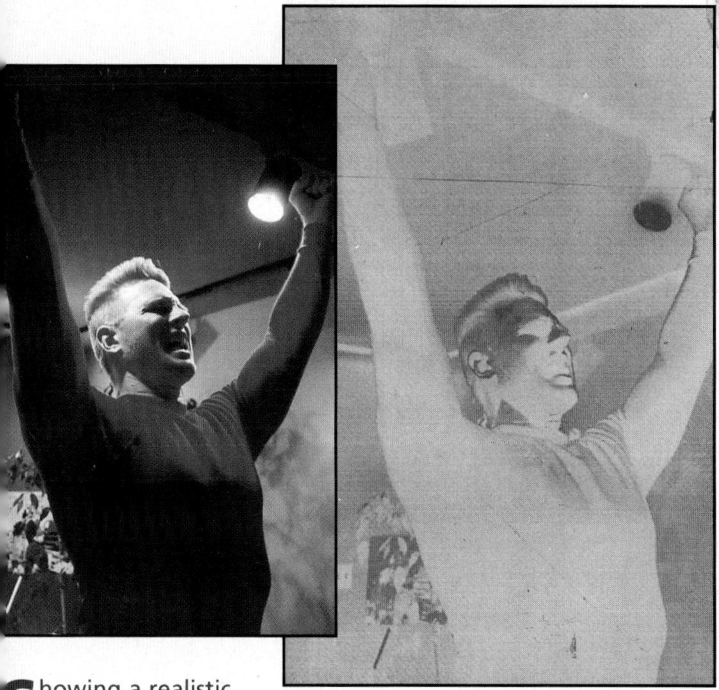

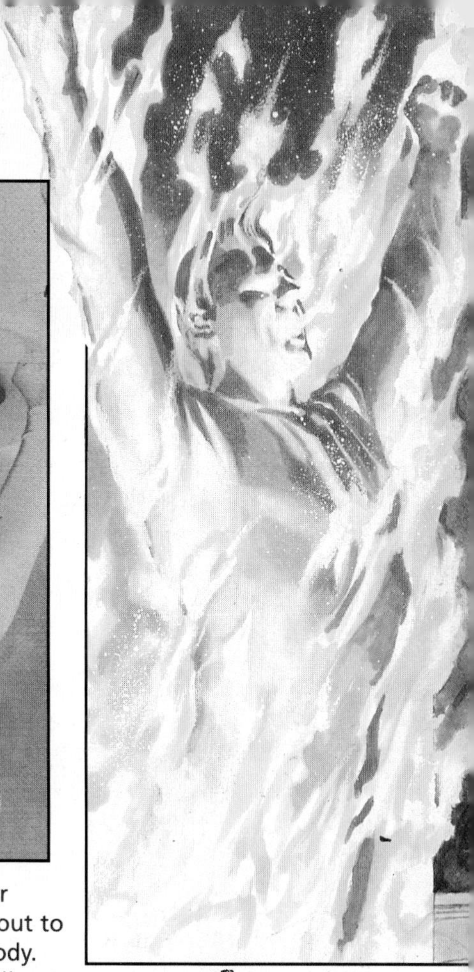

Showing a realistic Human Torch was my first inspiration for MARVELS. After shooting my model in extreme contrast, I took the negative out to study how light might appear to be coming from within a body. I also set a lot of stuff on fire and photographed that, too, till I fully understood the process (and had burned most of my belongings). ∩

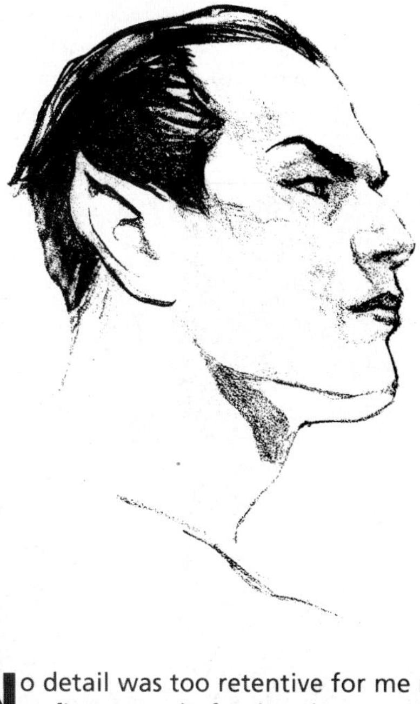

Having someone around who understood period clothing from firsthand experience made a big difference. My mother was a fashion illustrator of that era, and she helped design Doris's wedding dress. ⊃

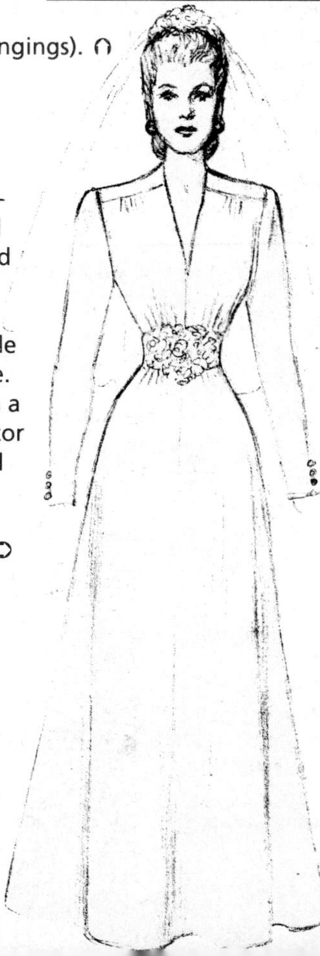

Drawing by Lynette Ross

No detail was too retentive for me not to figure out beforehand. In Namor's case, I tried to design a hairstyle somewhat appropriate to the time period, and show ears that differed from Mr. Spock's. ∩

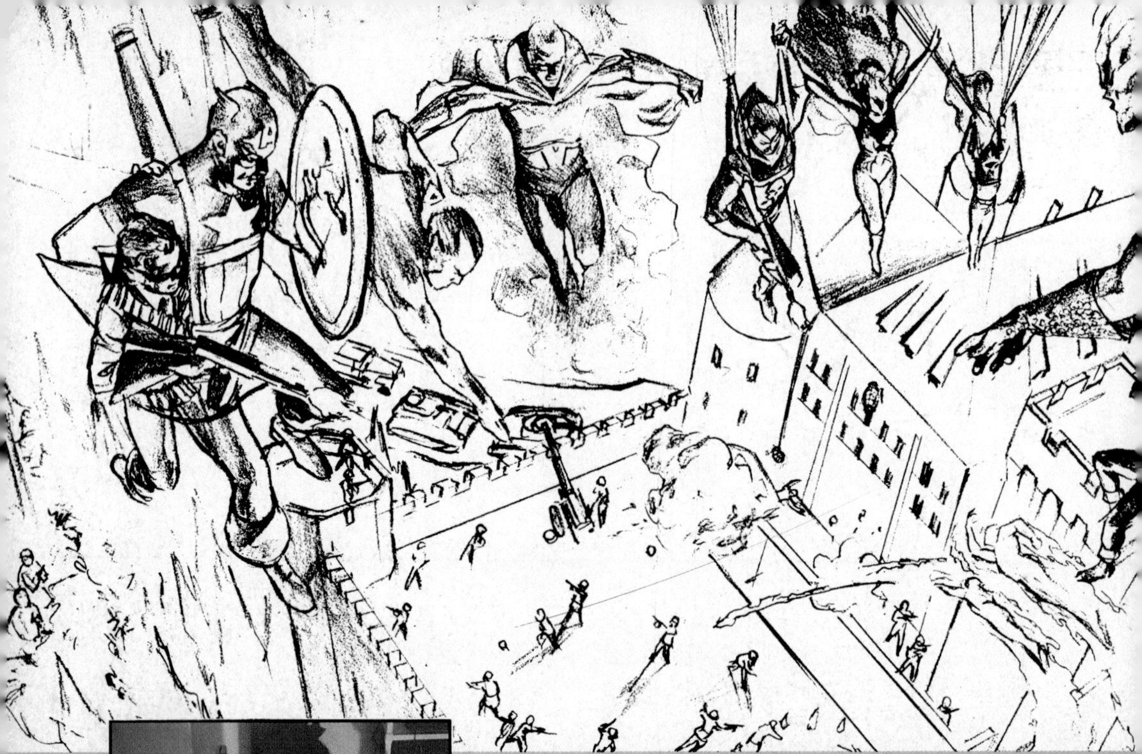

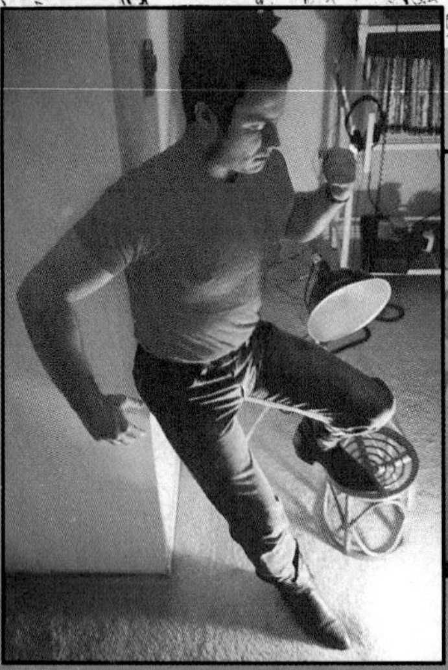

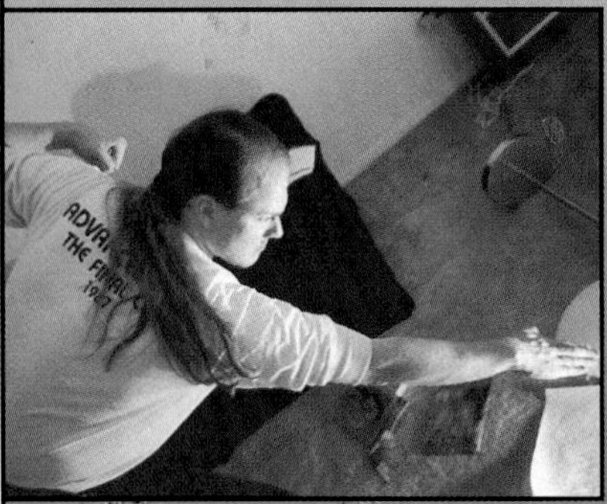

With an elaborate action shot, it was in my best interest to plan out the pencil "thumbnail" as much as possible, so that I wasn't completely at the mercy of how the photo references turned out. With the Nazi stronghold from this spread, I had the worst luck in finding anything that was even roughly accurate to refer to. ∩

Many times I would use a photo of someone to ground the realism of a scene through a dominant figure and then flesh out other people without reference (as with Bucky in this shot). ⊃ There was no time in the series, however, where I traced over any photograph to get the accuracy I needed.

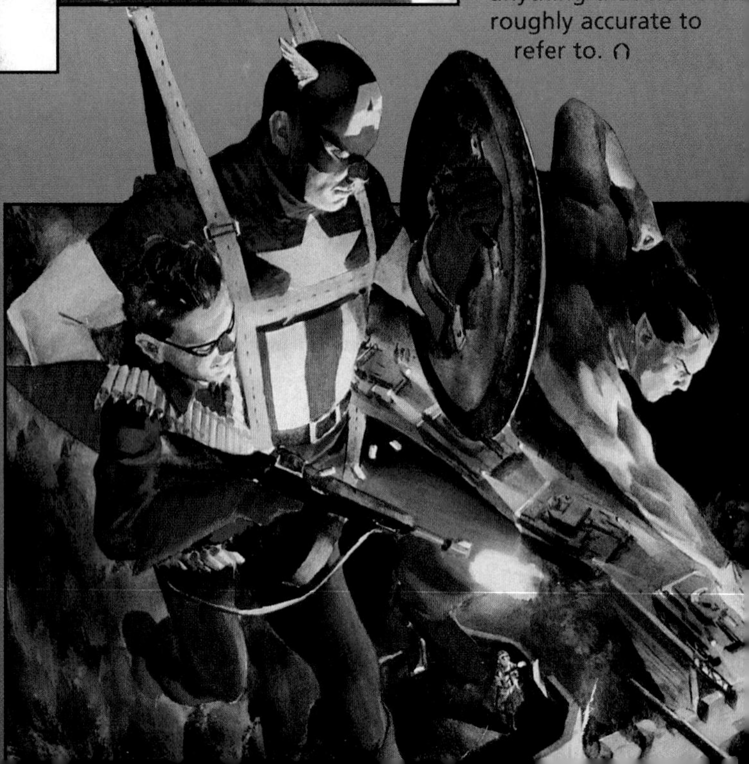

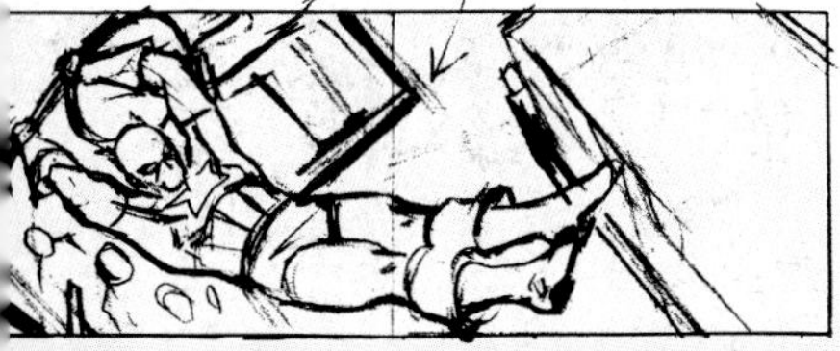

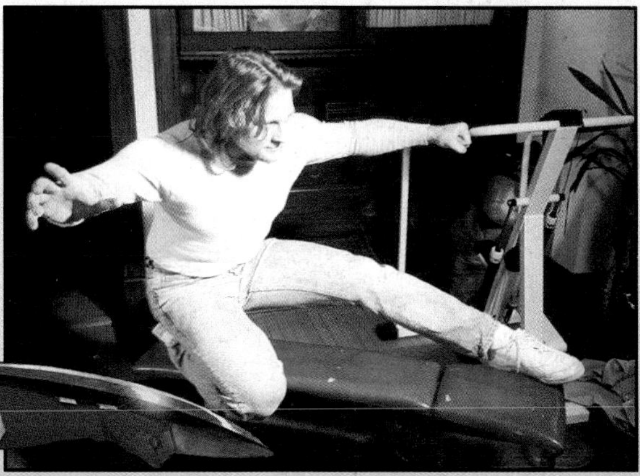

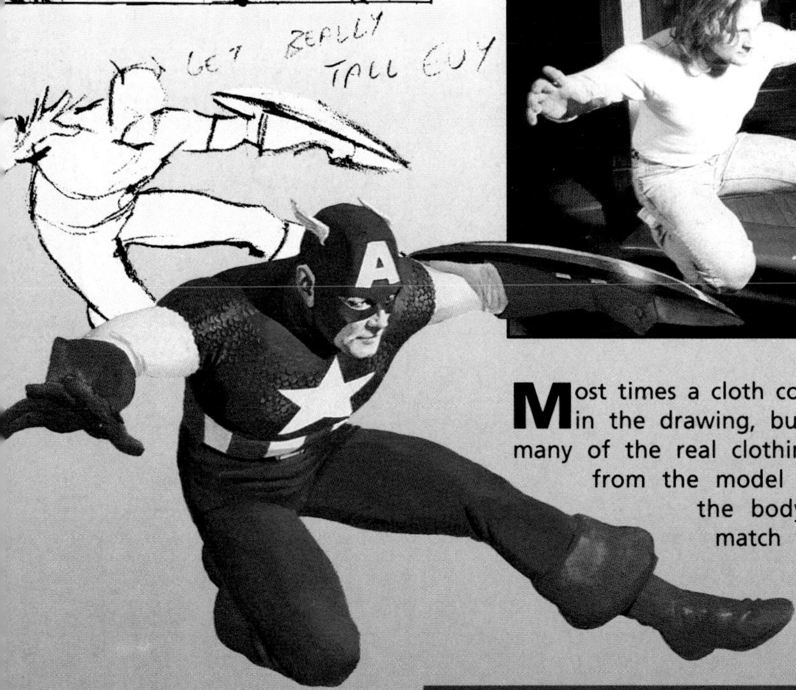
GET REALLY
TALL GUY

Most times a cloth costume was improvised in the drawing, but I liked to utilize as many of the real clothing folds and wrinkles from the model as I could. Pushing the body position farther to match what I'd done in the thumbnail was often necessary.

Pencil To Finish

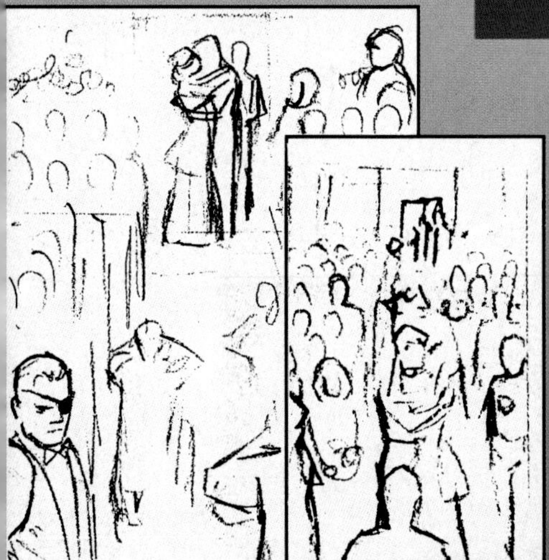

Sometimes a number of different thumbnails was needed to get the best angle on a scene. This was one of the most difficult scene structures, having figures interacting with a receding background. (Final thumbnail design reproduced here at actual size.)

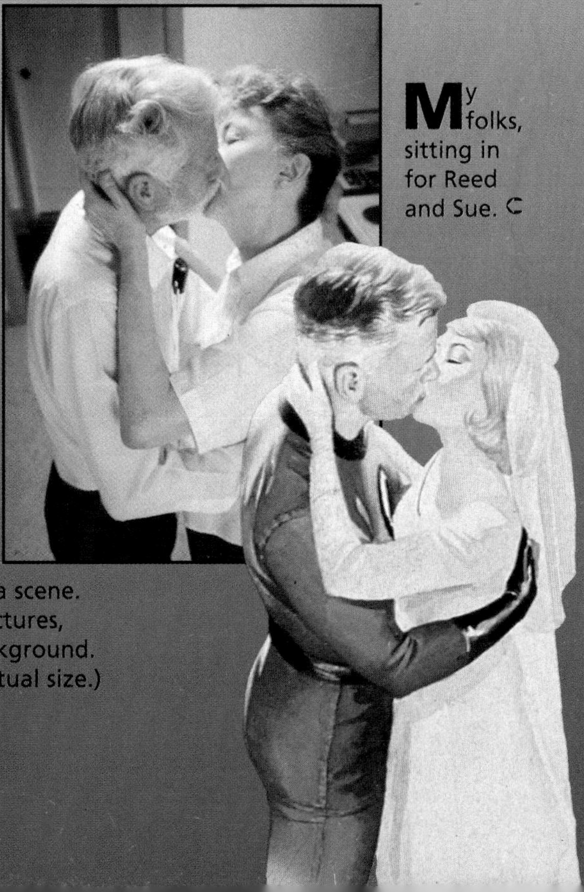

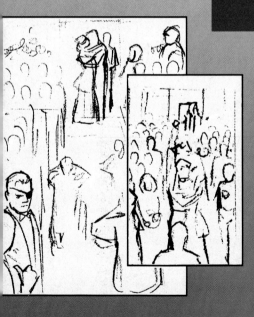

My folks, sitting in for Reed and Sue.

Every cover of this series called for a great deal of preparation in design, but few received more response than this one. I thought that I would be asking for a lot to have our big "X-Men issue" adorned with a single logo-riding X-Man from the original series. Luckily my editor and I saw eye-to-eye and it was a short step to the finished design.

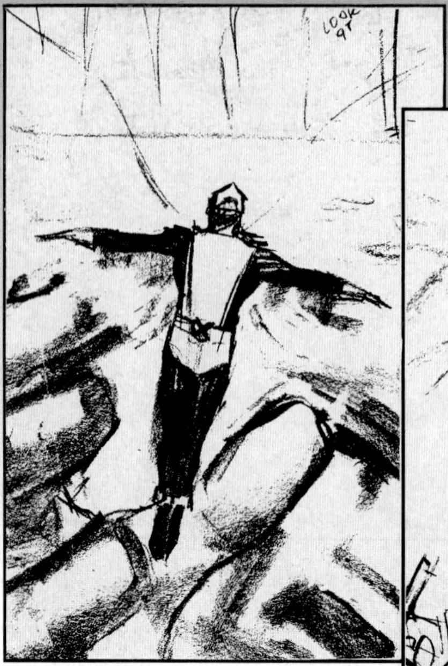

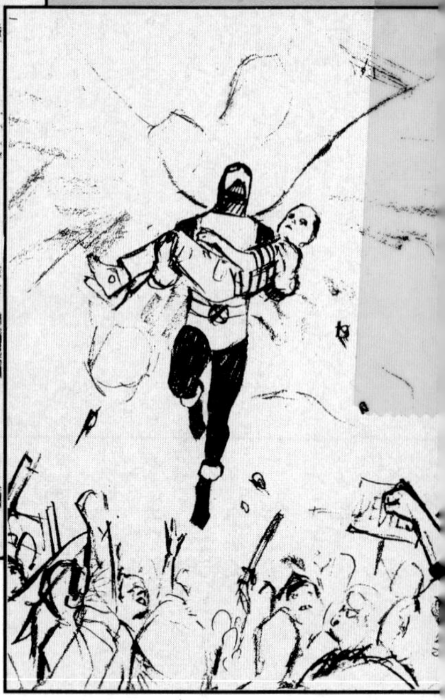

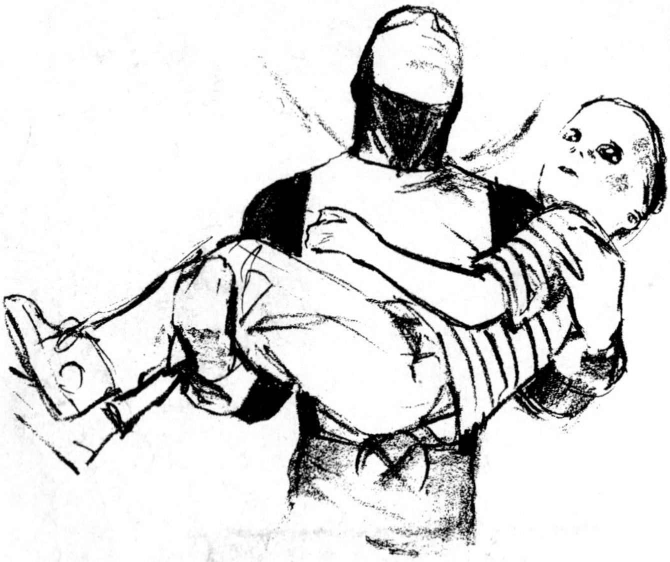

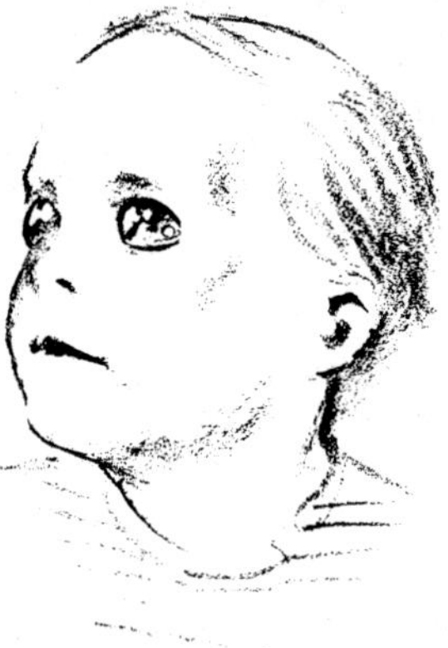

Kurt originally planned the mutant child to be a boy whose obvious mutant quality was that he was green. I had, in the back of my mind, an old Wally Wood EC comic from the fifties that had a frighteningly deformed little girl in it, and I proposed that the boy have something like that appearance to contrast with the more attractive mutation of the Angel. When I sent my design along with a page from the Wood story, Kurt liked the idea well enough to make the character a girl as well.

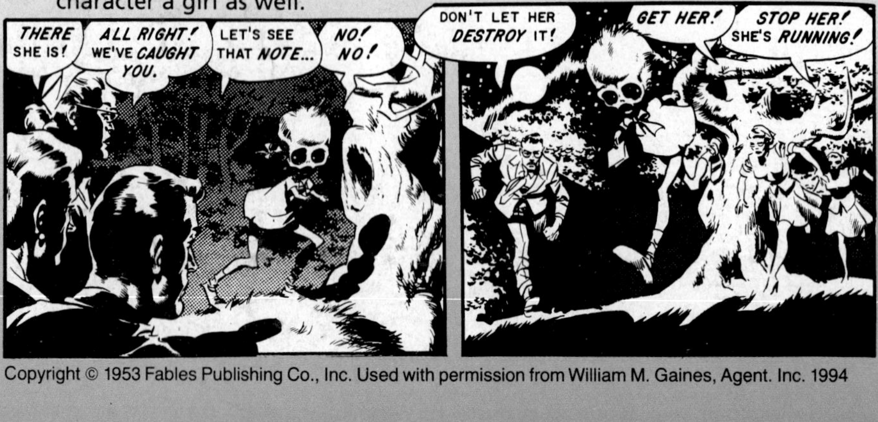
THERE SHE IS!
ALL RIGHT! WE'VE CAUGHT YOU.
LET'S SEE THAT NOTE...
NO! NO!
DON'T LET HER DESTROY IT!
GET HER!
STOP HER! SHE'S RUNNING!

Wally Wood art from
C "The Loathsor

MARVELS

Evolution of a Cover

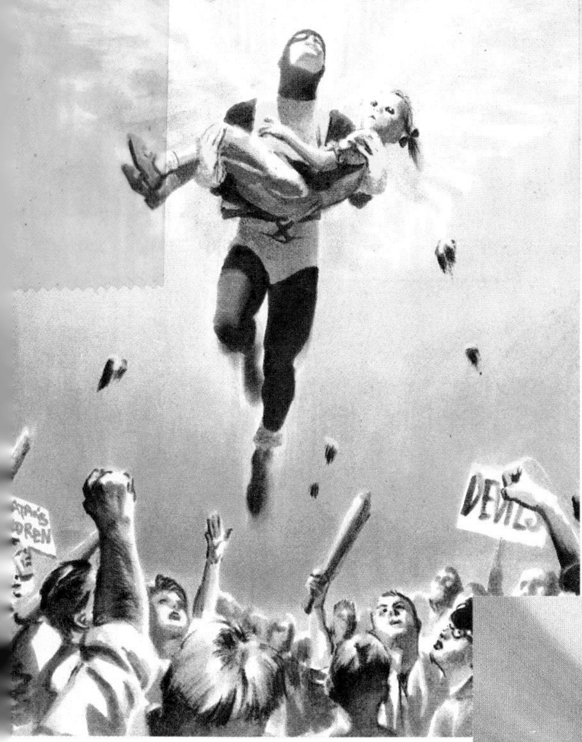
DEVILS

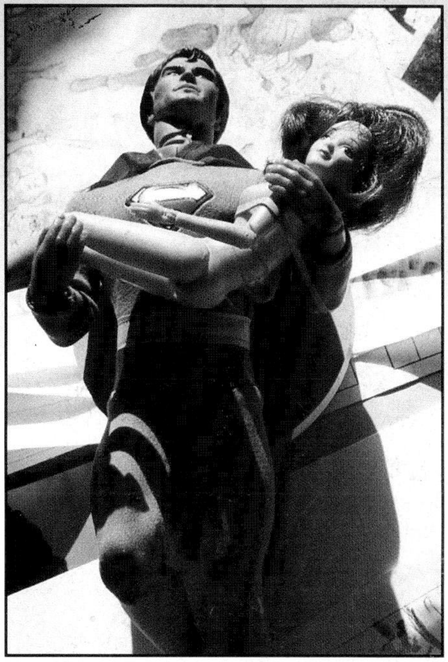

With the layout done (and the kid's gender determined) I could proceed to a color rough. This isn't a step I use often, but here I was unsure about how things would balance color wise, so the thing to do was a tight marker rendition.

For the next step I photographed the main figures. I usually stay away from toys and model kits since they can be too stiff to achieve the poses, but in this case a couple of dolls did the job perfectly. After the final pencil was done it took about a day or two to finish the painting.

Some touch-up with airbrush is used for the sky and angel's wings but mostly the medium was watercolor and gouache paints worked both transparent and opaque.

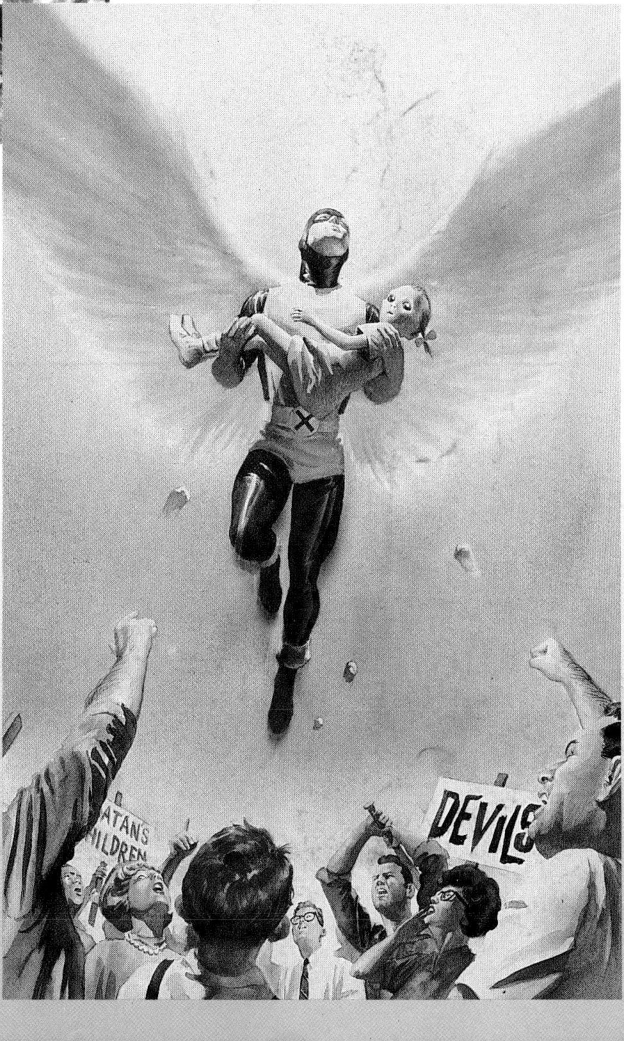
DEVILS

Costumes & Props

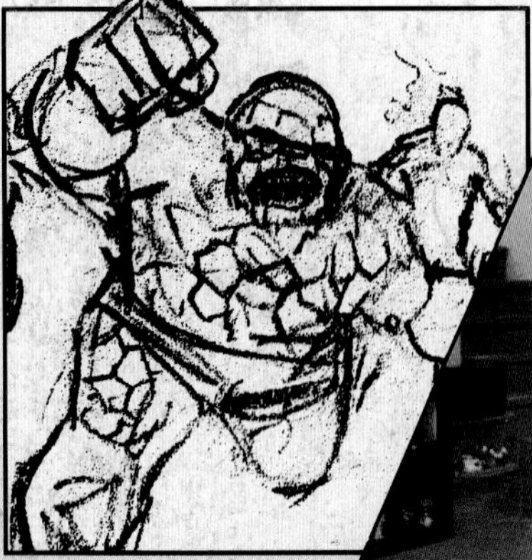

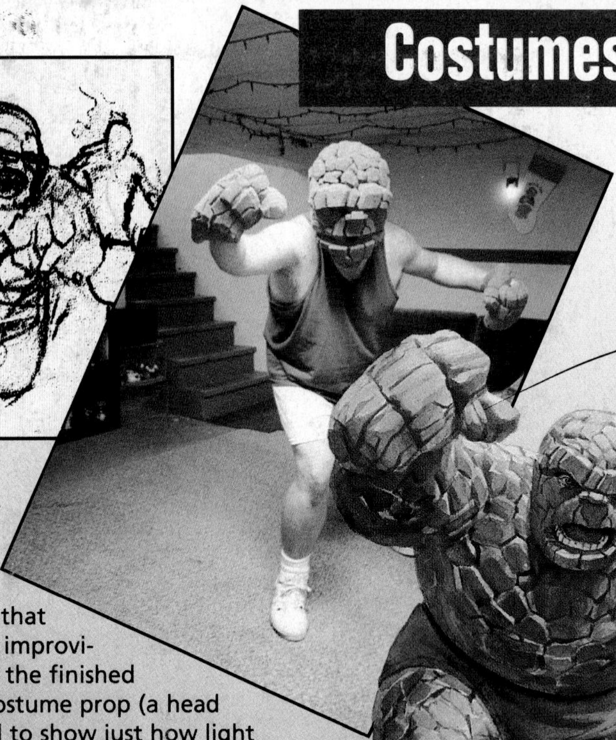

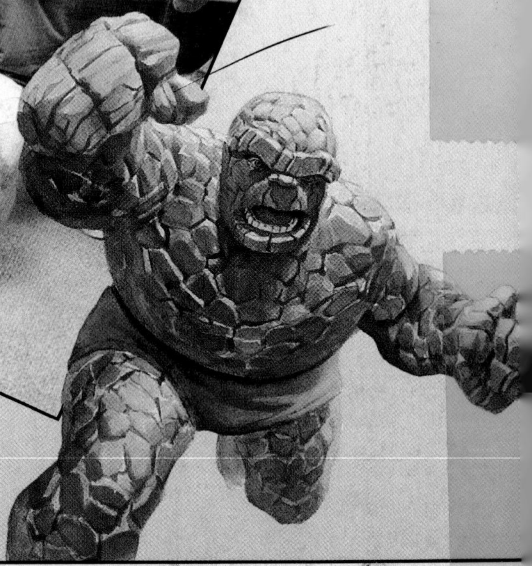

Believe me, just by chance I knew someone with a Thing costume. I'm not that nuts. Despite the improvisation needed for the finished illustration, this costume prop (a head and hands) served to show just how light would play across the Thing's rocky exterior.

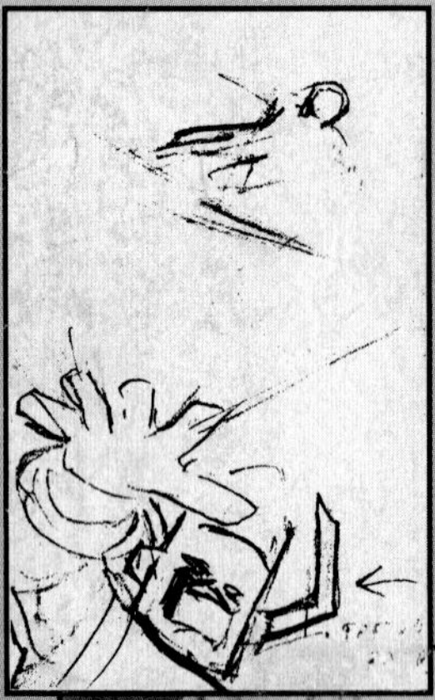

Sometimes a merchandised figurine of the character will give me what I want. A model kit of the Silver Surfer provided the chrome reflections I needed to capture his silvery hide.

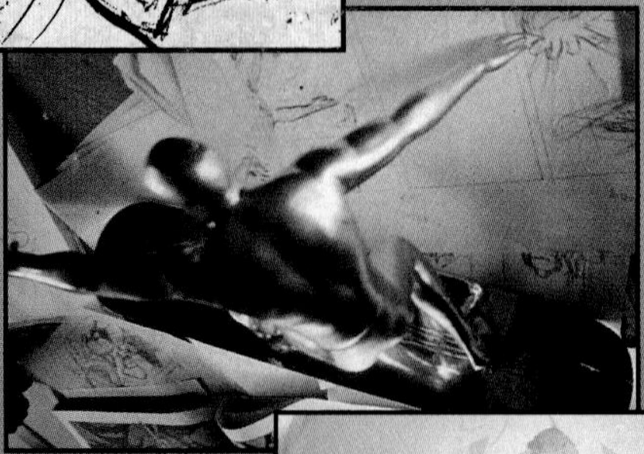

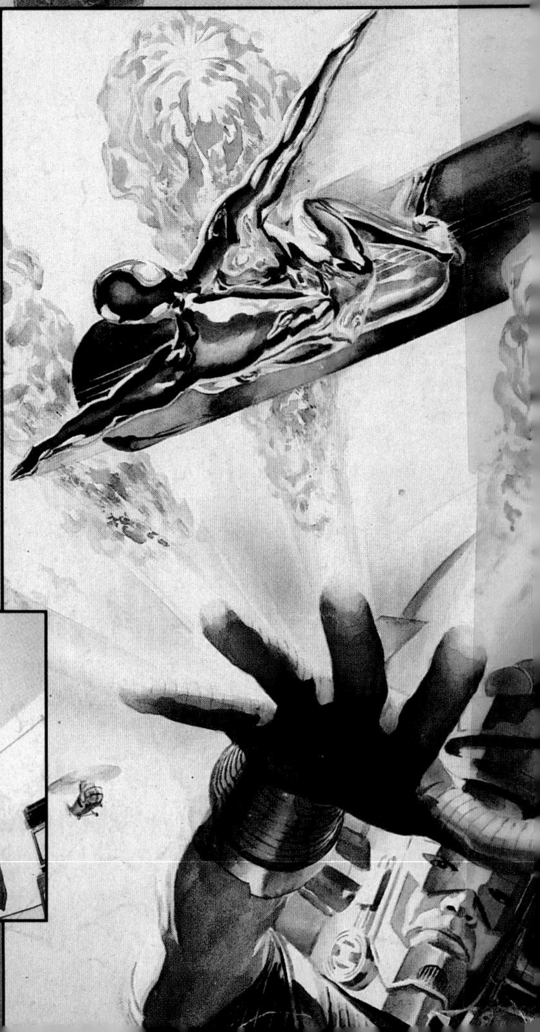

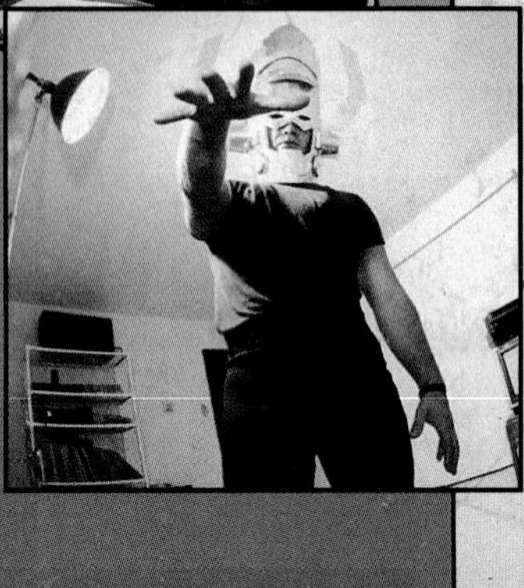

For Galactus, I constructed a cardboard helmet that gave me accurate shots of those tuning forks when seen from different angles.